THE MAKING OF MEDIEVAL ROME

Integrating the written sources with Rome's surviving remains and, most importantly, with the results of the past half-century's worth of medieval archaeology in the city, *The Making of Medieval Rome* is the first in-depth profile of Rome's transformation during the medieval millennium to appear in any language in over forty years. Though the main focus rests on Rome's urban trajectory in topographical, architectural, and archaeological terms, Hendrik Dey folds aspects of ecclesiastical, political, social, military, economic, and intellectual history into the narrative in order to illustrate how and why the cityscape evolved as it did during the thousand years between the end of the Roman Empire and the start of the Renaissance. A wide-ranging synthesis of decades' worth of specialized research and remarkable archaeological discoveries, this book is essential reading for anyone interested in how the ancient imperial capital transformed into the spiritual heart of Western Christendom.

Hendrik Dey spent years living and teaching in Rome, where he also held a two-year Rome Prize at the American Academy. His books include *The Aurelian Wall and the Refashioning of Imperial Rome, AD 271–855* (2011), and *The Afterlife of the Roman City: Architecture and Ceremony in Late Antiquity and the Early Middle Ages* (2015).

THE MAKING OF MEDIEVAL ROME

A New Profile of the City, 400–1420

HENDRIK DEY

Hunter College, City University of New York

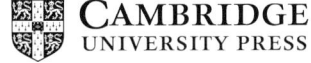

CAMBRIDGE
UNIVERSITY PRESS

University Printing House, Cambridge CB2 8BS, United Kingdom

One Liberty Plaza, 20th Floor, New York, NY 10006, USA

477 Williamstown Road, Port Melbourne, VIC 3207, Australia

314–321, 3rd Floor, Plot 3, Splendor Forum, Jasola District Centre,
New Delhi – 110025, India

103 Penang Road, #05–06/07, Visioncrest Commercial, Singapore 238467

Cambridge University Press is part of the University of Cambridge.

It furthers the University's mission by disseminating knowledge in the pursuit of
education, learning, and research at the highest international levels of excellence.

www.cambridge.org
Information on this title: www.cambridge.org/9781108838535
DOI: 10.1017/9781108975162

© Cambridge University Press 2021

This publication is in copyright. Subject to statutory exception
and to the provisions of relevant collective licensing agreements,
no reproduction of any part may take place without the written
permission of Cambridge University Press.

**Cambridge University Press gratefully acknowledges the generous support
of this book from Furthermore, a program of the J.M. Kaplan Fund.**

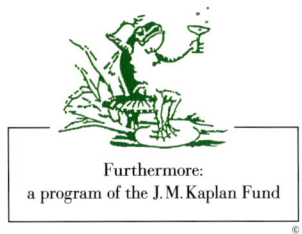

First published 2021

Printed in Singapore by Markono Print Media Pte Ltd

A catalogue record for this publication is available from the British Library.

Library of Congress Cataloging-in-Publication Data
Names: Dey, Hendrik W., 1976– author.
Title: The making of Medieval Rome : a new profile of the city, 400–1420 / Hendrik Dey, Hunter College, City University of New York.
Description: New York : Cambridge University Press, 2021. | Includes bibliographical references and index.
Identifiers: LCCN 2020058379 (print) | LCCN 2020058380 (ebook) | ISBN 9781108838535 (hardback) | ISBN 9781108971560 (paperback) | ISBN 9781108975162 (ebook)
Subjects: LCSH: Rome (Italy) – History – To 476. | Rome (Italy) – History – 476–1420.
Classification: LCC DG811 .D49 2021 (print) | LCC DG811 (ebook) | DDC 945.6/3201–dc23
LC record available at https://lccn.loc.gov/2020058379
LC ebook record available at https://lccn.loc.gov/2020058380

ISBN 978-1-108-83853-5 Hardback

Cambridge University Press has no responsibility for the persistence or accuracy of
URLs for external or third-party internet websites referred to in this publication
and does not guarantee that any content on such websites is, or will remain,
accurate or appropriate.

CONTENTS

Preface	*page* vii
Introduction	1
CHAPTER 1 *The Eternal City on the Brink: Rome in AD 400*	10
CHAPTER 2 *401–552: From Imperial Metropolis to Provincial Town*	33
CHAPTER 3 *552–705: Byzantine Rome*	69
CHAPTER 4 *705–882: A Papal "Republic of the Romans"*	102
CHAPTER 5 *882–1046: The Long Twilight of the Early Middle Ages*	137

CHAPTER 6
1046–1230: Church Reformed, Senate Reborn, Rome Renascent 170

CHAPTER 7
1230–1420: Barons, Babylonian Captivity, and Black Death: The Apogee and Agony of Late Medieval Rome 214

EPILOGUE
Rome and Pope Nicholas V (1447–55) 255

Notes 262
References 308
Index 332

PREFACE

THIS BOOK PURPORTS TO be the fullest treatment in any language of Rome's urban evolution across the full medieval millennium to appear in over forty years, since the publication, in 1980, of Richard Krautheimer's justly renowned *Rome, Profile of a City 312–1308*. As such, it has a staggering amount of ground to cover and needs to inform and (ideally) please a dauntingly wide range of prospective readers. It is a robust testament to the reach and quality of Krautheimer's book that it remains, even today, a standard resource for practicing scholars, for students, and – one assumes – for that legendary and much sought-after beast in academic publishing circles, the "educated general reader." Throughout the writing process, it has been my intent that all of the above likewise be able to use and profit from the present volume. I am aware of the risks inherent in trying to satisfy everybody and will make no apologies here for having made the attempt. I will, however, very briefly explain some of the editorial choices I have made.

Desiring to keep the text uncluttered by critical apparatus, I have remanded the notes to the end and reduced their number by placing them only at the end of paragraphs. Each paragraph or sequence of related paragraphs thus receives a more or less discursive endnote. Given that a mere list of all the bibliography relevant to the topics covered in the following pages, or even of the studies that have appeared since 1980 alone, would itself fill a book longer than this one, the sources that made the final cut are necessarily the survivors of a pitiless process of winnowing. My intention has been to permit students or less specialized researchers to find one or more, usually recent, starting points from which to begin exploring a topic in greater depth, and to provide experts with enough information to gauge who or what has done most to shape my thinking on a given subject. I include the syntheses that I find most valuable, of course, but tend to favor the primary sources, by which I mean both medieval texts and the reports produced by those responsible for the scientific excavation and/or analysis of medieval Roman sites in recent decades. More detailed or technical discussion than can comfortably fit in the main text may also appear in the notes.

I have not gone so far in catering to students and nonspecialists as to privilege English-language publications, though when something in English will do as well as anything else, I may opt for it. I have, however, fleshed out the primary sources in the bibliography by citing English translations of most of the editions listed. As I like to remind my students, and anyone else who will listen, it is almost always better to begin with the original sources – with what people (or, indeed, things) from the period in question have to tell us, rather than with what modern commentators say they said. As for the main text, I have tried to be clear enough to engage the novice, yet sufficiently precise to inform the expert, and withal to bore everyone as little as possible. Should tedium supervene nonetheless, the fault is probably mine, for it surely cannot lie with the city whose material riches and centrality on the world-historical stage combine to make it a uniquely fascinating place.

Nor, certainly, can the fault lie with those whose wisdom and generosity helped me bring this book to light. Special thanks are due to Paolo Squatriti, who toughened up a draft of the whole manuscript with his typically relentless critical acumen. Lucrezia Spera, Riccardo Santangeli Valenzani, and Nicoletta Giannini dissected smaller but still lengthy chunks and helped me in countless other ways besides. The two anonymous readers engaged by Cambridge Press likewise devoted a humbling quotient of care and critical acumen to the manuscript, suggesting improvements and corrections that far exceeded the common run of readers' reports in both quantity and quality. These kind, perspicacious counselors and I naturally do not agree on everything, and I have occasionally persisted in my own views despite suggestions to the contrary, undoubtedly at my own peril, which leaves them all the more blameless for whatever travesties of fact and good judgment remain. Their formidable erudition, unstintingly shared, has saved me from numberless errors of commission and omission, and sensibly enhanced whatever virtues this book has.

A host of others helped to sustain this project and its author across years of research, writing, and production. For sharing their knowledge (and written work, published and otherwise) of medieval Rome with me; facilitating access to sites and monuments, and memorable site visits in their company; invitations to speak on the book or topics integral to its conception; help with acquiring images and/or the rights to reproduce them; and a host of other acts of personal and professional kindness, large and small, I thank Marco Aimone, Franco Astolfi, Lia Barelli, Douglas Boin, Giulia Bordi, Nicola Camerlenghi, Robert Coates-Stephens, Lavinia Cozza, Alessandro Delfino, Valeria di Cola, Phil Ditchfield, Judson Emerick, Vincenzo Fiocchi Nicolai, Giorgio Fusconi, Federico Guidobaldi, Dario Internullo, Paolo Liverani, Manfred Luchterhandt, Daniele Manacorda, Maura Medri, Roberto Meneghini, Ian Mladjov, Alessandra Molinari, Fabrizio Oppedisano, Carlo Pavolini, Giorgio Rascaglia, Alessia Rovelli, Amy Russell, Michele Salzman, Rita Santolini, Mirella Serlorenzi, Sister Josepha and the nuns of the Fraternità di Gerusalemme at S. Sebastiano al Palatino; the Augustinian nuns of SS. Quattro Coronati; the Ministero per i beni e le attività culturali – Museo Nazionale Romano; the Sovraintendenza Capitolina ai Beni Culturali; the librarians and archivists at the American Academy in Rome, the Fototeca Unione at the American

Academy, the École Française de Rome, the British School at Rome; and the indefatigable ILL staff at the Hunter College library. Beatrice Rehl and her editorial team at Cambridge Press were, as always, a pleasure to work with. Finally, I gratefully acknowledge the institutional support that afforded me the time and resources needed for sustained intervals of research and writing, chiefly a fellowship in Byzantine Studies at Dumbarton Oaks during the 2016–17 academic year, and a second sabbatical year granted shortly thereafter by my home institution, Hunter College, which also generously helped to cover the cost of publishing my many color images. Without this teeming village of dear friends and esteemed colleagues, I would never have managed to raise my profile of Rome's medieval millennium to maturity, nor been half so delighted and inspired by the process of doing so.

INTRODUCTION

As Frederick I ("Barbarossa") approached Rome for the first time in 1155, on his way to be crowned Emperor of the Romans by Pope Hadrian IV, he was met by Roman envoys at Sutri, a day's journey north of the city. Nothing in the young German king's prior experience, even among the recalcitrant city communes of northern Italy, had prepared him for the blithe insolence of his visitors, who proclaimed themselves representatives of something called the Roman Senate. From the parchments they read aloud upon entering Frederick's presence, the majestically condescending voice of Rome personified rang out. Lady Roma spoke to the king as a mistress to a suppliant come to beg from her and the Senate the favor of an imperial coronation. The city, via the Senate that – this particular personified Rome suggested – embodied her will and incarnated her ancient glories, would deign to grant Frederick the imperial crown provided he obediently satisfy a long list of conditions, all punctually enumerated. He was to swear not to meddle with the ancient rights and privileges the Romans claimed to enjoy; to shed his own blood whenever necessary to prevent any injury befalling the Roman "republic"; and to pay the senators 5,000 pounds of silver for the trouble of acclaiming him emperor. This from a group of some fifty Romans who had first gathered in putatively sovereign assembly barely a decade before, without imperial consent, and in open defiance of the pope whom Frederick expected to anoint him emperor.

According to the German bishop and imperial chronicler, Otto of Freising, whose account we are following here, Frederick stressed to his importunate visitors that the key word with respect to Roman power and virtue was "former" (*quondam*), and dismissed them with a trenchant lecture on their shameful dereliction of their duties as imperial subjects. Frederick then moved decisively to cut the Gordian knot of local politics by dispatching 1,000 select troops that same night to join forces with the pope's faithful and occupy the walls of the Vatican, the *civitas Leonina*, where Frederick appeared the following morning with the rest of his army. Within hours of his arrival, he was duly crowned before the high altar at St. Peter's by Pope Hadrian IV, who welcomed the coming of a ruler as hostile to the sovereign pretensions of the independent-minded Romans across the Tiber as he was. The German troops of the new "Emperor of the Romans," meanwhile, guarded Ponte Sant'Angelo, the bridge that connected the Vatican with the city center, lest the Romans themselves attempt to interrupt the proceedings.

At the close of the ceremonies, Frederick paraded his army back to its camp outside the Vatican walls, at which point partisans of the Senate, enraged at the fait accompli, stormed across Ponte Sant'Angelo. They went rampaging into St. Peter's, where they found some imperial grooms still lingering and tore them to pieces. When he realized what was happening, Frederick rushed his troops back inside the walls to fight a pitched battle against a swelling crowd of Romans now pouring into the Vatican from two sides, from Ponte Sant'Angelo and also from Trastevere on the Vatican side of the Tiber. The emperor's heavily armed veterans tore into the Romans, repaying their "Arab gold" with "Teutonic steel," as Otto of Freising put it. The June heat, said Otto, posed a greater inconvenience to the steel-clad Germans than the hometown rabble they spent the remainder of the day slaughtering.[1]

And then, as everyone in Rome from the pope and the Roman senators on down knew would happen, Frederick headed back north after a few weeks, his army decimated by the usual afflictions of northern Europeans in Roman summer – malaria and dysentery, fever and flux – leaving Rome once more to the Romans. The partisans of pope and Senate settled back into their standoff, glaring back and forth between the senatorial stronghold on the Capitoline and the papal enclaves at the Vatican and the Lateran cathedral, more or less as though Frederick had never come. Within a decade, Hadrian's successor, Pope Alexander III (r. 1159–80), whose election Frederick had strenuously opposed, would himself side with the northern Italian communes in their struggle to break free of imperial domination. He provided crucial support to the Lombard League in the years leading up to the pivotal Battle of Legnano in 1176, where the allied communes' shocking victory over Frederick ushered in an age of civic autonomy in north-central Italy that lasted until the eve of the Renaissance.[2]

While both popes and leaders of local aristocratic factions frequently collaborated with external powers, the alliances they formed were endlessly fluid and never absolute. When Pope Hadrian sought to curb the political autonomy of the nascent Roman Senate in the 1150s, he found a natural ally in Frederick, who also considered his sovereign prerogatives threatened by the upstart assembly. Yet in 1160, Hadrian's successor, Alexander III, would excommunicate Frederick less than a year after becoming pope. When Frederick next came to Rome in 1166, Church and Senate jointly opposed him. Frederick again beat the Romans in battle, only to retreat north with his army once again ravaged by disease. Pope Alexander survived and returned to Rome, his stature if anything enhanced, to spend the remainder of his long pontificate supporting the northern Italian communes opposed to Frederick.[3]

In their different ways, popes Hadrian and Alexander and the Roman Senate all asserted the primacy of local, Rome-centered agendas and interests. They did so by invoking an image of Rome as an eternal and peerless capital, presenting themselves as the heirs to an unbroken tradition of Roman primacy rooted in the city's past glories. Papal claims to ecclesiastical preeminence throughout Christendom rested on the popes' special status as the apostolic successors of St. Peter, "Prince of the Apostles" and first bishop of Rome. Their assertion of temporal dominion over Rome and its environs derived from their claim to be the legal successors of the Roman emperors, a concept given lasting form in the Donation of Constantine, an 8th-century forgery purporting to represent emperor Constantine's (r. AD 306–37) cession to the papacy, in perpetuity, of all imperial lands in and powers over the western half of the Roman Empire. Meanwhile, the reborn Senate's competing claim to political autonomy and dominion over Roman territory derived from its self-identification as the rightful successor of the Senate of ancient Rome. It was the modern incarnation of "the indomitable Roman virtue that conquered all things," as the senatorial envoys put it to Frederick at Sutri.[4]

In topographical terms, too, Rome was as anomalous throughout the Middle Ages as it had been in antiquity, in ways directly connected to its erstwhile size and grandeur. From the 2nd century BC through the 4th century AD, Rome was the most populous city outside of China that the world had ever seen. No European metropolis would again rival imperial Rome in size and population until the 18th century. Its urban center, defined by jurists of the imperial era as the area covered by "contiguous roofs" (*continentia tecta*), housed close to a million souls. The 3rd-century walls begun by Emperor Aurelian (r. 270–5) were nearly 19 km (12 miles) long and encircled an area of some 1400 hectares, or 5.5 square miles, yet still failed to encompass all of its urban sprawl.[5]

This 'ancient' incarnation of Rome remained vibrant at the dawn of the 5th century AD, though the city in 400, like the empire as a whole, had changed and evolved in important ways since the halcyon days of the 1st and 2nd centuries. The construction of the Aurelian Wall itself was a dramatic moment. Busy neighborhoods were suddenly bisected by an impermeable barrier; countless buildings were leveled; traffic headed in and out of the city was constricted by the choke points of the city gates, and so on. Rome subsequently consisted of 'inside' and 'outside,' with the former becoming far more desirable as living space than the latter, for obvious reasons. The gradual Christianization of the empire following the promulgation of the Edict of Milan in 313 brought further changes, most visibly in the form of Rome's first monumental churches, most sponsored by the imperial family. But these earliest grand churches were all in peripheral locations; and the city center in the later 4th century did not look, feel, smell, or sound much different than it had a century or two earlier. A Roman alive in AD 200 could have felt at home there still in 400. But transported two centuries farther forward in time to AD 600, that same Roman would have materialized in a place transformed beyond recognition, and wept to see it.

Yet throughout the Middle Ages, Rome was always the most renowned city in Europe, the place that mattered most. As the seat of the papacy and epicenter of Latin Christendom, it remained better connected to the wider world than anyplace else. Over the course of the medieval millennium, more foreigners experienced Rome than any other European city. Many came and stayed, both clerics in the service of the Church and also laymen drawn by the lure of ecclesiastical wealth and patronage. Far more still, over the long term, passed through as pilgrims and tourists. Rome's reputation and prestige, its legacy of emperors long dead and popes past and present, proved irresistible also to a long succession of European potentates, Charlemagne and Barbarossa most famously among many others. From the 8th century on, rare was the Roman who lived to old age without seeing at least one foreign army camped outside the city, while its leader awaited imperial coronation at St. Peter's, or otherwise intervened more or less forcefully (and often disastrously) to assert some claim over the city and redirect the course of its local and ecclesiastical politics. Time and again, such outsiders underestimated the extent to which Rome was a world unto itself and overestimated their capacity to reshape Roman affairs in accordance with their ambitions.[6]

As in the case of Barbarossa's dealings with the Senate, and eventually also the papacy, ever-changing coalitions of urban power brokers passively resisted, balked, or outright foiled such *deus ex machina* attempts to meddle in the internal affairs of the city. (Native Romans tended to count the administration of the Church among the city's internal affairs, as did many popes, especially during the earlier Middle Ages.) The medieval Romans whose views appear in the surviving sources quite consistently considered themselves Romans first, and subjects of a usually distant sovereign at best a distant second. Civic patriotism and 'city-first' approaches prevailed in other Italian cities, too, particularly with the rise of independent-minded communal governments in the later 11th and 12th centuries, but at Rome the stakes were higher. It was the arena where the universalizing pretensions of popes and emperors collided most spectacularly with each other, and with the local agendas of Rome's perpetually restless and factionalized nobility and populace. These native Romans – very much the 'town' to the papal and imperial 'gown' – were emboldened by a persistent sense of Roman exceptionalism rooted in the city's imperial legacy and the physical remains of its staggeringly grandiose past. They were inspired by the cityscape itself.[7]

That cityscape lies at the heart of this book. Like urbanites everywhere, medieval Romans were products of their particular surroundings, but the experience of inhabiting medieval Rome was highly unusual insofar as the city itself was such an unusual place. Nowhere did the magnitude of past achievements more visibly surpass the scope of present capacities; nowhere was an urban population more dwarfed by the sweep and scale of the built environment. Within the 19 km (12 mile) circumference of the Aurelian Wall, several tens of thousands of people carved out an existence amid the crumbling hulks of a metropolis meant for many hundreds of thousands. They lived between ruins, inside ruins, on top of ruins. Even new buildings were mostly assembled with stones and bricks quarried from ancient piles. Lime for mortar was obtained by cremating marble and limestone building blocks, and countless thousands of marble sculptures besides. The intricate polychrome pavements of medieval churches were assembled with thousands of fragments of colored marbles that had once revetted ancient walls and floors; larger, round disks were harvested from thinly sliced columns. Other ancient columns and column capitals graced church interiors across the city, along with the porticoes and loggias of countless upscale houses. Meanwhile, enduring wonders such as the imperial palace on the Palatine, the Colosseum, the mausoleums of Augustus and Hadrian, the imperial bath complexes, the city walls, and even the sewers relegated the most ambitious efforts of medieval builders to comparative insignificance. Medieval Romans told fantastic stories about the original owners and builders of the city's architectural marvels, some of them real historical figures, others pure inventions. Monstrous, scaly things and demons were known to inhabit the darker recesses of these ancient piles.[8]

Monsters and myths flourish in the interstices between well-trodden paths, and Rome was full of such interstices from the 6th century on. Ancient landmarks and infrastructure sprinkled throughout the city continued to attract visitors and residents, subsisting as inhabited islands amid sweeping expanses given over to decay and abandonment, like the teeming pools left behind by an ebb tide. Many of Rome's most venerable churches, built during the 4th and early 5th centuries when much more of the intramural area remained thickly settled, stood distant from densely populated neighborhoods by the later Middle Ages, but they were rarely abandoned. The centrifugal pull of the Lateran cathedral on the eastern periphery, S. Maria Maggiore on the Esquiline, S. Stefano Rotondo on the Caelian, S. Sabina on the Aventine, and countless other churches, monasteries, and charitable institutions besides, as well as fortresses and residential compounds built into widely scattered ancient ruins, helps to explain why medieval Rome never fully contracted into a compact urban nucleus similar in size and shape to the other leading cities of medieval Italy. No attempt was ever made to create a smaller and more easily defended enceinte as an alternative to the walls of Aurelian, despite their being far too large to be defended in strength with the human resources available. From one end of the city to the other, there was too much of worth, materially and conceptually and symbolically speaking, to leave any of it out.

One result of Rome's diffuseness was a further diminution, or dilution, of the present in relation to the past. Medieval Romans were thinly spread across a sprawling landscape filled with resources and prizes over which to compete, which is in part why it became so difficult for anyone to control the whole city, especially from the later 9th century on. Various factions and families predominated in different regions, contributing to the gradual formation of discrete neighborhoods often centered on prominent landmarks and local strongholds. Many residents of these neighborhoods rarely left them. So balkanized was the cityscape by the later Middle Ages that people from different neighborhoods might speak perceptibly different varieties of Roman dialect. Those living just across the river in Trastevere, meanwhile, were understood to be something other than the residents of the city center.[9]

Rome's unparalleled size, its peerless inheritance of ancient monuments and infrastructure, and its scattered population made the experience of *being* there unique. Hence, while our main remit is historical topography and urbanism, we will touch variously on ecclesiastical, political, social, military, economic, and intellectual history, insofar as they are all intertwined with Rome's peculiar urban environment. The mental horizons, and thus also the behaviors, of Rome's medieval inhabitants were powerfully conditioned by their awe-inspiring surroundings. Both consciously and insensibly, they reacted to the physical contours of the spaces and places they negotiated on a daily basis, and the myths and memories, ideals and ideologies encoded therein. The lived experience of a place medieval Romans rightly believed to be one of a kind, in turn, informed the choices they made about how to configure those surroundings: what to raze or dismantle, what to abandon or ignore, what to preserve or repackage, what to create anew and how to situate it in relation to what was already there. It is these endless recursive loops created between human agents and inanimate matter that comprise the 'cityscape' at the heart of this book, as I intend the term: the totality of the built environment, populated by the human actors who animated and (partially) shaped it.

Our understanding of that built environment is rapidly transforming in all sorts of exciting ways. Until the 1980s, the archaeology of medieval Rome was pitifully sparse. Earlier excavators tended to rip through post-Classical remains in their haste to uncover the glories of the ancient city, often neglecting to make even a perfunctory pass at recording and processing the later materials they encountered. Cataclysmic visions of 'Dark Age' collapse following the dissolution of Rome's empire in the 5th century consequently, inevitably, became a kind of archaeological self-fulfilling prophecy: Excavators expecting nothing but desolation and a general impoverishment of culture, both material and otherwise, confirmed their expectations by failing to find what they chose not to seek in the first place. But the rapid growth of medieval archaeology in Rome over the past few decades has unleashed a flood of new information, and not a few outstanding discoveries. Archaeologists are steadily revealing layers of the city and facets of its medieval inhabitants' lives missing from the written sources and the preserved buildings and objects that underpinned older scholarship, in the process prompting historians, art historians, topographers, and others – themselves included – to return to the written sources with a more discerning eye.

As the most important synthesis of Rome's urban trajectory across the full sweep of the medieval millennium was published in 1980, before the revolution in postclassical archaeology began to bear fruit, it is high time for an update. That book is Richard Krautheimer's *Rome: Profile of a City, 312–1308*, surely the single most read work (in English and in translation into a number of languages) on medieval Rome written in the past century. It is a sweeping panorama of the city's material contours from the advent of Constantine until the papacy's temporary removal to Avignon, produced by a giant in the field who had already devoted some five decades to knowing Rome. Yet the discoveries made since its publication have expanded our understanding of the city in ways that would have been almost inconceivable to Krautheimer when he was writing his *Profile* in the 1970s. Krautheimer's Rome is basically a papal Rome, its topography a collection of churches, in large part because (surviving) churches were far and away the best-known component of the medieval cityscape in his day. Krautheimer naturally knew perfectly well that most Romans were not clerics, and that Rome did not consist primarily of ecclesiastical buildings, but he lacked reliable information about how and where most people were living and working throughout much of the Middle Ages.

For the early Middle Ages, c. 400–1000, some of the most important advances of the past few decades relate to settlement patterns, infrastructure, and residential or otherwise nonecclesiastical architecture. Whereas Krautheimer accepted the prevailing consensus that population clustered in the southern Campus Martius and Trastevere from the 6th century, we now know that settlement was spread widely, albeit sparsely, across much of Rome's intramural expanse for at least another 500 years. Krautheimer, in other words, was wrong about where Romans were living across roughly half the period he covers. As for how they were living, Krautheimer could say little about the places they inhabited prior to the 12th and 13th centuries, when the earliest standing examples of medieval houses were built. We now know more about the dwellings inhabited by both wealthy and humble Romans in the preceding centuries, thanks to extensive excavations such as those undertaken in the forums of Trajan, Nerva, and Caesar in the 1990s and 2000s – all areas where, in Krautheimer's day, few would have expected to encounter dense early medieval settlement.[10]

Correspondingly great strides have been made in identifying and dating the most common forms of early medieval masonry. One result of these advances is the realization that the popes intervened in the infrastructure of the city in the 8th and 9th centuries on a surprisingly grand scale, conducting extensive repairs of the city walls and several of the aqueducts, for example. Such discoveries have capillary effects, too: That multiple aqueducts were repaired into the 9th century and continued to function into the 10th and 11th helps to explain how and why relatively peripheral areas far from the Tiber, such as the Esquiline and Caelian hills, remained as frequented as they were at the time.[11]

With regard to the Roman economy, monetary circulation, the production and distribution of luxury goods and other commodities, and the city's connections with the wider world, a single watershed excavation at the Crypta Balbi in the 1980s and 1990s overturned centuries' worth of conventional wisdom on the early Middle Ages, much of which – the 7th and 10th centuries in particular – used to be treated as a time of unrelenting poverty and squalor. The quality, quantity, and sheer diversity of the finds unearthed there was revelatory. A limited slice of a single, rather undistinguished Roman neighborhood turned up more money and precious metals, more raw materials, and more high-quality finished goods than anyone expected. On the assumption that this neighborhood was not unusually vibrant (and further discoveries elsewhere suggest that it was not), these finds point to the existence of a surprisingly robust economy, still characterized in most periods by frequent monetary transactions and always by the production and circulation of high-quality goods.

In 1980, even the chronology of the most distinctive ceramics produced in the city between c. 800 and c. 1200, 'Forum Ware' and the later 'Sparse Glazed Ware,' remained controversial, with proposals for the introduction of Forum Ware ranging from as early as c. 600 to as late as the 9th century. This uncertainty deprived medieval archaeologists of their most common and distinctive class of diagnostic ceramics, and consequently of their ability to date closely the layers at the many sites where such pottery had turned up. Careful excavations at San Sisto Vecchio, the Crypta Balbi, and around the Palatine Hill, among others, provided the solution to the puzzle, and revealed in the process a resurgence of ceramic production in Rome from the later 8th century that reached quasi-industrial levels by the 11th. This pottery, moreover, traveled widely. Its presence in southern France, Sardinia and Corsica, and Byzantine southern Italy shows that Rome still participated in wide-ranging networks of trade and communications.[12]

It is probably fair to say that the past few decades have seen fewer revolutionary advances in our understanding of the later medieval cityscape, in part because it was better understood already in Krautheimer's day – structures and contours of the later Middle Ages persist more widely and visibly up to the present than those of the early Middle Ages. But real progress has been made in, for example, the study of construction techniques and the building industry. Étienne Hubert's now classic analysis of housing and settlement between the 10th and 13th centuries showed how much can be gleaned from Roman archival documents (simple contracts of sale and lease, etc.), anticipating a wave of studies by archaeologists and historians alike whose work is grounded in close study of the material remains. Architectural historians and 'archaeologists of architecture' (more on these later) have classified and dated characteristic types of masonry with greater precision than was possible only a few decades ago, in part via digital analysis and statistical sampling of medieval buildings. Studies of houses, towers and fortresses, shops and markets, and other forms of nonecclesiastical architecture have proliferated.[13]

Such material explorations have gone hand in glove with efforts by historians to open new vistas onto the social and economic structures of the city during the high and late Middle Ages. Landmark studies have appeared on the composition of the nobility and property-owning classes; networks of patronage and relations between laymen and the Church; the dynamics of land-tenure and property ownership; production and the sources of wealth. The result has been not so much to downplay the role of the Church as to contextualize it; to see more clearly both the reach and the limitations of ecclesiastical institutions in a city that remained a relatively wealthy and dynamic place in its own right. In a sense, later medieval Rome has been 'normalized' and brought into nearer rapport with other Italian cities, which it resembles more closely in social, political, and economic terms than used to be thought. Later medieval Rome was not a city of the Church, but rather – like other places – a city with a Church, albeit an unusually wealthy and influential one.[14]

This brief overview of recent developments barely samples the pile of work on medieval Rome produced since Krautheimer's *Profile of a City* and published in an endless array of monographs and papers. Syntheses are few and far between, and the best to appear so far, generally in Italian, rarely cover Krautheimer's full thousand-year arc. Hence the need for a new profile of the 'new' medieval Rome now emerging through the combined efforts of hundreds of researchers, whose work is transforming the city Krautheimer knew into something yet more complex and fascinating. My profile is designed to supplant its illustrious predecessor, to be sure, insofar as it accounts for sweeping gains made in knowledge and understanding, but also to complement it. Where I explicitly take issue with Krautheimer, it is because his views still underpin so many prevailing conceptions, and misconceptions, of medieval Rome. By indicating where his immensely influential *Profile* has been superseded, I hope also to aid those readers who will continue to read it and profit from all it contains of enduring value. Krautheimer's encyclopedic command of ecclesiastical architecture is still unsurpassed, and his mastery of the grand sweep of the Roman historical panorama remains a model of scholarly humanism to which all might aspire.[15]

In covering the years from 400 to 1420, I have chosen to begin and end roughly a century later than Krautheimer. In terms of Rome's topography and urban development, this seems to me the period that best corresponds with the literal meaning of 'medieval' as the interval between antiquity and early modernity; between the dissolution of the structures and systems characteristic of the ancient world and the rise of those characteristic of the Renaissance. I start in 400 because I want to emphasize that 4th-century Rome is not medieval – or rather, can be conceived as such only on the premise that Constantine's legalization of Christianity in 313 made Rome suddenly and profoundly 'medieval,' not only in religious or cultural terms but also in its physical configuration. This is not an argument I would want to make, implicitly or otherwise. Most Romans were not Christian for most of the 4th century, and intramural Rome in 400 was still in essence its ancient self: It looked, functioned, and bustled with life much as it had a century earlier. As systemic change occurred only from the early 5th century, we will begin there, after a glance at the 'ancient' city as it was around 400, on the cusp of the upheavals that would transform it into a very different sort of place.[16]

I close in 1420 in order to stress that 'medieval' Rome did not end when the papacy went off to Avignon at the beginning of the 14th century. To suggest otherwise is to imply that 14th-century Rome bereft of popes for seven decades was somehow no longer medieval. But the popes had largely avoided Rome for a century and more before Avignon, and even when present, their capacity to shape the city and the lives of its inhabitants was hardly absolute. The departure of the Curia depressed the local economy, to be sure, and seriously curtailed commissions for showy works of art and architecture; it also exacerbated an already worsening climate of political turmoil and civil strife, creating a partial power vacuum that left Rome's preeminent baronial families freer than ever to run amok in contending for wealth and influence. Yet these are recurring, even quintessential themes of Rome's medieval millennium. Time and again, the city traversed lengthy periods of sociopolitical – and material – entropy, when factional interests prevailed over centralized authority; when the putative leaders of the urban collective were too impoverished or ineffectual to steward the built environment or reshape it on a citywide scale; when control over existing monuments and infrastructure and the execution of new projects was left, if at all, to private individuals or local interest groups. Systemic change came only after the popes returned from Avignon, for good, as it turned out, and worked gradually but ultimately successfully to bring the nobility to heel, control municipal government, and exert a preponderant influence in the shaping of topography and infrastructure, architecture and the arts. This is the Rome of the Renaissance, the stable papal capital and magnet for artists and architects and humanists. As good a date as any for its inception is 1420, when Pope Martin V established himself at Rome after the close of the Great Western Schism.[17]

It is difficult and probably undesirable to try to impose a satisfying narrative, a cohesive plot, on a millennium of any city's history, much less a city so kaleidoscopically complex as medieval Rome. There is no one story, no unitary trajectory. If there is a guiding leitmotif in what follows, it is the persistence of the past. The material and ideological legacies of imperial and early Christian Rome loomed over the medieval present, ensuring the city's enduring centrality on the European scene but also creating constant *urbi et orbi* tension between Rome as city (*urbs*) and universal capital (*orbs*), between living place and transcendent ideal. The interests and ambitions of native Romans concerned with making their way in the only home they had kept butting up against the agendas of outsiders more concerned with the idea of Rome than its messy quotidian realities. All, however, locals and resident foreigners alike, daily confronted, negotiated, and took inspiration from the world's largest ensemble of ancient monuments and ruins. The built landscape inherited from antiquity remained the firmament on which medieval Romans operated, physically and mentally. Faced with an endless, often baffling jumble of Very Old Things, they made choices about what to notice and how to notice what they did. They selectively ordered the chaos to make sense of what they saw around them, and to make statements about politics and genealogy and beliefs and belonging. But they also daily adapted and reused the bricks and stones, roads and walls inherited from antiquity, simply because these things were unavoidably there.

Like medieval Romans, this book also makes endless choices about what to notice and how to notice what it does. A distillation of the surviving textual and material traces of the medieval city, it makes no pretense of exhaustiveness. The great challenge in writing it was deciding what to leave out, which had to be far more than it includes in order for it to pass the bathtub test, devised when a distinguished Roman archaeologist complained that issues of a leading journal had grown too hefty to allow for comfortable reading in the tub. But I hope some virtue may result from the necessity of writing a wieldy book. Instead of trying to cover everything, I focus on a selection of topics, sources, sites, and materials that seem (to me) most helpful in illustrating how and why the cityscape evolved as it did in the period c. 400–1420. I pay special attention to the advances made in the four decades since Krautheimer wrote, but also to the problems and uncertainties that remain. As usual, the great questions are how we know what we think we know, and how, if at all, we might go about learning what we don't.

Chapter 1

THE ETERNAL CITY ON THE BRINK

Rome in AD 400

During the first half of the 4th century, anonymous authors compiled a pair of very similar catalogs of Roman buildings and landmarks, the *Notitia* and the *Curiosum urbis Romae regionum XIIII*, the "Description" (*Notitia*) and "Gazetteer (*Curiosum*) of the fourteen regions of the city of Rome." Updated at least as late as the year 357, they listed noteworthy features of each of the city's fourteen regions, the administrative subdivisions, like Paris's arrondissements or London's boroughs, that had been introduced by Augustus in 7 BC (Fig. 1.1). The two Regionary Catalogs, as they are now called, are the most comprehensive resource we have for the names and places constitutive of Rome's urban fabric at the end of antiquity. For some areas, they are graphically supplemented by the surviving fragments of the Severan Marble Plan, a gigantic 1:240 scale map of Rome carved circa AD 203 into marble slabs mounted on a wall in the Forum of Peace (Fig. 1.2). Taken together with the surviving monuments and archaeological remains, these written and pictorial descriptions offer one way of imagining Rome at the end of the 4th century, in the last flush of its ancient grandeur.[1]

The three smallest and most central regions included a sweeping expanse of the city's most venerable and important public buildings and spaces, the heart of official Rome where the mighty posed and visitors gawked as vendors and touts hustled alongside beggars and pickpockets. The Roman Forum and the adjacent forum complexes built by Caesar, Augustus, Vespasian, Domitian/Nerva, and Trajan alone occupied an area the size of a middling provincial town, filled with temples, basilicas, porticoes, and open esplanades clad in gleaming marbles imported from North Africa, Asia Minor, Greece, and the Balkans: black and white, grey, purple, red, green, yellow, and speckled coralline pastels unfolded in long vistas teeming with statues, trophies, commemorative monuments, and historical memorabilia. The Capitoline Hill with its gold-roofed temple of Jupiter Optimus Maximus overlooked the forums from the west, the imperial palace on the Palatine Hill from the south, and from the east the Colosseum, a man-made mountain of travertine-faced concrete with seating for some 50,000 spectators. Here was ancient Rome's Champs-Élysées and Île de la Cité, its Westminster and St. James's, its midtown Manhattan; with Richard Krautheimer, we can call it simply the "Show Area."[2]

The Palatine Hill was a region unto itself (Region 10: *Palatium*), heart of the ur-Rome of Romulus and epicenter of Rome's earliest legends. On the western edge of the summit was the endlessly restored one-room thatched hovel where – ancient tradition insisted – Romulus lived in the 8th century BC, standing in the shadow of the marble-clad temple of Magna Mater, the "Great Mother of the Gods" brought from Syria to Rome in the dark days when Hannibal's Carthaginians rampaged through Italy. Next to it was Augustus' temple of Apollo, one of the first Roman temples built in white marble from the newly opened quarries at Carrara; original masterpieces of Greek sculpture filled the temple, and polished black statues of the fifty husband-murdering daughters of Danaus lined its colonnaded forecourt, interspersed among columns of yellow marble splotched with bloodred. The rest of the summit to the east was covered by the sprawling enormity of the imperial palace, built in stages between the 1st and 3rd centuries AD. It had its own aqueduct, the Aqua Claudia, which supplied hundreds of thousands of liters of water per day that gurgled in fountains and swam down walls sheeted in imported marbles polished to a mirrored sheen to prevent anyone sneaking up behind the paranoid emperor Domitian, as one Roman tradition had it (Fig. 1.3). At the eastern foot of the hill, facing those entering Rome from the south along the Via Appia, the Septizodium of Septimius Severus fronted the approaches to the palace: A three-story-high fountain with a columnar façade that symbolized the seven planets of the known universe, it hinted strongly that the palace itself was the center of that universe.[3]

Whereas access to the Palatine was tightly controlled, the two interlinked regions covering the low ground just to the north were the crossroads of the whole city, the symbolic heart of city and empire where Rome's main roads and human traffic converged. Region 8: "Great Roman Forum" (*Forum Romanum Magnum*) centered on the rectangular Forum plaza, Rome's central public space since it was drained and paved in the 7th and 6th centuries BC. A living museum of Roman history and legend, it was bounded on its short (east and west) sides by speakers' platforms, called *rostra* from the ships' rams (or "beaks" – *rostra*) that adorned them. The more ancient was the western Rostra in front of the Senate House, rebuilt by Julius Caesar and adorned with the rams captured in battle against Rome's Latin neighbors at Anzio in 338 BC; the one fronting the temple of the Deified Julius Caesar to the east sprouted rams from the fleet of Marc Antony and Cleopatra, taken at Actium in 31 BC. The Senate House itself, the Curia Senatus, was rebuilt in its current location by Julius Caesar and grandly reconstructed after the fire of AD 283. It adjoined the Atrium of Minerva (*atrium Minervae*), a portico where senators strolled under the gaze of venerable statues. More statues clustered in front of the Curia, among them the personified spirit (*genius*) of the Roman people and a golden equestrian statue of Emperor Constantine. Overtopping the western Rostra from behind was the temple of Concord – an elusive quality when it was rebuilt in 121 BC after the murder of Gaius Gracchus – and the adjacent temple of the deified Vespasian. Between the Temple of Vespasian and the Rostra, the

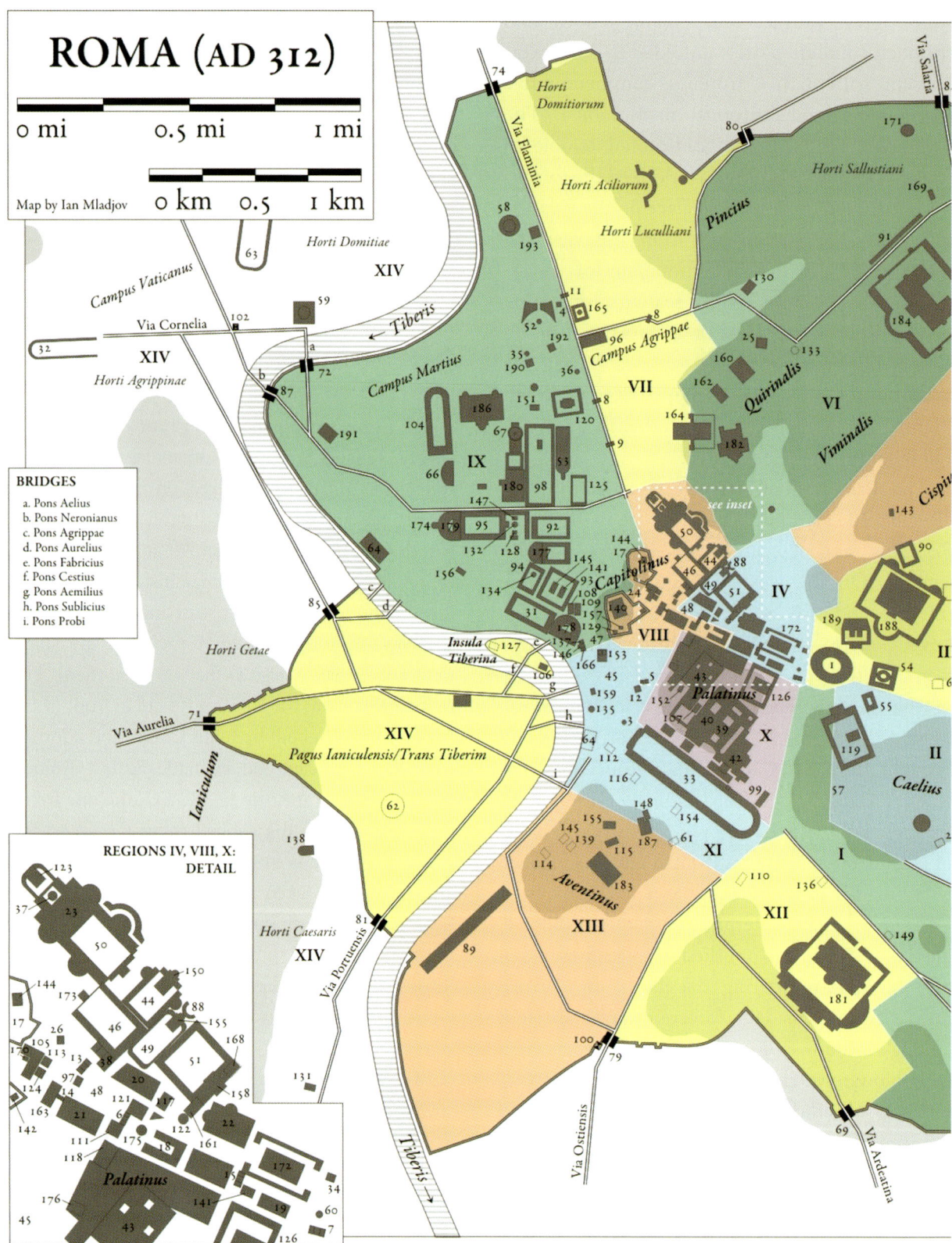

Figure 1.1 Rome in the 4th century: the fourteen Augustan regions and major features. (Map courtesy of Ian Mladjov.)

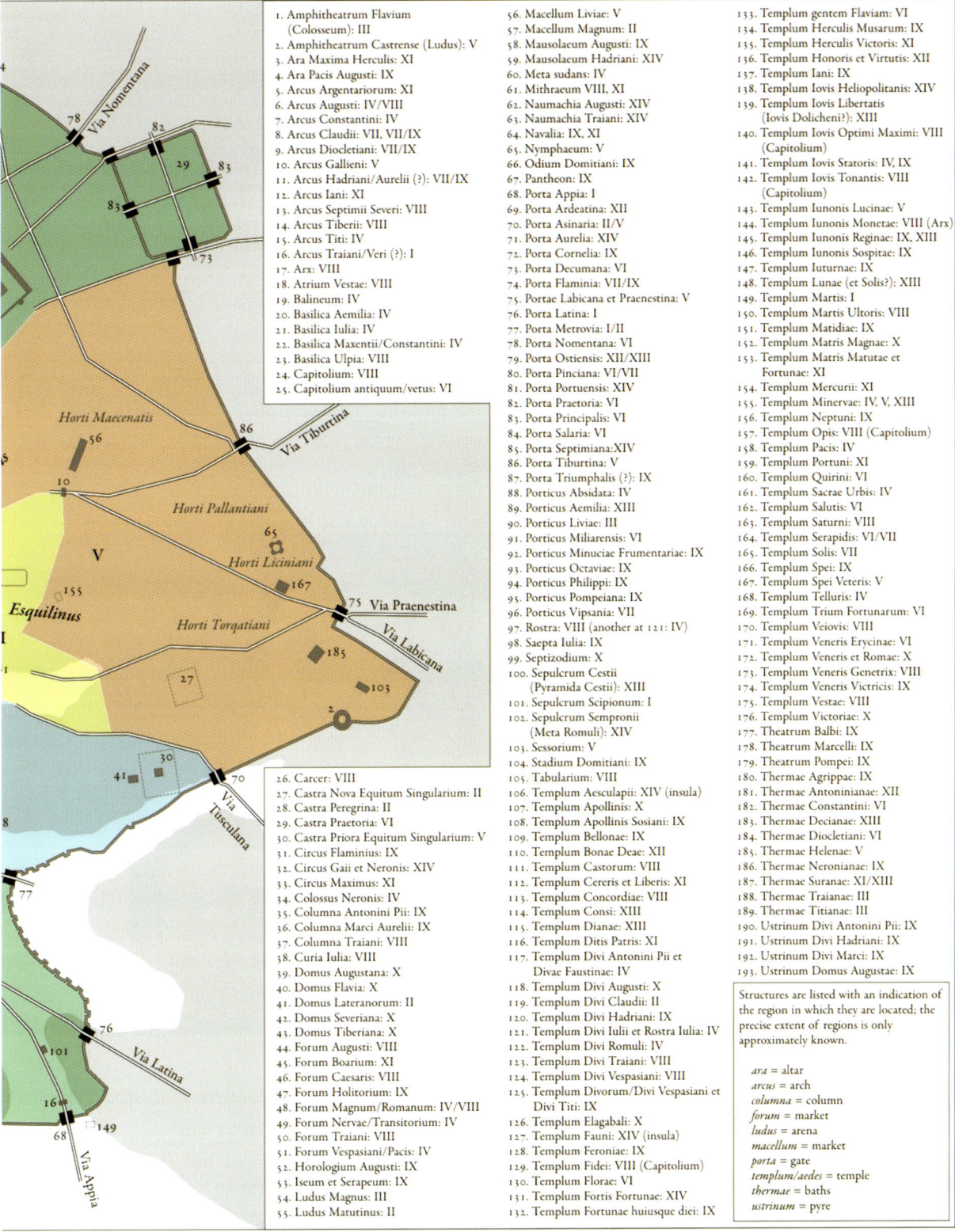

Figure 1.1 (cont.) (Map courtesy of Ian Mladjov.)

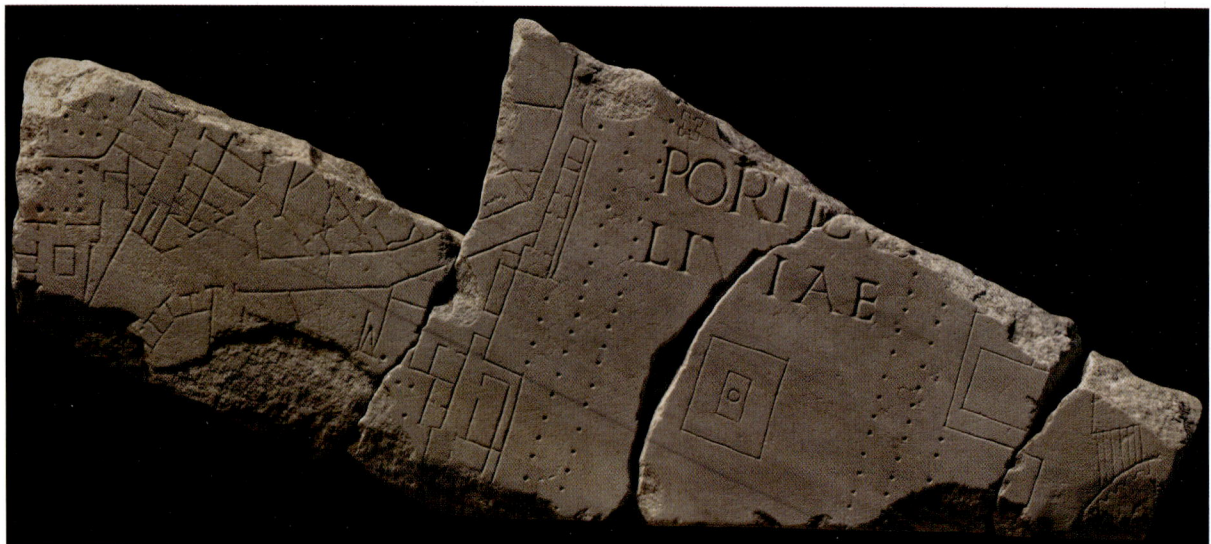

Figure 1.2 Fragments of the Severan marble plan showing the Porticus Liviae on the Esquiline. (Roma, Musei Capitolini, Antiquarium;© Roma, Sovrintendenza Capitolina ai Beni Culturali.)

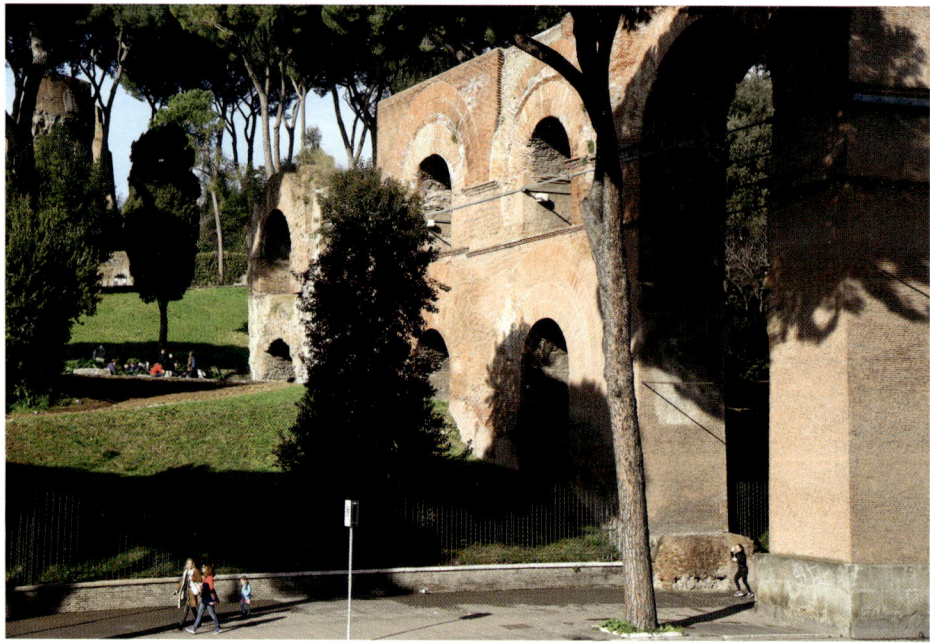

Figure 1.3 The Aqua Claudia at the foot of the Palatine Hill. (Author.)

"golden mile-marker" (*miliarium aureum*) listed distances to the far corners of the empire along all the roads that led to Rome: Fifteen major highways, paved with nearly indestructible blocks of volcanic stone and wide enough for two carts to pass abreast, radiated out from the metropolis, connecting the sole of the Italian boot to the shores of the English Channel and the Black Sea. High above on the crest of the Capitoline, the football-field-sized Temple of Jupiter Optimus Maximus (the Capitol) loomed over the western end of the Forum on a high podium built before 500 BC, its scintillating gilded roof tiles visible for miles around.[4]

The long south side of the Forum plaza was dominated by the very ancient Temple of Saturn on its high podium, lovingly restored by a pagan urban prefect in the 360s, at a time when Christian emperors were already abrogating the practice of traditional religion. Next came Caesar's Basilica Julia, a cathedral-sized hall with a cavernous nave flanked by statue-filled marble colonnades opening onto the plaza; and then the temple of Castor and Pollux, vowed after the Roman victory at Lake Regillus in 496 BC. Beyond was the little round temple of Vesta, goddess of hearth and household, whose eternal flame had burned for more than a thousand years under the care of a college of virgin priestesses, until the Christian emperor Theodosius extinguished it in 394. The temple still stood, like the rest of the pagan shrines in the Show Area, but its interior was dark, its doors locked, its college of priestesses dissolved (Fig. 1.4).[5]

Across the Forum plaza to the north, technically falling into Region 4: "Temple of Peace," the Senate House was flanked by the Basilica Aemilia, a close relative of the Basilica Julia, rebuilt many times since its founding in 179 BC, the last time after the fire of 283. Then came the Temple of the Divine Antoninus Pius (r. 138–61) and his wife, Faustina, perched on a high podium with six Corinthian columns across the façade. Continuing farther east along the Via Sacra, the main road leading from the Forum toward the Colosseum, still grander monuments loomed, starting with the *basilica nova*, the "new basilica" built by Maxentius (r. 306–12) but rededicated in the name of his conqueror, Constantine; the largest building in the immediate vicinity of the Forum, the concrete vaults of its central nave were 25 m across and soared 39 m above its marble floor (Fig. 1.5). Next came the *templum Romae*, the Temple of Venus and Rome built by Hadrian and rebuilt by Maxentius (r. 306–12). Its back-to-back cellas, one for each goddess, topped a high concrete platform, practically a forum in its own right, that bridged the slope between the Forum and the Colosseum.

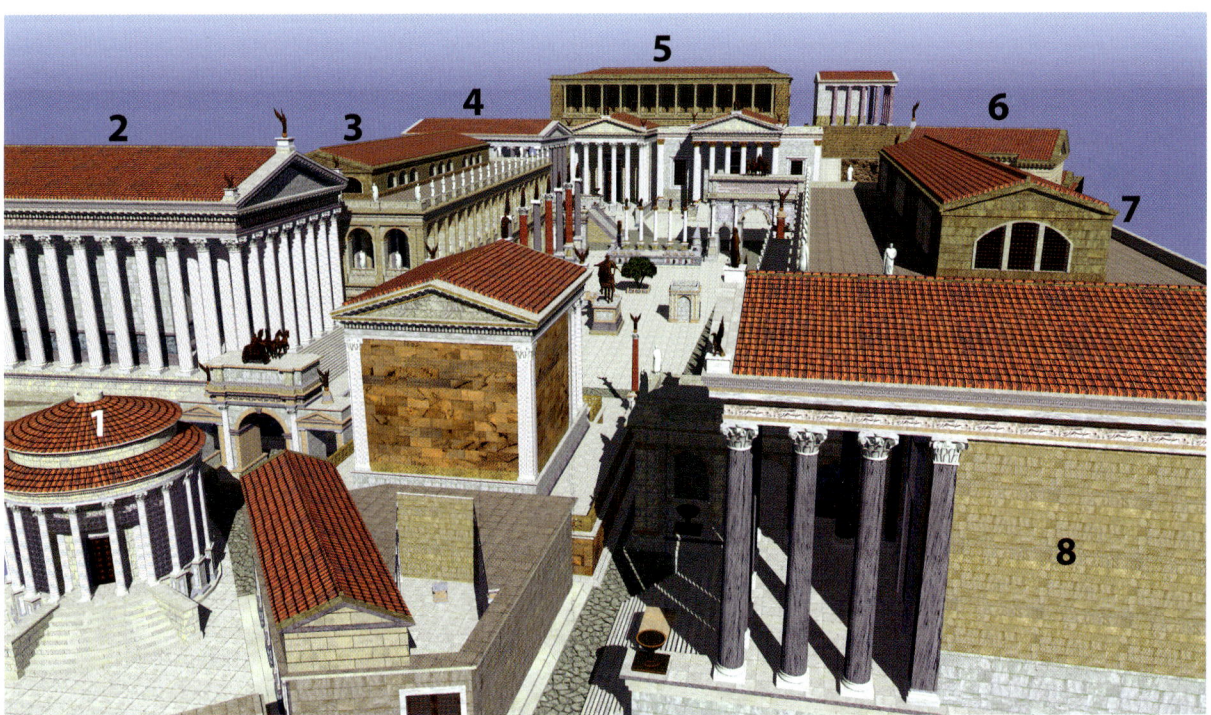

Figure 1.4 3D model of the Forum Romanum in the 4th century (compare with plan at Fig. 1.6). 1: Temple of Vesta; 2: Temple of Castor and Pollux; 3: Basilica Julia; 4: Temple of Saturn; 5: "Tabularium"; 6: Senate House; 7: Basilica Aemilia; 8: Temple of Antoninus and Faustina. (Wikimedia Commons/Lasha Tskhondia.)

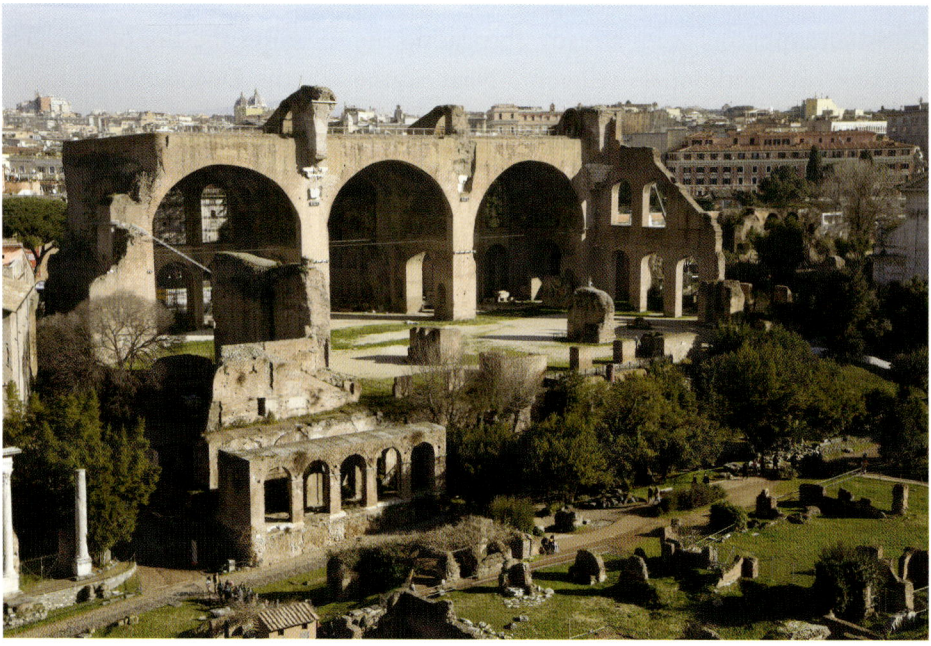

Figure 1.5 The lower, north aisle of the Basilica of Maxentius. Note the springing of the concrete vaults of the higher, central nave. (Author.)

Beyond was the biggest statue in Rome, the colossus erected by Nero in the image of himself, remodeled as the Sun after his death and repositioned – with a team of 24 elephants – adjacent to the Colosseum, which took its popular name from the colossal statue: "102 feet high," according to the *Curiosum*, "it has on its head seven [solar] rays, each one 22.5 feet long."[6]

North of the Forum and the Capitoline Hill, divided between Regions 4 and 8, stretched the newer forums built by Rome's early emperors (Fig. 1.6). The first, moving from west to east, was the complex built by Vespasian that gave Region 4 its name: a paved esplanade overlooked on its eastern flank by the "Temple of Peace" and surrounded by covered colonnades filled with statues attributed to famous Greek masters. Spoils from the sack of Jerusalem in AD 70 paid for the project; the gigantic golden menorah from the Second Temple was among the priceless trophies displayed here. Adjoining it to the west was the Forum of Nerva, also known as the *forum transitorium*, a narrow rectangle flanked by stately colonnades that connected the Forum with the heaving slums of the *Subura*, the neighborhood of densely packed tenements that climbed the slopes of the Quirinal and Esquiline hills. Then came the two forums built by Julius Caesar and Augustus, both colonnaded, rectangular enclosures with temples of Venus the Begetter (*genetrix*) and Mars the Avenger (*ultor*), respectively, at one end. One portico of Caesar's forum hosted the *basilica argentaria*, seat of Rome's silversmiths and silver merchants; the colonnades of Augustus' forum were packed with statues, Rome's legendary founders and heroes on one side and Augustus' family and ancestors on the other – Rome's new heroes and founders. An "apsidal portico" (*porticus absidata*) at the junction of the forums of Vespasian, Nerva, and Augustus marked the threshold between the glittering majesty of these public spaces and the chaos of the Subura just beyond; horseshoe-shaped and two stories high, it funneled traffic through the massive stone barrier built to block out the noises and smells of the slums and protect against the frequent fires that broke out there. Last came the Forum of Trajan, the largest and most spectacular of all. Here was the Temple of the Deified Trajan, its porch sustained by monolithic granite columns

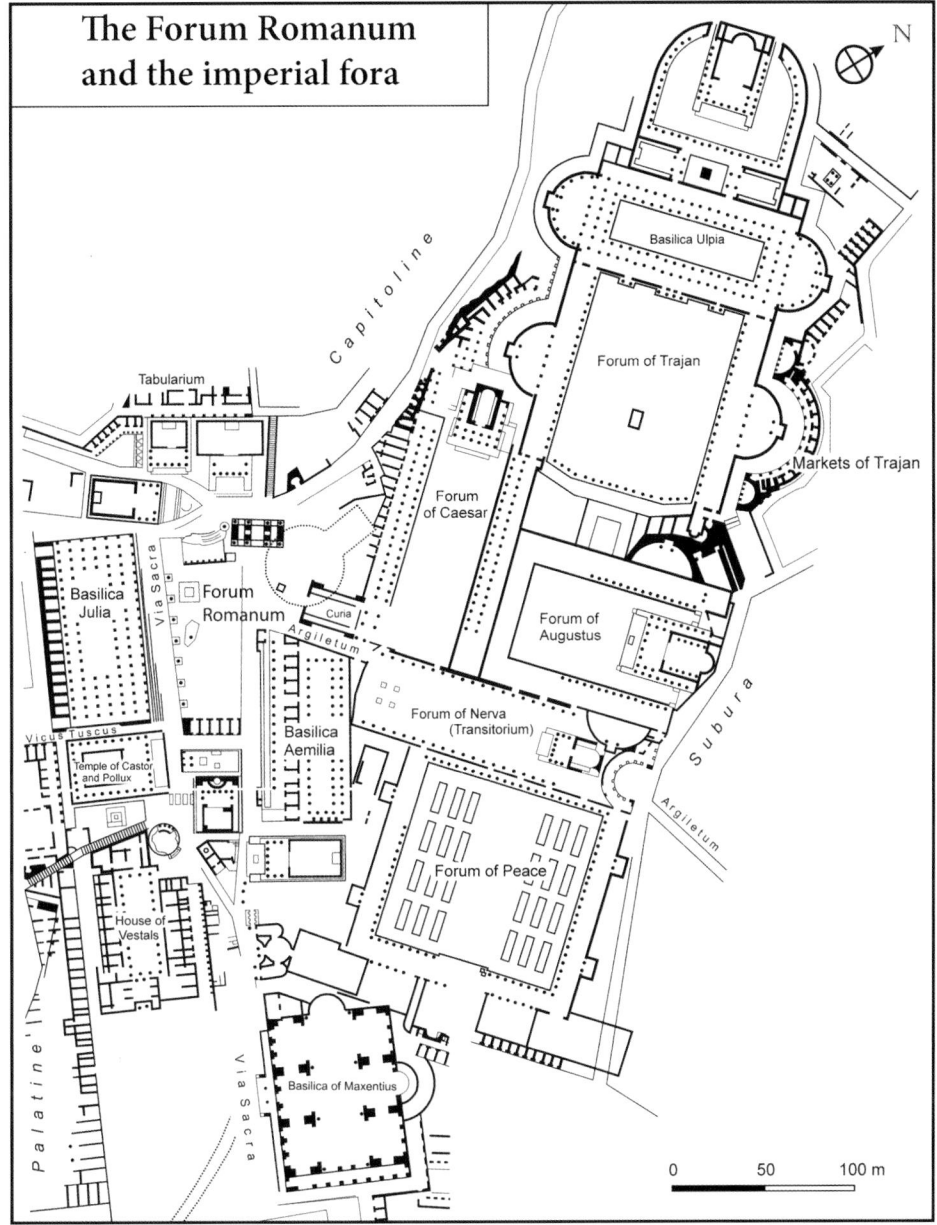

Figure 1.6 The Forum Romanum and the imperial fora (*regiones* IV and VIII). (Russell 2014, fig. 1, drawing by Joseph Skinner, adapted by Amy Russell.)

50 feet tall, each weighing over 100 tons. It fronted Trajan's column, the "spiral column 127.5 feet high with inside it 180 stairs and 45 windows," wrapped in a helical frieze depicting Trajan's Dacian wars that would stretch nearly 200 m if unwrapped and laid out flat. Behind it loomed the soaring Basilica Ulpia, the largest basilica in the city at c. 170 m long (including its two apses) by 60 m wide.[7]

The other region where monumental architecture sprouted thickest was the ninth: *Circus Flaminius*, which bordered the Show Area to the northwest. It encompassed all of the Campus Martius, the low-lying floodplain stretching across the cup-handle-shaped bend in the Tiber as far as the Capitoline Hill and the Via Lata, Rome's main northbound highway. The region took its name from the old racetrack by the Tiber at its southern extremity, just upstream of which were the "four stables of the six [circus] factions," the color-coded chariot teams that raced in the Circus Maximus. Julius Caesar encroached on the Circus Flaminius with the vast stone theater he began building, Rome's second after the one erected by his bitter rival, Pompey the Great, to celebrate his eastern triumph in 61 BC; Caesar's was finished under Augustus and named after the latter's nephew, Marcellus. After Pompey and Caesar, succeeding emperors and a few privileged collaborators filled the previously undeveloped plain with other sprawling vanity projects meant to enthrall the masses. Augustus' general, Balbus, added a third theater between those of Marcellus and Pompey, and emperor Domitian (r. 81–96) put the finishing touches on the city's theater district with the stadium that underlies today's Piazza Navona and an indoor theater, the Odeum. According to the Regionary Catalogues, "[the theater] of Balbus has 11,510 seats; that of Pompey has 17,580; that of Marcellus has 20,000; the Odeon holds 10,600. The stadium [of Domitian] holds 30,088." Rome's oldest palatial public baths were here, too, built by Augustus' henchman, Marcus Agrippa, and fed by a newly built aqueduct, the Aqua Virgo, which later supplied the even more opulent baths built by Nero and remodeled under Alexander Severus (r. 222–35).

Much of the rest of the Campus Martius was occupied by gigantic quadriporticoes, rectangular enclosures surrounded by covered colonnades. The theaters of Pompey, Balbus, and Marcellus all faced onto such enclosures, filled with paved promenades, statues, lush groves, and gardens watered by aqueduct. Along the northern flank of the Circus Flaminius, fronting the ancient Triumphal Way, there was the *porticus Philippi*, rebuilt by Augustus' stepbrother, L. Marcius Philippus, and the Porticus Octaviae, reconstructed around the same time and named for Augustus' sister, both enclosing venerable temples. Northward lay an even larger quadriportico (c. 145 by 115 m), the *Minucia vetus et frumentaria*, where until the 3rd century AD, some 200,000 Roman citizens entitled to a free grain ration had queued monthly, ration cards in hand, at forty-four windows. Nearby was the Saepta Julia, a huge rectangular enclosure surrounded by porticoes, begun by Julius Caesar on the site where citizens of the republic had gathered in their tribes to vote and be counted; completed under Agrippa, its long sides were called the "Portico of the Argonauts," for its frescoes of the mythological heroes, and the "Portico of Meleager," legendary killer of the Calydonian Boar and companion of the Argonauts on their quest for the Golden Fleece. Adjacent was yet another sprawling portico, the *Divorum*, built by Domitian in honor of his deified father and brother, Vespasian and Titus (Fig. 1.7).[8]

Sprinkled throughout were other marvels. There was the Pantheon with the world's largest concrete dome, 144 Roman feet (c. 43.5 m) across and constellated with gilded stars on a ground of midnight blue, a miniature cosmos unto itself. Its pendant was the imperial mausoleum that Augustus built facing it over a kilometer to the north, an even larger circular structure tapering upwards from a base 87 m in diameter. There was the *insula Felicles*, an apartment building (*insula*, or "island") so high even the African writer Tertullian knew of it. There was the double temple of Isis and Serapis, another of Minerva Chalcidica, and, overlooking the Via Lata to the east, temples for the deified Hadrian and Marcus Aurelius, the latter fronted by the twin of the spiral column in Trajan's forum, its helical sculptured frieze depicting Marcus Aurelius' bitter struggle against the Marcomanni on the Danube frontier: "175-and-a-half feet in height, it has 203 stairs inside, and 56 windows." Along the fetid and flood-prone riverbanks to the west, all this splendor was lapped by rougher and more utilitarian marvels such as the *ciconiae nixae*, "the perching storks,"

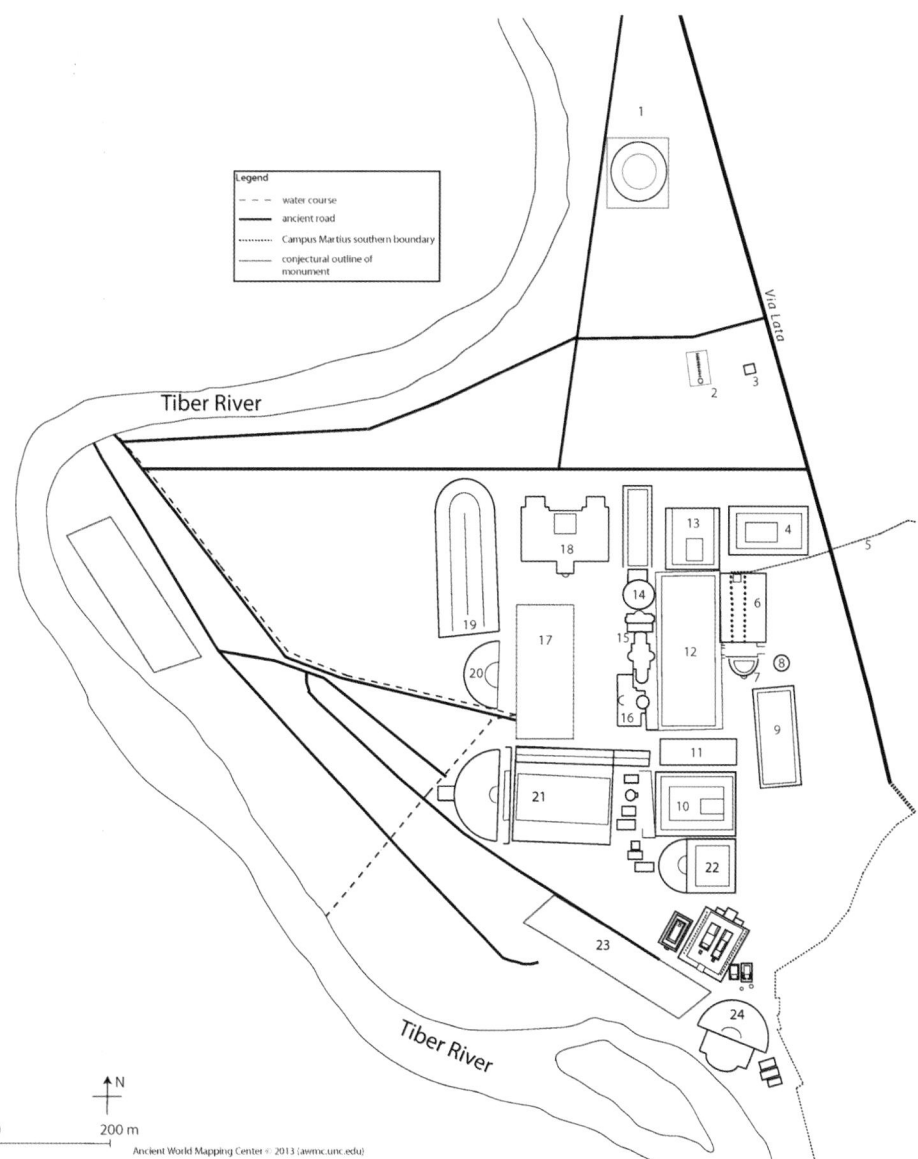

Figure 1.7 Plan of the Campus Martius. 1: Mausoleum of Augustus; 2: Horologium; 3: Ara Pacis; 4: Temple of Divine Hadrian; 5: Aqua Virgo; 6–7: Temples of Serapis and Isis; 8: Temple of Minerva Chalcidica; 9: Porticus Divorum; 10: Porticus Minucia Frumentaria; 11: Diribitorium; 12: Saepta Julia; 13: Temple of the Divine Matidia; 14: Pantheon; 15: Basilica of Neptune; 16: Baths of Agrippa; 17: Stagnum Agrippae; 18: Baths of Nero/Alexander Severus; 19: Stadium of Domitian; 20: Odeum of Domitian; 21: Theater of Pompey; 22: Theater of Balbus; 23: Circus Flaminius; 24: Theater of Marcellus. (Courtesy of the UNC Ancient World Mapping Center.)

a riverside quay studded with cranes used to unload barrels of wine from vast imperial estates upriver in northern Latium and Umbria that were distributed to the Roman plebs at subsidized rates.[9]

The heart of commercial Rome lay further south, however, where river traffic hauled upriver from Rome's ports at Ostia and Portus entered the city. Rome's earliest ports and markets were in Region 11: *Circus Maximus*, which included the riverbank and adjacent floodplain between the Capitoline and Aventine Hills. Here was the Ripa Graeca, the "riverbank of the Greeks," a neighborhood long distinguished by its communities of foreign merchants, and the Forum Boarium (Cattle Market) and Forum Holitorium (Vegetable Market), where warehouses and vendors' stalls jostled with temples and public buildings situated to greet those arriving by water: the Great Altar of Hercules; the round temple of Hercules, built in Pentelic marble from Attica, and the temple of Portunus, god of ports, both of which survive; the three closely packed temples now incorporated into the medieval church of S. Nicola in Carcere. Toward the Circus Maximus in the neighborhood called the *Velabrum* stood the *arcus Constantini*, a four-faced marble archway erected by Constantine athwart a crossroads, sheathed in white marble and pierced with ninety-six niches for sculpture. The rest of the region was dominated by the very ancient Circus Maximus, the chariot racing stadium situated at the foot of the imperial palace in the valley between the Palatine and Aventine hills. The largest spectacle building in the ancient world, by the 2nd century AD it had been expanded to hold perhaps 150,000 spectators.[10]

In the adjacent Region 13: *Aventinus*, docks and warehouses stretched south along the riverbank from the Aventine Hill to Monte Testaccio and beyond. Monte Testaccio is an artificial mountain composed entirely of broken pottery, the discarded remnants of the amphorae in which hundreds of millions of gallons of wine and olive oil arrived in the city between the 1st and 3rd centuries AD from as far afield as Spain and North Africa (Fig. 1.8). North of the hill stretched hypermarket-sized warehouses: the *Horrea Galbes et Aniciana*, the *Porticus Fabarius*, and, vastest of all, the Porticus Aemilia, or Emporium, a rectangle nearly 500 m long built entirely of fire-resistant concrete in the 2nd century BC. A kilometer and more of quays reconstructed under Trajan lined the banks of the river, from the Aventine on south beyond the perimeter of the Aurelian Wall. A half-day's downstream journey at the mouth of the Tiber, the largest artificial harbor built anywhere in the world until the modern era – a hexagonal basin of brick-faced concrete over 700 m across – received the ships that supplied the Romans with foodstuffs and commodities from every corner of the Mediterranean basin and beyond, as far as China and India. Nothing more powerfully captures the scale of the effort required to feed the population of imperial Rome.[11]

The docks and warehouses of Regions 11 and 13 continued across the river in Region 14: *Transtiberim*, today's Trastevere. The largest region by far, it stretched from the Vatican in the north to the riverbank facing the Emporium in the south, and inland as far as the summit of the Janiculum Hill. Much of it was open space: gardens such as those named for Geta, the murdered son of Septimius Severus, and fields for fairs and markets like the *campus Bruttianus et Codetanus*. Here too were both of Rome's aquatic arenas for naval battles, one north of Castel Sant'Angelo, fed by the waters of the Tiber, and the second far to the south at the terminus of the Aqua Alsietina, near today's Piazza San Cosimato. Atop the Janiculum were cascading sequences of water mills powered by Trajan's aqueduct, the Aqua Traiana, where the city's grain was milled before being baked into loaves and handed out to Roman citizens at hundreds of distribution points. In the floodplain below were the barracks of the seventh cohort of Rome's urban watchmen (the *vigiles*; there were seven cohorts in total, each staffed by 1,000 freedmen), and the *castra lecticariorum*, home of the paramilitary corporation of litter-bearers who muscled emperors and other VIPs through Rome's packed streets. Tanners plied their reeking trade along the riverbank at the *coraria Septimiana*, not far from residences and shops, and temples with mass appeal: here one to Hercules, patron of merchants and travelers, with a famous statue of the reclining god; there another to Fors Fortuna, the goddess of lucky chance, revered for her promise of rags-to-riches transformations.[12]

This cluster of contiguous regions held the bulk of Rome's grand public spaces, monumental

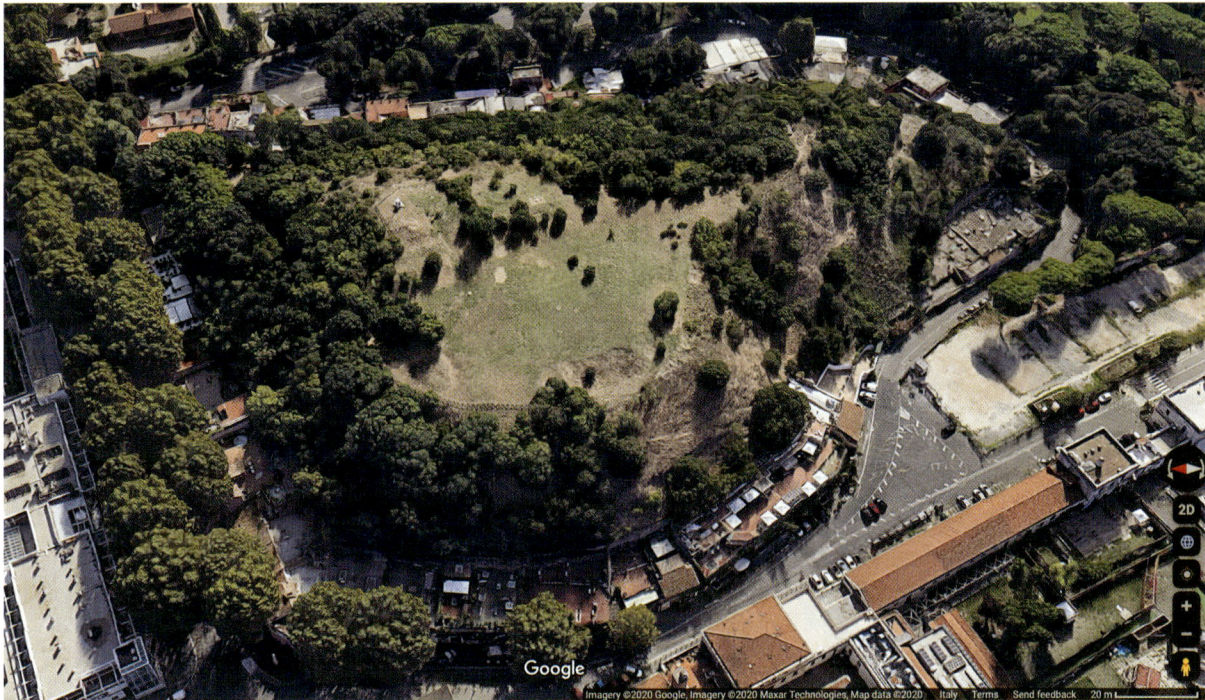

Figure 1.8 Satellite view of Monte Testaccio. (Google Maps.)

architecture, and commercial activity; as they also comprised the core of the city by the later Middle Ages, they will feature especially prominently hereafter. But they collectively represent less than half of the area enclosed by the Aurelian Wall. The urban core on the left bank of the Tiber was surrounded on all sides by an extensive "greenbelt" (Krautheimer's term) that traversed a wide arc of mostly high ground, sweeping clockwise from the Pincian Hill in the far north across the Quirinal, Esquiline, and Oppian Hills to the "Little Aventine" in the south. Less densely occupied than the rest, the remaining regions nonetheless contained many smaller cities' worth of monuments, infrastructure, and housing.[13]

The relatively central and built-up Regions 2 and 3 extended east from the Show Area across the crowns of the Caelian and Oppian Hills. Here, the Colosseum towered over everything. The amphitheater was surrounded by a constellation of service buildings linked to Rome's premier venue for blood sport. There were the four gladiatorial training schools established by Domitian: the partially extant *Ludus Magnus* with its 1:2.5 scale model of the Colosseum's oval arena, to which it connected via an underground passageway (Fig. 1.9); the "dawn school" (*ludus matutinus*) for the hunters of wild beasts, featured in early-morning shows; and the *ludus Dacicus* and *ludus Gallicus* for gladiators – named for the Dacian and Gallic prisoners who first occupied them. Nearby were the *spoliarium*, where dead gladiators were stripped of their arms and armor; the *saniarium*, where those that might be salvaged to fight again were treated; the *summum choragum* for the stage sets, tools, machines, and costumes needed for the spectacles staged in the arena; and the *Castra Misenatium*, the barracks for sailors detached from the fleet based at Cape Misenum near Naples, who manned the Colosseum's retractable awnings, or "sails" (*vela*), and helped choreograph the aquatic spectacles and naval battles once staged there.[14]

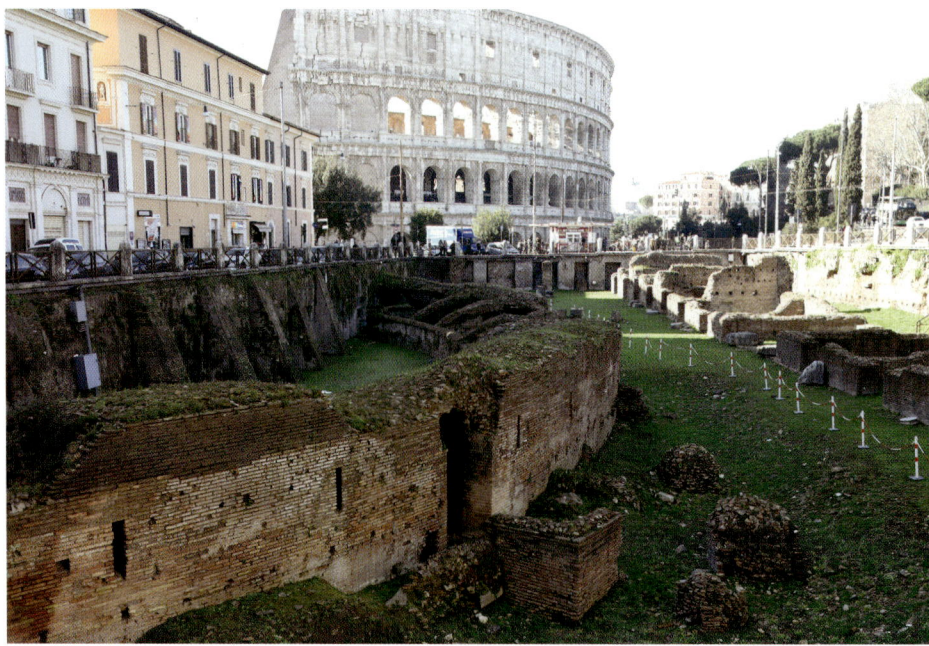

Figure 1.9 The excavated half of the arena (left) and barracks (right) of the Ludus Magnus, looking toward the Colosseum. (Author.)

Just south of the Colosseum on the Caelian was the Claudianum, the temple of the deified emperor Claudius (r. 41–54), built atop a gigantic rectangular platform larger in area than the Colosseum. Begun by Claudius' wife and possible murderer, Agrippina, incorporated by her son Nero (r. 54–68) into his extravagant palace, the "Golden House," and completed by Vespasian (r. 69–79), the surviving platform is an artificial mountain of brick-faced concrete rising over 15 m high in places. Its perimeter walls, measuring approximately 200 by 180 m, were Rome's hugest fountain, marble clad and pierced by alternating semicircular and quadrangular niches streaming with water supplied by Claudius' aqueduct, the Aqua Claudia. Just north of the Colosseum, on the Oppian Hill, loomed the Baths of Titus and, practically on top of them, the far larger Baths of Trajan. Constructed in brick-faced concrete at the beginning of the 2nd century AD, over parts of Nero's Golden House, Trajan's were the first of Rome's mega-baths, designed to cater to many thousands every day. Measuring over 300 m in length and width, they covered 10 hectares (almost 25 acres) of the hill in manicured gardens, libraries, gymnasiums; hot, warm, and cold plunge baths; and an over-Olympic-sized swimming pool (Fig. 1.10).[15]

Farther away from the city center on the summit of the Caelian, whorehouses (*luparii*) dotted the alleyways near the *macellum magnum*, the "great market" built under Nero; the barracks of the fifth cohort of *vigiles*; and the *castra Peregrina*, where visiting military detachments were quartered. As in so much of central Rome, grandeur and squalor, public and private, temples and fleshpots promiscuously intermingled. Along busy streets, the "African head" (*caput Africae*) leading to Porta Metronia and the Via Caelemontana to Porta Maggiore, shops and tenements jostled against senatorial mansions like the *domus Philippi* and the *domus Victiliana*: sprawling compounds with banqueting halls, reception rooms, and porticoes clad in exotic marbles, manicured gardens, fountains and pools brimming with running water channeled from the Aqua Claudia.[16]

The Greenbelt proper began in the north with Region 7: *Via Lata*, named for Rome's "Broadway," the urban tract of the Via Flaminia, today's Via del

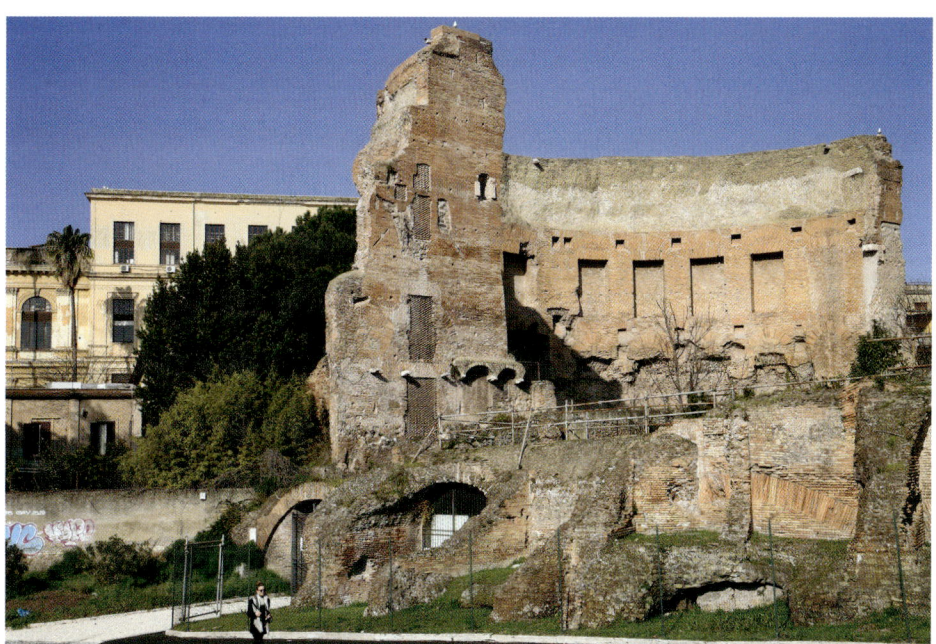

Figure 1.10 Baths of Trajan, exedra at the SW corner of the outer perimeter, by Via delle Terme di Tito. (Author.)

Corso. Its northern half encompassed the shady heights of the Pincian Hill, with its acres of manicured garden-estates named for owners long past: the Horti Domitiorum, the Horti Aciliorum, the Horti Luculliani… . Below, on the strip of low ground west of the Via Lata, imperial monuments overflowed from the Campus Martius across the way. The crowning monument rose from the *campus Agrippae*, the "field of Agrippa," which Augustus made into public gardens after Agrippa's death in 12 BC. Mostly undeveloped until the later 3rd century, Aurelian (r. 270–5) transformed it into an imperial showpiece to rival Trajan's forum. Its centerpiece was the temple dedicated to the Sun (*templum Solis*), Aurelian's special divine patron. One of the largest temples ever built in Rome, it was accessed from the Via Lata via two axially aligned quadriporticoes, each a forum in its own right; one of them served as Rome's principal wine market. Nearby was the pig market, the *forum suarium*, also rebuilt by Aurelian, along with the barracks of the first cohort of *vigiles*.[17]

Still more of Regions 6, 5, 1, and 12 (continuing east and south in clockwise order) was composed of imperial and senatorial estates and gardens: of Sallust, of Maecenas, of Pallas, of Torquatus. Here, opulent mansions in the guise of rural villas nestled among fountains and water-features, tableaux of statues, scenic shrines and sundry architectural caprices set among manicured fields and groves. Much of this land had entered the imperial domain over the centuries through bequests and confiscations alike: Emperor Honorius (r. 395–423) preferred to reside in a palace on the Pincian during his Roman visits, while Emperor Constantine's mother, Helena, dwelled in the Sessorian Palace just inside the walls in the far east of the city, near another imperial property where Constantine established the Lateran Cathedral. Most of Rome's aqueducts entered through the eastern greenbelt, supplying a congeries of building-sized fountains and waterworks. (Rome had a total of eleven aqueducts that branched into nineteen main lines, carrying spring water from sources dozens of miles away atop endlessly receding

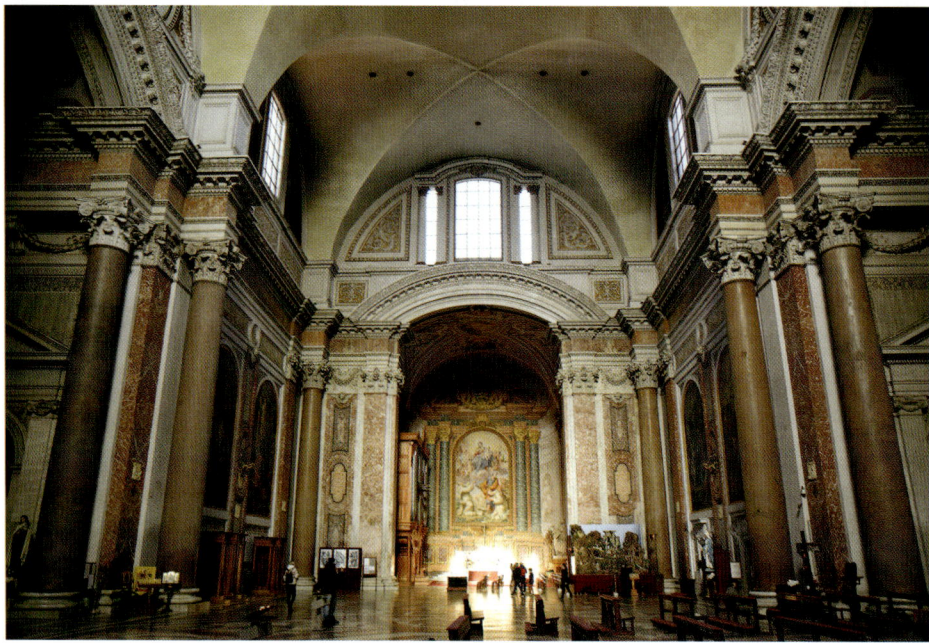

Figure 1.11 S. Maria degli Angeli: note the size of the adult humans relative to the columns! (Author.)

chains of stone and concrete arches to distribution tanks scattered across the city.) Region 1 included the over-Trevi-sized fountain of the *Camenae* and the "Pool of Prometheus"; Region 5 the "Lake of Orpheus" at today's Piazza San Martino ai Monti, with three circular collecting pools fronting a columnar façade, and the *nymfeum Alexandri* whose remains still tower over Piazza Vittorio Emanuele near Termini Station. Here also were the two hugest public baths of all. The Baths of Caracalla in the south (in Region 12), begun in the 210s, were supplied with water by a new, purpose-built aqueduct branch, the Aqua Antoniniana. They were carpeted in acres of mosaics and filled with colossal statues, among them those renowned since their rediscovery during the Renaissance as the "Farnese Hercules" and the "Farnese Bull." Northward in Region 6, looming high above the Horti Sallustiani, the Baths of Diocletian became the largest in the world when they were completed around 305. An entire neighborhood was razed to make way for the compound, which measured some 356 by 316 m and covered more than 11 hectares, or 28 acres. The swimming pool survives as the church of S. Maria degli Angeli, its concrete vaults still supported by monolithic columns of Egyptian granite so high that, as the Englishman Master Gregory noted around the year 1200, it was impossible to throw a stone at their capitals (Fig. 1.11).[18]

The Regionary Catalogues conclude with a still more condensed list of cumulative figures for the whole city. "28 libraries," the *Curiosum* begins. "6 obelisks, two in the Circus Maximus, the smaller 87-and-a-half feet tall, the larger 122-and-a-half. One at the Vatican 75 feet tall. In the Campus Martius one 72 and-a-half feet tall. 2 on the mausoleum of Augustus, each 42-and-a-half feet tall. 8 bridges … 7 Hills … 8 open esplanades (*campi*) … 11 forums … 10 Basilicas … 11 public baths … 19 aqueducts … 29 highways." Then, under a new heading, *breviarium* ("summary"): "2 capitols. 2 circuses. 2 amphitheaters. 2 colossal statues. 2 spiral columns. 2 meat-markets. 3 theaters. 4 training-arenas. 2 water-battle arenas. 15 monumental fountains (*nymfea*). 22 great equestrian statues. 80 golden gods; 79 ivory ones. 36 marble arches. 37 city-gates. 423 neighborhoods (*vici*). 423 neighborhood shrines. 672

neighborhood-supervisors (*vicomagistri*). 28 regional supervisors. 46,602 separate properties (*insulae*) throughout the whole city. 1790 private mansions. 290 warehouses. 856 private baths. 1352 fountains. 254 bakeries. 46 whorehouses. 144 public latrines. 10 praetorian cohorts; 4 urban; 7 of *vigiles*, divided into 14 detachments. 2 community banners (*vexilla communia*, whatever that means). Barracks of the horse-guards; of the foreign units; of the Ravenna fleet; of the litter-bearers; of the road-repair crews; of the Misenum fleet; of the postal service; of the sacrificial attendants. 2300 olive-oil distribution-points throughout the whole city."[19]

And on that rather anticlimactic note, the *Curiosum* and *Notitia* close. Their compilers faced the intractable questions familiar to anyone who has tried to describe Rome: Where to begin? Where to end? What to include and what to omit? In their dogged attempt to quantify the city, to break it down into manageable lists of facts and figures, they remind us of how unquantifiable it really was. What the Catalogs in fact succeed best in evoking – or mirroring – is the chaotic immensity of 4th-century Rome: its jumble of buildings and monuments, spaces and places and names, with all the myths and legends, histories and memories encoded therein. It had all accumulated willy-nilly over the better part of a millennium, shaped by numberless contingencies: largely unregulated private building activity, the whims of emperors and other fabulously wealthy and powerful individuals, laws and building codes, natural topography, chance, entropy, and so on.[20]

There were no strict zoning restrictions in the modern sense. Commercial and residential, public and private were all entangled. Residences permeated every region of the city and lapped right up to the center of the Show Area. Alongside the palatial *domus* with their fountains and colonnaded courtyards, their statues and imported marbles and polychrome mosaics, there were the *insulae* where most Romans lived: densely packed apartment buildings built of brick-faced concrete that were commonly five or six stories high, but might reach ten or more. Noisy, smelly, overcrowded, and fire-prone to be sure, many were as outwardly imposing as the *hôtels* of Haussmann's Paris or the residential *palazzi* of *Risorgimento* Rome. According to the Regionary Catalogues, every region was replete with both *domus* and *insulae*. Even in relatively exclusive neighborhoods atop the hills and in the more popular quarters of Trastevere and the Subura, rich and poor, great and small mixed. So too did the numinous and the mundane: Every region boasted whole pantheons' worth of temples and shrines, many with roots going back a half-millennium and more, housing deities sprung from all the territories known to Rome. Persian Mithras, Egyptian Isis and Serapis, Greek Asclepius mingled with Latin Salus, Flora, and Quirinus; with Jupiter, Juno, Minerva, Mars, the "Good Goddess beneath the rock," and countless others, plus a host of shrines dedicated to deified emperors and their dynasties.[21]

But while the Regionary Catalogues list all of the abovementioned temples and shrines to traditional deities, and dozens of others besides, there is not a word about any of the Christian churches built since Constantine took Rome in 312. The great (pagan) historian Ammianus Marcellinus, writing c. 390, likewise managed to recount the (Christian) emperor Constantius II's tour of Rome in 357 without once mentioning a Christian church. For those who wished to ignore visible signs of the Church's presence, Rome at the turn of the 5th century could be envisioned and described as though nothing at all had changed during the past century.[22]

Most of the monumental edifices built in 4th-century Rome, however, were Christian churches. To complete our inventory of the ancient metropolis on the eve of the 5th century, then, we turn to the Roman Church and its churches, which accounted for the most significant additions to the cityscape in the decades leading up to 400. In Rome and across the empire, Christians were a persecuted minority at the dawn of the 4th century. By century's end, they were a persecuting majority (or plurality) backed by the full weight of the imperial establishment, thanks in no small part to Constantine's early and energetic support for the faith from 312 until his death in 337. His descendants and successors, all Christians with the exception of the short-reigning "apostate" Julian (r. 361–3), continued to lavish resources and institutional support on the Church. The pace of conversion to Christianity consequently accelerated over the course of the 4th century, and purpose-built and often very grand churches began to supplant humble, mostly invisible house-churches in cities across the empire. But the empire-wide social and institutional ascendency of Christianity was slow to transform urban topography in Rome, where influential members of conservative senatorial families resisted conversion throughout the 4th century. A final paroxysm of local resistance to the Christian imperial establishment came in 392–4, when most of the Senate supported the pagan (or at best very lukewarm Christian) senator Eugenius, a champion of traditional and Roman values, in his attempt to overthrow the fanatically Christian Theodosius I (r. 379–95), who in 391 had issued the most sweeping prohibition yet on all public practice of pagan ritual. Reprisals following Theodosius' crushing victory over Eugenius' army, in 394, were swift. Prominent Roman supporters of Eugenius lost their lands and titles, and sometimes their lives. Those who remained found it politic, sooner or later, to embrace the new faith.[23]

Yet Rome's panoply of temples remained, preserved by imperial decree as "civic adornments." The city continued to look much as it had a century earlier – "through the 4th century, Rome remained to visitors, unless they came to pray at the Christian sanctuaries, an essentially classical, secular, and pagan city," as Krautheimer put it. In the monumental heart of the city, from the Colosseum in the east to the Capitol in the west, from the Circus Maximus in the south across the Palatine and the Forum Romanum to the imperial forums in the north, there was not a single church or other conspicuous physical trace of Christianity to be found, though two churches nibbled at the far western edge of the Show Area: S. Marco at today's Piazza Venezia, founded by Pope Marcus in 336, and S. Anastasia, established sometime in the 4th century near the northwest corner of the Circus Maximus.[24]

Those who did come to pray at the Christian sanctuaries headed for the outskirts of the city, where all the really monumental churches built starting under Constantine stood. Only one of Rome's nine biggest 4th-century churches sat inside the walls of Aurelian. This was the Lateran basilica, the *basilica Salvatoris*, cathedral of the bishops of Rome. Located just inside the walls on the eastern fringes of the city, it was constructed on imperial property, at Constantine's expense, starting soon after he took the city from Maxentius in 312. Constantine's other signature project rose later in his reign on the far side of the city at the tomb of St. Peter, Rome's premier martyr-saint. They were magnificent and massive edifices, roughly the size of a soccer pitch or an American football field, with room for several thousands in their cavernous interiors. (St. Peter's, at c. 120 m long by 64 m wide, was still larger than the Lateran, which measured c. 100 m by 53 m.) Both consisted of a high, central nave lit by clerestory windows, flanked on each side by two lower aisles supported by arcaded colonnades resplendent with recycled marble columns and wall-revetment in most of the colors of the rainbow. Rome's third great basilica, St. Paul's on the Via Ostiense, was built later, starting in the 380s,

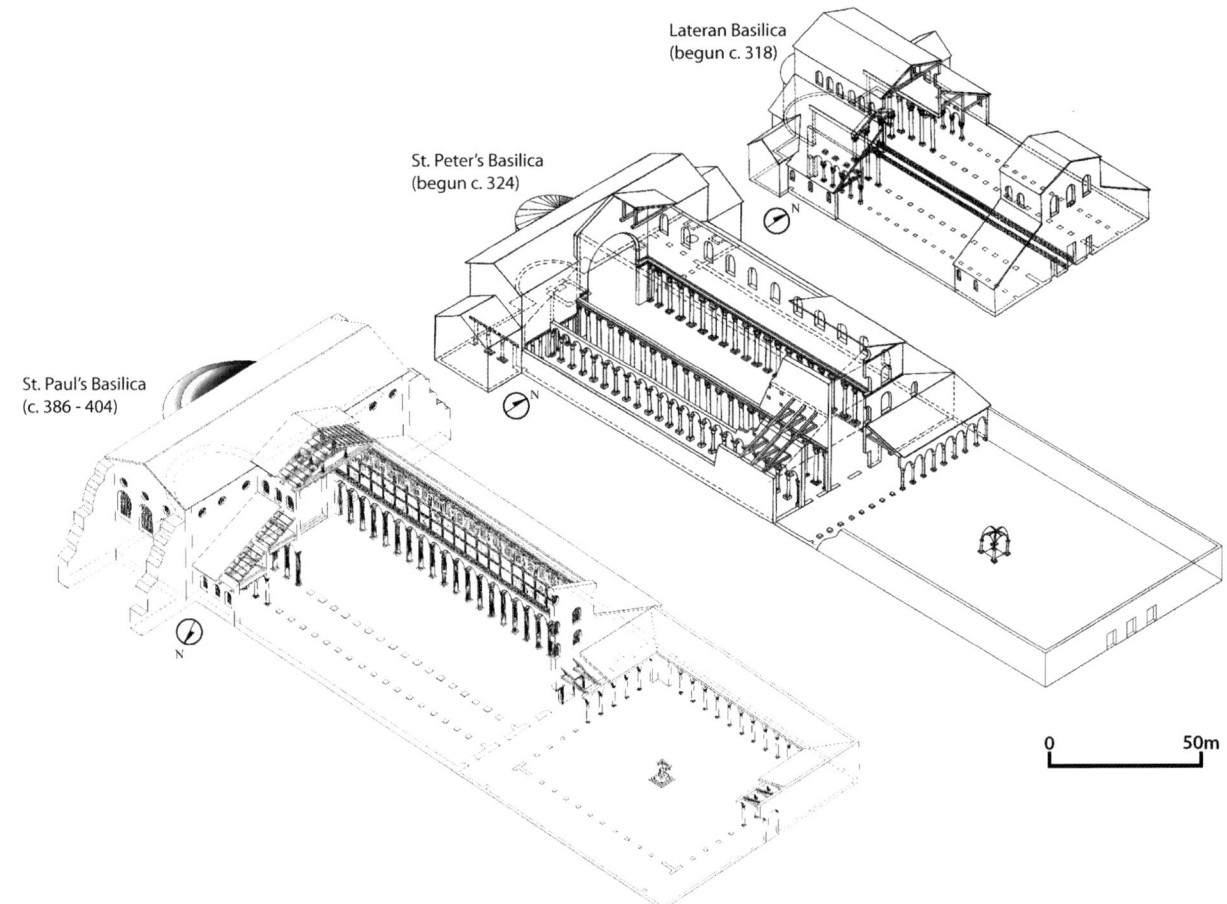

Figure 1.12 Comparative reconstructions (at scale) of the Lateran Cathedral, St. Peter's, and St. Paul's. (Camerlenghi 2018, fig. 2.2.)

replacing a much smaller Constantinian shrine at the grave of Rome's second leading apostle and martyr. At c. 128 by 65 m, it was the grandest of them all; and once again, imperial patronage was crucial to the completion of the gargantuan project (Fig. 1.12).[25]

Like St. Peter's and St. Paul's, the other six large basilicas stood well outside the city walls, amid the cemeteries and catacombs where all of Rome's dead, pagan and Christian, lay buried (burial inside the city limits had been forbidden since time immemorial; the custom would only begin to change in the 5th and, especially, the 6th century). These are the so-called "cemetery-basilicas," massive structures that rose at the graves of popes and Christian martyrs, whose remains exuded sanctity and consequently attracted throngs of burials. Rome's growing Christian population sought to be laid to rest as close as possible to the remains of the saints. Until 1991, there were thought to be five cemetery-basilicas: S. Agnese on the Via Nomentana, S. Lorenzo on the Via Tiburtina, SS. Marcellino e Pietro on the Via Labicana, one whose dedication is unknown, on the Via Praenestina, and the *basilica Apostolorum* (now S. Sebastiano) on the Via Appia. In 1991, a sixth was discovered a short distance from the Via Ardeatina, which has now been almost completely excavated (Fig. 1.13).

Like the others, the Via Ardeatina basilica resembles a Roman circus in plan (whence the name circiform sometimes applied to these structures), a

28 ⁓ THE MAKING OF MEDIEVAL ROME

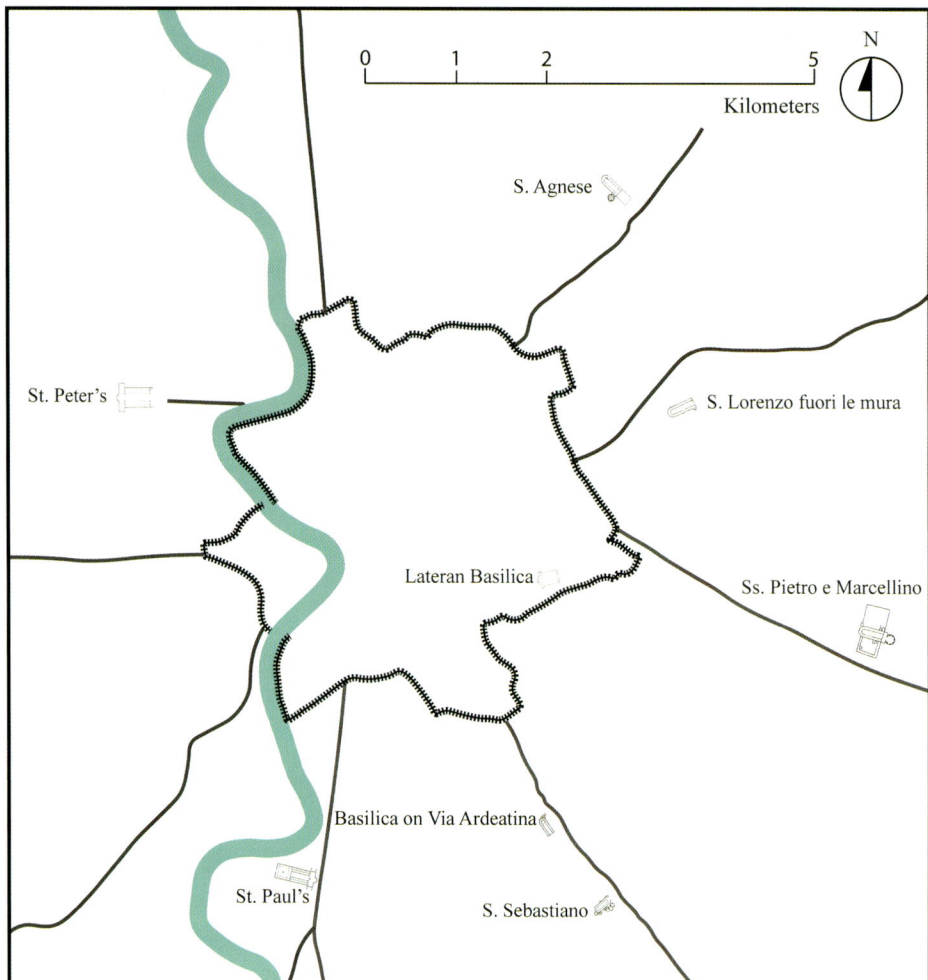

Figure 1.13 Principal 4th-century extramural basilicas. (Camerlenghi 2018, fig. 1.8.)

similarity that may not be coincidental, given the cosmic significance of circuses as symbols of cyclical time and eternity, rebirth and renewal. Built of brick-faced concrete with a timber roof, it measured 66 × 28 m. It was, in essence, a covered cemetery, its entire floor covered with tombs, some stacked one above the other, some 1,600 in all (Fig. 1.14). In the center of its curved end was the grandest tomb, a barrel-vaulted chamber that housed a hefty marble sarcophagus evidently reserved for its patron, presumably the short-reigning pope Marcus (r. 335–6), who is recorded in the *Liber Pontificalis* as the founder of the place. In this respect alone, the Via Ardeatina basilica is exceptional – it is the first Roman basilica known to have been founded by direct papal initiative, though Constantine probably contributed funds to the project and endowed the church with land. The other eight great 4th-century churches were all imperial foundations: Along with the Lateran and St. Peter's, the remaining five circiform churches were constructed on Constantine's initiative, though work in some cases continued under his sons (r. 337–61), while the construction of St. Paul's starting in the mid-380s was coordinated by Rome's urban prefects on behalf of the emperors Valentinian II, Gratian, and Theodosius.[26]

The churches located inside the walls by 400, scattered across the populous residential quarters beyond the Show Area, were humbler affairs. Most were *tituli*. Uncertainties remain about what exactly *tituli* were at the beginning, though nearly

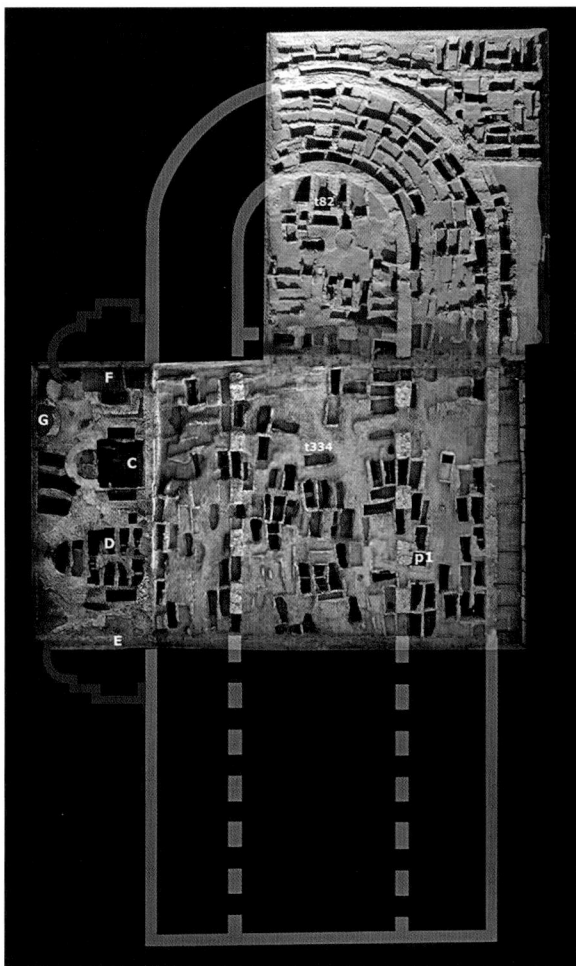

Figure 1.14 Photomosaic of the excavated portions of the Via Ardeatina basilica. The presumed founder-pope's tomb in the apse is marked t82. (Fiocchi Nicolai and Vella 2016-17, fig. 1.)

everyone has an opinion. They were certainly all inside the walls; the masses conducted in them partook of the host consecrated weekly at the Lateran by the pope; in the 5th century, many, if not all, of them had baptisteries installed. (In the 4th century, only the Lateran and, later, St. Peter's are known to have had baptisteries.) The most likely interpretation of the term *titulus* makes it a title of legal proprietorship. It indicates, that is, that the land and/or the building used to found a *titulus* had been donated to the Church, irrevocably, by individuals who therefore had no further claim to the property. The donors in turn were commemorated for their beneficence by the attachment of their names to the various *tituli*. Nearly all of the twenty-five *tituli* attested in the acts of the Church synod held at Rome in 499, the most comprehensive list available, took their name from what appear to be individual donors or patrons (Fig. 1.15).[27]

These *tituli* developed into Rome's main congregational churches, essentially urban parishes, staffed by resident clergy responsible for communion, marriages, last rites, and, increasingly over the course of the 5th century, baptism for their local flock. Those foundations listed in 499 proved resilient, too – most survived through the Middle Ages and have continued in use up to the present in one form or another. But although most of the twenty-five *tituli* present at the end of the 5th century existed as of 400 (at least eighteen of them), many remained unobtrusive to the point of near-invisibility – whatever functional and decorative modifications occurred were limited to the interiors of what remained, from the outside, ordinary private dwellings.[28]

Other *tituli* had been transformed into purpose-built churches since 312. Albeit with minor variations, they consistently followed the basilical plan that would remain standard at Rome for a millennium and more, a standard set and enshrined for the ages by the Lateran, St. Peter's, and St. Paul's, which together provided the templates for the large majority of all the monumental churches built at Rome through the 15th century – a striking example of Roman conservatism, and medieval Romans' inclination to look no further for inspiration than to their own imperial and early Christian past. (Even the Gothic, that trendiest and most cosmopolitan of late medieval styles, was only tardily and half-heartedly gestured at by Roman architects, as we will see.) The new *tituli* of the 4th and 5th centuries were thus rectangular basilicas with an apse at one end and either an enclosed atrium or a simple colonnaded porch (narthex) at the other. They were built in brick-faced concrete

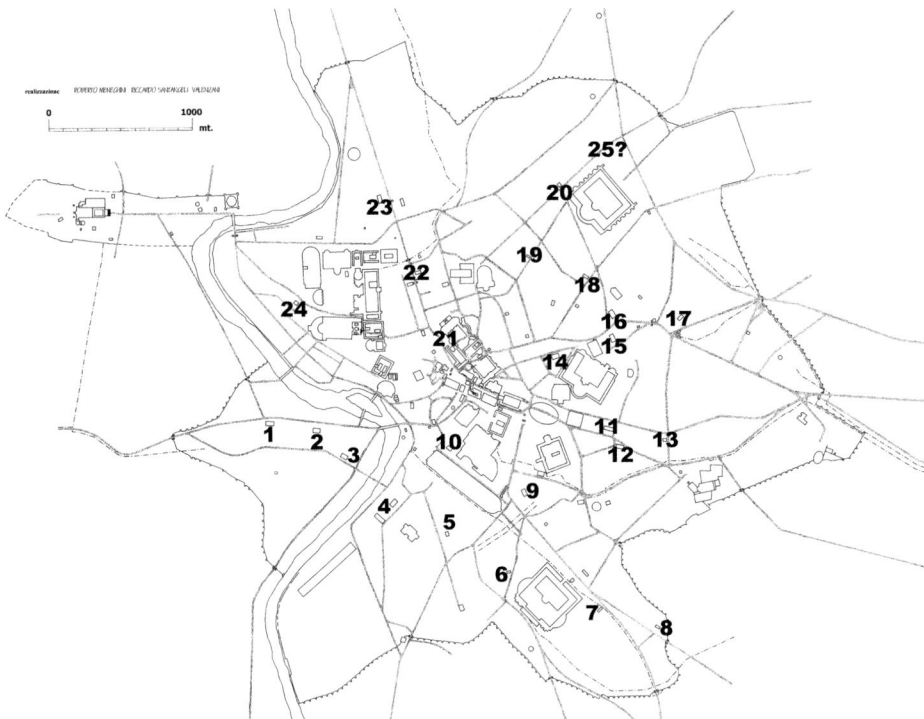

Figure 1.15 The twenty-five late antique titular churches: 1: S. Maria in Trastevere; 2: S. Crisogono; 3: S. Cecilia; 4: S. Sabina; 5: S. Prisca; 6: S. Balbina; 7: SS. Nereo ed Achilleo; 8: S. Sisto; 9: SS. Giovanni e Paolo; 10: S. Anastasia; 11: S. Cecilia; 12: SS. Quattro Coronati; 13: SS. Marcellino e Pietro; 14: S. Pietro in Vincoli; 15: S. Martino ai Monti; 16: S. Prassede; 17: S. Eusebio; 18: S. Pudenziana; 19: S. Vitale; 20: S. Susanna; 21: S. Marco; 22: S. Marcello; 23: S. Lorenzo in Lucina; 24: S. Lorenzo in Damaso; 25: S. Ciriaco (situated near the Baths of Diocletian, exact location uncertain). (Author.)

(*opus latericium*) or concrete faced in alternating bands of brick and tuff blocks (*opus vittatum* or *listatum*), with wooden trussed roofs covered with terracotta tiles. (The expensive, technically demanding concrete vaulting featured in many of Rome's most imposing public buildings during the imperial period, still used in the early 4th century in Maxentius' basilica in the Forum, was not used to roof churches.) Most featured a high, central nave lit by clerestory windows, flanked by lower, narrower side aisles. The aisles were divided from the nave by colonnades made from bases, column-shafts, and capitals usually recycled from older buildings. Reused marble slabs paved floors and revetted parts of the walls, which might also be decorated with frescoes and mosaics, with special attention paid to the apse-arch and apse that framed the altar and formed the visual and liturgical focal point of these buildings.

These new churches announced the growing Christian presence, surely, and provided communal gathering places for the people living in the vicinity, but they had not radically changed the face of the city in 400. The grandest of them were considerably smaller than many temples and comparable in scale to individual reception rooms and dining halls in the more opulent private mansions, some of which were in fact transformed into *tituli*. One of the newest and largest, likely still under construction in 400, was the basilica of S. Clemente near the Colosseum, built into the remains of a large public building, perhaps a warehouse, and a private house where a congregation had presumably met before the new church took shape. Not far away on the western slopes of the Caelian, the basilica of SS. Giovanni e Paolo – then called the *titulus Pammachii* after the wealthy senator who funded it – would soon

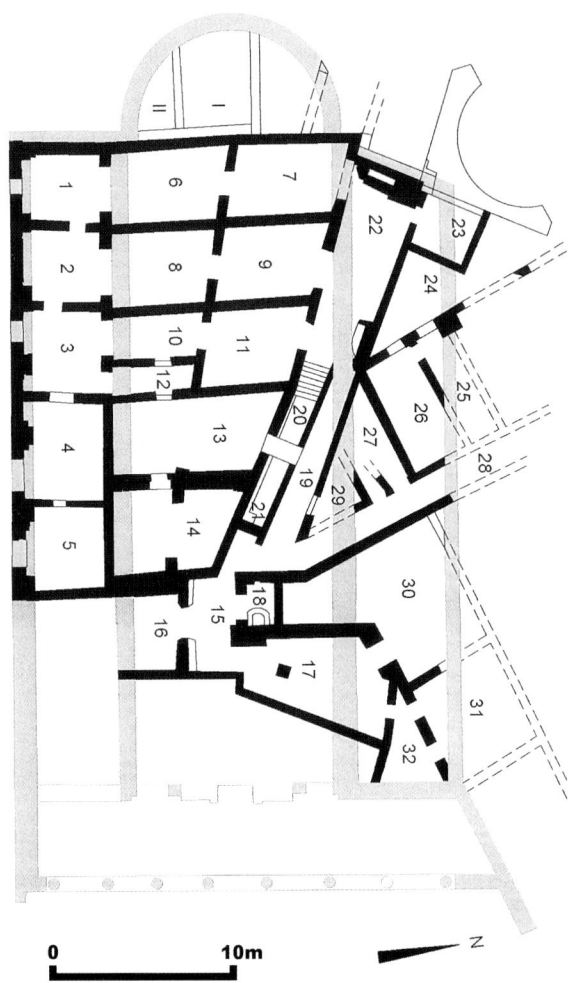

Figure 1.16 Plan of SS Giovanni e Paolo. The preexisting residential structures are in black; the outline of the church in grey. (Englen et al. 2014, p. 15.)

rise circa 410–20 atop the partially interred remains of another well-appointed house owned by Christians in the 4th century, whose unprepossessing exterior belied the richness of its frescoed interior (Fig. 1.16). Late in the 4th century, the house was furnished with a small shrine (*confessio*) whose walls were frescoed with some of the earliest unambiguously Christian imagery to survive outside of the catacombs, including scenes of martyrdom and an *orans* figure with arms outstretched in prayer (Fig. 1.17).[29]

Yet at c. 36 m long by 29.5 m wide (S. Clemente, exclusive of porch and apse) and c. 40 m long by 30 m wide (SS. Giovanni e Paolo), these leading examples of the new generation of purpose-built *tituli* were hardly larger than others inserted into single rooms or wings of existing building complexes, such as S. Pudenziana (c. 41 m by 19 m), the *titulus Pudentis* on the Viminal. Here, a porticated courtyard in a large apartment building was transformed into a basilica at the end of the 4th century. The rectangular courtyard was covered with a wooden roof and subdivided into side aisles and a central nave supported by arcaded pillars; a new entrance porch was installed at one end and an apse at the other. Following the sack of Rome in 410, the apse was decorated with the earliest surviving figural mosaic preserved in any Roman church, showing Christ seated in majesty among the apostles in Jerusalem, surmounted by Calvary with a jeweled cross and the four symbols of the evangelists (Fig. 1.18). From the outside, however, the shape of the building was little changed. Passersby might hardly have noticed the difference. Much the same applies to other early *tituli* such as S. Marco on Piazza Venezia, S. Balbina by the Baths of Caracalla, and SS. Quattro Coronati between the Colosseum and the Lateran, which largely preserved the contours of the apsidal halls in private mansions in which they were installed; and S. Anastasia by the Circus Maximus, which was inserted into the first-floor level of an older apartment complex, above the vaulted shops at street level.[30]

The topographical footprint of the Church, in short, remained small at the close of the 4th century, especially inside the walls, and most of all in the Show Area. It might further be stressed that in 400, and indeed for several centuries thereafter, Rome was not the 'papal' city it later became, in the sense that the popes were neither its rulers nor the principal owners and shapers of public buildings and infrastructure. Until the 8th century, the popes remained subordinate to the secular arm, which was represented at Rome by civic administrators in the service of Italy's duly constituted sovereigns:

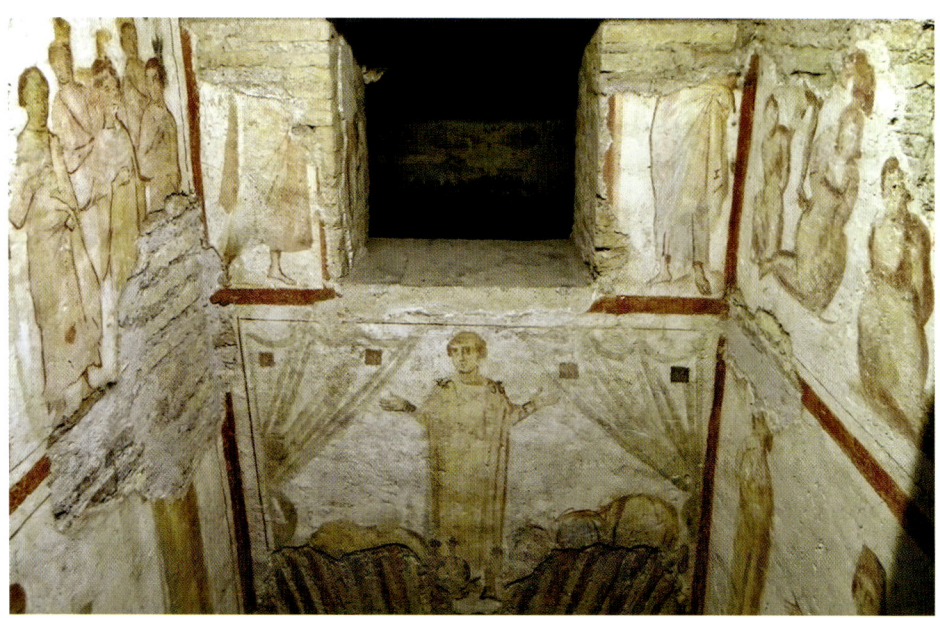

Figure 1.17 The *confessio* in the house beneath SS. Giovanni e Paolo; the aperture (*fenestella confessionis*) above the central *orans* figure communicated with a small chamber that presumably contained saintly relics, according to the interpretation of Fiocchi Nicolai 2019b. The martyrdom scenes on the side walls suggest the presence of two male and one female saints. (Author.)

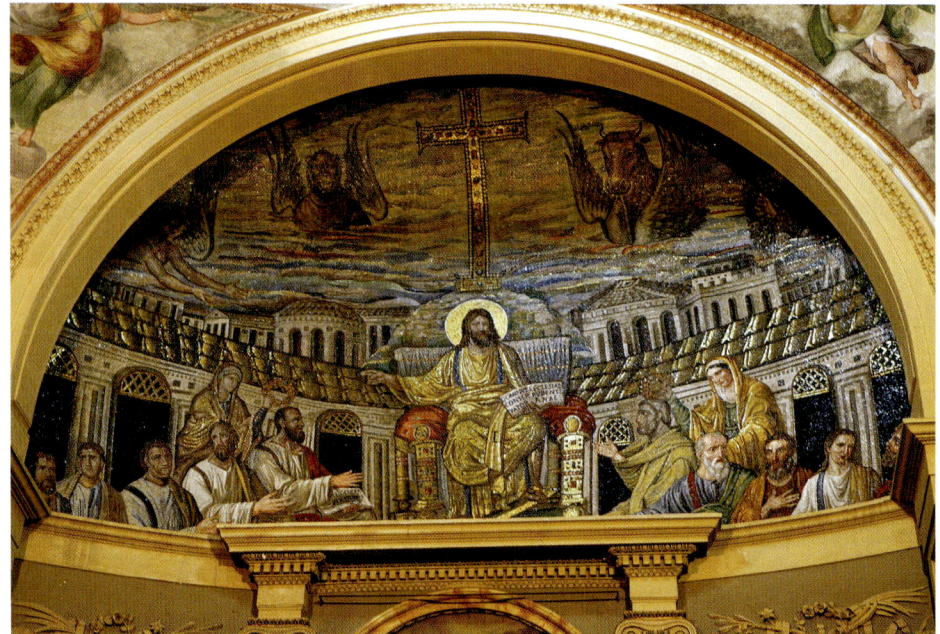

Figure 1.18 The apse mosaic at S. Pudenziana, c. 410–20, but heavily restored. (Author.)

western Roman emperors first, then 'barbarian' Germanic kings, and finally Byzantine emperors. In 400, they were not even the primary patrons of churches, many more of which were founded – and funded – by wealthy lay patrons than by popes and clerics. Rome featured a "Church in the city," as Federico Marazzi has put it, but was not yet by any means a "city of the Church."[31]

Chapter 2

401–552

From Imperial Metropolis to Provincial Town

WE BEGIN WITH THE CATACLYSMS, both local and systemic, that set Rome on a wholly new course. Between about 410, when Alaric's Goths became the first non-Roman army to capture and pillage Rome in 800 years, and the middle of the 6th century, when Byzantine and Gothic armies pulled the city apart in a murderous tug-of-war lasting almost two decades, the urban population declined by a full order of magnitude, from over a half-million to something like 50,000. A millennium would pass before the latter figure was again exceeded. Even at the height of Italy's communal age in the 13th century, when the mercantile and banking centers of Milan and Florence boasted 100,000 residents or more, Rome had maybe 50,000, a number equaled or exceeded also by Venice, Genoa, Bologna, Pisa, Siena, and Palermo.[1]

It is no exaggeration to say that the key to understanding Rome's urban trajectory in the 5th and 6th centuries is demography. A city ultimately consists in its inhabitants, whose cumulative exertions condition the evolution of the cityscape. Until the 5th century, Rome had hundreds of thousands living within the limits of its fourteen urban regions. The incarnation of Rome that emerged from the Gothic War in the mid 6th century had tens of thousands. Any notion of how much of the city could possibly have been occupied, maintained, or redeveloped depends on how many people we imagine to have been present at any given time. The question of demographic decline – its pace and extent – in the period between Alaric's sieges of 408–10 and the final expulsion of the Goths in 552 is the single most important problem confronting anyone seeking to understand Rome's transformation from a megalopolis into the sparsely inhabited shell of a megalopolis. It is worth facing the question head-on and trying to make some sense of the sparse and confusing evidence that historians and archaeologists use to arrive at the population estimates they often rather cavalierly propose.

As most of the city center can never be subject to close archaeological scrutiny, covered as it is by dense modern sprawl, estimates of population figures in late antiquity depend on a handful of laconic and frankly inscrutable texts pertaining (with one exception) to the city's pork supply. These texts offer ways of calculating either the total quantities of pork supplied to Rome each year, or the number of recipients eligible for the pork dole. All but one date to the period 367–452; the final one is a brief passage in a letter of Cassiodorus written in or shortly before 535. By any estimate, Rome's population was much lower in the first half of the 6th century than it had been in the 4th and earlier 5th centuries, but the documents present enough difficulties of interpretation that both the total numbers involved and the rate of decline over time are difficult to ascertain with certainty, such that divergent interpretations of the data persist. But it is worth pausing to peek into the cobwebby corners of these sources to give some sense of what they say, and what they do not say, if only because such an immense weight of historical interpretation depends on them. Difficult as they are, they remain the key to conceptualizing how large and populous Rome was at any given moment between the later 4th and the mid 6th century. They offer the only comprehensive, citywide picture currently available of the timing and trajectory of the reduction in population that took Rome from its full imperial grandeur to the relative emptiness that prevailed throughout the Middle Ages. If one wants to have an opinion on the maintenance of critical infrastructure, the condition of public buildings and spaces, or the distribution and density of residential settlement at any given time during these two centuries, one first has to decide how these texts are to be interpreted.

The earliest is an imperial decree of 367 that prescribes the compensation due to the *suarii*, members of the corporation charged with supplying pork to Rome, for the expenses they incurred in performing their duties. In short: the decree appears to say that the *suarii* are entitled to compensation worth 15 percent of the total value of the pork they supply. This payment is to come from the owners of the rural estates who supplied the hogs to the *suarii*, and is stated in terms of amphorae of wine: 17,000. Further, estate-owners who prefer to pay the *suarii* in meat instead of wine may do so at a rate of 70 pounds of pork per amphora. This allows the following calculations: If 17,000 amphorae of wine equal 15 percent of the value of all the pork supplied to Rome, then the total value of the pork equals 113,333 amphorae of wine, which, multiplied by the prescribed conversion rate of 70 pounds of pork per amphora, puts the total weight of the pork supplied to Rome each year at 7,933,310 pounds. This figure must then be treated together with a second decree of 419, which specifies that each recipient of the pork dole receives 25 pounds of pork per year, at 5 pounds per month for 5 months. 7,933,310 divided by 25 thus gives the equivalent of approximately 317,000 annual rations of pork. This, broadly, is the interpretation proposed by Santo Mazzarino in the 1950s and later defended by Elio Lo Cascio; I think it the most plausible, and it is probably fair to say that it now represents the majority view.[2]

But how large a total population might correspond with the figure of 317,000 annual rations of pork? As with the monthly grain ration (*annona*) distributed to adult male citizens in the early empire, so too with pork in the 4th century; the annual allotment of 25 pounds was likely meant to supply the needs not only of the citizen-recipient, but also of his underage and female dependents. The figures for 367, the equivalent of 317,000 annual rations or almost 8,000,000 pounds of pork, are high enough to suggest that they represent the total quantity of pork delivered to Rome by the *suarii*; certainly the text itself nowhere indicates that the quantities it presents are anything less than the annual totals. Mazzarino and Lo Cascio are consequently inclined to think that 317,000 corresponds roughly with the number of male adult citizens, which would give a total citizen population around 600,000–650,000, and a comprehensive total, including slaves, freedmen, and resident aliens, of at least 700,000–750,000 souls.[3]

To some, particularly those attached to the outmoded view of Rome as a city in inexorable decline from the 3rd century on, these figures seem unacceptably high, which has led to attempts to revise the totals downward. Jean Durliat's is the most rigorous. As there is no good way to question the amount of nearly 8,000,000 pounds given by the edict of 367, Durliat proposed instead that the quantity indicated refers to meat on the hoof, rather than the quantity of butchered pork actually available for consumption in Rome. He therefore suggested cutting the total by 40 percent, to 5,000,000 pounds of edible meat, thereby reducing annual rations to 200,000. But this will not do, firstly because the value of the meat, calculated at 70 pounds per amphora of wine, would be far too low if applied to living pigs: An amphora of wine is much more likely to have been worth 70 pounds of edible meat than 70 pounds of live pig, as Lo Cascio has pointed out. Secondly, there is the issue of the 15 percent compensation due to the *suarii* stipulated in the edict itself, which is calculated in amphorae of wine. Durliat believes that this sum, along with additional expenses mentioned in the law (together amounting to 40 percent), was subtracted from the total quantity of pork to be delivered. Were this the case, however, the mention of wine amphorae would be completely superfluous, as the *suarii* would simply have been compensated by a reduction in the quantity of meat they had to deliver to the authorities in Rome, not by some supernumerary delivery of wine. Hence, the 17,000 amphorae should be an additional quantity, separate from the almost 8,000,000 pounds of edible meat the *suarii* delivered to Rome, for which service they were compensated in wine.[4]

In any case, all of these commentators, Durliat included, concur that the quantities of food arriving in Rome in 367 were about as massive as always. In the later 4th century, population remained close to peak levels, and life went on much as before. The grain fleet, comprising hundreds of freighters, continued to arrive every year from Africa with the thousands of tons of grain distributed annually to Roman citizens. Rome's leading senatorial families still owned vast estates across the western Mediterranean, from Spain and North Africa to Italy and Gaul. With the fantastic wealth these estates produced, they staged lavish public entertainments in the city's principal theaters and arenas, all of which remained in service; they sponsored public buildings, commemorative monuments, and statues; and they progressively expanded and decorated their palatial urban residences – the *domus* occupied by scions of the illustrious Anicii, Valerii, and Symmachi families on the Caelian, the Junii Bassi on the Esquiline, the Caelii on the Quirinal, the Vettii on the Aventine, and many others came to rival or exceed the palaces of many provincial governors in size and opulence.[5]

The 5th century opened with one of the most ambitious building projects ever undertaken in Rome. This was the heightening of the city wall first built by Emperor Aurelian in the 270s, which in its original configuration was almost 19 km long, over 3.5 m wide, about 8 m high, and protected by close to 400 projecting square towers spaced at 30 m intervals, all of it realized in solid, brick-faced concrete. What emerged was essentially a new wall, nearly doubled in height to about 15 m, with correspondingly heightened towers and more imposing gates for the 15 major roads that traversed the circuit (Fig. 2.1). The dedicatory inscriptions placed on three of the rebuilt city gates survive to inform us that the project was undertaken between 401 and 403 under the auspices of the boy-emperor Honorius and Stilicho, his general and effective regent, under the supervision of the urban prefect Flavius Macrobius Longinianus. On the one hand, the new wall was a stark acknowledgement of Rome's vulnerability in an age when the frontiers were breaking down and imperial armies could no longer be relied on to keep enemies away from the ancient capital, for the project was launched in response to Alaric's first armed incursion into Italy, in 401. (Stilicho turned him back in the spring of 402, following two pitched battles in the Po plain in northern Italy.) On the other, however, the project speaks powerfully to the immense technical and financial resources the imperial administration still commanded at the beginning of the 5th century, and to the determination of its rulers to persevere in preserving and aggrandizing the ancient imperial capital. The wall they rebuilt would stand as Rome's most imposing monument throughout the medieval millennium and beyond, its first (and last) line of defense until 1870 (Fig. 2.2).[6]

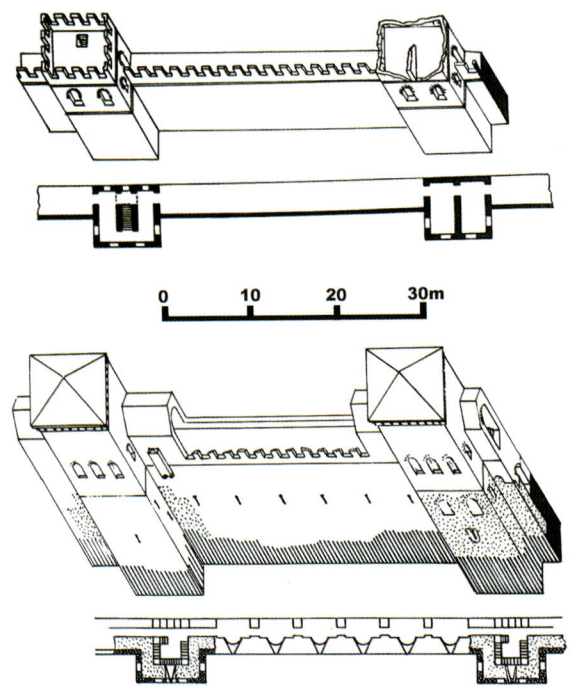

Figure 2.1 The Aurelianic (top) and Honorian (bottom) phases of the Aurelian Wall. (Adapted from Cozza 1987, fig. 30.)

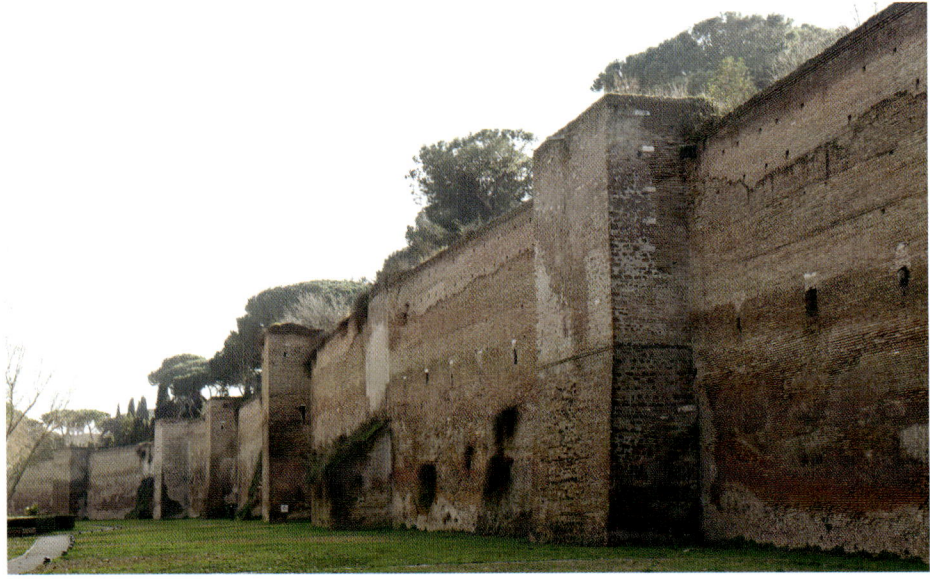

Figure 2.2 The Aurelian Wall in Sector J (Porta Metronia – Porta Latina), where it stands – albeit partially restored – to its full, early 5th-century height. (Author.)

The Show Area in the city center bustled with activity, too. In the Forum of Caesar, Virius Flavius Nicomachus the Younger, urban prefect in 399–400 and 408, installed as many as 21 statues inside the covered colonnades around its periphery: The statues are gone, but the bases they stood on, all recycled, survive. One bears an inscription from Nicomachus to Honorius' brother, the eastern emperor Arcadius (r. 395–408); another fragmentary inscription indicates that Nicomachus also restored or reconstructed part of the forum itself (Fig. 2.3). In the adjacent Forum of Trajan, the premier location for the display of honorary statues in late antiquity, Honorius' court-poet Claudian was honored with a statue at the request of the Senate, in 400. On the old rostrum in the Republican forum, the Roman people (*populus Romanus*) dedicated a silvered bronze statue of Stilicho, in 405/6, in thanks for his victory over a Gothic army under Radagaisus in 405/06, near another erected in the same year, in the name of the Senate and people of Rome, to the faithfulness (*fides*) and virtue (*virtus*) of Stilicho's soldiers. Two triumphal arches also commemorated the recent victories over the Goths, one over the Via Flaminia in the northern Campus Martius, the other on the main route from the city center to St. Peter's, just before the road crossed the Tiber at the Pons Aelius, dedicated by the Senate and People of Rome to the emperors Arcadius, Honorius, and Theodosius II, whose statues and "Gothic trophies" topped the archway. On the eve of Alaric's sack, Rome's ruling classes were still celebrating victories, commemorating themselves, and maintaining the décor of the city's central public spaces as they always had.[7]

Business as usual came to an end starting in 408, when Alaric descended unchecked on Rome and laid siege to the city. It was the first of three sieges that stretched over much of the following two years: two years of famine, sickness, and

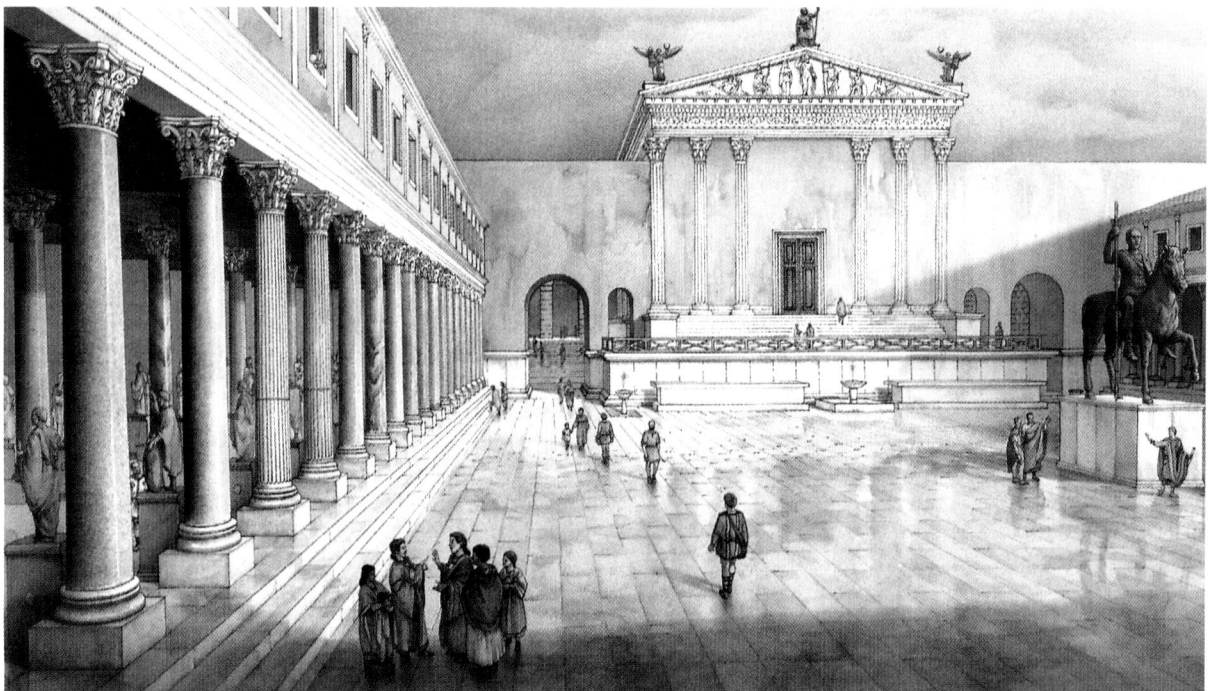

Figure 2.3 Reconstruction of the Forum of Caesar in late antiquity, following the installation of the transverse wall that shored up the façade of the Temple of Venus Genetrix at the beginning of the 4th century. Note the statues on tall bases inside the colonnade at far left. (Studio InkLink/Meneghini 2009, p. 54, fig. 53.)

privation for the people of Rome that culminated in the city's fall to Alaric's troops on August 24, 410. It is hard to overstate the importance of the sack, at least in symbolic terms, both for contemporaries and for generations of modern historians. The Roman world collectively recoiled in shock; St. Jerome histrionically wailed from distant Palestine while St. Augustine and his congregation prepared for a flood of refugees in North Africa. Christians blamed enduring crypto-pagan sacrilege for the catastrophe, pagans blamed the abandonment of the old gods, and the "fall of Rome" passed into history as a crucial turning point, the moment that heralded the beginning of the end of the Roman Empire and the inception of the European 'Dark Ages.'

For Romans living in the generation after the sack, however, the situation was less portentous. Damage had been, all things considered, light, and the Goths had spent only three days in the city. There was scattered destruction and burning, but nothing catastrophic; mostly the Goths had looted. They then left, heading south and taking with them only what they could carry: jewels and precious metals and other portable objects of value. Even statues were mostly too heavy and bulky to pillage, though Zosimus tells us that exceptionally valuable ones in silver and gold were taken and melted down. The Christian (albeit Arian) Goths even allegedly spared most churches from pillage on Alaric's command, though the several thousands of pounds of silver from the *fastigium* at the Lateran basilica, a sculpture-adorned columnar screen fronting the main altar, apparently proved too tempting a prize.[8]

But while most of Rome was not razed and most of its people not massacred, the sack and still more the disastrous two years that preceded it did have serious consequences, both immediate and longer term, for the appearance of the city and the lives of its people. There are scattered clues of upheaval in the archaeological record. A first one relates not directly to the sack, but rather to the sieges that preceded it: With the Goths surrounding the city and cutting off access to the cemeteries outside the walls, the ancient prohibition against burial within the city limits seems to have been at least partially abrogated. Out of a population of 600,000–800,000, some 5,000 deaths would be expected on a monthly basis during normal times; the epidemic, probably typhus, that broke out during the two-month siege in the fall of 408 could have added an additional 10,000 per month (based on urban mortality rates for documented epidemics in more recent times), leaving heaps of decomposing bodies requiring immediate disposal. One corpse was deposited in a flood-damaged storeroom by the Marmorata quay, on the Tiber-banks beneath the Aventine. Dozens more were placed in tombs installed both beneath and atop the paved esplanade surrounding the Colosseum, in the heart of the monumental city center(!). Parts of this *ad hoc* necropolis were preserved for posterity when the esplanade was raised and a road built along its periphery, covering some of the tombs, in the years 417–23 (Fig. 2.4). There are probably other contemporary burials yet to be discovered, but their relative scarcity suggests that most corpses, many thousands of them, still found their way to the extramural cemeteries: Perhaps burial parties were allowed to work during the sieges, or maybe the remains of the dead were transferred en masse when the Goths departed. Nonetheless, these first urban burials anticipated the onset of an epochal shift that would gain momentum over the course of the 6th and 7th centuries, when burial inside the walls became first common and eventually standard. Thereafter, medieval Romans shared the inhabited spaces of the city center with the remains of their dead, as they would until 1870.[9]

Some of the numerous hoards of precious objects, jewelry, coins, and even bronze statues buried or otherwise hidden in widely scattered points across the city can also be attributed to the

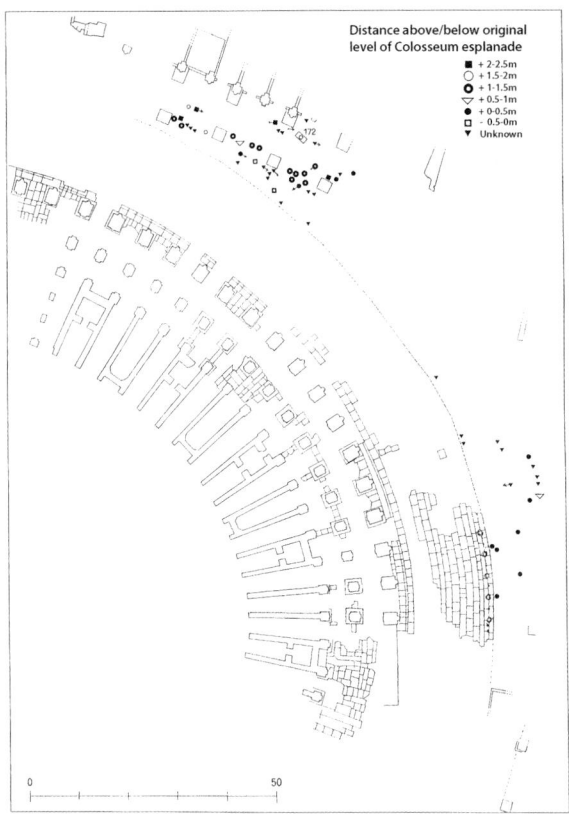

Figure 2.4 Distribution and levels of the 5th–7th-century burials outside the Colosseum. (Adapted from Rea [ed.] 2002, p. 87, fig. 3.)

period 408–10 (the best candidates are those containing numerous coins datable up to, and not beyond, the first decade of the 5th century). Others doubtless relate to other cataclysms that followed over the course of the 5th century, including the sacks of 455 and 472. Together, these hoards testify to the climate of fear and insecurity that prevailed during such periods of exceptional danger and hardship, leaving lasting scars on the city and the psyche of its residents alike.[10]

As for the sack itself, the textual and especially the archaeological evidence currently available suggests that instances of burning and destruction were sporadic and localized. The Goths entered the city through the Porta Salaria in the north, passing through the Horti Sallustiani on their way toward the city-center. Procopius says that houses inside the gate burned, including the mansion known as the 'House of Sallust,' whose blasted ruins remained visible in the 530s. But most of the Show Area was left intact, from the Palatine across the Forum to the imperial forums. A notable exception is the Senate House, which burned, apparently along with the adjacent Basilica Aemilia. It is possible that the Goths singled out this symbolic heart of civic governance for destruction in reprisal for the resistance they had faced. Otherwise, they seem mostly to have confined themselves to plundering, notably making off with some of the lavish spoils from the Roman sack of Jerusalem in AD 70 displayed in the Forum of Peace (the *templum Pacis*). It is worth noting that extensive excavations conducted in the 1990s and 2000s across the forums of Caesar, Trajan, Nerva, and Vespasian turned up no additional signs of burning or violent destruction attributable to the sack of 410, or for that matter to those of 455 and 472.[11]

From the Show Area, Alaric's troops apparently fanned out toward the wealthy residential quarters on the hills to the south and east. Some of the best material evidence for destruction directly connected to the Gothic army comes from mansions on the Caelian and Aventine hills. One of the most magnificent residences atop the Caelian belonged to the senatorial family of the Valerii. This property was excavated in the early 20th century under the Ospedale dell'Addolorata, where finds including lead pipes bearing the family name showed beyond reasonable doubt that the opulent *domus* uncovered there belonged to the Valerii. It was badly damaged by fire, traces of which appeared throughout the complex, and never reoccupied by upper-class residents. This may be the very house which the young Christian couple (Valeria) Melania the Younger and (Valerius) Pinianus famously tried to sell prior to leaving for the Holy Land, at the beginning of the 5th century. The asking price was so high that no buyer had been found by 410, when the house was totally destroyed, according to Gerontius' *Life of Melania*. The property in question was subsequently sold for almost nothing, presumably due not only to its ruinous condition but also to declining demand for luxury properties in the years after the Gothic sack.[12]

More recent excavations of an anonymous mansion on the Aventine, in Via del Tempio di Diana, paint a similarly dramatic picture of a quick and violent end. In the corner of one room, alongside a charred lock and chain, the excavators found a hoard of 259 coins dating from the 3rd century through the first decade of the 5th – but not one after 410. The metal objects remained on the floor after fire swept through the room and destroyed the locked wooden cabinet where the coins were stored. Other valuable metal artifacts found elsewhere in the house, mixed in with pottery and glass also datable up to the beginning of the 5th century, were likewise never recovered. It would seem that the house was destroyed so totally that no effort was made to rebuild it or salvage what had been lost, whether its owners survived or not. It is telling, too, that neither here nor at the House of the Valerii are there any signs of upper-class residents returning in the following generations, even in such formerly desirable neighborhoods. Property values evidently declined along with luxury housing after 410. Presumably, the population of wealthy aristocrats that had inhabited such dwellings was also in decline.[13]

Other excavated properties in the vicinity of the burnt mansions on the Caelian and Aventine, which were not violently destroyed but nonetheless wholly or partially abandoned by mid-century, strengthen the impression of partial dereliction of the built environment, and hint at demographic contraction extending beyond the ranks of the nobility. Another Aventine *domus* located almost immediately adjacent to the one that burned was simply vacated, and then systematically despoiled of its marble floor paving and wall revetments. The stripped floors in turn disappeared under a thin layer of dirt and detritus datable to the mid 5th century, suggesting that the house had been abandoned and then stripped somewhat earlier, perhaps as a direct or indirect consequence of the sack of 410. On the Caelian, the Castra Peregrina, erstwhile headquarters of the feared imperial special agents (the *agentes in rebus*), was filled with rubble around the beginning of the 5th century. (It would be tempting to posit another targeted Gothic reprisal against a hated arm of the imperial government, but there are signs of abandonment already in the years preceding the sack.) The area then remained mostly undeveloped for some decades until work began on the church of S. Stefano Rotondo somewhere around the mid 5th century (it was completed and dedicated by Pope Simplicius, r. 468–83). The nearby headquarters of the pagan priestly college of the *dendrophori*, the Basilica Hilariana, also decayed during the first half of the century: Some rooms became small workshops, and others filled up with rubbish (Fig. 2.5). While the direct cause in this case is probably the imperial edict of 415 that dissolved the *dendrophori* and arrogated their assets to the imperial treasury, the subsequent partial abandonment of the area again implies declining population pressure from the early 5th century.[14]

A similar picture begins to emerge also from scattered excavations in southern Trastevere, in the neighborhood of the 5th-century *titulus* of S. Cecilia. The church itself was built atop a 2nd-century apartment-building (*insula*) that was apparently partially ruined and abandoned by the early 5th century. Just to the north, across Via dei Genovesi, recent excavations beneath the Conservatorio di S. Pasquale Baylon show that the transformation of a preexisting *insula* into a private mansion was brusquely interrupted, again early in the 5th century. Work ceased while marble wall-revetments and pavements were still in

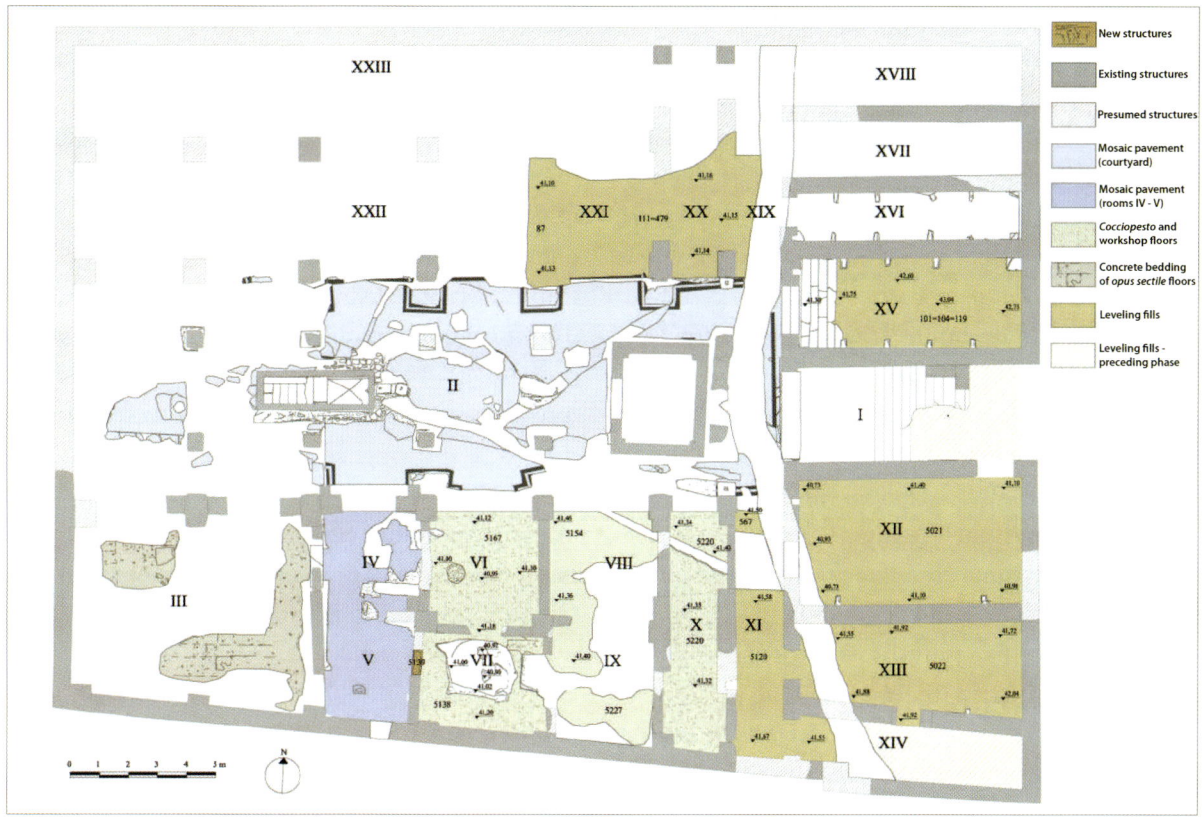

Figure 2.5 The Basilica Hilariana in the mid 5th century (Phase V). (Adapted from Palazzo and Pavolini 2013, fig. 111 on p. 90.)

the process of being installed, and layers of dirt and rubble began to accumulate on the floors of abandoned complex during the first half of the 5th century, growing to several meters in thickness over the course of the 5th and 6th centuries, when it was used as a tip for building rubble and refuse. Even a dump, of course, indicates some human presence; and the neighborhood around the new *titulus* of S. Cecilia was not wholly devoid of life after the early 5th century, but certainly it had more vacant, crumbling buildings than before, and fewer (if any) patrons of luxurious mansions.[15]

With regard to most buildings destroyed, abandoned, or converted to humbler uses in the earlier 5th century, however, it must be said that the precise date or cause of their dereliction will never be known for certain, no matter how diligently they are excavated. This uncertainty is worth considering. Rare and fortunate exceptions notwithstanding, archaeology is usually too imprecise a tool to connect signs of destruction or abandonment to the events of a particular year. Even in especially compelling instances of probable Gothic destruction, such as the house of the Valerii and the burned mansion in Via del Tempio di Diana, we cannot rule out a casual fire (a constant danger in any city), or the effects of an earthquake that struck in 408, or any number of other unknowable local contingencies. Serious floods recorded in 398 and 411, along with the earthquake of 408, may indeed have caused more material damage and disruption than Alaric's troops. What careful, scientific archaeology *is* good at, however, is documenting processes that unfold over time. In the case of residential buildings and settlement at Rome, there is an unmistakable pattern of partial contraction – but by no means total collapse – over the first half of the 5th century, which increases in intensity from mid-century on (more on this last point later).[16]

In order to integrate these scattered archaeological vignettes of destruction and vacancy into a more synthetic picture of demographic decline, we need to return to the pork dole. The next document after 367 is a constitution of 419 directed by Emperor Honorius to the praetorian prefect of Italy, Palladius. It presents the fewest problems of interpretation of the group and contains essential information. It shows, first, that each individual annual pork ration, called an *obsonium*, amounted to 25 pounds of pork, distributed in five-pound increments over five months. It further specifies that pork was distributed at Rome at a rate of 4,000 *obsonia* per day, or 120,000 per month; the latter figure should represent the total number of recipients of the pork dole at Rome. These recipients would then have received a cumulative total of 600,000 pounds of pork per month (120,000 × 5 pounds) over 5 months, for an annual total of 3,000,000 pounds. Assuming, as we have no choice but to do, that the quantity of the individual ration (25 pounds) and the nature of the recipients (all adult male citizens?) were the same as in 367, this gives a measure of relative population decline between 367 and 419 of over 60 percent (3,000,000 is approximately 38 percent of the 7,933,310 pounds attested in 367). In absolute terms, if we accept a population of 700,000–750,000 in 367, the same ratio of *obsonia* to total inhabitants would yield a population of about 275,000 in 419, a decade after the Gothic sieges and sack of the city. As the law of 419, however, pertains specifically to the number of daily rations distributed for free and in fact mentions that some additional quantity of pork was allocated to the imperial administration and unspecified others, it appears that the total quantity of pork delivered to Rome was a bit greater, and so might have sufficed for a somewhat larger population: 300,000? 325,000?[17]

Before proceeding, there is one more text to mention, a fragment by the 5th-century historian Olympiodorus, preserved in a 9th-century compilation, which reports for the year 414 that Rome's urban prefect, Albinus, feared there was insufficient grain available to feed the city, as "the number of 14,000 was being expended every day." The fragment shows that Rome's population was growing as the city recovered from Alaric's sack in 410, whence Albinus' worry that existing resources were insufficient to meet growing demand. The best interpretation of Olympiodorus' cryptic statement that the prefect was "expending 14,000 every day" should make it a reference to 14,000 *modii* of grain, or 420,000 *modii* per month (14,000 × 30); on the further assumption that the monthly grain dole still amounted to 5 *modii* per recipient, as it had in the 1st and 2nd centuries, dividing 420,000 by 5 would give a total of 84,000 recipients in 414. Though not all accept this view of Olympiodorus, it seems to me the most likely. If, then, the grain in question went to the same pool of recipients as the pork dole, it would result that Roman recipients of the dole grew from 84,000 in 414 to 120,000 in 419, an increase of almost 50 percent that is plausible for a city recovering from the trauma and depopulation of the years 408–10.[18]

These numbers fit well with the broader historical picture that emerges from the years after 410. In the decades immediately following the sack, the western empire and the integrated economic networks of the western Mediterranean endured, ensuring that considerable quantities of money, materials, foodstuffs, and human capital were available to underpin Rome's resurgence. The local aristocrats who sat in the Senate and held the leading administrative offices, the urban prefecture above all, remained exceptionally rich thanks to their landholdings across much of the western Mediterranean. The Roman Church possessed vast landed wealth, too, and its holdings continued to grow through both private bequests and imperial munificence. Emperors, imperial officials, and senators reacted to the sack by spending lavishly to restore public buildings and spaces. They also worked closely with the Church to restore older churches and erect magnificent new ones. After well over a century during which emperors had resided infrequently in Rome, the city even returned to prominence as an imperial residence after 410: Both Honorius (r. 395–423) and Valentinian III (r. 425–55) chose to spend almost as much time in the ancient capital as in Ravenna, and both were buried there in a new imperial mausoleum attached to St. Peter's, a remarkable choice given that not a single 4th-century emperor was buried at Rome. Romans in the decades following 410 might reasonably have expected their city to regain or even exceed whatever splendor it had lost in recent years.[19]

The material evidence points to real, albeit partial, resurgence. Emperors, urban prefects, and others among the senatorial elite restored many – but no means all – of the city's more frequented and symbolically charged monuments and public spaces. With population and resources still well below pre-408–10 levels, tough choices had to be made about what to restore and what to relinquish. One inscription shows that parts of the charred Senate House were being restored already in 412–14, when the urban prefect Flavius Annius Eucharius Epiphanius repaired the senatorial archives (the *secretarium Senatus*); and two more inscriptions indicate that the entirety of the Senate House had been refurbished by 423 at the latest. In the same years, the connecting portico on the short, eastern end of the Forum of Caesar, just behind the Senate House, was transformed into a basilica-like hall, suggestively named the Atrium of Liberty (*atrium Libertatis*), that was used for judicial proceedings. Yet by the mid 5th century, two of the rooms (*tabernae* X and XI) in the adjoining south portico of Caesar's forum had been stripped of their marble paving and turned into workshops for bone and metal, respectively, the latter complete with a furnace dug into the floor (Fig. 2.6). From the mid 5th century, then, we can imagine the

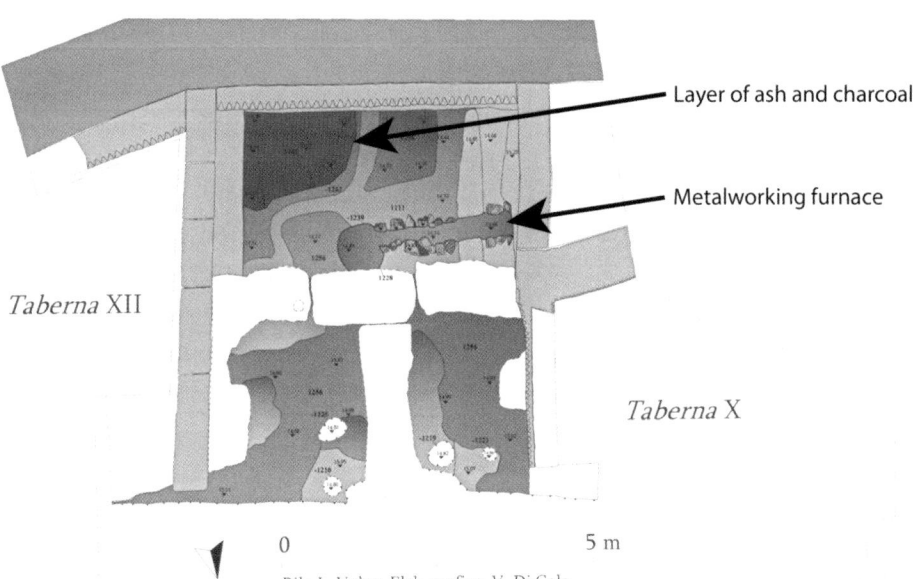

Figure 2.6 Plan of Taberna 11 in the Forum of Caesar (Corsaro et al. 2013, fig. 5 on p. 127; plan courtesy of Valeria di Cola.)

Senate meeting to the sounds, smoke, and smells of artisans at work just down the corridor.[20]

Meanwhile, the interior of the nearby Basilica Aemilia was never rebuilt after the fire, leaving a partial ruin in the heart of the Show Area. Yet in 416, the urban prefect Gabinius Vettius Probianus restored the facing Basilica Julia, located just across the Forum plaza, and filled its portico with an assemblage of statues, some attributed to famous Greek masters (Polykleitos, Praxiteles, Timarchos). Probianus thus created a kind of museum of statuary that also conspicuously proclaimed his and the Senate's ongoing concern for the décor of the city's most representative public spaces. As the 5th century progressed, such contrasts became more and more common in Rome's monumental center. Senators met in solemn conclave cheek-by-jowl with artisans at work. Restored public buildings abutted hulks that had been stripped of their ornaments and adapted to more utilitarian ends.[21]

The architectural bones of the Show Area remained solid, however. Even when parts of buildings were repurposed for distinctly humbler activities or stripped of their marbles, the structures themselves mostly stood through the 5th century, and often long thereafter. From a distance, an observer might have noticed little change. Farther west in the monumental heart of the Campus Martius, too, urban prefects continued actively to restore grand public buildings, even as others crumbled or filled with workshops and humble dwellings – the huts or shacks (*casae seu tuguria*) that an edict of 397 had expressly forbidden in the Campus Martius. At the Theater of Pompey, already repaired under Arcadius and Honorius between 395 and 402, Aurelius Anicius Symmachus, urban prefect in 418–20, dedicated a statue to Emperor Honorius, plausibly in connection with additional architectural restorations. Just beyond the theater portico, the esplanade around the four republican temples at Largo Argentina was repaved around the same time. Another inscription found close to the Theater of Balbus records the reconstruction of a building, possibly a portico, said to have been "toppled by fatal misfortune" (*subversa fatali casu* – Flood? Earthquake? Goths?) under Anicius Acilius Glabrio Faustus, urban prefect three times between 425 and 437.[22]

Other grand public monuments in the neighborhood, however, were left to decay or adapted to more utilitarian functions. The most detailed archaeological picture of urban transformation comes from the so-called Crypta Balbi excavations conducted in and around the portico of the Theater of Balbus, starting in the 1980s and continuing up to the present. In the first half of the 5th century, the floor of the portico's huge quadrangular enclosure was covered with a layer of dirt and garbage, becoming in essence a trash-strewn vacant lot. The semicircular exedra at the east end, opposite the theater, was then reoccupied, around 450, by a workshop for the production of glass vessels, complete with a small furnace (Fig. 2.7). The adjacent, still-larger colonnaded enclosure of the *Porticus Minucia* was also growing dilapidated: A cart track wended its way along the line of the dismantled southern colonnade in the first half of the 5th century (see below, Fig. 4.19), while the temple at the center of the enclosure crumbled. The travertine paving slabs of the plaza and parts of the temple were removed and stored for reuse, and workshops took over parts of the precinct (Fig. 2.8). Workshops also began to occupy the perimeter of the Stadium of Domitian in the 5th century, when games and shows were evidently no longer held there, as they had been through the end of the 4th.[23]

On the whole, however, considerable effort and resources still went into maintaining public amenities all across the city in the first half of the century, especially entertainment venues and baths. The Colosseum and Circus Maximus

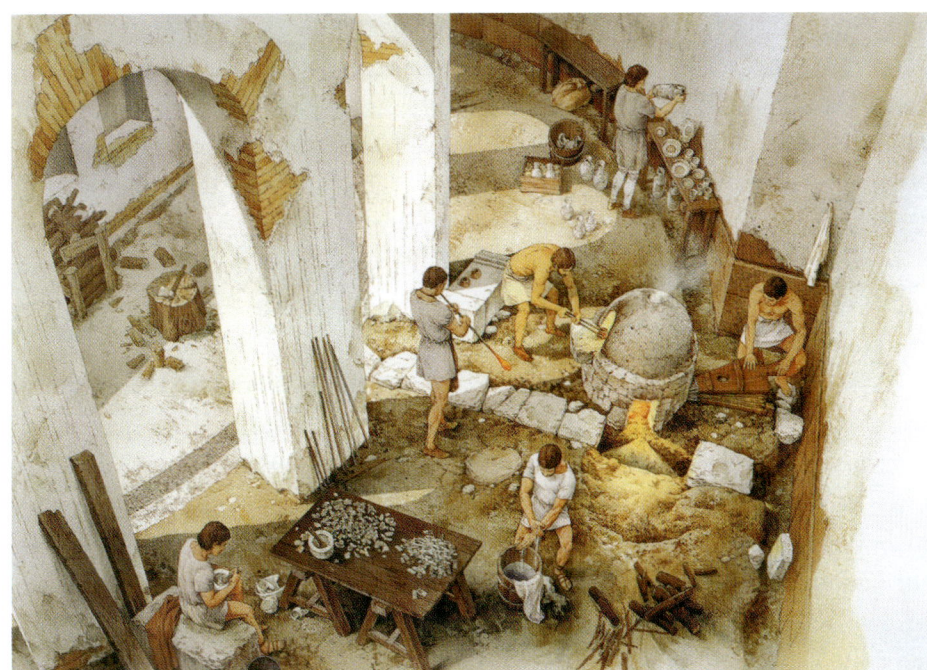

Figure 2.7 Reconstruction of the 5th-century glass workshop in the exedra of the Crypta Balbi. (Studio InkLink/Manacorda 2001, p. 43, fig. 45.)

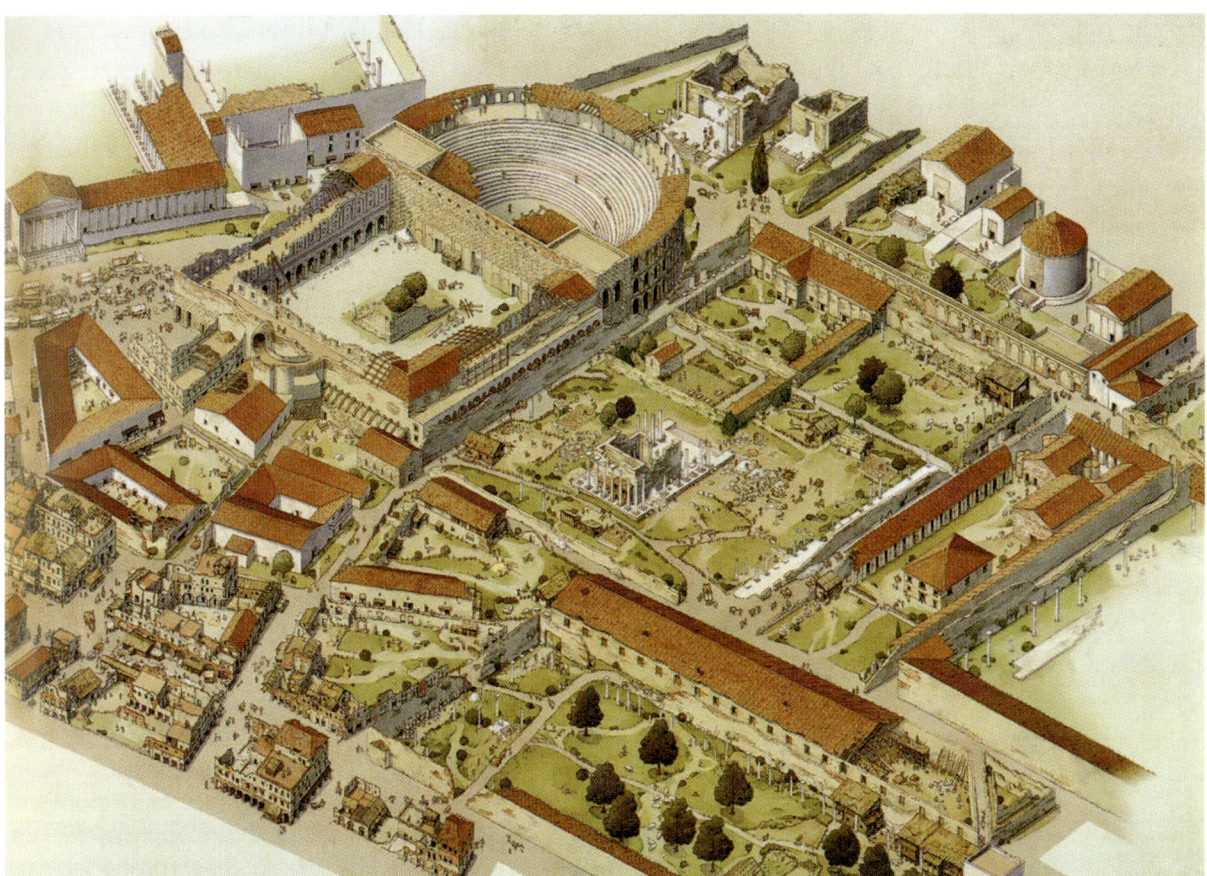

Figure 2.8 Reconstruction of the area of the Crypta Balbi (upper left) and Porticus Minucia (middle right) in c. 500. (Studio InkLink/Manacorda 2001, p. 45, fig. 47.)

were regularly repaired and continued to host bloody spectacles and other entertainments, including chariot races at the Circus Maximus, into the 6th century. The major imperial bath complexes likewise functioned through the 5th century, thanks to assiduous efforts to maintain and restore them. The urban prefect of 414 repaired the Baths of Decius on the Aventine, which the earthquake of 408 or Alaric's Goths (or both) may have damaged. The urban prefect of 443 restored the Baths of Constantine on the Quirinal, damaged as a result of what the inscription calls "civil, or rather beastly, slaughter." The even more massive baths of Caracalla and of Diocletian continued to function, too, as did the older baths of Agrippa and those of Nero in the Campus Martius, which Sidonius Apollinaris mentioned in the 460s. The aqueducts that supplied water to these baths, and to much of the city besides, were naturally also kept in good working order.[24]

Even pagan temples survived both natural and manmade disasters, not to mention the advent of Christianity, quite well. They comprised a significant chunk of the city's most ornate and prominent public structures, to the point that their wholesale destruction would have left gaping holes in the urban fabric. Long after they were closed to all forms of traditional religious practice in the 390s, they were preserved as civic adornments, urban landmarks redolent of Rome's storied past and repositories of venerable statues and other works of art. Still in the late 5th century, we find the traditionalist aristocrat and urban prefect Acilius Anicius Aginatius Faustus restoring a statue of Minerva in the *atrium Minervae*, behind the Senate House, after the roof of the building burned and collapsed probably during Ricimer's sack in 472. Some temples, among them the Pantheon and the Hadrianeum in the Campus Martius, the temple of Antoninus and Faustina in the Forum, and the temples of Portunus and of Hercules in the Forum Boarium, survive mostly intact even today. Countless others endured well into the Middle Ages.[25]

As for the Church, it seems in one important respect to have benefited from declining population pressure, which increased the availability of property in choice locations. The decades following Alaric's sack were a golden age for church construction, spurred on by a succession of ambitious and assertive popes eager to enhance the physical presence of the Church in the city. It is important to note that the task of these popes was facilitated by strong imperial support. The *Liber Pontificalis* presents Valentinian III and members of his family as the most avid patrons of Roman churches since Constantine. During the pontificate of Sixtus III (432–40), Valentinian donated thousands of pounds' worth of precious liturgical vessels and altar-furnishing to St. Peter's, St. Paul's, and the Lateran, presumably to replace what the Goths had taken, explicitly so in the case of the 2,000-pound silver altar-screen (*fastigium*) he gave to the Lateran to replace the one "which had been removed by the barbarians." The LP also reports another donation, apparently of property, made by Valentinian to a church of S. Lorenzo, which must be either the funerary basilica by the martyr's extramural grave, or the intramural church of S. Lorenzo in Lucina, one of Rome's eight new 5th-century *tituli*. His wife, Eudoxia, funded the rebuilding of the *titulus Apostolorum* (S. Pietro in Vincoli), and his mother, Galla Placidia, sponsored new mosaics for the triumphal arch at St. Paul's in the 440s, evidently in conjunction with Pope Leo I's efforts to restore the basilica after it was damaged early in his pontificate, probably by both fire and earthquake. The dedicated effort made by popes and rulers to banish memories of 410 and burnish Rome's image as a resurgent Christian capital culminated in three of the largest and most ornate basilicas erected since the age of Constantine, all built in

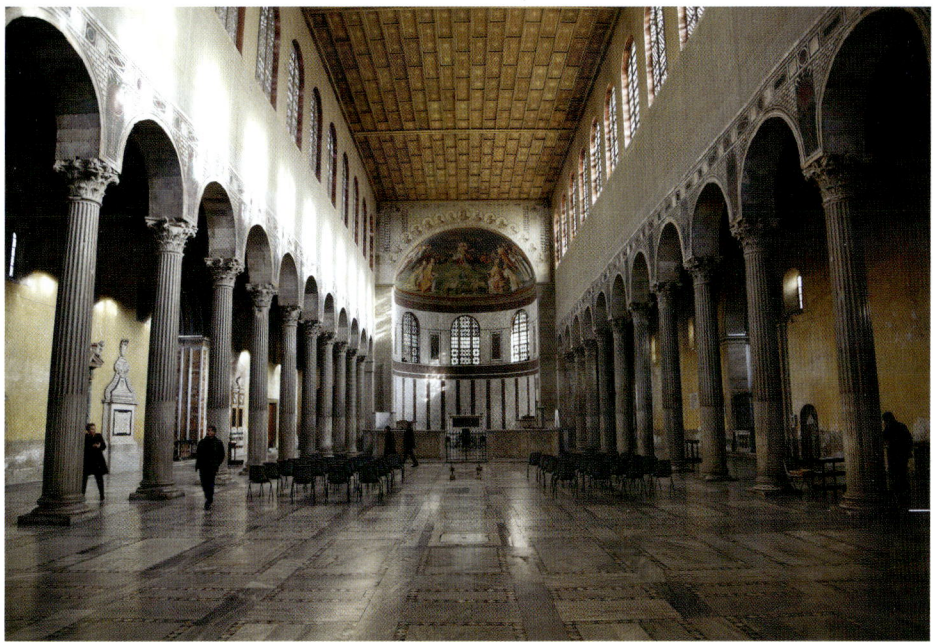

Figure 2.9 S. Sabina. (Author.)

prominent locations where they stood out for all to see, towering above the urban sprawl.[26]

The earliest was the *titulus Sabinae*, now S. Sabina, prominently situated on the crest of the Aventine. Begun under Pope Celestine II (r. 422–32), as the surviving dedicatory mosaic on the interior of the façade states, it was completed in the 430s under Sixtus III. In 1936–9, Antonio Muñoz removed medieval, renaissance, and baroque accretions to return the church to something resembling its pristine form. Though the restoration is too heavy-handed for some, the effect is nonetheless stunning and gives a better sense of a 5th-century church interior than any other building in Rome (Fig. 2.9). "That basilica," as Krautheimer said, "remains the most graceful and splendid Early Christian church to survive in Rome." It is larger than most *tituli*, at 53 m long, and features a high central nave, well lit by unusually large clerestory windows. (The stone tracery set with small, alabaster panes is Munoz's invention but should approximate the original scheme.) The clerestory rests on a set of 24 perfectly matched 2nd-century columns with Corinthian capitals, topped by an arcade revetted with polychrome marble inlays depicting Eucharistic chalices and bowls (Fig. 2.10). The apse and clerestory walls were once covered by colorful figural mosaics, now lost. Papally sponsored, large, light-filled, covered in shining marbles and mosaics, S. Sabina belongs to a new generation of churches designed to transform the intramural heart of the city into a Christian showpiece.[27]

S. Maria Maggiore, the largest of all Rome's intramural churches after the Lateran, was designed to similar effect. Also completed under Sixtus III, it rose on the summit of the Esquiline, looming over the Subura and easily visible from as far away as the Forum and the Lateran. It was built over the remains of two houses that had lain abandoned and partially ruined for some years, possibly since the time of Alaric's sack. It was not a *titulus*, but rather a devotional basilica, a church without resident clergy that depended directly on the pope, who presided in front of the crowds of the faithful that congregated there on special occasions in the Church calendar. S. Maria Maggiore would become the focus of Roman devotion to Mary, whom a Church council at Ephesus had

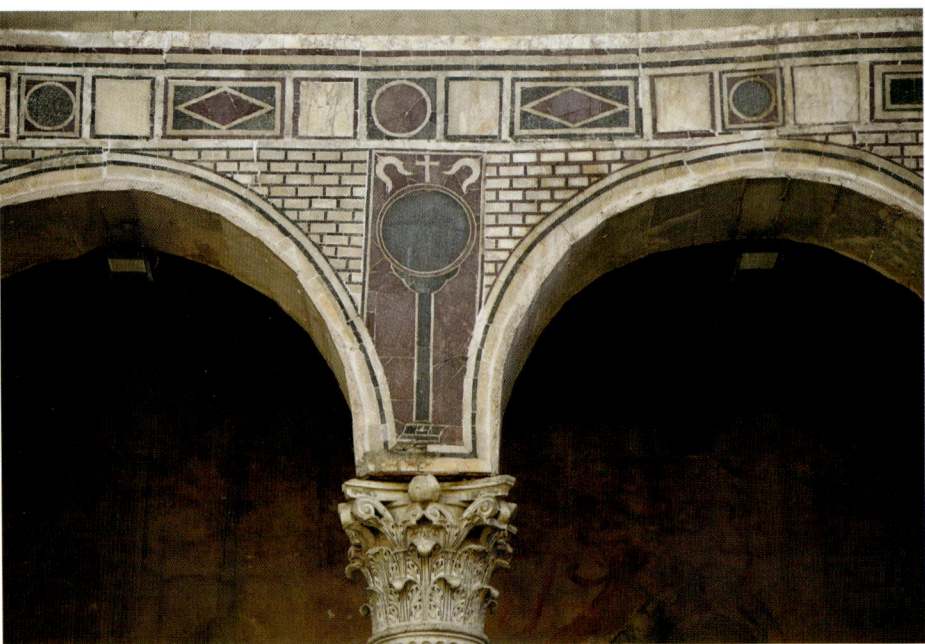

Figure 2.10 S. Sabina, interior: detail of *opus sectile* decoration of the nave arcade. (Author.)

proclaimed "Mother of God" (*theotokos*) in 431, just before construction began. At 79 by 35 m, it dwarfed even S. Sabina, which it otherwise resembles in shape, with its high central nave lit by large clerestory windows and separated from the side aisles by 20 matched pairs of reused columns in Proconnesian and cipollino marble. An extensive cycle of brilliantly colored figural mosaics covers the apse (redone at the end of the 13th century), the apse arch, and the lower register of the clerestory, depicting Christ in majesty, scenes from the New Testament, and scenes from the Old Testament, respectively (Fig. 2.11). New Ionic capitals, a form rarely seen in Rome after the 2nd century, were carved for the nave colonnades. Instead of arcades, the colonnades bore a trabeated (flat) entablature reminiscent of grand imperial buildings from centuries past, like the Basilica Ulpia in Trajan's forum, but also the Constantinian churches of St. Peter's and the Lateran (Fig. 2.12). This was a classicizing marvel designed to rival the works of Rome's pagan emperors, dedicated to the people of Rome by a pope eager to evoke the legacy of the emperors he had come, in a purely spiritual sense, to supersede: "Sixtus III to the people of God" (*Xystus episcopus plebi Dei*), the mosaic dedication over the apse proudly proclaims.[28]

A third great church dedicated under Sixtus III was built overlooking the Subura from atop the Oppian Hill, near the baths of Trajan. The new basilica, the *titulus* of apostles Peter and Paul (now S. Pietro in Vincoli), occupied the site of an existing apsidal hall plausibly associated with the *Curia athletarum*, the headquarters of a sporting association whose strongly pagan religious associations would have led to its closure by the 390s. Within two decades of the hall's initial conversion into a church in the 420s, thanks (probably) to an imperial bequest of the property, the old building was replaced by a much larger, three-aisle basilica whose construction was patronized by the empress Licinia Eudoxia, wife of Valentinian III. At 61 × 29 m, with a central nave supported by a pristine

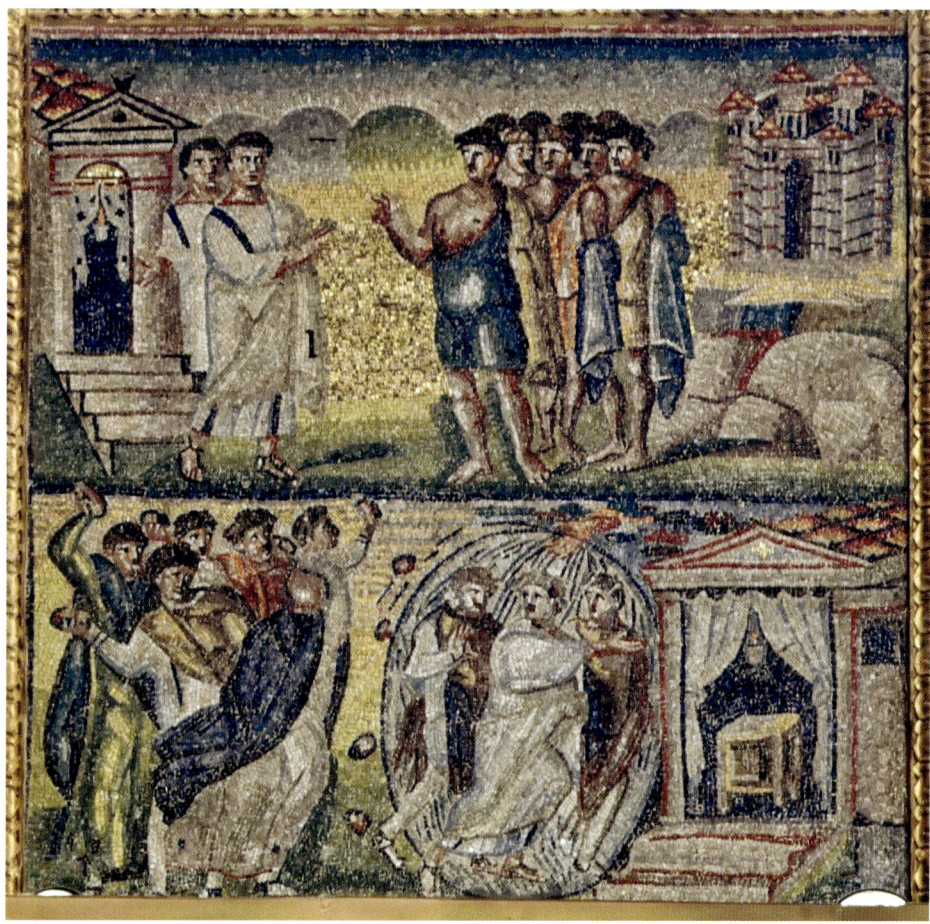

Figure 2.11 Santa Maria Maggiore, S wall of nave, mosaic panel. Top register: Moses sends spies into Canaan (*Num.* 13:17–20); bottom register: God protects Moses, Joshua, and Caleb from stoning (*Num.* 14:9–10). (Author.)

set of fluted Doric columns, it was a building worthy of its distinguished founders, a monument to cooperation between 'Church and state,' imperial family and popes, in the shaping of Christian Rome (Fig. 2.13).[29]

What all of these churches had in common, in addition to their size and their prominent hilltop locations, was their establishment on sites previously occupied by luxurious dwellings in prestigious neighborhoods. S. Sabina rose among the ruins of a temple and several houses destroyed by fire shortly before its construction, very possibly in 410. S. Maria Maggiore was built over the remains of two large houses, both of which went out of use shortly before the church was built, not far from 410. The walls were razed down to the floor level of the church and the substructures filled with rubble in order to provide a solid foundation for the new building (Fig. 2.14). S. Pietro in Vincoli incorporated standing walls of an earlier apsidal hall that formed part of the presumed *Curia athletarum*, itself a partly residential complex that occupied parts of an older *domus* on the site. In all three instances, whether the existing dwellings were put out of commission during Alaric's sack or simply abandoned, sold, or donated by their owners in the ensuing couple of decades, Church authorities capitalized on the growing availability of extensive tracts of prime real estate. That they were so readily able to do so, however, owes much to the active support not only of the imperial establishment but also of local elites, in an age when Christianity was firmly established and the

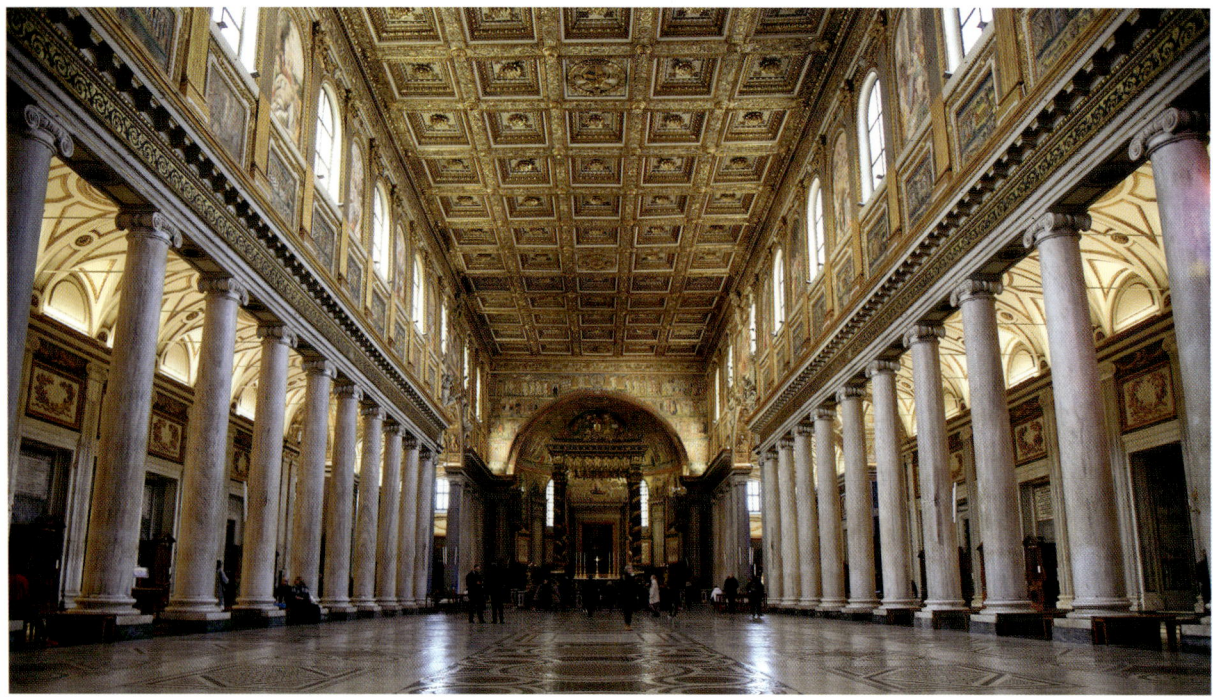

Figure 2.12 Santa Maria Maggiore. (Author.)

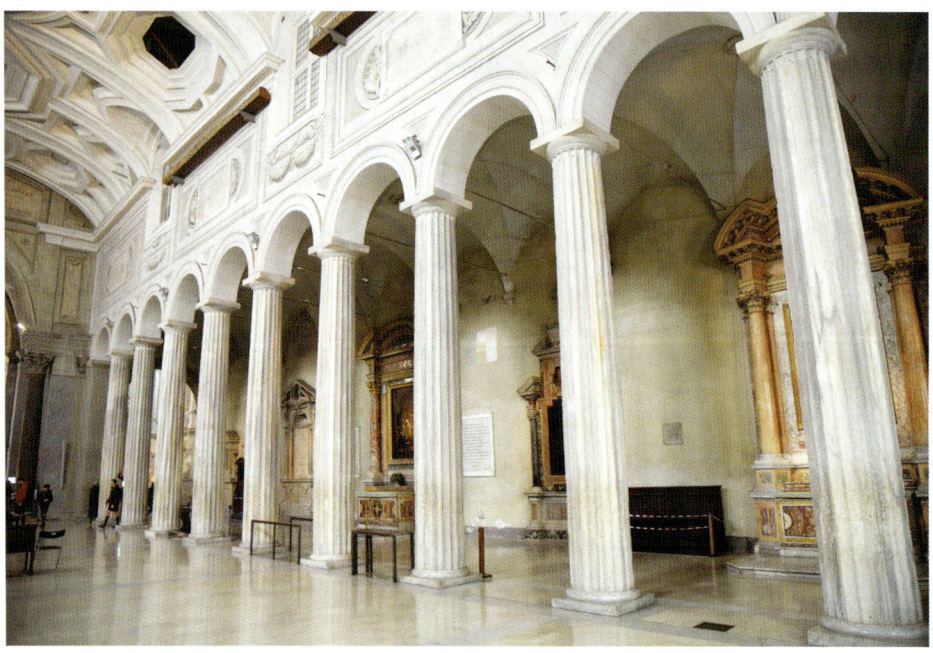

Figure 2.13 S. Pietro in Vincoli, nave colonnade featuring matched set of spoliated (and very unusual, in a Roman context) Doric columns. (Author.)

performance of ecclesiastical patronage had become common practice among the upper classes, from the senatorial aristocracy on down.[30]

Another point of comparison between the three churches is their incorporation of high-quality architectural *spolia*, especially columns,

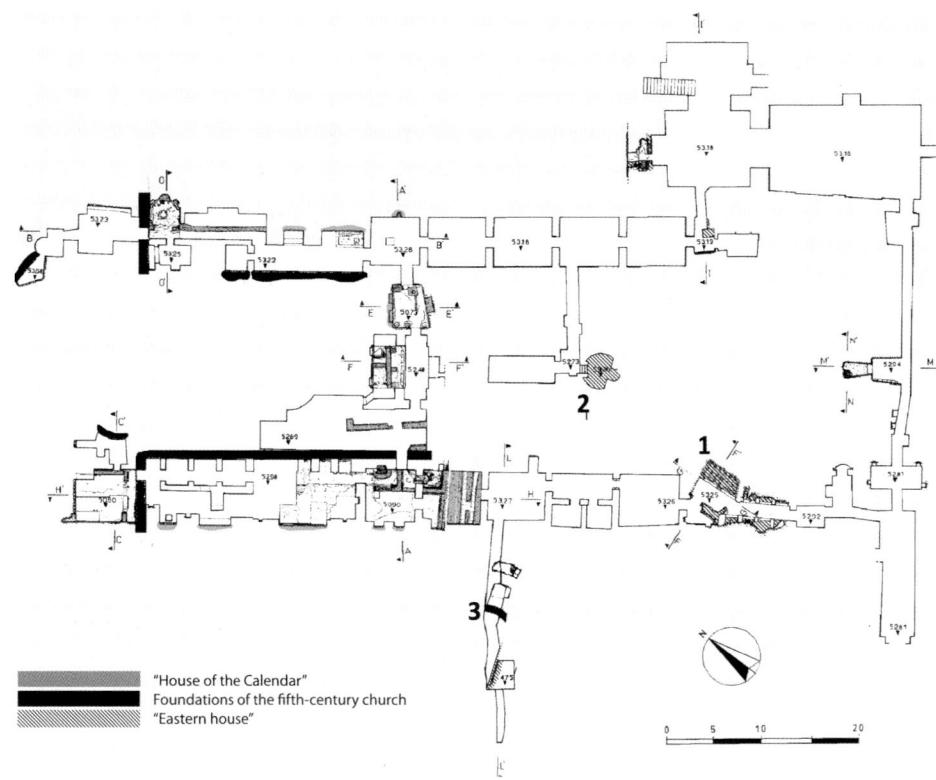

Figure 2.14 Plan of the two houses beneath Santa Maria Maggiore. (Courtesy of Paolo Liverani, modified by author.)

the ready supply of which again hints at changes in the cityscape. Surely the buildings these columns once belonged to were not, as some have imagined, destroyed by Alaric's Goths or any other violent catastrophe. S. Sabina's 24 matched columns and Corinthian capitals, the 20 deeply fluted Doric shafts at S. Pietro in Vincoli, and the 40 more heterogeneous marble columns at S. Maria Maggiore are too pristine to have come from structures reduced to rubble by hostile hands, fires, or earthquakes. In all of these cases, and others besides, the best assumption is that the source buildings were methodically dismantled and their components carefully collected. If the components were not harvested with specific projects already in mind, they might have been stored in 'spare-parts depots' while awaiting future use. A column shaft from S. Sabina and another from S. Maria Maggiore were in fact both inscribed with the name of a certain Rufenus, whom it is tempting to imagine as a sort of dealer in *spolia*. While permission to demolish public buildings was required from the imperial administration, as several edicts demonstrate, the pious emperors of the 5th century likely raised few objections in the case of derelict structures whose parts could be reused in new churches. In any case, although the dismantling of large, well-preserved buildings for their materials again suggests a certain contraction of the built environment, it hardly bespeaks chaos and wholesale urban disintegration. There seems to have been an orderly, well-regulated market for recycled building materials, which also presumes demand for these materials – eager architectural patrons, in other words, among them the builders of Rome's great 5th-century churches.[31]

This period of Roman resiliency evidently continued up to mid-century, when the penultimate document relating to the city's pork supply was issued. This is a law (*novella*), appended to the Theodosian Code, that was issued by the western emperor Valentinian III in 452. The crucial passage states explicitly that the total quantity of pork rations (*obsonia*) provided by the pork dealers (*suarii*) during the five months of the annual pork dole in Rome amounted to 3,628,000 pounds of meat. Dividing this figure by the 25 pounds of a single *obsonium*, we get a total of about 145,000 individual rations. The key point here is that this figure, like that of 367, appears to represent the total quantity of pork supplied to Rome; it should thus be directly comparable to the earlier figure. The change from 317,000 rations in 367 to 145,000 rations in 452 represents a decline of 54 percent. In absolute terms, this would mean Rome's 700,000–750,000 inhabitants in 367 were reduced to about 320,000–340,000 in 452.[32]

What is worth noting here is the apparent stability of Rome's population over the three-plus decades since the previous edict of 419, when 3,000,000 pounds of pork was earmarked for free distribution. Even if we increase that figure by 20 percent to account for the unspecified additional quantity diverted to the imperial administration and others (perhaps to be sold on the open market), the total quantity of pork sent to Rome in 419 was no greater than the 3,629,000 pounds delivered in 452. The apparent conclusion is that in the intervening period, the Roman population had stabilized, and probably even grown slightly (on the assumption that the unspecified additional quantity in 419 amounted to less than 20 percent of the total supply).[33]

To give a better sense of what is at stake in the interpretation of these texts, note again the alternative population figures proposed by Jean Durliat, who starts from the premise that the total number of pork rations distributed in 367 was 200,000 instead of 317,000. He accepts 120,000 pork rations for 419, but wants the quantity of pork in 452, like that of 367, to be some 40 percent lower than the text would appear to indicate – 80,000 *obsonia* instead of 140,000–145,000. Thus, instead of 317,000 (367) to 120,000+ (419) to 140,000–145,000 (452), his progression goes from 200,000 (367) to 120,000+ (419) to 80,000 (452). The result is a distinctly different picture of Rome's urban trajectory in the years 367–452. According to Durliat's model, population was steadily, inexorably declining, which makes it look as though the Roman scene was bleak and getting bleaker after the sack of 410. The Mazzarino/Lo Cascio model, on the other hand, makes Rome in the four decades after 410 a relatively vibrant place, only about half as populated as in 367, to be sure, but which rebounded from Alaric's sack and stabilized at several hundred thousand inhabitants from c. 420 into the 450s. For all the reasons outlined above in connection with the law of 367, I think the latter scenario comes closer to the truth. Rome in 452, then, was doing about as well as it had at any point since the sack of 410.[34]

But it was on the cusp of new calamities. An initial blow had already fallen with the Vandal occupation of North Africa, breadbasket of Rome, in the 430s, culminating in the fall of Carthage in 439. The North African provinces had been the richest still under western imperial control, the source of much of Roman senators' wealth and, crucially, most of the free grain distributed in the city. In 443, a powerful earthquake struck Rome, at a time when the Vandals had already begun raiding the coasts of Italy from their new African bases. Emperor Valentinian III and his very competent military commander, Aëtius, held the line for another decade, though resources were stretched critically thin: One law issued in 440 provided for the citizenry of coastal towns to arm themselves against Vandal incursions; another of the same year set Rome's population to work maintaining and guarding the walls.[35]

Then, in 454, court intrigue led to the murder of Aëtius at the hand of Valentinian himself, who was in turn murdered at Rome in the following year. Under their ambitious and dynamic king, Genseric, the Vandals took advantage of the ensuing chaos to seek the biggest prize of all. Less than three months after the death of Valentinian, Genseric led a fleet up the Tiber and easily occupied the city. (Petronius Maximus, Valentinian's hapless successor, had been dismembered by a mob in the tumult preceding the arrival of the Vandals.) The Vandals in 455 were able to be much more thorough in their pillaging than the Goths in 410. They plundered systematically and kept at it for weeks, presumably until the many ships in their fleet were filled with spoils: gold and silver ornaments and liturgical vessels from churches; metal statues; even the gilded bronze roof tiles – many tons of them – from the Capitol. Fires, whether set intentionally or otherwise, broke out in various places. They also took Valentinian's wife and two daughters back to Africa, along with all the Roman senators they could lay their hands on. Contemporaries perceived the event as especially disastrous; some even equated it with the end of imperial government in the West.[36]

This time, the prospects of recovery were more daunting than in 410. The immediate effects of the Vandal sack were bad enough: portable wealth irretrievably gone, buildings in ashes, food scarce, inhabitants scattered to the countryside or, for those with means, farther abroad, many never to return. Worse, the means to rebuild and repopulate the city on anything like its former scale were lacking. The last western emperors were impoverished, having at their disposal mainly the dwindling resources of peninsular Italy, much of which was subject to continuing Vandal raids. (The Vandals followed up their Roman success with the conquest of Sardinia, Corsica, and Sicily, turning much of the western Mediterranean into a 'Vandal lake' and depriving Rome of more resources and revenues.) Rome's remaining senators naturally also lost their African (and Sardinian, and Corsican, and Sicilian) estates to the Vandals. Many of their remaining Italian properties were ravaged, as were those of the Church. Most of Spain and Gaul, too, were lost to other occupiers.[37]

Worse yet, the state-subsidized African grain (and oil) that had, for centuries, fed hundreds of thousands was a thing of the past after 455. Just when the state had less money than ever to pay for imports of foodstuffs, that is, the supply of grain that it had formerly collected as taxes, in kind, from the African provincials for distribution at Rome dried up. It is probable that the African grain supply had persisted more or less uninterrupted right up until 455, even after the initial Vandal conquest of North Africa in the 430s. In 442, Valentinian III had signed a treaty with Genseric, betrothing his eldest daughter to Genseric's son in return for the continued sailing of the grain-fleet from Africa. But this arrangement ended when Petronius Maximus murdered Valentinian and immediately married his daughter. While Genseric got the princess when he took Rome, there is no reason to think that he continued the consignments of food thereafter. Though some African grain and oil doubtless still went to Rome for sale on the open market, they no longer came free of charge, for distribution free of charge to the urban plebs. The archaeological record in fact shows a measurable decline in the quantities of African transport-amphorae coming to Rome in the second half of the 5th century, evidently because trading connections between Africa and Rome were curtailed, while a larger percentage of the dwindling imports that still arrived came from southern Italy/Sicily and the eastern Mediterranean. The loss of Africa practically ensured that the urban population not only failed to rebound after the disasters of 455, but probably indeed declined further and faster than before.[38]

Near-constant political and military turmoil compounded Roman miseries, the more so as Rome was again the main imperial residence between 450 and 474 – the center of the maelstrom. No western emperor after Valentinian III reigned for more than five years, and a total of nine were recognized at Rome in the 20 years following his death, six of whom reigned for less than two years. Effective power lay with the troops and their commanders. The Gallic aristocrat Avitus succeeded Petronius Maximus at Rome, where he remained for close to a year with the Gothic troops from Gaul who had proclaimed him emperor. To pay this 'friendly' army, he resorted to stripping bronze fixtures and statues from the city's public buildings, enraging Romans who helped overthrow him in 456. From then until 472, the real power behind the throne was Aëtius' successor as Master of the Soldiery (*magister militum*), the Germanic commander Ricimer, who was instrumental in making (and unmaking) a series of short-reigning "shadow emperors." When he fell out with the last of them, Anthemius (r. 467–72), he besieged Rome in 472, taking it after five (or perhaps nine) months that dramatically compounded the miseries of the dwindling survivors left in the city. Those who endured through the long months of famine and disease saw Ricimer's troops pillage and burn for days after they entered the city. In 474, Julius Nepos (r. 474–5) overthrew Glycerius (r. 473–4) with the help of yet another army that was allowed to occupy the city for months. Relief came only after 476, when another Germanic general, Odoacer, deposed the child-emperor Romulus Augustulus and ended the western imperial line. Odoacer ruled Italy from Ravenna for over a decade, until a Gothic army under King Theodoric arrived in Italy in 489; after four more years of conflict, Theodoric overthrew (and murdered) Odoacer in 493.[39]

From a Roman perspective, it is easy to agree with near-contemporaries who saw 455 and its aftermath as a watershed moment. A growing body of material evidence at Rome points to 455 as a tipping point, a moment when local cataclysms combined with the systemic failure of the western Roman empire to leave the city irreparably diminished. Though the archaeological findings are (inevitably) scattered and circumstantial, they cumulatively suggest that processes of decay and abandonment already sporadically visible in the first half of the century were accelerating.[40]

There are enough documented cases of houses either abandoned or violently destroyed from the middle of the 5th century to suggest that the pace of residential contraction was increasing. The two senatorial residences discovered under today's Ospedale Militare on the Caelian Hill, for example, were vacated in mid-century and never reoccupied by upper-class tenants. Most of the sprawling *domus* in Piazza dei Cinquecento, near Termini Station, also fell vacant in the second half of the 5th century; only the former service quarters stayed inhabited, presumably because their cramped chambers were easier to maintain and keep covered than the big rooms, whose roofs, once ruined, were beyond the remaining occupants' capacity to repair. The grand halls were walled off from the small inhabited wing and turned into a garbage dump. The aristocratic residence beneath today's Palazzo Altemps likewise seems to have decayed from the mid-5th century. In the further case of the house at the Vicus Caprarius, near the Trevi Fountain, which was gutted by fire in mid-century and never rebuilt, the temptation to attribute the damage to the Vandals is very strong, particularly in light of the recent excavations nearby along Via del Tritone that point to a more widespread pattern of mid-5th-century destruction and/or abandonment of upper-class houses in this neighborhood, among them the *domus* uncovered in the basement of the new Rinascente department store in Via del Tritone, and another farther east under the padiglione Pio Piacentini, in Via Francesco Crispi.[41]

Similar processes of decay lapped at public buildings. Some burned or collapsed, but most of Rome's most imposing monuments were robust enough to stay standing for centuries after they had lost their original function. Those not abandoned entirely were often stripped of their ornaments and fine marbles and adapted for humbler uses. We have already mentioned the installation of craftsmen in the porticoes of the *Porticus Minucia*, and the transformation of the exedra at the Crypta Balbi into a glass workshop, and of two *tabernae* in the Forum of Caesar into metal- and bone-working spaces, all around the middle of the 5th century. In other cases, restoration involved the street-facings alone of otherwise derelict buildings, whose grandiose facades concealed the desolation that lay just behind. A notable example is the fire-damaged Basilica Aemilia, where only the facades along the Via Sacra and the Argiletum were restored after the fire of 410, leaving a ruin at its core (Fig. 2.15).[42]

We might cite many more picturesque tableaux of transformation and dereliction at various sites across Rome, but the panorama they present remains impressionistic and, often, fuzzy in its chronological outlines. It may be more productive instead to seek ways of gauging the progression of Rome's 5th-century contraction that are more systematic than recourse to the scattered glimpses offered by excavations. One is the epigraphic record, the (usually datable) inscriptions that record maintenance and construction on public buildings, for example, or the dedications of commemorative monuments and statues. Taken in their entirety, various categories of inscriptions found throughout the city can show something about the intensity of various activities over time, or at least the intensity with which such activities were epigraphically recorded.

Statue dedications (known mostly through inscriptions, though there are also a few surviving statues) can be conveniently studied and statistically analyzed thanks to the database of the "Last Statues of Antiquity" project at Oxford. By my count, there are 19 dedications at Rome (including statues either erected new, restored, or moved) from the years 395–406; unsurprisingly, none at all from 407 to 411; 38 from 412 to c. 450; 18 from 455 to 484; and 7 from 485 to

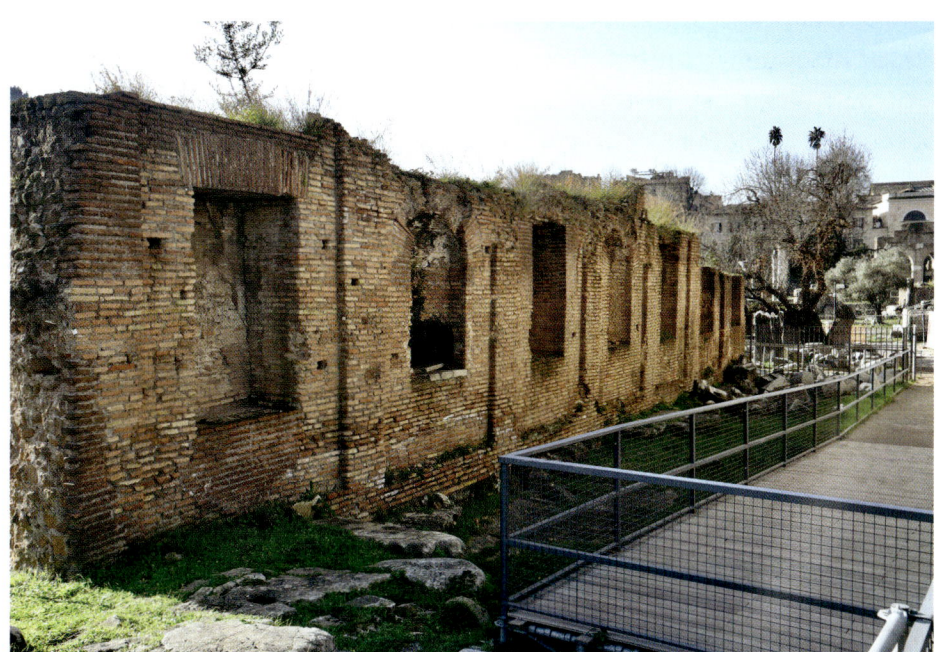

Figure 2.15 The late antique façade along the short (west) flank of the Basilica Aemilia, facing onto the Argiletum, with niches for sculpture. (Author.)

526, after which there is nothing save a single dedication in 608 (the statue of the Byzantine emperor Phokas atop a column in the forum). Thus: for the dozen years before the Gothic sieges and sack, we have an average of 1.58 dedications per year. For the period 412–50, the average is almost exactly one per year (38 dedications in 39 years), though over some shorter intervals, such as the first rush of renewal after the Gothic sack, it is somewhat higher (11 dedications in the nine years 412–20). The decline after 455 is considerably sharper: for 455–84, it is 0.6/year; for 485–526, it is 0.17, and thereafter it drops essentially to zero.[43]

What to make of these numbers? Outside of Rome, statue dedications throughout the western provinces had mostly ceased already by the beginning of the 5th century, for whatever combination of reasons: conflict and unrest, changes in taste and customs, and so on. One might therefore say that Rome merely followed the general trend, albeit with a good century of delay relative to most of the Italian peninsula. But my sense is that there is more to it than this. Throughout the first half of the 5th century, emperors, imperial officials, and senators continued to dedicate statues at Rome with gusto, hewing in this respect, as in many others, to centuries of tradition. That only about half as many statues were dedicated in the decades following the sack of 455 as in the decades after 410 seems unlikely to result wholly from a sudden change in taste. More probable, I think, is that the reduction reflects a real disturbance in established mechanisms of commemoration: a decrease in the number of wealthy dedicators (and dedicatees?) of statues, and in the resources or capacities of those who might still have wished to make such dedications. Given also that an increasing percentage of 4th- and earlier 5th-century inscriptions already commemorated restorations or moves of existing statues, as opposed to newly commissioned pieces, it may also be the case that there were simply fewer older statues left to move or rededicate after the multiple episodes of pillage in the period 455–72.[44]

Building inscriptions corroborate the impression that we are dealing with systemic shifts that run deeper than changes in epigraphic culture. As in the case of statues, so too with regard to epigraphic commemoration of building activities, the Romans tenaciously persevered well into the 5th century with a practice that was elsewhere in wholesale decline. Silvia Orlandi has pointed out that there is, once again, a marked difference between the decades after 410 and those after 455. While the city teemed with restoration work after 410, as we have seen, far fewer inscriptions record repairs made after 455. But perhaps more tellingly, the language of the inscriptions carved after 455 breaks with centuries of precedent: For the first time, conquering barbarians are explicitly acknowledged to have been the cause of the damage being repaired. "Barbarian incursion," "enemy attack," and even "Vandal fury" all occur after 455, whereas damage remedied after 410 was more elliptically attributed to "fatal chance," "fatal fire," and so on. The reality of defilement by invaders was evidently too pervasive to ignore by the later 5th century, also because the Vandals caused more damage than Alaric's Goths, much of which was never repaired. Signs of destruction and decay were more pervasive, and inscriptions made little further effort to conceal that reality. As Orlandi puts it, they describe "a cityscape composed of ruins and teetering buildings, of piles of rubble needing to be removed and squalid, abandoned places, certainly in order to emphasize the pressing importance of the remedial action, but with a frankness that speaks to a different relationship with the city's present and its past."[45]

Another broader proxy for Roman contraction in the later 5th century is the declining frequency of really enterprising construction projects, churches included. Already by the beginning of the century, churches were the main focus of ambitious Roman patrons. Older basilicas, theaters, porticoes, and so on might be restored, but were rarely built new – Rome had more than enough of such traditional building types already! Popes, emperors, and aristocrats all invested heavily in church-building during the first half of the 5th century, when all three of the largest and most opulent intramural churches (after the Lateran) were constructed: S. Sabina, S. Pietro in Vincoli, and S. Maria Maggiore, along with a healthy group of other, still very impressive, foundations: SS. Giovanni e Paolo (the *titulus Pammachii*), S. Vitale (the *titulus Vestinae*), and the lower church at S. Clemente, among others. In the second half of the century – in fact for a full century after 455 – only one church of comparable magnitude appeared in the city. This is S. Stefano Rotondo on the Caelian, "the last grand building of antiquity in Rome" (Fig. 2.16). But although it was probably completed around 470, it may in fact have been under construction already before 455, in which case the contrast between the pre- and post-455 generations would be yet starker. Otherwise, none of the Roman churches founded in the century 455–555 approached the size and magnificence of the grand basilicas of the earlier 5th century.[46]

While the urge to build churches never fully waned, it is striking how modest in scale and few in number were the projects attempted in the decades after 455. A general scarcity of human and financial resources surely helps to explain the drop-off, but we might also posit a partial breakdown in established mechanisms of patronage during these years of armed strife and ensuing political and social upheaval. It seems a telling sign of the times that the two intramural foundations of the later 5th century that we know most about resulted not from the initiative of Roman clerics or senators, but rather Germanic warlords. The first is today's S. Agata dei Goti, an edifice built from scratch on the south slope of the Quirinal in the Subura. Its apse mosaic, now lost, featured a mosaic inscription, datable to between 459 and 470, that proclaimed Ricimer himself the patron of the edifice. The almost square plan comprised a central nave, lit by clerestory windows, flanked by single side aisles supported by reused columns (Fig. 2.17). The

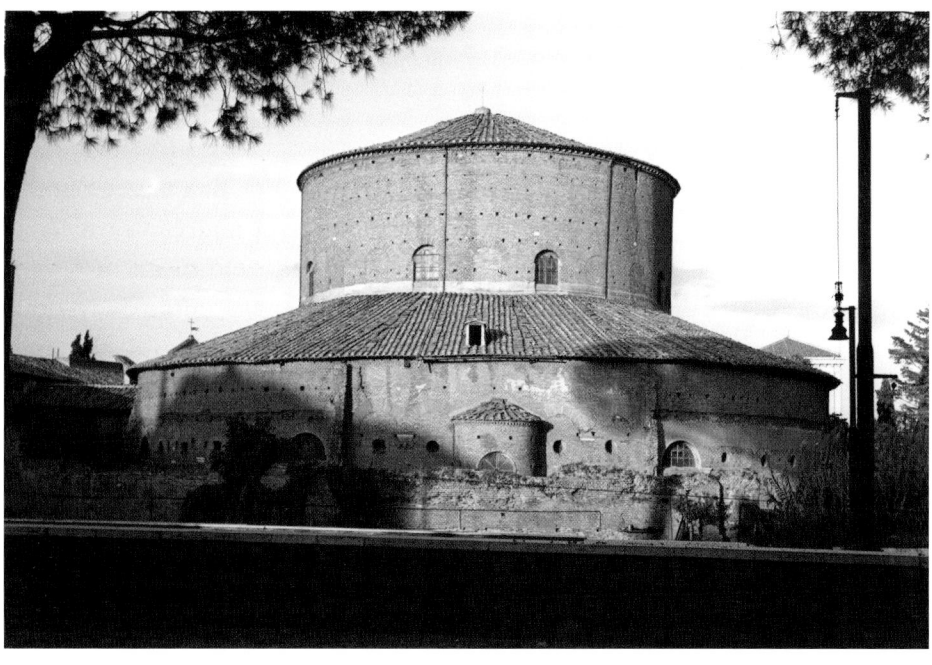

Figure 2.16 S. Stefano Rotondo, c. 1950s. (American Academy in Rome, Fototeca Unione, Roma. CHSSR.3.)

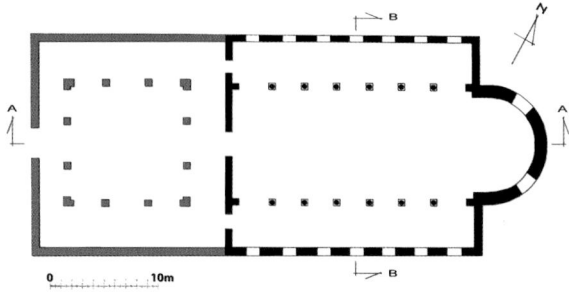
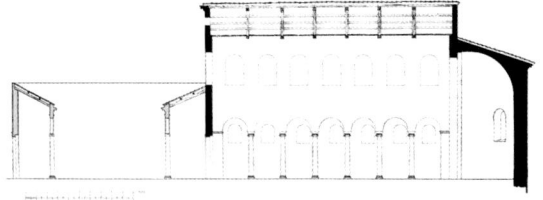

Figure 2.17 S. Agata dei Goti. (Plan and elevation by Marco Aimone, courtesy of the author.)

quality of its mortared brick masonry and internal marble furnishings is comparable to that of churches built earlier in the century, such as S. Sabina and S. Maria Maggiore. At 22.5 m long by 18.5 m wide (exclusive of the apse), however, it is considerably smaller even than the most modest of the 4th- and early 5th-century *tituli*.[47]

The second well-documented intramural church of the later 5th century was implanted in an existing building. This is S. Andrea in Catabarbara on the Esquiline, demolished in 1930, which occupied the former audience hall of the mansion on the Esquiline once owned by the Junii Bassi family. This so-called "Basilica of Junius Bassus" was willed to the Church by another high-ranking Germanic general, the *magister militum* (and self-fashioned Roman aristocrat) Flavius Valila, and consecrated by Pope Simplicius (r. 468–83). The older apsidal hall was repurposed with a minimum of structural modifications – even the superb 4th-century *opus sectile* wall revetments with their decidedly profane themes (Egyptianizing scenes, tigers attacking prey, pagan myths) were left untouched, though a new mosaic was installed

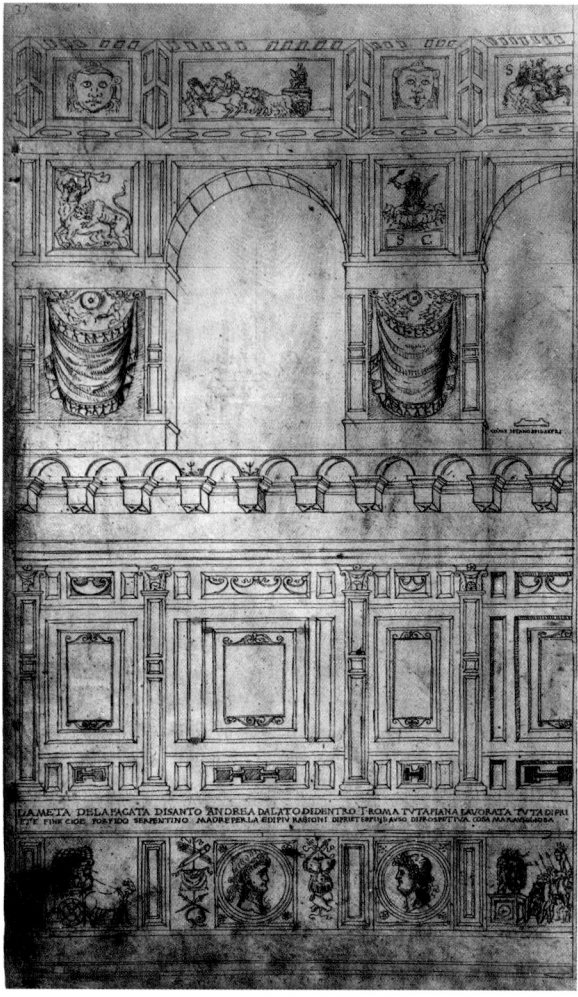

Figure 2.18 S. Andrea in Catabarbara, 16th-century drawing of nave, with its 4th-century *opus sectile* revetments, by Antonio Da Sangallo. (American Academy in Rome, Fototeca Unione, Roma.BASIU.11.)

in the apse (Figs. 2.18–2.19). At a time when the city was fuller than ever of unoccupied halls in mansions, bath complexes, and so on that were suitable for churches, the decision to convert an old building instead of putting up a new one would in any case have made good sense. But for the aspiring church-founder of the late 5th century, conversion was probably the most feasible choice anyway, given the diminished resources available to even the wealthiest Romans of the day.[48]

In the end, it is almost a moot point whether any localized instance of decay, destruction,

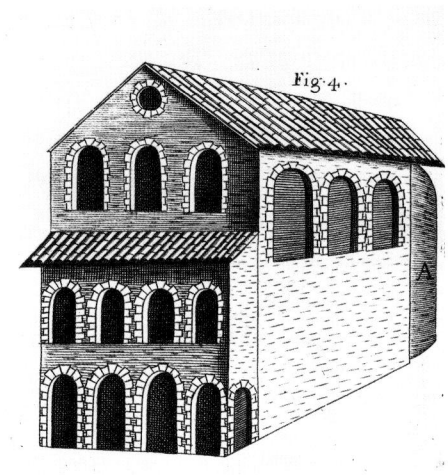

Figure 2.19 17th-century drawing of S. Andrea in Catabarbara. (American Academy in Rome, Fototeca Unione, Roma.BASIU.6.)

abandonment, or transformation results from Goths in 410, or Vandals in 455, or Ricimer's army in 472, or rather from earthquakes in 408, 443, and circa 484, or fires and floods and other casual misfortunes, or simply from the slow wear of time. In the grand historical scheme of things, the essential points are that population was declining at a steep and increasing rate, including the wealthy and influential citizens whose houses are larger and easier to identify archaeologically, and that decrepit properties were rebuilt and reoccupied less regularly than they had been in earlier centuries. After all, Rome had suffered fires, floods, earthquakes, plagues, and sieges in the past and always rebounded. What changed over the course of the 5th century was the capacity to recover. As the attractions of urban living diminished, notably the gargantuan distributions of food and the economic opportunities that derived from proximity to wealthy patrons and consumers, there was a corresponding drop in the steady influx of immigrants needed to maintain population levels in a pestilential pre-modern metropolis such as Rome, where deaths reliably outnumbered births. Further, Italy's rural population, whence so much of Rome's fresh blood had always come, was also declining in the 5th and 6th centuries, thus drying up much of the capital's traditional demographic reservoir. With the crumbling of the empire-wide networks that had sustained and protected – and fed! – Rome, in short, the city's capacity for regeneration declined, too.[49]

The confluence of local catastrophes with the structural failure of the western empire, then, was far more damaging than the end of the western imperial line per se. Indeed, after the chronic violence and instability of the years 455–76, the inception of Odoacer's reign in 476 came as something of a reprieve. Unlike Stilicho and Ricimer, the Germanic generals who had controlled Italy in all but name before him, Odoacer chose to dispense altogether with the fiction of the sovereign western emperor. He sent Romulus Augustulus' imperial regalia to Constantinople and ruled Italy as king (*rex*) and – he half-heartedly claimed – regent of the emperor in Constantinople. His eventual conqueror, Theodoric (r. 493–526), would likewise claim to rule as the regent of the eastern emperor. And while Romans knew perfectly well that they were living in a post-imperial order, under barbarian rule (Odoacer and Theodoric are never called "emperor" in surviving inscriptions), not much changed in legal and administrative terms. Both Church and Senate accommodated themselves quite smoothly to the rule of barbarian kings nominally representing the eastern emperor in Constantinople.[50]

In fact, though Romans in 476 had little reason to suspect it, the half-century that followed turned out to be one of relative peace and prosperity, a period that has been described as an "Indian summer" for Rome and Italy. The new Germanic rulers of the peninsula, first Odoacer and then Theodoric, strove to assert the fundamental Roman-ness of their regimes, and their faithfulness to imperial tradition, in part by stressing their respect for the history and prerogatives of the ancient capital. Rome would also stay clear of warring armies for some 60 years, including during the four years of conflict between Odoacer and Theodoric in 489–93, until the Byzantine reconquest of Italy began in 535.[51]

With both Odoacer and Theodoric preferring to reside in northern Italy, closer to the frontiers of the kingdom, Rome was mostly left to its own devices. The Senate continued to play the leading role in local governance. Senators still regularly assembled in the old Senate House in the Forum, where they gave speeches, deliberated, and issued proclamations and official correspondence as a corporate body. The Senate maintained regular exchanges of written communications and embassies with the royal court at Ravenna, providing an essential channel of communication with Rome's barbarian overlords. Senators continued to act as civic patrons, sponsoring games and distributing largesse to the masses. Mimes and actors still performed in the theaters, hunters killed wild beasts in the Colosseum, chariots raced in the Circus Maximus. And senators still poured money into the royal coffers. In return, Odoacer and Theodoric allowed the Senate considerable autonomy and honored its most prominent members, scions of leading families such as the Symmachi, Decii, and Anicii, with consulships and urban prefectures and other traditional dignities and emoluments.[52]

Although the literary sources are naturally less kind to Theodoric's defeated predecessor, the material record suggests that Odoacer treated Rome much as Theodoric later would. At the Colosseum, eminent senators inscribed their names and titles with renewed care on their reserved seats in the front rows of the arena. The most distinguished were the consuls whom Odoacer still appointed each year, as had his imperial predecessors. Among the inscribed names are the consuls of 480, 481, 483, 485, and 490, and probably of 482 and 486 also. The urban prefect of 484, another senator, repaired parts of the amphitheater in the wake of an "abominable earthquake." But these proud assertions of continuity, physical and institutional, unfolded against a backdrop whose cracks were inconcealable. The colonnade that had encircled the uppermost story of the seating area until the earthquake was never repaired after it collapsed; instead, its shattered remains were buried beneath the arena floor, filling the warren of corridors and chambers whence animals and men had once waited to spring forth.[53]

Rome's ruling elite, including surviving members of ancient families and new men promoted to high office by Odoacer, were too few and too limited in their means to maintain more than a fraction of the monumental fabric. Hard choices had to be made about what to restore and what to abandon or dismantle, even in the heart of the Show Area. The Forum of Trajan was kept up as a privileged venue for ceremony and elite self-representation, while the adjacent Forum of Augustus was possibly being dismantled already in the decades around 500. One column-drum from the Augustan temple of Mars bears the crude inscription "of [i.e. belonging to] the patrician Decius," obviously carved when the column was in pieces (Fig. 2.20). If Meneghini and Santangeli Valenzani are right that the Decius mentioned is one of the three members of the Decii family who held the consulship between 486 and 529, it would follow that this personage was presiding in some capacity – whether official

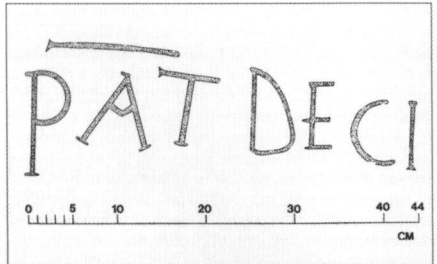

Figure 2.20 Inscription on a column-drum from the Temple of Mars in the Forum of Augustus. (Meneghini and Santangeli Valenzani 2004, p. 71, fig. 48.2.)

or private – over the transformation of the Forum of Augustus into a scrapyard for building materials. On the far (east) side of the Forum of Augustus, the paved esplanade of the Forum of Peace had already been occupied by a busy, rather grubby market in the 4th century, where merchants plied their wares in the shadow of the Greek sculptural masterpieces installed there by Vespasian, many of which still stood well into the 6th century. Across the Forum on the Palatine, the main residential and reception spaces of the *domus Augustana*, overlooking the Circus Maximus, retained much of their antique splendor, even as parts of the *domus Tiberiana* and the precinct of the Temple of Elagabalus on the Forum side of the hill fell into disuse and decay, with burials occurring in some vacant areas by the 6th century (Fig. 2.21).[54]

We are better informed for the period of Ostrogothic rule at Rome under Theodoric and his successors (c. 493–536), thanks mostly to the collection of state papers, the *Variae*, written and

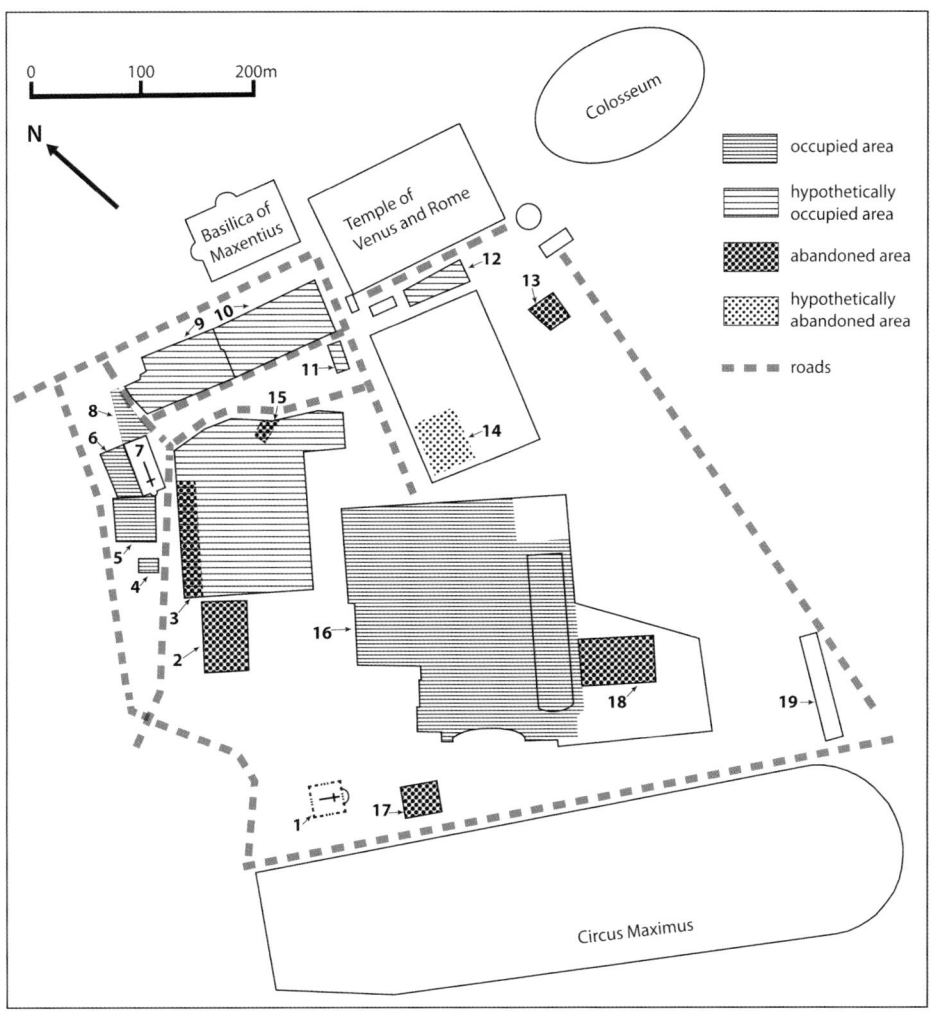

Figure 2.21 Schematic plan of the Palatine and its surroundings in the 6th century. 1: S. Anastasia; 2: Temple of Magna Mater (burials); 3: Bastione Farnesiano (abandoned section of the *domus Tiberiana* – burials); 4: building under S. Teodoro; 5: *horrea Agrippiana*; 6: hall adjacent to S. Maria Antiqua; 7: S. Maria Antiqua; 8: area fronting S. Maria Antiqua; 9: *atrium Vestae*; 10: shops/storerooms along the Via Sacra; 11: *tabernae* along the *clivus Palatinus*; 12: building by Arch of Titus; 13: *domus Tiberiana*; 14: Vigna Barberini (many burials); 15: abandoned section of *domus Tiberiana* (burials); 16: main palace block (*domus Flavia/Augustana*); 17: so-called *Schola Praeconum*; 18: Severan wing of palace; 19: Septizodium. (Redrawn and adapted from Augenti 1996, fig. 2.)

later assembled for publication by Theodoric's chancellor, the Roman senator Cassiodorus. Cassiodorus' letters and the decrees he issued in Theodoric's name paint the Gothic king as an eminently Roman ruler keen to respect tradition and renew the glories of the ancient past, a sovereign who indeed cared more for Romans and the city of Rome than the last 'Roman' emperors who had preceded him. Theodoric dispensed considerable sums for the maintenance of the city's public buildings and infrastructure, and underwrote the continued distribution of grain and pork to the urban plebs. During his one visit to Rome, in 500, he processed in majesty through the streets, addressed the Senate, and prayed at St. Peter's. In short, in his dealings with the Romans, Theodoric strove to emulate emperors long past. For their part, the Senate, people, and popes of Rome were by and large willing to accept Theodoric as emperor in all but name.[55]

We have hard evidence for some of Theodoric's restoration projects at Rome thanks to another Theodorican archaism: As no Roman ruler had done since the 4th century, Theodoric produced bricks and roof tiles stamped with his name. (A letter in the *Variae* in fact shows Theodoric recommissioning a defunct tile factory, the *Portus Licini*, and charging it with producing 25,000 pieces per year for use in restoring Roman monuments.) For Theodoric, this studied revival of an ancient imperial tradition made for good publicity; for us, it corroborates some of the restoration projects mentioned in textual and epigraphic sources and adds others to the list. Theodoric's stamps have turned up in several sectors of the Aurelian Wall; the imperial palace on the Palatine; the Baths of Caracalla; the Baths of Constantine on the Quirinal; and in the Forum, at the Senate House and the Basilica Aemilia.[56]

The *Variae* attest to restorations at the Theater of Pompey (4.51) and the Senate House (9.7.2). Additional work was done to clean and maintain the city's vast sewer system (3.30) and aqueducts (3.31.3–4; 7.6.1). An inscription adds the *secretarium Senatus* and *atrium Libertatis* by the Senate House, and possibly also the temple of Jupiter Optimus Maximus on the Capitoline. Another inscription found in the exedra of the Crypta Balbi may record repairs to the Theater of Balbus. These projects were carefully chosen to serve very specific ends. Theodoric concentrated on crucial infrastructure (walls, aqueducts, sewers); on the amenities lavished on the Roman people from time immemorial (entertainment venues and baths); and on some of Rome's most ancient and symbolically pregnant monuments: the heart of imperial power on the Palatine; the Senate House; and possibly even the most prominent temple in the city, the Capitol.[57]

But there was also clear-eyed acknowledgement that much of Rome was depopulated and dilapidated beyond the capacity of the urban authorities to repair. Some vacant structures were privatized, granted to new owners who might restore and reoccupy them. A partially ruinous warehouse below the Aventine was bestowed on a new owner for reconstruction as a private dwelling (*Var.* 3.29). Even the *porticus curva*, the horseshoe-shaped vestibule connecting the forums of Augustus and Nerva with the Subura, was given gratis to a senatorial family to become the nucleus of a new – and very centrally located – townhouse (*Var.* 4.30). In some cases, the concession of monumental buildings to individuals clearly backfired; *Var.* 3.31.4 laments that public buildings and even temples were being scrapped by their new proprietors instead of restored, as Theodoric had intended.[58]

The recovery and reuse of materials from irreparably ruined buildings is another recurring topic in the *Variae* (see esp. 7.44), where Theodoric/Cassiodorus stressed the importance of dismantling unsightly ruins and reusing their *spolia* to embellish other buildings whenever possible, in a sort of architectural triage. "Rome herself, that great mother of cities, rejuvenates by amputating the parts that are rotten with age," as Ennodius of Pavia put it in his panegyric for Theodoric. The great problem was the illegal harvesting of valuable materials from buildings that were *not* ruined, but (presumably) unfrequented enough to be easy prey for robbers who specialized in stripping valuable metals such as bronze and lead: the clamps that held stone masonry together, lead roofing, sculptural decoration, and so on. Theodoric protested vigorously against such depredations that threatened to compromise the décor and structural integrity of urban monuments, and threatened dire consequences for obstinate offenders (*Var.* 3.31.4), as he did for those who absconded with statues (*Var.* 7.13). One imagines the robbing continued all the same, as certainly did authorized spoliation. A remarkable example of the latter comes from the Colosseum, where an inscription shows that parts of the outer ambulatory were being dismantled in the early 6th century (Fig. 2.22), even as the arena remained in use and senators continued to have their names carved on their seats. Another dramatic episode of spoliation occurred in 532–3, when Queen Amalasunta authorized sending eight gigantic columns from the porch of Aurelian's Temple of Sol to Constantinople, where they were installed at Hagia Sophia.[59]

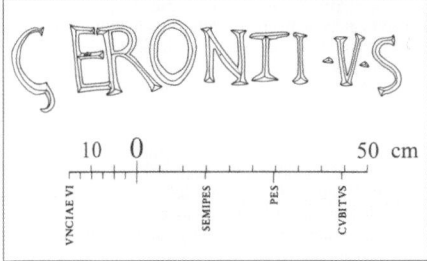

Figure 2.22 Inscription from the partially dismantled outer ambulatory of the Colosseum, with the name of the senator Gerontius in the possessive case. (Meneghini and Santangeli Valenzani 2004, p. 71, fig. 48.1.)

Given the Ostrogothic rulers' understandable focus on maintaining, restoring, or otherwise regulating the use (or reuse, or disuse) of Rome's enormous existing architectural patrimony, it may come as little surprise to learn that neither the *Variae* nor any other source mentions a single new monumental edifice erected anywhere in the city. Still, the total silence is striking. The *Variae* says nothing even about church-building at Rome, this at a time when sumptuous churches were being erected in northern Italy – projects undertaken in Theodoric's reign at Ravenna alone included S. Apollinare Nuovo, S. Apollinare in Classe, S. Vitale, and the Arian baptistery. The *LP* does attribute a few new churches to Pope Symmachus (r. 498–514), but we may wonder how impressive these projects were, given that all were supplanted by new structures already during the early Middle Ages, leaving little trace of whatever Symmachus built. These are a "basilica" at S. Pancrazio, outside the walls on the Via Aurelia; another extramural "basilica" of S. Agnese on the Via Nomentana, both of which were replaced, assuming they existed at all, by the extant basilicas built at both sites under Pope Honorius I (r. 625–38); and an intramural "basilica" on the site of the 9th-century church of S. Martino ai Monti. Otherwise, Symmachus confined himself to improving and embellishing existing foundations, as did his successors for the rest of the first half of the 6th century, albeit on a more limited scale. Probably neither the Ostrogothic sovereigns nor the popes saw much need for new churches in a place whose tens of thousands of remaining inhabitants were served by a collection of churches built to serve hundreds of thousands.[60]

The lone extant church certainly founded between 493 and the start of the Gothic War in the mid-530s looks to have been more a (very potent) symbolic gesture than a practical necessity. This is the church dedicated to the eastern healer saints Cosmas and Damian, installed in one wing of Vespasian's Forum of Peace but accessible from the Forum proper via the small rotunda on the Via Sacra built under Maxentius (the so-called "Temple of Romulus"), which became a kind of entrance vestibule. The apsidal hall occupied by the church, already richly appointed with marble wall revetments, was left more or less unaltered – the installation of liturgical furnishings and a splendid apse mosaic sufficed to transform it into a Christian shrine (Fig. 2.23). It may not be by chance that the space was made available to Pope Felix IV (r. 526–30) only after Theodoric's death in 526, presumably on the initiative of Theodoric's daughter, Queen Amalasunta, who seemingly sought to establish closer relations with the Church of Rome. In any case, as the first church installed anywhere in the central Show Area, SS. Cosma e Damiano marks a critical milestone in the Christianization of the cityscape. Even sandwiched between much grander temples, it gave the Church its first foothold in the Forum, setting the stage for a wave of ecclesiastical foundations that swept the city center starting in the mid 6th century.[61]

To conclude on Ostrogothic Rome: with all due allowance for the positive bias of the surviving sources and the effectiveness of Theodoric's propaganda of renewal, both in his time and later, it still seems safe to say that, relative especially to the difficult decades from the 450s to the 470s, more effort was made by the sovereign and Roman notables alike to maintain infrastructure and conserve important monuments. But the basic fact remained that much of the urban sprawl exceeded the ability of its rulers and its remaining population to care for, as Cassiodorus well knew: "It is clear how great Rome's population must have been," he began a memorable document on the city's pork supply (*Var.* 11.39), citing as proof "the vast enclosure of the city walls, the sprawling embrace of the spectacle buildings, the marvelous size of the baths, the numerousness of the grain mills specially dedicated to feeding the people."[62]

Thus, we return one last time to the quantitative analysis of Rome's demographic decline, which may be our best way of gauging how extensive Theodoric's much-touted program of renovation really was. When we left off in 452,

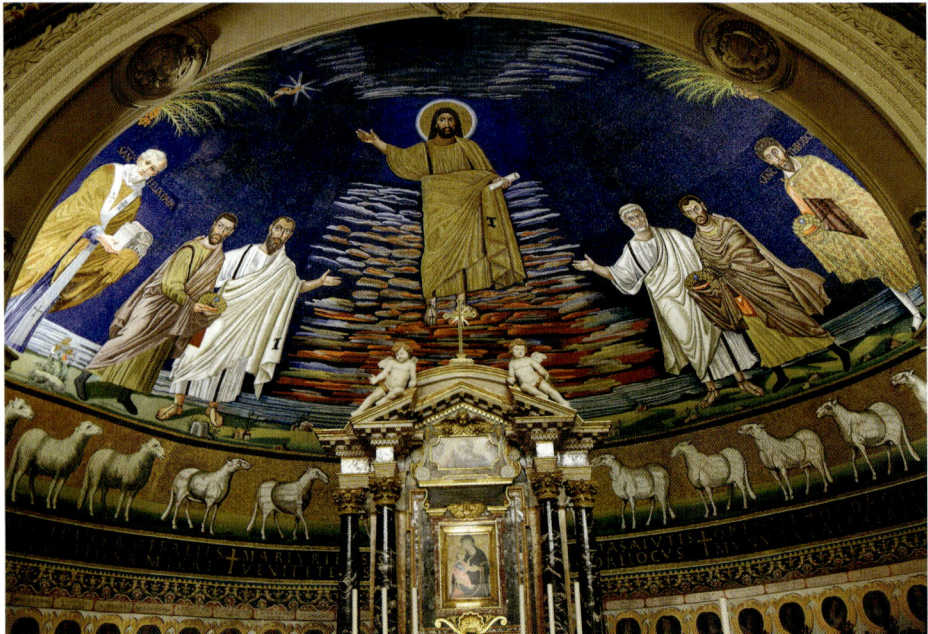

Figure 2.23 SS. Cosma e Damiano, apse mosaic, heavily restored. (Author.)

Rome had lost about half its inhabitants relative to 4th-century levels but had seen population stabilize somewhere in the neighborhood of 300,000–350,000 during the decades after 410. It bears emphasizing that at this size, it was still one of the greatest cities in the Roman world, maybe surpassed only by Constantinople.

But the last word on Rome's pork supply, *Variae* 11.39, of circa 535, shows that a dramatic, even cataclysmic, demographic collapse had occurred at some point over the eight decades separating it from Valentinian's *Novella* of 452. Cassiodorus tells the estate owners of the southern Italian provinces of Lucania and Bruttium that the value of their annual mandatory contribution to Rome's supply of pork and beef would thenceforth be reduced from 1,200 gold *solidi* to 1,000. At the rate of 240 pounds of pork to the *solidus* given in the prior edict of 452, this makes for a total of 240,000 pounds of meat, or 9,600 yearly rations of 25 pounds each. In 452, those two provinces had provided approximately 40 percent of the total quantity of meat delivered to Rome; if they still did in 535, the total quantity of meat delivered to Rome would have been 9,600 rations / 40 percent, or 24,000 portions. This, further, is the highest reasonable estimate that the figures allow, and most prefer other ways of doing the arithmetic that make the total still lower, in the range of 15,000–20,000 portions. I will retain 24,000, however, both to give a conservative estimate of the magnitude of demographic collapse, and also because this figure may find corroboration in the one other text that gives hard numbers for food distribution in Ostrogothic Rome. According to the 6th-century Anonymous Valesianus, Theodoric funded an annual distribution of 120,000 *modii* of grain for the people of Rome; at the traditional 5 *modii* per individual portion, this would equal exactly 24,000 recipients.[63]

Thus, following our preferred Mazzarino/Lo Cascio scenario, even at 24,000 *obsonia*, the pork dole in the 530s only amounted to about 1/6 of the total in 452. This makes Rome's rate of population loss drastically higher in comparison to the period 367–452. In the earlier period, population declined by a factor of two. In the later period, it declined by a factor of six (140,000 to 24,000), if not more. In absolute terms, a sixfold decline would have seen the c. 300,000–350,000 inhabitants of 452 reduced to something like 50,000–60,000.

This figure seems so low that one is tempted to reject it. Possibly Lucania and Bruttium were providing a smaller percentage of Rome's meat than they had a century earlier, in which case the total quantity of *obsonia* would be somewhat higher. Possibly a lesser fraction of Rome's populace was receiving free pork under the Ostrogoths than in the 5th century. (Maybe, in other words, 15,000, or 20,000, or 24,000 pork rations were all that reached Rome by the 530s, for a range of possible reasons, in which case the amount of available pork, rather than the total number of eligible recipients, might have been the determining factor in the number of rations distributed.) But there is no way of knowing for certain, and the simplest and least conjectural assumption is that the same category of eligible beneficiaries received the same individual rations they had in the 5th century. In any case, it is clear that Rome's population plummeted between 452 and 535. The numbers for the dole, taken in concert with the more circumstantial literary, epigraphic, and archaeological indicators discussed above, conduce to no other conclusion.[64]

Probably the process of demographic collapse was still more abrupt, with the bulk of the decline unfolding not gradually across the full period 452–535, but rather within a much shorter span. Given that Rome experienced a long period of tranquility from the accession of Theodoric in 493 until the arrival of a Byzantine army in 536, and that Theodoric was investing at least as much as (and probably more than) his immediate predecessors in restoring Rome and feeding its people, the population seems unlikely to have diminished under Ostrogothic rule. If anything, it may have risen somewhat. The bulk of the demographic collapse would then fall before 493, and probably before 476, since Odoacer's reign, too, brought at least relative calm to Rome – relative, that is, to the years 455–76, when political turmoil following the murders of Aëtius and Valentinian, coupled with Rome's renewed political centrality as the main imperial residence in the West, involved the city in a sequence of sieges, sacks, and further disastrous occupations by 'friendly' troops. Many of those who did not die of violence, starvation, or sickness aggravated by malnutrition during these two decades doubtless simply fled. They had all the more reason to do so after 455, when shipments of subsidized grain from Vandal North Africa were interrupted, probably for good. The loss of the productive surplus of North Africa would alone have reduced Rome's population well below the levels of 452 over the long term. Coming as it did at the beginning of perhaps the two most traumatic decades in Rome's long history, it practically ensured that most of the inhabitants lost during this period were not recouped in the more tranquil decades that followed.

All things considered, then, it looks as though most of the demographic collapse that unfolded between 452 and 535 happened in the years 455–76. In 535, on the eve of Rome's involvement in the Gothic War, following four decades of peaceful and quite benevolent Ostrogothic rule, population was probably stable and possibly even growing. It may have been as low as 50,000, and probably did not exceed 100,000, though there is no way to know for certain. In any case, it is reasonable to assume that Rome in 535 had somewhere between one-fifth and one-tenth of the population it had had in 400, dwelling thinly scattered across the cityscape. One obvious implication is that however many public buildings Theodoric repaired, and however many private dwellings were occupied and maintained, their numbers were dwarfed by the quantity of those left derelict. The drastic drop in population also helps to account for the lack of new construction attested under Theodoric, including churches. It must have seemed almost perverse to attempt new projects in a mostly empty city flush with old but basically sound structures available to be restored and repurposed. The smaller, more densely settled towns of northern Italy (Pavia, Verona, Ravenna), where Theodoric readily launched ambitious new projects, make for a particularly revealing contrast with Rome.[65]

But while Rome under Ostrogothic rule was sparsely inhabited and filled with crumbling buildings, optimists might nonetheless have envisioned modest growth and reasonable prosperity to come. By the 520s and 530s, after several decades of peaceful and largely benevolent Ostrogothic rule, there was at least the prospect of an upward trend in the ancient capital's urban trajectory. Instead, another two cataclysmic decades followed. After Theodoric's death in 526, his daughter, Amalasunta, and her young son, Athalaric, struggled to hold the throne against a succession of rivals and pretenders. When Amalasunta was assassinated in 535, her friendly diplomatic ties with Constantinople gave Emperor Justinian the pretext he wanted to invade Italy. Later in that same year, a Byzantine army led by Belisarius arrived in the south, capturing Naples and moving north toward Rome, which Belisarius occupied in 536. From 537 until 552, when the Byzantines took it for good, Rome was contested between Byzantine and Gothic armies, changing hands repeatedly and spending a total of several years under siege. Procopius claims that by late 546, when the Goths entered after a siege lasting nearly a year, there were only 500 men left in the whole city (*Wars* 7.20.19). Over the preceding year, the Romans had slowly starved. When grain ran out, they ate nettles, with results best left to the pen of Procopius:[66]

> But this food was insufficient for them, for it was utterly impossible to satisfy themselves with it, and consequently their flesh withered away almost entirely, while their color, gradually turning to a livid hue, gave them a most ghostly appearance. And it happened to many that, even as they walked along chewing the nettles with their teeth, death came suddenly upon them and they fell to the ground. And now they were even beginning to eat each other's dung. There were many too, who, because of the pressure of the famine, destroyed themselves with their own hands; for they could no longer find either dogs or mice or any dead animal of any kind on which to feed. (*Wars* 7.17.17–19, trans. Dewing.)

Regarding the figure of 500 adult male inhabitants, one might suspect some exaggeration on Procopius' part (though he was with Belisarius in Rome and witnessed firsthand much of what he reports), but there is no doubt that Rome's population reached an all-time low during the conflict, far below what it had been under Theodoric. The population undoubtedly rebounded when relative peace returned in the early 550s, but it is impossible to know by how much. From the time of the Gothic War on, all estimates of medieval population figures for Rome are basically pure guesswork, and it is best to say so frankly from the outset. The best guesses suggest, in any case, that numbers probably never much exceeded 50,000–60,000 at any point between the later 6th century and the 15th, and may at times have dipped as low as 20,000–30,000.[67]

Rome's physical plant likewise reached new lows after fifteen years of continuous conflict during which episodes of violent destruction, along with the failure to attempt even basic maintenance under wartime conditions, compounded the slow attrition of time. Procopius describes various instances of destruction, among them the cutting of all the city's aqueducts when the Goths under Vitigis first besieged Rome in 537 (*Wars* 5.19.13). Belisarius then walled up the empty water channels to keep out Gothic infiltrators (*Wars* 5.19.18). Later that year, the rich collection of marble statuary that still adorned Hadrian's mausoleum, on the Vatican side of the Tiber, was smashed to pieces by its Romano-Byzantine garrison during a determined Gothic assault. The defenders thwarted the attackers by raining shattered hunks of statues down on them as they tried to scale the perimeter wall with ladders (*Wars* 5.22.25). Ten years later, the Gothic king Totila tried to render the city indefensible by razing large stretches of the Aurelian Wall, which Belisarius promptly repaired by filling the breaches with heaps of unmortared stone (*Wars* 7.22.67; repairs 7.24). Rather in passing, Procopius mentions also that Totila had burnt large swaths of the city, especially in Trastevere (*Wars* 8.22.3).[68]

But despite it all, Rome endured. Procopius hints at parts of the explanation for this persistence (*Wars* 8.22.5–8, trans. Dewing):

> Yet the Romans love their city above all the men we know, and they are eager to protect all their ancestral treasures and to preserve them, so that nothing of the ancient glory of Rome may be obliterated. For even though they were for a long period under barbarian sway, they preserved the buildings of the city and the most of its adornments, such as could through the excellence of their workmanship withstand so long a lapse of time and such neglect. Furthermore, all such memorials of the race as were still left are preserved even to this day, and among them the ship of Aeneas.

It is not only that there was too much physically left, too many historic monuments and serviceable buildings, too much superb infrastructure, for

Rome to disappear, though certainly there were these things, too. For Rome's new Byzantine overlords, control over the ancient capital was essential both for reasons of imperial prestige and for their ambitions of reconstituting the Roman Empire across as much of its former extent as possible. For the Church, rootedness in the *caput mundi* and seat of St. Peter's ministry was the rock on which papal claims to spiritual dominion over all of Christendom were founded. For Roman elites and commoners alike, a Roman pedigree was the last and most unbreakable token of their exceptionality, at a time when the institutional advantages and material privileges of being Roman were mostly a thing of the past. Together, Empire and Church, civic leaders and ordinary Romans, went about picking up the pieces of the shattered city as best they could after the Gothic War.

Chapter 3

552–705

Byzantine Rome

ROME IN THE CENTURY and a half after the Byzantine reconquest is characterized both by deep structural continuities with the past and by often profound ruptures and innovations that pointed toward the future. In purely topographical terms, however, the past prevailed. Some old monuments and infrastructure were retained in something close to their original condition, others were altered and/or repurposed, and many more were left to decay for want of sufficient human and material resources. In all cases, though, the physical contours of the 'Byzantine' present mostly consisted of features first created centuries earlier. Streets and piazzas, walls and aqueducts, housing and churches inherited from the imperial era still defined the parameters of the material environment in which Romans lived and worked.

In administrative terms, too, there was substantial continuity with the late antique past, insofar as Rome was still subject to the local representatives of a distant ruler to a decidedly greater degree than to the popes who did reside stably in the city. It is a point worth stressing, belabored as it is by the weight of past misconceptions. Richard Krautheimer himself declared that in the years following the sack of 410, Rome passed from imperial to papal control: "The emperor had been unable to safeguard the city. Its safety now rested with its Christian heroes, Peter and Paul, with its bishops, the successors to Saint Peter. They were the only effective power left. Rome was the papacy and the papacy was Rome." All of this is demonstrably false. Rome was the premier imperial residence in the West for much of the three generations after 410, when western emperors still existed; and as we have seen, it was precisely Rome's favored status under the last western emperors that brought upon it the disasters of the years

455–76. As for the popes, they had no legal authority to involve themselves in, much less control, civil administration. Like bishops generally, Rome's bishops mostly concerned themselves with the affairs of the Church. They were ecclesiastical administrators and spiritual guides. Emperors and imperial functionaries, along with the Senate, ran 5th-century Rome. What the popes did assert more and more stridently over the course of the 5th century, especially from the time of Leo I (r. 440–61), was the spiritual primacy of the Church of Rome, and the popes themselves, over all other churches and prelates in the Christian world. As the self-proclaimed heirs of St. Peter, Leo and his successors strenuously maintained their right to have the final word on matters of ecclesiastical administration and the definition of orthodoxy. While this claim applied in theory to all of Christendom, in practice it was more effectively asserted in the West than in the East, where the popes butted up against emperors and patriarchs in Constantinople who bowed reluctantly at best to Roman pretensions of primacy.[1]

Even after 476, it is only true in the most narrow, technical sense that Rome was no longer an 'imperial' city. There were no more emperors in the West, and Italy's rulers thereafter based themselves primarily at Ravenna – first Odoacer and Theodoric, and then, after the Byzantine reconquest, the chief Italian representatives of the emperor in Constantinople, the (military) exarch and the (civil) prefect of Italy. The absence of resident western emperors aside, however, Rome was not much less imperial, or more papal, in the 7th century than it had been in the 5th – it belonged to the Byzantine emperor as much as any other city in the empire and was administered by the emperor's local representatives. Imperial functionaries were the city's duly constituted rulers, from the prefect of Italy and (later) the Exarch in Ravenna, down through the subordinate duke (*dux*) and "judges" (*iudices*) and building supervisors (*curatores*) based in Rome. The military units stationed at Rome were captained by Byzantine generals. The criminal courts were appendages of the state. The minting of coins, a crucial prerogative of sovereign rulers, occurred in state-run workshops. Public buildings and urban infrastructure were supervised by government-appointed *curatores* who administered them on behalf of the state that owned them. The Senate, meanwhile, never recovered from the dispersion (or worse) of its members during the Gothic War. The last remotely plausible reference to the Senate gathering as a corporate body comes in 603, when a group of notables identified as "senators" joined the pope and clergy at the Lateran to acclaim the arrival of the official portraits of the new Byzantine emperor, Phokas, and his wife, Leontia. The transformation of the Senate House in the Forum into the church of S. Adriano, around 630, merely accounted for an established fact: The ancient Senate was no more. Thereafter, the remaining scions of Rome's old senatorial families had two possible career choices: the Byzantine civil/military administration or the Church.[2]

As for the popes, they, like all bishops in the Byzantine Empire, remained imperial functionaries subordinate to the emperors in Constantinople. Their election was subject to imperial confirmation, and popes who displeased Constantinople could be summarily recalled. As of 553, the reigning pope, Vigilius, had been under house arrest in Constantinople for six years because of his refusal to sanction the eastern position in the Three Chapters Schism. An imperial official at Rome had given him a peremptory summons to appear, packed him aboard a ship, and sent him off to face Justinian's displeasure in person. A century later, in 653, Pope Martin I was hauled off to Constantinople, tried, and exiled to the Black Sea for opposing the Constantinopolitan position on Monothelitism. Though the Roman clerics who wrote the *Liber Pontificalis* biographies of both Vigilius and Martin lamented the strong-arm tactics, they never questioned the emperors' right to deport recalcitrant popes. As late as the 680s, newly elected popes still had to be confirmed by official decree from Constantinople before they could take up their office, and the successful candidates paid accession fees like other imperial officials appointed to high office.[3]

None of this is to say that popes were not prominent figures on the Roman scene, or that their activities were wholly confined to ecclesiastical affairs. The Church played a growing role in feeding and ministering to the needy, at a time when the state was ever less ready to do so. As semiofficial members of the Byzantine apparatus of state, popes might also fill in for absent or otherwise occupied officials, usually in times of war or other pressing emergencies. Such emergencies came more frequently after the Lombards invaded the Italian peninsula in the late 560s, subtracting much hard-won territory from Byzantine control. The Lombards never took Rome itself, though they besieged it several times; but Rome-based officials and troops were often called away to meet Lombard threats over the next two centuries, while the popes resided stably in the city. The emperors and their local subordinates therefore sometimes allowed popes to fill in when the state was, for whatever reason, unwilling or unable to perform its usual functions. But the operative term here is "allowed" – suggestions that popes usurped prerogatives formerly reserved to the state, against the will of the Byzantine authorities, are badly misguided for any period prior to the 8th century, as we will see.[4]

The process of reconstructing the role of non-Church actors in Byzantine Rome is complicated by the strong ecclesiastical bias of the written sources, the most important of which is the Roman *Liber Pontificalis* (hereafter *LP*), a collection of papal biographies first compiled in the early 6th century and regularly updated through the 9th, probably by clerics attached to the Lateran palace. This bias has made it all too easy for past historians, including but hardly limited to those whose own confessional inclinations led them to favor 'Church triumphant' narratives, to imagine that the popes took the lead in governing the city and shaping its physical contours from an early date – if not by the 5th century, as Krautheimer had it, then at any rate by the later 6th. In so doing, they have perpetuated a modern corollary of the medieval fiction enshrined in the "Donation of Constantine." This late 8th-century fabrication was probably produced in Rome under papal auspices and designed to legitimate ex post facto the position of autonomy the popes had then achieved by claiming that Constantine, after his conversion to Christianity, conceded to Pope Sylvester in perpetuity all imperial rights and privileges in the western half of the empire. In fact, the forgery – it has been recognized as such since the 15th century – was necessary precisely because the de facto autonomy of the later 8th-century papacy was a novelty, a recent innovation without justification or precedent in Romano-Byzantine law.[5]

Interestingly, much of the recent work that has been most instrumental in setting the record straight relies on written sources that traditionalists have used all along. It sometimes suffices to recognize that one cannot make uncritical use of texts written for, about, and sometimes by the popes themselves to argue that the papal administration had supplanted the very civic leaders whose role those texts programmatically underreport or ignore. The ecclesiastical sources themselves contain revealing hints of the limits of papal authority, which awaited notice by scholars prepared to evaluate them with greater critical detachment. But when specific information about nonecclesiastical actors is omitted entirely, as it so often is, more creative and frankly speculative approaches are required. It is often a question of learning to read between the lines of our texts in order to recognize, for instance, that what the *LP* does not mention can be as revealing as what it does. Among the important information the *LP* tends to omit are initiatives sponsored by laypeople, including not only public buildings and infrastructure, but also churches and other religious foundations (monasteries, hostels, etc.).[6]

Material evidence has an essential and constantly expanding part to play in redressing the historiographical imbalance between Roman Church and Byzantine state. The recent excavations at the Crypta Balbi and elsewhere give the lie to the old view of a 'Dark Age' Rome in which churches, and the Church, were lonely shining lights in a void – in a cityscape otherwise characterized by almost universal squalor, inhabited by technologically challenged rubes cut off from the wider world and reduced to conditions of extreme material poverty. It turns out that 'Byzantine' Rome was not nearly so poor, backwards, and isolated as all that. Through the 7th century, it was well integrated into trans-Mediterranean political and commercial networks that linked it closely with the rest of the Byzantine world. Its economy was surprisingly robust, raw materials and imported commodities were plentiful, and technical knowledge inherited directly from antiquity flourished, allowing skilled artisans to keep catering to the needs of a sizeable group of urban consumers.[7]

With these preliminaries in mind, we can now take a broadly thematic approach to the century and a half when Rome was firmly under Byzantine rule, moving from infrastructure and public buildings, to churches and other ecclesiastical foundations, and finally to residential architecture, settlement patterns, and the material culture of everyday life. By reexamining old evidence and integrating the new findings, it becomes possible to treat all of these topics in more granular detail than before, and in the process to show that Rome was much more than a "city of the Church" throughout the period in question.

In the summer of 554, when Byzantine forces under Narses had mostly completed the conquest of Italy, Emperor Justinian issued a proclamation whose twenty-seven short chapters laid out the legal framework for Italy's reintegration into the Byzantine empire. Addressed to Narses, commanding general and "Head of the Sacred Bedchamber" (*praepositus sacri cubiculi*), and Antiochus, prefect of Italy, it was issued, according to Justinian, at the prompting of Pope Vigilius. As such, it is a close proxy for the institutional rapport that developed between the papacy and the civil authorities in Byzantine Italy: The pope could and did take it upon himself to petition the emperor to remedy pressing problems and intercede in difficult times, but effective action depended on the involvement of imperial officials. They alone had the legal and institutional mandate, not to mention a monopoly on the armed force and coercive authority, necessary to govern.

Much of this "Pragmatic Sanction" (a modern title; it is called the *constitutio pragmatica* at Ch. 27) sought to redress the worst of the problems caused by almost two decades of warfare: proprietors exiled or hauled off into captivity who sought to recover their lands and possessions; legal transactions and other contractual obligations complicated by the loss or destruction of all relevant documentation; the restitution of stolen or fugitive slaves and animals; nuns carried off from their convents and raped and/or married, and so on. Justinian also stipulated that "the annual food distributions (*annona*) that Theodoric used to give" be renewed, and that special benefits go to language teachers, orators, doctors, and lawyers, such that there might be enough of these skilled professionals to teach the next generation. The one chapter devoted

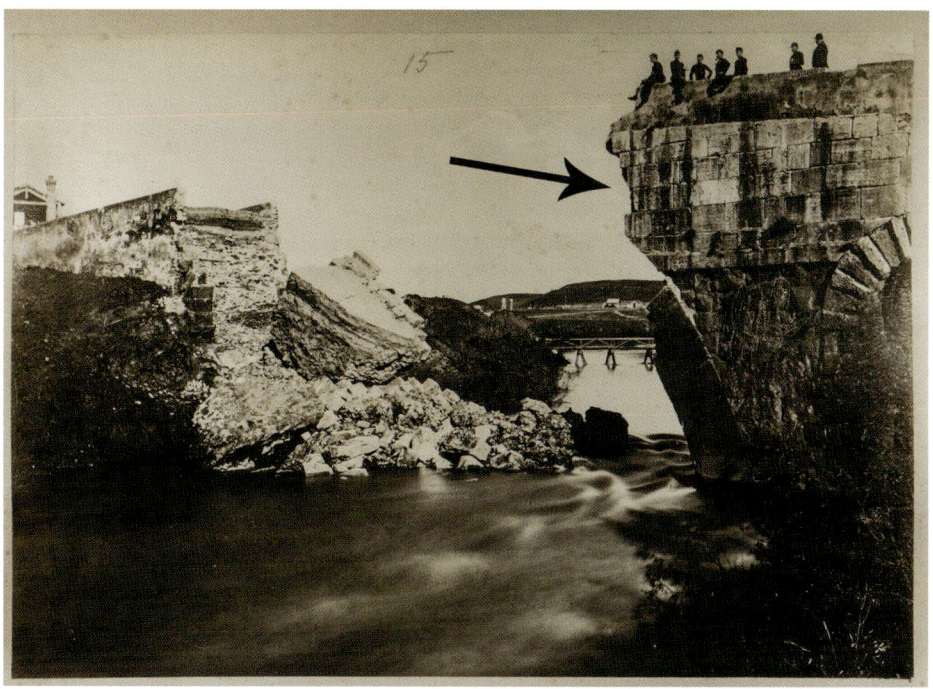

Figure 3.1 Gioacchino Altobelli's photo of the Ponte Salario in late 1867, after demolition by French troops. The arrow indicates the 6th-century reconstruction of the superstructure in travertine ashlars.

specifically to Rome deals entirely with the stewardship of its monuments and infrastructure. Headed "That public buildings be preserved," it continues "We command that the customs and concessions pertaining to the repair of the public buildings of the city of Rome, the banks of the Tiber, the Forum, and the Roman harbor, and to the repair of the aqueducts, be maintained, in such a way, that is, that they be financed only from those same sources formerly earmarked for them." In legal and administrative terms, in other words, things at Rome were supposed to run much as they had until the upheavals of the Gothic War.[8]

As under the late Roman emperors, and under Theodoric and his heirs, the state owned Rome's public architectural patrimony and was responsible for maintenance and public works. And insofar as resources permitted, Rome's Byzantine administrators did try to restore the sorts of critical infrastructure indicated in the Pragmatic Sanction. In 565, Narses rebuilt a bridge over the River Aniene just north of the city that had been destroyed by the Goths, the Ponte Salario, in fine ashlar masonry (Fig. 3.1); similar repairs at other bridges over the Aniene, the Ponte Nomentano, Ponte Mammolo, and Ponte Lucano (all likewise put out of action by Totila in the 540s), probably date to the same period. The Aurelian Wall was probably also renovated under Narses. One possible example of work done at the time is the fine marble facings added to the towers and gate curtain of the Porta Appia, which include an inscribed keystone (in Greek) dedicated to Conon and George, two eastern soldier-saints unfamiliar in Rome before the Byzantine reconquest (Fig. 3.2). And Paolo Vitti has recently made a strong case that the reconstruction of the brick vaulting in at least one tower (J-17, near Porta Latina) is the work of Byzantine craftsmen of the age of Justinian.[9]

The civic administration employed lay officials called curators (*curatores*) to maintain and, when necessary, repair other essential structures. The

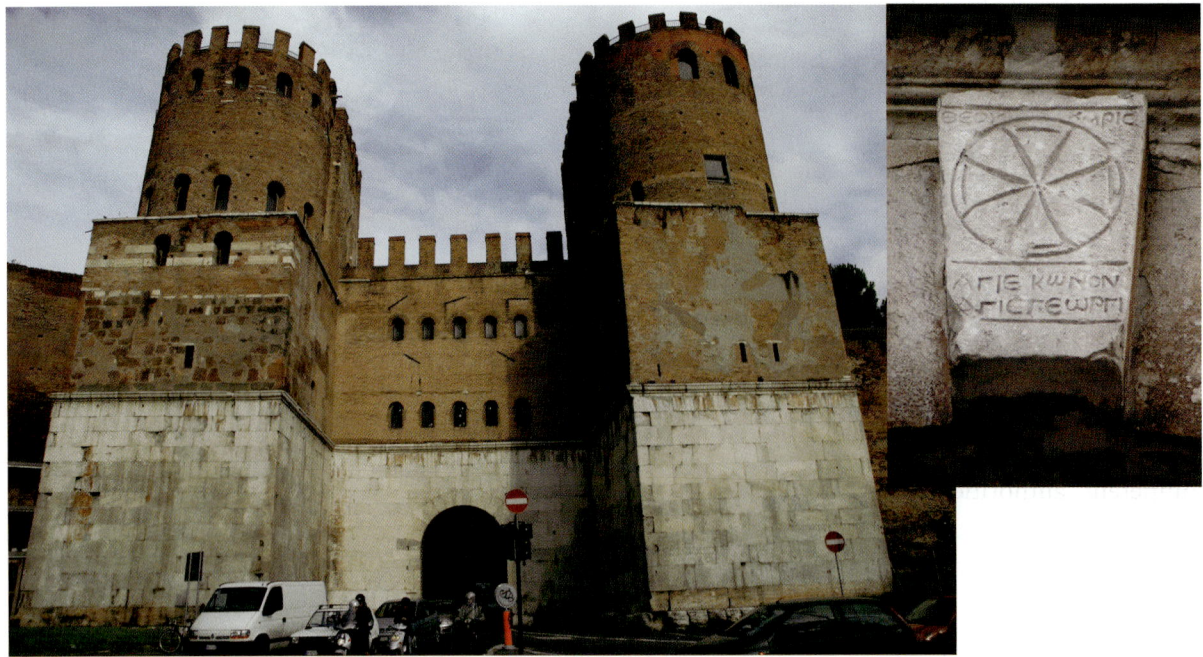

Figure 3.2 The Porta Appia with (inset) the inscribed keystone from the interior of the archway. (Author.)

aqueducts were still supervised by a curator in the 7th century, as they had been under the emperors and the Ostrogoths. The imperial palace on the Palatine, too, had a dedicated curator. Toward the end of the 7th century, the post belonged to a man called Plato, father of the future pope John VII, who carried out restoration work while in office, according to his epitaph at S. Anastasia. The palace was always the primary seat of the Byzantine administration. Portraits of the reigning emperors were kept in the palatine chapel of Saint Caesarius. It was the regular residence of the governor (*dux*) of Rome and hosted other luminaries during their Roman sojourns: Narses stayed there in the 550s and 560s, as did an exarch visiting from Ravenna in the 650s, and probably also Emperor Constans II himself when he visited Rome in 663.[10]

The *LP* itself shows that the emperors, via their local representatives, maintained full jurisdiction over Rome's physical plant through the 7th century and into the 8th. In the year 609, Pope Boniface IV needed the explicit consent of Emperor Phokas to convert the Pantheon into a church. Pope Honorius I (r. 625–38) sought and received special permission from Emperor Heraclius to use bronze roof tiles from the temple of Venus and Rome to repair the roof of St. Peter's. When Emperor Constans II visited Rome in 663, he treated Rome as what it was: his possession. His agents spent two weeks methodically pillaging all the valuable metals they could get their hands on. They hauled off statues, architectural ornaments and fittings from public buildings, and even the bronze roof tiles of the Pantheon, consecrated church though it was. The *LP* biographer of Pope Vitalian (r. 657–72) was appalled, but never questioned Constans' sovereign right to act as he did. Even as late as the 730s, Pope Gregory III still relied on the exarch's goodwill to reuse six old columns in the chapel he was building inside St. Peter's.[11]

It is worth considering how weak the case for papal involvement in civil administration prior to the 8th century really is, taking the aqueducts as a representative example. In 602, Pope Gregory I wrote a letter to his representative in Ravenna, a subdeacon called John. Among other matters, he entreated John to prevail upon the praetorian prefect of Italy to appoint a new curator for Rome's aqueducts, whose poor condition Gregory lamented. Gregory's preferred candidate for the job was a layman of senatorial rank, presumably a Roman, named Augustus. What this passage shows, of course, is that the pope had the authority neither to maintain the aqueducts himself nor to appoint the curators who were supposed to care for them. As pastor of the Roman flock, Gregory's role was primarily to advocate for the population under his care. He could alert the competent authorities to matters of concern, admonish them to remedy the situation, even offer advice on whom to appoint. But he had no legal mandate to administer civic affairs on his own, as he clearly recognized. Otherwise, why beg the praetorian prefect to install a new curator of aqueducts?[12]

Yet scholars continue to use this text to contend that 7th-century popes were responsible for Rome's water supply. They support the claim by recourse to one additional source, a line in the *LP* Life of Honorius I (r. 625–38), which alleges that this pope repaired an aqueduct on the Janiculum Hill (evidently the Aqua Traiana) and built an associated water mill. Apart from the fact that the passage itself is garbled, the bigger problem is that it is a much later interpolation that first appears in the manuscript tradition in the late 11th century. Not one of the many earlier *LP* manuscripts contains it. The interpolated passage makes perfect sense in the 11th century, when the Church manifestly did have charge of Rome's water supply, but none whatsoever in the 7th, when it would be a strange anomaly – there is not a single other mention in the *LP*, or anywhere else, of popes maintaining Rome's aqueducts until the time of Hadrian I (r. 772–95). By then, the aqueducts were under papal control; in the 7th century, they were not.[13]

The point holds more broadly. As Robert Coates-Stephens has pointed out, the clearest sign that the Church had little or nothing to do with the maintenance of Rome's nonecclesiastical buildings through the 7th century is the simple fact that the *LP* makes no mention of any such papal activity (the anachronistic interpolation regarding Honorius and the aqueducts aside). When the popes did undertake significant building projects, the authors of the *LP* rarely neglected to mention the fact; and when the popes began to take responsibility for Rome's civic buildings, starting early in the 8th century, the *LP* diligently proclaimed their works. The silence of the *LP* through the 7th century is thus a good indication that nothing of the sort was happening at the time.[14]

It is true that hard evidence of interventions on civic monuments sponsored by the Byzantine administration is not particularly abundant, either. From 552 through to the beginning of the 8th century, we have a couple of mentions of curators for the imperial palace and the aqueducts, one rebuilding of a bridge proved by inscriptions, and more circumstantial signs of attention to several other bridges and the city walls. Gregory I's letter of 602 makes it clear that at least some aqueducts had been put back into working order after the Ostrogoths cut them in 537. Archaeology adds some work in the Roman Forum, the one area singled out for mention in the Pragmatic Sanction, which included the remodeling and rededication of an older honorary column. In 608, this 4th-century monument located along the south side of the Forum plaza received a new stepped base in marble and a culminating statue of Emperor Phokas (r. 608–10), dedicated by the exarch, Smaragdus. The administration should probably get credit also for the opulent polychrome marble pavements installed, in the later 6th century, in several of the rooms along the façade of the Basilica Aemilia (Fig. 3.3). The rooms' prominent position in a prestigious public building suggests that they may have served as offices or reception

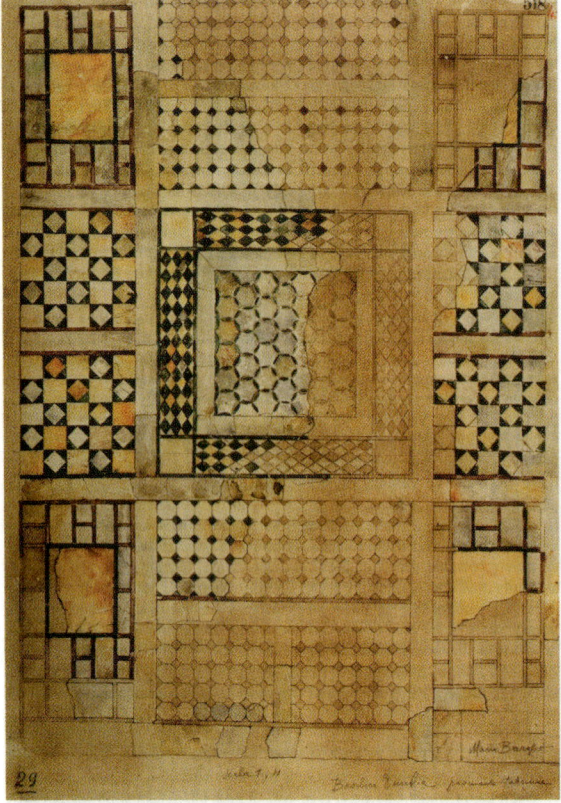

Figure 3.3 Late 19th-century watercolor by Maria Barosso of the 6th-century *opus sectile* pavements in one of the *tabernae* fronting the Basilica Aemilia. (Coates-Stephens 2011, p. 391, fig. 1.)

spaces for government officials. But with only this smattering of projects to show for 150 years and more of Byzantine rule, some have understandably concluded that the civil administration accomplished little work on public buildings and infrastructure.[15]

Yet even the known initiatives are hardly negligible, especially given that there is no 'secular' equivalent of the *LP* dedicated to exalting the civil administration's accomplishments, and that the practice of epigraphically commemorating repairs to public buildings had mostly ceased by this period. Few inscriptions attest to the grand papal initiatives of the 8th and 9th centuries, either, though they certainly occurred. More to the point, work on Rome's town-sized palace and Forum, its 19 km of walls, and its hundreds of kilometers of surviving aqueducts might collectively represent a massive investment of effort and resources. It all depends on the physical extent of the areas involved in any such restoration projects and the nature of the work involved, which might range from minor patching to complete reconstruction. The problem is that nobody has been able to determine how much was actually accomplished. Physical traces of Byzantine-era work have proven difficult to identify in surviving structures, in part because 6th- and 7th-century masonry can be similar enough to the stuff produced in preceding centuries as to be almost indistinguishable.

But this basic continuity in ways of building at Rome is itself noteworthy, the more so because that continuity ruptures from the late 7th century, just as Byzantine governance began to vacillate and the Church took its first tentative steps toward administrative autonomy. From the early 8th century, new and different construction techniques prevailed, as we will see in Chapter 4. Before then, ancient traditions persisted. The cut stonework in the Ponte Salario as restored in 565 is very high-quality stuff, as are the facings of the Porta Appia – the materials and workmanship would not be out of place in imperial Rome (Figs. 3.1–3.2, above). The marble pavements in the *tabernae* fronting the Basilica Aemilia feature top-quality colored marbles assembled with consummate skill; though the patterning is distinct from older *opus sectile*, the quality of the workmanship is comparable. As for mortared masonry, the most common technique in late antique Rome is *opus vittatum* (also called *opus vittatum mixtum* and *opus listatum*): alternating bands of brick and small, roughly rectangular blocks of local stone (usually varieties of tuff) called *tufelli* in Italian. The materials used are fairly homogenous, though they are invariably recycled from older buildings, and the horizontal courses tend to be reasonably level and evenly spaced. Usually one, but sometimes two or more courses of tuff blocks alternate with one or more courses of brick, generally in repeating sequence.

This technique rivaled brick facings in popularity from the 3rd century and predominated by the 6th (Fig. 3.4).[16]

At present, Byzantine-era *opus vittatum* is best attested in churches known to have been built in the later 6th and 7th centuries, which account for most of the new building projects (as opposed to restorations) undertaken at the time, or at least for the relatively monumental constructions that survive today. They include San Lorenzo *fuori le mura* on the Via Tiburtina, from the 580s, and San Pancrazio on the Janiculum and S. Agnese on the Via Nomentana, both erected during the pontificate of Honorius I (r. 625–38); there is also the smaller S. Venanzio chapel adjacent to the Lateran Baptistery, created in the 640s by remodeling an earlier structure (Figs. 3.5–3.6). What these places together show is that the building industry in Rome was still functioning basically as it always had – that there was unbroken continuity with centuries of tradition. Rome's vast stock of dilapidated, empty buildings was still systematically mined for valuable building materials, which in turn were reassembled into new structures by seasoned professionals

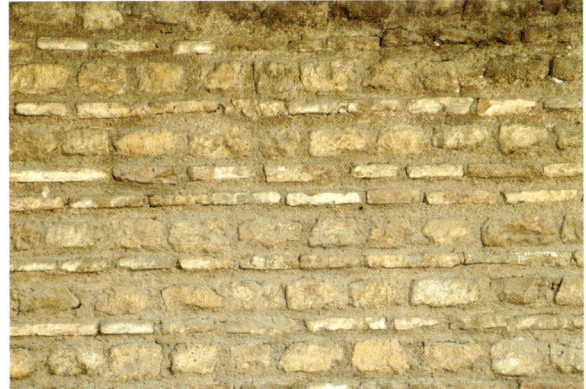

Figure 3.4 S. Vitale, narthex, facade: *opus vittatum* of the early 5th century. (Author.)

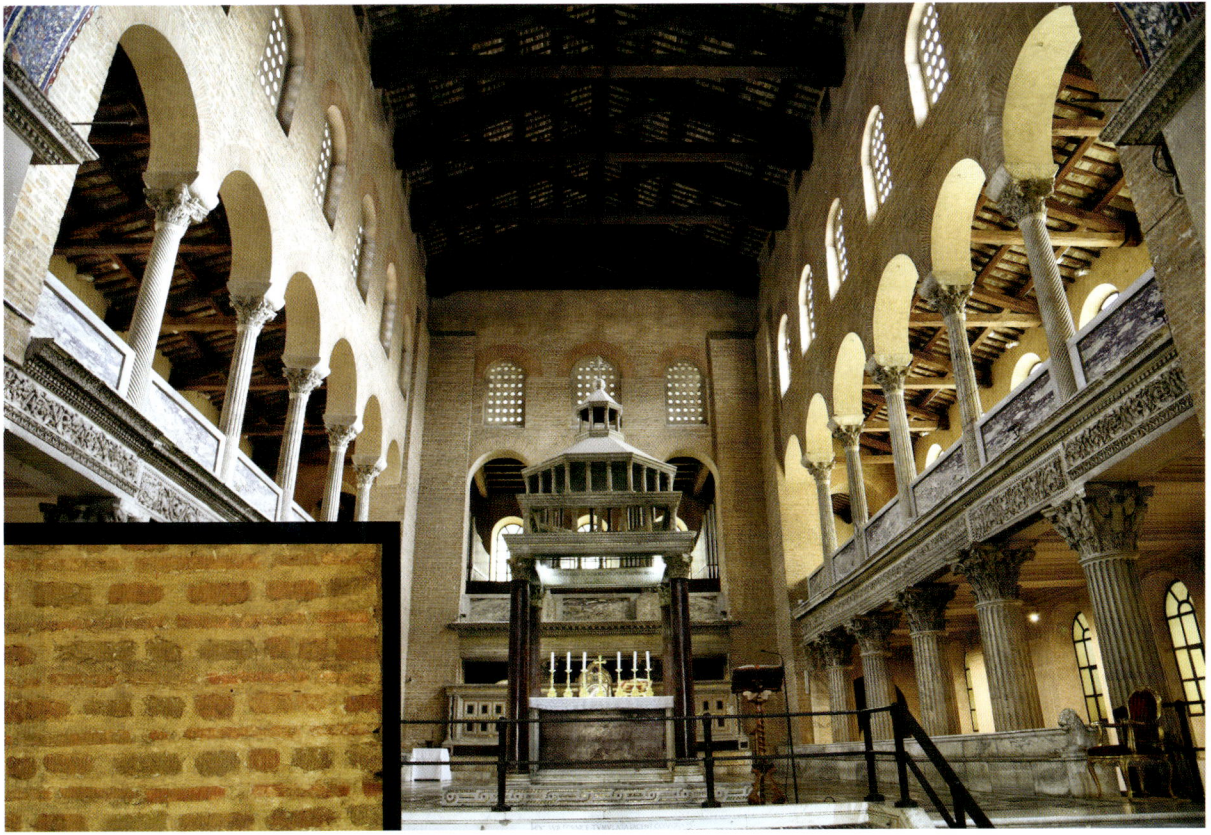

Figure 3.5 The 6th-century basilica of S. Lorenzo *fuori le mura* with inset detail of *opus vittatum* from the S wall of the nave. (Author.)

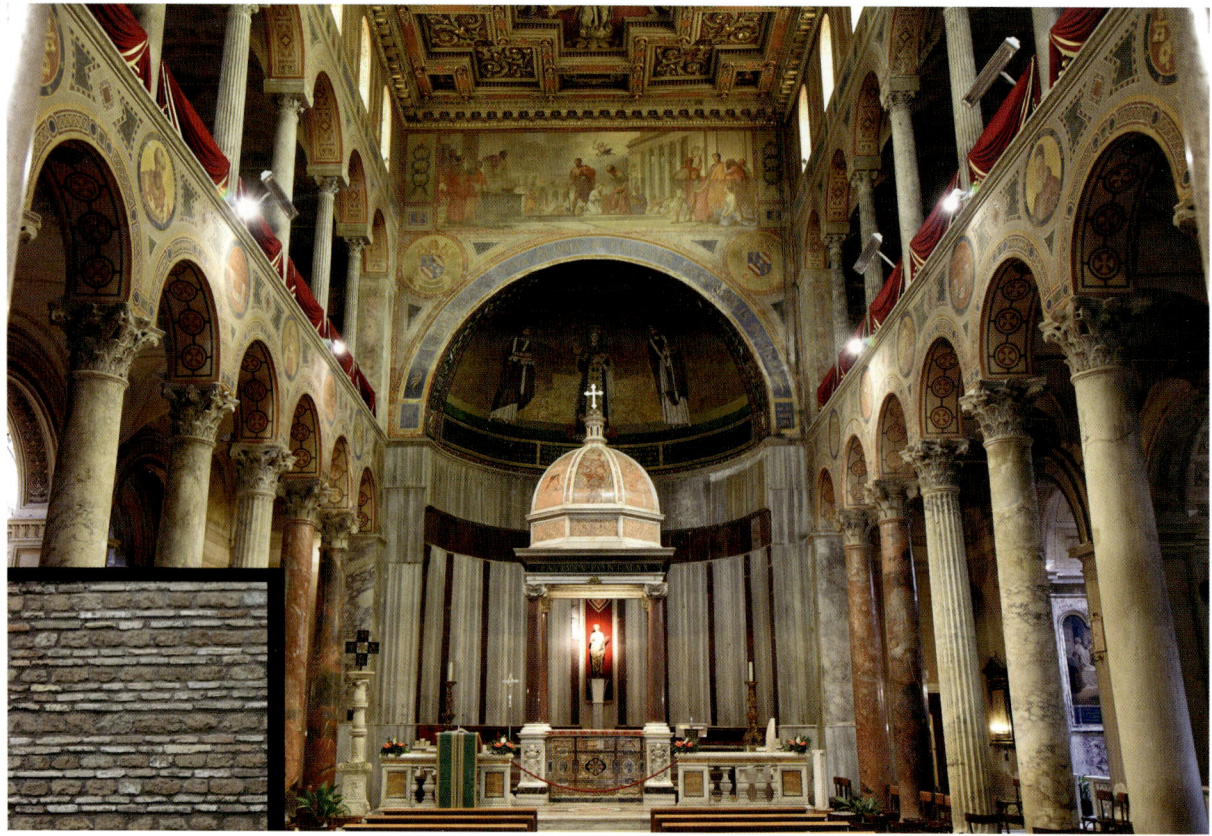

Figure 3.6 The 7th-century basilica of S. Agnese on the Via Nomentana, with inset detail of *opus vittatum* from the exterior of the façade. (Author.)

working to similar standards. The quality of the work is undoubtedly professional; it was done, that is, by people who worked full time as builders, using skills passed down from generation to generation of trainees. This continuity was presumably possible because there was more or less constant demand for skilled builders at Rome. Enough projects were consistently under way to provide steady work for architects, masons, suppliers of building materials, and so on.[17]

These professional builders would have worked on both civic and ecclesiastical commissions – there is no reason to think the Church and the Byzantine administration drew on different groups of building professionals. The technical characteristics of civic and ecclesiastical foundations are similar enough to suggest that much the same workforce was involved; certainly nobody has claimed that the masonry of Rome's late antique churches differs so markedly from that of coeval civic constructions as to suggest the existence of separate labor pools. It being unlikely that the relatively few substantial papal commissions of the era sufficed to provide regular work – not one big church is known to have been built between S. Lorenzo in the 580s and S. Pancrazio and S. Agnese around 630 – Roman building professionals must often have concentrated on other projects, among them commissions sponsored by Byzantine administrators and private patrons. Some were churches, such as S. Maria Antiqua, built into an older hall at the foot of the entrance ramp leading from the Forum to the Palatine around 570. But others doubtless involved the city walls, aqueducts, roads and bridges, and select public buildings, and may well have been quite extensive.[18]

The best hope of identifying Byzantine-era work on the city walls, the aqueducts, and other public buildings will come via improved methods for dating common types of mortared masonry, *opus vittatum* in particular. Using the well-dated churches as a baseline, computer-aided comparative analysis (statistical tabulations of the size and shape of the bricks and *tufelli*, the number of pieces per square meter of facing, the thickness and composition of the mortar beds, etc.) can help to identify similar masonry in repairs to older structures. This approach is already showing promise for the Aurelian Wall, where it has turned up several probable instances of 6th/7th-century restorations.[19]

In short: It looks as though professional builders in Rome had regular work for a good century after the Pragmatic Sanction of 554, involving both religious commissions and state-sponsored maintenance of critical infrastructure. But while some of the churches are still there to see, we will not find any more newly built civic monuments and infrastructure produced under Byzantine rule than under Ostrogothic rule, and for much the same reason: There was no need for brand-new structures when so many older ones remained to be occupied and readapted, far more in fact than Rome's remaining inhabitants, public officials included, could possibly use. The Byzantine ruling establishment consequently tended to establish itself in select, relatively limited areas; but in those zones it did occupy, it was active enough to make a lasting impression.

The Byzantine presence is thickest in the heart of the ancient city, from the Palatine across the Forum to the Capitoline, and from there down to the Tiber by the old cattle and produce markets (the Forum Boarium and Forum Holitorium, respectively), an area known throughout the Middle Ages as the *Ripa Graeca*, the "Greek riverbank." This concentration across the zones most closely associated with the ancient imperial establishment indicates that the Byzantine civil authorities consciously positioned themselves as the heirs of the ancient Roman emperors. It was a simple and natural thing to do, because they were in fact the direct legal descendants of the emperors by virtue of being the local surrogates of the current 'Roman' emperor residing in Constantinople. Rome's monumental center continued to pertain to the state, whose functionaries layered a web of 'Byzantine' names and places over it. With a bit of effort, parts of that web can still be traced.[20]

One especially active strand looks to have been the initial segment of the route that ran all the way from the southwest corner of the Palatine, by the Circus Maximus, to St. Peter's. Already one of the most important avenues in the ancient city, it had hosted triumphal processions in the Republican and early imperial periods, and then grown again in importance from the 4th century with the emergence of St. Peter's as Rome's premier martyrial shrine. Its defining feature was the covered porticoes that lined most of its course and gave the street its common name: the *porticus maximae*, or "greatest porticoes." These ancient porticoes along the main trunk of the route had been extended, starting around 380, to the Tiber at Ponte S. Angelo, and eventually all the way to St. Peter's (Fig. 3.7). The basilica was thereby linked to the city center by one of the most grandiose streets in Rome, a magnificent backdrop for the processions (and the everyday traffic) that traversed it. What is interesting is how many features along the route bear the stamp of Rome's Byzantine administration, principally in the initial stretch between the Palatine and the Theater of Pompey.[21]

The first is S. Anastasia, situated adjacent and parallel to the west end of the Circus Maximus, just north of the "Greatest Portico," as the route was still called in the 8th century. By the first half of the 7th century, the old 4th-century *titulus* had morphed into a central node in the liturgical topography of Byzantine Rome. After centuries

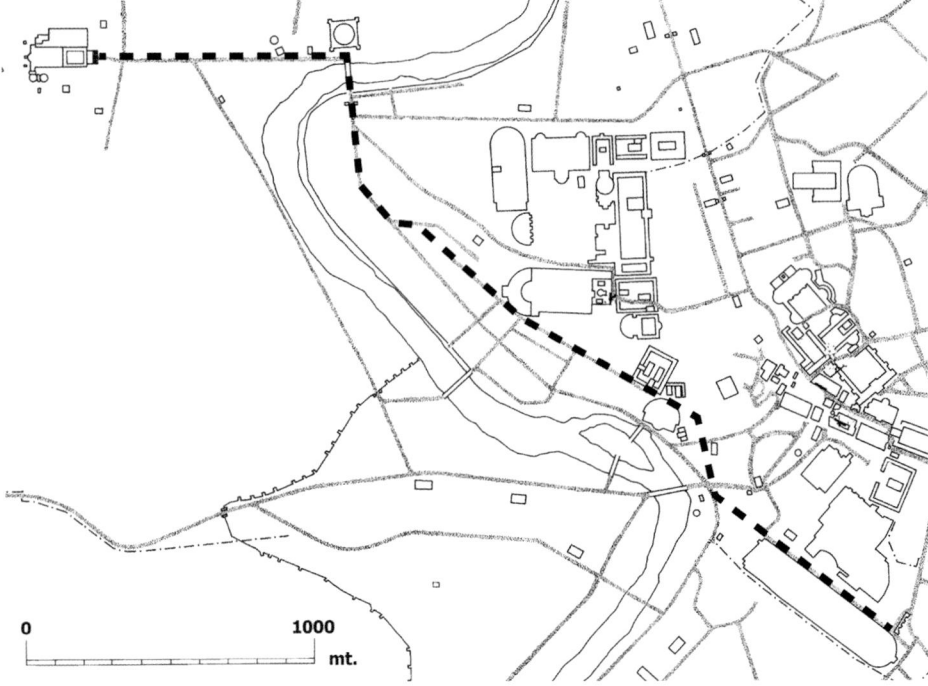

Figure 3.7 The colonnaded route (*porticus maximae*) between St. Peter's and the Circus Maximus/Palatine. (Author.)

of relative obscurity, it suddenly appears ranked third among all Roman churches, behind only St. Peter's and St. Paul's, in the so-called *Itinerarium Salisburgense* (or *Notitia ecclesiarum urbis Romae*), a list of Roman churches probably compiled under Pope Honorius I (r. 625–38). By then, it seems to have functioned as a kind of palace-church frequented by the Byzantine officials stationed in and around the Palatine, some of whom were buried there, among them the Plato we have already met as curator of the palace in the late 7th century. The *Itinerarium Salisburgense* is also the first source to say that S. Anastasia was where the seven regionary crosses were kept. These ceremonial crosses, one representing each of Rome's seven ecclesiastical districts, were carried in all the major processions of the annual liturgical cycle. Hence, before any ecclesiastical procession, the crosses first had to reach the day's starting point from S. Anastasia, whose proximity to the Forum and Palatine, seat of the Byzantine administration, likely favored its 'promotion' after the Byzantine reconquest. The regents of Byzantine Rome thereby ensured that liturgical processions all, in a sense, began with a church located in the shadow – literally – of the Palatine.[22]

For the next features along the route we have to rely on place-names recorded in later medieval sources, chiefly the *Ordo* of Canon Benedict, written c. 1140. The section of portico just past S. Anastasia (heading toward St. Peter's) was called the *porticus Gallatorum*. The best explanation of the otherwise unknown term *Gallatorum* is Giuseppe Marchetti Longhi's old idea that it derives from the *kalatores* formerly based in the Roman Forum, who once served as heralds for the pagan priests at the Regia. In the Byzantine period, following the suppression of traditional cult, the *kalatores/gallatores* would have moved the short distance from the Forum to the *porticus maximae*, but retained their job of proclaiming official decrees and judicial verdicts.[23]

Some corroboration comes from the next medieval landmark along the road, which also looks like a legacy of Byzantine government in

Rome. This is the *porticus Crinorum*, located across the road from a prison and site of public judicial assemblies by the church of S. Nicola in Carcere. A passage in the *LP* Life of Hadrian I (r. 772–95) shows that the prison definitely existed at the beginning of his reign, and that public judicial proceedings were held there at the time. But it should be older still, as Roman saints' lives written no later than the 6th century mention a place of imprisonment and trial in the same area. It was probably established there by the beginning of the Byzantine period, when the original *Tullianum* in the Forum was no longer used as a prison (whence, perhaps, the transfer of the name to the new prison). As for the name *porticus Crinorum*, given its location just across the street from the prison and site of judicial assemblies, Marchetti Longhi's suggestion that it derives from the Greek word for the Byzantine "judges" who presided in or near this portico becomes almost inevitable. While the arguments for the *Gallatorum* as "heralds" – even "judicial heralds" – and the *crinorum* as "judges" would be weak in isolation, the close connection between the two porticoes, and their mutual proximity to the site of a prison and public judicial assemblies, together make it look as though the judicial apparatus of the Byzantine state clustered in this area.[24]

Farther along the *porticus maximae*, between the theaters of Marcellus and Pompey, there was the *insula militena et drachonarii* near today's church of S. Carlo ai Catinari. The *milites drachonarii* ("dragon-soldiers," from the kitelike dragons they bore aloft on standards) were a unit of the Roman militia tasked with carrying the banners (*banda*) and standards (*signa*, possibly including the regionary crosses) that featured in civic and religious processions. They first appear in the Byzantine period, when the early 8th-century set of liturgical guidelines now known as *Ordo Romanus* 1 mentions them as participants in the city's grand Easter Sunday procession. Flag bearers called *drachonarii*, based in the same place, still featured in papal processions during the 12th century. The *insula* itself should thus be the barracks or headquarters of this elite military formation.[25]

Under Byzantine rule, it seems, institutions representing both the civil administration and the Church clustered along the porticoes of what was arguably Rome's grandest and most heavily trafficked avenue, where it traversed the "Greek riverbank" on its way between the Palatine and St. Peter's. This initial tract from the Palatine through the *Ripa Graeca* was bookended by twin poles of processional ceremony: S. Anastasia with its regionary crosses and the barracks of the military corps of ceremonial flag bearers, both of which are first attested in the Byzantine era. In between clustered other appendages of the civil bureaucracy: judges and town criers (or judicial heralds), and a prison where public judicial assemblies occurred. It is tempting to think that Byzantine officialdom saw the *porticus maximae* as the local equivalent of the Mese, the central, colonnaded avenue that linked Constantinople's most important churches and civic monuments and hosted the city's grandest processional ceremonies.[26]

There are also a number of churches and charitable centers (*diaconiae* – complexes staffed by monks that fed and cared for the needy) situated directly on or very near this stretch of the *porticus maximae* that were probably or certainly established under Byzantine rule. We cannot know exactly when they were founded because the *Liber Pontificalis* says nothing, which strongly implies that the popes were not directly involved. This suggests private or state patronage, which in the case of places dedicated to eastern saints previously unknown or at least uncommon in Rome likely originated with members of the 'Byzantine' ruling elite, including Greek-speaking transplants but possibly also local adopters of eastern fashions. There is the church and *diaconia* of S. Maria in Cosmedin, named for the Cosmidion monastery in Constantinople. The latter, restored by Justinian, also adjoined a church dedicated to Mary that was renovated by Emperor Justin II (r. 565–78), which makes the Roman complex of Mary in Cosmedin look very much like a recreation of the Constantinopolitan pairing. We might presume that the Roman 'copy' was sponsored by a Byzantine patron not long after the rejuvenation of its eastern exemplar. Nearby was the church and *diaconia* of S. Giorgio in Velabro, dedicated to the Byzantine soldier-saint George; it was not new at the time of its first mention in the *Liber Pontificalis* in the time of Pope Zacharias (r. 741–52) and thus should also date to the later 6th or 7th century. Farther on toward the Theater of Marcellus was the church and *diaconia* of S. Nicola in Carcere, already mentioned in connection with the nearby prison. The dedicatee of the church, Nicholas of Myra, was in fact a popular patron saint of prisoners in the early Middle Ages. Various hints (in addition to its association with the prison and the "Greek" dedication to another imported eastern saint) point to its also being established under Byzantine rule (Fig. 3.8).[27]

But these three are only the tip of a much larger iceberg of religious foundations apparently sponsored by nonecclesiastical actors. Although the *LP* says almost nothing about it, it looks as though laymen, notably including members of the Byzantine ruling establishment, played a crucial role in Christianizing the Forum and surrounding areas of the city center, founding a slew of churches and other religious institutions that transformed the Show Area into a showpiece of imperial Christianity under the patronage of the city's ruling elite. Following SS. Cosma e Damiano, the lone church established in the Forum before the reconquest, at least seven more were installed in Forum alone in the century or so after 554. Five of the seven are dedicated to eastern, Byzantine saints: S. Adriano in the

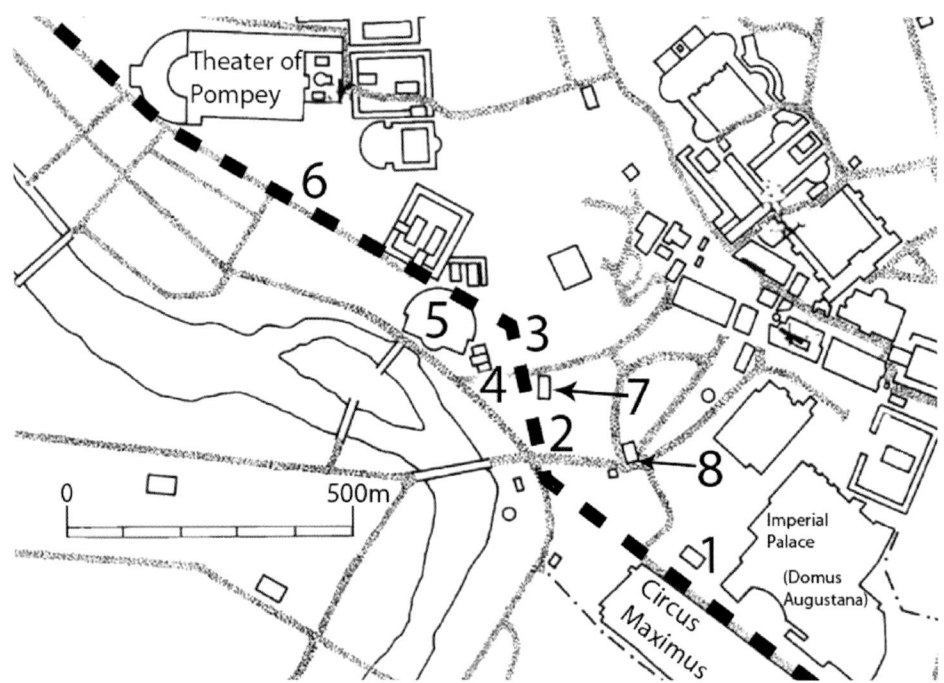

Figure 3.8 The *porticus maximae* from the Circus Maximus/Palatine to the Theater of Pompey, with main sites mentioned in the text. 1: S. Anastasia; 2: *Porticus Gallatorum* (approximate); 3: *Porticus Crinorum* (approximate); 4: S. Nicola in Carcere/prison; 5: Theater of Marcellus; 6: *insula militena et drachonarii*; 7: S. Maria in Cosmedin; 8: S. Giorgio in Velabro. (Author.)

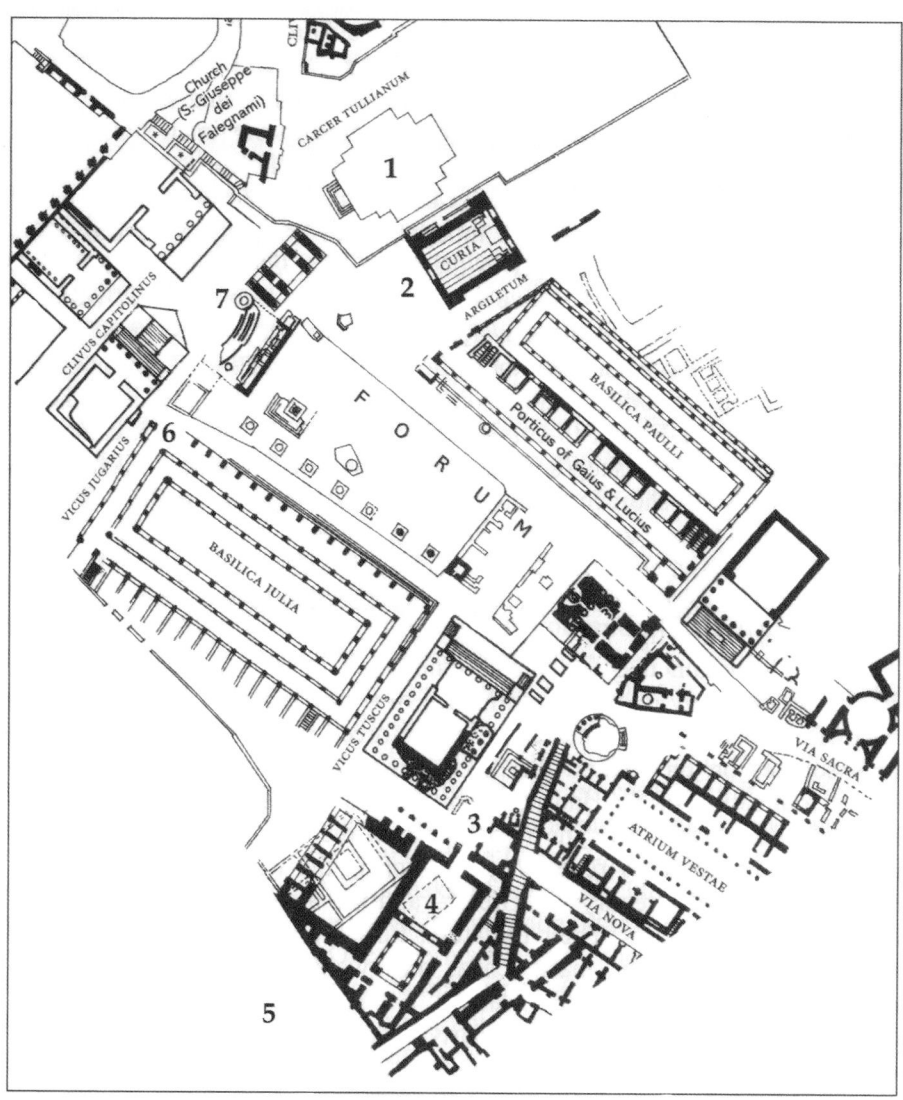

Figure 3.9 Forum plan with Byzantine-era church foundations. 1: S. Martina; 2: S. Adriano; 3: Oratory of the Forty Martyrs; 4: S. Maria Antiqua; 5: S. Teodoro; 6: S. Maria in Cannapara; 7: SS. Sergio e Bacco. (After Coates-Stephens 2011, p. 406, fig. 7.)

former Senate House, SS. Sergio e Bacco, S. Teodoro, the forty martyrs of Sebaste, and S. Martina (whose 'Byzantine' character is more questionable than the others); the other two (S. Maria Antiqua and S. Maria in Cannapara) are dedicated to Mary, the special patroness of the Byzantine emperors, whose popularity in Constantinople surged from the later 5th century on (Fig. 3.9). Yet neither the *LP* nor any other ecclesiastical source mentions the founding of any of them except for S. Adriano at the Senate House, for which Pope Honorius I gets credit (a public building as important as the Senate House was presumably granted to the pope himself by special imperial concession, as the Pantheon had been under Boniface IV in 609). While we will never be sure of who was responsible for the others, the probability of a Byzantine founder is high in each case. The dedications to typically 'Byzantine' saints are already suggestive, but more telling is the fact that five of the six were established in public buildings formerly under state control: S. Maria Antiqua and the Oratory of the Forty Martyrs at the entrance to the Palatine, in late 1st-century annexes of the palace; S. Maria in Cannapara in the Basilica Julia; S. Martina in an annex of the Senate House; and S. Teodoro in the remains of a warehouse along the western foot of the Palatine; the sixth, SS. Sergio e Bacco, stood between the temples of Vespasian and Concord on the paving of the Forum itself, also clearly still in the public domain in the Byzantine period.[28]

Certainly Rome's first two Byzantine regents, Belisarius and Narses, set an example for pious commissions that later lay patrons might have followed. Shortly after he first arrived in Rome in 536, Belisarius built a *xenodochium* (a charitable center similar to a *diaconia*) with an attached oratory dedicated to Mary just east of the Via Lata, on the site of today's S. Maria in Trivio near the Trevi Fountain – his is the one act of Byzantine lay patronage the *LP* does record. His successor, Narses, was renowned for his piety and his devotion to the Virgin Mary in particular; later writers called him a great founder and restorer of churches. In the 10th century, Benedict of Soracte plausibly claimed he founded the monastery of the Tre Fontane (*ad aquas salvias*) near St. Paul's. Modern commentators have also proposed Narses as a likely candidate for the founder of S. Maria Antiqua, which does look to have been transformed into a church while he was in Rome, c. 552–71, and based nearby on the Palatine.[29]

Like SS. Cosma e Damiano before them, the new churches in and around the Forum were mostly adapted from older buildings that were often little altered apart from the addition of new liturgical furnishings (altars, chancels, etc.) and devotional images in fresco or mosaic. S. Adriano got a new apse. S. Maria Antiqua was converted from an unroofed atrium, part of a late 1st-century complex built by Domitian at the Forum entrance to the Palatine, which was covered and divided into nave and side aisles with the installation of arcaded colonnades; three coins of Emperor Justin II (r. 565–78), placed under one of the columns, provide the best dating evidence for the project (Fig. 3.10). The Oratory of the Forty Martyrs was established

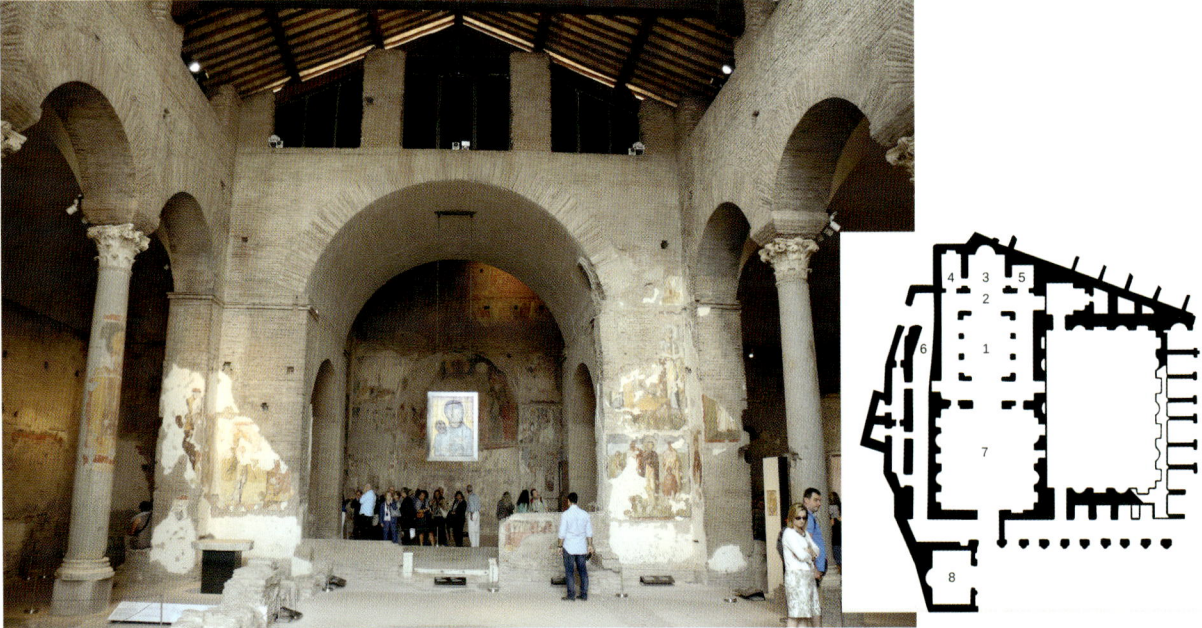

Figure 3.10 S. Maria Antiqua, interior facing apse (Wikimedia Commons/Sailko). Inset plan: 1: nave; 2: presbytery; 3: apse; 4: Theodotus chapel; 5: chapel of healer saints; 6: ramp to Palatine; 7: open-air atrium; 8: Oratory of the Forty Martyrs. (Wikimedia Commons/Afternand74.)

next door by redecorating another chamber in the Domitianic suite of rooms. The only one of the seven likely to have been a new building was SS. Sergio e Bacco, sited at the west end of the Forum between the temples of Vespasian and Saturn.[30]

All of this indicates that the heart of the city in the Palatine-Forum-*Ripa Graeca* area first developed a monumental Christian presence during the period of Byzantine rule, starting very soon after the reconquest. What needs stressing is that the process looks to have been shaped at least as much by the Byzantine administration, which controlled and maintained most of the spaces and buildings where the new foundations took root, as by the Church. This is by no means to say that the state, or the individual patrons it helped to transform public spaces and places into churches, were working at cross-purposes with the papacy, or that the Christianization of the Show Area was not sanctioned and supported by the Church. At least through the first half of the 7th century, rather, it looks as though the Church and the civil administration cooperated constructively to shape religious topography. The transformation of civic monuments as iconic as the Pantheon and the Senate House into churches is one sign of this entente; the continued participation of the city's professional builders in the most important ecclesiastical commissions of the age (S. Lorenzo, S. Agnese, S. Pancrazio, etc.) is another. But the fact remains that nonpapal, nonclerical actors established many (most?) of the churches founded in the Show Area of Byzantine Rome, and doubtless many others elsewhere in the city.[31]

Far from being a novelty, this prevalence of nonecclesiastical actors is another instance in which Byzantine Rome looks to have operated in the tradition of late imperial and Ostrogothic Rome. Ever since the days of Constantine, lay patrons had shouldered much of the burden of establishing new churches by giving land and/or buildings, paying construction costs, and providing the landed endowment necessary to maintain and staff churches in perpetuity. We have seen the role of the imperial family in founding and endowing Rome's greatest late antique churches (the Lateran, St. Peter's, and St. Paul's in the first place); but similar processes of lay patronage also saw less exalted patrons sponsoring less exalted churches, notably the *tituli* established in the 4th and 5th centuries. The *LP* attributes five to direct papal involvement (S. Silvestro, S. Marco, S. Lorenzo in Damaso, S. Maria in Trastevere, and a *titulus Crescentianae* founded by Pope Anastasius, r. 399–401), and only one to a lay patron, the *titulus Vestinae* (now S. Vitale), built under Innocent I (r. 401–17). It says nothing about who founded the remaining 19. The best bet is that laypeople sponsored many of them, as in the case of the *titulus Pammachii*/SS. Giovanni e Paolo on the Caelian, the brand-new basilica built after 410 on the property of the Christian senator Pammachius, whose patronage is attested by an inscription contemporary with the foundation. Elsewhere, 5th-century inscriptions record lay patronage at S. Agata dei Goti (Ricimer), S. Andrea in Catabarbara (Valila), and S. Pietro in Vincoli (Empress Eudoxia), as we have seen. Surely lay patrons also sponsored many (most?) of the more than 60 churches and monasteries in existence at the beginning of the 9th century whose foundation the *LP* says nothing about.[32]

There is a simple explanation for how Rome's ecclesiastical topography came to be so profoundly conditioned by lay patrons from the 4th century through the 7th. Across this period, most of the Romans with the most money and property (both urban real estate and rural landholdings) were not popes or clerics. This is especially true for the 4th and 5th centuries, when the senatorial aristocracy remained fantastically wealthy and continued to prefer traditional service in the Senate to a career in the Church – until well into the 6th century, in fact, no son of a senatorial family ever became pope. Even in the later 6th and 7th centuries, when the Senate dissolved and scions of senatorial families, Pope Gregory I among them, did start to gravitate toward ecclesiastical careers, there were always many more wealthy, property-owning laymen in the city than popes, including but not limited to holders of high office in the civil administration.[33]

The property-owning qualification is particularly important, for the obvious reason that substantial parcels of urban real estate – ideally with a suitable structure already present – were required in order to establish churches, monasteries, and charitable institutions. In the case of the land and buildings in the Show Area, the state was the primary owner and therefore very probably the main orchestrator of the process of Christianization, by determining which locales were made available for ecclesiastical foundations, and who was permitted to sponsor them. Meanwhile, clerics who wished to undertake work without the active assistance of the civil administration had to build either on private property or on Church property. Most such properties, naturally, were located outside the Show Area. It thus happens that, with the exception of public monuments granted to the popes by imperial concession for conversion into churches, most of the substantial papal building projects in Byzantine Rome occurred on the urban periphery, at cemeteries and martyrial shrines outside the walls.

In fact, for the 150 years from the reconquest through the end of the 7th century, spanning the pontificates of Vigilius (r. 537–55) through Sergius I (r. 687–701), the *LP* mentions but one important intramural church plausibly built (more or less) from scratch and on papal initiative. This is the "basilica of the apostles Philip and Jacob," now SS. Apostoli, a sizeable, three-aisled basilica located north of the Forum of Trajan, which the *LP* says was begun by Pelagius I (r. 556–61) and completed and dedicated by John III (r. 561–74). Every other intramural church whose creation and dedication the *LP* attributes directly to papal initiative was installed in an old building. Meanwhile, all of the six churches the *LP* says popes built "from the ground up" (*a solo* or *a fundamento*) in those 150 years stood outside the city center, at the graves of martyrs in suburban cemeteries, as did the couple of other churches mentioned that might also be new buildings. Otherwise, the popes mostly limited themselves to restoring or enhancing existing buildings, both inside the walls and in the suburbs.[34]

A number of more general patterns emerge: outside the walls, the popes took the lead in building new churches, transforming existing buildings into churches, and repairing or improving older foundations. Outside is also where most new construction happened, largely because of the need to transform old, unprepossessing cemeteries into showpieces of devotion to local martyrs. From the mid 5th century, the popes also paid special attention to developing the three premiere martyr shrines at St. Peter's, St. Paul's, and S. Lorenzo, the preferred destinations for the growing numbers of pilgrims and religious tourists flocking to Rome. There they built some of the city's earliest monasteries, to ensure the constant presence of caretaker monks at the basilicas, along with facilities for the poor, the sick, and visitors. Leo I (r. 440–61) founded the first monastery at S. Peter's, the *monasterium maior sancti Petri*; by c. 800, four more had joined it. Hilarus (r. 461–8) established the first monastery by S. Lorenzo. Pope Symmachus (r. 498–514) erected "dwellings for the poor" (*pauperibus habitacula*) at all three places. The expanding constellations of shrines and service buildings around the martyrial basilicas began to resemble small towns in their own right, urban satellites spaced at roughly equal intervals around the city center, staffed by resident monks and clerics and populated by the needy poor who came for care, and the devout who gathered to partake of the holy aura exuded by the bones of Rome's leading martyrs. Concentrations of monasteries and service buildings also formed around prominent intramural churches such as S. Maria Maggiore and the Lateran, each of which was served by three nearby monasteries by the 9th century.[35]

Inside the walls, on the other hand, relatively few churches were built *ex novo* under Byzantine rule. Founders, both clerics and laypeople, understandably preferred to repurpose existing structures. In the Show Area itself, Byzantine officials look to have been almost as predominant as the popes were outside the walls, as far as patronage of religious institutions is concerned. In the intermediary zone between the Show Area and the walls, something approaching parity probably prevailed, with clerics and lay patrons alike doing what they could where resources and circumstances allowed.[36]

One category of foundations whose architecture and location alike depended heavily on chance and circumstance were the monasteries and charitable centers installed in private dwellings, among them a number established by Roman popes in their family houses. The first papal house foundations reported in the *LP* are the hostel (*ptochium*) for elderly poor installed in the house of Pelagius II (r. 579–90), and Gregory I's transformation of his ancestral mansion on the Caelian into the monastery of S. Andrea in the 570s, before he became pope. From then on, the *LP* makes it sound as though this sort of thing became standard practice: Boniface IV (r. 608–15), Honorius I (r. 625–38), and Adeodatus (r. 672–6) are all supposed to have made monasteries out of their family residences.[37]

In choosing to consecrate personal property to the service of the Church, these aristocratic prelates did nothing particularly unusual for members of their class, and indeed quite conventionally followed along in a tradition long established among pious Romans of similar wealth and standing. The papal initiatives that the *LP* deigns to record undoubtedly comprise only a small fraction of a much wider phenomenon largely shaped by lay actors. The earliest known ascetic communities in Rome occupied the houses of Roman noblewomen in the later 4th century, and nobles also established the first attested charitable institutions, again shortly before 400: a *hospitale* by Fabiola and a *xenodochium* at Portus by Pammachius, the same Christian senator who provided the land and funding for SS. Giovanni e Paolo on the Caelian. Up to the time of the Gothic War, Rome's still-vibrant senatorial aristocracy kept on installing monasteries and charitable centers on property they owned or otherwise obtained for the purpose; and when Byzantine potentates arrived in the city, they did likewise, starting with the already-mentioned examples of Belisarius and Narses. The apparent conclusion, as Riccardo Santangeli Valenzani has put it, is that "in late antiquity the activity of providing aid to foreigners and pilgrims seems to have been a monopoly of the senatorial aristocracy." By the 7th century, the Senate was defunct, but Roman aristocrats, including those who now chose instead to pursue careers in the Church, kept up with the performance of religious benefaction.[38]

The locations where such benefactors continued to establish churches, monasteries, and, especially, charitable institutions have important implications for the broader question of settlement and population distribution in early medieval Rome, to which we now turn. Most of the known charitable foundations postdate the Byzantine reconquest, when population already approached its nadir; and we can safely assume that *xenodochia* and *diaconiae* tasked with aiding the sick and needy tended not to be established in uninhabited areas. Many doubtless developed into focal points for their surrounding neighborhoods, possibly even helping to attract denser

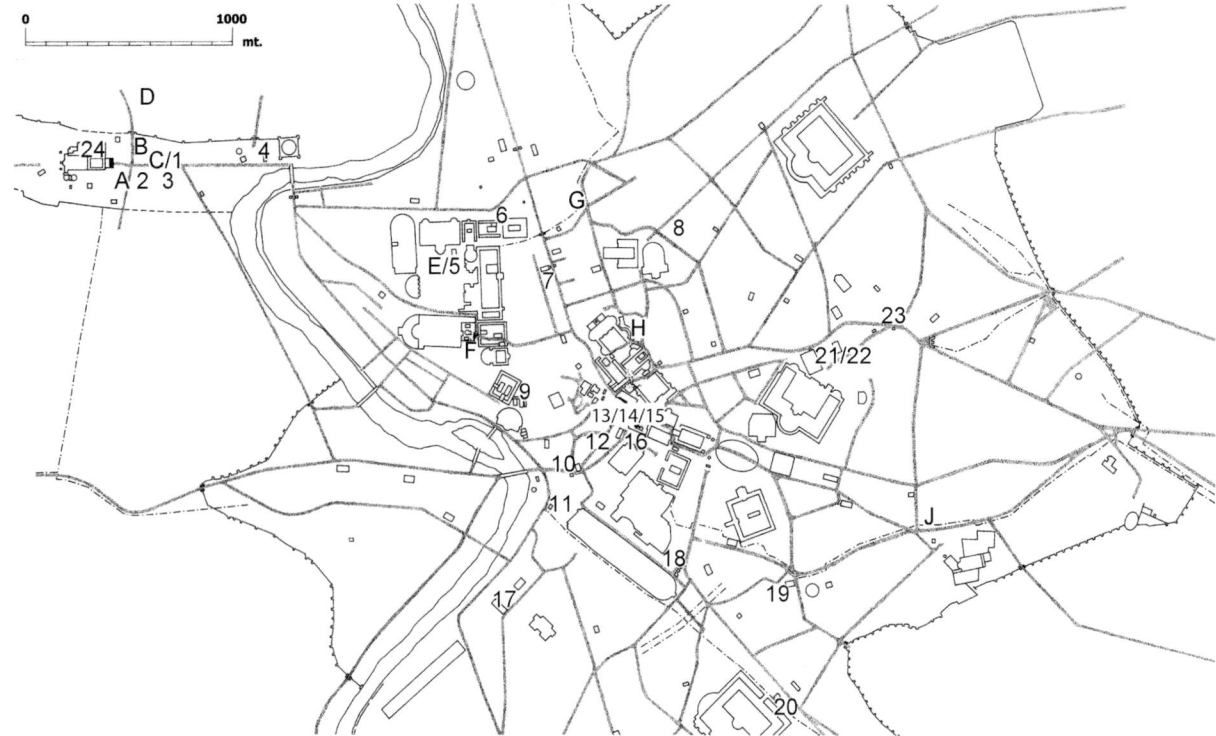

Figure 3.11 *Diaconiae* and *xenodochia*, 9th century and earlier. Letters = *xenodochia*; numbers = *diaconiae*. A: S. Gregorio; B: S. Pietro; C: S. Maria; D: S. Pellegrino; E: *xenodochium in platana*: F: *xenodochium Aniciorum*; G: *xenodochium in via Lata*; H: *xenodochium Valeriorum*; J: Schola cantorum. 1: S. Maria *in caput portici*; 2: S. Silvestro; 3: S. Martino; 4: S. Maria *in Adriano*; 5: S. Eustachio; 6: S. Maria in Aquiro; 7: S. Maria in Via Lata; 8: S. Agata *de Caballo*; 9: S. Angelo in Pescheria; 10: S. Giorgio in Velabro; 11: S. Maria in Cosmedin; 12: S. Teodoro; 13: SS. Sergio e Bacco; 14: S. Adriano; 15: SS. Cosma e Damiano; 16: S. Maria Antiqua; 17: S. Bonifacio; 18: S. Lucia *in septem viis*; 19: S. Maria in Domnica; 20: SS. Nereo e Achilleo; 21: S. Lucia in Selce; 22: SS. Silvestro e Martino; 23: S. Vito; 24: SS Sergio e Bacco. (Author.)

concentrations of people thanks to the services they provided. A glance at the distribution map of those in existence in 807, when the most complete surviving list was included in the *LP* Life of Leo III, shows them spread across a broad swath of the city center, though there is again a relative dearth in the Tiber bend (Fig. 3.11). They cluster along busy roads that connect the city center with its surrounding territory, especially from the Forum down to the docks and marketplaces of the *Ripa Graeca*. Close proximity to land- and water-routes helped ensure the ready availability of commodities such as wine, oil, and grain that were distributed at *xenodochia* and *diaconiae* (more on this below).[39]

As for churches, it is the parishes (*tituli*) that should correspond most closely with populated zones, though the calculus in this case is complicated by the fact that they were almost all established in the 4th and earlier 5th centuries, when population remained far higher than it was by the 6th century. Nonetheless, most *tituli* probably did still serve a reasonable number of local residents in the early Middle Ages. Like the charitable foundations, they provided essential services that encouraged people to live nearby: From baptism to marriage to last rights and burial, medieval Romans depended on their local parish church. At least some *tituli* also owned clusters of nearby houses, occupied by tenants whose rents supported the church. The distribution of the *tituli* corresponds reasonably well with the areas of early medieval settlement documented by texts and archaeology: They were scattered widely across the intramural area, save for the far north and south, and (again!) the Tiber bend, the entirety of which was served by the lone *titulus* of S. Lorenzo in Damaso (Fig. 1.15, above).[40]

The elephant in the historical room here is Krautheimer's assertion that by the later 6th century, Rome's remaining inhabitants (he guessed they numbered around 90,000) mostly clustered in the cup-handle-shaped bend of the Tiber in the Campus Martius and across the river in the adjacent sections of Trastevere, from about the Tiber Island up to the Vatican. He called this populated nucleus of settlement the *abitato*, as it was known by the 16th century. I suspect that Krautheimer went so badly astray in part because of his tendency to overestimate the Church's impact on Rome's urban trajectory prior to the 8th century, in this case perhaps by imagining that the Vatican was a stronger pole of attraction than it was. The reality, now broadly recognized, is that Romans occupied much of the intramural area throughout the early Middle Ages, and only really began to concentrate in the areas indicated by Krautheimer from about the 11th century, as we will see.[41]

This brings us to the material contours of the residential fabric. It should first be said that documented remains of dwellings erected in the early Middle Ages almost all date after the Byzantine period, when new and distinctive building techniques came into widespread use. There are in fact no well-dated examples of early medieval houses built anywhere in Rome prior to the 9th century. For the period c. 550–750, archaeological evidence for residential building is almost nonexistent, leaving us dependent on texts and certain other proxies for our sense of how and where people were living. The causes of this lack are important, and revealing in their own right about the nature of settlement in post-reconquest Rome.

The main reason we are unlikely ever to find many houses built c. 550–750 is – I think – that very few new residences were wanted at a time when Rome remained chock-full of hundreds of hectares' worth of still-serviceable ancient buildings. When we recall that Rome's population after the Gothic War never exceeded 5 to 10 percent of its imperial-era peak, it is evident that only a small fraction of Rome's imperial-era housing stock needed to survive to accommodate everyone, both in terms of mansions for the elites and apartment blocks (*insulae*) for the rest. There is little doubt that well over 10 percent of Rome's usually very solidly built stock of ancient housing remained inhabitable in the 6th and 7th centuries, and many *insulae* in fact survived far deeper into the Middle Ages, and sometimes beyond – the so-called *insula* of the Aracoeli at the foot of the Capitoline Hill, for example, was inhabited into the 20th century (Fig. 3.12)![42]

Thus, the vast majority of Romans were almost certainly living in old buildings throughout the Byzantine period and beyond, which presents archaeologists looking for them with terrible problems. Archaeology is good at documenting change and destruction: collapses, accumulations of dirt and debris on floors, extensive remodeling or redecorating of existing spaces. But early medieval residents of an *insula* who kept their floors swept and made only the most essential repairs (to leaky roofs, for example) necessary to stay reasonably sheltered will leave hardly a trace for modern archaeologists to find. An additional difficulty is that the kinds of mortared masonry employed in Rome in the 6th and 7th centuries, usually some variety of *opus vittatum*, are hard to distinguish from the more numerous constructions of the 4th and 5th, as we have seen. Further, many of whatever such later bits once existed were summarily dismantled by past generations of archaeologists, who were generally content to refer generically to an ill-defined "late" or "post-classical" period, generally meaning "somewhere from the 4th century on." Even with more care and more refined techniques, it will never be easy

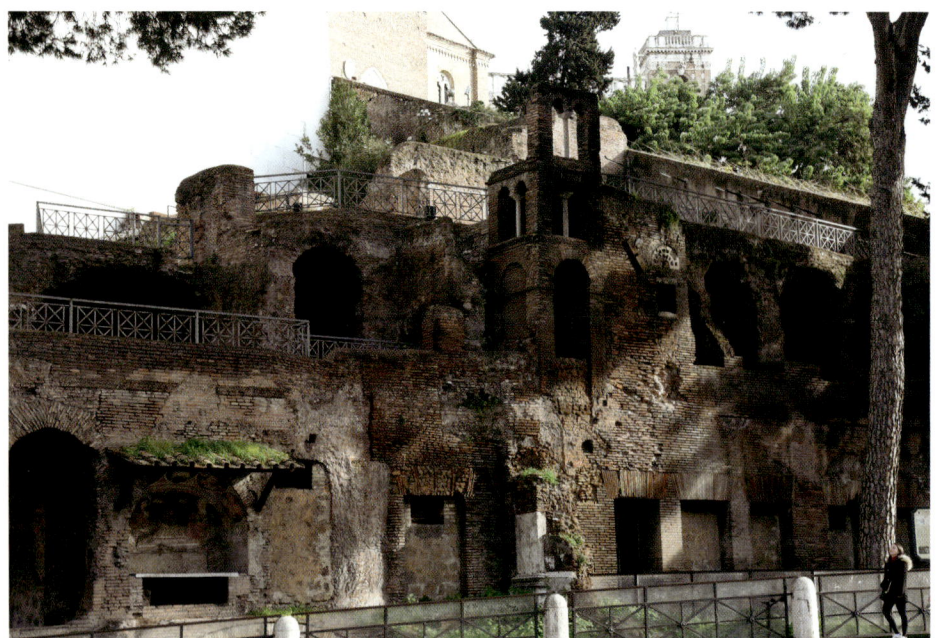

Figure 3.12 The 2nd-century *insula* at the foot of the Capitoline, beneath S. Maria in Aracoeli. Note the later medieval (c. 12th-century) bell tower built in connection with a chapel installed inside the *insula*. (Author.)

to date many of the isolated bits and pieces (patches, blocking of older apertures, partition walls) that must often constitute the most durable traces of Byzantine-period habitation of older structures.

But the written sources alone might have sufficed to show that people were scattered much more widely around early medieval Rome than Krautheimer suggested, as the subsequent reassessment of the textual record spearheaded by Étienne Hubert and Robert Coates-Stephens demonstrates. For the period 500–1000, Coates-Stephens identifies eighteen popes whose family houses have known locations, often thanks to the monasteries established in them. Not one of them is in Krautheimer's *abitato* (Fig. 3.13). Hubert's careful study of Roman archival documents (contracts of sale and lease, etc., many for relatively humble properties) makes it clear that Rome's less exalted classes also spread widely, from the Esquiline all the way across town to the Aventine and Trastevere. Until at least the 11th century, however, few of them can be shown to have occupied the Tiber Bend. Archaeological traces of early medieval habitation are also sprinkled fairly consistently across a wide band of the city center, absent the far north and south and – again – the western portions of the Tiber bend, as a glance at Coates-Stephens' plan shows (Fig. 3.14).[43]

In short: There is less written and material evidence for people actually living in the Tiber bend than in most other areas of the early medieval city. It has no *diaconiae*, few *xenodochia*, and only one of the city's twenty-five *tituli*. It was emphatically not the most densely settled region of Rome at any point between 400 and 1000.

There is now broad consensus that Byzantine Rome's remaining tens of thousands of inhabitants tended to collect in settled 'islands' scattered across much of the intramural area and separated by more or less vacant stretches of abandoned buildings and ruins, some of which sprouted gardens and orchards and pastures. Like the leopard-skin pattern to which they are often compared, the inhabited 'spots' were widely distributed, but cumulatively occupied well under half of the total intramural area. The location of any given cluster was conditioned by any number of factors, most rooted in ancient

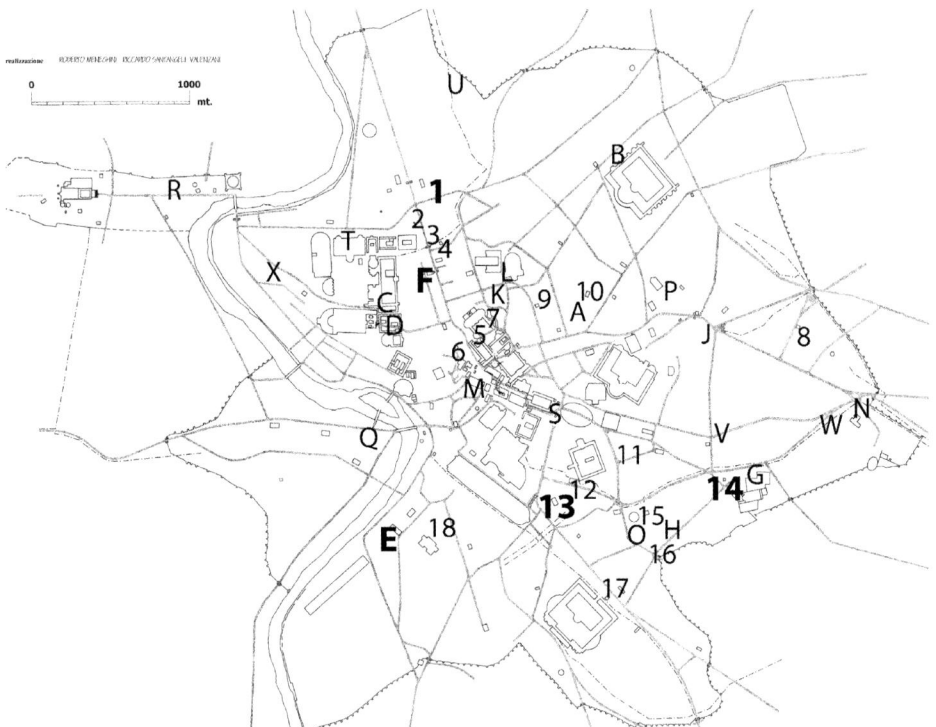

Figure 3.13 Locations of textually attested early medieval residences, through the 10th century. Numbers = houses of popes; letters = other houses; large characters = certain locations; small characters = approximate. 1: Stephen II/Paul I; 2: Hadrian I; 3: Valentine; 4: Stephen V; 5: Leo VIII; 6: Benedict VI; 7: John XVII; 8: Anastasius II; 9: Gregory II; 10: John XV; 11: John II; 12: Agapitus; 13: Gregory I; 14: Honorius I; 15: Deodatus; 16: John XVIII; 17: Leo IV; 18: Eugenius I; A: *ad Gallinas Albas*; B: *iuxta Thermas Diocletianas*/S. Susanna; C: *iuxta Thermas Agrippianas*; D: *Pallacenis*; E: Alberic II; F: Marozia, Stefania, Teodora, cousins of Alberic; G: Campus Lateranensis; H: Crescentius *murcapullo*; J: John of Albano; K: Alberic II; L: *Crescentius a caballo marmoreo*; M: *Cannapara*; N: Porta Maggiore cluster; O: S. Erasmo cluster; P: S. Maria Maggiore cluster; Q: Piscinula cluster; R: Vatican cluster; S: S. Maria Nova cluster; T: *Crescentii*; U: *Domus Pinciana*; V: *Domus Merulana*; W: *Domus Pilati*; X: *Palatium Cromatii*. (Redrawn from Coates-Stephens 1996, fig. 1.)

topography. Proximity to main roads was desirable, especially those that led through the gates and connected the city center with the surrounding countryside. Running water from surviving aqueducts also was important, not only for drinking, bathing, and irrigation, but also, particularly on the Janiculum, for powering grain mills. While some were never repaired after the Gothic War, a number clearly were, among them the four again restored in the late 8th century after being cut during the Lombard siege of 756: the Jovia/Iobia in the south, the Claudia in the east, the Virgo in the north, and the Sabbatina (Traiana) in the west (see Fig. 4.9, below). More localized stimuli to settlement included the presence of especially large or well-preserved structures; markets and commercial areas; zones of high symbolic or administrative significance; and religious foundations. Prominent among the latter were the great devotional and martyrial basilicas, both inside the walls and out, with their halos of monasteries, charitable centers, and hostels; the intramural *tituli* serving various neighborhoods; and, at least from the later 7th century, the places the *LP* calls "monasteries of the *diaconia*."[44]

Diaconia is the Latin form of a Greek singular noun used since the 4th century as a blanket term for the charitable services offered at monasteries, which included providing food, lodging, and medical care for travelers and the indigent. The term appears in Rome with an apparently similar meaning starting in the 680s, when the *LP* starts

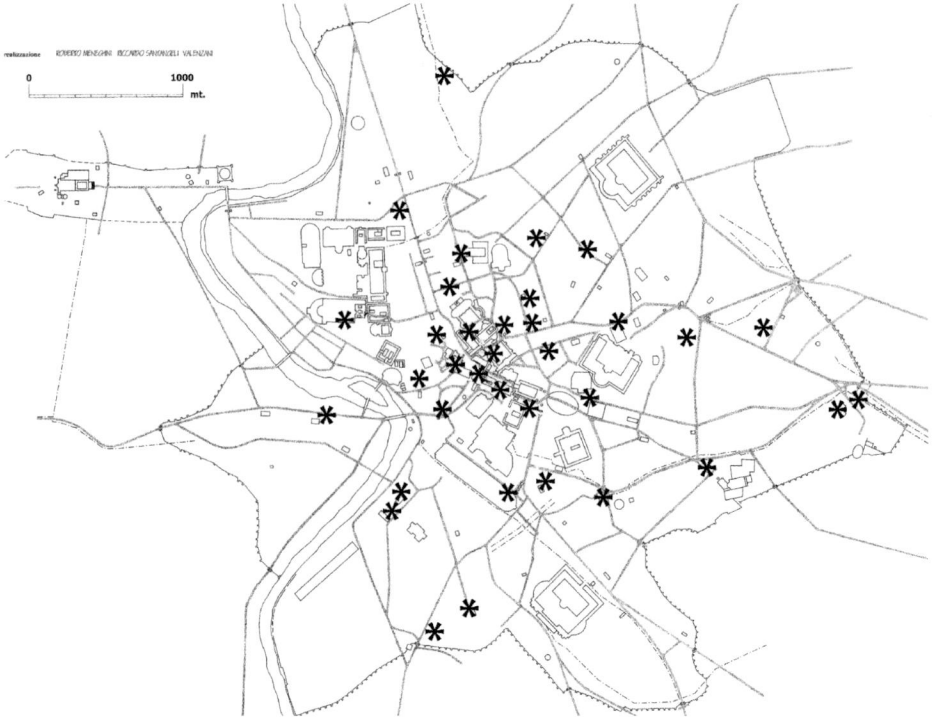

Figure 3.14 Locations of archaeologically attested early medieval housing, through the 10th century. (Redrawn from Coates-Stephens 1996, fig. 2.)

to mention papal donations to the "monasteries of the *diaconia*." Though debate over its meaning continues, the phrase is best taken to show that by this time, the Church had begun to assume responsibility for funding and administering various types of charitable centers, which were staffed by monks and jointly placed under papal supervision. By the 730s, the term *diaconia* was applied to specific Roman locales where charity was administered, though it may well have been used in this way earlier, as individual *diaconiae* are known at Naples and elsewhere in Italy already by the time of Gregory the Great. In any case, the sudden appearance in the 680s of the collective term *diaconia* for a network of Roman charitable centers patronized by the popes looks significant. Though plenty of institutions such as "hostels" or "hospitals" (*xenodochia*) and "poorhouses" (*ptochia*) had already been established in the 5th and 6th centuries, most of the early examples were founded and endowed by noble patrons, as we have seen, apparently without much in the way of centralized coordination. The *LP*'s mentions of papal patronage of "monasteries of the *diaconia*" from the 680s is the first plausible sign of any such coordination.[45]

These textual references show, at the very least, that the Church was more visibly asserting itself as the leading provider for Rome's needy by the 680s. Thereafter, the *LP* makes popes the founders of all new charitable centers and also the stewards of the existing ones, including those originally founded by laypeople: The popes provided for their upkeep and installed the administrators, called "supervisors" (*dispensatores*) or "fathers" (*patres*), responsible for running each institution. The key point regarding the larger question of how and where Romans were living, however, is that from the second half of the 7th century on, the various *diaconiae*, *xenodochia*, and so on are the only places known to have provided free food (along with other services) for the urban populace. In this sense, they are the only attested successors of the *annona*, the state-sponsored distribution of foodstuffs that had continued under Theodoric and under the terms of the Pragmatic Sanction of 554.[46]

We will never know exactly when the *annona* as such ceased to exist. Scattered hints, such as an episode in which Emperor Justin I (r. 565–78) redirected Egyptian grain normally reserved for Constantinople to Rome to alleviate a famine in the later 570s, suggest that it continued for some time after the Byzantine reconquest, but there is general agreement that government-sponsored distributions of foodstuffs at Rome petered out by the 7th century, perhaps as early as 618, when the *annona* was discontinued at Constantinople. The apparent chronological coincidence between the end of the *annona* and the rise of an articulated system of charitable institutions under direct papal supervision has led some, notably Jean Durliat, to propose that the Church simply replaced the secular administration as the nourisher of Rome. Once again, however, this would be to exaggerate the role of the Church on the Roman scene. While the Church may to some extent have supplanted the civic authorities in the matter of feeding, it looks as though it was supplying a much more restricted segment of the population than had the *annona*.[47]

The *annona* had been a perquisite granted by the emperors to the *plebs Romana*, the collective of Roman citizens, but not to slaves, foreigners, and vagrants – the most rootless and disenfranchised of the urban masses. It was precisely these latter groups who were the main recipients of Christian charity from the beginnings of the organized Church. With the legalization of Christianity in the 4th century, Church charity came to supplement the civic *annona*, but by no means to supplant it. Throughout the early Middle Ages, the ecclesiastical sources consistently claim that Church distributions of food continued to be targeted toward the desperately poor and homeless, the sick, and foreigners or pilgrims. Hence the exaggeration in proposing that Church-directed charity replaced secular largesse in its classical form: As far as we can tell, the popes, unlike the emperors, never intended to feed the bulk of the citizenry on a regular basis. That the *LP* presents Pope Hadrian I's provision to feed 100 beggars daily at the Lateran in the late 8th century as an act of extraordinary magnanimity implies that the scope of the Church's charitable efforts remained quite limited.[48]

On the other hand, we cannot know exactly who qualified as sufficiently poor and needy to be eligible for the services provided at *diaconiae* and *xenodochia*, and it may be that a larger subset of the populace benefitted from Church charity after traditional forms of public assistance were discontinued. And the fact remains that by the end of the 7th century, ecclesiastical 'social services' were all that was left. In addition to food, *diaconiae* were also supposed to provide occasional baths for their needy 'clients,' thus (very partially) prolonging another service no longer furnished by the imperial administration. By the time of the reconquest, the gigantic imperial-era baths were all mostly or totally defunct, and restoring them to service was not a viable proposition – the daily operation of any one of Rome's mega-baths at its original capacity, for c. 10,000–15,000 daily users, required tons of firewood, tens of thousands of gallons of aqueduct water, small armies of service personnel, and so on, all of which far exceeded the means of Rome's Byzantine civil administrators, not to mention the needs of its remaining population. Whatever bathing still happened took place on a much-reduced scale, generally in smaller, private baths like those attached to charitable centers and churches. Finally, in its provision of lodging and medical care for select recipients, the Church offered something the imperial authorities had never given to ordinary citizens. It is fair to conclude that the "monasteries of the *diaconia*" played a large and growing part in the lives of many Romans, in the process helping to conserve or expand many of the spots on the "leopard-skin" of Roman settlement.

But it is also fair to conclude that the Church's charitable organs served a much narrower slice of the populace than the old civic *annona*. From the 7th century on, most Romans could count on neither state nor Church to feed (and house, and bathe, and cure) them.[49]

The citizenry also had much less in the way of public entertainments. After the Gothic War, no more traditional spectacles are reported to have taken place in any of Rome's entertainment venues. No chariot races in the Circus Maximus; no blood sport in the Colosseum; no mimes and plays in the theaters and auditoriums. In part, the Roman situation tracks with a broader decline in traditional mass spectacles across the Byzantine Empire by the later 6th century. Procopius actually claims that Justinian, a notoriously pious killjoy, terminated funding for all public games and spectacles, leaving entertainment venues empty and derelict throughout his dominions. Procopius may exaggerate, but the basic point stands that government support for traditional public entertainments was drying up by the later 6th century, when the abandonment (and sometimes dismantling or repurposing) of spectacle buildings across the empire was more or less universal, with the notable exception of the hippodrome at Constantinople. At Rome, there was also an especially vast disparity between the capacity of the ancient arenas and the size of the post-reconquest population. At its original capacity, the Colosseum alone might have seated, roughly speaking, everyone left in town by the 7th century. Even if public entertainments did not cease entirely, it would have been highly impractical to maintain gargantuan arenas for the (depressingly tiny) crowds left to occupy them. Already before the Gothic War, Cassiodorus had cited the size of the arenas as evidence of how drastically Rome's population had shrunk; and by his time, if not somewhat earlier, parts of the Colosseum were being dismantled for scrap, even as it continued to host games.[50]

Still, we should be wary of assuming that nobody was having any fun anywhere. To take but one example, the old Stadium of Domitian in the Campus Martius offers tantalizing signs of functional continuity, despite the fact that the stands of the hairpin-shaped enclosure were already being transformed and repurposed during the 5th and 6th centuries. Workshops or storerooms occupied some of the vaulted chambers under the seating area, 6th-century burials occupied others, and the western flank of the superstructure eventually sprouted a church dedicated to Agnes, later called S. Agnese in Agone, "Saint Agnes in the sports-field." Yet the arena floor was kept open and practicable throughout the Middle Ages, as it remains up to the present, as the Piazza Navona. From at least as early as the 10th century, its common name was the "field of competition" (*Campus Agonis*), and by the later Middle Ages, it was definitely hosting tournaments and other popular entertainments. While the nature of the spectacles held there changed over time – from gladiators to jousts, as it were – the arena may well boast a more or less unbroken history of use as a place of recreation and competition. In one way or another, Romans found ways to indulge in public games and entertainments throughout the Middle Ages, albeit on a much humbler scale than their imperial-era predecessors. But the fact remains that, by the Byzantine period, government-subsidized mass spectacle was no longer a perk of Roman citizenship.[51]

The end of the civic *annona* and the transformation of both games and bathing from large-scale, state-sponsored institutions to (at best) smaller-scale, more ad hoc affairs are all ruptures with traditions characteristic of ancient Rome that point the way toward the Middle Ages. Another such rupture that transpired under Byzantine rule involves Romans' changing approaches to their dead. Even as churches began to multiply in the Show Area (yet another rupture), burials were proliferating across all of the city. This was an epochal shift. Until the 5th century, ancient tradition had dictated a strict separation between the city of the living and the necropolises, the "cities of the dead" outside the city center where human remains were deposited. The dividing line between the two spheres was the *pomerium*, the ancient religious and legal boundary that distinguished the urban 'inside' from the nonurban 'outside,' and which probably coincided with the newly built Aurelian Wall after the 270s. Even after the coming of Christianity, the prohibition against intramural burial was broadly observed until the Gothic sieges and sack at the beginning of the 5th century, when a first smattering of corpses was inhumed inside the walls, presumably because the besieging Goths complicated access to the extramural cemeteries.[52]

But these initial burials were an exceptional measure necessitated by exceptional circumstances, and extramural burial in fact remained the norm for some time thereafter. Few 5th-century graves have been found inside the walls, while many hundreds of inscriptions (and other datable objects and furnishings) from extramural cemeteries testify to ongoing deposition of corpses on a considerable scale. It was only from the time of the Gothic War in the mid-6th century that deposition inside the walls became common. By the 7th century, the extramural burial grounds were clearly being used less, though of course people never entirely stopped being buried – and living! – outside the walls. This shift reflects a broader revolution in the relationship between the living and the dead that swept Christian Europe in the 5th and 6th centuries, where burials also became common in old town centers, for reasons that no early medieval author explains. It is partly a matter of strands of Christian theology and eschatology that overturned the traditional view of corpses as polluting and encouraged regular graveside prayers as helpful to the souls of the deceased, prayers that were more conveniently said when bodies were close at hand instead of miles away on the periphery. But there were more prosaic and utilitarian causes at work, too, such as the increasing availability of unused land in old town centers that had lost much of their Roman-era populations.[53]

Both the theological and utilitarian motives will have loomed especially large at Rome. On the one hand, the extramural catacombs and open-air cemeteries were mostly located in a band stretching some three miles out from the Aurelian Wall, which put most bodies buried there literally miles away from living relatives inside the city. On the other, the city center was replete with unoccupied spaces and buildings by the mid 6th century – no other city in Europe had as much intramural space available for interring corpses. From the 6th century into the 8th, Romans made very broad use of all this space, depositing burials singly or in small groups in both built-up and vacant areas scattered across the city: inside the ambulatories of the Colosseum and the Stadium of Domitian; in derelict mansions on the Caelian, Esquiline, and Aventine hills; in the great imperial bath complexes, and so on (Fig. 3.15). Others were buried in and around churches, and at cemeteries administered by the various *tituli* on behalf of their parishioners, but this was only one option among many until the later 8th century. Only then did burial in churches and associated cemeteries develop into the standard procedure for

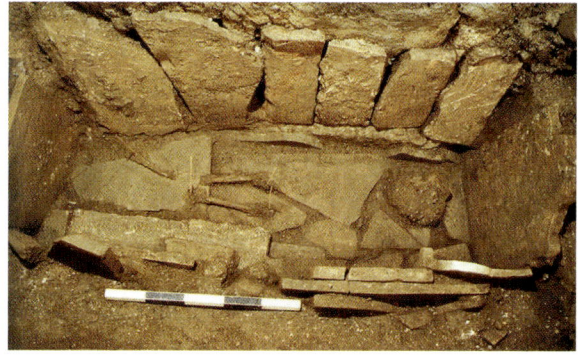

Figure 3.15 6th-century burial at the Crypta Balbi, installed inside the perimeter wall of the portico. (Manacorda 2001, p. 49, fig. 53.)

Romans that it remained for the rest of the Middle Ages. The presence of early medieval graves across the city center is probably the single best argument for the widespread distribution of population throughout the early Middle Ages, and against any early concentration of settlement in the Campus Martius, where relatively few early medieval burials have turned up (Fig. 3.16). (Intramural burials are, after all, a sign of continuing urban life and tend to cluster in neighborhoods where people still lived.)[54]

Where Byzantine-era graves are not found, on the other hand, is encroaching on public spaces maintained by the civil administration, such as streets and piazzas. So, for example, while there are burials at the churches in the Show Area, the paving of the Roman Forum and the adjacent imperial forums was kept free of graves, as were certain parts of the palace complex on the Palatine, even as burials began to occupy more peripheral areas. The most common location for cemeteries is, in fact, in old public buildings (baths, entertainment venues, etc.) that underwent what looks to have been a relatively orderly, regulated transition into designated funerary spaces after losing their original functions. Most corpses were not randomly or haphazardly buried in Byzantine Rome, in short. It is another telling sign that the civil administration exercised effective control over the urban fabric, enforcing restrictions on what could and could not be done with various spaces, and distinguishing between the public patrimony and the rest.[55]

After this extended discussion of breaks with longstanding tradition, it is fitting to close by returning to another of the continuous threads that linked Byzantine Rome with an ancient past that remained, in many respects, alive and vital in the post-reconquest period. We thus turn to material culture: to the stuff of everyday life that opens a window onto the 'standard of living,' as we would now say, enjoyed by Romans in the later 6th and 7th centuries. Among the many groundbreaking excavations of early medieval sites in the past forty years or so, still the most surprising and illuminating is the Crypta Balbi. With regard to the Byzantine period, the most exceptional finds came in the early 1990s during the excavation of the exedra at the rear of the rectangular portico attached to the Theater of Balbus, which we have already seen transformed into a glass workshop around the middle of the 5th century. At the end of the 7th century, the exedra was piled high with a thick layer of intentionally deposited detritus, apparently in the wake of one of the catastrophic floods that periodically inundated this low-lying area of the Campus Martius. The occupants of some nearby complex, possibly the inhabitants of a monastery located just north of the exedra, evidently shoveled out their dwellings and work-spaces and dumped the soggy mess in the abandoned exedra (Fig. 3.17; see also Fig. 4.2, below). Whatever the neighboring facility was, it obviously included a large workshop engaged in making a broad range of consumer and luxury goods, whose variety and quality of both materials and workmanship came as a revelation. Nearly every major category of finds from the late 7th-century deposit forced a reassessment of prevailing, overly pessimistic assumptions about the material conditions of Roman life in this period.[56]

As usual, the bulk of the deposit was pottery. Most was in the form of amphorae, transport containers used to ship liquids such as wine, oil, and fish sauce. Even more startling than the sheer quantity of the many thousands of amphorae recovered was the fact that the majority still originated from the far shores of the Mediterranean: Some 40 percent of the total came from North Africa, and another 30 percent from the Levant. This cache alone sufficed to dispel the notion that 7th-century Rome was impoverished and isolated, cut off from overseas bounty and reliant on local produce for its survival. Still at the end of the 7th century, Rome was about as deeply implicated in

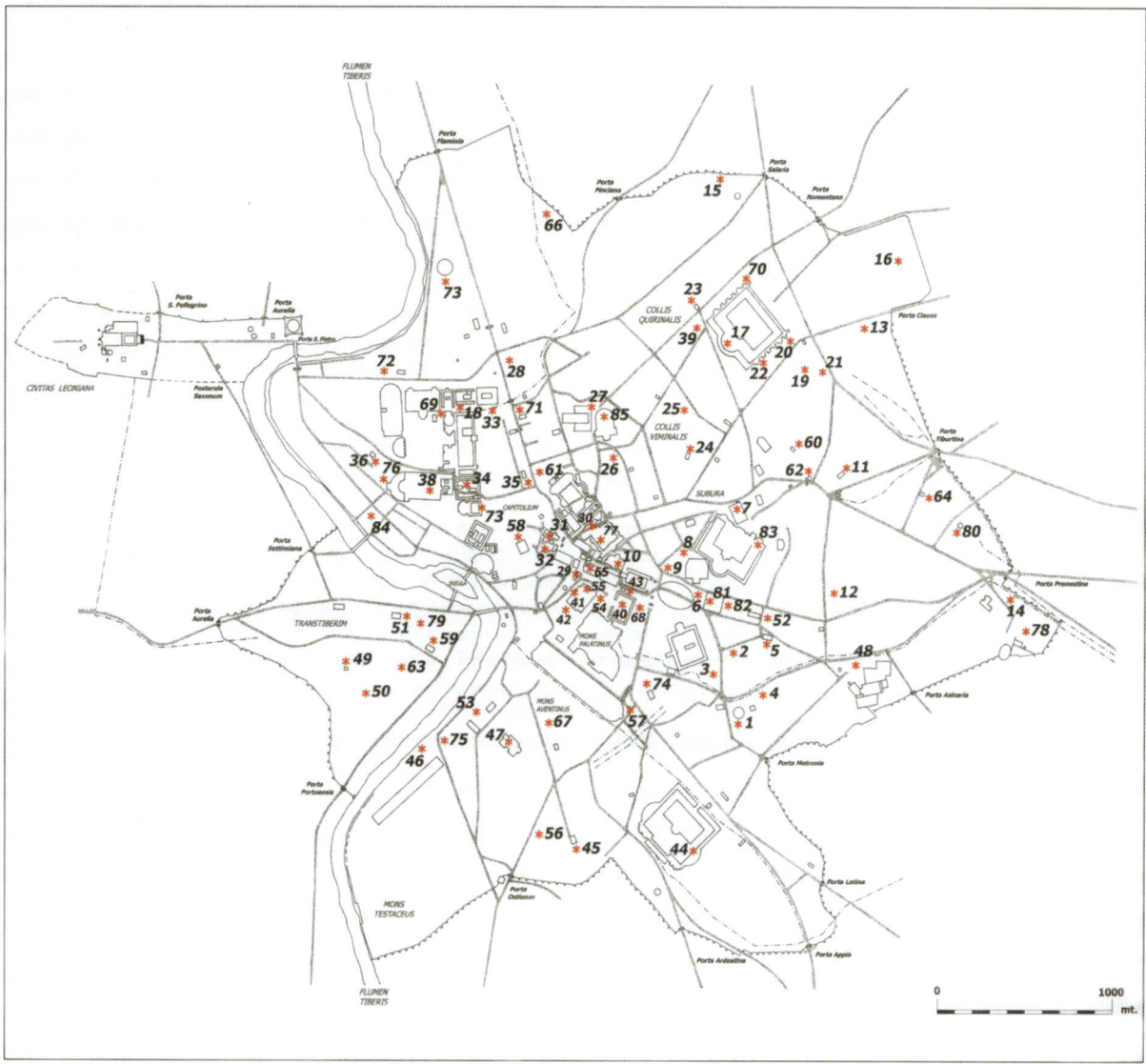

Figure 3.16 Locations of intramural burials, 5th–10th century. 1: S. Stefano Rotondo; 2: Ospedale Militare; 3: Via dei Simmachi; 4: Ospizio dell'Addolorata; 5: SS. 4 Coronati; 6: Colosseum; 7: *Porticus Liviae*; 8: Via della Polveriera; 9: Via degli Annibaldi; 10: Basilica of Maxentius; 11: S. Eusebio; 12: Via Ariosto; 13: Via Varese; 14: Terme Eleniane; 15: Via Campania; 16: Praetorian Camp; 17: Baths of Diocletian; 18: Via del Seminario; 19–20: Piazza dei Cinquecento; 21: Termini Station; 22: Piazza dei Cinquecento; 23: S. Susanna; 24: S. Lorenzo in Panisperna; 25: Interior Ministry; 26: Via Mazzarino; 27: Piazza del Quirinale; 28: Via del Mortaro; 29: S. Maria Antiqua; 30: Forum of Nerva; 31: Tabularium; 32: *Clivus Capitolinus*; 33: Piazza San Macuto; 34: *Porticus Minucia*; 35: S. Marco; 36: Palazzo della Cancelleria; 37: Mausoleum of Augustus; 38: Theater of Pompey; 39: Via Torino; 40: Vigna Barberini; 41: Bastione Farnesiano; 42: Temple of Magna Mater; 43: Baths by Arch of Titus; 44: Baths of Caracalla; 45: S. Saba; 46: Lungotevere Testaccio; 47: Baths of Decius; 48: Piazza San Giovanni in Laterano; 49: S. Cosimato; 50: Via San Francesco a Ripa; 51: S. Crisogono; 52: S. Clemente; 53: Giardino degli Aranci; 54: *Clivus Palatinus*; 55: *Domus Tiberiana*; 56: Via della Piramide Cestia; 57: Piazza del Circo Massimo; 58: Via del Campidoglio; 59: S. Cecilia; 60: S. Andrea in Catabarbara; 61: Piazza Venezia; 62: S. Vito; 63: Via Anicia; 64: S. Bibiana; 65: House of the Vestals; 66: Villa Medici; 67: Largo Arrigo VII; 68: east slope of Palatine; 69: Baths of Nero/Alexander Severus; 70: Finance Ministry/Baths of Diocletian; 71: Palazzo Sciarra; 72: Palazzo Altemps; 73: Crypta Balbi; 74: S. Gregorio al Celio; 75: Testaccio; 76: Palazzo Righetti; 77: Forum of Peace; 78: S. Croce in Gerusalemme; 79: S. Pasquale; 80: nympheum of the *Horti Liciniani*; 81: Ludus Magnus; 82: Via di San Giovanni in Laterano; 83: Baths of Trajan; 84: Palazzo Spada; 85: Vicolo Mazzarino. (Meneghini and Santangeli Valenzani 2004, p. 104, fig. 82.)

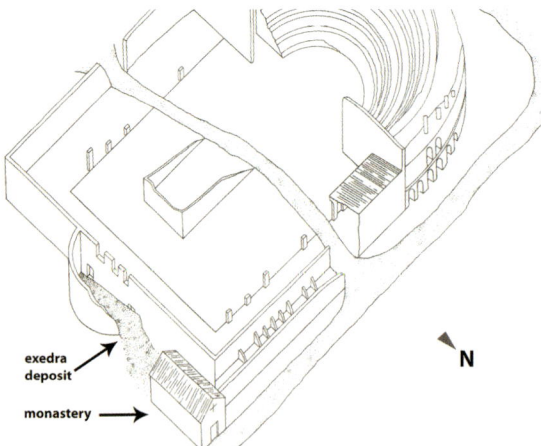

Figure 3.17 The "monastic hypothesis" for the source and formation of the deposits in the exedra of the Crypta Balbi. (Adapted from Saguì and Rovelli 1998, fig. 2.)

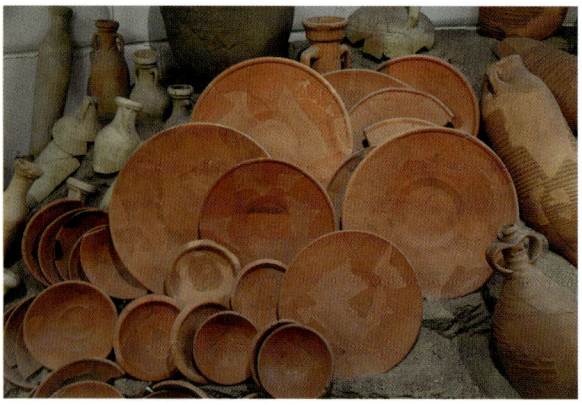

Figure 3.18 ARS plates and bowls from the 7th-century deposit at the Crypta Balbi. Note also the slender North African amphorae (*spatheia*) at upper left, and the ribbed Levantine amphorae at far right. (Author.)

Mediterranean-wide networks of trade and exchange as it was under the last emperors, as other recent finds elsewhere in the city also show. Whoever produced the waste dumped in the exedra was eating and drinking about as well, and consuming the same sorts of imported products, as well-off Romans in the time of Constantine, say. They were also eating and drinking from similar plates, bowls, and cups. In the 4th century, Rome's preferred upscale terra-cotta tableware was the glossy, reddish-orange "African Red-Slip" (ARS) ceramics imported from North Africa, primarily Tunisia and western Libya. At the end of the 7th century, Romans were still eating off of glossy wares imported from Africa, as the thousands of fragments of ARS in the deposit at the Crypta Balbi show (Fig. 3.18).[57]

The community that deposited the trash in the exedra might also have paid for their tablewares in small-denomination bronze coinage, which also would have come as a surprise to historians and numismatists of Krautheimer's generation. Until the Crypta Balbi excavations, it was understood that the Roman economy was mostly demonetized by the 7th century, with only a few high-denomination gold and silver coins in circulation that were far too valuable for use in everyday transactions, and negligible quantities of small-denomination bronzes. But the hundreds of coins recovered from the exedra alone sufficed to show that Rome in fact continued to have a fully functioning trimetallic monetary system into the early 8th century, with gold, silver, and large numbers of bronze coins in all the standard Byzantine denominations – and still featuring the names and portraits of the Byzantine emperors, of course (Fig. 3.19). Coins were still minted at Rome, the bronzes in a state-run facility that may now have been located at the three adjoining 2nd-century auditoriums recently excavated at Piazza Venezia. Romans in the later 7th century were emphatically not reduced to a barter economy: Like their imperial-era ancestors, they had money in denominations suitable for transactions large and small, in the same denominations used throughout the lands still under Byzantine control.[58]

Moreover, Romans still had access to all sorts of low- and high-value goods on which to spend their multidenominational coins. The 7th-century material from the deposit in the exedra includes an exceptional array of expertly crafted manufactures, including arms (swords, daggers, tips for spears and arrows); personal accessories (brooches, pins, belt buckles, spurs); jewelry in gold, silver, and semiprecious stones; furniture, including an inlaid ivory bishop's throne; plaques, combs, and pins in

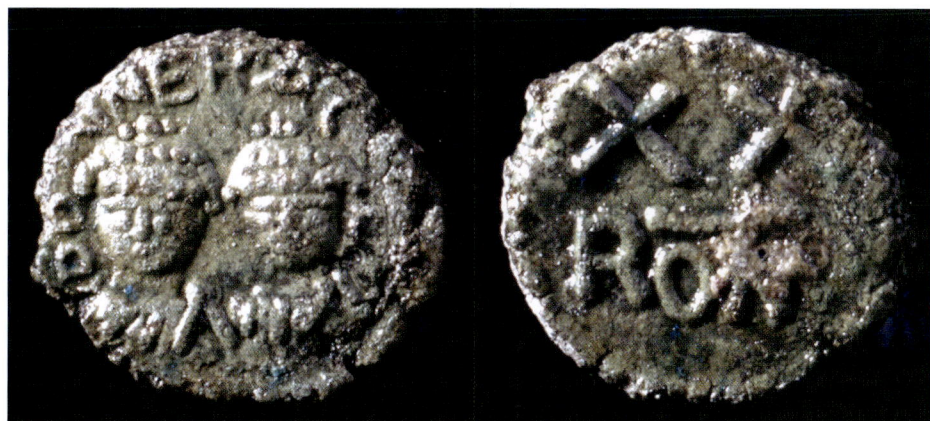

Figure 3.19 Bronze 20-*nummi* coin from the 7th-century deposit at the Crypta Balbi, 613–621/22, Rome mint. The obverse features frontal busts of (left) Emperor Heraclius (r. 610–41) and (right) his son, Heraclius Constantine. (By concession of the Ministero per i beni e le attività culturali e per il turismo – Museo Nazionale Romano.)

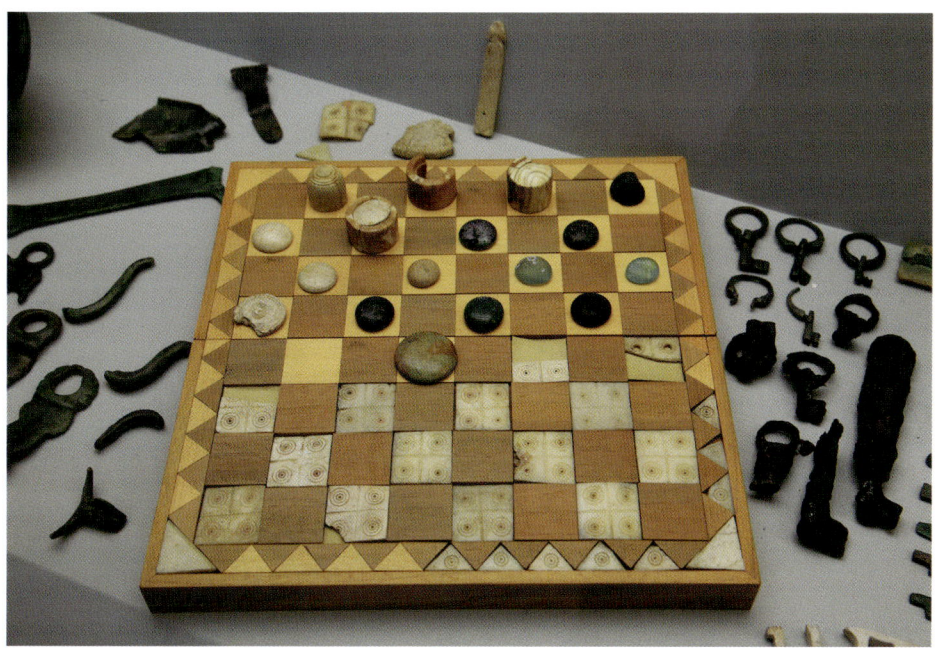

Figure 3.20 Game-board in bone and (modern) wood; disparate gaming-pieces in bone, horn, ivory, glass, and stone; and metal objects from the late 7th-century deposit at the Crypta Balbi. (Author.)

bone and even ivory; inlaid game-boards; blown and fused-glass objects; and the list goes on (Figs. 3.20–21). These are products made to high standards, with the best and most expensive materials (some coming from as far away as Africa and Asia), by trained professionals: experts in glassblowing, metalworking, carving, inlaying, carpentry, and other crafts. Nothing about this squares with notions of 'Dark Age' regression into ignorance and squalor. Just the opposite, in fact: There was clearly demand for the goods being produced in semi-industrial quantities by the skilled craftsmen in the Crypta Balbi workshop, which is to say there was a relatively sophisticated clientele with the resources (and coin) necessary to pay for the nice things they continued to consume.[59]

The obvious conclusion from all of this is that Byzantine Rome was not nearly as isolated,

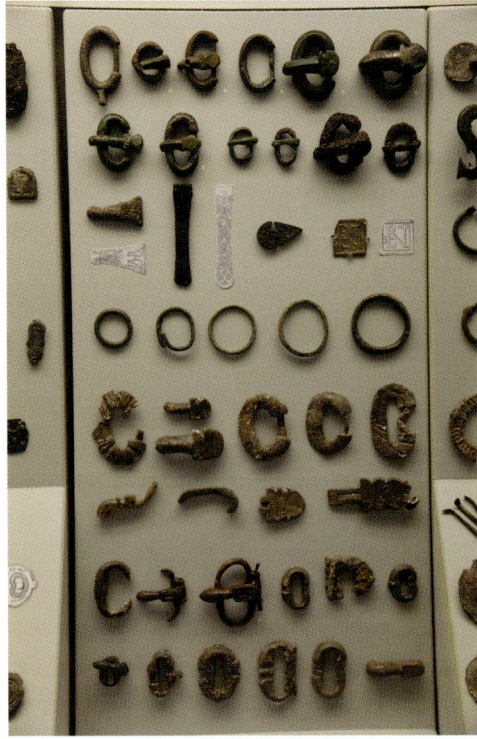

Figure 3.21 Buckles and other metal fittings from the late 7th-century deposit at the Crypta Balbi. (Author.)

technically retrograde, or impoverished as nearly everyone assumed until the 1980s. The rich harvest of finds from the Crypta Balbi is the more remarkable for coming from one of the first excavations undertaken in the city center that made finding and documenting medieval remains a priority. More Crypta Balbi–like sites undoubtedly exist, though finding them will be difficult since most of central Rome is too densely occupied to be easily excavated. It is already clear that the Crypta Balbi is better imagined as the tip of a material-cultural iceberg than as the one flourishing island in all of Byzantine Rome. Other recent excavations have produced multidenominational coins and imported pottery that corroborate the findings at the Crypta Balbi, and new wonders continue to emerge. One is the metal-working facilities installed in the 2nd-century auditoriums discovered during the construction of the new Metro C stop at Piazza Venezia, where more than 100 furnaces of different types

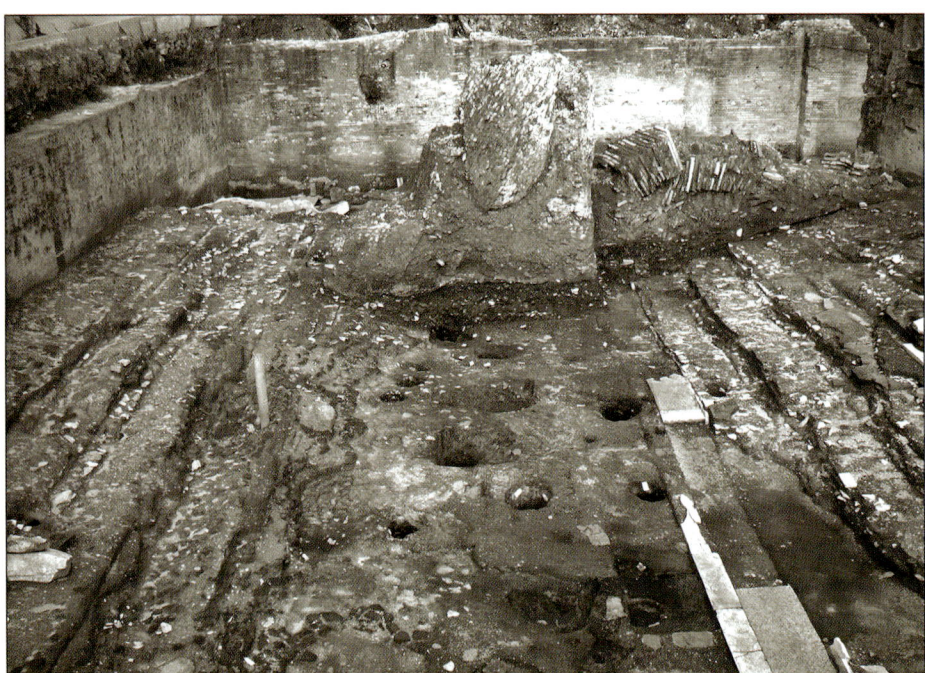

Figure 3.22 The middle chamber of the three adjoining auditoriums at Piazza Venezia. The holes hacked into the concrete under-bedding of the (mostly stripped) marble flooring at the center of the room all belong to metalworking furnaces used in the period c. 550–700. Note also the rising rows of seats at right and left, and, at the rear of the chamber, the remains of the ceiling vaults that collapsed onto the floor, probably during the earthquake of 847. (Serlorenzi et al. 2017, fig. 3, photo courtesy of the authors/SSABAP di Roma.)

occupied the floors of the three connected auditoriums during the 6th and 7th centuries, in what may be another instance of state-sponsored conversion of old public buildings to new uses (Fig. 3.22). Here, sophisticated and diversified metalworking techniques, inherited from antiquity, were used to produce a wide range of bronze and iron objects on a semi-industrial scale, among them, perhaps, much of Byzantine Italy's bronze coinage.[60]

The bustling artisanal activity in the auditoriums would come to an abrupt end around 700, however, when the metalworking apparatus was quickly and thoroughly dismantled, and the floors of the empty halls turned into a burial ground for humble folk deposited there in simple tombs. This abrupt local transformation might be read as a symptom of broader changes afoot in the decades around 700, when Rome gradually diverged from the Byzantine orbit in both political and economic terms. As Constantinople looked to its own survival against the Islamic armies sweeping the eastern Mediterranean, it devoted fewer resources to Italy. In the growing power vacuum that ensued, the popes emerged as the preeminent champions of local, Roman interests and began, tentatively at first, to take a more prominent role in civic governance and administration. By the later 8th century, after the final collapse of Byzantine power in Italy, they would come into their own as the first effectively sovereign rulers to reside in the ancient imperial capital since the last emperors in the 5th century, and set out to reshape the cityscape accordingly, as we shall now see.

Chapter 4

705–882

A Papal "Republic of the Romans"

OVER THE COURSE OF the 8th century, Rome finally became what papal apologists (medieval and modern) claimed it had been centuries earlier: an effectively autonomous polity ruled by popes and administered by bureaucrats and functionaries employed by the Church. After a lengthy gestation period stretching back into the 7th century, this papal "Republic of the Romans" (*respublica Romanorum*) matured in the second half of the 8th, under Frankish protection, and flourished into the later 9th. It comprised the city itself and a surrounding territory, roughly coextensive with the modern region of Lazio, that fell under direct Roman jurisdiction. During the century and more of the papal Republic's apogee, the popes claimed, and flaunted, privileges and prerogatives previously reserved to Romano-Byzantine emperors, becoming in the process the first sovereign rulers to reside stably in Rome since the 5th-century emperors. Only at this point does it finally become proper to speak of a 'papal' Rome where the Church, led by the popes, was the dominant force in shaping the cityscape (Fig. 4.1).[1]

Our start-date of 705 is basically arbitrary, in the sense that Rome did not pass from Byzantine to papal control in that year, or for that matter in any single year. There was no clean break, no definitive moment of rupture. The year 705 represents an approximate midpoint in the protracted, messy separation between Rome and Constantinople that had already begun by the mid 7th century, and only passed the point of no return in the mid 8th. The causes of the rupture were many. From the 640s on, worsening doctrinal disputes between the Church of Rome and the authorities in Constantinople opened a growing rift between the

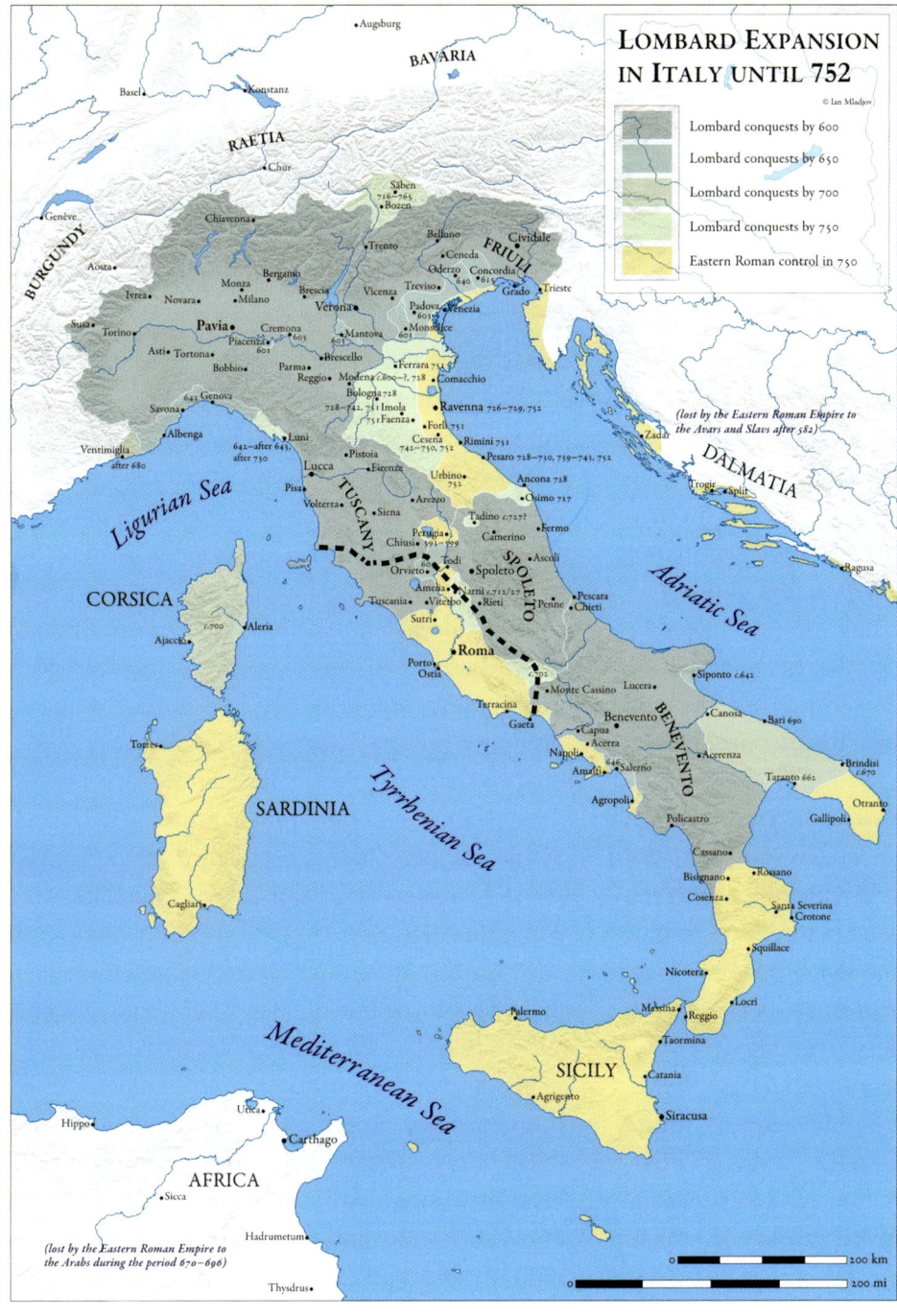

Figure 4.1 Italy in the 8th century. The yellow area around Rome marks territory under papal/Byzantine control in the first half of the 8th century; the dotted line marks the approximate boundary of territory under papal control at the end of the 8th century. (Map by Ian Mladjov, modified by author.)

popes and the Byzantine emperor's representatives in Italy. (It was Pope Martin I's staunch support of the anti-Monothelite decrees issued by the Lateran Council of 649 that led to his arrest and deportation to Constantinople in 653, where he was tried and exiled to the Black Sea.) At the same time, the resources and attention that Constantinople could devote to Rome and Italy declined sharply in the wake of the Muslim conquests in the eastern Mediterranean from the 630s on, which left the empire in a fight for its life that consumed most of its dwindling resources. One result was that troops based in Italy were drawn increasingly from local levies, thereby coming gradually to identify more closely with local, Italian interests.[2]

Already by the pontificate of Sergius I (r. 687–701), a pronounced shift toward papal, Roman, and Italian independence is evident. After Sergius repudiated the canons of the Church Council "in Trullo" held in Constantinople in 692, the imperial envoy dispatched to Rome to arrest him was lucky to escape lynching at the hands of the Roman people and the Italian troops. Whether or not he was forced to take refuge under the pope's bed in the Lateran palace, as the *LP* gleefully claims, the mere fact that the *LP* could make such an assertion shows how much had changed in the four decades since the deportation of Martin I. It is undoubtedly true that Byzantine plans to deport the pope were thwarted by local elements, including much of Italy's 'Byzantine' standing army, whose loyalty lay more with the pope than with the distant emperor. Pope Sergius also minted low-denomination bronzes bearing his monogram that are the first coins ever struck in the name of a pope. Papal patronage of "monasteries of the *diaconia*," starting in the mid-680s, looks to be another foray into territory (food distribution on a citywide scale) previously occupied by the civil administration and individual lay patrons. Thus, a book on Roman history might well put the origins of 'papal' Rome in the 680s, as Tom Noble did in his fundamental *The Republic of St. Peter*. But for a profile of Roman urbanism, the brief papacy of John VII (r. 705–7) works better, for reasons rooted in both textual and material evidence.[3]

We can begin where we left off in Chapter 3, with the exedra at the Crypta Balbi, where a second deposit of waterlogged flood debris was deposited atop the first in the mid 8th century (probably c. 740), to the joy of present-day archaeologists and historians. This second layer seems to have been shoveled out of the same place as the first, and contains as rich and varied a sample of materials from the first half of the 8th century as the first one does from the second half of the 7th, permitting direct comparison between the two. The later deposit captures Rome in a moment of rapid and dramatic change (Fig. 4.2).[4]

The Muslim conquest of North Africa, culminating in 698 with the fall of Carthage, seems finally to have put a serious dent in the networks of overseas trade that had uninterruptedly converged on Rome for a millennium, leading to increased reliance on Italian resources and products. Imports from North Africa and the Levant, which comprised the majority of the transport amphorae present in the 7th-century deposit, disappear in the early 8th, as does the high-quality African Red Slip tableware (ARS). Transport amphorae from southern Italy and Sicily become more prevalent, while locally made plates, cups, and bowls supplant the Tunisian ARS.[5]

From the 730s, Sicilian and southern Italian imports also declined, such that Rome became still more isolated from the wider world and more dependent on local produce for its sustenance. At the same time, Rome's trimetallic monetary system broke down completely: Emissions of bronzes slowed and then stopped completely between c. 720 and 740; the purity of locally minted gold and silver coins plummeted after c. 730; and by the 740s, stocks of precious metals were evidently exhausted to the point that the Roman mint ceased to function altogether. Older, more valuable coins were melted down or removed from circulation, such that by the pontificate of Zacharias (r. 741–52), Romans were mostly reduced to a barter economy. These trends recur at sites across the city, though the contrasts between the later 7th century and

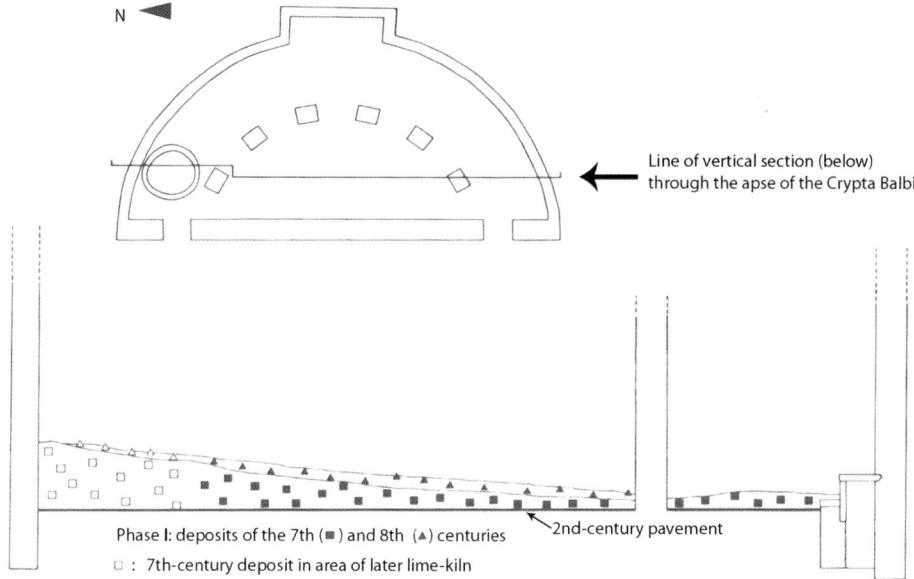

Figure 4.2 The late 7th- (c. 690) and mid 8th-century (c. 740) deposits in the exedra of the Crypta Balbi; note the diminishing thickness of the layers from north (toward the presumed source of the discarded materials) to south. (Adapted from Saguì and Rovelli 1998, figs. 1a–b.)

the first half of the 8th are especially clear in the two, superimposed levels at the Crypta Balbi.[6]

This systemic reorientation of Rome's material horizons reflects the collapse of relations between Pope Gregory II and Byzantine emperor Leo III that began in the mid 720s. A first clash over Leo's decision to increase taxes on the Church's Italian landholdings was followed almost immediately by Gregory's repudiation of iconoclasm, the rejection of religious imagery supported with growing fervor by both the emperor and the ecclesiastical authorities in Constantinople. Leo retaliated by appropriating the Church's vast estates in southern Italy and Sicily, along with the considerable revenues those lands produced, which explains why the Rome-ward flow of southern produce and precious metals alike dried up when it did. In response, the popes took the lead in promoting Roman economic self-sufficiency, attempting to compensate for the shortage of hard currency by stimulating local production and favoring exchanges in kind. Zacharias began the process of consolidating Church-owned lands in the Roman countryside into vast, centrally administered agricultural estates called *domuscultae* that supplied the city with food and other essentials.[7]

The expanding corpus of archaeological finds makes it increasingly clear, in short, that the material record closely tracks Rome's growing isolation from the rest of the Byzantine Mediterranean, and its political estrangement from Constantinople, over the first half of the 8th century. By 751, when the Lombards took Ravenna and ended the Byzantine presence in north-central Italy for good, the popes were well placed to fill the ensuing political void after a half-century and more of defending Roman interests against a distant, often outright hostile, imperial administration. During that same half-century, the popes had also begun to play a larger role in stewarding and at times actively shaping Rome's physical fabric, including select public monuments that remained at least nominally under state control. This brings us back to John VII at the beginning of the 8th century.[8]

The pope's terse biography in the *LP* contains the eye-opening revelation that he built himself a new papal residence on the Palatine, located above the church of S. Maria Antiqua (which he also redecorated), where he spent the remainder of his pontificate. John's biographer, presumably a cleric at the Lateran little pleased by the move to the Palatine, notes tartly that "above the same church [S. Maria Antiqua], he built the *episcopium* he very much wanted for himself, and there he finished the time of his papacy and his life." The pope whose father, Plato, had been curator of the imperial palace thus abandoned the Lateran to install himself on the Palatine, in the part of the *domus Tiberiana* that overlooks the Forum. Recent excavations have revealed parts of three masonry structures installed inside a courtyard of the imperial palace that date to the beginning of the 8th century and might well belong to John's *episcopium* (Fig. 4.3). His successors may have stayed in the new residence up until the pontificate of Zacharias, who allegedly found the Lateran complex neglected and decayed enough to require extensive renovations when he occupied it in the 740s. Probably the move to the Palatine was made with the sanction of the Byzantine administration to whom the palace still belonged, but the project is no less significant for all that. For a time in the early 8th century, the papacy installed itself in the very center of the Show Area, in the building that embodied like no other the exercise of temporal authority in Rome.[9]

Pope John's other projects included an oratory inside St. Peter's that was richly decorated with mosaics and ancient marble reliefs, and new fresco cycles at S. Maria Antiqua and the next-door Oratory of the Forty Martyrs. His portrait features prominently in all three locations, in mosaic at St. Peter's and in fresco at the other two, framed by the square halo that signified a living likeness. John is the first pope known to have exalted himself with public portraits while still living and reigning, in the traditional manner of kings and emperors. His biographer was apparently conscious of the novelty, which he again reported with a fillip of irony: "He also commissioned scenes in various churches, where whoever wants to know will find his face depicted in them." By focusing on locations as crucial as the imperial palace, the shrines at the Forum entrance to the Palatine, and St. Peter's, and inserting himself into these hallowed venues by plastering his portraits across them, John visibly and materially enhanced the profile of the papacy, and proclaimed its (and his) growing prominence in civic government and administration.[10]

Subsequent developments show John VII's successors following his lead. After his move to the Palatine, the popes started behaving more like civil administrators (or rulers), in part by assuming a more active role in shaping the cityscape. John's immediate successor, Sisinnius, died after

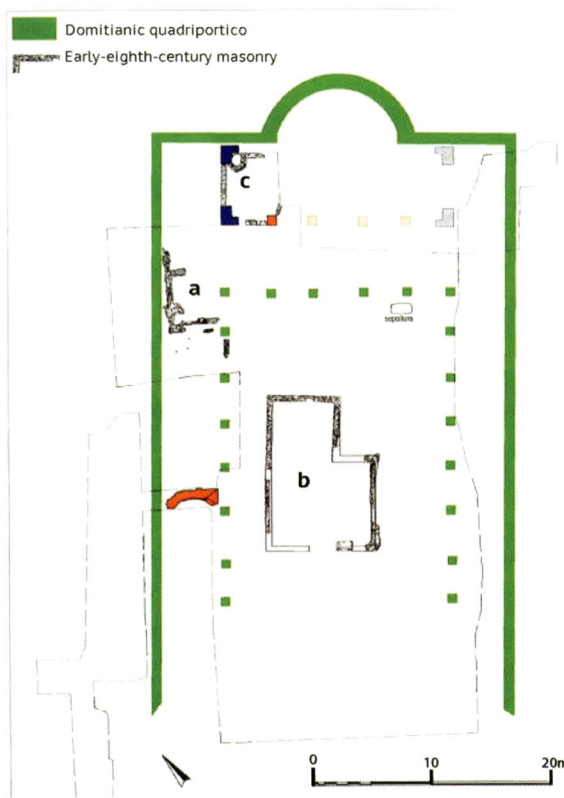

Figure 4.3 Plan of the early 8th-century structures (marked a, b, and c) built inside the quadriportico of the *domus Tiberiana*. (Plan courtesy of Lucrezia Spera, modified by author.)

20 days in office; his four-line biography contains exactly one substantive bit of information, to the effect that he ordered the preparation of mortar to be used in repairing the city walls. As the very first instance in which the *LP* says anything about a pope taking charge of maintaining of civic infrastructure, it is a clear sign that something had changed in the mechanisms of civic governance. Whether prior popes had perhaps attempted something similar is a moot point – regardless, it is from the time of John VII's immediate successor that it became acceptable and evidently desirable to proclaim papal stewardship of Rome's most critical piece of infrastructure.[11]

If Sisinnius' successor, Constantine I (r. 708–15), used the mortar for the wall, the *LP* says nothing about it, but Gregory II (r. 715–31) began his pontificate by launching a restoration of the entire circuit, starting at Porta Tiburtina. He was unable to complete the project because of "emerging inconveniences and various tumults," among them presumably the several attempts on his life by the Byzantine duke of Rome and the exarch acting on behalf of Emperor Leo III, who hoped to be rid of the uncooperative pontiff. (The loyal Roman militia protected Gregory, thus making him effectively both master of the city walls and commander-in-chief of the local military garrison.) Gregory III (r. 731–41) finished the job, restoring the majority of the circuit and "providing food for the workers and money for buying mortar from his own funds." He did so, according to the *LP*, when the Lombards under their expansionist king Liutprand (r. 712–44) were threatening Roman territory, which prompted Gregory to take another unprecedented initiative by sending envoys to the Franks to petition for aid against Liutprand. If pressed, Gregory would doubtless have explained that he did so only out of dire necessity, at a time when Byzantine forces elsewhere were too hard-pressed to help, but he was nonetheless acting as something very close to an independent ruler, both in his restoration of Rome's defenses and his diplomatic outreach to a foreign power. Though nothing came of this first mission to the Franks, it pointed the way toward the Franco-papal alliance of the 750s, a development that would reshape the political landscape in Rome and Italy for centuries.[12]

The popes in the first half of the 8th century were undoubtedly operating in difficult, legally ambiguous circumstances as they gradually expanded their governing portfolio. Through the 740s, it bears emphasizing, there was both a Byzantine duke (*dux*) in Rome and an exarch in Ravenna, who retained full legal title to imperial lands and public buildings in the name of the emperor in Constantinople. Right up to the fall of the exarchate of Ravenna in 751, the Roman Church consciously acknowledged the juridical distinction between imperial and Church property, as in the case of Pope Zacharias' successful petition to Emperor Constantine V to transfer two landed estates south of Rome from the imperial domain (*ius publicum*) to the Church. In the case of their work on the city walls in particular, Gregory II and III were acting without a strict legal mandate, which may partly explain why Gregory III's biographer is at pains to stress that the pope paid for the work out of personal funds, as if to say that he was making an extraordinary (in both senses of the word) contribution to the defense of Rome. From John VII through Zacharias, the popes were something like renters tempted to make expensive improvements to properties owned by a landlord who might someday reoccupy them.[13]

Nevertheless, popes from John VII on did start investing more in public buildings and infrastructure. In addition to the new Palatine residence and the city walls, their projects included a growing number of churches, monasteries, and charitable centers. Starting under Gregory II and especially Gregory III, popes again began to sponsor ambitious works, erecting new churches and extensively restoring older ones after many decades during which their predecessors had mostly limited themselves to essential maintenance – fixing roofs in particular – and redecorating. Gregory III was the first pope since Honorius I a century earlier to erect several large churches from the ground up (S. Maria in Aquiro, SS. Sergio e Bacco at the Vatican, SS. Marcellino e Pietro near the Lateran), and the pace of work increased under succeeding popes. It will not be coincidence that papal patronage of both churches and civic infrastructure picked up under Gregory III, just as the rift with Constantinople was expanding into a soon-to-become insurmountable chasm. By building more frequently and grandly, the popes displayed their growing independence in the most visible possible way. They made physically manifest their role as Rome's primary patrons and protectors.[14]

The novelty of what John VII and his successors were attempting comes through clearly in the appearance of the buildings they sponsored – in the technical characteristics of the masonry itself. By the beginning of the 8th century, Roman builders had mostly stopped working in the classical tradition that had continued unbroken into the mid 7th century, when S. Pancrazio and S. Agnese were still done in basically the same kind of *opus vittatum* masonry used in the 3rd and 4th centuries. Two samples of early 8th-century walls from recent excavations starkly illustrate how much had changed in the interim. The first comes from the sector of the imperial palace overlooking the Forum, the *domus Tiberiana*, where archaeologists uncovered the remains of structures built around 700, in a courtyard of the old palace, that very possibly belong to John VII's new papal residence. Instead of regular, repeating courses of brick and tuff blocks bonded with tenacious lime mortar, these walls consist of what is best called rubble: ragged bits of reclaimed stone and brick, even chunks of old concrete, in a variety of shapes and sizes, bonded with a clay-based mortar of inferior quality (Fig. 4.4). The second sample comes from the monastery Gregory II built along the south flank of St. Paul's *fuori le mura* in the 720s, also newly excavated. Once again, the irregularity and variety of the materials contrasts sharply with the relative homogeneity of the components used for *opus vittatum* in previous centuries. Though late antique *opus vittatum* had also made extensive use of recycled brick and stone, its bricks and stone blocks (*tufelli*) tended to be carefully selected from large stockpiles of salvaged components, presumably obtained by methodically dismantling, cleaning, and sorting entire buildings' worth of materials. The masonry consequently tended to be quite regular in appearance. But the builders at St. Paul's, like those at the *domus Tiberiana*, manifestly used whatever random bits came to hand, a bucket- or cart-load at a time – there is no attempt to sort pieces by size, shape, or material, nor to reshape or refinish them. The result is something that looks more like a jigsaw puzzle than a masonry wall (Fig. 4.5; contrast with Figs. 3.4–3.6, above).[15]

I would suggest that the technical swerve of the early 8th century happened in large part because

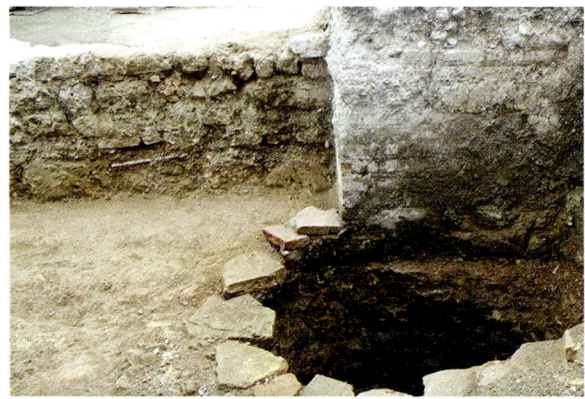

Figure 4.4 *Domus Tiberiana*, early 8th-century wall in rubble masonry (upper left) attached to Severan-era pillar in brick (c. 200 AD, upper right); this is building "c" in the plan at fig. 4.3. (Photo courtesy of Lucrezia Spera.)

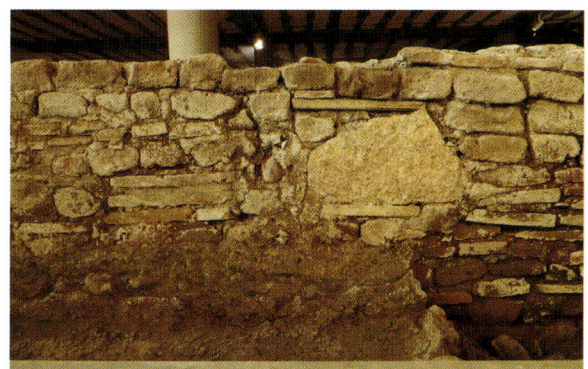

Figure 4.5 Wall in mortared rubble belonging to the first phase of the monastery built by Gregory II (r. 715–31) along the S flank of St. Paul's. (Author.)

the popes needed to recreate a construction industry practically from scratch, after a building slump lasting several generations. Probably fewer large masonry structures were built in Rome during the second half of the 7th century than in any other half-century in the preceding millennium. Textual sources, the LP in the first place, report far less activity than they do for the immediately preceding and following periods; no mosaics or inscriptions record anything of note; and excavators have failed to uncover substantial constructions datable to the time, despite the surge of recent attention devoted to the early Middle Ages. There was, in other words, a real collapse in architectural patronage at Rome, apparently due to the unsettled economic and political conditions that prevailed during the period when the popes and the Byzantine emperors were at doctrinal loggerheads, even as Constantinople was already investing less in Rome and the West because of the critical situation in the eastern Mediterranean. Cooperation between Romans and Byzantines, between the Church and the civil administration, broke down, and evidently neither popes nor civil administrators were willing or able to do much on their own.[16]

Hence, when the early 8th-century popes chose to go it alone, they needed to assemble a workforce along with all the tools and building materials required to build such things as papal residences, monasteries, sections of the city walls, and, eventually, monumental churches, too. The workforce was already a problem: as trained construction workers in Rome had been chronically underemployed for generations, there must have been very few left, even to train a new cohort in the skills and techniques that had formerly been passed down from generation to generation. But building materials presented an equally thorny challenge, if the recently discovered walls at the *domus Tiberiana* and the monastery at St. Paul's are any indication. Though Rome had thousands of derelict buildings and public monuments, it is obvious that none were dismantled to provide relatively homogenous, high-quality building components for this first generation of papal projects.

The reasons, I think, are both logistical and legal. They mirror the ambiguities and uncertainties of a transitional period when Rome hung in the balance between a civil administration in decline and a Church bureaucracy not yet fully empowered to rule in its own right; a time when the popes yet lacked both the institutional mandate and the human and material resources to take full control of Rome's monuments and infrastructure. In purely logistical terms, whatever organized, regulated system for scrapping old buildings and stockpiling their materials had existed through the mid 7th century must have broken down for want of use by the early 8th. But even had John VII and Gregory II (for example) wished to hire, train, and pay new teams of skilled demolitions and salvage crews, they would not have done so for the simple reason that the Church as yet had no legal claim to most of the buildings and ruins available to be mined for architectural *spolia*. Land and buildings in Rome that were not privately or Church owned belonged to the *ius publicum*, the patrimony of the state, a juridical construct that still applied in the 740s, as we have seen. Strict laws in the Theodosian and Justinianic codes governed the circumstances under which damaged or abandoned buildings could be dismantled for scrap; and imperial dispensation was needed for substantial demolitions. In the first half of the 8th century, such authorization was evidently not forthcoming from the civil administration, possibly as a result of worsening relations between the popes and the emperors, or simply because the Byzantine authorities judged it inexpedient to relinquish control to the popes.[17]

The best support for this conjectural state of affairs comes in the abrupt and dramatic reversal that occurred from the 750s on, which is to say from the moment the popes finally achieved effective sovereignty over Rome. In the second half of the 8th century, vast quantities of well-sorted bricks and masonry blocks (not small *tufelli* but large, quadrangular pieces weighing hundreds of kilograms), all obtained from substantial ancient edifices dismantled for scrap, suddenly became ubiquitous in the masonry of Church-sponsored building projects. The abundant presence of such spoliated materials imparted to Roman masonry the distinctive characteristics it would retain for the next couple of centuries, a period when the popes left a lasting mark on the cityscape, constructing or reconstructing dozens of churches and religious foundations and performing critical interventions on civic infrastructure such as the Aurelian Wall and the aqueducts (see below, Figs. 4.10–11). The evident conclusion is that from the mid 8th century on, the popes took advantage of their new-found autonomy to scrap decrepit structures in the public domain and use the materials for their own building projects. They thus put Rome's vast stock of ruinous buildings to good use and ensured that new walls would employ higher-quality materials than those built by their predecessors in the early 8th century. In the process, they also ostentatiously advertised their ownership of Rome's public patrimony, their sovereign right to dispose of it as they pleased.[18]

The rise of the staunchly papal Rome that flourished from the later 8th century into the later 9th was catalyzed by a well-known series of events that need not be rehashed here in detail. Byzantine power over north-central Italy, including Rome, collapsed once and for all with Ravenna's fall to King Aistulf's Lombards in 751. Emboldened by his success, Aistulf next sought to subjugate Rome and impose a tax on its inhabitants, threatening the Romans with annihilation if they failed to meet his demands. In response, Pope Stephen II (r. 752–7) crossed the Alps in 753 and sealed what turned out to be a durable alliance with the Franks, anointing Pippin II King of the Franks in early 754 and thereby exchanging Rome's spiritual imprimatur for Frankish military protection against the Lombards. More difficulties followed in the short term, beginning with the enraged Aistulf's three-month siege of Rome in 756. Aistulf's army burned and pillaged outside the walls, cut the aqueducts, and looted churches and martyrs' shrines in the extramural cemeteries before Frankish pressure forced it to retire. In 772, when the Lombards under their new king, Desiderius, again threatened to attack Rome, the newly elected Pope Hadrian I appealed for assistance to the young king of the Franks, Charlemagne, son of Pippin II. In 773, Charlemagne led a Frankish army across the Alps, overthrew Desiderius, and subdued all of Italy north of Rome by 774. With Charlemagne guaranteeing papal rule over Rome and its territories, and pilgrims and money pouring in across a newly peaceful Italian peninsula, Hadrian was free to spend his long reign (772–95) transforming Rome into a papal capital worthy of the name.[19]

In the chaos and uncertainty of the first two decades after the final collapse of Byzantine power in 751, however, the public works undertaken by the popes were relatively limited in scope. The recurring Lombard threat aside, it was also not at all clear that the Byzantine withdrawal would be permanent, and Byzantine emissaries indeed kept appearing in Italy to connive at recovering their lost territories. The vacuum left by the final dissolution of the civil administration, in turn, led to growing strife between various local factions and families, which exploded into open hostility in the years 767–72. Following the death of Pope Paul I in 767, Duke Toto of Nepi entered Rome with an armed retinue and installed his brother, a layman named Constantine, as pope. A coalition of Roman nobles and clergy supported by the Lombard duke of Spoleto eventually deposed Constantine after a year (he was first blinded, then tried, excommunicated, beaten again and left in the street), but the bad blood unleashed by the conflict spilled over into the four years of Stephen III's papacy (768–72): the *LP* reports a series of vendettas, mutilations, and extrajudicial murders at a new pitch of gory intensity.[20]

In the 750s, Pope Stephen II concentrated his efforts on the Vatican: for the benefit of the growing crowds of pilgrims there, he founded two *xenodochia*, which he "associated" with two existing *diaconiae*. He also created a fourth monastery to supplement the existing three, whose monks were meant to serve the basilica, maintaining and guarding it and performing constant litanies of prayer. He began to transform the old imperial mausoleum on the south side of St. Peter's into a chapel dedicated to St. Petronilla, as he had promised the Frankish king he would. He also restored the colonnaded atrium in front of the main basilica, where he also built what was probably the first monumental bell tower at Rome. Elsewhere in the city, he restored four old *xenodochia* and built a new one *in Platana* by today's S. Eustachio, near the Pantheon, where 100 paupers were supposed to be fed daily. Taken with his immediate predecessor Zacharias' institution of the first *domuscultae* in Church-owned estates outside the city, Paul's charitable centers look to be part of a coordinated papal initiative to better provide for Rome's needy and indigent, and generally to supply the city without reliance on long-distance imports or expenditures of hard currency.[21]

Traces of at least one, and very possibly two, charitable centers built during the papacy of Stephen II survive. The clearest example is the church and *diaconia* of S. Angelo in Pescheria, which an extant dedicatory inscription in the church shows was founded in 755 by Theodotus, identified as *primicerius* (lay administrator) of the Roman Church as well as the director ("father") of the new *diaconia*. The church itself was installed just behind the entrance-porch of the Porticus Octaviae, along the Via Triumphalis/*porticus maximae* just west of the Theater of Marcellus. A three-aisled basilica with three semicircular apses, it is one of the first of the new generation of ecclesiastical projects constructed with massive quantities of high-quality recycled materials: the typical early medieval *opus quadratum* in large blocks of tuff in the foundations and lowest courses of the walls, with undulating brickwork above. The service-buildings associated with the *diaconia* abutted the rear of the podiums of the still-standing temples of Apollo and Bellona, transforming the portico that ran behind the two temples into a kind of covered sleeping porch, to which were annexed storage rooms and a small bath for the ritual ablutions of the needy (Fig. 4.6).[22]

In its reuse of valuable materials taken from existing structures and its occupation of public buildings, as the two temples of course were, the S. Angelo project reveals the impressive political clout of its patron, a nobleman named Theodotus whose career spans the critical period of transition from Byzantine to papal rule. He is almost certainly the same Theodotus, "former *dux* and now *dispensator*," who included his family portrait in the chapel he redecorated at S. Maria Antiqua

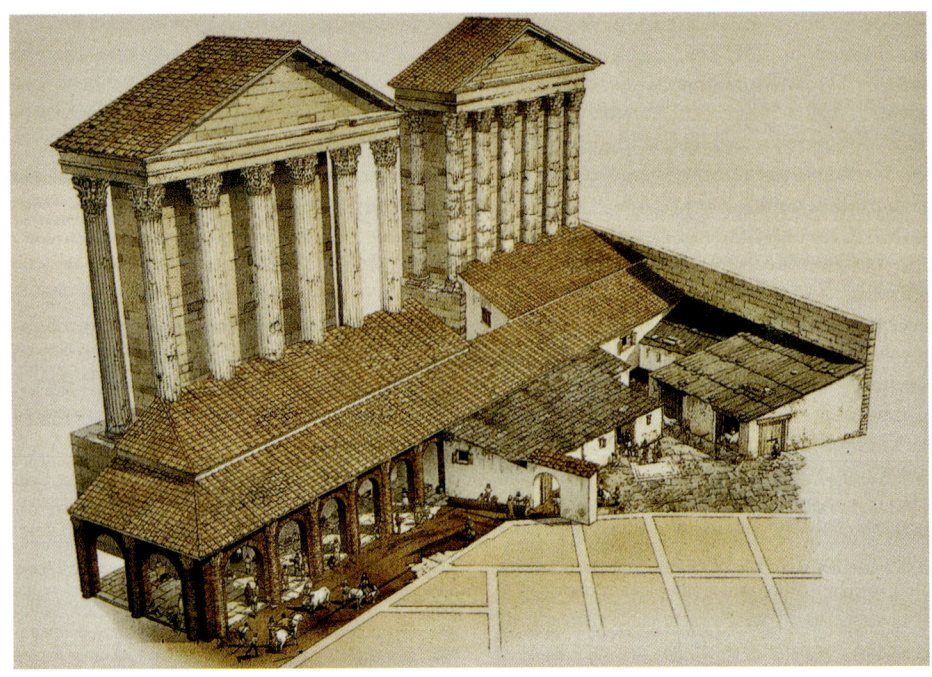

Figure 4.6 Reconstruction of the *diaconia* of S. Angelo in Pescheria, built abutting the rear façades of the temples of Apollo and Bellona. (Studio InkLink/Meneghini and Santangeli Valenzani 2004, p. 90, fig. 73.)

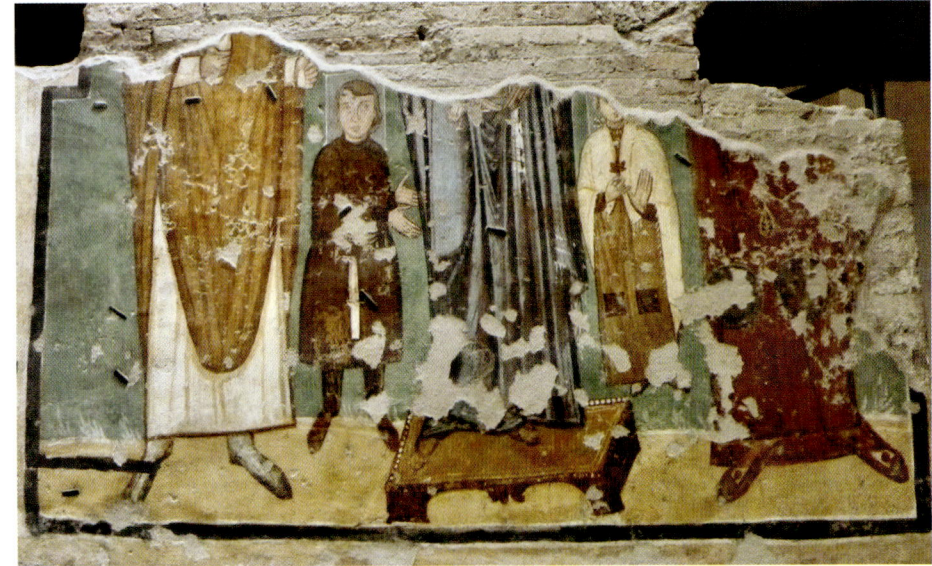

Figure 4.7 Detail of donor portrait from the Theodotus Chapel at S. Maria Antiqua. L – R: Theodotus, his young son, Mary, his young daughter, his wife. (Author.)

under Pope Zacharias, in the 740s, and whom the *LP* later mentions, again as former duke turned *dispensator* of the Roman Church, as the uncle of Pope Hadrian I (Fig. 4.7; see also Fig. 3.10, above). Following a career at the summit of the Byzantine administration in Rome, then, this Theodotus evidently passed into the service of the Church just as the popes were taking effective control in Rome. There were undoubtedly other such influential insiders, some from old Roman families and others (very possibly including Theodotus) descended from 'Greeks' installed in Rome during the centuries of Byzantine rule. Their offspring blended and intermarried, producing wholly 'Roman' descendants able to weather the transition to papal rule with the aplomb of Theodotus, whose nephew and ward, Hadrian I, the *LP* can claim as a blue-blooded Roman. As the Church took control of Rome, men from leading local families sought and obtained high Church offices up to and including the papacy, and they did so as 'Romans': after seven decades during which popes were almost invariably Greek-speaking easterners or southern Italians, those elected from Stephen II on are usually given a resoundingly Roman pedigree by their biographers in the *LP*.[23]

Stephen II's younger brother succeeded him as Pope Paul I (r. 757–67). He transformed the family house into a monastery dedicated to Saints Stephen and Silvester, to which he annexed a new church, today's S. Silvestro in Capite, situated just off the Via Lata. He completed his brother's chapel of St. Petronilla in the old imperial mausoleum at the Vatican; installed another oratory inside St. Peter's, where he would later be buried; and built a small church in the Forum, across the Via Sacra from the Temple of Venus and Rome. But Paul's most ambitious project was to begin transferring the bones of Rome's saints and martyrs from their suburban resting places inside the city walls. The Lombard siege of 756 provided the immediate impetus for this novel initiative by demonstrating how vulnerable to theft and vandalism the precious relics scattered among ruined, neglected extramural shrines had become. Many bones, including those of Stephen and Silvester, ended up at the new monastery in his house; those of Petronilla graced the new oratory at the Vatican; and uncounted others went to "the titular churches (*tituli*) and *diaconiae* or monasteries and the remaining churches" inside the city. Under Paul's successors, the process gathered momentum. The more bones were transferred into the city, the lonelier and more neglected those left outside became, which prompted still more translations of the leftovers. By the mid 9th century, what amounted to an inversion of Rome's saintly topography was approaching completion. The relics that had once surrounded the walls in a kind of protective cordon now mostly clustered within them: what had been a doughnut around the city became a doughnut-hole roughly coextensive with the inhabited parts of the city-center itself.[24]

As topographically (and socially) impactful as the mass translations of relics would eventually become, however, they began as a limited, ad hoc response to an immediate threat. The building projects of the 750s and 760s, too, still look to be localized efforts on a limited scale to improve scattered corners of the cityscape. They collectively pale in comparison to the transformational building boom of the following decades. Between 772 and 816, Hadrian I and his immediate successor, Leo III (r. 795–816), launched the most intensive campaign of papal building yet seen in Rome. Nobody since the emperors had acted so decisively to renew and reshape the cityscape, as both men clearly realized: as the self-proclaimed heirs of the emperors, they built to exalt themselves and their office, and to proclaim Rome's transformation into the capital of an effectively sovereign papal state. Tom Noble's careful sifting of the *LP* provides some simple figures that strikingly capture the unparalleled magnitude of Hadrian and Leo's initiatives. Of the 263 individual construction projects he counts for the years 715 to 891, fully 147, or 56 percent, date to the 45 years from 772 to 816.[25]

These projects were financed mostly by a wave of gold and silver that came pouring into the papal coffers at the Lateran in these years, much of it from the Frankish domains. Carolingian royals donated lavishly, other grandees gave more, and crowds of northern pilgrims arriving in Rome in unprecedented numbers brought still more. But the resources of the Roman Church were also greatly – and much more lastingly – enhanced, after the end of Byzantine rule in Italy, by its absorption of vast tracts of fiscal land previously under imperial control. Directly descended from the late Roman imperial patrimonies in Italy, these lands passed wholesale under Church control in the decades after 751. Some were located as far afield as the territory of Ravenna, but the lion's share lay in that area of central Italy, roughly corresponding with the modern region of Lazio, that thenceforth formed the core of the papal dominions – the *patrimonium Sancti Petri*. Coupled with the extensive properties the Church had already accumulated since the 4th century, the new possessions made the Church by far the largest landholder in Rome and its environs, as it would remain throughout the Middle Ages, profiting handsomely from rents delivered both in kind and in coin.[26]

A telling index of this surging papal wealth comes via the donations of precious metal objects and furnishings (but also embroidered silks: curtains and altar cloths and tapestries) that the popes made to churches and other religious institutions at Rome, according to the *LP*'s detailed accounting. From the minimum totals of 45,867 pounds of silver and 4,480 pounds of gold reported for the years 715 to 891, Hadrian and Leo between them distributed 68 percent of the gold, and Leo alone gave 48 percent of the silver. (Leo's lengthy biography in the *LP* consists mostly of a punctilious and frankly tedious list of the donations he made to well over 100 churches, monasteries, and charitable centers.) Only a few decades after Zacharias' pontificate, when supplies of precious metals had hit rock bottom, the popes were again flush with cash. Hadrian promptly began to mint silver coins in his own name, tellingly pegged to the standard of the Carolingian silver *denarius* rather than any Byzantine denomination (Fig. 4.8). These monodenominational silver coins minted by the popes, along with those minted to the same standard by Charlemagne and his heirs, became the main vehicle for monetary payments at Rome; too valuable to be used for most everyday transactions, they doubtless helped pay for the supplies and labor that underpinned the local building boom. They were also, of course, a crucial token of the popes' pretensions to sovereignty.[27]

The projects funded by this newfound wealth went well beyond churches and monasteries. Though infrastructure and public works make up only a small fraction of the reported papal

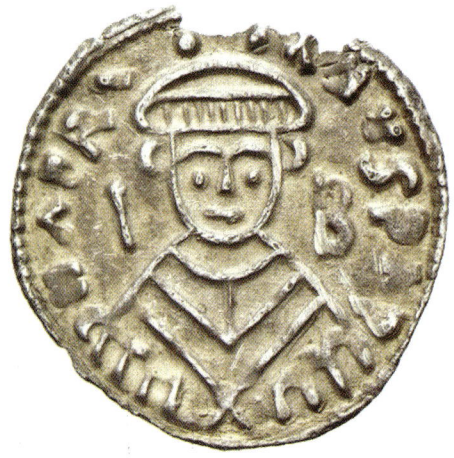 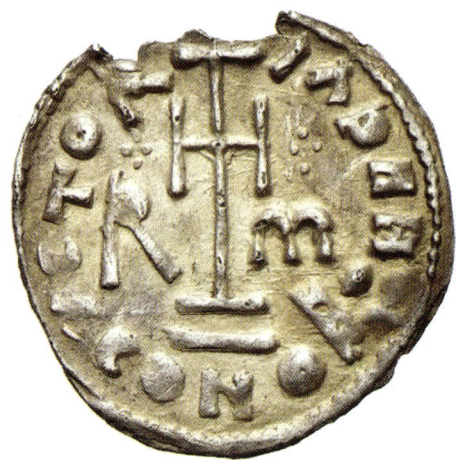

Figure 4.8 Silver *denarius* of Pope Hadrian I, later 780s or early 790s: L: obverse; R: reverse. (Image courtesy of Giorgio Fusconi.)

initiatives, the actual extent of the work in terms of, say, square meters of masonry might rival or exceed all the churches and religious institutions combined. This is especially true for Hadrian, who launched a sweeping program of urban renewal starting early in his pontificate. In about 776, he spent the princely sum of 100 pounds of gold to repair the Aurelian Wall (which, again, was almost 19 km long), and in addition restored four aqueducts that cumulatively comprised dozens of kilometers of water channels raised on monumental arcades built in brick, concrete, and stone. He later recycled thousands of blocks of tuff (the *LP* says over 12,000) from the ancient embankments of the Tiber in order to reconstruct the covered portico that ran for over a kilometer between St. Peter's and the Tiber bridge at Castel S. Angelo, and then also rebuilt the covered porticoes of similar length that connected Saint Paul's and S. Lorenzo with their respective gates in the city walls. Around 790, he undertook a second campaign of repairs to the Aurelian Wall, conscripting workers throughout the papal domains and setting them to work in teams all around the circuit. This second restoration is particularly noteworthy for coming at a time when Rome was less threatened than it had been in centuries, thanks to the peace that prevailed throughout north-central Italy under Frankish dominion. It seems an essentially cosmetic project intended to give Rome a mural crown befitting the citadel of the papacy, and put Hadrian's stamp on the city's largest and most visible civic monument.[28]

As for the aqueducts, Hadrian began with the Aqua Traiana (by then called the Aqua Sabbatina), which carried water 40 km from Lake Bracciano to the Janiculum and Trastevere, and from the Janiculum to the Vatican via a branch line made of lead pipes that was repaired at the same time. The Vatican channel provided water for the famous bronze *pigna* (pinecone) fountain in the atrium of St. Peter's, as well as for a bath-building where the poor got weekly baths. The repairs to the main line included rebuilding 100 arched bays of the raised channel, according to Hadrian's biographer. Next to be fixed was the Aqua Iobia (Jovia), a branch of the Aqua Marcia (or maybe the Claudia) that served the southern part of the city, from the Porta Appia on past the Baths of Caracalla, and then down to the Tiber through the teeming neighborhood of the *Ripa Graeca*. The third was the Aqua Claudia, which served the Lateran and its surroundings, but continued on over the summit of the Caelian Hill and on to the Palatine. Finally, attention turned to the Aqua Virgo, which entered the city from the Pincian Hill in the north, descended past today's Trevi Fountain (part of the channel is now visible in the basement of the new Rinascente department store in Via del Tritone) and terminated in the Campus Martius; Hadrian's biographer enthused that its repaired channel "put forth water in such abundance that it satisfied practically the whole city." The four aqueducts singled out for restoration look to have been strategically chosen to serve the city center on all sides: the Traiana/Sabbatina from the west, the Claudia from the east, the Virgo from the north, and the Iobia in the south. They provided water for churches and religious foundations, the Vatican and Lateran in the first place, but also for a population of ordinary Romans who, clearly, still lived widely scattered around the intramural area. The presence of these functioning aqueducts through the 9th century and beyond must indeed be one of the factors that encouraged early medieval Romans to spread across as much of the ancient city center as they did (Fig. 4.9).[29]

Some sense of the scale of these public works is now possible thanks to Robert Coates-Stephens, who in the 1990s finally called attention to the fact that both the city walls and the four aqueducts in question show abundant traces of repairs in mortared masonry typical of the 8th/9th

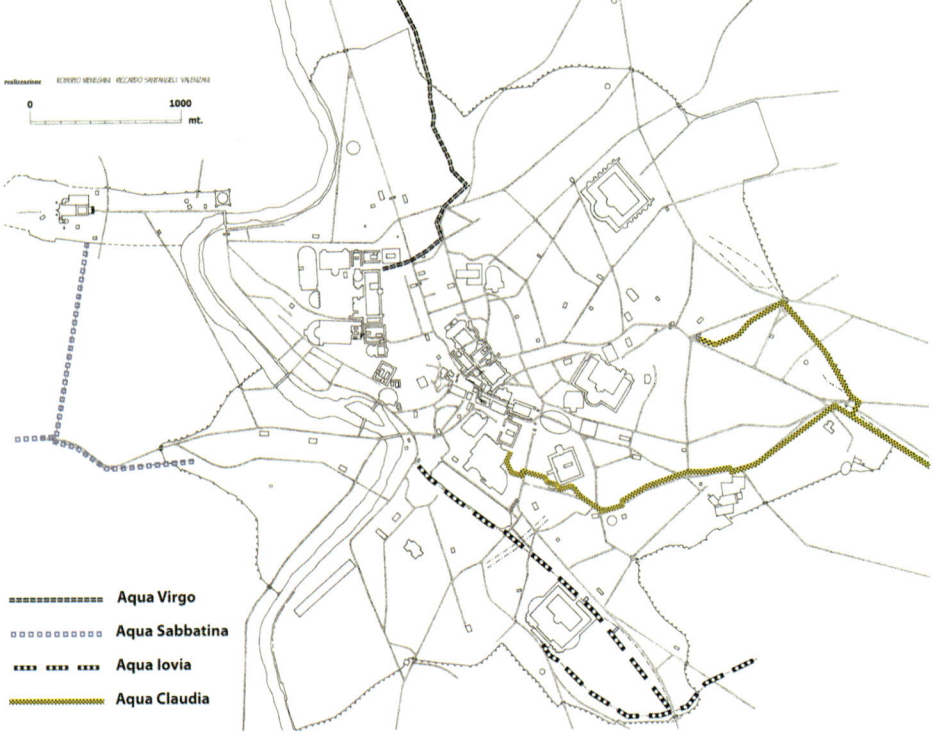

Figure 4.9 The four aqueducts restored in the 8th–9th centuries. (Redrawn from Meneghini and Santangeli Valenzani 2004, p. 55, fig. 30.)

centuries. Two principal styles predominated, one featuring reused brick and the other large, worn blocks of tuff also recycled from ancient structures. Not all of the sections executed in these techniques belong to Hadrian, as 9th-century popes conducted further repairs on the wall and aqueducts that are indistinguishable from the later 8th-century work, but the extant repairs, taken together, are in any case widespread and substantial enough to substantiate the *LP*'s claims of extensive papal restorations of sensitive and symbolically potent urban infrastructure. Two towers of the Aurelian Wall, one reconstructed in tuff blocks below shifting to brick above (Fig. 4.10), the other rebuilt completely in brick (Fig. 4.11), represent well the two prevailing typologies. The quality of the materials and workmanship undoubtedly surpasses the standards of the early 8th-century work at the *domus Tiberiana* and Gregory II's monastery at St. Paul's, but nobody would mistake any of this masonry for its ancient antecedents. The reused tuff blocks were worn and irregular enough that thick beds of mortar mixed with brick fragments were often required to fill the seams between them, while the presence of blocks of different sizes and shapes made it still harder to achieve the perfect horizontal coursing of ancient masonry. Brick facings, too, comprise heterogeneous assemblages of reused and frequently fragmentary pieces laid in slanting or undulating courses. The horizontal level that had allowed ancient Roman masons to build with almost mechanical precision was apparently absent from the tool kit of papal builders in the later 8th and 9th centuries.[30]

Yet at least some of these builders must have been full-time professionals, the sort of "master builders" (*magistri*) mentioned as traveling in teams available for hire in 9th-century Italy. The constant stream of commissions at Rome in the peak years c. 780–860 undoubtedly sufficed to

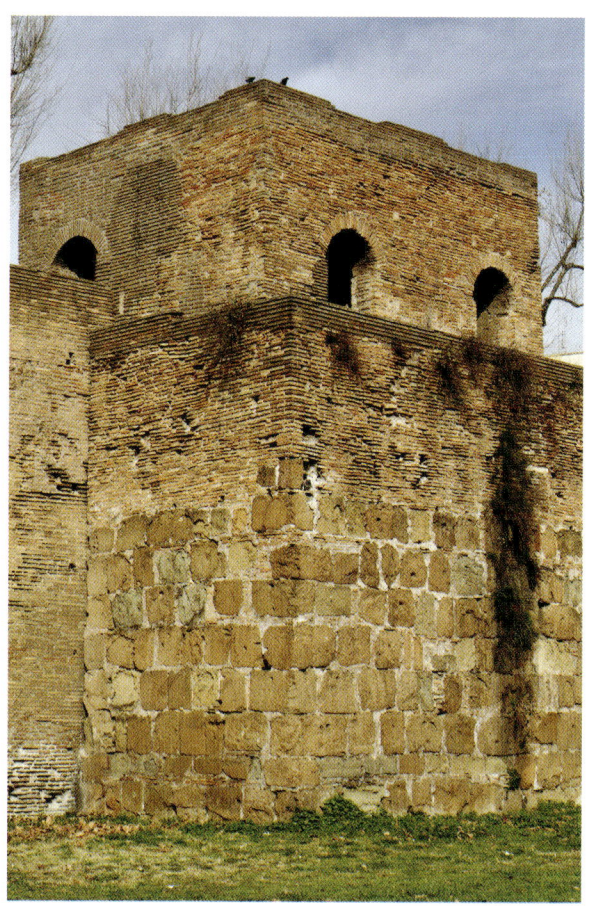

Figure 4.10 Tower H14, near Porta Metronia, reconstructed in the late 8th or 9th century. (Author.)

attract and provide steady employment for skilled outsiders and home-grown specialists alike. Their efforts were supervised by another professional, the *vestiarius* or *vestararius*, a top-ranking official based at the Lateran whose broad portfolio of responsibilities included the financing and coordination of important building projects. Much of the manual labor, however, was clearly done by unskilled workers, especially on the largest, most labor-intensive projects, such as the repairs to the Aurelian Wall and the aqueducts. The *LP* alludes to levies drawn from across the papal dominions; and two inscriptions from the circuit wall built around the Vatican in the mid 9th century record discrete sections built by teams of laborers (farm-workers, presumably) drawn from two papal estates.[31]

A higher percentage of skilled professionals perhaps attended to churches and other prestigious commissions inside the city, where the quality of workmanship is generally higher. In addition to his renewal of infrastructure, Pope Hadrian also repaired, rebuilt, and founded more churches and religious foundations than

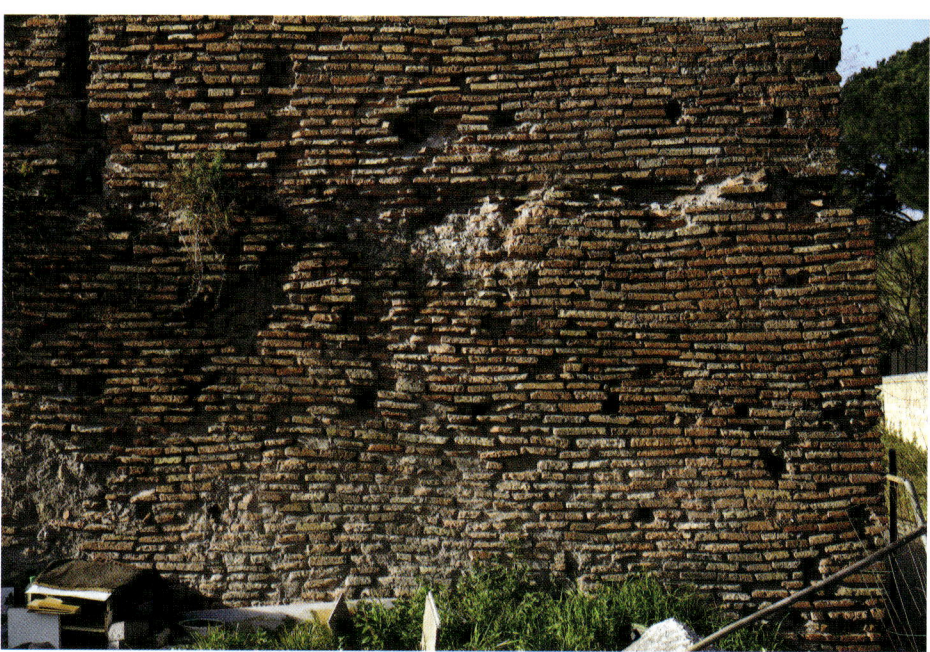

Figure 4.11 Tower M14, between Porta Ostiense and the Tiber, detail of late 8th/9th-century brickwork. (Author.)

any previous pope, dozens of which are listed in his *LP* biography. He endowed these and others with prodigious quantities of furnishings and liturgical vessels in gold and silver, and altar cloths and tapestries in silk and other fabrics, starting with the five patriarchal basilicas (St. Peter's, St. Paul's, S. Lorenzo, the Lateran, and S. Maria Maggiore) but including many more located both inside and outside the city walls. He paid special attention to the Vatican, founding and renovating monasteries and charitable foundations that catered to the tourists, pilgrims, resident foreigners, and beggars who were turning the area between St. Peter's and the Tiber into one of Rome's busiest neighborhoods. So many pious English "Rome-seekers" (*romipetae*) thronged the Vatican that the local community had a kind of national clubhouse and residential quarter there in the 8th century, a *schola*, as would the Franks, Lombards, and Frisians by century's end. By the early 9th century, the bustling English quarter by the river around today's S. Spirito in Sassia was called the "burg" (*burgus* in Latin) from the Old English word for a town; in the later Middle Ages, the Italianized "Borgo" would come to denote the entirety of the Vatican neighborhood. Frankish royalty also stayed at the Vatican during their visits, in a palace built by Charlemagne where the permanent Frankish representative (*missus*) in Rome resided. The palace should remind us, as it doubtless did the early medieval popes, that a Frankish presence always loomed over 'papal' Rome. As much local autonomy as pontiffs as assertive as Hadrian I and Leo III enjoyed, they worked in partnership with the Frankish kings, on whom they depended heavily both for protection and financial support.[32]

The pendant to this extramural pilgrims' town was the intramural complex on the far side of the city at the Lateran, where the popes continued to be based, along with the bureaucratic apparatus of the Roman Church. Within the sprawling papal residence and administrative center, there were the popes' living quarters, of course, several chapels, and dining and reception rooms, but also schools to prepare youngsters for ecclesiastical careers, archives and offices where old documents were stored and new ones produced, fiscal offices and the treasury, a bathhouse, storerooms and magazines for foodstuffs supplied by the *domuscultae* that fed the city's clergy and many of its poor, and a portico where some of this food was distributed to beggars, decorated with a fresco of the popes doing just this. Elsewhere in the vicinity stood the Lateran baptistery and its annexes, and several monasteries where the monks who served in the cathedral dwelled.

Unfortunately for posterity, almost all the surviving parts of the main residential/administrative complex (the *patriarchium*, as it was called in the 8th century) were razed in the late 16th century, leaving modern scholars free to play endless games of "imagine the Lateran Palace." But although much remains uncertain, both textual descriptions and early modern plans do shed light on the location and general appearance of many principal features. After centuries of silence, the *LP* reports a first campaign of improvements to the Lateran complex under Zacharias: in addition to a general refurbishment after a long period of neglect, he added an imposing new front entrance consisting of a gate tower and portico, and also a grand dining/reception room (*triclinium*) decorated with sumptuous mosaics and frescoes that included a depiction of the known world. This last image is the sort of thing a ruler with sovereign pretensions would commission, but so too is the *triclinium* itself: such grand dining/reception halls were essential features of palace architecture (the imperial palace in Constantinople was full of them), and Zacharias' is the first reported example built in Rome since the days of the emperors (Fig. 4.12).[33]

The next pope credited with work at the papal residence is Hadrian, who added a second tower

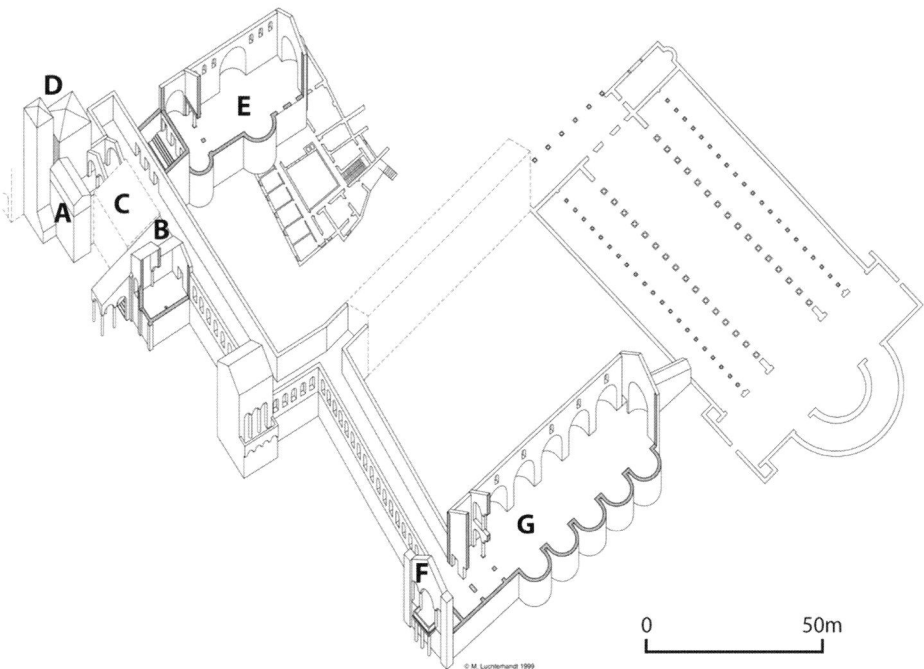

Figure 4.12 Provisional reconstruction of the Lateran palace complex in the early 9th century, after the additions of Leo III. A: Sancta Sanctorum chapel; B: Zachary's entrance vestibule and stairway leading to elevated portico; C: Zachary's *triclinium*; D: towers of Zachary and/or Hadrian I(?); E: Leo III's (first) *triclinium maius*; F: Leo III's raised loggia overlooking the *campus Lateranensis*; G: Leo III's second *triclinium* (the *aula concilii*). (Adapted from Luchterhandt 2014, fig. 3.)

"next to the portico that goes down to the baths," and decorated both the upper-story room of the tower and the portico with new marble revetments and frescoes. Probably also in the second half of the 8th century, possibly under Hadrian himself, an assortment of venerable and symbolically pregnant ancient bronzes was transferred to the open esplanade, the *campus Lateranensis*, along the north side of the Lateran palace, where they would stay for the rest of the Middle Ages. The most celebrated among them were a statue of a she-wolf, though apparently not the celebrated one now in the Capitoline Museum, and the gilded equestrian statue of Marcus Aurelius transferred to the Capitoline in the 16th century. The she-wolf was, of course, the symbol *par excellence* of Rome, "the mother of the Romans," as two 10th-century authors put it. But the equestrian statue made if anything an even more pointed political statement. Believed to represent Constantine, it inevitably called to mind that emperor's alleged transfer to the papacy of all his sovereign rights and possessions – the Lateran palace prominent among them – in Rome and the West, as described in the Donation of Constantine, itself forged around the time when the statues presumably migrated to the papal palace.[34]

But it was left to Leo III to launch the next really ambitious restructuring of the *patriarchium*, a project he made into one of the defining initiatives of his papacy, in the process turning the Lateran into "the biggest permanent construction-project in the city," as Antonella Ballardini recently put it. He began c. 797/98 by installing another *triclinium*, the *triclinium maius*, a massive, two-story complex that measured some 50 m long from end to end. The principal feature was a palatial throne room and audience chamber on the second floor, 26 m long (exclusive of the apse) and accessed via two colonnaded antechambers. The main apse at the rear was

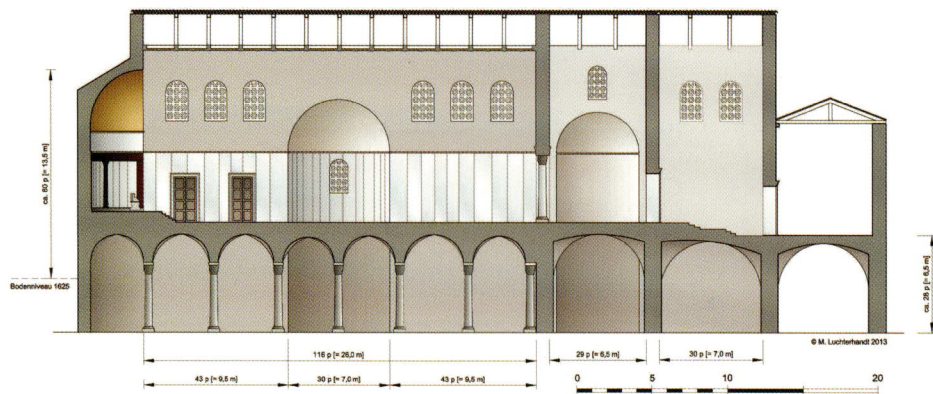

Figure 4.13 Sectional reconstruction of Leo III's *triclinium maius*. (Luchterhandt 2014, fig. 8.)

decorated in mosaic (it survives, much restored and moved from its original location, on the façade of the Sancta Sanctorum chapel); frescoes covered the two apses projecting from each sidewall (one in the main chamber, one in the antechamber). The chamber's floor and walls were sheathed in precious marbles, and columns in porphyry and white marble marked the entrance, facing which was a papal throne beneath the main apse (Fig. 4.13). Remarkably, less than five years later, around 801/02, Leo commissioned a still larger triclinium complex, the *aula concilii*, located (literally) just down the hall from the first, the hall being a raised portico or loggia on two levels that Leo also reconstructed. This second structure was c. 53 m long by 13 wide, exclusive of its eleven apses, each of which housed a dining couch in the single chamber that occupied all of the upper floor. The central apse was again decorated in mosaic, while the five on each side were frescoed with stories of the apostles. In the middle of the room, a porphyry basin spouted jets of water supplied by pressurized pipes from the restored Aqua Claudia, a technical marvel guaranteed to impress any early medieval visitor.[35]

As many others have noted, the popes beginning with Zacharias who expanded the Lateran residence, Leo III certainly most of all, were transforming the old bishops' residence into a palace, a palace modeled mainly on the example of the imperial palace in Constantinople – among whose famous halls was a gigantic *triclinium* with 19 apses/dining couches that manifestly inspired Leo's second *triclinium* at the Lateran. Both palaces had equestrian statues of Christian emperors ('Constantine' at the Lateran and Justinian at Constantinople) near their main entrances, and so on. The basic point is clear: by the time of Leo III, the popes were assuming – and constructing – the trappings of imperial pomp and splendor formerly reserved for the emperors, as the Donation of Constantine insisted the popes were authorized to do in the western provinces outside of Constantinople's control. Leo and his immediate successor, Paschal I (r. 817–24), also refitted the private papal chapel inside the palace, the *Sancta Sanctorum* ("Holy of Holies"), with new jeweled reliquaries and a reliquary chest modeled on the Ark of the Covenant, within which Rome's most precious relics were stored, including wood from the true cross and the foreskin of Christ. Not even the palace of the Byzantine emperors could compete with the trove of relics in the popes' inner sanctum at the Lateran. The remodeled Lateran residence represented papal pretensions to both temporal and spiritual preeminence, and it is no coincidence that the *LP* first starts to call the erstwhile *patriarchium* a "palace" (*palatium*) beginning in the 820s.[36]

Leo III and his immediate successors were also avid builders and restorers of churches, monasteries, and charitable centers, many of which continued to be enriched with the saintly bones that continued to migrate from the suburbs into the city. Three unusually well-preserved churches built or restored under Paschal I can serve as representative examples of ecclesiastical architecture during the so-called "Carolingian Renaissance" of c. 780–860: these are the rebuilt *tituli* of S. Prassede on the Esquiline and S. Cecilia in Trastevere, and the diaconal church of S. Maria in Domnica on the Caelian. All three exemplify the point made long ago by Krautheimer that the churches built during the heyday of the papal "Republic of the Romans" consciously evoke the architecture of Rome's Christian glory days under Constantine and his successors in the 4th century, St. Peter's above all. The difference, of course, was that Pope Paschal was now the patron, playing the imperial role of Constantine.[37]

S. Prassede is a typical three-aisle, 'T-type' basilica in the traditional style of St. Peter's and St. Paul's, with a wide central nave, capped by an apse the width of the nave, separated from narrower side aisles by colonnaded arcades. Its transept is configured like those at St. Peter's and St. Paul's, flush with the rear wall of the basilica (hence T-type). S. Cecilia is similar in size and configuration to S. Prassede, but lacks a transept, as does S. Maria in Domnica, which has three apses, a wider central semicircle flanked by two smaller ones in correspondence with the side aisles (Fig. 4.14). All three churches feature annular crypts. The annular crypt was introduced at the end of the 6th century by Gregory I, who remodeled and raised the area around the high altar at St. Peter's (and probably also St. Paul's) in order to allow a constant stream of pilgrims to approach and circulate around the relics beneath the altar without getting in the way of clergy and congregants in the nave above. The altar was raised several steps above the nave on a platform that was flanked on each side by stairways leading down to the crypt below,

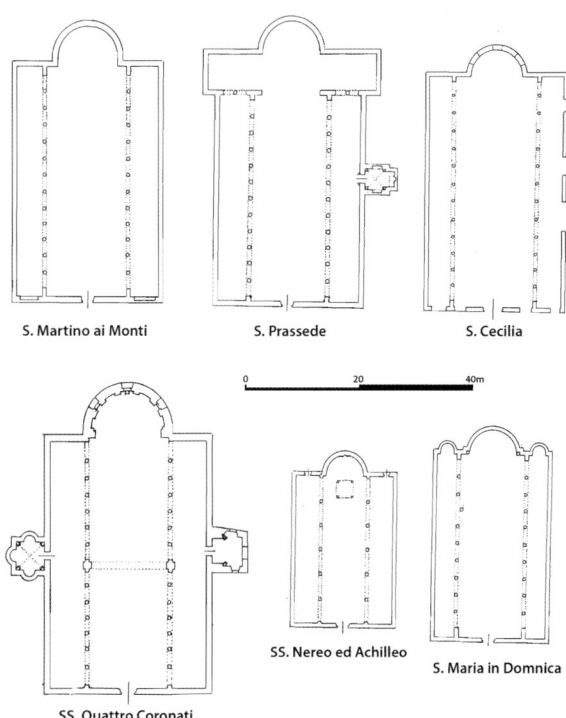

Figure 4.14 9th-century Roman churches, drawn to scale. (Matthiae 1954, p. 66.)

where a horseshoe-shaped corridor hosted a one-way flow of traffic, starting down one staircase and reappearing into the nave via the other. This very logical solution to crowd control was copied at other Roman churches already in the 7th and early 8th centuries (S. Pancrazio, S. Crisogono), but became really common in the churches sponsored by those popes from Hadrian I on who pointedly tried to evoke St. Peter's in their new buildings (Fig. 4.15).[38]

The most dazzling feature in all three of Paschal's surviving churches is the brilliant polychrome mosaics that cover their apses and apse walls, which again evoke the glories of late antiquity. Though the art of mosaic-making never disappeared completely in the difficult times of the 7th and earlier 8th centuries, really ambitious mosaic programs returned only from the end of the 8th century. They reached a peak of brilliance – if the extant examples are any indication – under Paschal. In the case of the

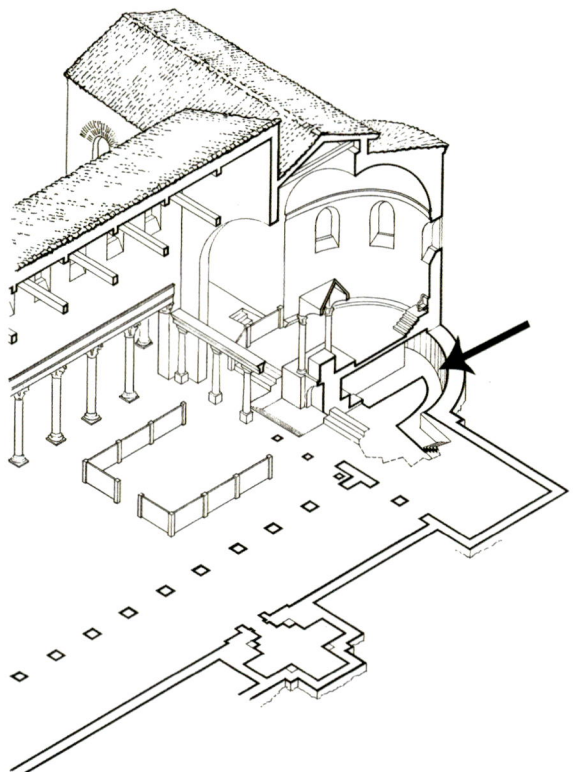

Figure 4.15 S. Prassede: the arrow indicates the annular crypt. (Reconstruction of the choir and presbytery by Judson Emerick, isometric drawing after Krautheimer, *CBCR*, by Johannes Knoops.)

two titular churches, the local Roman saints Praxedis (Prassede) and Cecilia are protagonists in the heavenly scenes that adorn the conch of the apse, where they stand at the right hand of Christ seated in majesty between Saints Peter and Paul (Fig. 4.16). In both, square-haloed Paschal embraces the titular saint, proclaiming in no uncertain terms that he, as pontiff, is the living bridge between the Roman collective on Earth and its legions of saintly protectors in heaven. Paschal reinforced his connection to both martyrs by recovering their remains from extramural cemeteries and transferring them to the churches dedicated in their names. Cecilia, said Paschal, gave him her special stamp of approval by appearing in a dream and leading him to her bones, which were supposed to have been stolen by the Lombards in 756. In the apse at S. Maria in Domnica, Paschal courts an even more exalted celestial intercessor in the figure of Mary herself, Rome's special patroness and protector. He kneels at her feet, holding one foot in both hands as though to kiss it, while gazing straight out toward the congregation (Fig. 4.17). At the

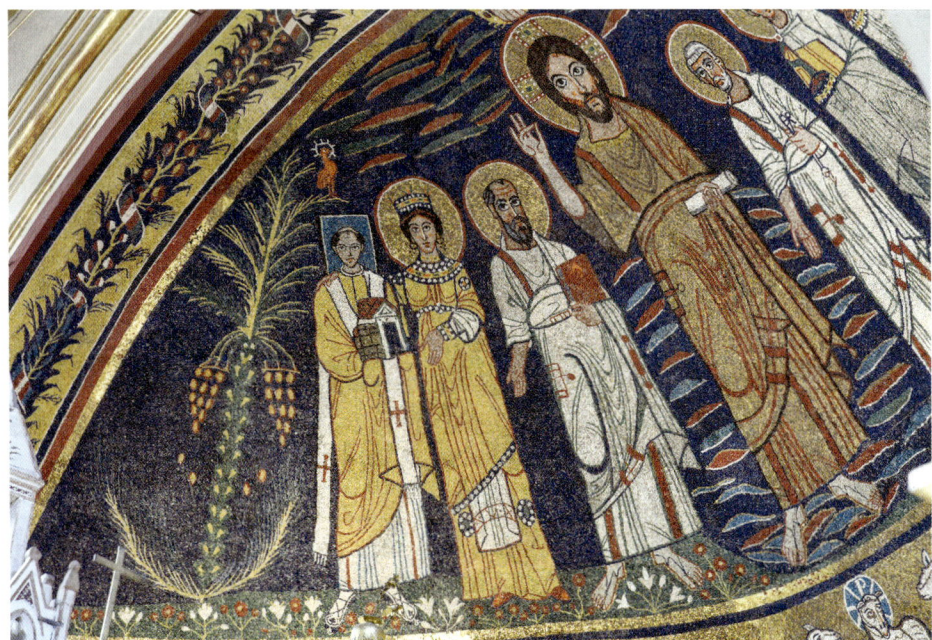

Figure 4.16 S. Cecilia in Trastevere, apse, detail. L – R: Paschal I, St. Cecilia, St. Paul, Christ, St. Peter. (Author.)

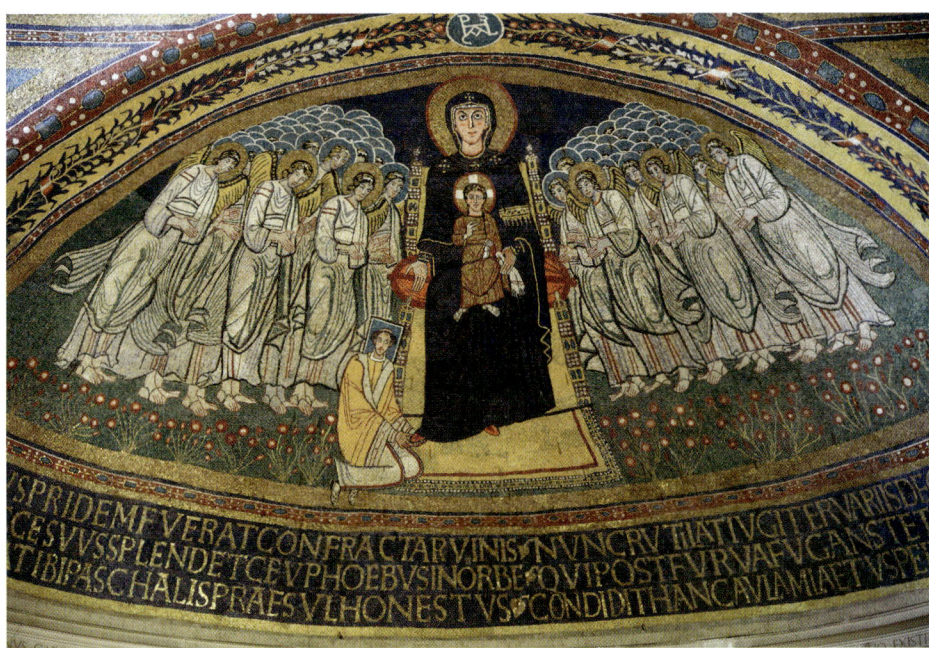

Figure 4.17 S. Maria in Domnica, apse mosaic. (Author.)

springing of the apse, mosaic texts in brilliant gold on a dark blue background, again modeled on 4th- and 5th-century exemplars, commend Paschal's works in all three churches. The words combine with the imagery, the relics, and the rebuilt churches themselves to proclaim Paschal the regent of heaven on Earth, the leader of the Roman collective, the privileged intermediary between the living and the divine. Coming as it did at a time of renewed controversy over iconoclasm, the strident iconicity of these apses reads also as a militant affirmation of Rome's traditional embrace of religious imagery.[39]

The papal resuscitation of the glories of early Christian Rome continued apace through the mid 9th century. Almost constant work on churches went on through the pontificate of Leo IV (r. 847–55), and frequent additions and renovations to the Lateran "palace," as it was now regularly called, are reported into the time of Nicholas I (r. 858–67). Yet the popes' most extensive and costly projects in the mid 9th century were not religious commissions, but rather fortifications and (very) small cities. These initiatives must cumulatively have far exceeded in scale and cost all the ecclesiastical buildings undertaken in the period c. 840–80, and left still more physically imposing marks on the landscape. By constructing walls and even proclaiming themselves the founders of new "cities," the popes again impersonated the emperors of old, while also very practically acting as the rectors and protectors of Rome and its surrounding territory.[40]

The immediate impetus for the wave of walling was the appearance of the "Saracens," Muslims from north Africa, Spain, and southern France who established permanent footholds in the islands (Sicily, Sardinia, and Corsica) and southern Italy in the first half of the 9th century, within easy sailing distance of Rome. Like the Vikings, they used their ships to make lightning raids on coastal populations, pillaging and then disappearing long before any coordinated response could be mounted. The *LP* first acknowledges their existence under Gregory IV (r. 827–44). With Saracen depredations increasing, around 842 Gregory collected the residents of Ostia, at the Tiber mouth, and put them to work building the circuit wall that now forms the nucleus of the medieval *borgo* of Ostia Antica, on the inland edge of the sprawling ancient port city. The surviving traces of the wall suggest a perimeter no longer than 400–500 m, enclosing an area of only c. 1 ha (2.47 acres), but Gregory blessed the wall and proudly christened the little place Gregoriopolis. He thus became the first pope to claim another privilege traditionally associated with Romano-Byzantine emperors, the founding of eponymous towns (e.g. Hadrianopolis, Philippopolis, Diocletianopolis, Marcianopolis, Justiniana Prima, and Constantinople itself).[41]

Four years later, in the late summer of 846, a "Saracen" raiding party sailed from Sardinia to the mouth of the Tiber, where it defeated the ragtag band of Romans and locals from Ostia sent to oppose it. From there, the Muslim raiders sailed up the Tiber and ransacked the suburbs of Rome, including St. Peter's and St. Paul's, which were stripped of their precious furnishings. The profanation of Rome's famous martyrial shrines resonated throughout western Europe almost like Alaric's sack of 410. It was a humiliation both for the papacy and for Rome's Carolingian protectors, the Emperor Lothar himself in the first place. A new and energetic pope, Leo IV, went to work to shore up Rome's defenses and bolster the morale of its people soon after taking office at the beginning of 847. He restored the Aurelian Wall and completely rebuilt 15 of its towers, including two on opposite banks of the Tiber that could be connected by a chain to bar passage to ships coming upriver from Ostia. Then, starting in 848, he launched the most ambitious civic project attempted in medieval Rome: a 3 km-long circuit of walls around St. Peter's and the Borgo.[42]

Construction began after Leo obtained the consent of the Roman nobility (the *LP* has them beseeching Leo to protect the Vatican) and the support of Emperor Lothar, Charlemagne's grandson, who financed much of the project with funds raised from parishes throughout his dominions. Leo then assembled laborers and materials from all the cities under papal control, from monasteries, and from the Church's rural estates (*massae* and *domuscultae*), and set them to work in teams around the perimeter of the new defenses. After another Saracen attack in 849 was repelled with the help of the Neapolitans and Gaetans, those Saracen prisoners not hanged immediately were sentenced to hard labor on the new fortifications. By 852, the circuit was largely complete: Starting at Castel S. Angelo, where the new fortification joined the old walls via the "Bridge of St. Peter"/ Ponte S. Angelo, the wall went straight west to enclose St. Peter's, turning south behind the church and then back east to the river, which it rejoined by today's S. Spirito in Sassia, forming a roughly rectangular perimeter (Fig. 4.18; see also Fig. 7.10, below). It was a kind of reduced-scale

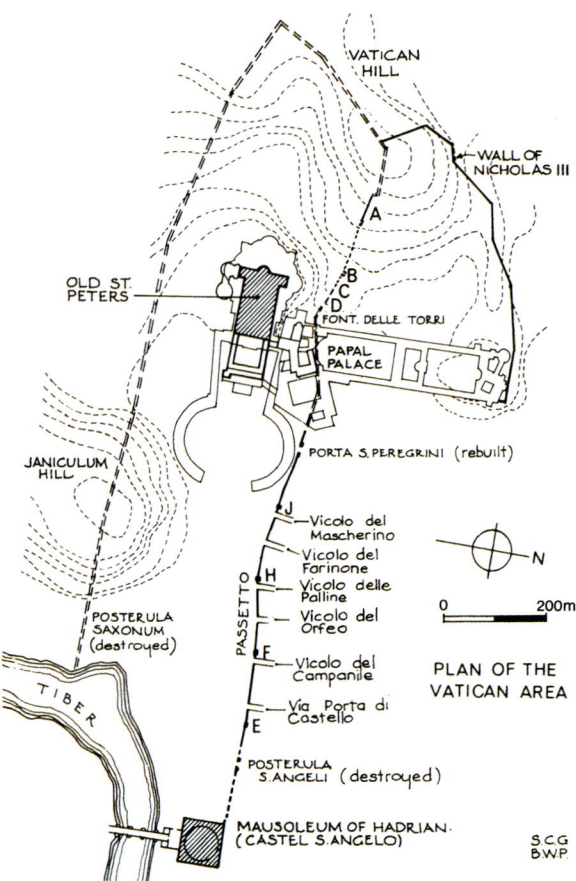

Figure 4.18 Leo IV's wall around St. Peter's and the Borgo, with Nicholas III's 13th-century extension. (Gibson and Ward-Perkins 1983, p. 223, fig. 1.)

version of the Aurelian Wall, lower and thinner than the original, but – like Aurelian's wall – built mostly in brick-faced concrete and reinforced with rectangular projecting towers.[43]

The wall's consecration in 853 was celebrated as the inauguration of a new city: Leo led a procession of the Roman clergy, nobles, and people around the perimeter, pausing to asperse the three main gates with holy water. He christened the place the *civitas Leonina* ("Leo-ville"), and had inscriptions installed over the three gates, which acknowledged Carolingian assistance even as they left no doubt that the wall, and the new city it constituted, were his creation. The Leonine wall is the supreme testament to the logistical and technical capacities of the papacy as it approached the centenary of its effectively autonomous governing mandate; it also made Leo look like the undisputed, and very regal, leader of the Roman collective.[44]

This impression was reinforced by two other initiatives launched while the building of the Leonine wall was ongoing. Leo repaired the late antique walls of Portus, Rome's other port city at the mouth of the Tiber, and repopulated the place with Corsican refugees from Muslim incursions who swore their allegiance to Leo and to Rome. Soon thereafter, he founded another little city to replace the old town of *Centumcellae*, modern Civitavecchia, whose inhabitants had scattered to the countryside after a devastating Saracen raid in 813. Leo built a new circuit of mortared stone blocks on a hilltop some 20 km inland from the old site, well away from the perilous coastline, and settled the refugees and their descendants there. Once again, a classicizing marble inscription over a gate named Leo the city's founder and patron. After another inaugural parade that featured Leo aspersing the gates and distributing money (like an emperor) to the new town's inhabitants, he christened the place Leopolis.[45]

Thirty years later, around 880, the charismatic and assertive Pope John VIII (r. 872–82) created another eponymous "city" by enclosing St. Paul's and its surrounding cluster of monasteries and dwellings within a new walled circuit. Though nothing of the wall survives, inscriptions originally placed over its two gates are still preserved at St. Paul's. According to the more prolix of the two:

> This wall stands forth as a savior, and the unconquered gate / which forbids the reprobate and takes in the pious. / Enter here you young and old togate nobles / and the blessed plebs seeking the holy threshold of God / duly created by John, the regent of the Lord / who radiates with shining morals and merits. / Built in the name of John, regent of God, the eighth of that name / behold the venerable city Iohannipolis flourishes.

John's address to the Roman nobles and commoners as joint beneficiaries of his project invokes the ideal unity of the three pillars of Roman society – nobility, people, and, implicitly, the Church – united and protected under the pontiff. The reality was always more complicated, and often contentious, but the fact remains that he was able to marshal the resources, the labor, and the consensus necessary to turn the existing cluster of settlement around St. Paul's into a fortified mini-city. It was the last of the really enterprising public works attempted in early medieval Rome, far grander than anything undertaken during the following two centuries. As such, it is as good a sign as any that John really was, as historians tend to suggest, the last pontiff whose international connections and local prestige allowed him at least partially to transcend the vicissitudes of local factional politics and make a plausible show of representing the city as a whole.[46]

We can leave the causes and effects of the waning of the papal "Republic of the Romans" for Chapter 5, and return for now to the topography and material culture of 'papal' Rome at its early medieval apex. The state of knowledge has progressed so far in the past few decades, thanks both to new archaeological discoveries and to critical reevaluations of existing written and material evidence, that all of the following points might be made without reference to any scholarship available when Krautheimer published his *Profile* in 1980.

Most of the cityscape continued gradually along the trajectory of slow decay that characterized the Byzantine era. If population still reached or exceeded 50,000 in the first half of the 7th century, it had probably declined further by the 8th, as Rome fell out of the trans-Mediterranean economic and commercial networks that had formerly helped sustain its inhabitants. Meneghini and Santangeli Valenzani may well be right to estimate no more than 20,000–30,000 residents, but there is simply no way to be sure. Certainly the large majority of the structures inherited from antiquity were unoccupied and unmaintained, and so kept falling to pieces. Recurring natural disasters accelerated the constant effects of weather and time. The most common were floods, ranging from minor events that regularly swamped low-lying areas near the river, to major catastrophes that could inundate nearly everything from the Tiber as far east as the Via Lata, and on southward across the *Ripa Graeca* and Velabrum and inland into the Forum and Circus Maximus, along with the populated parts of Trastevere across the river. Events extraordinary enough to make it into the *LP* occurred c. 716, 791, 845, 856, and 860, and other substantial floods went unreported, among them those presumed responsible for the late 7th- and mid 8th-century cleanup deposits at the Crypta Balbi.[47]

Rome had always flooded, of course, as it continued to do until the erection of the modern river embankments starting in the late 19th century, but the ancient city was considerably better prepared to confront the problem. First, stone embankments had protected the more exposed sections of riverbank and helped to mitigate the effects of ordinary flooding; by the 780s, when Pope Hadrian harvested over 12,000 blocks from the erstwhile embankments to rebuild the portico to St. Peter's, whatever protection they once offered was waning fast. Worse, the elaborate system of drains and subterranean sewers that had speeded the retreat of receding floodwaters from the ancient city center fell progressively into disrepair. There are signs of unremediated clogging and spotty maintenance in some areas already in the 4th and 5th centuries, and the situation was clearly much worse by the 8th and 9th. Floodwaters consequently lingered for longer in low-lying areas, leaving thicker deposits of silt and filth, and weakening many structures that did not collapse outright under the impetus of the surging water by saturating their foundations and ground floors. Further, whereas there had been more than enough available manpower in ancient Rome to scour the city of muck and debris after floods, a bad flood left behind far too much filth for the few, thinly spread Romans of the 8th and 9th centuries to handle. Cleanup efforts were inevitably partial, leaving flood deposits to fester and accumulate in many areas.[48]

Even in low-lying areas such as the Campus Martius and the *Ripa Graeca*, however, the city's crucial connective arteries still functioned in the form of the larger and more trafficked roads inherited from antiquity. The so-called Einsiedeln Itineraries, a series of guided walks through the city compiled somewhere around 800 for the benefit of northern pilgrims in Rome, offers the best textual evidence of the persistence of ancient street networks. The various itineraries begin and end at famous churches such as St. Peter's and St. Paul's, or at city gates. They direct readers along streets that can usually be identified, pausing to point at landmarks, churches but also many ancient monuments, located (sometimes far) off to the left and the right. Most of the routes are ancient: the Via Triumphalis/*porticus maximae* from the Vatican to the *Ripa Graeca*; the Via Lata leading straight north from the Capitoline; the *via maior* from the Colosseum to the Lateran, the Via Tiburtina on the Esquiline, and so on. Four of the walks traverse the Forum Romanum itself, still the focal point on which Rome's radiating network of main roads converged.[49]

While the Einsiedeln Itineraries do not reveal the condition of these streets, archaeology now often does. Some roads long remained at their original levels, with their Roman paving exposed and practicable. In many other cases, roadbeds rose together with surrounding ground levels more generally, as sediment, trash, and rubble built up over the centuries. The new surfaces almost invariably consisted of poorer, less resistant materials than the closely fitted stone pavers favored in antiquity: for main roads, a rough conglomerate composed of small stones and potsherds compacted by constant use was common, while the subsidiary alleys that branched off of them were often little more than dirt paths that turned to mud when wet. In the 8th and 9th centuries, levels along much of the *porticus maximae* in the Campus Martius were gradually rising, even as the course of the road remained unchanged and large tracts of its flanking porticoes still stood. In the Forum area, both the Via Sacra and the Argiletum kept their ancient levels into the 9th century, as did the southern extremity of the Via Lata nearby at Piazza Venezia. In all three of these cases, however, the roads and their underlying drains and sewers ceased to be cleaned and maintained over the course of the 9th century: rubbish and dirt started to accumulate, leading to rising, superimposed sequences of roadbeds in compacted gravel and potsherds (Fig. 4.19). Particularly on higher ground, some ancient road surfaces continued in use longer

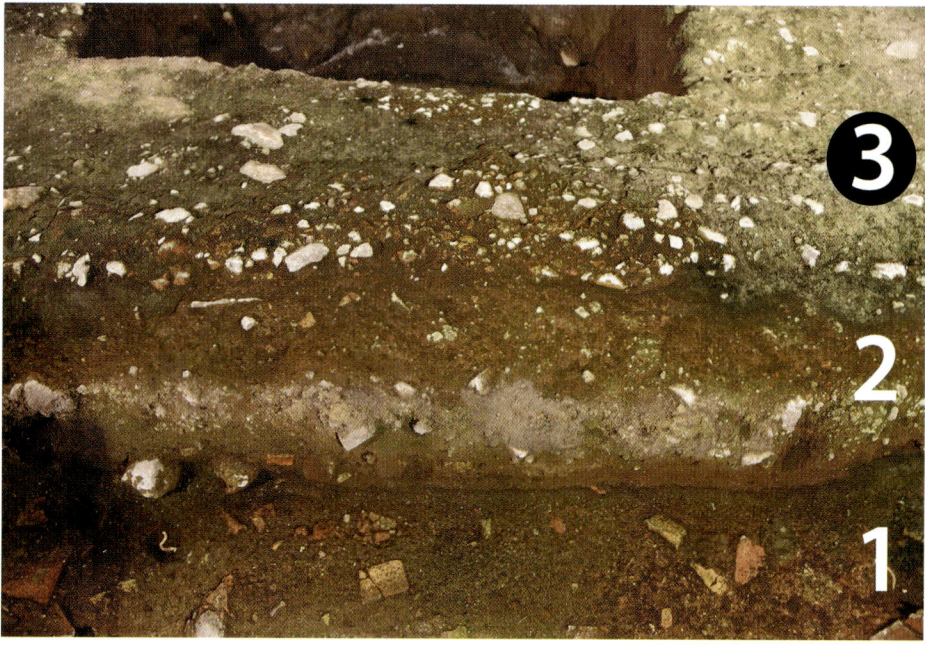

Figure 4.19 Three successive elevations of the surface of the early medieval street, composed of potsherds, gravel or small chunks of stone, and dirt (marked 1, 2, and 3; c. 9th–10th century), which formed along the S flank of the *Porticus Minucia* in the 5th century and gradually rose over the centuries (now visible on the bottom floor of the Museo Nazionale della Cripta Balbi). (Author.)

still, into the high Middle Ages (and beyond), when the writers of contracts and other archival documents used phrases like *in silice* to call attention to roads still paved in *silex*, the black volcanic leucite favored by ancient Roman road builders.[50]

Those parts of the city above the reach of floodwaters were not spared from Rome's other recurring natural disaster, earthquakes. The *LP* singles out for notice quakes in 618 and 801, the latter of which collapsed the roof of St. Paul's, and in 847. Widespread archaeological evidence of damage at various sites points to 847 as the most destructive of these events. The damage it caused to S. Maria Antiqua was severe enough to prompt Leo IV to build an entirely new church across the Forum on the podium of the temple of Venus and Rome, in a spot that was also considerably higher and drier than the boggy, ill-drained corner of the Forum where the old church stood. At the Crypta Balbi, it collapsed the half-dome of the exedra, putting an end to its long and varied history as indoor space. At the recent Metro C excavations at Piazza Venezia, the concrete vaults of the Hadrianic auditoriums came crashing down, burying the floor under a jagged carpet of rubble a couple of meters thick that remained unfrequented thereafter for two centuries and more (Fig. 3.22, above). One of the two 9th-century quakes also damaged the centerpiece of the nearby Forum of Trajan, the magnificent Basilica Ulpia, scattering columns and chunks of its concrete apse vaults across the forum paving.[51]

Like floods, earthquakes were hardly new; again, what had changed by the early Middle Ages was Romans' capacity to clean up afterwards and rebuild. In the case of imposing public monuments such as Hadrian's auditoriums at Piazza Venezia and the Basilica Ulpia, the resources and technology to rebuild or repair them to their original specifications no longer existed. Nobody in 9th-century Rome was quarrying and carving (or otherwise importing) columns big enough to replace the African marble monoliths of the Basilica Ulpia when they fell and broke. Nobody was building massive concrete vaults, such as those that collapsed at the Basilica Ulpia and the auditoriums of Hadrian. In the wake of such catastrophes, there was nothing left to do but abandon the ruins completely, or raze and level them, or build humbler structures into or around surviving sections.

If comparable accommodations were wanted to replace those lost through attrition, the best option was to use other ancient monuments in better condition. Over time, the great disparity between Rome's relatively tiny early medieval population and its vast store of old buildings would thus gradually have resolved itself: as time, weather, and natural disasters steadily diminished the number of functional edifices that remained, people occupied a growing proportion of those that were left. In the case of residential structures, we might imagine both aristocratic inhabitants of single-family *domus* and ordinary dwellers in multifamily *insulae* tending to exchange buildings damaged beyond repair for 'new' old structures in better condition, for as long as usable buildings survived in desirable locations. Only when supply was no longer sufficient to meet demand will there have been a substantial move toward alternative forms of housing – either via extensive reconstruction of old buildings, or the creation of entirely new habitations.[52]

Until the 9th century, there is little sign that such a tipping point was reached. Only then do new houses, freestanding and independent of older remains, begin to appear in some numbers. All of the best-documented examples occupied public spaces that had been maintained in something approaching their original form since antiquity. This brings us to conclude on residential architecture, public monuments, and infrastructure (including piazzas/forums and also streets), and the regulation and use of space. These topics are inseparable, as recent excavations have made clearer than ever, nowhere more so than in the Show Area from the foot of the Palatine across the Forum Romanum to the imperial forums. We will concentrate on this zone, where revolutionary discoveries have been made since the 1990s, with occasional glimpses farther afield to help illustrate broader patterns of continuity and change in the papal Rome of the later 8th and 9th centuries. Unlike the Forum proper, most of which was cleared down to ancient levels by the early 20th century, large expanses of the Forums of Caesar, Nerva, Trajan, and the Temple/Forum of Peace were excavated only in the 1990s and 2000s. The early medieval levels there are incredibly rich and complex. Revelatory in their own right, they also help to reconstruct and interpret the extensive medieval remains found in the past in the Forum and elsewhere that were only (at best) summarily recorded and photographed before removal.

The full papal takeover of civic governance in the mid 8th century set the stage for the transformation of the imperial forum complexes, which changed more drastically in appearance in the years c. 750–900 than in the preceding half-millennium. Initially, from the mid 8th century until the early 9th, the governing authorities selectively and very methodically set to stripping valuable materials for reuse in the new wave of Church-sponsored building projects. In the Forum of Caesar, the travertine pavement was removed all at once in the mid 8th century. Not long after, the white marble revetment was stripped off the walls in the Forum of Trajan, and then also in the Forum of Peace. It is notable that a far larger percentage of the colored marbles once present in these complexes has been found than of the calcareous white marbles and limestone, which have almost totally vanished. The reason is simple: The calcareous stones were burned to produce lime, much of it produced on-site in kilns such as the 8th-century examples discovered in the Forum of Trajan. The quantities of mortar that resulted were prodigious: the paving of Caesar's forum would have provided 600–700 tons of lime; the marbles of Trajan's forum, ten times as much (c. 7,000 tons!). The mortar that held together all that was new or restored in the resurgent papal Rome of the later 8th and 9th centuries came from the incinerated wall and floor coverings of some of the city's most prominent and well-preserved ancient monuments, now come under Church control.[53]

The standing structures of the imperial forums mostly remained, however, and there was no encroachment on their open plazas during this initial phase of dismantling, whether they remained paved (Trajan, Nerva) or had been stripped to their concrete underbedding (Caesar, Peace). There was evidently nothing chaotic or anarchic in the treatment of the Show Area in this period. In the Forum of Peace, orderly piles of architectural bits and pieces were made in various places, where they remained undisturbed until their discovery in the excavations of the early 2000s (Fig. 4.20). The monuments were firmly under the control of the governing authorities, who enacted what looks like

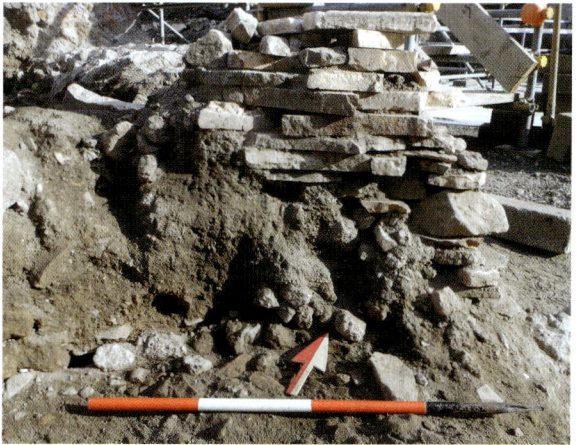

Figure 4.20 One of the neat piles of calcareous marble fragments assembled inside the Forum Pacis in the later 8th century, presumably in anticipation of being cooked into mortar. (Photo courtesy of Riccardo Santangeli Valenzani and the Parco Archeologico del Colosseo.)

a deliberate and closely regulated process of partial spoliation, while leaving the structural and spatial integrity of the forum areas largely intact. Like the Forum Romanum proper, the forums of Nerva, Trajan, and Caesar preserved their ancient contours into the 9th century: their main temples (of Minerva, Divine Trajan, and Venus Genetrix, respectively) and surrounding porticoes and perimeter walls still stood, and the still-paved esplanades of the forums of Nerva and Trajan were kept clear of dirt and debris. In this respect, they differed markedly from the Forum of Peace, for example, parts of which had been covered since the 6th century by a thick deposit of soil and rubble that was partly occupied by a cemetery possibly connected to the church of SS. Cosma e Damiano.[54]

Over the course of the 9th century, along with further spoliation came, for the first time, a marked impulse toward the parcellization and privatization of hitherto unitary public spaces. The Forum of Caesar begins an accelerated process of de-monumentalization already in the first half of the 9th century, for reasons that can only be guessed at. Not long after 800, at least two small shacks in wood and other perishable materials were built inside the open, pavement-free enclosure, and most of the area was given over to intensive cultivation, beginning with herbs and vegetables: cabbage, lettuce, coriander, white mustard, mint, and green anise, according to the paleobotanical analysis. Within a few decades, these first gardens and shacks were covered with a thick deposit of earth that permitted the cultivation of more substantial crops: grapevines were planted in one section, and an orchard of fruit trees (cherries, plums, hazelnuts, figs) in another, turning the whole precinct into a kind of enclosed garden orchard (Fig. 5.10, below).[55]

At the Forum of Trajan, the marble flooring was all very suddenly torn up and carted away in the mid 9th century. It was a staggering quantity of stone: Trajan's pavement had comprised more than 3,300 rectangular slabs of white Luni marble, each more than a meter wide by two meters long, covering an area of over 9,000 square meters, for a total of some 1,300 cubic meters of material. Over the ensuing few decades, silt and dirt washed down from the slopes of the Quirinal Hill began to accumulate on the underlying concrete bedding (Fig. 4.21). By century's

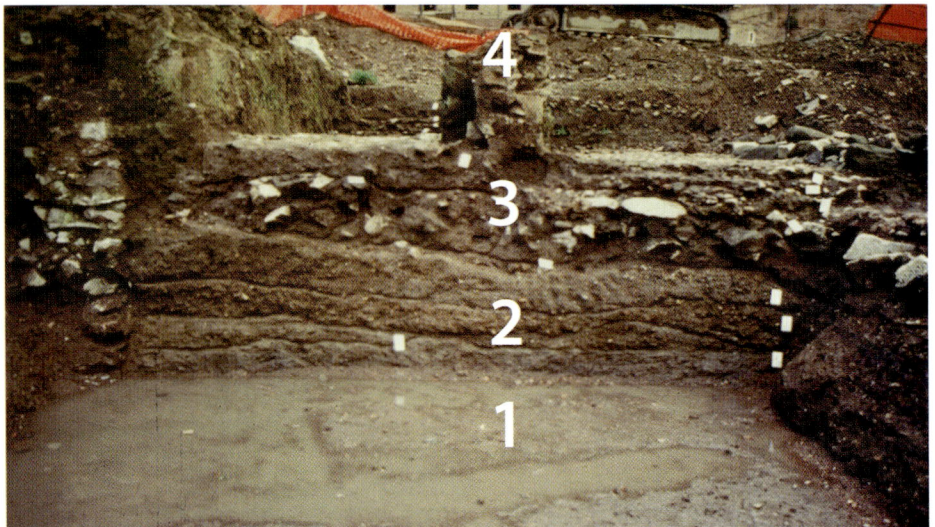

Figure 4.21 The stratigraphic sequence in the Forum of Trajan. 1: concrete bedding of the paving stones (removed mid-9th century); 2: natural formations of alluvial sediments (late 9th–early 10th centuries; 3: rubble fill and levelling layer (mid 10th century); 4: wall erected atop the fill (later 10th–11th century). (Adapted from Meneghini and Santangeli Valenzani 2004, p. 184, fig. 174.)

end, the erstwhile marble-paved esplanade of the grandest imperial forum was a field choked with weeds and brambles, a kind of monumental vacant lot. By way of explanation for the sudden dismantling of this grandest of all imperial forums, whose pavement had been kept clean and unobstructed for more than seven centuries, Santangeli Valenzani has suggested that Leo IV requisitioned the paving slabs to produce the exceptional quantities of lime mortar needed for his repairs to the Aurelian Wall and the construction of his new, 3 km-long circuit around the Vatican. The idea is certainly plausible, particularly if we imagine the earthquake of 847 damaging parts of the forum (including the huge Basilica Ulpia) beyond hope of repair, leading to the decision to cook its pavers into lime in the following year.[56]

The pavers of the neighboring Forum of Augustus may have met the same fate. They were also removed apparently during the 9th century, from which point alluvial deposits datable to the 9th–10th centuries began to accumulate on the concrete bedding underneath. Here, too, a new form of occupation took shape by the 9th century, when the compact monastery of S. Basilio was installed atop the podium of the Temple of Mars, in the shadow of the few remaining Corinthian columns of the Augustan edifice (Fig. 4.22).[57]

In the Forum of Nerva, the really exciting discovery is the well-preserved remains of two substantial houses of the mid 9th century, whose construction was part and parcel of a profound transformation of the forum as whole. The ancient travertine pavement, which had remained clear and in use until then, was removed, and a half-meter-thick deposit of soil spread across the concrete underbedding to facilitate the planting of vegetables and eventually trees. At about the same time, work on the two excavated houses began. They were built with their foundations resting directly on the

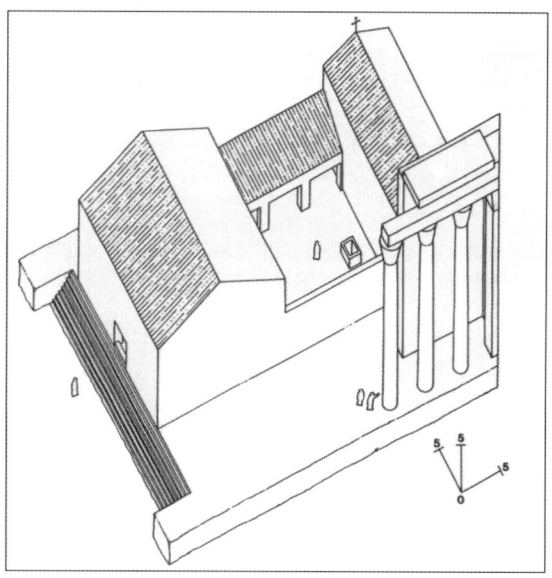

Figure 4.22 The monastery of S. Basilio on the podium of the Temple of Mars. (Meneghini and Santangeli Valenzani 2004, p. 100, fig. 81.)

underbedding of the forum pavement, both facing onto the Argiletum, the busy throughway that ran diagonally across the Forum of Nerva on its way between the Forum and the Subura. This had also kept its ancient level until the 9th-century restructuring, when it was raised by a half-meter in correspondence with the rest of the area and resurfaced with a packed layer of small stones and sherds (Fig. 4.23).[58]

The larger of the two houses backed directly onto the forum's high perimeter wall. It forms a rough rectangle measuring c. 19 × 10 m, with a ground floor built in *opus quadratum* masonry of reused, worn blocks of peperino (a soft, volcanic stone similar to tuff) laid in irregular courses with rough joints and crevices that were filled in with raw clay. A dividing wall bisecting the ground floor lengthwise supported the beams for the floor of an upper story built in mortared brick and probably roofed with wooden shingles. A few decades later, still before the end of the 9th century, the surviving arcaded porch facing onto the Argiletum was added. The second house, on the other side of the street, has basically the same

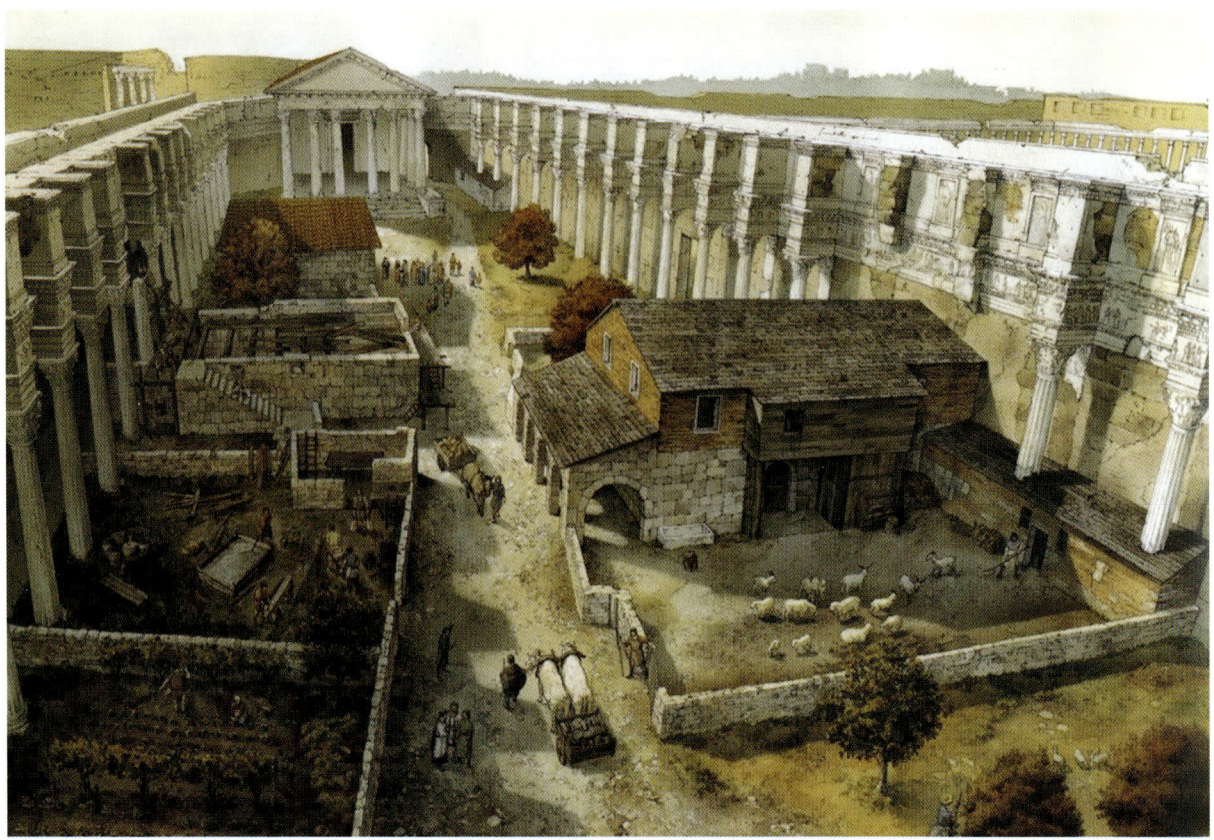

Figure 4.23 Reconstruction of the Forum of Nerva in the mid-9th century. The larger of the two excavated houses is at right; the smaller, at left, is shown still under construction. (Studio InkLink/Meneghini and Santangeli Valenzani 2007, p. 130, fig. 137.)

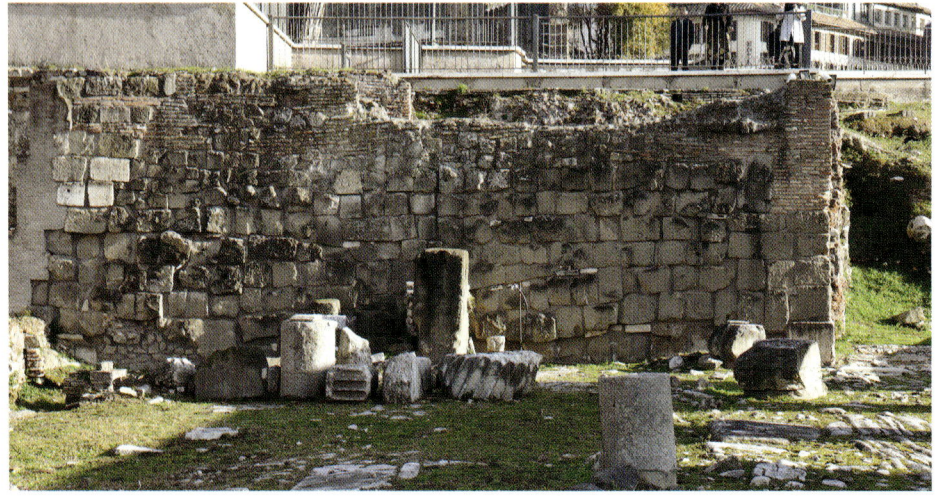

Figure 4.24 The S wall of the smaller of the two houses in the Forum of Nerva. Note the beginnings of the upper story in brick, interspersed with smaller blocks of tuff. (Author.)

plan. It was somewhat smaller, at c. 17 × 8 m, but more carefully built. Here the peperino blocks of the ground floor were recut to fit somewhat more closely together, and joined with thick beds of high-quality lime mortar (Fig. 4.24). The upper floor was again built in mortared brick, with a heterogeneous assortment of recycled bricks laid in the undulating courses typical of the period. The absence of any remains of roof tiles again suggests a wooden shingled roof. Both houses had external staircases leading to the upper story and were surrounded by enclosed yards containing gardens, stables, wells, and cesspits.

What to make of all this? First, the Forum of Nerva ceased to be maintained as an open public space and was subdivided and in some sense privatized toward the middle of the 9th century, nearly eight centuries after its creation. The area was covered by planting soil, though the main structures of the old forum, from its colonnaded perimeter walls to its crowning temple of Minerva, remained mostly in place. The houses' size, expensive materials, and prominent location all indicate they belonged to relatively important people, but there is no way of knowing just who the owners were, or how they were authorized to build where they did.

The houses themselves are nothing like the spatially extensive *domus* inhabited by wealthy Romans since late antiquity, with their sprawling assortments of apsidal halls and *triclinia*, service quarters, and even baths arrayed around open courtyards. The residences in the Forum of Nerva belong to a new, early medieval residential paradigm attested across much of Italy. They are compact and square and solid, and extend upward rather than out. They are considerably more utilitarian and less luxurious than late antique *domus*, too: the ground floors, accessed directly from the yard, functioned as stables, storerooms, kitchens, and possibly sleeping quarters for servants, while even the upper floors where the proprietors lived had few architectural flourishes. Such dwellings are basically urban farmhouses that resemble actual rural residences, built at a time when parts of Rome's monumental center were taking on a semirural appearance, such that even members of the nobility lived among domestic animals and gardens and orchards. Not coincidentally, such upper-class houses with their surrounding property and outbuildings were sometimes called *curtes*, "courts," a term borrowed directly from rural estates.[59]

Bits and pieces of other early medieval dwellings have turned up across the city over the years, though most were summarily removed by their 19th- and earlier 20th-century excavators. Several of the most complete examples came to light in the Forum Romanum itself, which evidently underwent its own process of privatization and parcellization. Much of this residential construction faced onto the Via Sacra, the road running along the north side of the Forum plaza from the Basilica of Maxentius to the Arch of Septimius Severus. The one preserved structure was inserted into the front portico of the Basilica Aemilia, and is now confidently identified as a house based on its close resemblance to those next door in the Forum of Nerva: a rectangle with a ground floor in tuff blocks, divided lengthwise by an internal wall to support an upper story in brick that was accessed by an external staircase. Farther east, early 20th-century photos and plans show that a large house made from recycled brick abutted the Temple of Caesar and the eastern rostra; and other walls in tuff blocks and brick inserted into the Regia suggest that this, too, was converted to residential use by the 9th century. It looks as though the main road through the Forum became more built-up than ever by the 9th century, as new houses filled in the spaces between ancient monuments to create a dense sequence of facades.[60]

The road running parallel to the Via Sacra along the south side of the forum plaza had a more workaday character: Sockets for posts and roof beams chiseled into the bases of the Tetrarchic-era honorary columns and the surrounding pavement indicate that small shops or workshops built in wood clustered here from the 7th century or so, extending all the way to the old

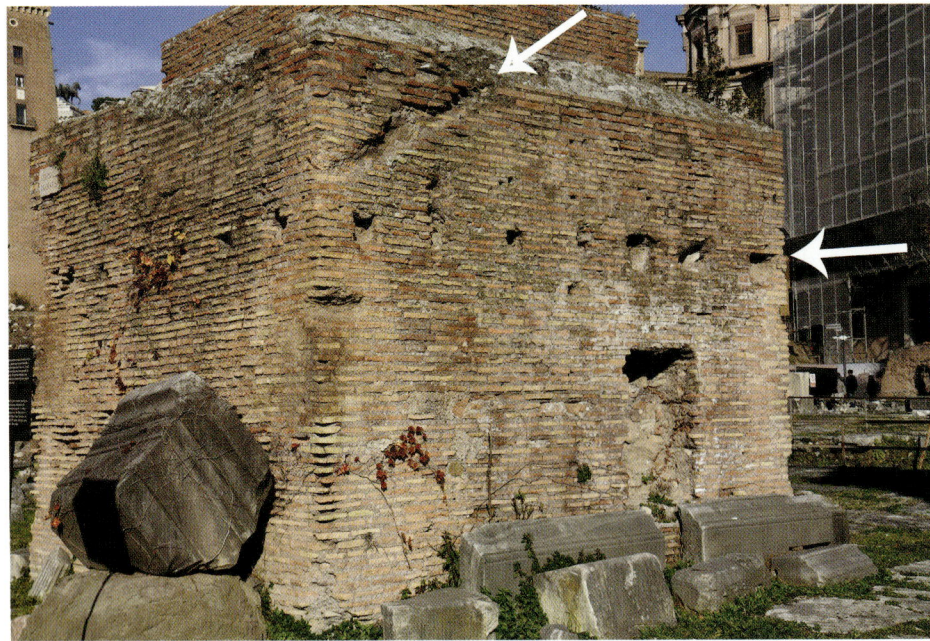

Figure 4.25 The base of one of the late antique honorary columns along the S side of the Forum plaza. The horizontal arrow at right points to a row of sockets for roof timbers hacked into the brick; the upper arrow points to a diagonal cut evidently intended to support a pitched roof. Their placement at little more than head height above the ancient paving shows that the wooden shacks to which these sockets belonged predate the rise of ground-levels after the 9th century. (Author.)

speaker's platform (rostra) at the west end of the Forum plaza (Fig. 4.25). More workshops specializing in stone and metalwork occupied much of the floor of the adjacent Basilica Julia, further accentuating the artisanal, productive character of this southern flank of the Forum, which later medieval sources call the *Cannapara*. By the beginning of the 10th century, several centuries' worth of such activities had raised levels inside the west end of the Basilica Julia by nearly a meter, at which point the adjacent stretch of the Vicus Iugarius was repaved in coarse rubble at the higher level, and a substantial dwelling measuring some 8 m square was built at the same level, abutting the west side of the basilica and opening onto the road (Fig. 4.26).[61]

But it needs to be stressed that, notwithstanding the adaptation of older buildings to new and often humbler uses, and the construction of new houses, workshops, and so on around the periphery of the Forum plaza, Rome's most ancient and central public space still looked, well into the 9th century – at least from a distance, or in mist – much as it had at the end of the Empire four centuries earlier. The ancient (early 3rd-century AD) paving of the central plaza remained mostly clear and unobstructed, and every important ancient monument in the immediate vicinity still stood, with the lone exception of the Temple of Vespasian, which collapsed late in the 8th century, flattening the adjacent *diaconia* of Sergius and Bacchus in the process. The temple of Concord and the Arch of Septimius Severus still defined the western edge of the Forum-plaza; the Basilica Julia and the Temple of the Dioscuri the south; the Temple of Caesar the east; and the Senate House/S. Adriano, the front portico of the Basilica Aemilia, and the Temple of Antoninus and Faustina the north. Farther up the Via Sacra toward the Colosseum, there was the Maxentian rotunda incorporated into SS. Cosma e Damiano, and the biggest monument of all, the Basilica of Maxentius/Constantine. Monumental additions to the area,

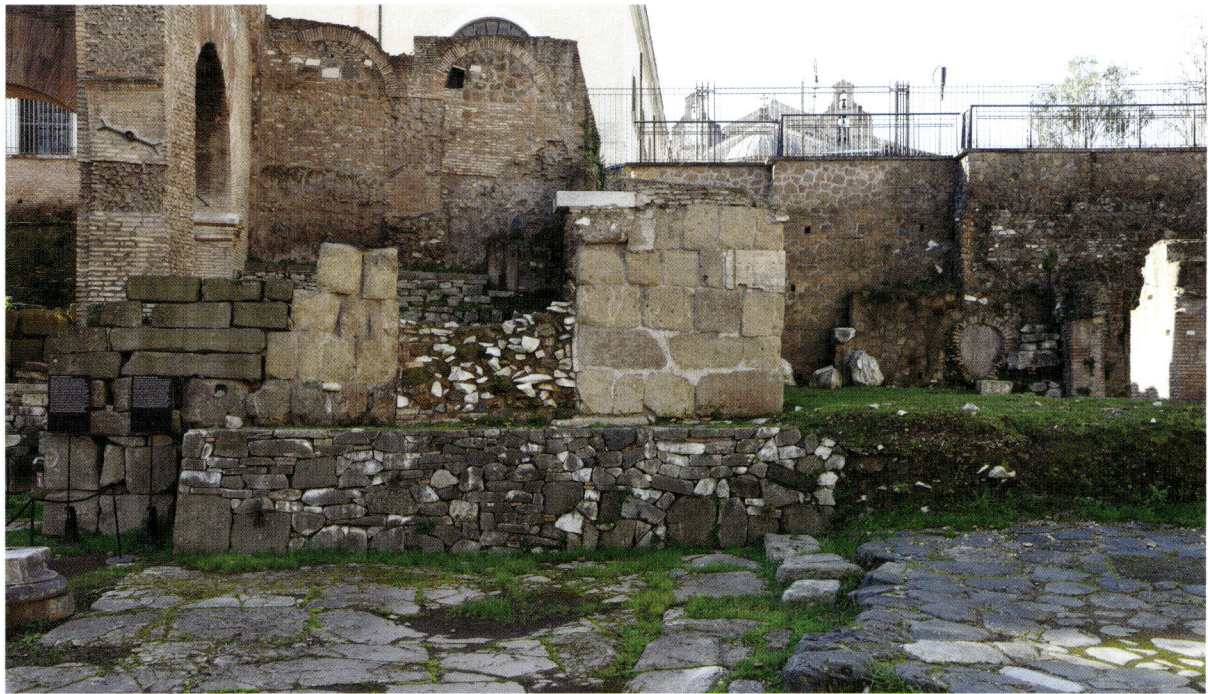

Figure 4.26 The early 10th-century house built between the west façade of the Basilica Julia (at far upper left) and the Vicus Iugarius (note the ancient pavers at lower right). The foundations of the house were cut down to the ancient paving, while its floor matched the level of the new roadbed, some 70–80 cm above the ancient pavers. (Author.)

meanwhile, were nonexistent until Leo IV built the church of S. Maria Nova (now S. Francesca Romana) on the podium of the Temple of Venus and Rome. This "new" church of Mary, which replaced in a higher and dryer location the "old" S. Maria Antiqua shivered by the earthquake of 847, was the first and only really sizeable new construction installed in the environs of the Forum throughout the early Middle Ages.[62]

It is from the late 8th through the mid 9th century, then, when the papacy stood at the apex of its prestige and power, that dramatic change finally overtook those last public spaces in the Show Area that had been cleaned and maintained since antiquity. The forums of Caesar, Augustus, and Trajan were spoliated and 'ruralized' – either cultivated (Caesar) or temporarily abandoned to accumulations of dirt and wild vegetation (Trajan and Augustus); the Forum of Nerva was divided into housing lots and gardens; the Forum of Peace was stripped of its valuable materials; and dirt and debris finally started to accumulate across parts of the central plaza of the Forum Romanum itself. Nearby drains and sewers were failing at what looks to be an increasing rate, such that the ancient paving of principal roads also disappeared beneath rising ground levels. There is no unequivocal explanation for why these transformations occurred when they did, and probably no single cause. Possible contributing factors include a growing need for mortar and building materials for expansive papal projects such as Leo IV's Vatican walls; and the two earthquakes of 801 and 847, the second of which especially looks to have provoked widespread damage to buildings and infrastructure that was beyond reasonable possibility of repair.

Age-old constants such as need for materials and natural disasters seem insufficient to explain what occurred, however. Rather, new and different choices were apparently made about how to treat the monumental heart of the city. It is not only that venerable civic spaces were finally disassembled en masse to furnish materials for new projects, but also that these formerly communal monuments were then subdivided, privatized, and given over to housing and agriculture. Given that the systematic dismantling began within a few decades of the popes' assumption of ownership over public buildings and spaces formerly under imperial control, it is very likely that the dismantling, at least, occurred under papal auspices and served to meet the immediate needs of the Church. It would follow that the privatization and parcelization of these areas also occurred with the consent, and very possibly the active encouragement, of the ecclesiastical authorities. Once the decision was made to strip the forums of their adornments and thereby compromise their (relatively) pristine monumentality, it would have made good sense to open them up to occupation rather than leaving an empty wasteland in the heart of the city; and the Show Area's centrality, its converging network of roads, and its heaps of surplus building materials surely all appealed to prospective owners and tenants. Difficult and probably unanswerable questions remain, however, about how and why this process unfolded. Did the popes make bequests of property to favored subordinates, lay or clerical, and allies? Did they offer it to the highest bidders, or allocate it according to the presumed need of potential beneficiaries? Or did powerful families and interest groups perhaps take the initiative on their own, leaving the popes to accede to the fait accompli?

In any case, for all that the Church is likely to have catalyzed the transformation of the Show Area, the sudden and widespread 'rezoning' of central public spaces betokens changing social and political dynamics on a scale well exceeding the purview of the popes and their functionaries. It may not be coincidence that textual hints of increasing factionalism and internecine strife multiply during the second half of the 9th century, pointing to the emergence of a more fractious political climate that may have complicated cooperative stewardship of communal architectural patrimony. But whether such fractures are a symptom of the privatization of strategically located former public spaces and monuments, or rather the partial cause thereof, or a parallel but largely unrelated phenomenon, at least initially, it is difficult to say. Whatever the causal sequence, however, the subdivision and occupation of formerly public buildings and infrastructure ultimately did contribute to processes of retrenchment, political and topographical, that gained momentum after the mid 9th century. As central authority receded, less was invested in civic building projects and upkeep, while the spots of Rome's leopard-skin pattern of settlement grew starker and more defined, taking on more of their own local character and identity, as we will now see.

Chapter 5

THE LONG TWILIGHT OF THE EARLY MIDDLE AGES

882–1046

THE PERIOD COVERED IN this chapter, from the death of Pope John VIII in 882 until the beginnings of the papal reform movement in the mid 11th century, has traditionally been treated as the blackest of the early medieval 'Dark Ages' at Rome. The perspective is understandable, and not entirely wrong. The written sources decline markedly in quality and quantity from the second half of the 9th century, while the few 10th-century narratives that survive tend to present the Roman scene in bleak terms. Historians of art and architecture have had still less to go on. Not a single monumental edifice survives from the years 882–1046. As far as we know, in fact, not a single really monumental edifice was built for two centuries after the fortified circuit erected circa 880 by John VIII around the peri-urban nucleus at St. Paul's: no imposing civic monument or piece of infrastructure, nor a single church comparable in size or opulence either to those built or rebuilt by John's 9th-century predecessors (S. Susanna, S. Prassede, S. Maria in Domnica, S. Cecilia, S. Martino ai Monti, S. Marco, S. Maria Nova, etc.), or to those that would again be constructed starting in the first half of the 12th century (S. Clemente, S. Crisogono, S. Maria in Trastevere, etc.).[1]

Even repairs and basic maintenance on existing monuments tailed off considerably. Leo IV's restoration of the Aurelian Wall around 850 is the last recorded for over 300 years, until 1157. Pope Nicholas I (r. 858–67) is the last person credited with repairs to the aqueducts (the Aqua Iobia and the branch of the Traiana leading to St. Peter's); thereafter, all remaining aqueducts went out of use for good by the 11th century, with the lone exception of the Aqua Virgo. Nicholas I also made the last important addition of the early Middle Ages to the

Lateran palace, a residential wing (*domus*) with an attached oratory whose interior decoration was completed by his successor, Hadrian II. As for churches, Leo IV's S. Maria Nova was the last big project of the early Middle Ages, and the last mentioned in the *LP*, with the exception of Nicholas I's presumably small oratory at the Lateran.[2]

The sparseness of textual and material traces of building activity naturally made the period seem all the bleaker to past observers of Roman topography and urbanism, who in turn tended to write it off as hopeless and leave it at that. In his *Profile of Rome*, Krautheimer essentially threw up his hands. He followed his lengthy chapter on "Carolingian" Rome, circa 760–860, with a sort of interlude in the form of a brief survey of Roman history from the later 9th century to the beginning of the 14th, resuming his in-depth analysis of art and architecture only from around 1100. The 10th and 11th centuries disappear.

In fairness to Krautheimer, it should be said from the outset that, after some 40 years of dedicated archaeological exploration, there is hardly more evidence for monumental urban interventions, churches or otherwise, in the period 882–1046 than there was when he was writing. Yet this is itself an important result. Recent excavations provide intriguing glimpses of what was happening in various locales across the city, but also of what was not happening. The findings tend to support the textual record in suggesting that municipal leaders made little effort to embellish or reshape the cityscape on a grand scale. In its broad contours, we can imagine that the city in 1000 or 1050 looked much like the city in 850, albeit with much of its infrastructure and monuments somewhat more dilapidated through lack of maintenance. The important exception is domestic architecture: Houses and residential compounds, notably monasteries, continued to be built or renovated, and in some cases whole new residential quarters were created. And in marked contrast with the preceding centuries, the driving force behind what initiatives did occur was no longer popes (and Byzantine regents before them) publically empowered to govern the urban collective, but rather local notables, both lay and clerical, acting in pursuit of more parochial ends. As the signal novelty of the period, these innovations in Rome's residential and social geography will feature prominently in our discussion; but this focus on the new should not distract us from the fact that Romans otherwise largely made do with what they already had.

It should be stressed, however, that what Romans had in the 10th century was still very substantial, and that relative stasis need hardly betoken a period of unmitigated disaster, an urban 'Dark Age' as black as its absence from Krautheimer's survey – and many others besides – makes it seem. On the all-important question of how many inhabitants Rome had, we simply have no hard information of the sort that would conduce to a close estimate. The best-informed recent guessers suggest something like 20,000–30,000 for the 9th and 10th centuries, down from maybe double that number in the 7th, when Rome was still integrated into the political and economic networks of the Byzantine Mediterranean and well supplied with imports from North Africa and the Levant. In any case, there is general agreement that even at 20,000–30,000 inhabitants, or whatever the actual number was, Rome remained the most populous city in Italy, and for that matter in all of Latin Christendom, into the 11th century. It had more producers, artisans, educated professionals, and clerics, a more diversified economy, and more landed wealth controlled by urban proprietors than anyplace else.[3]

As it had since antiquity, this urban population continued to live widely scattered across much of the intramural area, excepting much of the far north and south. But this continued residential diffusion means that the density of settlement was inevitably lower than in any subsequent era, when Rome's population rose stably above its 9th/10th-century nadir, and began to cluster in the Campus Martius and adjacent regions across the Tiber. Never did Romans lie more lightly on the land; never were Rome's inhabitants so few and scattered in relation to the scale and sweep of the built environment inherited from the past. This underlying reality helps to explain why Romans were often content to use and conserve what parts of the existing urban fabric they could, instead of attempting ambitious new projects.

Hence the "long twilight of the early Middle Ages" of this chapter's title. If there is a guiding leitmotif for Rome's long 10th century, c. 882–1046, it would seem to be relative stasis – substantial continuity with the past, though of course the cityscape and its inhabitants naturally never stood still, and localized corners of the city continued to be reconfigured. These years encompass the final stage in the long demographic slide that had continued mostly uninterrupted from the 5th century on, but also the first, tentative beginnings of the recovery. They are the last moment when settlement still persisted across much of the ancient city center; when multiple ancient aqueducts still functioned; when Roman congregations still overwhelmingly assembled in churches first established in late antiquity. The old took precedence over the new even in the continued use of the fourteen Augustan administrative regions of the city to locate properties, in notarial documents if perhaps less in the popular imagination. (By the mid-11th century, these regions would disappear once and for all, to be supplanted by a new constellation of urban quarters – *regiones*, or *rioni/contrade* in the vernacular – that bore no relation to the older system, and conformed more closely to the contours of the denser, more nucleated distribution of settlements that emerged from the later 11th century in the low-lying ground in the west of the city.) It is, in short, the last interval of comparative quiet, in topographical/urbanistic terms, before the drastic changes that would reshape the map of the city in the 12th century. Rome coasted along, topographically and also in some respects socially and administratively, albeit at a low ebb relative both to the immediate past and to the future that began to take shape from the mid-11th century and built toward the revolutionary developments of the 12th.[4]

Before turning to the urban fabric in detail, we should return to Rome's political and institutional evolution, which points to a range of additional factors that likely contributed to the sharp decline in building activity and urban upkeep. The beginning of our period, c. 880–910/20, does represent a turning point of sorts, a tumultuous moment that upset the institutional framework of the papal "Republic of the Romans" as it had been during its heyday from the later 8th century through the mid 9th. The autonomy, wealth, and prestige of the papacy diminished, and with them the popes' willingness and capacity to shape the cityscape.[5]

One notable symptom of these dislocations – and the one most inconvenient for historians – is the waning of the textual record itself. After well over three centuries of relatively continuous updating, the early medieval compilation of the *Liber Pontificalis* breaks off after 891. Subsequent papal lives tend to be shorter, and were usually written well after the events they purport to recount. Only from the later 11th century would there be a new sequence of papal biographies written by near-contemporaries. There is a gap already with the pontificate of John VIII, presumably because of the posthumous machinations of his enemies, but in this case the surviving collection of John's voluminous correspondence compensates for the loss and reveals much about the turbulent decade of his papacy. No comparably expansive collections of letters illuminate the activities of any of his successors up to the mid 11th century. Further, none of the sources that do survive from the 10th and 11th centuries are nearly as attentive to architecture and material culture as was the early medieval redaction of the *LP*.[6]

Already for several decades before it breaks off, the *LP* frequently hints at increasing dysfunctionality in the mechanisms of civic governance at Rome. After the pontificate of Leo IV (847–55), it has much less to say about papal largesse and architectural patronage, and much more about current events and worrisome developments in local politics. There are endless accounts of contested papal elections, riots and civil disorders, and simmering feuds between the partisans of various families and factions. The biographer of Hadrian II (r. 867–72) referred outright to "the tyranny of the hyper-partisan raging more fiercely than usual," while the correspondence of his immediate successor, John VIII, reveals a pope chronically hampered by internecine rivalries and challenges to his authority. It is not that the *LP* omits acts of papal patronage after Leo IV; papal biographers indeed eagerly commemorated the most trifling contributions. Rather, there was less to talk about because less was in fact being done. After a century and a half when they were the prime shapers of the cityscape, the popes radically scaled back their efforts, and there is no indication that anyone else stepped in to fill the void, neither local grandees nor Carolingian royals faced with growing problems of their own.[7]

When the newly elected pope Stephen V (r. 885–91) went to take up residence at the Lateran, he found that the complex had been systematically looted after the death of his predecessor, in an early instance of what soon became the established custom whereby Roman mobs ransacked the papal palace upon the death of the reigning pontiff. Among the losses were treasures that had been kept safe there for hundreds of years, including a gold cross donated by Belisarius more than three centuries earlier. Stephen's biographer lamented that Stephen was for all intents and purposes broke as a result; in his dutiful effort to laud the pope's acts of beneficence over the six years of his reign, the biographer was reduced to praising him for providing incense to St. Peter's, oil to illuminate nocturnal services at S. Maria Maggiore, and a smattering of books (manuscripts, not jeweled bindings!) and silks to a few other churches and monasteries. It was a far cry from Leo III's far-reaching program of urban renewal at the beginning of the century, or even Leo IV's at mid-century.[8]

The turmoil continued in the following decades, when shifting coalitions of Roman nobles and their central-Italian allies competed to install, and sometimes remove, a succession of popes whose tumultuous and usually brief tenures diminished the prestige of the office and compromised their ability to transcend partisan divides at home. In 897, Rome was treated to the sight of the corpse of Pope Formosus (r. 891–6) exhumed by his enemies and hauled off to the Lateran palace, where it was dressed in papal vestments and tried for high crimes and heresies in the presence of Pope Stephen VI (r. 896–7). The condemned skeleton was ritually mutilated and thrown in the Tiber. In 898, a new pope (John IX, r. 898–900) sympathetic to Formosus had the skeleton alleged to be his reburied at St. Peter's, after it was purportedly (miraculously!) found washed up on the banks of the Tiber; one tradition has the bones exhumed and discarded a second time when another bitter enemy of Formosus acceded to the papal throne as Sergius III in 904. By the time this struggle between the 'pro-Formosan' and 'anti-Formosan' contingents played itself out, effective power in Rome resided with the lay aristocrats who had made the Lateran bureaucracy, and the papacy with it, into an extension of their political and economic ambitions.[9]

Political instability at Rome was exacerbated by the more unsettled conditions that prevailed in Italy upon the waning of Carolingian power. The symbiosis between a solid Carolingian polity in north-central Italy and a stable papal administration, which had brought Rome a century of relative peace and prosperity, faltered on both sides from the 870s on. After the death of Charlemagne's grandson, Charles the Bald, in 877, neither the last Carolingians nor the regional actors, notably the House of Spoleto, who advanced their own claims to rule, managed to consolidate power over the lands between Rome and the Alps. In the absence of strong central rule, the principalities, duchies, and counties of north-central Italy squabbled endlessly among themselves, in the process opening the door to opportunistic foreign invaders because of their inability to organize a coherent response. After the more sporadic raids of the earlier 9th century, bands of Muslim adventurers established permanent footholds later in the century, raiding throughout central Italy from the base they established at the estuary of the River Garigliano in Campania. Great monasteries such as San Vincenzo al Volturno, Subiaco, and Farfa were sacked and temporarily abandoned – the ruins of Farfa became another permanent Saracen encampment for years after they burned it in 898 – while large swaths of the countryside were repeatedly devastated. (10th-century property documents from the archives of Roman churches and monasteries include telling references to rural properties pillaged and ruined by these "Saracens.") Peasants were chased from their fields and villages, some were captured and sold into slavery, and many more of the displaced turned to brigandage to survive. Travel by road and by sea was dangerous for all but the largest and best-armed contingents. Matters slowly improved after 915, when a coalition of Romans allied with the Christian polities of south-central Italy (including the dukedom of Spoleto under Alberic I, father of the future Roman *princeps* Alberic II) broke the back of Muslim power at the battle of the River Garigliano, though "Magyars" from central Europe would make more ephemeral but nonetheless damaging incursions into central Italy in the period c. 927–42, plundering right up to the walls of Rome on at least one occasion.[10]

These interrelated phenomena inevitably had serious repercussions at Rome. The power vacuum that ensued upon the death of Charles the Bald in 877 also badly weakened the papacy, which had derived much of its local influence and prestige from its role as power-player in Carolingian geopolitics, and primary intermediary between the Roman collective and north-central Italy's Frankish sovereigns. Meanwhile, Italian political fragmentation provoked economic dislocations and breakdowns in law and order, which in turn diminished the flow of visitors, pilgrims, and merchants on the roads to Rome, along with the heaps of foreign cash that had sustained much of Rome's Carolingian-era 'renaissance.' Foreign raiders can only have compounded the problem; worse, they caused real damage – just how much is impossible to know – to the rural holdings that were far and away the most important and reliable source of wealth for the Church and nobility of Rome, and which supplied most of the foodstuffs that fed the Roman populace. Seaborne commerce, meanwhile, was severely limited by the strong Muslim presence in the Tyrrhenian Sea. As for the cityscape, the years around 900 cannot have been kind: Lack of central leadership, chronic shortages of funds, and the unsettled situation in Rome's rural hinterland all boded ill for the effective stewardship of urban monuments and infrastructure. The Lateran Cathedral itself was open to the elements for years after its roof collapsed "from the altar to the front entrance" in 896/97; in 898, Pope John IX complained that he was unable to fix it because "malicious people" (*malitiosi homines*) had made it impossible to obtain new roof beams from the forests of the

Appenines. The essential repairs were accomplished only a decade later under Sergius III (r. 904–11).[11]

However, while the period circa 880–910 in particular was manifestly difficult – unusually so – at Rome, it would be unwise to exaggerate the severity and especially the duration of the crisis. The old conception of the whole 10th century as a period of unremitting chaos and misery both in Italy and at Rome has rightly been revised in more recent scholarship. Whatever they did outside the walls, no "Saracen" or "Magyar" raiders ever made it inside, nor did the Italian and German sovereigns who periodically descended on the city engage in wholesale pillage or destruction. As for civic governance, for all that the independence of the papacy may have declined as Rome's leading families turned the power of the office to parochial ends, this is not to say that Rome was ungoverned, nor even necessarily worse governed than previously. All signs indeed point to considerable administrative continuity throughout the 10th and earlier 11th centuries, much of which saw lengthy periods of stable rule under lay leaders capable of achieving a high degree of consensus, beginning with the family of Theophylact, the leading political power-player of his day on the Roman scene, who was instrumental in ensuring the election of Pope Sergius III in 904.[12]

Already a ranking member of the Lateran bureaucracy as "Palatine judge" (*iudex Palatinus*), Theophylact became both *vestararius*, a kind of high chamberlain of the Lateran Palace, and *magister militum*, head of the Roman militia, upon the elevation of Sergius III. He later took the additional titles "most glorious duke" (*gloriosissimus dux*) and "senator of the Romans" (*senator Romanorum*), while his wife, Theodora, styled herself *vestararissa*. After the death of Theophylact, around 925, his family retained its primacy in Roman affairs, first under his and Theodora's daughter, Marozia, who married in succession a duke of Spoleto, a margrave of Tuscany, and a king (Ugo of Provence, king of Italy from 927 to 46), deposed one pope, made another pope of one son from her first marriage, and was finally deposed and imprisoned by another son, Alberic II. As "prince" (*princeps*) and "senator" of the Romans, Alberic ruled Rome largely free of external interference from 932 until his death in 954. The long years of his hegemony were a time of unusual peace, stability, and perhaps gradually increasing prosperity in Rome and the surrounding territories under Roman control. On his deathbed, he swore the Roman nobility to make his young son Octavian (note the ringing antiquarian pretentions of the name!) his successor as *princeps*, and to appoint him pope upon the death of the incumbent. Octavian thus became Pope John XII in 955, at about 20 years of age, and reigned supreme until the arrival of the Saxon king Otto I at the head of an army in 963. After Octavian/John died in the following year while Otto and his troops remained in Italy, he was replaced by pontiffs more congenial to the Saxon monarch (Leo VIII, r. 964–5, and John XIII, r. 965–72). Under the Ottonian/Saxon dynasty (until 1024) and their Salian successors, Rome again passed under the nominal suzerainty of sovereigns based north of the Alps, most of whom came to the city at least once, to be anointed "Emperor of the Romans" at St. Peter's, but rarely stayed long. (The exception was the young Emperor Otto III, who spent much of the years between 998 and his premature death in 1002 in Rome, which he seems to have envisioned as his imperial capital – another sign of Rome's enduring symbolic appeal, and the pull it exerted on ambitious foreign potentates.)[13]

Otherwise, day-to-day rule remained in the hands of Roman nobles, in particular the descendants of Theophylact, from whose ranks both popes (often) and the holders of the leading civic dignities such as the urban prefecture (usually) came. In the late 10th century, an interrelated group oversimplistically identified as the "Crescenzi" family predominated, taking titles such as "patrician" and "senator of all the Romans," and using their close links with a series of popes (notably John XIII, r. 965–72; and Benedict VII, r. 974–84) to obtain concessions on Church properties across Lazio, transforming them into rural strongholds and sources of wealth. After the death in 1012 of Giovanni di Crescenzio, the last of the line to rule as "patrician" of the Romans, local primacy passed to another branch of Theophylact's descendants, the counts of Tusculum, a clan with roots, and extensive landholdings, in the countryside southeast of the city. The so-called "Tuscolani" family monopolized the papacy by installing three of its own on the pontifical throne: two sons of Gregory of Tusculum as Benedict VIII (r. 1012–24) and John XIX (r. 1024–32), and their nephew as Benedict IX (r. 1032–45). Only following the civil strife of 1044/5, and the "German coup" that put a series of foreign-born popes on the throne from 1046, was the local nobility's virtual monopoly of the papacy, the higher ranks of the clergy, and the Lateran bureaucracy seriously curtailed.[14]

But, again: for much of this long span, notably during the primacy of Theophylact, the 22 years of Alberic's hegemony, and most of the three decades of Tuscolani ascendancy after 1012, there is no reason to think that Rome was not as stably and efficiently governed as it had been under the powerful popes of the 8th and 9th centuries. Further, while popes and lay rulers came and went, Rome's administrative and military hierarchies, and the upper crust of aristocratic families that dominated them, went on much as they had for centuries. The bureaucratic apparatus at the Lateran palace was run by a cadre of seven senior officials (*primicerius, secundicerius, sacellarius, arcarius, primus defensor/primicerius defensorum, nomenclator, protoscriniarius*) collectively referred to as the *iudices de clero* or *iudices palatini*. Their counterparts outside of the Lateran administration were the *iudices de militia*, the commanders of the Roman militia and leaders of the citizenry, which since Byzantine times had been grouped into perhaps ten or twelve local subdivisions, the *scholae* of the *militia*. Both the "clerical" and the "military" offices were, in practice, filled by members of the same constellation of noble families that collectively constituted Rome's quasi-hereditary ruling class, often generically called the *primates romani*. The parallel hierarchies were closely intertwined, and at times nearly indistinguishable, with the same individuals often holding offices both *de clero* and *de militia*, sometimes even both at once, as Theophylact did after 904. From the 8th century through the first half of the 11th, the composition, titles, and powers of this group remained quite consistent, as far as we can tell: they were the 'deep state' that persisted despite whatever transient events ruffled the surface of Roman politics. Systemic change came only later, from the mid 11th century.[15]

This, then, is the historical background against which we have to evaluate Rome's urban evolution in the 10th and earlier 11th centuries, as we try to make sense of the limited written sources and the expanding body of archaeological material. By way of preface to the more detailed topographical excursus that follows, I would again stress that the evidence currently available, the material record included, suggests that "conservatism and stasis" is a better way to conceptualize the Roman situation in this period than "Dark Ages and crisis." Further, I suspect that the first, tentative beginnings of economic and demographic recovery after the real crisis years c. 880–910 were occurring already in the mid to late 10th century. This is by no means to say that Rome was a prosperous, well-connected place in the later 10th century – the apparent scarcity of precious metals in circulation and, still more, the almost total absence of imported ceramics show that the city was surviving predominantly on its own, local resources. Nonetheless, I think there are signs that at Rome, as elsewhere in Italy and western Europe, the economic and demographic expansion that all agree was underway by the 11th century had roots stretching farther back into the 10th. Such signs, discussed below in more detail, include the apparent expansion of areas under intensive cultivation, especially vineyards, in the urban periphery; the existence of bustling neighborhoods given over to productive activities and commerce that appear in documents by the early 11th century, which presumably did not materialize from nowhere after c. 1000; and the substantial and probably growing quantities of thick-glazed ceramics being produced in the city and its environs.[16]

When possible, I will rely on the results of recent archaeological work, which, however, involves only a tiny portion of the city, comprising a smattering of sites that are limited in area and scattered about more or less at random. In Rome, one generally excavates not where one would most wish to dig, but rather where and when it becomes possible to do so, in open areas or in connection with construction projects. Most of the medieval city will always be hidden beneath the crowded sprawl of the modern metropolis. Thus, for all its capacity to offer genuinely new and often surprising insights, archaeology mainly provides suggestive vignettes, scattered windows onto a diffuse urban organism whose connecting tissues remain mostly invisible.

Much the same can be said for the written record, the more so in our period because of the increasing prevalence of a new type of material that helps compensate for the deficiencies of the narrative sources: documents preserved in the archives of Roman churches and monasteries. They are mainly contracts involving the sale, lease, or donation of properties, or records of legal actions stemming from disputes over ownership and rights of use. After a bare handful in the 8th and 9th centuries, their numbers increase gradually but steadily over the course of the 10th and 11th – another sign that not all was doom and gloom – though they become really plentiful only starting in the 12th. (The increase in preserved 10th-century acts relative to the preceding period must be treated with caution, however, as it was precisely then that parchment gradually replaced the far less durable papyrus previously used; nonetheless, real growth in documentary output was clearly occurring by the late 10th/early 11th century, a steadily rising curve that may well begin still earlier.) These contracts are extremely useful in that they tend to describe the property being transacted in some detail, along with its confines, including the other properties or features that bounded it on all sides. Most of Rome's medieval archives are lost, however, such that coverage across much of the city center and the surrounding countryside is poor or nonexistent. As with the material remains, we get scattered islands of light separated by larger voids: because the holdings of religious institutions tended to be concentrated in discrete areas, the loss of an archive frequently casts a pall of invisibility over the entire zone where the properties of the parent institution clustered. The flip side of the coin, fortunately, is that those collections of documents that do survive often present a fine-grained panorama of a particular region. Such zones are few and far between in the 10th and earlier 11th centuries, however, which puts the handful that do exist front and center of any attempt to reconstruct the appearance of the cityscape.[17]

We now turn to that attempt, concentrating on several of the zones best attested in the documents and/or the archaeological record, all located in a broad swath across the central, more densely inhabited portion of the walled circuit. We begin with two zones in the far east situated in close proximity to the city walls: the neighborhood of Porta Maggiore on the Esquiline, and the Caelian Hill to the south, including the area around Porta Metronia at the foot of its eastern slopes. Moving west from there, we will pause in the vicinity of the Colosseum and the eastern end of the Forum, around the old temple of Venus and Rome. Next comes the contiguous area of the imperial forums and the northern foot of the Capitoline Hill, where the most extensive recent excavations have occurred. Finally, we will continue west into the Campus Martius and on across the Tiber to the Vatican and Trastevere.

What we know about the surroundings of Porta Maggiore in the 10th and early 11th centuries comes almost exclusively from the fortuitous survival of property documents from the archive of the great monastery of Saints Benedict and Scholastica at Subiaco in the Sabina, c. 50 km east of Rome, whose records happen to be preserved and remarkably complete precisely for the period in question. The monastery acquired a number of properties inside and outside the gate starting in the second quarter of the 10th century, and these possessions and their environs are described in enough detail to give a reasonable idea of the general pattern of settlement and land use. It should be stressed from the outset, as Robert Coates-Stephens has done, that the only obviously remarkable thing about this small sector of the city is the quality of the surviving documentation that relates to it, which makes it look like a flourishing island in the midst of a void. But the void is one of evidence – if archives of documents pertaining to the surrounding areas survived, some might well look similarly vibrant.[18]

The land immediately outside the gate, bordering the city walls and extending across the widening triangle of land between the Via Praenestina and Via Labicana, was devoted to agriculture and pasturage. It was divided into parcels of widely varying size that belonged

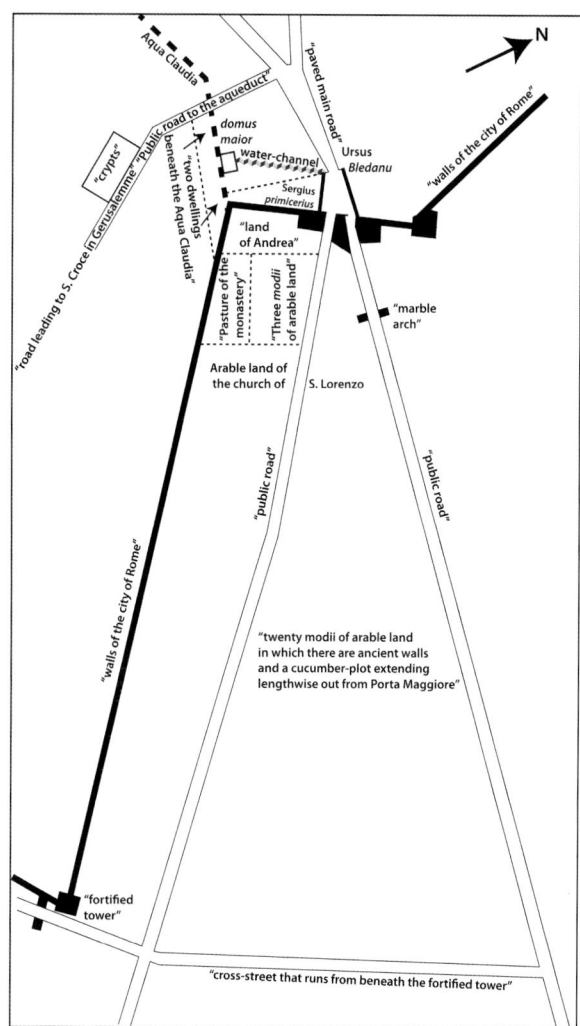

Figure 5.1 The vicinity of Porta Maggiore around the year 1000, based on the Subiaco documents. (Redrawn from Coates-Stephens 2004, fig. 92.)

both to individual proprietors and religious institutions (Subiaco, the nearby church of S. Lorenzo *fuori le mura*, the Lateran *schola cantorum*), and interspersed with standing remains of ancient structures (*parietinis desertis*). Most of it was given over to cultivation of grain (*terra sationale/sementaricia*), though we also hear of a pasture (*pratum*) and a cucumber plot, both owned by Subiaco (Fig. 5.1).[19]

Inside the walls, the landscape was distinctly different. Much of the area was occupied by adjoining or proximate residential lots, consisting

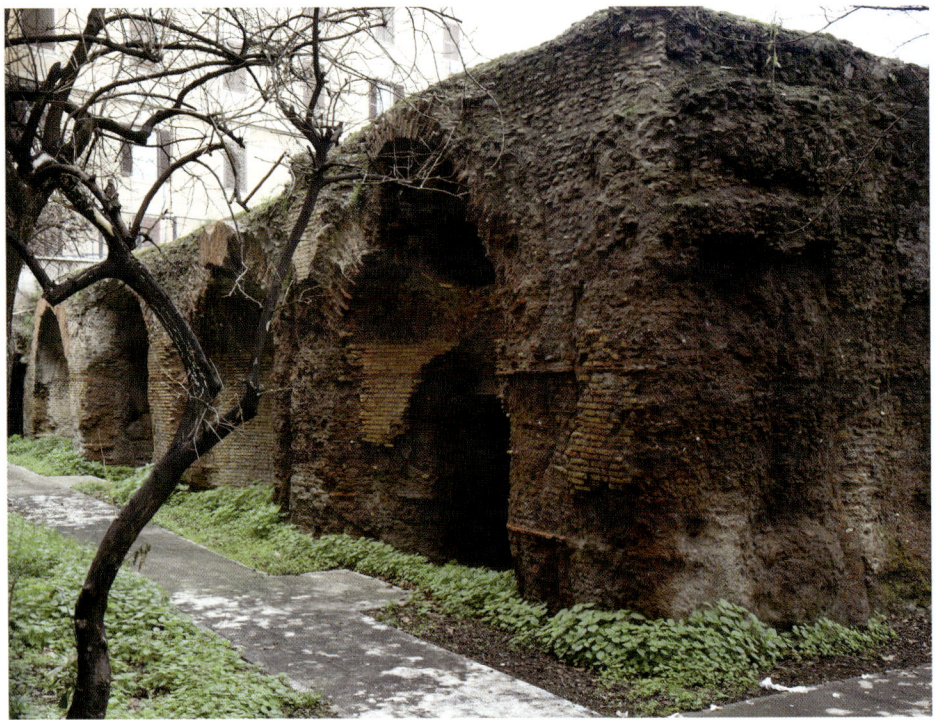

Figure 5.2 The concrete-vaulted cisterns of the Terme Eleniane (*thermae Helenianae*), built in the later Severan period but restored by empress Helena, mother of Constantine (see Palladino 1996). Located along the road leading from the area of Porta Maggiore to S. Croce in Gerusalemme (today's Via Eleniana), they may be those "crypts" (*griptis*) mentioned in the Subiaco documents that are marked on fig. 5.1. (Author.)

of freestanding houses with enclosed yards at front and/or rear, surrounded and separated from each other by a patchwork of gardens, orchards, and vineyards. Throughout ran prominent pieces of infrastructure inherited from antiquity: the city walls and the Porta Maggiore itself, with its fortified interior courtyard; the main Roman road leading through the gate and a smaller cross street that ran south toward S. Croce in Gerusalemme; and, towering over the houses, the arcades of the Aqua Claudia, which entered the walls by the gate and from there turned south, running toward the Lateran and on over the summit of the Caelian Hill on its way toward the Palatine. Repaired by Hadrian I in the 770s, it was still flowing in 1006 in sufficient quantity to power a water mill located just inside the gate; the runoff from the mill was channeled through a conduit mentioned as the boundary between two properties. Lesser vestiges of the ancient city were scattered throughout this landscape, crumbling walls (*parietinis*) and still-usable chambers covered by concrete vaults (*cryptis*) (Fig. 5.2).[20]

The most prestigious residential holding was the so-called *domus maior*, a compound occupying an irregular quadrilateral bounded on two sides by the intersecting Roman roads, on the third by the arcades of the aqueduct, and on the fourth, nearest the city walls and gate, by gardens and houses that belonged to the *primicerius* Sergius. It first appears in 924, when Sergius and his wife bequeathed it to Florus, a priest attached to the nearby monastery of S. Vito. The complex featured a main house consisting at least partially of an ancient structure in concrete (*signino opere*), which contained or adjoined an oratory dedicated to St. Theodore. There was an enclosed yard in front, while at the rear it was abutted by ruinous ancient walls and a garden with fruit trees. In 937, this complex passed to a certain Marozia, a nun evidently of very elevated social standing, who subsequently acquired adjoining properties to create a substantial contiguous holding. By 952, when Marozia in turn gave it all to Subiaco, there were "four conjoined dwellings" (*quattor ... domoras iunctas*) along with the oratory of Theodore and two enclosed yards, a smaller and a larger said to contain an oven and various subsidiary buildings; the adjoining garden plot by then had grapevines as well as fruit trees. The property also included the water mill mentioned in the document of 1006, which Coates-Stephens tentatively locates on the podium of a large, circular mausoleum whose remains abutted the aqueduct; the runoff channel would then be the vaulted passageway lined in waterproof plaster (with medieval graffiti incised in the plaster) that opens out of what remains of the podium of the mausoleum. The description of the *domus maior* of 924 as containing concrete construction (*signino opere*) and abutting prominent ruins at the rear may mean that the chapel and the "four conjoined dwellings" of 952 were all located on the podium of the mausoleum itself, which would then place the vineyard-orchards and courtyards between it and the Porta Maggiore, roughly along the line of the channel (Fig. 5.1, above).[21]

This compact ensemble of ancient ruins and monuments, houses, oratory, gardens, vineyards, and orchards bordered on other residential properties on at least three of its four sides. To the east, toward Porta Maggiore, there were the houses that once belonged to the *primicerius* Sergius, mentioned above. To the north, along the main road through the gate, there was, by 952, the house of a certain Ursus *bledanu*. And to the south, on the far side of the aqueduct arcade, there was another family compound that had once belonged to two members of the same family, Iohannis and Stephano *de grifi*, both dead by 958. Here were two houses with attached yards containing gardens and a grape arbor (*pergula*); the property also had an enclosed vineyard with fruit trees, and, nearby, other ancient vaulted structures (*criptis*). It is possible that these houses (marked on Fig. 5.1) are the two mentioned in 937 as being situated "under" – in immediate proximity to – the Aqua Claudia, said to be two-story *domus solaratae* roofed with both tiles and wooden shingles (perhaps a tiled central block with shingled additions or annexes?), presumably of the same basic type as the 9th-century examples in the Forum of Nerva.[22]

The panorama that emerges from these documents is one in which the skeleton of the ancient city deeply conditioned the contours of life in the neighborhood of Porta Maggiore. Its residents still moved along the zone's two principal ancient roads, much of whose Roman-era paving remained intact and visible, at least in the case of the main road running through the gate, which is invariably called the *silex publica* for its black leucite pavers. The Aurelian Wall was the clear line of demarcation that separated the cultivated fields outside it from the residential quarter located just inside. The Aqua Claudia supplied the whole zone with running water, sufficient not only for the domestic needs of the residents but also to power at least one grain mill, and presumably also to irrigate both the farmland immediately outside the walls and the gardens and orchards within. To the extent that this quarter was privileged relative to most of intramural Rome, it was by virtue of its proximity to one of the very few functioning aqueducts, which probably did make it more densely settled and prosperous than other peripheral zones near the city walls that had no access to aqueduct water.

The ancient skeleton, however, had put on new and distinctly medieval flesh. The crumbling hulk of the circular mausoleum inside Porta Maggiore housed a water mill, and perhaps also had the oratory of Theodore with its four conjoined dwellings sprouting from its podium. All of these structures, like the rest of the houses in the neighborhood, were evidently new constructions of the early Middle Ages, though many undoubtedly incorporated some of the ubiquitous remains of ancient masonry that dotted the area. These remains must originally have belonged more to tombs and mausolea than to houses, however: in antiquity, this was primarily a zone of cemeteries, and seems not to have had much in the way of residential construction. So it is that by the 10th century, a sparsely inhabited fringe of the ancient city had transformed into a vibrant residential quarter populated by clerics, monks, and reasonably well-off small landowners, whose dwellings grew up amid the imposing relics of antiquity like mushrooms on a decaying stump.[23]

We now follow the arcades of the Aqua Claudia and the main ancient road that paralleled it, the *via Caelemontana*, southward to the Caelian Hill, the second part of the eastern periphery that can be reconstructed in some detail thanks to the Subiaco archive. In 938, the derelict monastery of S. Erasmo on the Caelian was annexed to Subiaco on the urging of Alberic, along with all of its properties. The monastery, itself located on the summit of the hill near S. Stefano Rotondo and adjacent to the Aqua Claudia, owned numerous properties in the vicinity, extending east down the far slopes of the hill to Porta Metronia and beyond; and more were acquired after its annexation to Benedict's prestigious foundation at Subiaco. Once again, settlement shaped itself around the contours of surviving antique infrastructure, chiefly the Aqua Claudia and the intersecting axes of two main ancient roads. The first was the roughly east–west line of the *via Caelemontana – clivus Scauri*, which paralleled the brick-faced arcades of the aqueduct all the way from Porta Maggiore in the east to the foot of the Palatine in the west, passing the Lateran palace along the way and then traversing the summit of the Caelian.

The second was the "Africa Head" street (*via/vicus capitis Africae*) running north–south across the crown of the hill, from Porta Metronia toward the Colosseum (roughly corresponding to today's Via della Navicella – Via Claudia).

The Caelian as a whole is much better documented archaeologically than Porta Maggiore, especially for the centuries leading up to the period covered by the Subiaco archive. Numerous excavations conducted over the course of the past century collectively indicate that population declined steeply during the 5th century, leading to the virtual abandonment of some areas and progressive decay in others, as we have seen. The remaining inhabitants tended to collect in the vicinity of the two primary street axes, whose importance relative to other roads had already increased markedly after the construction of the Aurelian Wall in the late 3rd century, and the blocking of its subsidiary gates from the beginning of the 5th, which naturally privileged the streets connected with the fifteen-odd main gates that remained open. The few new monuments erected from the 5th century on also clustered along these two roads, including all three of the monumental churches in the area. S. Stefano Rotondo, built in the mid 5th century, and S. Maria in Domnica, built in its current form by Paschal I around 820, were situated at the most strategic point of all, by the junction where the *capitis Africae* road toward Porta Metronia intersected the *via Caelemontana* and the aqueduct. The monastery of S. Erasmo itself, which is first securely attested in the 670s, was also here. Farther west down the *clivus Scauri* was the early 5th-century *titulus Pammachii*, now SS. Giovanni e Paolo (Fig. 5.3). These foundations all persisted in the 10th and early 11th centuries, when the Subiaco documents open their window onto the human and material contours of the region. Abandoned, overgrown fields and expanses of crumbling ancient ruins were a common sight, to be sure, but there were also

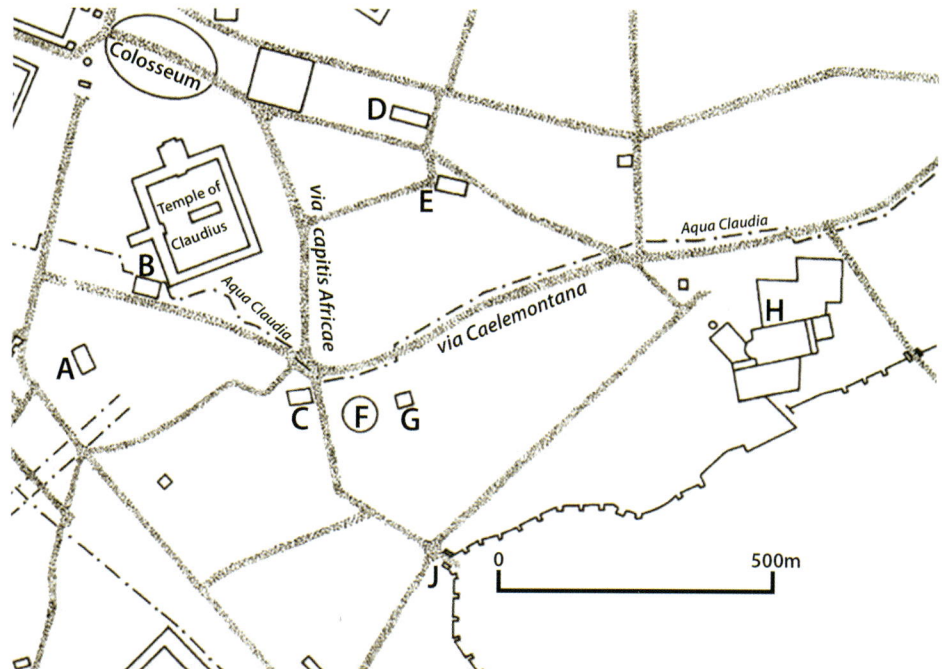

Figure 5.3 Plan of the Caelian in the early Middle Ages. A: S. Andrea/S. Gregorio Magno; B: SS. Giovanni e Paolo; C: S. Maria in Domnica; D: S. Cecilia; E: S. Clemente; F: S. Stefano Rotondo; G: S. Erasmo; H: Lateran cathedral and palace; J: Porta Metronia (Plan by R. Meneghini and R. Santangeli Valenzani, modified by author.)

ample tracts of cultivated land, gardens, olive and fruit trees, and eventually vineyards, which commingled with dwellings ranging from solidly constructed two-story houses to humble one-story hovels, all usually located along the main roads.[24]

S. Erasmo is most fully described in the document of 938 that annexed it to Subiaco, "with its cells or dwellings, and its perimeter-walls and with all its buildings and gardens or grain-fields with olive-trees and other kinds of fruit-trees around the monastery." On one side it was bordered by the *curtis*-complex of the nobleman (*magnificus vir*) Georgius, a road, the house of the middling citizen (*vir honestus*) Petrus, still more (*plures*) houses belonging to unidentified others, ancient walls and "crypts," and a plot of arable land. On the second side were the fields of the priest Leo and the road to Porta Metronia; on the third, the grainfields of the heirs of a certain Hadrian, deceased, who lived near the Markets of Trajan, and the garden/vineyard of the noblewoman Sergia; and on the fourth, another road

and a residential complex that included an oratory of Saints Cosmas and Damian. We learn more about this last property from another document that records its donation to S. Erasmo in 978 by the legatees of a deceased couple: there was a two-story house roofed with tile and shingle, the oratory, an interior courtyard, a garden in front with a fig tree, and an enclosed yard with a grape arbor, all in close proximity to the Aqua Claudia. One striking thing about this description is the density of habitation along one side of the monastery, where there must have been some five or six houses, given the mention of "several" more in addition to the large *curtis*-compound of Georgius and the house of Petrus. The diverse group of named individuals also suggests a rather vibrant local society that included noblemen and -women, property owners of lesser stature, members of the clergy, and surely also the peasants and day laborers who worked the fields, though not surprisingly they are scarcely represented in the property documents.[25]

A number of other houses in the neighborhood of S. Erasmo were very substantial. In addition to the *curtis* of Georgius and the complex with the oratory of Cosmas and Damian, we hear in 965 of another place on the road to Porta Metronia, "two stories high with a tile roof … with an enclosure in front with a grape-arbor [*pergula*], a well, and a marble staircase" that sounds very much like the houses in the Forum of Nerva, which also had external stairways leading to the upper story, one in reused marble blocks. Even some of the one-story houses were apparently quite solid, enough so to be roofed at least partially in tile, the weight of which can only have been supported by stone walls and strong roof timbers.[26]

The mixture of abandoned fields and ruins, cultivated plots, and houses – even clusters of houses – along the principal roads is a consistent feature of the Subiaco documents throughout the period they cover. One of the earliest texts in the collection, from 857, records the lease of another property that faced onto the road to Porta Metronia, "a reasonably-sized vacant plot of land with an enclosure suitable for building a house, and a little garden with running water in the middle among the crypts, and another empty plot." It was bordered on one side by abandoned buildings belonging to S. Erasmo, on the second by the road to Porta Metronia, on the third by a pipe or conduit carrying running water from the aqueduct, and on the fourth by additional derelict ruins that belonged to a woman called Theodula. Note again the steady availability of fresh water from the Aqua Claudia![27]

Activity in the area seems to pick up from the mid 10th century. The sequence of documents grows progressively denser, suggesting that demand for land was increasing, and we hear of land being put under more intensive cultivation than before. Especially notable is the proliferation of vineyards, labor-intensive enterprises that need constant attention over a period of years even before they start to produce. They require a level of long-term planning and investment, in other words, considerably beyond what is involved in tending the gardens and arable fields prevalent in the earlier texts. On the Caelian proper inside the walls, they become common from the 960s, being mostly located in the vicinity of a field (*campus*) along the road to Porta Metronia called *decenniae* (*ad decennias*, etc.) and said in 952 to belong to the nearby church of SS. Nereo ed Achilleo. S. Erasmo itself became a producer of wine on a substantial scale around the same time: while it had no vineyards at the time of its transfer to Subiaco in 938, by 997 vineyards had been planted on the monastery's grounds, where there was also a dedicated building (*cella vinaria*) for wine production. Such concerted investment in vines, which was not limited to the Caelian, makes sense only if there was a substantial, and apparently increasing, market for wine, and presumably also a growing population of consumers.[28]

The increasing desirability of vineyards (and demand for wine) apparently then prompted grape cultivation to expand farther out, beyond Porta Metronia, from the late 10th century. Early descriptions of land outside the gate, in 943 and 968, refer exclusively to pastures and fields of grain. Vineyards make their first appearance in 993, when S. Erasmo leased to Crescentius *murcapullo* a swath of gardens and existing vineyards outside Porta Metronia. Thereafter, wine production outside the gate surged, such that by the 1020s and 1030s, there are multiple mentions of vineyards surrounded by other vineyards on three or all four sides.[29]

The broad similarities between the Caelian and the neighborhood at Porta Maggiore will by now be apparent. As at Porta Maggiore, settlement (mixed with cultivation and ruins) was invariably located inside the Aurelian Wall, in close proximity to a gate that gave access to the exclusively agrarian sector outside. The most frequented roads were again the ancient ones connected to nearby gates (the Porta Asinaria/S. Giovanni near the Lateran, just off the *Caelemontana*, and the Porta Metronia by way of the *capitis Africae*), along which the majority of local inhabitants also lived. (Unlike the Via Praenestina-Labicana at Porta Maggiore, however, the *capitis Africae* had lost its ancient pavement, replaced by around 800 with a superimposed roadbed in coarse gravel and potsherds.) As at Porta Maggiore, so too on the Caelian, fresh water supplied by the Aqua Claudia was integral to the life of the neighborhood. Along with the Claudia itself, which directly supplied properties along the *via Caelemontana*, there was also the branch line that diverged to follow the intersecting axis of the *via capitis Africae* to Porta Metronia. Attested as early as 857 and as late as 1011, this pipe or conduit (*fistula*) surely contributed to the relatively intensive exploitation of the land along the road, supplying both houses and, increasingly, vineyards. The flow presumably continued on to Porta Metronia and perhaps beyond, where it might have helped irrigate the new vineyards. In 993, we hear of a marsh and fishpond located just outside the gate in direct proximity to the walls – one wonders if the old defensive ditch outside the wall had become a catchment basin for the runoff.[30]

It is hard to escape the conclusion that the Aqua Claudia was a lifeline across a long stretch of Rome's eastern suburbs during the period covered in the Subiaco archive. Among all the residential properties represented, the proportion located in direct communication with the aqueduct or a branch line thereof is strikingly high. This is surely significant: At a time when Rome's population was near historic lows, most of the extensive tract from the Caelian north to Porta Maggiore – the linear distance between S. Erasmo and Porta Maggiore is about 2 km – cannot have been densely occupied. Rather, it looks as though the aqueduct itself was a real attraction, sufficient to entice Romans with the means to own property and build dwellings, including some very substantial ones, to establish themselves nearby and – somehow, by hook or by crook – tap into it.[31]

The Subiaco archive unfortunately peters out in the mid 11th century, such that it reveals neither when the Aqua Claudia finally went out of use, nor what became of the adjacent neighborhoods around Porta Maggiore and S. Erasmo once it did. Still flowing in 1006 (and probably 1011), the aqueduct was presumably defunct by the early 12th century, when pope Callixtus II (r. 1119–24) diverted water from broken aqueducts miles outside the city into a newly dug canal, the Acqua Marana, to furnish the Lateran palace and its annexes with running water. This substantial project must have been undertaken after the failure of the Claudia, one of whose main functions in the early Middle Ages was to supply the Lateran; the aqueduct will therefore have ceased flowing sometime during the 11th century. The best guess is that the neighborhoods around it began to empty out at about the same time. Archaeological remains of later medieval settlement are almost nonexistent at Porta Maggiore and on the Caelian, and as we will see in Chapter 6, indicators across the city point to the 11th century as the inflection point when Rome's previously diffuse settlement landscape began to contract into a denser nucleus in the low-lying plains between the slopes of the Capitoline Hill and the Tiber in the west, leaving the hills in the eastern half of the intramural area mostly uninhabited. The failure of the Claudia, and the Iobia, too, which together had supplied much of Rome's eastern and southern periphery, may thus be among the factors that contributed to the westward – riverward – shift of settlement, though it was hardly the only one.[32]

We jump now to the ancient Show Area in the city center, from the Colosseum across the

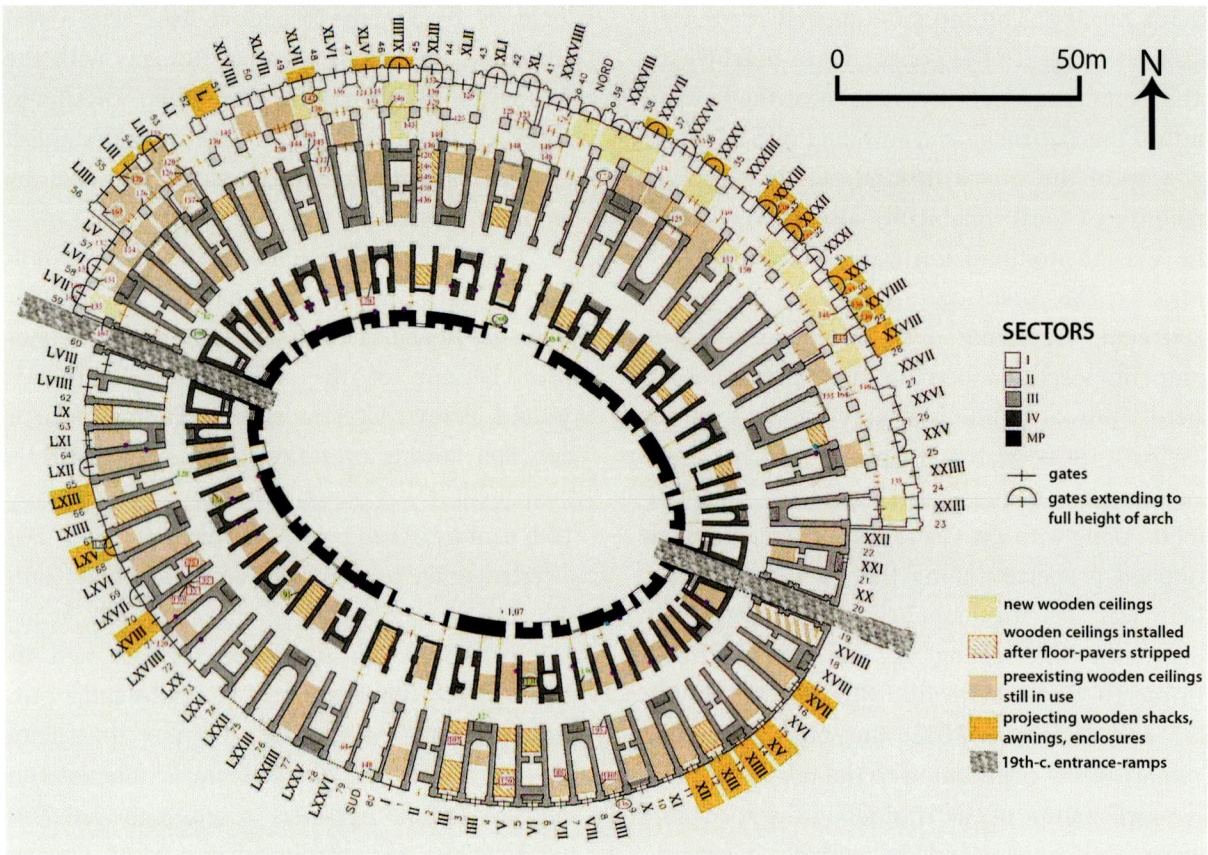

Figure 5.4 The ground floor of the Colosseum in the 11th century. The reconstruction of features is based mostly on cuttings made in floors and rising walls, and the elevations of the wall cuttings, which rose gradually over time along with ground levels, but might again drop suddenly where the ancient travertine pavers were dug out and stripped. (Modified from Rea [ed.] 2002, p. 310, fig. 40.)

imperial forums to the slopes of the Capitoline Hill, on the eastern edge of what would develop into the heart of the later-medieval *abitato*. Then as now, the Colosseum was the preeminent landmark. By the 11th century, it was subdivided into a warren of properties partly owned by two nearby churches, S. Maria in Pallara on the Palatine and S. Maria Nova on the podium of the Temple of Venus and Rome. Thanks to the archive of S. Maria Nova, the only entity near the Forum to preserve a substantial collection of medieval documents, we know quite a lot about the tenants of S. Maria who occupied the substructures of the amphitheater, which were already bustling with activity by the first half of the 11th century. The vaulted, wedge-shaped chambers and passageways radiating out from the oval of the arena, always called *cryptae*, were held by individual tenants and used variously as workshops, stables and hayricks, storerooms, and (probably occasional) living quarters for service personnel (Fig. 5.4). Chambers on upper floors may have been more continuously inhabited. Already in 1038, the first *crypta* mentioned was surrounded on three sides by other tenanted *cryptae*, while the fourth opened onto the external esplanade; the whole wedge must therefore have been divided crosswise, with another occupant holding the innermost portion. The arena itself remained at least partially unobstructed, serving as a kind of common yard for the tenants of the *cryptae* that opened onto it, via apertures cut into

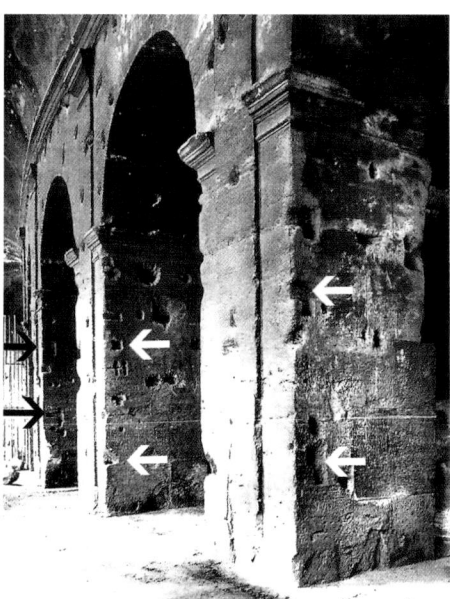 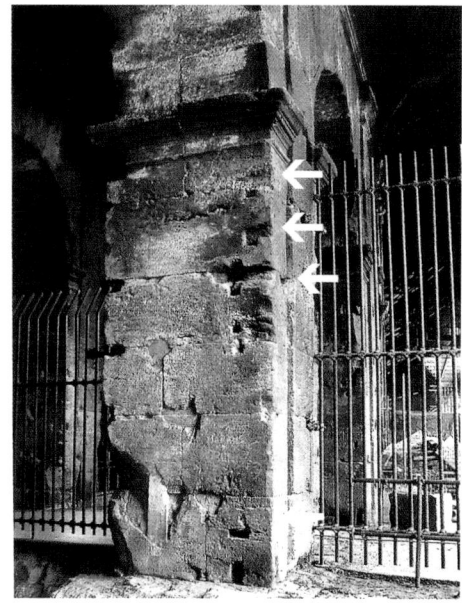

Figure 5.5 Left: sockets for the crossbeams of the removable wooden barriers enclosing bays XXXII, XXXIII, and XXXIIII in Sector 2 (the inner face of the outer ambulatory). Right: bay XLVI in Sector 2: successively rising sockets for the crossbeams of the wooden partition. (For locations of sectors and bays, see fig. 5.4.) (Rea [ed.] 2002, p. 309, figs. 37–8.)

the podium wall. Surviving scars on the masonry throughout the edifice show that the 'crypts' were provided with wooden lofts and ceilings laid on rafters socketed into the walls, while gates, fences, and flimsy stone partitions were used to subdivide or close off interior spaces (Fig. 5.5). Abundant quantities of 10th- and 11th-century ceramics found in three ground-floor 'wedges' in the SE sector of the building (III, VIIII, and X on Fig. 5.4), excavated in 2011–15, provide tangible signs of a dense human presence that substantially predates its earliest appearance in the documents. Little more can be said archaeologically, unfortunately, because the ancient travertine pavers on the ground floor of the Colosseum were removed during the later 11th and 12th centuries, obliterating the stratigraphy of the older deposits.[33]

This towering bastion of 'pagan' Rome was surrounded by a halo of at least six small churches and oratories; yet another, S. Salvatore *in rota Colisei*, sat somewhere inside the arena. None of them survive, and though they only appear in written sources from the 12th century on, some of them surely existed by the 10th. One of the most suggestive extant traces is a reused travertine block from the Colosseum, discovered just north of the building in 1895, bearing a high-quality fragment of fresco depicting two male saints, probably the martyred Roman deacons Lawrence and Stephen (Fig. 5.6). Giulia Bordi dates it to the third quarter of the 10th century, based in part on its close stylistic affinities with the fresco cycle of S. Maria in Pallara on the Palatine, co-owner of the Colosseum in this era; the church by the Colosseum that it once decorated may even have been an affiliate of the mother community, located but a few hundred meters away on the northeast slopes of the Palatine and easily visible from the Colosseum. In any case, as there are no traces of older painting under the visible fresco, the logical assumption is that the church to which the frescoed block belonged was built around the time the painting was done.[34]

S. Maria in Pallara (now S. Sebastiano al Palatino) is itself the only extant 10th-century church in Rome. The building was heavily

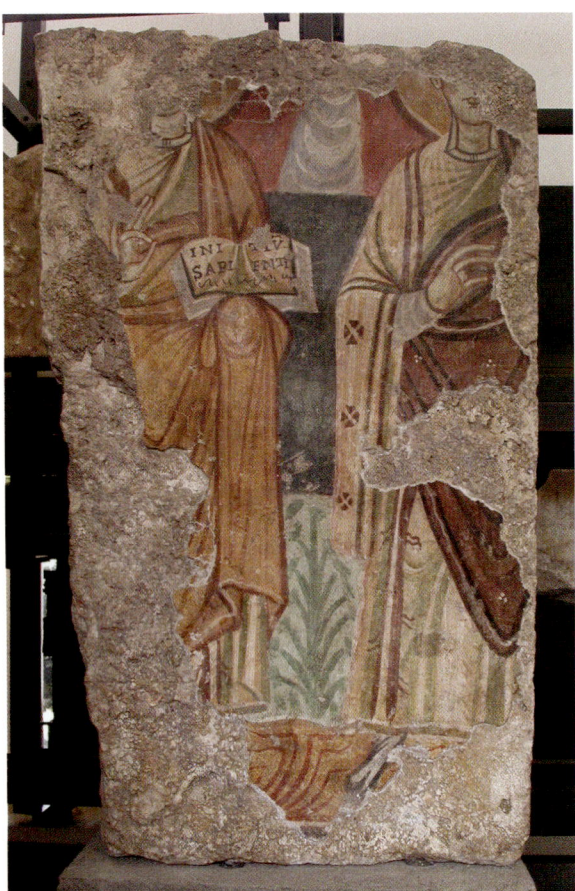

Figure 5.6 10th-century fresco on a reused block from the Colosseum: Saints Lawrence and Stephen? Maximum dimensions 109 × 66 cm. (Photo courtesy of Giulia Bordi.)

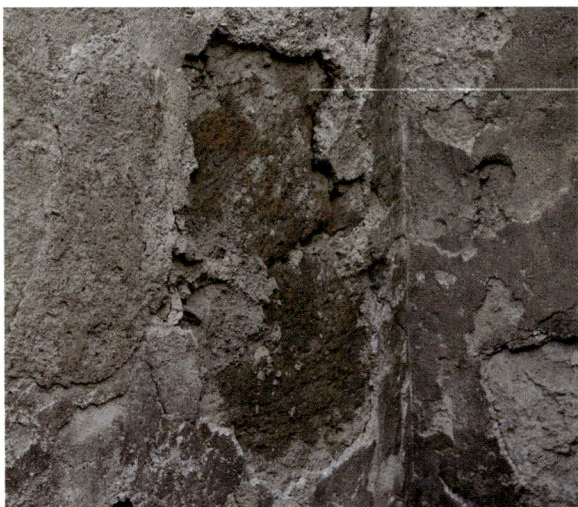

Figure 5.7 The exterior of the apse of S. Maria in Pallara (now S. Sebastiano al Palatino), masonry in large blocks of reused tuff visible beneath modern plaster. (Photo by author, thanks to the kindness of the sisters of the Fraternità Monastica di Gerusalemme.)

restored in the 17th century, concealing much of the original structure and hindering a proper architectural study, but the walls are built partly in a rough *opus quadratum* of recycled blocks that cannot predate the mid 8th century. As there are no signs of any decoration beneath the late 10th-century fresco cycle, it is best to imagine the building as a whole as a product of the later 10th century, for the church cannot have remained undecorated long after its construction. The patron was a prosperous physician, Petrus *medicus*, whose name appeared twice in painted inscriptions included with the frescoes of the apse and apse arch; he and his wife Johanna endowed both the church and the new Benedictine monastery to which it was attached. He was certainly dead by 999, and possibly as early as 973, which puts the construction of the church and monastery around the third quarter of the 10th century.[35]

As Rome's only surviving 10th-century church, S. Maria in Pallara offers a crucial, albeit very limited, perspective on religious architecture and church decoration. It was a small building, c. 15 × 7.5 m according to descriptions that precede the 17th-c. remodeling, with a single nave capped by a semicircular apse. In terms both of its structure and its decoration, it accords well with our characterization of the 10th century as an era connected more closely to the early medieval past than the high medieval future. The sections of masonry in recycled tuff blocks, such as the apse and surrounding rear wall, are so similar to the characteristic stuff of the later 8th and 9th centuries that some have been tempted to antedate its construction primarily on this basis alone (Fig. 5.7). But it is important to note that such masonry continued in regular use at least through the 10th century, giving way to new techniques only during the 11th. (The abundance of extant structures erected during the early medieval building boom c. 780–860 hardly justifies the *a priori* dating of all similar walls to the same period; such *a priori* assumptions are likely in fact to make the 10th century seem darker relative to the 9th than it really was, and should be avoided!) As for its decoration, Laura Marchiori has shown that the preserved frescoes of the apse and apse arch have more in common, in terms of style and iconography, with the decorative programs in Rome's 8th- and 9th-century churches than with those of the later 11th and 12th, and fit well on stylistic grounds in the later 10th century (Fig. 5.8). For all that it is smaller and less opulent than the grand churches built in the 9th century and again in the 12th, S. Maria in Pallara nonetheless represents a significant investment in the ecclesiastical geography of the neighborhood, an investment made, be it also noted, by a lay patron, at a time when evidence of papal patronage is very scant. Indeed, Robert Coates-Stephens has stressed that not a single one of the churches he counts as possibly or certainly built during the 10th century "was the result of papal funding or even papal initiative."[36]

The rest of the neighborhood between the Colosseum and the eastern end of the Forum also seems to have been a fairly vibrant place by the late 10th/early 11th century, insofar as we can tell from the handful of documents in the S. Maria Nova archive (a total of 15 for the period 982–1052). The church owned much of its surroundings, from the Colosseum westward into the Forum, past the Basilica of Maxentius and on down the Via Sacra, which remained the primary artery connecting the Forum to the Colosseum and, along the *via maior*, to the Lateran complex beyond, gaining new importance during the early Middle Ages as the setting

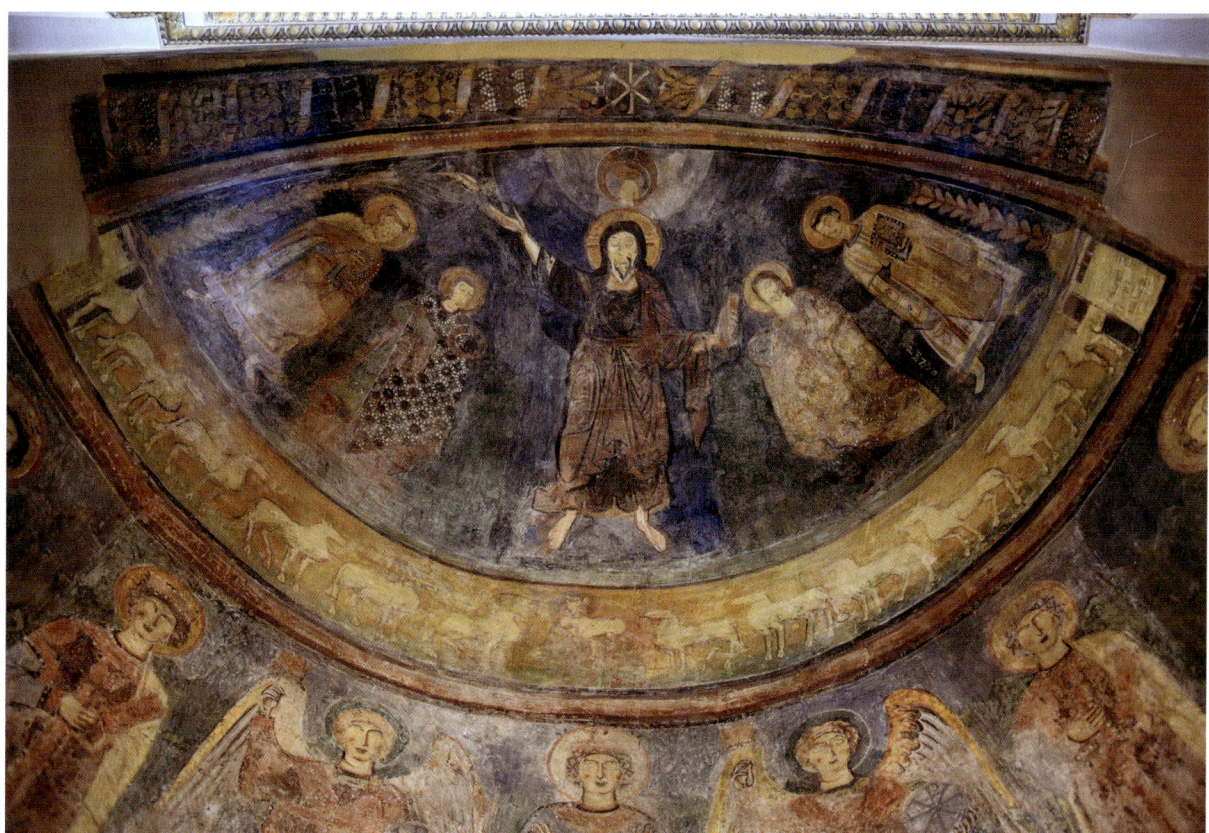

Figure 5.8 The late 10th-century fresco program in the apse of S. Maria in Pallara/S. Sebastiano al Palatino. (Photo by author, thanks to the kindness of the sisters of the Fraternità Monastica di Gerusalemme.)

for papal processions that passed back and forth between the Lateran and St. Peter's. People lived among and atop the ancient monuments, in houses surrounded by gardens, orchards, and vineyards. The Basilica of Maxentius, most of which had already collapsed, probably in the earthquakes of the 9th century, was surrounded by gardens and house plots. More houses and gardens bordered the podium of the adjacent Temple of Venus and Rome, which also belonged to S. Maria Nova. By 982, there were at least three residences *in templum quod vocatur Romuleum*, thus possibly atop the podium itself, on the half facing the Colosseum that was not occupied by the church; one at least was two stories high, with a tile roof and marble staircase. Other tenants of the church rented vaulted 'crypts' nearby, some facing onto the Via Sacra itself and others inside or near the temple podium. These crypts now sprouted wooden-shingled roofs, possibly to extend the usable area, or to keep water from infiltrating the exposed, perhaps cracking concrete vaults beneath.[37]

The inhabitants who appear in the documents were reasonably prosperous professionals, artisans, and small landowners, typical representatives of a Roman "medium elite," as Chris Wickham has recently termed them, that was growing in wealth and numbers from the later 10th century on, as we have already seen on the Caelian. The leading profession in the area before 1050 was metalworking: we encounter a number of people who specialized in bronze and iron, including in 1025 the head (*prior*) of the association of bronzesmiths (*scola errariorum*). The metalworkers would later be joined by members of other professions, notably cobblers and money changers. In 1039, we also get our first glimpse of resident members of the Frangipane family, the potent noble clan that would dominate this sector of the city in the 12th century.[38]

Thus, by the decades around 1000, there was already a sizeable and variegated community around S. Maria Nova that occupied ancient monuments and colonized the interstices between with new housing and cultivated plots. As at Porta Maggiore, a zone characterized in antiquity by public monuments and infrastructure, with little residential occupation, became a living part of the urban fabric in the early Middle Ages, evidently populated by more people than ever before. The group of specialized metalworkers established there must have been producing for a substantial market of consumers drawn from well beyond the immediate neighborhood, and other skilled craftsmen would soon arrive, making the area still busier. More tenants filled the Colosseum. Older religious foundations thrived on growing rental income from their lands and were joined by new or rejuvenated churches and monasteries. This rising tide of population, economic specialization, and – consequently – prosperity cannot have materialized from nowhere around 1000; rather, the process must have its roots earlier, before the widespread advent of documents written on durable parchment that would allow us to see it. Fortunately, the recent excavations just to the west in the imperial forums reveal much more about the evolution of ample swaths of the city center over the course of the 10th century.[39]

After the common upheavals at the forums of Caesar, Augustus, Peace, Nerva, and Trajan from the late 8th to the mid-9th century, when most of their ancient paving was finally removed and their thitherto reasonably pristine enclosures variously transformed into cultivated plots and residential lots, these complexes followed strikingly different trajectories from the late 9th century on. In the Forum of Augustus, after the marble pavement was stripped and the monastery of S. Basilio went up on the podium of the temple of Mars by (probably) the first half of the 9th century, there was little change and few signs of human activity for several centuries thereafter. No permanent structures were built around the temple podium, nor even do the vineyards and orchards present in the other forums seem to have been planted during the 10th and 11th centuries. Sediments washed down from the slopes of the Quirinal gradually accumulated, while the monks on the temple podium went about their daily routines. The Forum of Nerva also preserved the aspect it took on upon becoming a residential neighborhood in the mid 9th century, with continuing occupation of the original houses and garden plots into the 11th century.[40]

The remaining three imperial forums experienced more significant transformations. At the Forum of Peace, already since the 6th century mostly covered by an earthen fill, a massive new deposit of soil around a meter thick was spread across much of the enclosure in the later 9th century, kept in place by a system of retaining walls in drystone masonry. The evident intention was to create better cultivable land. Never built up, the open expanse inside the still standing perimeter walls was given over to the sorts of gardens, vineyards, and orchards that appear around the adjacent Basilica of Maxentius in the S. Maria Nova archive. Unlike the casual accumulations in the Forum of Augustus, the c. 1500 cubic meters of fill deposited here represent a planned and very labor-intensive urban intervention: There was a guiding authority behind the project with a substantial workforce at its disposal, and considerable logistical capabilities.[41]

At the Forum of Caesar, the 9th-century gardens and shacks were buried, in the first half of the 10th century, beneath another thick, intentionally deposited layer of earth, atop which a new residential quarter quickly arose. Five houses of what was probably once a larger cluster turned up in the excavations of the late 1990s, all of them small and ragged one-story affairs, with one or at most two interior rooms separated by a flimsy partition. The largest measured c. 10 × 4 m, and the rest were smaller still. The lower parts of their walls, up to about a meter above ground level, were in rough fragments of stone bonded with a 'mortar' of liquid clay, with the occasional column drum or larger block thrown in for reinforcement at the corners and midpoints of walls. The upper portions, or sometimes the full height of the wall, were in mud-brick or possibly a sort of wattle-and-daub consisting of a light wooden framework slathered with raw clay. Roofs were of wood or thatch (Fig. 5.9). All five lay along a cart path with a bed in compacted cobbles and sherds set atop the same fill the houses were built on, running lengthwise down the middle of the forum and connecting the Via Lata to the west with the Argiletum in the Forum of Nerva to the east. It all looks to have been a sort of low-rent housing development, with roads and small lots laid out in a single, coordinated intervention (Fig. 5.10).[42]

Still more dramatic changes overtook the Forum of Trajan, which had lain vacant for several generations after the removal of its pavement in the mid-9th century, as is clear from the several tens of centimeters of alluvial sediments that gradually collected, as in the neighboring Forum of Augustus, over the concrete underbedding of the missing paving slabs. Toward the middle of the 10th century, the entire area was covered by a layer of fill around 30 cm thick, composed mostly of many tons of ground-up pottery, some 3000 cubic meters in all. The pottery is far older (2nd–4th centuries), and must have been taken from large ancient deposits elsewhere that were systematically mined to provide the necessary material for the job. A new neighborhood soon grew up atop this compact, well-drained surface (Fig. 4.21, above). Cobbled roadbeds were laid out that, though rising gradually over the centuries, would remain the principal thoroughfares in the neighborhood until all was demolished in the 1920s. They were lined with houses more substantial than those in the Forum of Caesar: the most complete examples (only the foundations remain) were evidently of the two-story *domus solarata* type, with ground floors in mortared masonry of reused tuff blocks

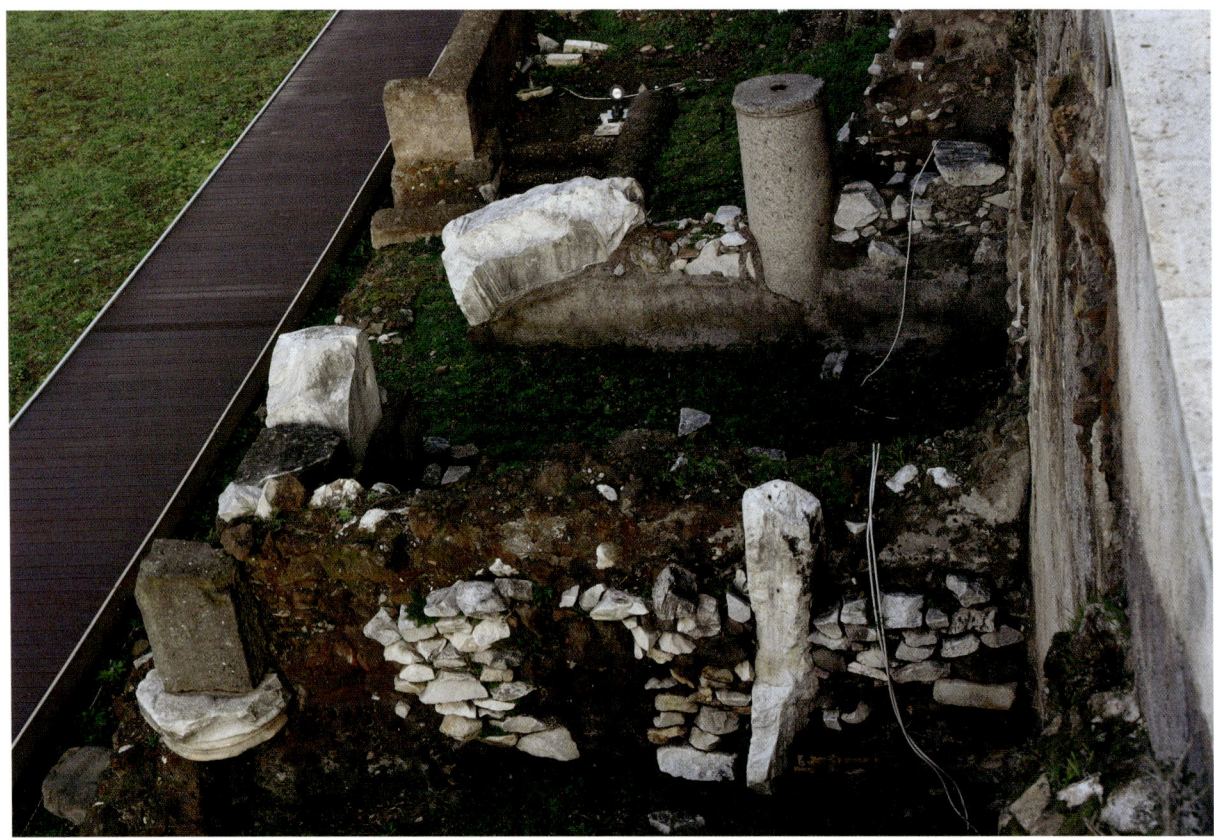

Figure 5.9 One of the 10th-century houses in the Forum of Caesar. Note the abundant use of ancient spolia, including the column drum and the marble slab at the midpoint of the two facing walls, which served to bear the weight of a crossbeam supporting the roof. This is the leftmost house shown on the drawing in Fig. 5.10. (Author.)

mixed with smaller fragments that recalls some of the poorer-quality 9th-century work in the Forum of Nerva, whose houses they also approximate in size. At the rear of the houses, on the interior of the residential blocks, was open space for the sorts of enclosed yards with trees, vines, and domestic animals that we see in the property documents (Fig. 5.11; see also Fig. 7.3).[43]

From the late 9th century, then, the forums of Peace, Caesar, and Trajan followed markedly divergent trajectories, with intensive agriculture at the first, peasants' hovels and gardens at the second, and more substantial residential lots at the third. There is, however, a common thread that connects them. All three were transformed, at around the same time, by carefully coordinated interventions that must have been promoted by powerful people, presumably members of that top tier of Roman nobles who controlled the Lateran bureaucracy and the urban *militia*.

We can put a name to the Forum of Trajan, which by 1004 was being called the "*campus of the former Kaloleus*." This Kaloleus was a top-tier aristocrat in the immediate circle of the *princeps* Alberic in the mid-10th century. In action in 942, when we see him at a gathering of Alberic's close associates held in Alberic's *curtis* next to the nearby church of SS. Apostoli, he died between 963 and 967. Riccardo Santangeli Valenzani has therefore proposed Kaloleus as the motivating force behind the coordinated intervention that birthed the new neighborhood in the mid 10th century. Working presumably with the support of Alberic, Kaloleus would have acted to establish a nucleated network of (rent-paying)

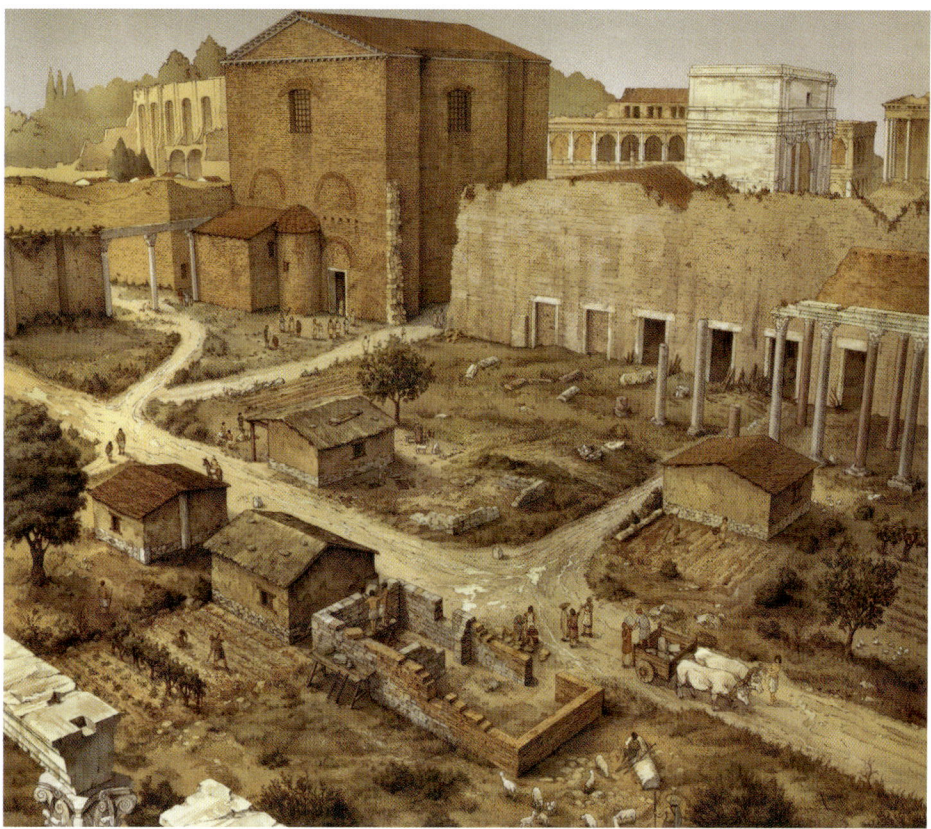

Figure 5.10 Reconstruction of the 10th-century neighborhood in Forum of Caesar in the 10th century; note that there may have been more houses in soon-to-be-excavated areas beneath the walkway along the Via dei Fori Imperiali. (Studio InkLink/ Meneghini and Santangeli Valenzani 2007, p. 147, fig. 157.)

tenants and clients probably in the vicinity of his own *curtis*-compound, thereby creating a solid local power base and ensuring for Alberic that this area close to his own residence at SS. Apostoli was controlled by a loyal ally. In a similarly hypothetical vein, Roberto Meneghini suggests that the instigator of the settlement in the Forum of Caesar was none other than the future pope Leo VIII (r. 964–5), who lived nearby when he was still *protoscriniarus* at the Lateran, and from whose title the toponym later associated with the area, the "slope of the Protoscriniarius" (*ascesa Proti*), would then derive.[44]

By way of closing on the Show Area, we should note that the rich archaeological data give real substance to the (more tenuous) impression of 10th-century growth offered by the S. Maria Nova documents. Settlement was expanding in the imperial forums during the 10th century, when the neighborhoods in the forums of Caesar and Trajan joined the existing one in the Forum of Nerva. Indeed, as Meneghini has said, the 10th century evidently represents the peak of medieval residential occupation in the area as a whole. (While the neighborhood in the Forum of Trajan persisted and indeed grew thereafter, those in the forums of Caesar and Nerva declined in the 11th century – more on this in Chapter 6.) The 10th-century expansion is notable also for following a period of accelerated decay around 900: it was then that alluvial sediment began accumulating in the forums of Augustus and Trajan, unchecked and unshaped by persistent human activity. When we recall that it was also toward the end of the 9th century that substantial

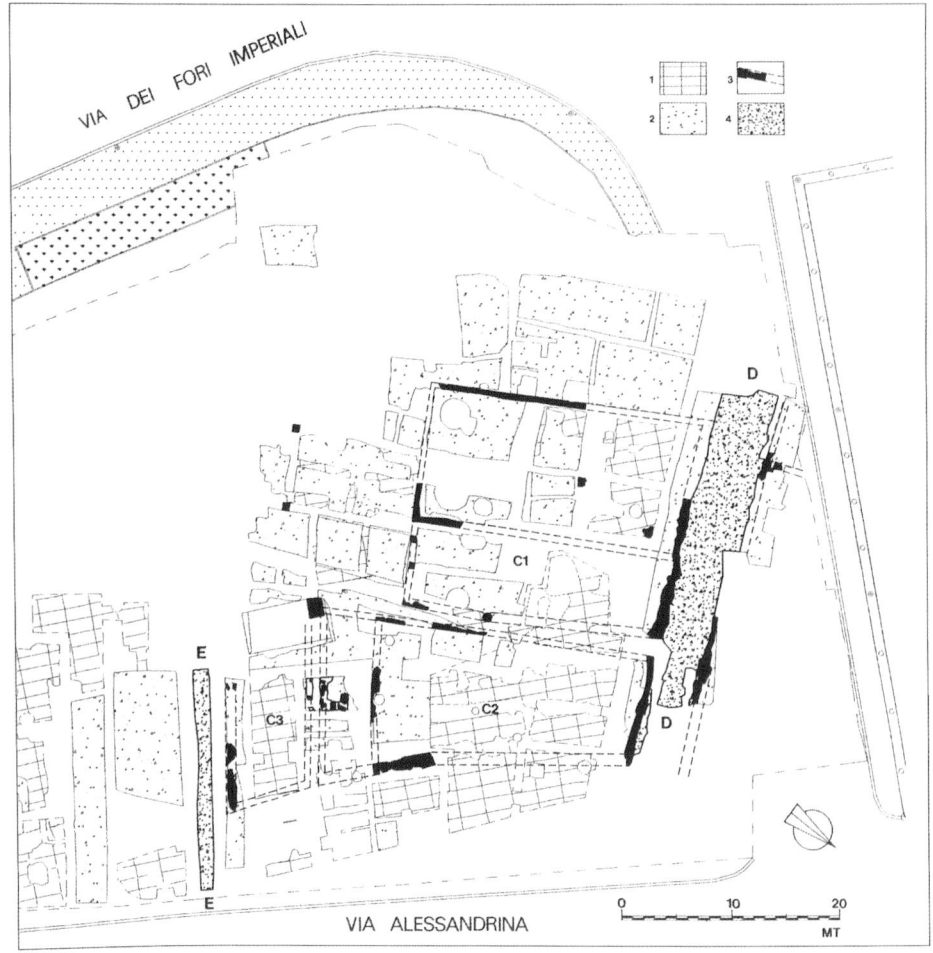

Figure 5.11 Forum of Trajan: the area excavated in 1998–2000, showing both ancient (Trajanic) and 10th-century levels. Legend: 1: impression of ancient pavers in concrete bedding; 2: leveling fill of mid-10th century; 3: 10th (or perhaps early 11th)-century walls; 4: roadbeds. C1-2-3: building lots; D – D: street; E – E: street (both streets survived until the 1920s demolitions). (Meneghini 2009, p. 213, fig. 278.)

deposits first began appearing in parts of the Forum Romanum itself, the impression of stagnation and decay grows stronger. It becomes tempting to associate the moment when dirt and rubbish first began to accumulate – permanently, as it turned out – across ample tracts of the Show Area with the unusual difficulties of the period c. 880–910.[45]

Interestingly, similar signs of dereliction begin around the same time in another of Rome's premier public spaces, the piazza fronting the Pantheon. Through all the floods that had periodically inundated this section of the Campus Martius (a massive one had struck as recently as 860), its 2nd-century marble paving had always been maintained and cleaned. Improvements were still being made at the beginning of the 9th century, when a new fountain was installed adjacent to the front stairs of the Pantheon. But this continuous history of renovations and diligent stewardship ended around 900, when the marble paving began to disappear under deposits of mud and refuse that thereafter grew steadily thicker, reaching several meters in depth by the end of the Middle Ages. In this case, too, the decades around 900 marked an irreversible turning point. The relatively pristine contours of formerly well-maintained ancient monuments began to give way, sometimes to abandonment, but sometimes also to new, messier forms of occupation.[46]

The rest of the Campus Martius can be treated more briefly than the preceding regions for the simple reason that its urban trajectory still broadly paralleled theirs into the 11th century. The low floodplain in the bend of the Tiber was still dominated by the towering piles of ancient public buildings: the baths of Agrippa and of Nero, the theaters of Pompey and of Balbus, the stadium of Domitian, the Temple of Hadrian, and so on (Fig. 1.7, above). Its thinly scattered residents established their dwellings and service buildings, wells and cisterns, orchards, and cultivated fields inside and among the ubiquitous relicts of antiquity. Rare are the properties described in surviving documents whose buildings and boundaries are not composed at least partly of ancient structures and ruins.

Much of our information comes from the copious archives of the Sabine monastery of Farfa, which had a local branch inside the Baths of Nero/Terme Alessandrine and owned many properties nearby, in the neighborhood that was already being called by the name it would keep throughout the Middle Ages, *scorticlaro/scorticlari*, for the tanners who clustered there. The monks and some of their tenants lived inside the sprawling rectangular precinct of the baths (it covered c. 3.4 ha, over 8 acres!), which was still defined by perimeter walls that soared above all the neighboring medieval constructions. Within or just outside its precincts were several small churches, and the usual two-story *domus solarate* and one-story *domus terrinee* with their attached yards and orchards. Ancient buildings and ruins were everywhere, bracketing properties on multiple sides and sometimes defining the full perimeter of houses or residential plots. In one case, an entire *curtis* comprising a two-story house and its attached yard, with a well and fig trees, occupied a single chamber of the baths. Stables, hayricks, storerooms, and the like were also installed in the ancient vaulted *cryptae* that persisted everywhere.[47]

The important point is that, while clusters of settlement in the central Campus Martius in the 10th and early 11th centuries may not have been *less* dense than in other neighborhoods we have seen (at Porta Maggiore and in parts of the Caelian, for example, as well as the Show Area), on the current state of the evidence there is no reason to think they were any denser, either. Interspersed among the region's widely spaced houses surrounded by ample yards, there were pastures and arable fields, and plenty of vacant plots, too. By the early 11th century, to be sure, there are signs of demographic expansion here, as there are elsewhere, but nothing out of the ordinary. The most striking illustration of a growing population comes from the eastern fringe of the Campus Martius by the Via Lata, around the convent of SS. Ciriaco e Nicola, founded adjacent to S. Maria in Via Lata in the 10th century. A sequence of documents starting in 1019 shows the convent dividing its vacant landholdings into contiguous, street-facing lots, similar in size to those at the Forum of Trajan, which it rented out to tenants for renewable nineteen-year terms. These tenants were expected to build houses on their plots, which also had plenty of room for gardens and orchards, and to pay the convent a small annual fee in addition to a larger sum owed upon entering into the lease. Here we have a documentary corollary to the phenomenon detected archaeologically at the forums of Caesar and Trajan: a structured process, directed by a large landowner (in this case, a religious institution rather than an eminent aristocrat), that transformed a previously undeveloped stretch of fields and ruins into a residential neighborhood populated by rent-paying tenants. With population and demand for housing clearly on the rise, Rome's leading landowners, churches and monasteries prominent among them, were quick to meet the demand, ensuring for themselves a stable source of revenue in the process.[48]

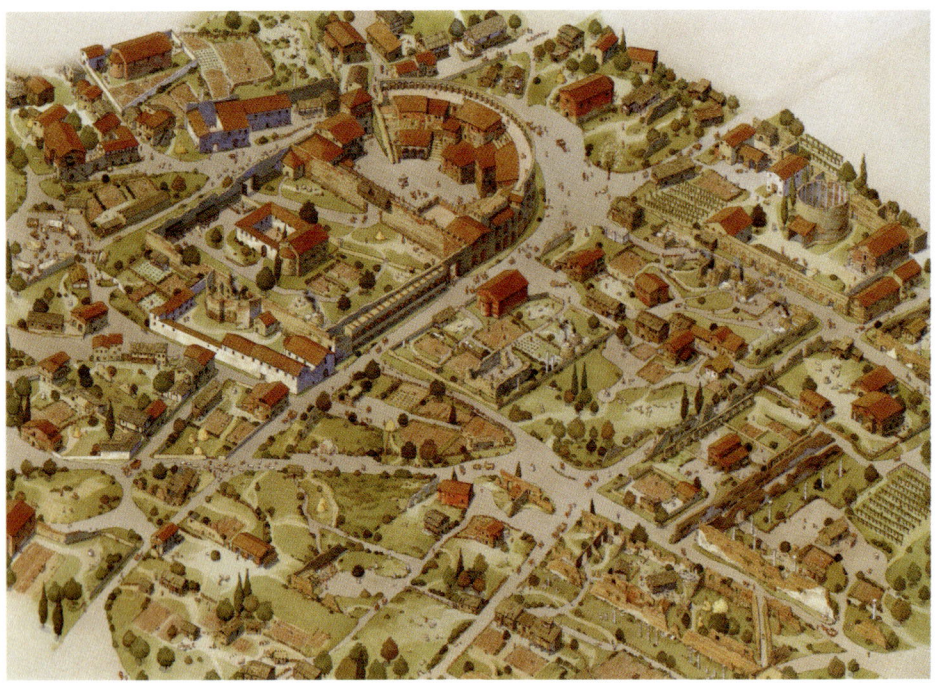

Figure 5.12 Reconstruction of the sparsely inhabited neighborhood of the Crypta Balbi around the year 1000. Compare with fig. 2.8, above. (Studio InkLink/Manacorda 2001, p. 64, fig. 71.)

But, again: The new development by SS. Ciriaco e Nicola is part of a rising tide of population that extended well beyond the Campus Martius, much of which remained sparsely inhabited through the first half of the 11th century and beyond. The area of the Crypta Balbi, for example, which was quite densely built up by the 13th century, stagnated through the 10th and 11th, as the recent excavations have shown. Until the 12th century, the porticoes of the theater and those of the adjacent *porticus Minucia* continued their slow decay amidst relative solitude. There are no signs of substantial new construction, and only slight traces of any stable human presence, apart from some burials (Fig. 5.12). Farther west toward the Tiber, in the bend of the river beyond Piazza Navona, there are still fewer indications of residential occupation. While this void may partially be attributable to the sparseness of reliable excavations, when coupled with the scarcity of textual signs of activity, it suggests that the region had made little progress on its way to becoming the dense core of the late- or post-medieval city. It seems significant that not one of the known *curtes* belonging to leading aristocrats in the period before 1050 can be located west of Largo Argentina on either textual or archaeological grounds; and most of those that can be pinpointed with any precision were in fact east of the Via Lata and the Capitoline, between SS. Apostoli, the markets of Trajan, and the Forum. Still other nobles (and their clients and retainers) resided yet farther away to the south, atop the Aventine Hill (Fig. 5.13).[49]

Finally, we move from this western extremity of the Campus Martius toward the Vatican along the final stretch of the processional route between the Lateran and St. Peter's, the "Papal Way" as it was already called by 1017, crossing the Tiber on Ponte Sant'Angelo, the old Roman bridge to Hadrian's mausoleum. Here was a region much closer than the Campus Martius to attaining the density of settlement it would reach in the later Middle Ages. We have seen

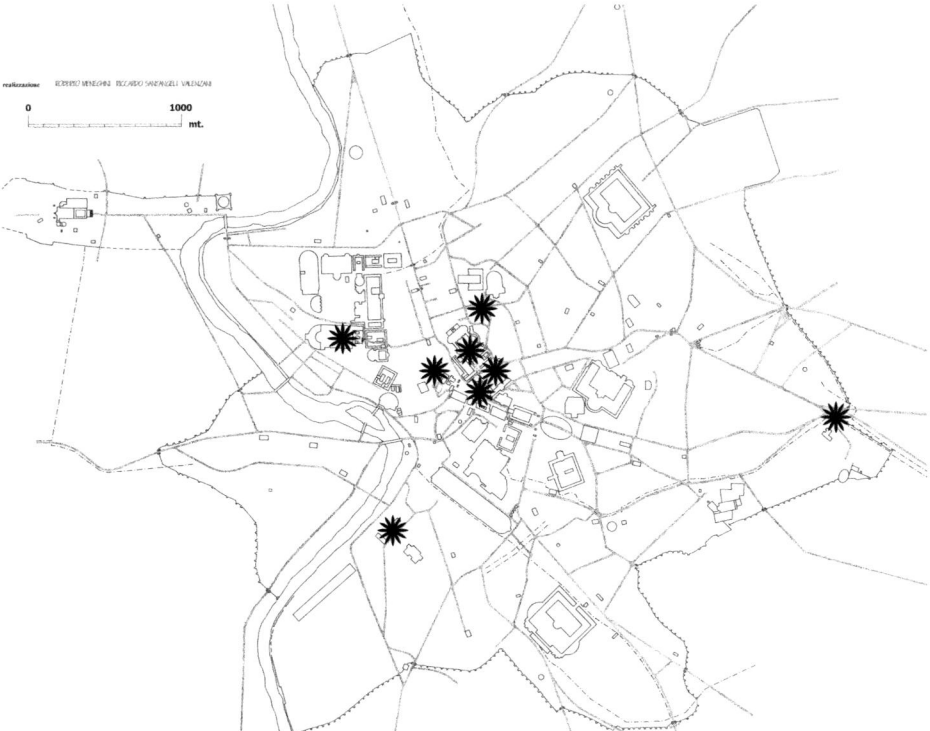

Figure 5.13 Locations of 9th-10th-century *curtes* of leading noble families attested on the basis of written and archaeological evidence. (Plan based on Santangeli Valenzani 2011, fig. 6.2; Aventine residence of Theophylact's family added by author.)

that the "burg" between St. Peter's and the river was a busy neighborhood already by c. 800, featuring a constellation of churches and monasteries gravitating around St. Peter's; the four *scholae* for foreign pilgrims; the residence of the Carolingian emperors and their local representatives, and so on. The fire that leveled much of the neighborhood at the beginning of the 9th century is a telling sign of the density of settlement already attained by then. The building of the encircling Leonine walls in 848–52 thus responded to what was already an urban success story, a zone experiencing growth unparalleled elsewhere in early medieval Rome (Fig. 4.18, above). But the presence of the new walls undoubtedly provoked a wave of further development, such that this "new" or "Leonine city" (*civitas nova/Leonina*) became perhaps the city's most densely occupied region by c. 1000.[50]

The neighborhood centered on the road and the covered portico, rebuilt by Pope Hadrian I in the 770s, that ran from Castel Sant'Angelo to St. Peter's. Long files of houses ranged two (or more?) ranks deep in places ran along this "Great Portico" (*porticus maior*), from the Saxon *borgo* near the Tiber all the way to the atrium of St. Peter's. Still more houses jostled up against the façade of the atrium. The houses adjoining the portico often owned one or more stalls in the portico itself, prime retail space fronting the busiest road in the area, thronged by clerics, visiting pilgrims and tourists, and ordinary Romans who gravitated toward the shrine of Rome's premier martyr. Many of these properties were owned by the four monasteries attached to St. Peter's, whose extensive possessions in and around the *civitas Leonina* had been confirmed by Leo IV immediately after the completion of the Vatican walls in the 850s, but other Roman churches and monasteries also had a foothold in this prestigious area. Land was at a premium and rents were high, making property in the *civitas Leonina* an especially valuable commodity.[51]

We have little archaeological documentation of the material contours of settlement in the *civitas Leonina* in the 10th and 11th centuries, however. Intense population pressure here at the doorstep of St. Peter's ensured that the smaller, flimsier, less tightly packed buildings of the early Middle Ages were more or less completely replaced in later centuries. The extensive demolitions undertaken in the 1930s to create the Via della Conciliazione involved structures built from the later Middle Ages on; and if any earlier scraps were encountered, nobody bothered to examine them closely. In any case, while existing churches, the circuit walls, and the main portico from Castel Sant'Angelo were built in durable stone and brick, the documents leave the impression that domestic architecture was mostly still in wood and other perishable materials, as it clearly had been at the time of the fire under Leo III. With one exception, the houses described prior to 1050 had roofs with wooden shingles, the two-story *domus solaratae* included. When exterior staircases leading to upper floors are mentioned, they are also in wood. There is thus a perceptible contrast with the Campus Martius and other areas across the river, where a higher proportion of houses had roofs wholly or partly of tile and also stone exterior staircases, features that can only have been employed in conjunction with walls of solid masonry.[52]

This different material environment can be explained by the fact that the Vatican was not a densely built neighborhood in antiquity, such that builders of early medieval dwellings were less conditioned by the vestiges of the past. In marked contrast to the situation across the river, property boundaries here are rarely defined in relation to ancient ruins; houses likewise are not said to incorporate such ruins; and the *cryptae* commonly used elsewhere as service buildings are also rare. In the absence of standing remains and heaps of solid building components that could be conveniently recycled, early medieval builders evidently made do with less durable materials.[53]

The contrast is equally marked in relation to the heart of Trastevere, downstream along the Tiber to the south. Most of the old built-up area inside the transtiberine salient of the city walls was sparsely populated and distinctly suburban in our period, but still crowded with *cryptae* and other remains of antiquity. In the earliest surviving 10th- and 11th-century property documents, the residences we encounter seem to have been scattered among "crypts," gardens, and open fields. What habitation there was clustered close to the riverbank near the Tiber island, roughly from S. Maria in Trastevere in the northwest to S. Cecilia in the southeast, not coincidentally near the only two river crossings that survived downstream of Ponte Sant'Angelo (the Pons Cestius – Pons Fabricius across the island, and the Pons Aemilius, the medieval Pons Maior, just to the south). The main area of docks along the Tiber, the Ripa Romea/Ripa Grande, was also nearby, just downstream of the Pons Maior (Fig. 7.32, below). Here was a neighborhood of merchants and artisans, and millers, too: both banks of the river, especially around the island where the current divides and quickens, were lined with floating water mills. Such mills had appeared in Rome at least as early as the 6th century, and we see them clustering densely along the riverbanks in the early documents of the 10th and 11th centuries. With the failure of the Aqua Traiana, whose flow had turned mills on the slopes of the Janiculum since the 2nd century, these floating mills on the Tiber became all the more essential to the production of flour for the Romans' daily bread. Fishponds along the riverbank provided locals with another source of calories, and income. A few minutes' walk inland from the river, however, settlement dwindled to near-rural levels. The area around today's S. Cosimato, for example, was mostly fields and derelict ruins for generations after Alberic's henchman Benedetto *campanino* founded the monastery of SS. Cosma e Damiano *in mica aurea* there c. 936–44.[54]

It is time to conclude by zooming back out to the wider urban panorama that Rome presents in this most poorly documented period in its medieval history. As more research is done, it becomes ever harder to avoid the conclusion that the scarcity of both textual and material traces of ambitious building projects reflects a real decline in activity in comparison to what was occurring both before and after. So too does the lack of evidence for basic maintenance of infrastructure as critical as the city walls and the aqueducts. While this total silence does not necessarily mean that nothing whatsoever occurred (localized damage to the walls was surely repaired, for example), it surely betokens reduced investment in important elements of the urban fabric inherited from antiquity. So too does the fact that public spaces as prestigious and central as the forums of Trajan and Augustus, parts of the Forum Romanum, and the plaza fronting the Pantheon were first allowed to be buried under sediment and refuse in the decades around 900.

Equally striking is the scarcity of surviving churches and other religious foundations datable to this period, and here it is worth pausing on the implications of "surviving." As we will see, churches and monasteries were in fact established with some frequency, at least from the mid-10th century on. The fact that so little of them remains, however, suggests that they were generally less ornate and solidly constructed than the many large and lavish churches built in the 9th century, and again from the 12th. Those built in the interim, that is, must either have been too poorly built to stand the test of time, or otherwise too unimpressive to be thought worth preserving in later centuries. For the period from the death of John VIII in 882 up to the mid 10th century, nothing remains, while the one extant foundation of the later 10th century, S. Maria in Pallara, does little to dispel the impression of a general decline in the scale and opulence of religious architecture. Again: It is small, roughly built in recycled blocks and brick, has no side aisles that would have required the use of columns, and is decorated with frescoes instead of mosaics or marble revetment. Other sparse survivals point in a similar direction, among them the fresco fragment presumably from a minor church by the Colosseum, discussed above, and the atrium of S. Maria Antiqua in the Forum, which was lightly modified and adorned with new frescoes probably in the later 10th century, when a Benedictine community took up residence there (Fig. 5.14).[55]

We have already noted that S. Maria in Pallara was established by a lay patron, as were most of the other 10th-century foundations about which anything is known. It bears stressing that there is no indication of popes founding new urban churches from the end of the 9th century through the 11th. S. Maria in Pallara thus exceeds, on its own, the known extent of papal building activity in all of 10th-century Rome, with the lone exception of the Lateran! Even at the Lateran, the only really substantial project we know of was Sergius III's (r. 904–11) restoration of the extensive damage caused to the basilica by the earthquake of 896/97, which entailed rebuilding the roof and probably additional work on the upper portions of the walls and parts of the nave colonnades. As everything of value had been pillaged from the church during its decade of dereliction, Sergius also provided an extensive new set of liturgical furnishings and implements, according to the 12th-century *Descriptio Lateranensis Ecclesiae*. Elsewhere in Rome, the sum total of attested 10th-century papal projects consists of a possible tomb or honorary monument for John XIII at St. Paul's, now lost; some pictures added to the chapel of S. Maria *in gradibus* at

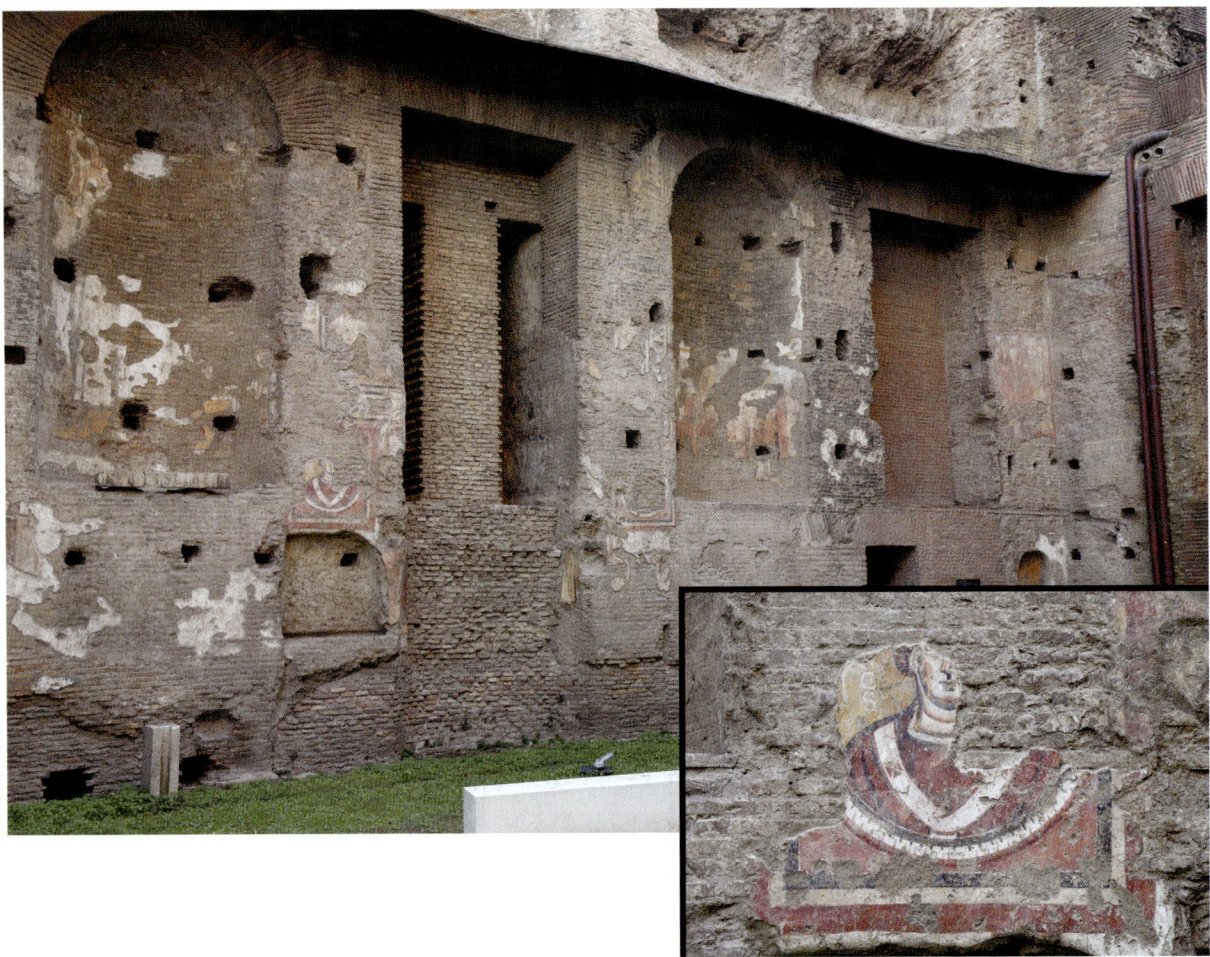

Figure 5.14 The east wall of the atrium fronting S. Maria Antiqua, with its 10th- and 11th-century frescoes. Osborne (1987, pp. 200–19) dates the decoration of the two domed niches and the flat panel at far right to the mid to late 10th century, and the fragmentary medallion portraits (see inset detail) between the two domed niches to the late 10th or, more probably, the 11th century. (Author.)

St. Peter's under John XV (r. 985–96), also now lost; and fragmentary frescoes of uncertain but probably late 10th-century date at S. Adriano in the Forum. Even allowing for deficiencies in the sources and the vagaries of preservation, this is strikingly little. For two centuries after the crisis of the late 9th century, the popes, impoverished and politically weakened, generally confined themselves to essential maintenance and minor improvements on Rome's already vast stock of religious architecture.[56]

The real driving force behind most of the religious architecture commissioned in the 10th and early 11th centuries looks to have been lay patrons, prominent nobles in the first place. That so little of what they sponsored survives is a function of the simple reality that no individual or family, not even the descendants of Theophylact, ever controlled more than a tiny fraction of the resources available to the papacy in the 9th century, and again from the 12th. These individual nobles or noble families thus naturally operated on a more modest scale commensurate with their limited wealth and ambitions; with the local, as opposed to citywide, bases of their power and income. Instead of dazzling architectural marvels designed to incarnate the majesty of the Church universal and its supreme pontiffs, Roman nobles focused on humbler projects that rarely stood the test of time, but which sufficed in the moment to enhance their personal prestige and consolidate their control over little corners of the cityscape.

In practice, this meant they did two things. First, they founded monasteries on family properties, which seemingly functioned as a sort of land trust to ensure that these patrimonies would be transmitted to posterity undivided, or better yet augmented via subsequent pious donations, papal gifts, and so on. Relatives or trusted associates of the founding family were installed as abbots and supervisors of the new monasteries, whose lands, now technically the property of the Church, could not be sold off or subdivided among competing heirs. Ways were presumably found by which the founding families continued to profit from revenues generated by the inalienable, often growing possessions of these 'family monasteries.' Alberic himself appears to be a key figure in this development. Although he brought in Odo of Cluny to lend that famous monastic reformer's spiritual imprimatur to a comprehensive reform of Roman monasteries under stricter Benedictine observance, the main beneficiaries of the monastic revival look to have been Roman aristocrats, prominent among them members of Alberic's inner circle. In addition to the restoration or reoccupation of older monasteries (e.g. S. Erasmo on the Caelian), some six new ones were founded during Alberic's 'principate,' including three by Alberic and his close associates: SS. Ciriaco e Nicola near S. Maria in Via Lata by his cousins Theodora, Marozia, and Stefania; SS. Cosma e Damiano *in mica aurea* by his close collaborator Benedetto *campanino*; and S. Maria in Aventino by Alberic himself, in one of his family's houses on the Aventine Hill. While some of these foundations made use of older residential buildings and churches (S. Maria in Aventino in Alberic's house, SS. Ciriaco e Nicola at S. Maria in Via Lata), others were substantially new, such as Petrus *medicus*' church and monastery of S. Maria in Pallara, and probably also Benedetto *campanino*'s new monastery amidst the fields and ruins in suburban Trastevere.[57]

Second, the upper crust of the Roman elite attached churches to their family *curtis*-compounds. These were publicly accessible chapels, with (naturally) relics in the altar and officiating clergy, that served their surrounding neighborhoods. The congregants in these family churches brought in tithes, and furnished besides a pool of prospective clients and supporters grouped in the immediate vicinity of the leading family's residence. The earliest grand residence mentioned in writing, a *domus* probably located near the Trevi fountain that was purchased by Emperor Louis II from a Petrus *consul et dux* in 868 for 800 pounds of silver, included both a bath building and a church dedicated to S. Biagio. The presumed *curtis* excavated at Largo Argentina also included within its confines a church, the predecessor of the 12th-century S. Nicola *de Calcarario*.

As the best (probable) example of such a compound yet uncovered, the complex at Largo Argentina deserves close attention. Excavated in the 1920s and only summarily recorded before most of the medieval structures were demolished, its outlines have been reconstructed by Riccardo Santangeli Valenzani (Fig. 5.15). It occupied nearly all of the excavated expanse of the Area Sacra, making extensive use of the ancient perimeter wall but completing the circuit at various points in typical early medieval *opus quadratum* of recycled tuff blocks. Within was an *opus quadratum* house larger than those in the Forum of Nerva, abutting the perimeter wall at the rear and with two marble columns flanking the main entrance at the front. A second structure also attached to the old perimeter looks to have been a stable or service building. The church itself was built onto the podium of the

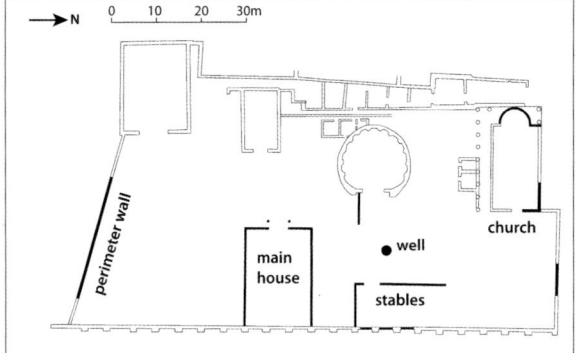

Figure 5.15 Reconstructed plan of the presumed 9th-10th-century *curtis* in Largo Argentina. Segments in solid black indicate sections of early medieval *opus quadratum* masonry revealed (and mostly removed) during the excavations of the 1920s. (Redrawn from Meneghini and Santangeli Valenzani 2004, p. 42, fig. 20.)

republican-era Temple A, with an apse and bits of nave wall added in similar *opus quadratum* masonry. Pieces of architectural sculpture found in the church suggest a 9th-century date for its construction, and so perhaps for the complex as a whole. A sprawling enclosure (.55 ha, well over an acre) furnished with a large residence, service buildings, and a substantial church as well: This is as close as we can currently get to a paradigm of the places inhabited by Rome's upper elites in the 9th and 10th centuries.[58]

Though we cannot reconstruct other such *curtes* in similar detail, many certainly contained churches. Roberto Meneghini has proposed that the presumed *curtis* of Kaloleus at the Forum of Trajan included the church later known as S. Maria in Campo Carlèo (whose remains were uncovered in the 1930s and again in the 1990s); and that the church of S. Lorenzo *de ascesa*, possibly to be identified with walls of plausibly 10th-century masonry cleared in the 1930s, might have pertained to the *curtis* of the founder of the settlement in the Forum of Caesar. Be this as it may, some of the many churches attested later in the Middle Ages with epithets such as *de curte* and *in curtis* must once have been attached to the *curtes* of leading Roman nobles of the 9th–11th centuries. Many were surely built by these same nobles, to dimensions and standards, however, which ensured that most would be reconstructed, built over, or simply removed in later centuries, leaving precious few traces.[59]

The scattered pieces (written and material) of the surviving *curtes* of Rome's upper nobility barely hint at the scope of the far-reaching transformation of residential architecture and settlement patterns that occurred between the 9th and 11th centuries. The local magnates who owned these *curtes* inhabited what were becoming, more and more, inward-looking residential islands, increasingly self-sufficient entities equipped with stables and service buildings, chapels, wells, and even baths, in addition to living quarters. They in turn lived surrounded by dependents and tenants, grouped into circumscribed neighborhoods that gravitated around the residence (and church) of the patron/landlord. The apparent parallels with *incastellamento* in the countryside, the process whereby more scattered rural populations moved, or were moved, to nucleated settlements centered on the residence of the local lord, have been remarked by more than one commentator. In Lazio, this process began in earnest from the 920s, as aristocrats and ecclesiastical landlords sought to extend their control over sectors of the countryside where they had landed interests, following the chaos and dislocations of the late 9th and early 10th centuries.[60]

In Rome, the consolidation of discrete residential nuclei becomes very pronounced after the beginning of the ecclesiastical reform movement after 1046, as we will see in Chapter 6; and it is then that we have the first clear proof of compounds fortified with towers and proper defensive circuits. But the roots of this phenomenon lie farther back in time, in the 9th and 10th centuries, when nucleated holdings were already taking on a stable and lasting form, as proprietors aggregated properties, established *curtes* or monasteries there, gathered clients and tenants in the vicinity, and generally acted to ensure that they control and profit from their nucleated urban patrimonies over the long term. Even if the Largo Argentina *curtis* originally had no towers or imposing fortifications, it did have a solid and apparently continuous perimeter wall that gave it a distinctly 'closed' physical profile. In this sense, it was very different from the sprawling mansions of late antiquity, and even from the 9th-century upper-class houses in the Forum of Nerva and the Forum Romanum. Slowly but surely, from the 9th century to the 11th, the essentially 'open,' community-oriented architectural paradigms that had prevailed in Rome since antiquity began to transform into something more self-contained and inward-looking.[61]

Any attempt to explain the origins and causes of this evolutionary process must be strictly hypothetical. I suspect it has something to do with the strife and factionalism that grew from the mid 9th century toward a crescendo in the period c. 880–910, on the evidence of texts such as the *LP* first, and later the various papal letters, conciliar decrees, and partisan screeds that show the Roman nobility and clergy deeply divided between 'pro-' and 'anti-Formosan' parties in the years around 900. There were doubtless many other factors, personal/familial economic self-interest not least among them, that helped push both lay and ecclesiastical proprietors to carve out territorial enclaves centered on *curtes* and also monasteries. But it strikes me that this process of circling the wagons, as it were, could not have occurred when and as it did without the weakening of the sovereign papacy, the relative detachment of transalpine rulers, and the fragmentation of the Roman body politic that ensued.

Certainly turmoil at home and rising politico-military instability elsewhere in Italy, which also peaked in the decades around 900, combined to make Rome poorer, more isolated, and generally dingier than before. The assertive and well-financed popes of the 8th and 9th centuries who had worked to renovate and beautify Rome as befitted the capital of Christendom were a thing of the past. Thereafter, despite long periods when one family or individual did exercise effective authority over the city and its surrounding countryside, as under Theophylact and his heirs c. 906–63 and the Tuscolani in the first half of the 11th century, civic leaders lacked the means or the will (or both) to undertake projects on a city-wide scale – to build or maintain on behalf of the collective. Rather, urban magnates acted more locally, investing in their own residences and neighborhoods, or in select churches and monasteries in which they had a particular interest. Discrete neighborhoods consequently embarked on increasingly individualized trajectories shaped by the initiatives of local power brokers, leading aristocrats and clerics from the same restricted group of interrelated noble families, who began to divvy up the cityscape into 'personal' neighborhoods inhabited by loyal clients and centered on family compounds that grew gradually more imposing. The parcellization of the residential fabric that gained momentum between the 9th and 11th centuries would condition urban topography, and politics, for the remainder of the Middle Ages.

Chapter 6

1046–1230

Church Reformed, Senate Reborn, Rome Renascent

THE RELATIVE TEXTUAL AND archaeological invisibility of the 10th and 11th centuries at Rome is especially vexing for coming at a critical transitional period, just when the early medieval city began to metamorphose into the very different sort of place it became in the later Middle Ages. The later medieval city as it emerged from the 12th century on broke with its ancient roots in a number of ways. At least as late as the 9th century, upper-class residences like the ones in the Forum of Nerva retained a distinctly unfortified profile; though these houses were smaller and more compact than the aristocratic mansions of imperial Rome, they nonetheless prolonged a tradition of accessible, 'civilian' residential architecture that had continued unbroken for a thousand years. By the 12th century, however, Roman nobles lived in fortified compounds, complete with defensible outer walls and tall towers. As late as the 10th and 11th centuries, very few churches had bell towers, either; the soaring, graceful *campanili* attached to surviving medieval churches only proliferated in the 12th. In the 9th and 10th centuries, patches of settlement still extended across much of the intramural area. By the 12th, population was clustering in a nucleus roughly centered on the Capitoline Hill, from the *Ripa Graeca* and riparian Trastevere in the south to the Pantheon and SS. Apostoli in the north. In the 9th and even the 10th centuries, although ancient public spaces and monuments across much of the city center were being despoiled of materials and abandoned or put to new uses, ground levels often remained fairly close to where they had been at the end of antiquity – a meter or less of increase is common. But in the 12th century, thick deposits of soil and rubble covered widely separated areas of low-lying terrain, raising the ground across parts of the Show Area, the southern Campus Martius, Trastevere, and elsewhere several meters above late ancient and early medieval levels. Together, these developments redrew the map of medieval Rome. And though some of them surely originate in the period covered in the last chapter, they become visible as established realities only from the mid-11th century, where this chapter begins.

The nominal start date of 1046 derives from high geopolitics. It is the year when, following civic disturbances and insurrection in 1044/5 against the last Tuscolani pope, Benedict IX (r. 1032–45), the Salian king Henry III crossed the Alps and descended on Rome with an armed retinue, deposed three Italian claimants to the papacy at a synod he convened at Sutri, and installed a German bishop on the throne of St. Peter as Pope Clement II (r. 1046–7). Thus ended the *Adelspapsttum*, that most provincial incarnation of the Church of Rome wherein the papacy and the Lateran bureaucracy were appanages of a coterie of Roman noble clans, latterly the Tuscolani family. Thus began in earnest the period of ecclesiastical reform that eventually produced a more assertive and ecumenical Church: a Church as a sovereign power, headed by popes who reigned in the imperial style of the ancient Roman and Byzantine emperors, absolute in their own sphere, putatively above and independent of lay rulers, and empowered to shape the spiritual trajectory of all Latin Christendom. This "Great Reform" is among the most studied subjects in all of medieval history. It unfolded in a litany of conflict and recrimination that festered for generations between the reform popes and the German kings whose dominions included north-central Italy, as the former strove to assert the spiritual supremacy of Church over state, of *sacerdotium* over *regnum*. It requires some discussion here insofar as these transformational events bear very significantly upon the evolution of the cityscape, and the sharp swerve in Rome's urban trajectory that gained momentum during the first century of the reform period.[1]

In wresting control of the papacy from the local nobility, the pious Emperor Henry III and the four German popes he helped install before his early death, in 1056, returned Rome to center stage on the European scene. The success of the reformers in enhancing the Church's prestige and asserting its ecumenical mandate ensured that Rome would ever after remain deeply entangled in European power dynamics. Local and ecclesiastical politics were subsequently played for higher stakes than before, among players who included powerful actors with interests and allegiances that extended far beyond Rome. Between 1046 and 1187, just two of the popes remembered as legitimate came from Rome and its environs, and they reigned for only 15 of those 141 years, this after Romans had occupied the papal throne for well over half of the three centuries prior to 1046. The foreign popes (the first five were all German) were accompanied by other eminent prelates who occupied leading positions in the ecclesiastical hierarchy. After 1046, most of the cardinals – cardinal bishops, priests, and deacons, a newly important dignity whose standing was elevated by the reformers – whose origins can be ascertained were also non-Romans. Thus, although the assertive, internationalist Church that emerged after 1046 was based in Rome, it was less 'of' Rome than before. It was a power unto itself, pursuing policies and interests distinct from those of its lay supporters and rivals alike. These included diverse, and shifting, coalitions among the local nobility, as well as the Italian and European powers whose interests and ambitions converged on the seat of the papacy.[2]

First among the external powers was the confederation of German and northern Italian states under Salian suzerainty (hereafter simply "the Empire"), under whose ruler and senior clergy the initial purge and impetus for reform had come. Until Henry III's death in 1056, at only 39, the reform popes and the emperor worked toward a common purpose. They were the twin poles of the divinely appointed order on Earth, the emperor as steward of his domains and supreme defender of the Church, the pope as the spiritual guardian of the Empire and its subjects. After Henry's death, however, relations between the reform papacy and the Empire deteriorated under the weak regency that ruled in the name of the boy-king Henry IV (r. 1056–1106). The situation was further complicated by the advent of the Normans, who gobbled up the mosaic of Lombard- and Byzantine-controlled enclaves south of Rome, starting in the 1040s, and melded them into a Norman polity spanning the lower third of the Italian boot. With the establishment of this new force in the Italian peninsula, the Empire confronted a strong competitor, which it naturally viewed with suspicion. Rome henceforth found itself sandwiched between two powerful rivals, both eager to intervene on the Roman scene, where they inevitably found accomplices among the welter of competing local factions, both lay and ecclesiastical.

Turmoil ensued, punctuated by episodes of open warfare that peaked in intensity during the second half of the 11th century. In 1058, the leaders of Rome's old aristocracy made a bid to restore their fortunes by installing a local protégé of the Tuscolani as Pope Benedict X in 1058. The reform faction under archdeacon Hildebrand, supported by rising noble families based inside the city, elected its own candidate later in the same year as Pope Nicholas II. Lacking effective support from the Empire, the partisans of Nicholas II turned to the Normans to their south, with whose help Benedict X was chased from Rome and deposed. When Nicholas II died in 1061, Hildebrand's party again relied on the force of Norman arms to elect Alexander II (r. 1061–73), despite fierce opposition by supporters of the Tuscolani and other elements of the Roman 'old guard.' The alliance of convenience between the Hildebrandine reform faction and the Normans outraged the Germans, who in turn made common cause with Roman notables to invest Bishop Cadalus of Parma as (anti-)Pope Honorius II later in 1061. Though Cadalus was deposed in 1064, relations between Alexander II and the Empire remained strained, and when Hildebrand himself became Pope Gregory VII following Alexander's death in 1073, the rupture was total.[3]

Under Gregory VII, the vision of papal theocracy adumbrated in the Donation of Constantine was stated more forcefully and explicitly than ever before. Gregory envisioned a Church independent of and supreme over the Empire, and popes as crowned sovereigns in the trappings of a latter-day Roman emperor. Open conflict with the Empire ensued: The beginning of the investiture controversy (1075–1122) over the emperor's right to sanction ecclesiastical appointments; the vigil at Canossa and Gregory VII's multiple excommunications of Henry IV; Henry IV's support for the long-lived (anti)pope Guibert of Ravenna/Clement III (r. 1080–1100); the sack of Rome in 1084 by a Norman army summoned by Pope Gregory to save him from the forces of Henry IV and Guibert/Clement III – all sprang from the surging strength and confidence of the reform faction under the direction of Hildebrand/Gregory VII. When the Church that Henry III had worked to purge of its parochial Roman entanglements grew into a spiritual colossus beyond the power of the Empire to control, it rebounded spectacularly against his son. By the death of Gregory VII, in exile, in 1085, the tone was set for the next two centuries, including the Roman adventures of Barbarossa with which we began this book. Rome was betwixt and between a papacy with international ambitions, German rulers intent on asserting their sovereign rights, Norman kings eager to subvert imperial designs with gold or force of arms, and, last but hardly least, the clans and coalitions of influential Romans who, in the relentless pursuit of their own designs, readily made and broke alliances with all three.[4]

The enduring presence, of course, was the Romans themselves who dwelled stably in and around the city while foreign influencers came and went. They need further introduction here, insofar as sweeping changes in the composition of Roman society were afoot by the 11th century, which in turn reshaped the cityscape. A growing population and a flourishing economy brought new groups to prominence, and gradually eroded an entrenched social order in place for centuries – that 'deep state' of interrelated noble families, with extensive landholdings across much of modern Lazio, that had controlled the Lateran bureaucracy and led the Roman militia since the 8th century. Already in the first half of the 11th century, old families such as the Crescenzi and Tuscolani were gravitating toward their rural estates, and they largely dropped off the urban stage after the mid-century upheavals. Meanwhile, as we saw in Chapter 5, a rising middle class of artisans, professionals, and small landowners, based firmly inside the city walls, starts to appear already in the later 10th and early 11th centuries. By the mid 11th century, the more successful among this emerging "medium elite" had amassed enough wealth and landed possessions to emerge as nobles in their own right, willing and able to challenge the older families for control of the city center. Some of these arriviste clans, evidently with considerable support from the medium elite, played an important part in provoking the disturbances of 1044–5 that led to the deposition of Benedict IX, the end of the *Adelspapsttum*, and the emergence of the reform movement. 'New' families such as the Pierleoni and Frangipane later supported the reform faction of Hildebrand/ Gregory VII against its imperial rivals, offering bases in the city and money to pay for Norman support. They profited handsomely from their alliance with the papacy, and with the eventual triumph of the Gregorian line over the imperial side, their place at the apex of the urban nobility was solidified for generations.[5]

Alongside the reform Church, these urban nobles and medium elites were the key protagonists in the topographical transformations that reconfigured the urban fabric almost beyond recognition from the later 11th century into the 13th, to which we now turn. We begin with two early, perhaps related developments that first become clearly visible in the second half of the 11th century: first, the growing concentration of population in the low-lying areas in the west, on both banks of the Tiber; and second, the appearance of new forms of middle-to-upper-class housing.

The population shift was a gradual, long-drawn-out process – the diffuse, polyfocal clusters of early medieval settlement did not morph all at once into the more compact nucleus of settlement in the Campus Martius, Trastevere, and the Vatican Borgo that appears in the 15th and 16th centuries, when the earliest informative drawings and maps were produced. But it would seem that the shift gathered momentum after c. 1050, spurred on by a range of factors that can be only partially accounted for. Some are 'negative' developments that made the high ground in the east less desirable. By some point in the 11th century, for example, the two aqueducts (the Iobia and the Claudia) that still supplied the eastern periphery for some time after they were last repaired in the 9th century had ceased to function. There is also the Norman sack of 1084, which looks to have hit the environs of the Caelian Hill especially hard.[6]

But probably the more influential factors are 'positive' developments that made the area between the Capitoline and the Vatican more desirable. Rome's newly flourishing merchants and artisans were less concerned about being close to cultivable land, and more interested in having ready access to resources and raw materials, good communications, and the Tiber. The roads that led to the nearest seaports, along with the essential salt-pans at the Tiber mouth, were the Ostiense, Portuense, and Aurelia, all in the west of the city. The Tiber itself was the most efficient means of transporting both raw materials and finished goods in bulk between the city center and the ports at the river mouth, from which Roman merchants ranged up and down the Tyrrhenian coast of Italy in growing numbers. Maritime commerce came and went from the main river-port of Ripa Grande, in southern Trastevere, and crossed into the city center via two of the three surviving river-crossings: the Pons Aemilius (called the Pons Maior or Ponte S. Maria in the later Middle Ages), just south of the Tiber Island, and the Pons Fabricius-Pons Cestius (Pons Iudaeorum/Ponte Quattro Capi) across the island itself (see below, Fig. 7.32). More goods and materials came downstream from upper Lazio and Umbria to the Ripetta port in the northern Campus Martius. With the aqueducts defunct, the Tiber was also the last remaining source of power for water mills, which crowded thickly along its banks. Its waters were essential also for fulling and dying and tanning and a host of other water-intensive industries. Further, from the mid 12th century until the end of the 14th, the Capitoline Hill was the seat of communal government, the center of Roman political life and thus a powerful pole of attraction.[7]

There was also the proximity of St. Peter's and the Borgo, which were easily accessible from both Trastevere and the neighborhoods along the left (city center) bank of the Tiber. The Vatican neighborhood throve with Rome's return to international prominence during the reform period, a time when, moreover, wealth and population were steadily rising across much of Europe.

More clerics and lay potentates came to Rome, and the flow of visiting pilgrims grew, as did the influx of (paying) petitioners seeking judgments in papal courts of canon law. There was good business to be done in feeding and lodging and generally catering to the needs of these visitors, which encouraged Romans to gravitate to nearby neighborhoods in Trastevere and the Campus Martius. For medium elites and nobles anxious to expand their urban holdings and build new and more imposing dwellings, the Campus Martius in particular offered further advantages: much of it was relatively undeveloped; it had not been bought up and occupied by the established elite families of the early Middle Ages, who mostly lived elsewhere; but yet it was, after the Show Area itself, the part of the city with the greatest concentration of ancient monuments that might either be adapted to residential use or dismantled for building materials.[8]

One can see, in short, why a growing proportion of up-and-coming families might have found it expedient to settle in what eventually became the late and postmedieval *abitato*, and it is striking how many newly prominent clans established themselves there from the 11th century on. The Papareschi dwelled in Trastevere, close to the Tiber and the bridges leading to the city center. The Pierleoni were based just across the river in the vicinity of the Theater of Marcellus, not far from the Berardi and Tebaldi families, who had residences in what is now the Jewish ghetto, in the *contrada* that became known from the later 11th century as the Calderario after the cauldron-makers who practiced their trade there. The Sant'Eustachio inhabited the eponymous *contrada* near the Pantheon. Other families established early on in the Campus Martius include the Buccapecora, the Boboni, the Tignosi, and the Bonfiglioli, and the list goes on. Indeed, it would be shorter to list the upstart noble clans based elsewhere, most important among them the Frangipane, who controlled a wide swath of territory stretching southward from S. Maria Nova and the Colosseum, across the northern slopes of the Palatine, and on to the Septizodium at the east end of the Circus Maximus.[9]

The reconfiguration of the Roman settlement map also manifests in the emergence of new neighborhoods and administrative subdivisions starting in the 11th century, just as the 14 ancient districts (*regiones*) established by Augustus finally disappeared for good from the vocabulary of the notaries who compiled the surviving archival documents. By the end of the 11th century, some 30 of these new regions are attested. They took their names from prominent monuments (Colosseo/S. Maria Nova; Ponte), from streets (Arenula; Biberatica; Trevi/*tribii*) or topographical features (Campus Martius; Pallara for the Palatine), from prevailing activities or professions (Scorteclari, Caccabarii), and so on. In contrast to the 14 Augustan *regiones*, which encompassed the entirety of the intramural area and more, most of the new regions were relatively small and clustered in those areas in the west where the population was concentrating. In the 12th century, these dozens of neighborhoods would coagulate into a new set of 12 larger *regiones*, *rioni* in the vernacular, each subdivided into smaller *contrade*. In the 13th century, the number rose to 13 with the addition of Trastevere. With the exception of the largest *rione*, Monti, which encompassed most of the hills in the east (the Quirinal, Viminal, Esquiline, and Caelian), they all occupied the low-lying ground in the west. For the rest of the Middle Ages, these *rioni* would define the administrative geography of the city (Fig. 6.1).[10]

Suggestive as it is, however, the picture of Rome's settlement map that results from archival documents and narrative histories that happen to mention names of neighborhoods, and the locations where members of a few prominent families

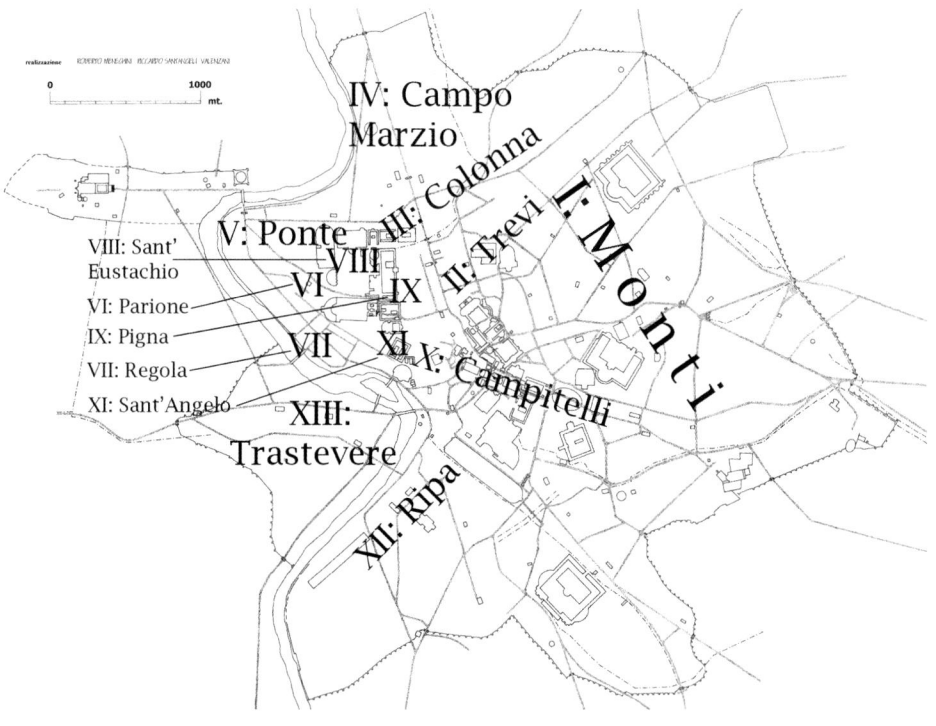

Figure 6.1 Rome's later medieval *rioni*; I–XII are attested in the 12th century, Trastevere in the 13th. (Author.)

resided, is impressionistic and very incomplete. Fortunately, the archaeological record is at last becoming robust enough to offer alternative ways of gauging where medieval Romans were living, and how the distribution of settlement changed over time. Distinctive, closely datable types of ceramics in everyday use provide the single best proxy for human presence. Where people use ceramics, they also regularly break them, and the useless fragments of shattered vessels tend to be discarded near where they were used and broken. One of the most ubiquitous and easily identified kinds of pottery produced in Rome and its surroundings in the period c. 800–1200 is the so-called Forum Ware, or thick-glazed ware (*ceramica a vetrina pesante*), and its later stylistic offshoots (sparse-glazed ware, or *ceramica a vetrina sparsa*), all of which can now be dated with some precision. As this typological sequence comfortably spans the critical transitional phase when the diffuse early medieval settlement map contracted into a more compact nucleus, its spatial distribution offers valuable clues about when and how the change occurred.[11]

The first phase of production is the thick-glazed ware proper, which has a heavy coat of vitreous glaze, usually greenish but shading also into hues of dull yellow and brown, applied fairly evenly over the visible surfaces of the vessel (Fig. 6.2). (The vessels themselves were usually closed shapes like pitchers and jugs that were suitable for holding and storing liquids; plates and bowls are much rarer, evidently because such open shapes were usually made of wood in this period.) After occasional initial appearances shortly before 800, production ramped up steadily over the course of the 9th and 10th centuries, building toward quasi-industrial levels by the 11th. As of c. 2014, examples typical of the period c. 800–950 had turned up in more than 40 discrete locales inside the city walls, in sites excavated anytime from the later 19th century to the present. While (naturally) far from comprehensive, this is a considerable

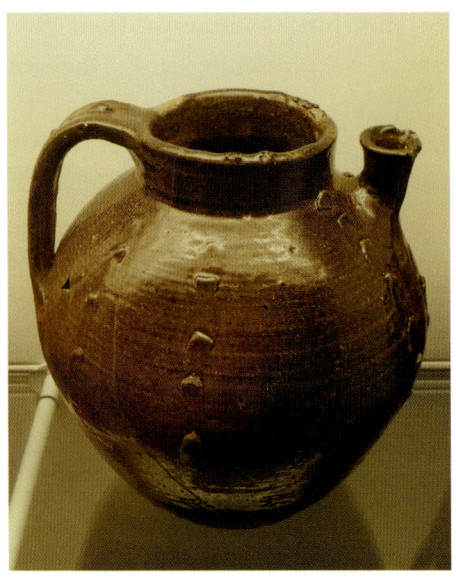

Figure 6.2 Thick-glazed pitcher from the Crypta Balbi excavations, late 9th or 10th century, Museo Nazionale della Cripta Balbi. (Author.)

sample of useful data. As one might hope, the distribution of thick-glazed ware tracks quite closely with the patterning of settlement traced, in the preceding two chapters, on the basis of textual references to and material traces of early medieval housing c. 800–950. Much the densest concentration occurs all across the Show Area and its immediate surroundings, from the *Ripa Graeca*/Forum Boarium and the slopes of the Capitoline to the Palatine, northward across the Forum and imperial forums, and onward to the initial tract of the Via Lata and the neighborhood of Alberic's stronghold at SS. Apostoli. A more diffuse but still considerable scatter of sites extends south and east from the main nucleus, from the Aventine in the west, through the valley of the Via Appia, via the Baths of Caracalla and S. Sisto Vecchio, and on across the summit of the Caelian (S. Stefano Rotondo, the former Basilica Hilariana, and S. Clemente). As for the Campus Martius, there is conspicuously little, and only a single site in all the large expanse west of the Crypta Balbi and S. Lorenzo in Damaso. Thus, the Forum Ware proxy test for population, too, suggests that the centripetal flow of inhabitants

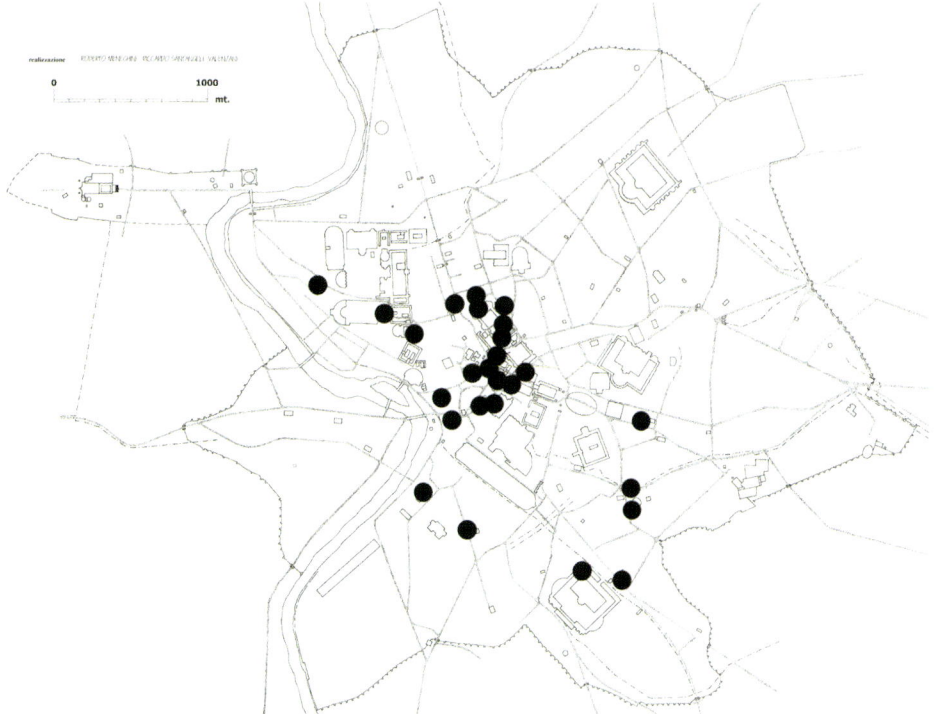

Figure 6.3 Intramural distribution of thick-glazed ceramics, c. 800–950. (Redrawn from Rascaglia and Russo 2015, fig. 3.)

toward the Tiber bend had yet to occur by the mid 10th century, when the next ceramic phase begins (Fig. 6.3).

After the mid 10th century, the vitreous coating of thick-glazed ware began to thin and recede from parts of the surface, exposing areas of unglazed clay. This transitional style spanned the years c. 950–1075, emerging as the mature sparse-glazed ware (*ceramica a vetrina sparsa*) of the period c. 1075–1200, which has bands or splatters of glaze on the body of the vessel, much of which remained unglazed (Fig. 6.4). The sites where transitional and sparse-glazed ware occur correspond to a considerable extent with the find-spots of thick-glazed ware from the preceding period, and the environs of the Show Area still predominate. But where there are divergences in the post-950 record, they are suggestive. In the 'transitional' phase, c. 950–1075, the few preexisting sites in the Campus Martius, all of which continue, are joined by others, notably

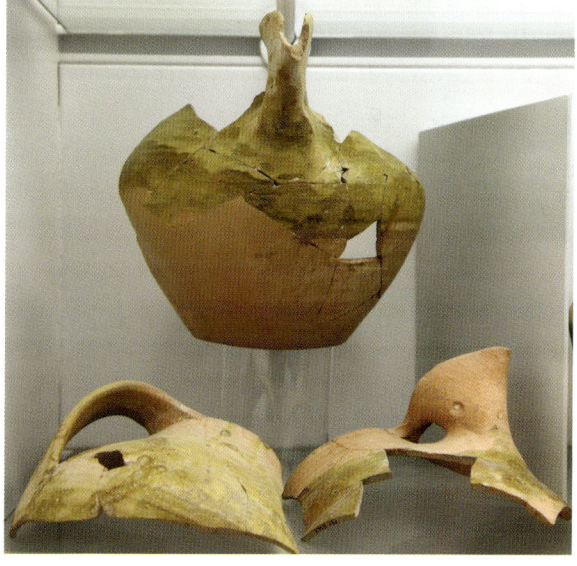

Figure 6.4 12th-century sparse-glazed pitchers from the Crypta Balbi excavations, in the Museo Nazionale della Cripta Balbi. (Author.)

around Piazza Navona, where transitional pottery turns up in multiple locations. It also occurs a short distance to the south in Via dei Chiavari,

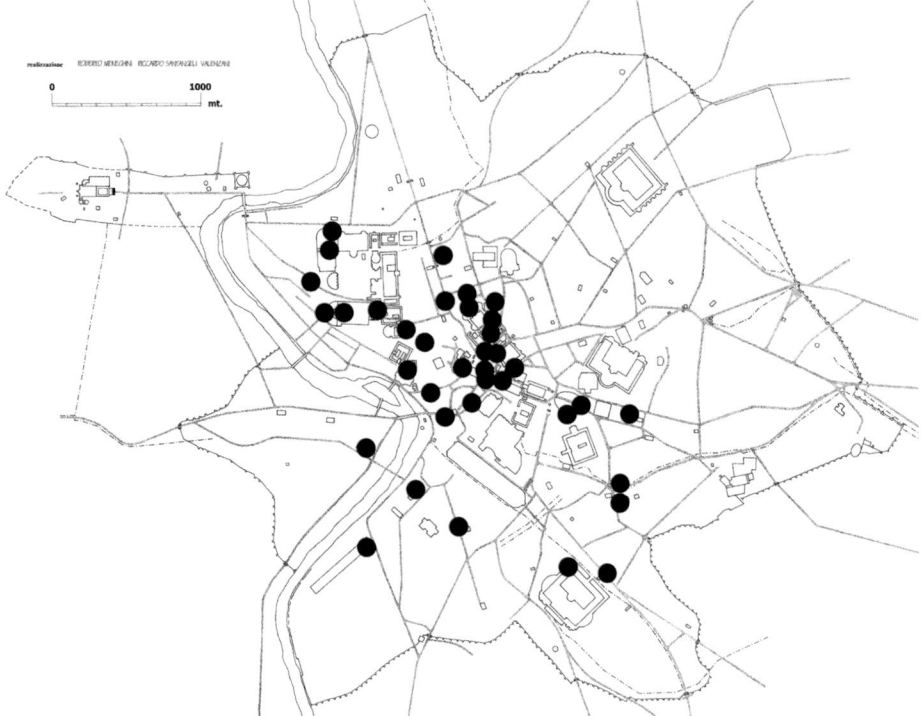

Figure 6.5 Intramural distribution of transitional-period ceramics, c. 950–1075. (Redrawn from Rascaglia and Russo 2015, fig. 5.)

and in multiple locations along the river toward the *Ripa Graeca*, at the Theater of Marcellus and Tor de' Specchi (Fig. 6.5). From the late 11th century, glazed pottery spreads to other locations in the Tiber bend, from Palazzo Altemps all the way to the river by the mausoleum of Augustus. It also shows up in growing quantities in central Trastevere. But – and this is important – the easternmost sites atop the Caelian (the Basilica Hilariana, S. Stefano Rotondo) where the earlier styles were found drop off the map by the late 11th century, prior to the transition to mature sparse-glaze, none of which has yet been found there. The ceramic record on the Caelian thus supports the case outlined in Chapter 5 for declining 11th-century settlement on the eastern edge of the city (Fig. 6.6).[12]

Though the map of ceramic finds is far from complete, the evidence so far available presents a fairly coherent picture. Throughout the years c. 800–1200, and indeed for the rest of the Middle Ages, the tightest grouping of diagnostic glazed ceramics – and presumably the population that used them – occupies a nucleus roughly centered on the Capitoline Hill and the Forum area, extending from the *Ripa Graeca* in the south to SS. Apostoli and S. Maria Nova in the north. This density is partially a function of the intense archaeological coverage of this zone, to be sure, but there can be no doubt that there was always a consistent human presence here. What is interesting is the ways in which patterns of settlement around that central nucleus shift over time. From the 11th century on, the Campus Martius gains steadily in prominence, though there is still very little in the far western tip of the river-bend. Meanwhile, there is correspondingly less happening in the east from the 11th century, certainly by the start of the mature sparse glazed period after c. 1075, from which point nearly all the new ceramic find-spots crop up in the west.

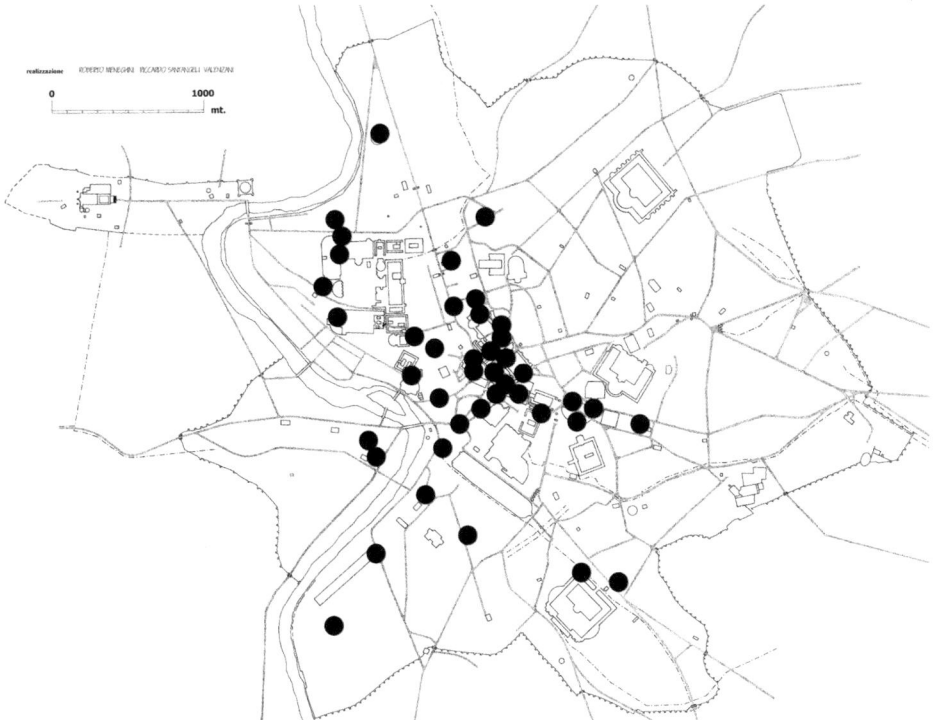

Figure 6.6 Intramural distribution of sparse-glazed ceramics, later 11th to early 13th century. (Redrawn from Rascaglia and Russo 2015, fig. 7.)

Thus, into the 11th century, the main nucleus around the Show Area was roughly at the center of a more diffuse constellation of other sites. From the 12th century, by contrast, that nucleus marked the eastern periphery of the main zones of settlement, though it still had an eastern 'tail' extending to the Lateran via the Colosseum and S. Clemente. Subsequent expansion of settlement came chiefly on the low ground to the west, on both sides of the Tiber. Were the intensity of archaeological investigation in these areas to match that devoted to the Show Area, the westward shift might well become considerably more pronounced. The current void in the Borgo, for instance, where little has been done in the era of conscientious medieval archaeology, would probably be filled in.

The gradual westward migration continued across the 13th–15th centuries, when sparse-glazed pottery was supplanted on Roman tables by new and more colorful types of glazed wares derived from Islamic productions. First came the so-called *ceramica laziale*, or Roman proto-maiolica, in the 13th and early 14th centuries (Fig. 6.7), followed by early forms of maiolica in the later 14th and 15th centuries. The distribution map of the ceramic finds from these later years can largely speak for itself (Fig. 6.8). The eastern 'tail' to the Lateran persists, but finds otherwise cluster overwhelmingly in the low-lying ground in the west, including much of the Campus Martius.[13]

It may not be coincidence that the westward-moving users of these high-quality tablewares started to build new and different kinds of residential complexes after c. 1050, as they began to cluster more thickly and jostle up against each other in the low-lying neighborhoods north and west of the Capitoline. The tensions and rivalries that naturally arose as Rome's refractory property-owning classes

180 ~ THE MAKING OF MEDIEVAL ROME

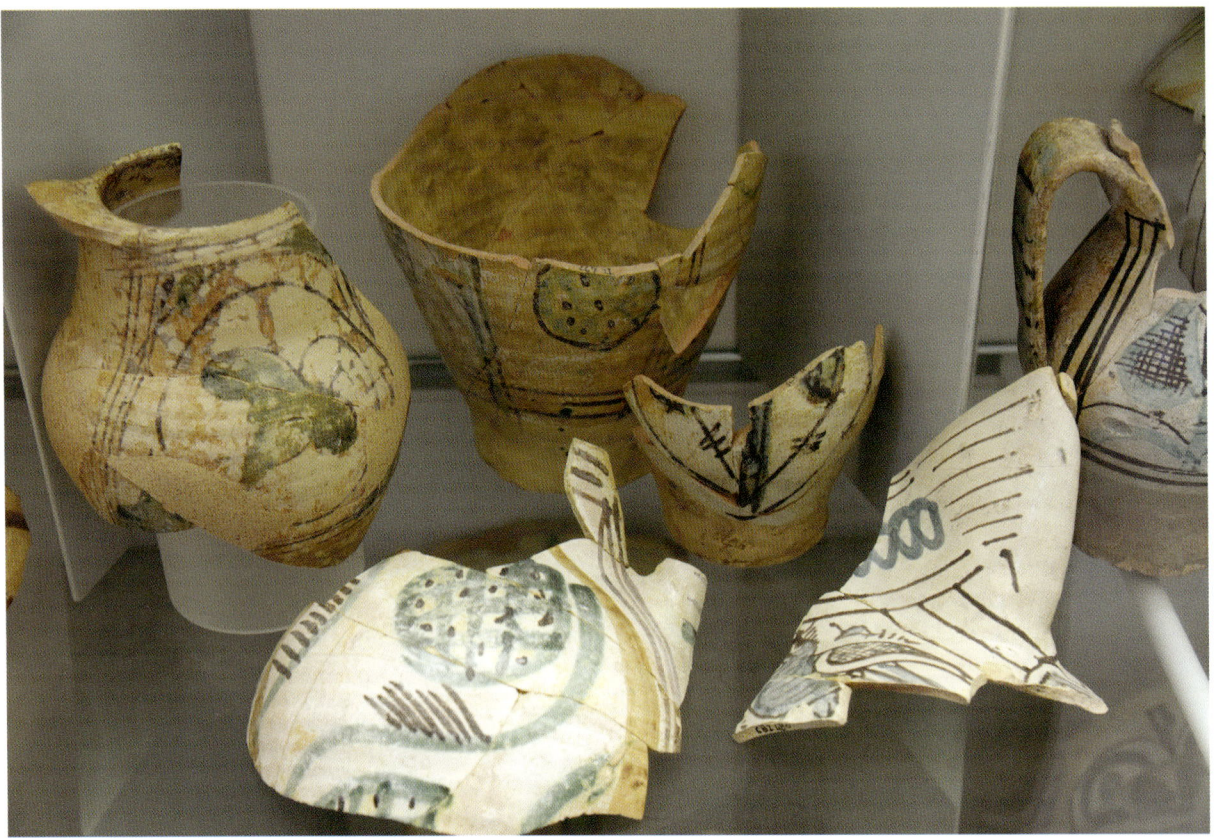

Figure 6.7 Roman proto-maiolica (13th – early 14th century) in the Museo Nazionale della Cripta Balbi. (Author.)

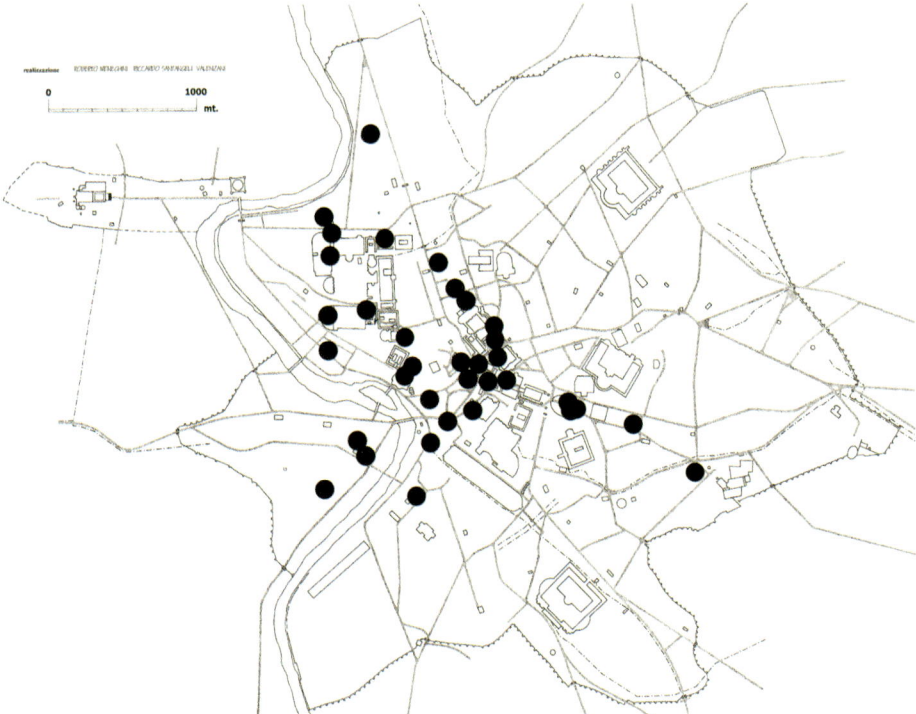

Figure 6.8 Intramural distribution of glazed ceramics (Roman proto-maiolica, etc.), 13th – early 14th century. (Redrawn from Rascaglia and Russo 2015, fig. 9.)

grew in numbers, wealth, and ambition were exacerbated by the simmering conflict that subsisted between the 'Gregorian' and 'imperial' factions across the early reform period. It is against this background that the signal architectonic development of the later 11th century should be seen: the militarization of the residential landscape. The circumscribed but seemingly not overtly militarized *curtes* and town houses characteristic of the 9th and 10th centuries began to transform into more heavily fortified compounds, complete with towers that were both a proclamation of status and a practical means of prosecuting conflicts against rivals – a last refuge against attack and a commanding vantage from which to rain down missiles on adversaries.

The first archival appearance of a tower associated with a residential compound comes in a rental contract of 1069 for a property near S. Maria in Trastevere. Thereafter, others appear in contracts of 1073, 1076, 1086, 1094, 1117, 1129, 1145, 1149, 1155, and 1192. Most, as we might expect, are located in the Campus Martius. But these dozen-odd mentions of towers in documents predating 1200 can only hint at the tower-building craze that swept the city in these years. Though their sudden appearance in multiple documents in the later 11th century is surely significant, towers are nonetheless badly underrepresented in the archival sources. In part, this is because the preserved archives are overwhelmingly ecclesiastical: since Romans rarely gave towers to the Church, they naturally occur infrequently in contracts preserved by religious institutions. Further, towers were often internal features of properties, incorporated into other structures or surrounded by perimeter walls, such that they did not mark the confines of a property and were therefore not cited in descriptions of boundaries.[14]

The timing of the earliest documentary reference to a tower in 1069 is closely paralleled in narrative histories and chronicles, which also start to feature towers – prominently – in the second half of the 11th century. In 1062, the staunchly anti-Gregorian nobleman, Cencius (*Cencius praefecti Stephani*), hosted (anti-)pope Cadalus/Honorius II in the tower he himself had built athwart Ponte Sant'Angelo, thus in an exceptionally strategic location on the single bridge connecting the city center to the Vatican. The *LP* explicitly calls the place a tower (*turris*). Thirteen years later, after the same Cencius spectacularly abducted Gregory VII from Christmas mass at S. Maria Maggiore, he locked the pope in his "house" (*domus*) in the Campus Martius, located near the bridge with his tower. This "house" too was presumably well fortified, in order to be chosen as a place of confinement for a popular pope, though it was promptly "taken" by a throng of enraged Romans, who freed Gregory and leveled his place of imprisonment. In 1093/94, the Frangipane would protect Urban II against the partisans of Guibert/Clement III by hosting him in a "most solid fortress" (*firmissima munitio*) near S. Maria Nova. By the early 12th century, the Frangipane neighborhood stronghold between S. Maria Nova and the Palatine included multiple fortified residences held by various family members, and at least three imposing towers. In 1145, the family acquired yet another tower, the *turris de Arco* at the center of a fortified enclosure in the curved end of the Circus Maximus, which still stands today, albeit in considerably altered and lowered form (Fig. 6.9).[15]

Most of Rome's medieval towers do not survive, however, and most of those that do date to the 12th century and (especially) later, such that the textual sources remain the best way of understanding the distribution and configuration of the earliest towers. The very few "towers" mentioned before 1000 (Katermaa-Ottela counts 11 in all) were established inside or atop imposing ancient monuments, such as Castel Sant'Angelo and the Septizodium, thus enhancing the already considerable defensive and visual profile of these looming piles. The thirty-four

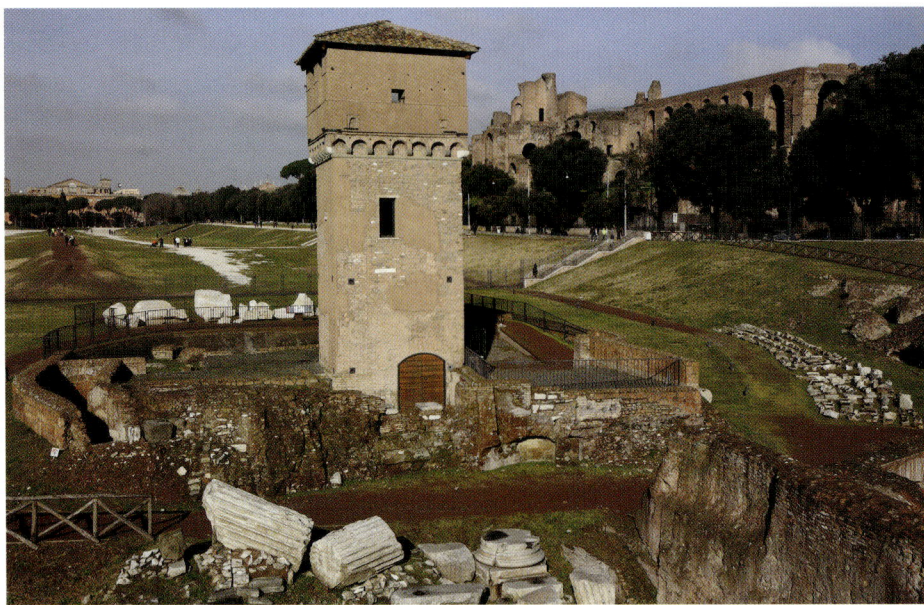

Figure 6.9 The *turris de Arco* in the Circus Maximus, acquired by the Frangipane in 1145. (Author.)

new towers attested in the 11th century – already a steep increase – were commonly still placed atop ancient structures: solid concrete vaults, triumphal arches, and so on. They thus tended to be separate from residential buildings, and it is important to stress, as Hubert has, that these early towers served only as occasional refuges, and were usually neither inhabited nor directly incorporated into the houses of their proprietors. They were established in the most commanding locations possible within easy reach of their owners' residences.[16]

This all makes a certain amount of a priori sense. Into the 12th century, enough ancient edifices suitable for the erection of towers were available to satisfy the needs of most tower-building families. They acquired the desired structure, raised a tower on it for protection and puffing of family pride, and dwelled nearby. Some proprietors in the period c. 1050–1150 probably indeed chose to establish residences wherever they managed to acquire a promising ruin on which to found a tower, often with an eye to controlling busy streets and strategic junctions. But from the later 12th century on, the supply of suitable ruins in desirable locations was diminishing, while the population continued to grow. The calculations of Katermaa-Ottela give a sense of the saturation process that occurred over time: eleven towers built before 1000; thirty-four in the 11th century; forty-one in the 12th; eighty-eight in the 13th (more than the combined total of all earlier towers!); sixty-five in the 14th, and fifty in the 15th. As towers became *de rigueur* for any ambitious family of means, more families will have had to make do with erecting them on whatever property they happened to occupy, such that towers were increasingly incorporated into the residential units themselves. Thus emerged the "house-tower" (*casatorre* in Italian) typical of the 12th and 13th centuries: a compact ensemble of living and service spaces with an attached tower, whose outer walls formed a more or less defensible perimeter. This paradigm has close parallels in north-central Italian cities (Florence, Siena, Bologna, Milan, etc.), whose densely packed centers approximated the crowded conditions now developing in Rome's most populous neighborhoods in the west, where most of the new *casatorri* were built.[17]

Most of the extant towers, a small fraction of the total that once existed, belong to this second

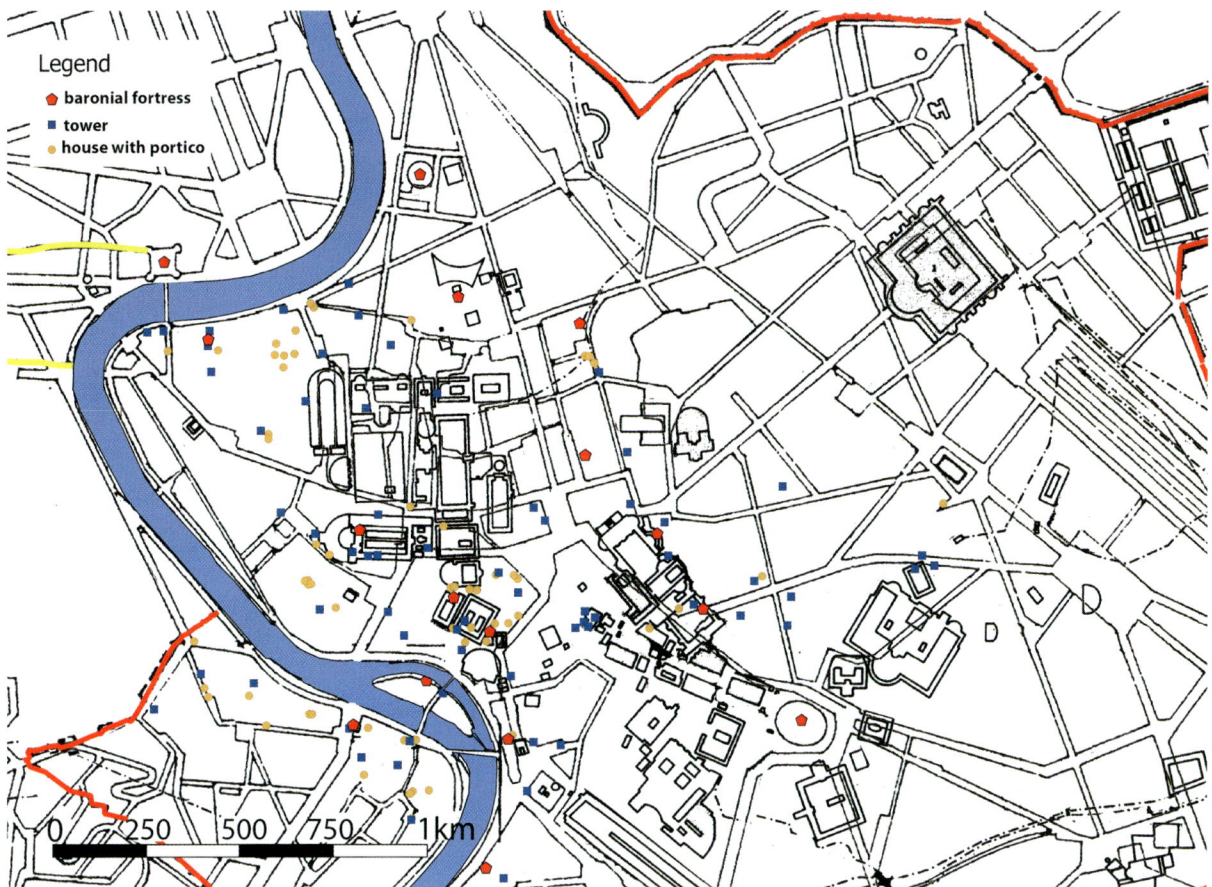

Figure 6.10 Distribution of baronial fortresses, towers, and houses with street porticoes, based on the digital *Forma Urbis* of medieval Rome. (Image courtesy of Nicoletta Giannini.)

phase, from the later 12th century on. We now finally have a means of cataloguing and analyzing systematically their surviving remains, thanks to Nicoletta Giannini's new digital *Forma Urbis* of medieval Rome, a GIS database that includes entries for (among other things) all extant medieval buildings inside the city walls. The count currently stands at eighty-nine towers, most of which can be dated to the 12th and, especially, the 13th centuries. Less than 10 percent of the sample clearly postdates the 13th century, while only one or two towers plausibly predate the 12th. Unsurprisingly, they cluster thickly across the populous neighborhoods in the west, though a substantial group also extends father east into the Subura in the *rione* Monti (Fig. 6.10). The model of the house-tower, the residential complex that grew up alongside or around a fortified nucleus, increasingly predominated by the 13th century, as the text-based analyses of Hubert and others had already suggested.[18]

These towers were typically built either in masonry of recycled ancient brick, more common in the 12th and early 13th centuries, and later also in *petit appareil* stonework of small, roughly rectangular *tufelli*. Well-preserved examples include the two Capocci family towers by S. Martino ai Monti on the Esquiline; the Torre del Grillo and Torre dei Borgia in the Subura; the Torre dei Grassi attached to the inside of the propylon of the Porticus Octaviae in the Ghetto and the nearby Torre dei Margana in Piazza Margana; the Torre del Papito at Largo Argentina; and the Torre della Scimmia/Torre degli Scapucci

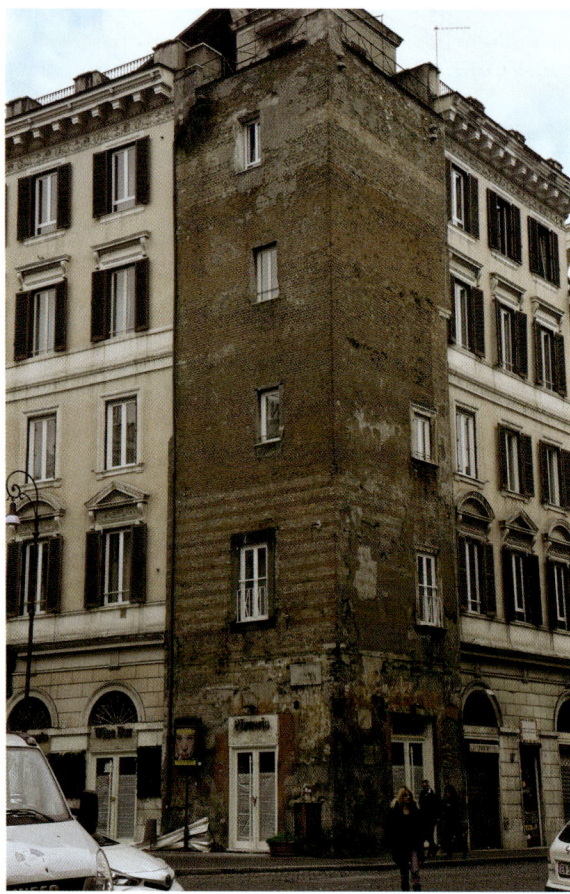

Figure 6.11 The 13th-century Tor Sanguigna in the Campus Martius, located just north of Piazza Navona. Note the decorative bands above ground-floor level. (Author.)

and Tor Sanguigna in the Campus Martius (*rione* Ponte) (Fig. 6.11). But by far the most impressive of the extant towers, which dominates the skyline of the Subura in today's *rione* Monti almost as much as it did in 15th- and 16th-century *vedute*, is the Torre delle Milizie, built atop the Markets of Trajan. In its initial phase, datable to the early 13th century, it was a slender beanstalk well over 50 m high; later in the 13th century, perhaps because of structural problems, the original structure was encased in the two massive, tapering stages, over 3 m thick at the base, that it features today, above which project remnants of the square top of the original tower, ruined in the earthquake of 1349 (Figs. 6.12–13). This tower was once rivaled by the nearby Tor de' Conti, probably erected during

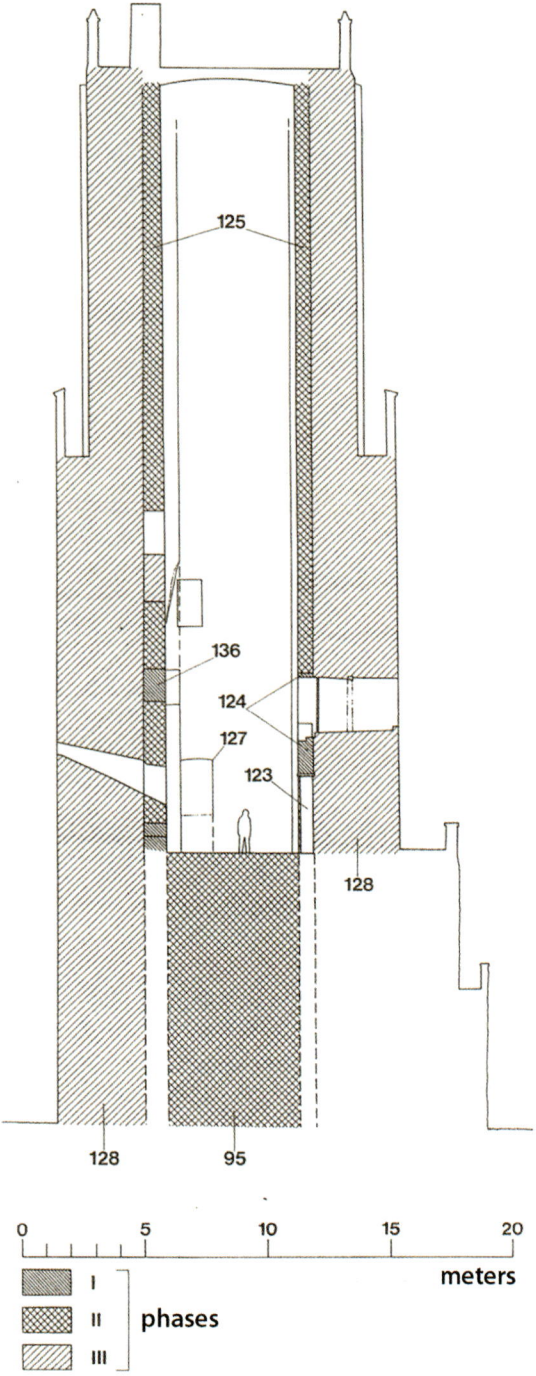

Figure 6.12 Section drawing of the Torre delle Milizie, with its two primary construction phases (phases II and III, respectively early and late 13th century) and the remnants of the preexisting 12th-century residential hall (Phase I). (Bernacchio and Meneghini 1994, fig. 4.)

the pontificate of the great Conti pope, Innocent III (r. 1198–1216). Judging by the dimensions of the surviving base and the thickness of its walls, it

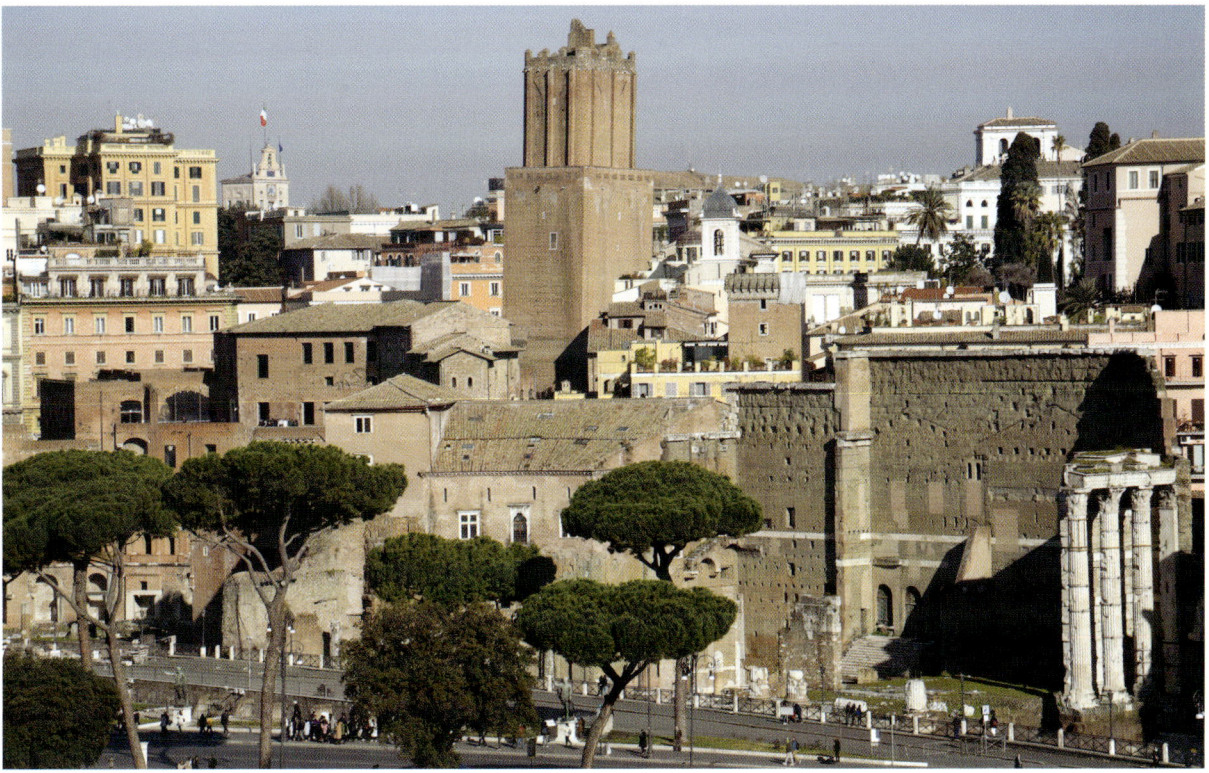

Figure 6.13 The Torre delle Milizie rising about the Forum of Augustus (lower right) and Markets of Trajan (lower left). (Author.)

would have been still higher and more massive than the Torre delle Milizie. It had more aesthetic pretensions, too, evident in the elegant bands of black and white stonework at the base (Fig. 6.14). Originally surrounded by fortified enclosures, proper urban castles, these two towers bracketed the zone dominated by the Conti family in the early 13th century, making it a nearly impregnable clan stronghold.[19]

These and the dozens of other extant family towers can only hint at the extent to which the process of urban *incastellamento* transformed the cityscape in the later Middle Ages. As of 1050, there were few towers anywhere, and none incorporated into ordinary residential compounds, as far as we know. Yet around the beginning of the 13th century, the English pilgrim Master Gregory's first view of Rome from atop Monte Mario called to mind nothing so much as a field of grain, each of whose countless stalks was a tower. By then, ample swaths of intramural Rome must have looked like the Tuscan town of San Gimignano does today, only on a far greater scale, and more towers were being built every year, so many that in 1257, the ruling senator Brancaleone degli Andalò reportedly had about 140 private towers razed, which still left many others standing (Fig. 6.15).[20]

On a general level, as noted above, the 'encastling' of the cityscape looks to have roots in the rivalries and violent factionalism that divided the Roman populace during the reform period, and festered thanks in part to the interference of competing external powers involved in the struggle for control over the Church. But the reform movement set into motion other processes that helped urban clans to build fortified residences complete with imposing towers, and to maintain and often expand these familial strongholds over the long term. Tommaso di Carpegna Falconieri

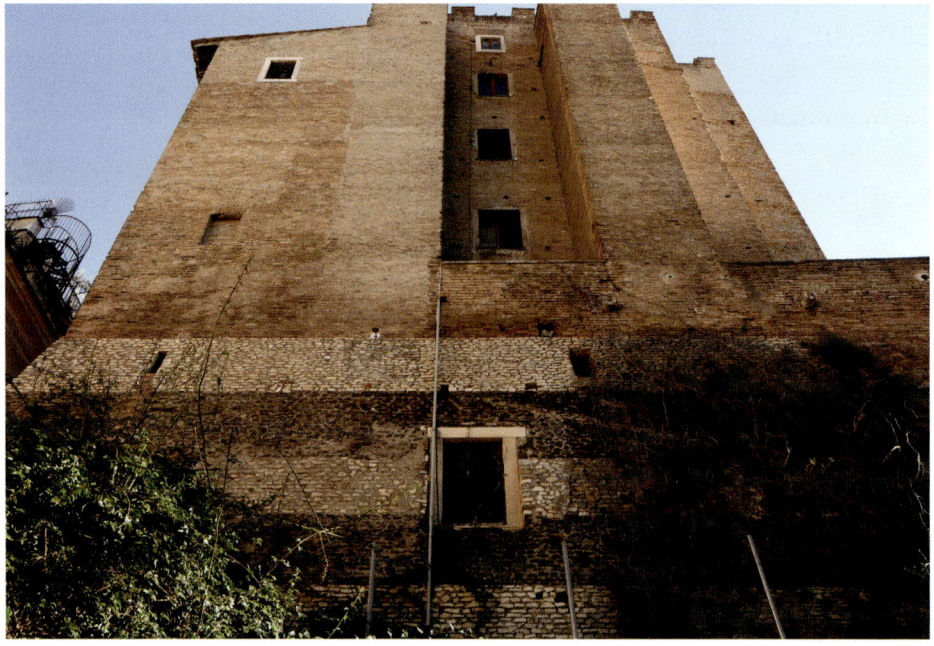

Figure 6.14 The west face of the Tor de' Conti. (Author.)

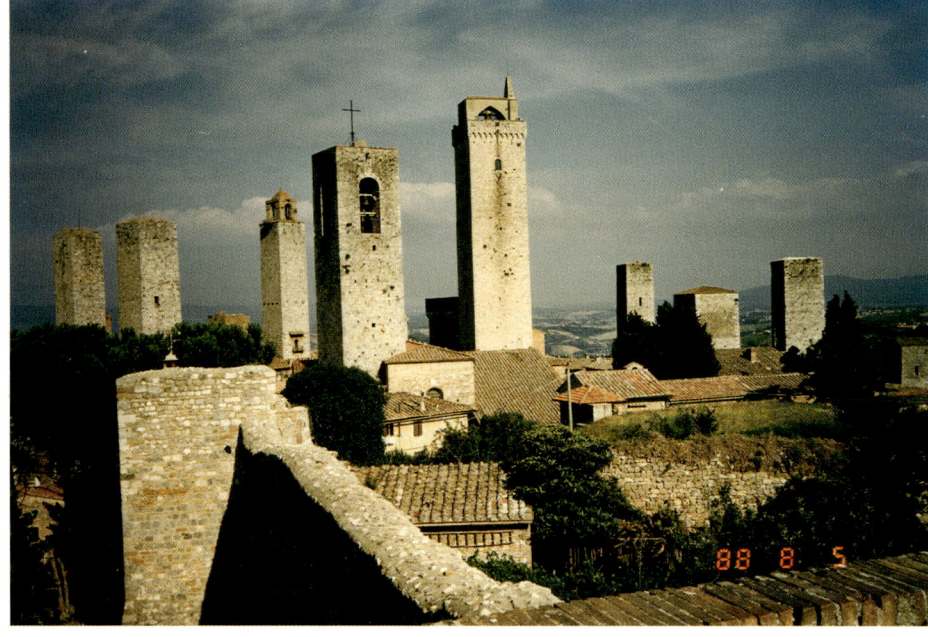

Figure 6.15 The skyline of San Gimignano today. (Wikimedia Commons/Friviere.)

points to two in particular. First, after c. 1050, wealthy Romans largely stopped donating or willing valuable properties to the Church. They did so for the very simple reason that, after the suppression of the *Adelspapsttum* in the 1040s, the Church of Rome no longer belonged to them. In the 10th century, as we have seen, upper-class Romans were only too happy to, for example, turn family properties into monasteries or charitable institutions. They maintained close ties with their foundations, had a say in who ran them – often relatives or clients – and continued to profit from them in various ways. Such 'gifts' to the Church often served to consolidate family possessions by rendering them inalienable by sale or inheritance. But in the reform period, wealthy proprietors had far less incentive to turn over prized possessions to a Church now staffed and ruled by zealous foreigners. They had to find alternative ways to avoid dissipating family patrimonies through marriage and divided inheritances.

This led to the second process adduced by Carpegna Falconieri, one that slowly gathered momentum in the period c. 1050–1200. Legal structures governing inheritance and legal title to property evolved to favor male heirs in patrilineal line of descent, and specifically eldest sons, such that family holdings were not dispersed among multiple heirs. By also discouraging the alienation of property via wives and daughters, through marriage or inheritance, this emerging agnatic system allowed real estate to be transmitted undivided from one generation to the next in the male line. True dynastic clan holdings thus came into being, stable agglomerations of property that successive generations could consolidate, expand, and improve with new buildings and amenities, including towers – investments both for the present and the future. So it was that by c. 1200, many influential families had come to be firmly rooted in their particular corners of the city. Some would derive their family names from their locales of origin, like the Sant'Eustachio or later the Annibaldi *de Rota* ("from the Colosseum"), while others would lend their names to features located within their sphere of influence (the Arcionii to the churches of S. Nicola and S. Stefano *de Arcionibus* in the Trevi *rione*, the Mellini to another church of S. Nicola, the Baroncini to S. Salvatore *de Barunciniis*, and so on), or even to a whole neighborhood (*contrada*) in the case of the Arcionii and the *contrada de Arcionibus* in the Trevi *rione*.[21]

The diminished access of local Romans to the upper echelons of the ecclesiastical administration during the reform period, then, provided part of the impetus for the creation of the *contrade* into which the city's thirteen late medieval *rioni* were subdivided (Fig. 6.1, above), some of which were lastingly shaped by the presence of the powerful families that stably resided in them. In 'disinheriting' the Church and moving to agnatic modes of inheritance, these families were able to maintain lasting control over urban properties that were well worth furnishing with fortified residences built to last, complete with towers to protect and exalt the families who built them.

As for the less elevated members of Rome's propertied classes, who crowded in cheek by jowl with the magnates in the more populous neighborhoods, we are mostly dependent on the property documents for an understanding of how and where they were living, especially prior to the 13th century. Here it suffices to summarize some of the salient points in Étienne Hubert's superb survey of the archival records. In the 11th century, settlement density everywhere remained relatively low. Houses tended to be bordered on at least one and often on multiple sides by vacant plots. As in the preceding centuries, most had only a single story, and even the grander residences rarely exceeded two. They were virtually always freestanding, sharing no walls with neighboring dwellings, and occupied a limited portion of the housing plot, leaving space for yards and gardens at both front and back. After an initial period of expansion in the first half of the 11th century, when monasteries such as S. Ciriaco in Via Lata started dividing their holdings into building lots, new development slowed until the 1120s, a pause that corresponds suggestively with the years of turmoil that followed the advent of the reform papacy. From the 1120s until the late 13th century, however, the quantity and density of housing in the prime residential zones grew considerably. It was in these years that the crowded center of late- and post-medieval Rome began to take shape in the low-lying regions on both sides of the Tiber: from the *Ripa Graeca* and the foot of the Capitoline in the south to the top of the Tiber bend in the north; from the Via Lata and Trevi Fountain in the east to Trastevere and the Borgo in the west.

Land-rich churches and monasteries were among the primary drivers of residential development: S. Silvestro in Capite in the Trevi *rione*; S. Ciriaco along both sides of the Via Lata; S. Maria in Campo Marzio farther west in the Campus Martius; SS. Cosma e Damiano in Trastevere, and many others. They marked out housing plots and leased them to tenants who were responsible for putting up houses, generally required to be done within the first few years of the lease. The plots were usually rectangular, disposed in continuous files that fronted on a road, and tended to be between 50 and 150 square meters in area (though plots as small as 20 m^2 and large as 370 m^2 are known). By 1194, S. Maria in Campo Marzio would own and rent to paying tenants more than 150 houses in its neighborhood, and it was hardly the biggest of Rome's ecclesiastical landowners.[22]

But while the division of land into contiguous lots in the western nucleus of the later medieval *abitato* was well advanced by c. 1200, it is important to note that the houses built on these plots were still rarely attached so as to present an unbroken sequence of street-facing façades. The earliest documentary mention of a common wall shared between two houses appears only in 1199, though rows of contiguous houses undoubtedly existed in some places by then. References to connected houses gradually increase over the course of the 13th century, but even by 1300 contiguous dwellings were hardly ubiquitous.

Apparently it was only from the 13th century that rising population pressure, and the steadily growing value of both land and housing that ensued, compelled most property owners to build across the full width of their plots, and generally to make more intensive use of the land they had available – it is also in the 13th century that houses regularly started to be built out as far as the streets that fronted them, dispensing with the open-air courtyards prevalent until then. Thereafter, the preferred intermediate space between domestic interiors and streets was the covered portico, usually supported by ancient column shafts, whose immured remains persist across the late medieval *abitato* (Figs. 6.10 and 6.16). (It is not coincidence that most preserved medieval houses date to the 13th century and later, when they attained their mature proportions; those built earlier were replaced or swallowed up by wider houses that spanned the full width of the available street frontage and rose higher, too, often to three or four stories (see below, Fig. 7.17). But, again, even by 1300, this transition from separate to attached housing was far from complete. The contiguous, densely packed facades crowding forward onto narrow streets that still characterize much of the Campus Martius and Trastevere, for example, in many cases only reached full saturation in the 15th and 16th centuries, after a substantial pause in the 14th.[23]

Turning back now from the *longue durée* to the beginning of the reform period, we can say that the acceleration of the westward population shift and the first appearances of fortified houses and towers are the two signal topographical developments of the later 11th century. Otherwise, there was relative stasis. The climate of political instability and partisan strife that provided much of the initial impetus for building the first family towers and fortified houses ensured that little else was attempted, least of all by the contending pontiffs, who were too busy confronting

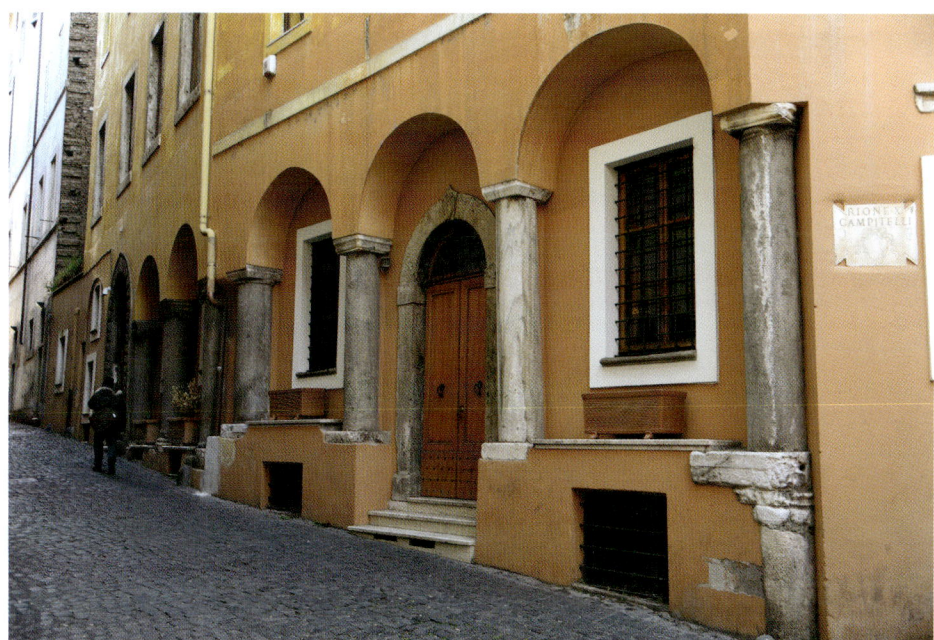

Figure 6.16 Immured street-portico in Via di S. Angelo in Pescheria. (Author.)

their opponents to concern themselves much with church-building and public works in general.

In fact, there is no evidence of a pope (or antipope) as the main sponsor or funder of a single important architectural commission in the second half of the 11th century. Few churches were built at all, and those that were tended to be small and undistinguished. One is the vanished S. Maria in Portico in the *Ripa Graeca*, along the porticoes of the old Via Triumphalis/*porticus maximae*, dated to 1073 by an inscription on the surviving altar. The inscription does not say who sponsored the work, but it seems not to have been Pope Gregory VII, who is only said to have consecrated the place upon its completion. Another is S. Maria in Cappella in Trastevere, erected around 1090 and hardly bigger than a chapel; its patron is unknown (Fig. 6.17).[24]

Most of the work attributable to identifiable clerics was done by cardinal priests on their titular churches, and abbots on their monasteries. One of the most ambitious projects was a thorough renovation of S. Pudenziana by its cardinal priest, Benedict. An inscription preserved in the left-hand aisle explicitly credits him with the work, which occurred under Gregory VII. At S. Cecilia, the cardinal priest Desiderius of Montecassino oversaw the installation of a new altar in the *confessio* around 1080, which Pope Gregory was again present to consecrate. At S. Cosimato, a preserved inscription records abbot Odmundus' restoration of the cloister c. 1069, when Alexander II presided over the reconsecration of the church. The monastic church of S. Biagio alla Pagnotta was likewise renovated by its abbot, Dominic, in the twelfth and final year of Pope Alexander II's reign (1072); a second inscription of the same year mentions work on a porch, a (bell?) tower, and a residential *domus*.[25]

As in the preceding two centuries, it was still lay patrons who sponsored much of the important work done in the later 11th. Probably in the 1080s, Beno de Rapiza and his wife, Marozia, donated a new fresco cycle in the lower church of S. Clemente, featuring scenes from the life of

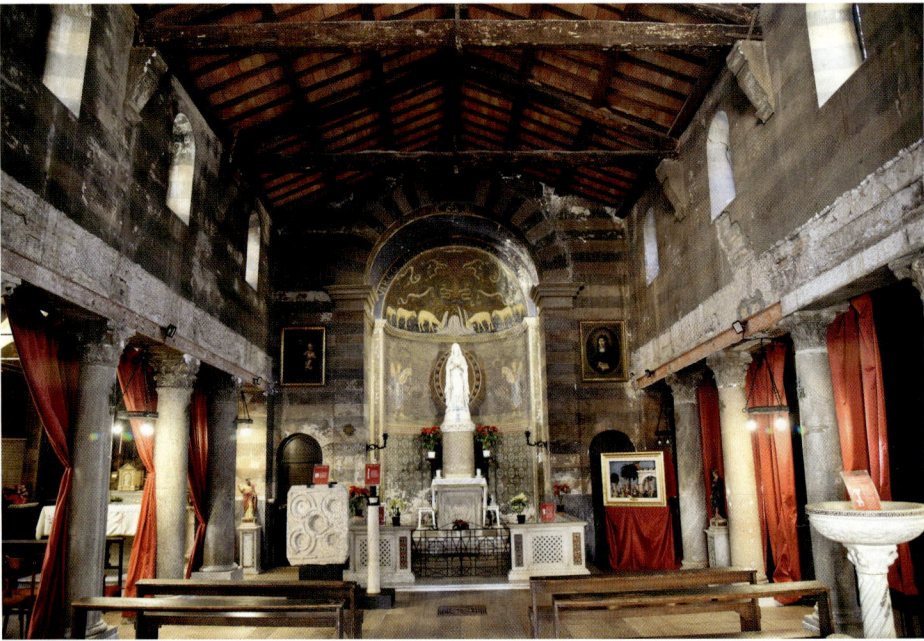

Figure 6.17 S. Maria in Cappella. (Author.)

the titular saint. Donor portraits of the couple are preserved, along with the painted text of their dedication (Fig. 6.18). Outside the walls on the Via Appia, S. Urbano alla Caffarella, which occupied a 2nd-century temple, also got an extensive new cycle of frescoes on all four interior walls, perhaps around the same time. The frescoes are badly damaged but preserve traces of the donor portraits of another lay couple, more of which was visible when they were drawn in the 17th century, along with the accompanying painted dedication. While obviously well-off, the donors at both S. Clemente and S. Urbano do not seem to have come from the crème de la crème of the Roman nobility – they were not scions of old-regime families like the Tuscolani and Crescenzi, nor of rising powers like the Frangipane and Pierleoni. Their works bear further witness to the steadily rising tide of medium elites and minor nobles that continued apace throughout the 11th century, notwithstanding the political dramas of the time. By the middle of the 12th, many such families would take the lead in the bid for control over civic government that culminated in the establishment of the Senate and commune of Rome in 1143–4.[26]

They would butt up against a resurgent Church, however, whose powers had grown immensely in the first half of the 12th century, following the triumph of the Hildebrandine/Gregorian faction over the imperial. The ascendancy of the Church began in earnest during the long pontificate of Paschal II (1099–1118), whose election was shortly followed in 1100 by the death of Guibert/Clement III, the longest-reigning and most formidable of the antipopes, who controlled Rome for most of the period 1084–99. In 1111, Pope Paschal reached an initial compromise on investitures with the new German emperor, Henry V (whom Paschal was reluctantly convinced to crown at St. Peter's as part of the bargain), which paved the way for a final resolution in the Concordat of Worms of 1122, signed between Henry and Pope Callixtus II. If Gregory VII had prepared the ideological template for an imperial papacy, independent of

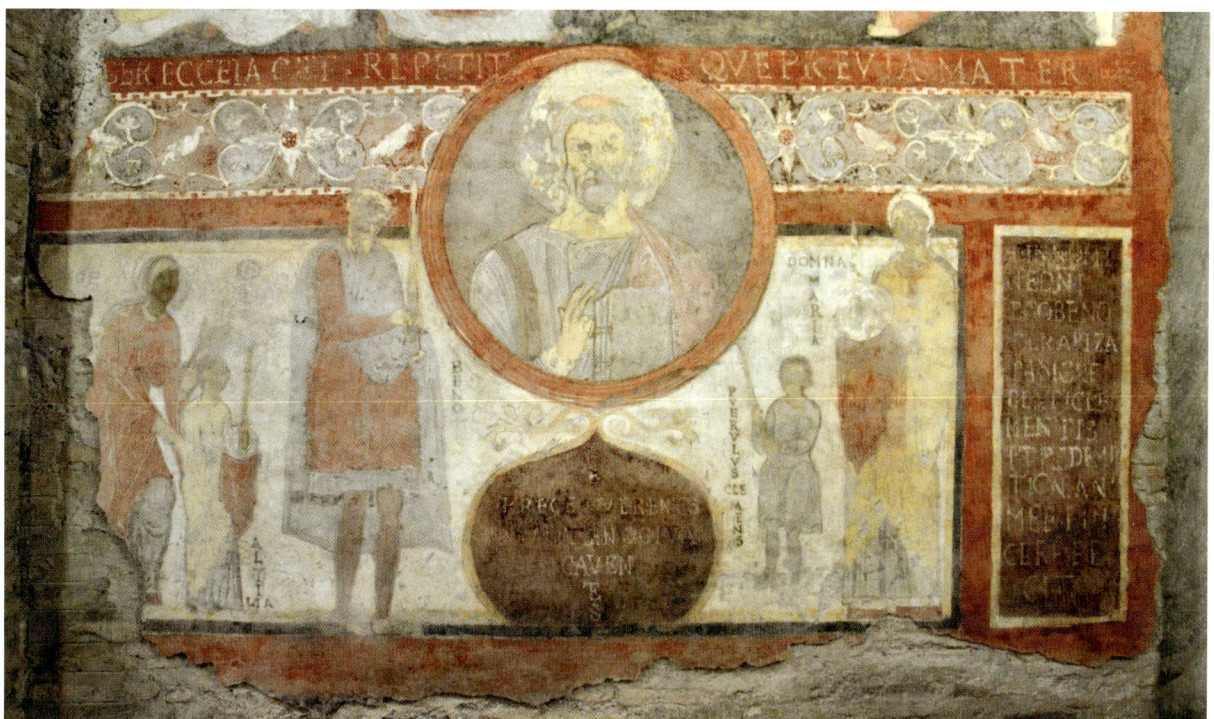

Figure 6.18 S. Clemente, lower level: donor portraits of Beno (left) and Marozia (right) with their two children, flanking a central medallion of Christ. (Author.)

the secular arm and empowered with the rights and privileges embodied in the Donation of Constantine, it was left to Paschal II and his successors to translate the vision into reality. For the first time since the 9th century, popes ruled triumphant in Rome, and once again, they turned seriously to putting their stamp on the city. To do so, they deployed a cohesive, mutually reinforcing battery of ceremony and symbols, images and architecture.[27]

Paschal and his leading allies in the Curia set about transforming the resurgent papal capital into a new incarnation of imperial and early Christian Rome, with the pope in the guise of a latter-day emperor, both spiritually and temporally supreme. There was much to do, in general to compensate for two centuries of neglect of religious architecture, and more immediately to remedy the scars of the past half-century of conflict, prominently including those left by the Norman incursion of 1084. This had caused localized but still substantial damage, notably on the Caelian Hill between the Lateran and the Colosseum. But the first site chosen for renewal was a place with few rivals in terms of both visibility and symbolic impact: the church of S. Adriano in the old Senate House at the Forum. Within two years of Paschal's accession in 1099, the ancient building morphed into a three-aisle basilica with the addition of internal arcades supported by ancient column shafts. Its floor was raised more than 3 m over its original level, and a new apse was built. Elsewhere, the early medieval church of S. Bartolomeo on the Tiber Island was replaced by the current building, probably by as early as 1113; and the new church of S. Maria in Monticelli rose a few hundred meters away in the southern Campus Martius.[28]

The epicenter of activity under Paschal II was the fire-scarred Caelian, where three substantial projects unfolded more or less simultaneously. (One might see here an attempt on Paschal II's part, ultimately unsuccessful, to prevent the Lateran complex from becoming what it eventually did by the end of the Middle Ages: an isolated enclave separated from the populous zone in the west by mostly deserted expanses of crumbling ruins.) On the western slopes of the hill facing the Palatine, the heavily damaged monastery of S. Andrea was repaired, beginning with the monastic church itself, today's S. Gregorio Magno, and its adjacent cloister. Nearer the Lateran, the 4th/9th-century titulus of SS. Quattro Coronati, gutted by fire in 1084, was rebuilt at about half its original size. The surviving apse and parts of the nave walls in the west were incorporated into the new, narrower basilica, while the eastern half of the old building became an atrium, open to the sky; the columns of the former nave were incorporated into the side walls to form a kind of false gallery (Fig. 6.19; see also the plan at Fig. 7.19). Despite its reduced dimensions, the early 12th-century church was an impressive building. Its nave arcades rest on multicolored ancient columns and capitals, and are topped at the clerestory level with a dwarf gallery made up of carefully selected ancient colonettes. Its intricate *opus sectile* floor, a geometric carpet composed of thousands of pieces of meticulously cut colored marble, is an early example of the stunning pavements installed in dozens of Roman churches in the 12th and 13th centuries, called cosmatesque after the Cosmati, one (but only one) of the groups of highly skilled *marmorarii* working in later medieval Rome. The new church was adjoined by an elegant cloister along its south wall, one of the first in a wave of quadrangular porticoes annexed to Roman basilicas in the 12th and 13th centuries (other well-preserved examples include those at S. Pudenziana, S. Cosimato, St. Paul's and S. Lorenzo *fuori le mura*, and the Lateran Cathedral) (Fig. 6.20).[29]

The supreme achievement in the program of renewal launched under Paschal II is the new S. Clemente, situated less than 200 m down the

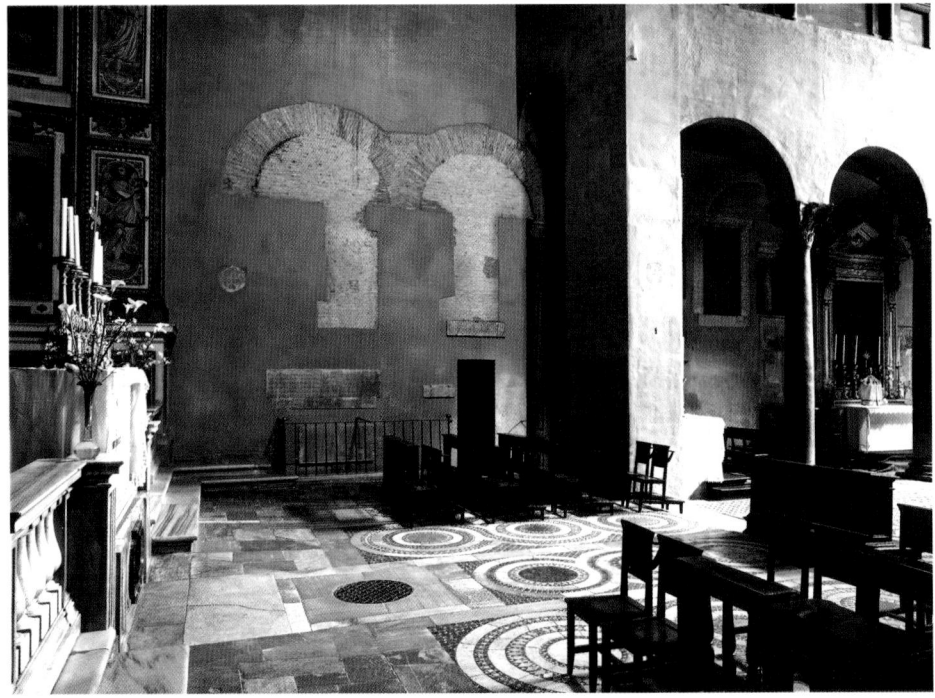

Figure 6.19 The north wall of the nave of the 12th-century church of SS. Quattro Coronati. Note at left-center the immured arcades of the colonnade that divided the nave of the wider, 9th-century church from the side aisle; also the intricate cosmatesque pavement. (American Academy in Rome, Fototeca Unione, no. 10965.)

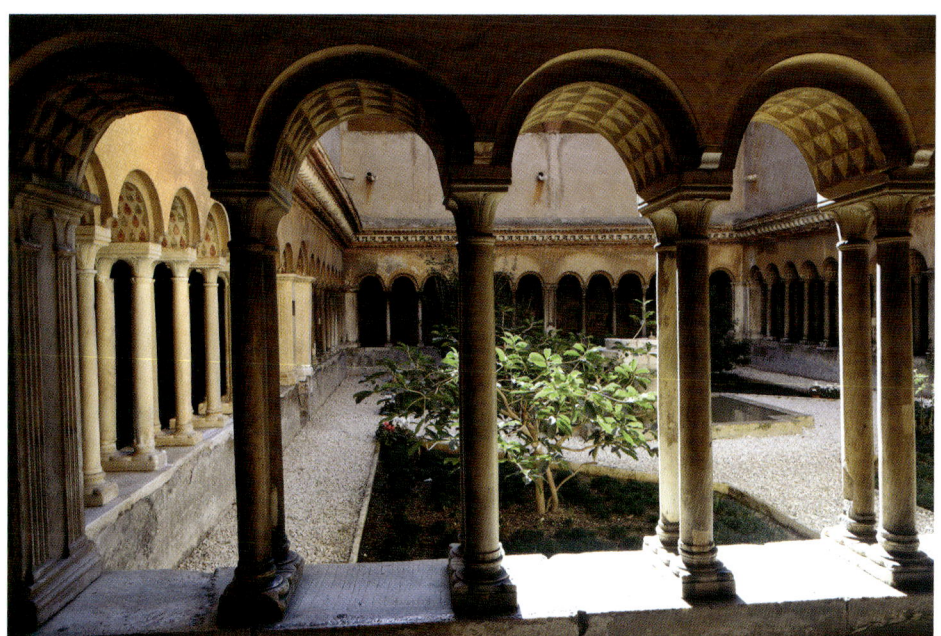

Figure 6.20 The 12th-century cloister at SS. Quattro Coronati. (Author.)

north slope of the Caelian from SS. Quattro Coronati, along the main road (*via maior*) linking the Lateran with the Colosseum and the city center. A wholly new church was built some 4 m above the level of the late antique basilica, parts of whose walls were incorporated into the foundations of the new one that rose atop it. The project was begun and probably completed under the auspices of Cardinal Anastasius, an ally of Paschal II who became cardinal priest of S. Clemente after the latter's accession in 1099, and died in 1125. Anastasius' basilica was the same length as the original, but narrower by the width of the old north aisle, which was left outside the footprint of the new building, which thus followed the line of the northern nave colonnade of the lower church, whose arcades were incorporated into the base of the outer, north wall of the upper church (Fig. 6.21). Like its predecessor, the new building was fronted by a full-fledged atrium surrounded by covered colonnades, unlike most 12th-century churches, which made do with a colonnaded porch. Its luxurious carpet of cosmatesque pavement, intricately carved marble chancel with polychrome inlays, and nimbate papal throne installed in the apse, bearing an inscribed dedication of Cardinal Anastasius, all proclaim the surging ambition of the Church and its leading functionaries under Paschal II.[30]

The crowning glory of Anastasius' basilica, however, was its apse mosaic, the first of its kind known to have graced a Roman church since the papal glory days of the 9th century. Inspired by early Christian prototypes, most explicitly the mosaics in the Lateran baptistery and the apse of the cathedral, it features a central crucifix surrounded by lush arabesques of green acanthus, all set against a gold background. The head of the serpent is crushed beneath the foot of the cross, under which flow the four rivers of paradise whose waters form the lower border of the composition, where deer and birds drink while herdsmen pasture flocks and women feed chickens. In the interstices between the acanthus scrolls are saints and Church fathers, monks and clerics, laymen representing various classes of

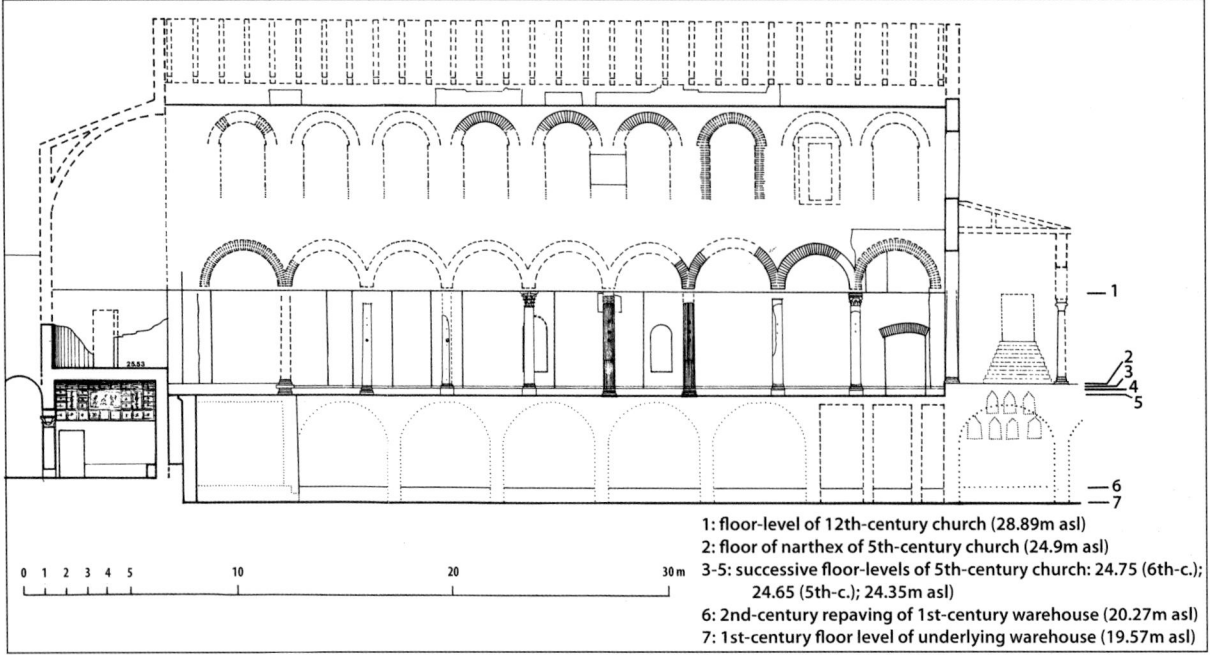

Figure 6.21 S. Clemente, longitudinal section. The 12th-century church (level 1) was built more than 4 m above the floor of the 5th-century church (levels 3–5), which was covered with fill up to the springing of the nave arcades. (Adapted from Guidobaldi 2014, fig. 2.)

society, putti, dolphins, peacocks, cranes, and so on (Fig. 6.22). There is a whole Christian cosmos here, blending history and prophesy, past and present, secular and profane, into a coherent vision of a world reborn and exalted under the aegis of the reform Church and its leaders, through whom the glories of the early Church were to be resuscitated.[31]

The wholesale renovation of Christian, papal Rome gathered steam under Paschal's successors, and the triumphalist tone set by popes and leading clerics went up another notch after the Concordat of Worms in 1122, which was treated at Rome as a substantial vindication of the Church over the secular arm – nowhere more baldly than in the frescoes that Callixtus II installed in a new wing of the Lateran palace between 1122 and his death in 1124, which showed the "legitimate" popes trampling the antipopes of the past half-century beneath their feet, and Callixtus II himself, enthroned in majesty, receiving a scroll with the imperial concessions granted at Worms from a standing Henry V, who thus appeared in what any medieval viewer would have recognized as the position of a suppliant or vassal. Around the same time, the church of S. Maria in Cosmedin, in the *Ripa Graeca*, was restored by the papal chamberlain (*camerarius*), Alfanus. The early medieval church was transformed with the addition of a cosmatesque pavement, wall frescoes, a colonnaded porch, and a soaring bell tower (Fig. 6.23). Just up the road toward the Theater of Marcellus, the current church of S. Nicola in Carcere was erected straddling the remains of three Roman temples, two of whose surviving colonnades were prominently incorporated into the exterior walls of the new basilica (Fig. 6.24). It looks as though the patron, perhaps a Pierleoni cardinal, wanted literally to absorb the remains of ancient Rome and demonstratively turn them to the glory of the Church, and his church in particular.[32]

In Trastevere, the 1120s saw the late antique basilica of S. Crisogono razed and new church

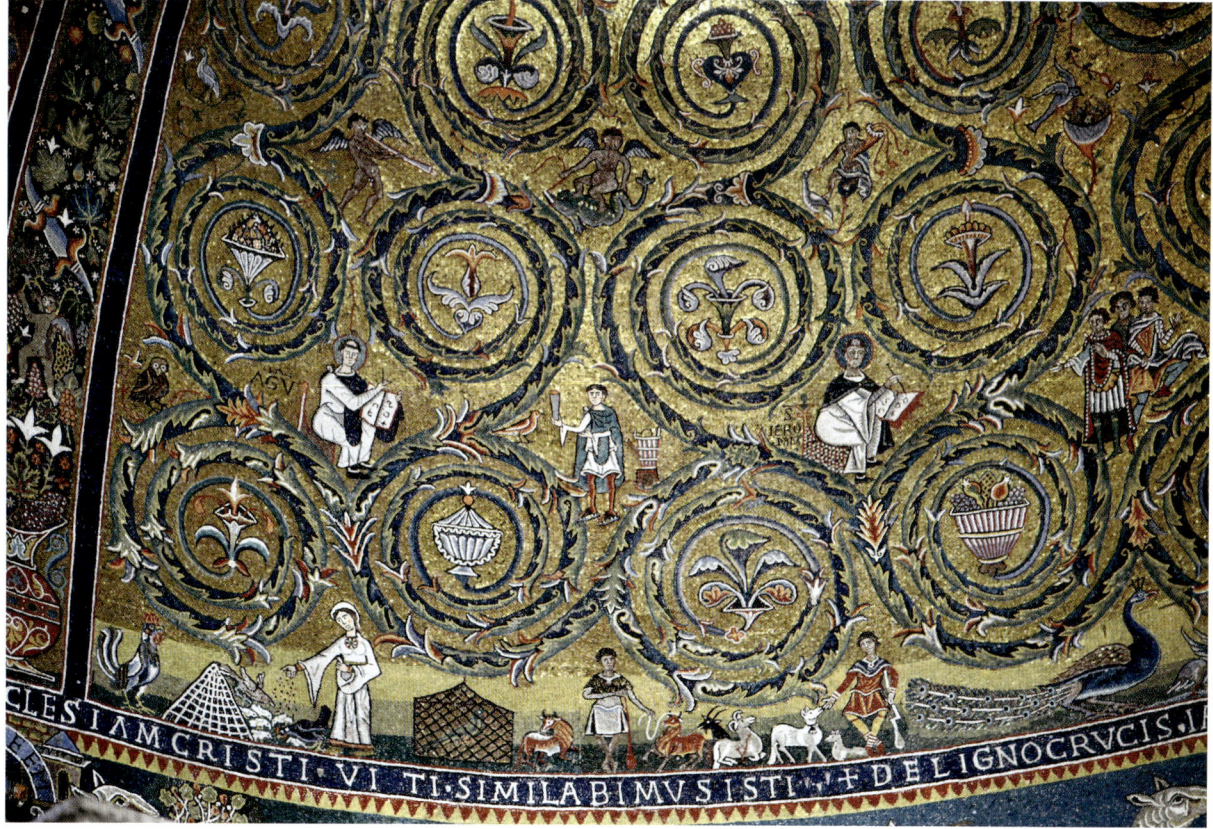

Figure 6.22 S. Clemente, apse-mosaic, detail. The two seated writers are St. Augustine at center-left and St. Jerome at center-right. (Author.)

built adjacent to the old site, some 4.5 m higher up. The new building aimed to rival in size and grandeur the surviving monuments of early Christian Rome. A typical three-aisle basilica with transept, its nave colonnades consist of eleven pairs of massive, matching columns of grey granite; they carry a trabeated architrave composed of elegantly carved blocks of ancient *spolia* that recalls, surely intentionally, the flat entablatures of early Christian basilicas such as S. Maria Maggiore and St. Peter's itself (Fig. 6.25). The austerity of the grey, unfluted columns is counterbalanced by a matching pair of porphyry columns supporting the triumphal arch, and the kaleidoscopic profusion of the cosmatesque pavement. The patron was John of Crema, cardinal priest of the church from 1116 to 1136/37, who served both Callixtus II (r. 1119–24) and Honorius II (r. 1124–30) as a kind of secretary of state *ante litteram*. His immense wealth and influence are manifest in the size and opulence of the new church, especially in the quantity and quality of its spoliated columns and architrave blocks. As in the later 8th and 9th centuries, the riches of the ancient city were again conspicuously appropriated by the leaders of the Church that again ruled supreme, albeit not uncontested, at Rome.[33]

Though the years c. 1110–30 saw an especially concentrated burst of activity, other superb churches followed, if with diminishing frequency as the 12th century progressed. When Innocent II Papareschi (r. 1130–43) outlasted the rival pope Anacletus II/Petrus Pierleoni (r. 1130–8), he razed the latter's cardinal *titulus* of S. Maria in Trastevere and replaced it with the present

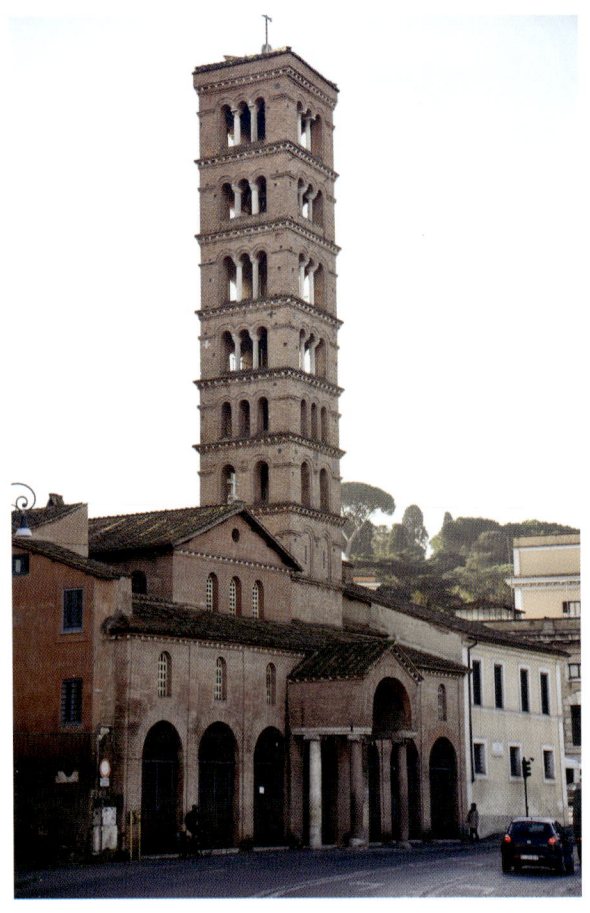

Figure 6.23 S. Maria in Cosmedin, with its 12th-century porch and soaring bell tower. (Author.)

structure c. 1140–3. Or perhaps, as Alison Perchuk now argues, Petrus Pierleoni began the new basilica as early as the 1120s while still its titular cardinal, in which case Innocent II would merely have substituted his own apse mosaic in the otherwise completed structure – and very successfully consigned the memory of his dead rival's great project to oblivion (Fig. 6.26). S. Maria was another three-aisle basilica with a transept, similar in size and form to S. Crisogono. Its nave also has a matching set of spoliated columns taken from the Baths of Caracalla, topped by ornately carved marble architraves, and a fine cosmatesque pavement. The decorative scheme culminates in the mosaics of the triumphal arch and apse; in the latter, Christ and Mary sit enthroned side by side in majesty on a gold ground, flanked by a bevy of local saints and Pope Innocent himself, who appears uncharacteristically large and prominent. A final blaze of artistic splendor came in 1161, when Pope Alexander III (r. 1157–81) remodeled Leo IV's S. Maria Nova/S. Francesca Romana at the Forum. He added a new choir and apse, narthex, cosmatesque pavements, and

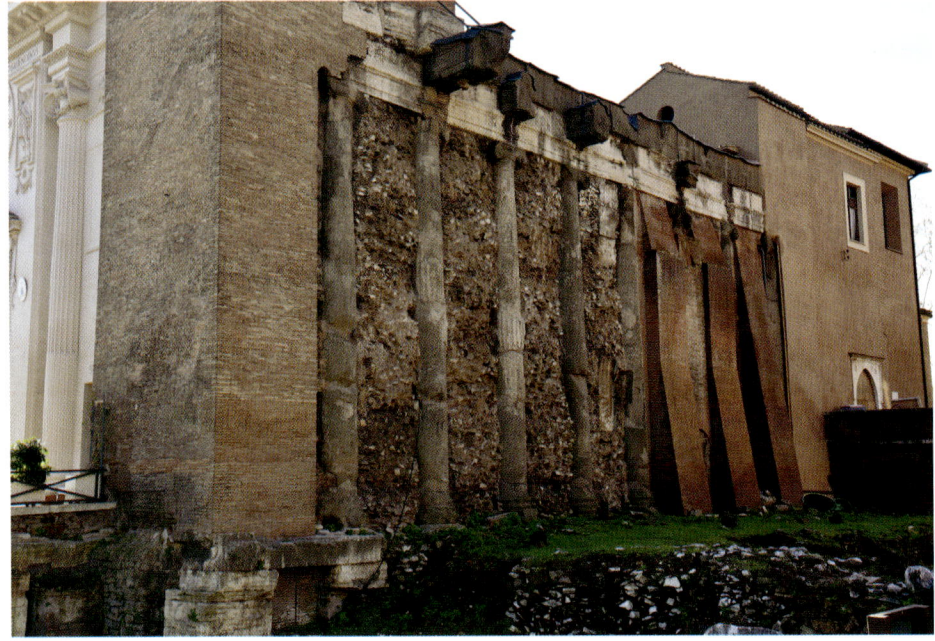

Figure 6.24 The N wall of S. Nicola in Carcere, incorporating the colonnade of the Republican temple of Juno Sospita. (Author.)

1046–1230: CHURCH REFORMED, SENATE REBORN, ROME RENASCENT ~ 197

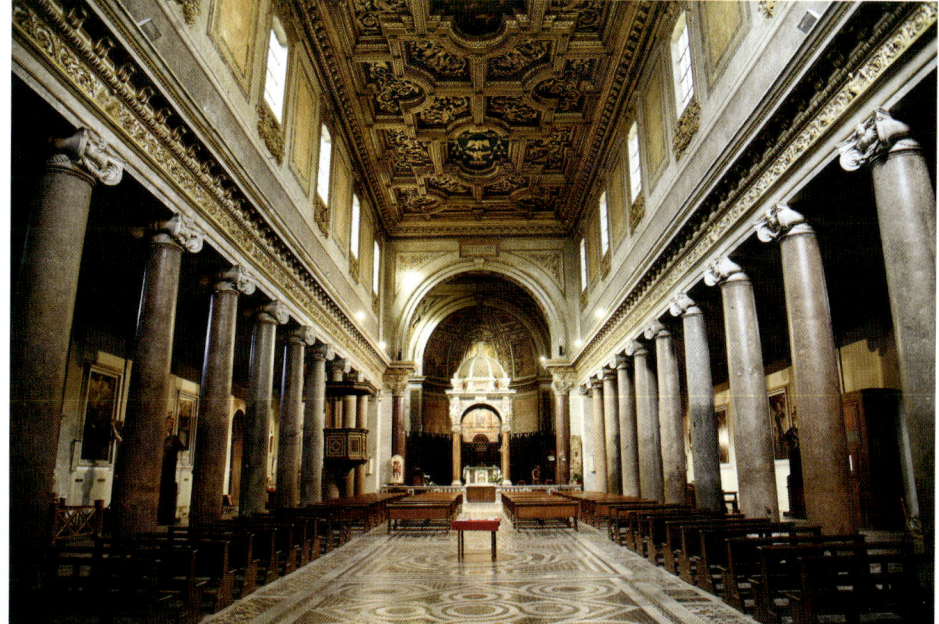

Figure 6.25 S. Crisogono. (Author.)

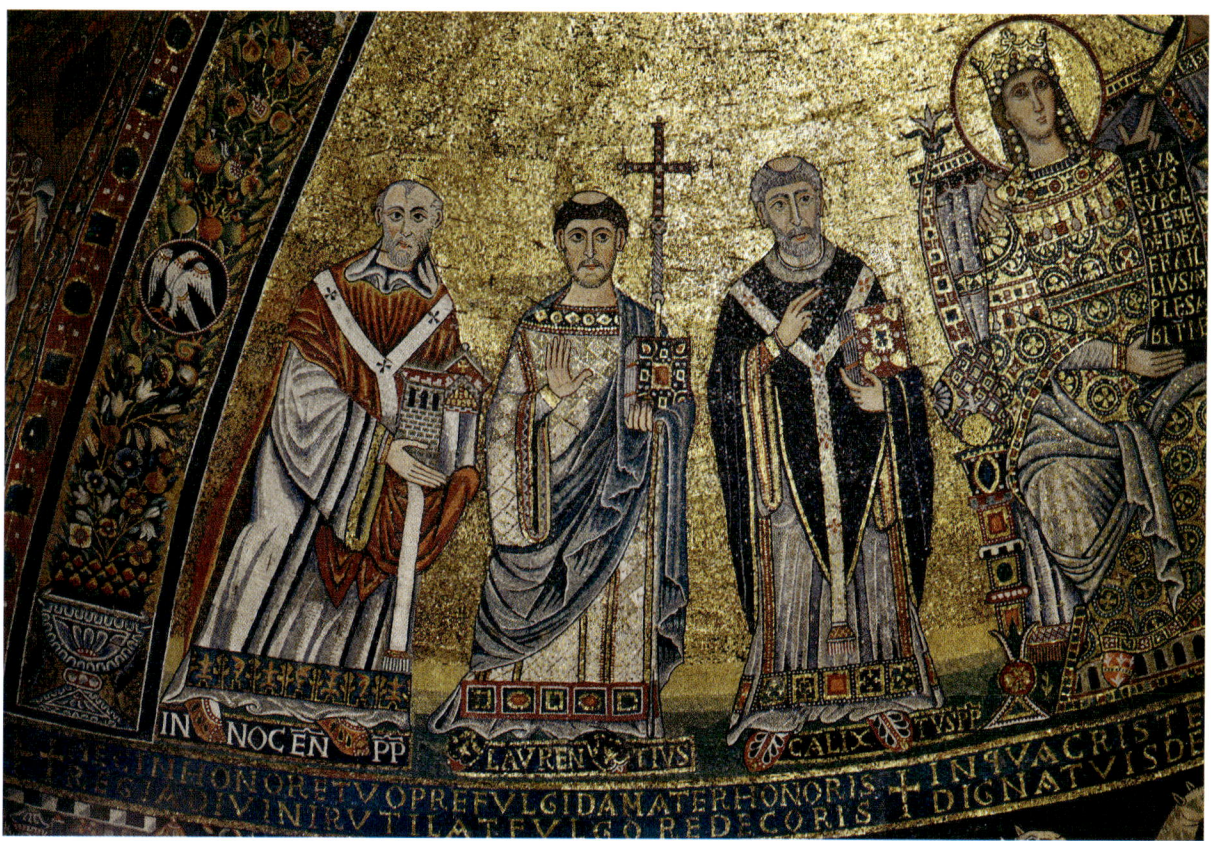

Figure 6.26 S. Maria in Trastevere, apse, detail. Flanking Mary and Christ appear (R – L) Pope Callixtus I (r. c. 217–22), the putative founder of the first house-church on the site; St. Lawrence; Pope Innocent II, offering a simulacrum of the new church. (Author.)

a soaring bell tower. The dome of the apse features the third and last of Rome's surviving 12th-century apse mosaics, showing a central Madonna and Christ-child in majesty flanked by the apostles John, James, Peter, and Andrew, on the usual gold ground (Fig. 6.27).[34]

But the most profuse and (literally) eminent architectural manifestation of the proudly imperious Church that emerged after 1100 is Rome's unparalleled collection of Romanesque bell towers. The thirty-one *campanili* that survive mostly intact are the Middle Ages' most striking contribution to today's skyline, and these are but a fraction of the (at least) 100-odd that once existed. The seven that can be closely dated by literary and epigraphic evidence all rose in the century between 1120 and 1220, and most of the other extant examples are attributable to the same period on the basis of the technical characteristics of their masonry and decorative elements. In her important survey of Roman *campanili*, out of a sample of thirty-five towers (thirty-one standing and four partially preserved), Ann Priester attributed fully twenty-six to the years 1120–1200, and six of the remaining nine to the 13th century. Thanks to advances in the understanding of masonry techniques and refined methods of technical analysis, Nicoletta Giannini is now able to date several surviving towers firmly to the second half of the 11th century, thus anticipating by a half-century or so Priester's proposed dating for the beginnings of the wave of *campanile*-building that swept Rome. The earliest examples, such as S. Biagio de Mercato, S. Benedetto in Piscinula, and S. Maria in Cappella (all later 11th century), are small-scale but stylistically full-formed versions of the 12th-century towers (Fig. 6.28). Written evidence adds a couple of other towers now vanished: an inscription now at S. Silvestro in Capite commemorates the building of what is explicitly called a *campanile* (*turrem quam campanilem*

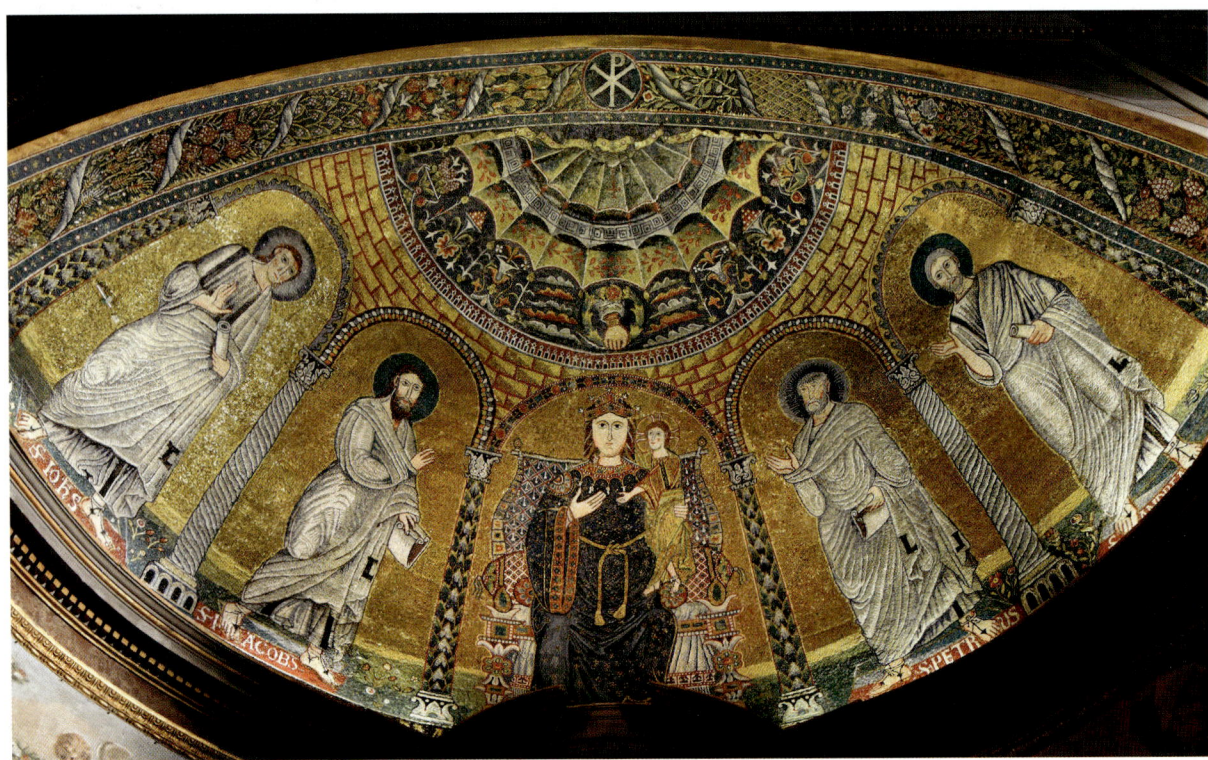

Figure 6.27 S. Francesca Romana, apse mosaic. L – R: John, James, Mary/Christ, Peter, Andrew. (Author.)

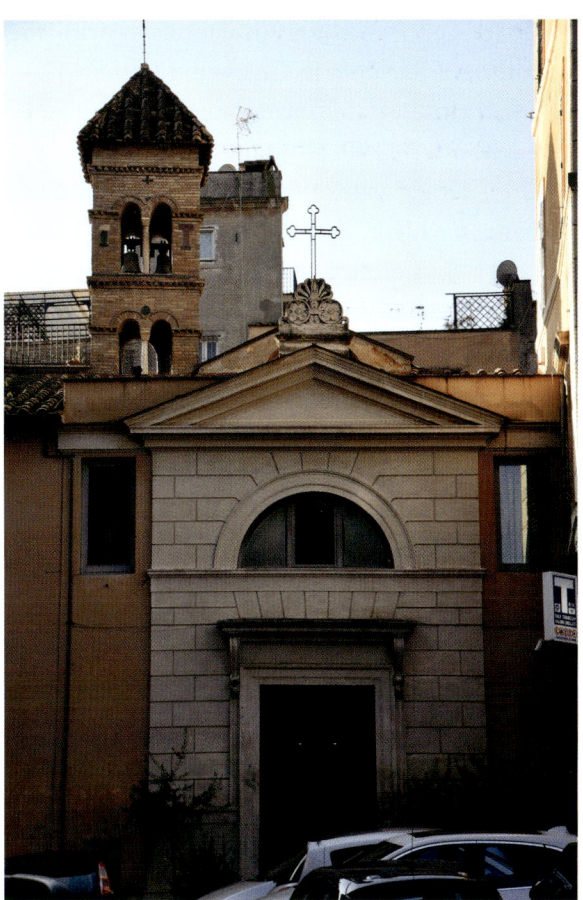

Figure 6.28 S. Benedetto in Piscinula, with its pint-sized bell-tower. (Author.)

dicimus) at S. Valentino on the Via Flaminia by Pope Nicholas II (r. 1059–61), while another was erected at S. Biagio alla Pagnotta, in Trastevere, in the early 1090s. But the essential point stands that the 12th and early 13th centuries were the golden age of Roman bell towers, which transformed both the visual and auditory horizons of the cityscape in little more than a century. In 1100, only a handful of Roman churches had them, while by 1250, rare was the urban church that had not been furnished with a monumental bell tower.[35]

Though they differ in size and decorative details, the towers comprise a remarkably coherent and distinctly Roman stylistic grouping. As Priester says, "They are essentially hollow brick towers, more or less square in plan. They consist of a series of superimposed, roughly cube-shaped stories, resting on a tall base. The divisions of the stories are marked by cornices, and the stories themselves are pierced with arched openings of one, two or three lights." They mostly have sides 4–6 m long, and typically range from 25 to 35 m in height, though a couple exceed 40 m (S. Croce in Gerusalemme and S. Maria Nova/S. Francesca Romana, both at 42 m), and others are dwarfs, as with the 11th-century examples mentioned above, or S. Rufina in Trastevere. They are usually placed to one side of the façade, either abutting or installed within the side aisle, attached to the church yet formally independent of it (Fig. 6.23, above).[36]

It bears repeating that none of the extant examples appears to have existed by 1050, and only a handful before 1100, though church bells, known north of the Alps already during late antiquity, had definitely made their way to Rome by the 8th century. Rome's earliest known bells were installed at St. Peter's by Stephen II (r. 752–7), maybe not coincidentally after returning from his historic trip to France in 753/54. Leo IV mounted bells at the nearby church of S. Andrea in the mid-9th century, and the Lateran cathedral had them by 968 at the latest, when Pope John XIII named a new bell he provided for the church after himself. Some of these early Roman bells, like those beyond the Alps, were presumably hung from simple wooden gantries perched atop church roofs, but others seem to have been housed in proper towers. The *LP*'s description of Stephen II's *turris* at St. Peter's suggests that it was a full-fledged, freestanding tower in solid masonry, very probably the first of its kind built in Rome. Some support for such an early masonry-built *campanile* at St. Peter's comes from St. Paul's, where recent excavations in the 8th-century monastery on the south flank of the basilica have revealed the foundations of what was clearly a small tower, a rough square built in masonry of tuff blocks with sides

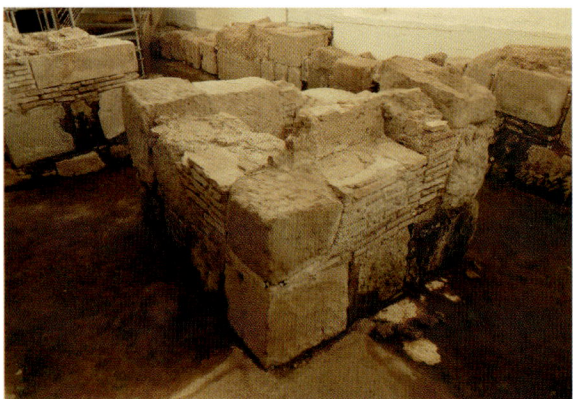

Figure 6.29 The foundations of the proposed bell tower in the courtyard of the monastery at S. Paolo, dated to the pontificate of Hadrian I. (Author.)

only about two meters long that appears to date to the pontificate of Hadrian I (r. 772–95) (Fig. 6.29). As it was located inside the courtyard of the monastery and has no appreciable defensive function, the excavators think it likeliest to have been a bell tower. We might then assume that the Lateran *campanile* where John XIII's bell was installed in 968 also followed the precedent set at St. Peter's and St. Paul's, though there is no proof. Still, if the presumed *campanile* at St. Paul's is any indication, these earliest Roman bell towers were considerably smaller and less imposing than those built from the 12th century on, as indeed are the surviving examples of the 11th century.[37]

On the whole, in fact, Rome was relatively slow to embrace grand bell towers. Monumental towers similar in size and solidity to the 12th- and 13th-century ones in Rome had started to proliferate in Italy already from about 1000, beginning in the far north and making their way to central Italy in the mid-to-late 11th century, when splendid specimens were erected at the great abbeys of Subiaco, Farfa, S. Vincenzo al Volturno, and Montecassino. The scarcity of imposing Roman *campanili* in the later 11th century is not so perplexing, given the turbulence of the period and the resulting scarcity of ambitious architectural projects undertaken at the time. But, as Priester has pointed out, the Roman hesitation persisted well into the 12th century – with the exception of S. Maria in Cosmedin in the 1120s, the other closely dated, monumental *campanili* all appeared after 1140: S. Maria in Trastevere c. - 1140–3, along with the church; S. Francesca Romana c. 1161; S. Giovanni a Porta Latina c. 1191; S. Lorenzo in Lucina c. 1196; and S. Sisto Vecchio in the 1210s. Further, most of the churches built or rebuilt c. 1100–40 seem to have lacked *campanili* at first, getting them only some decades later; likely examples include S. Adriano in the Forum, S. Bartolomeo all'Isola, S. Clemente, S. Nicola in Carcere, S. Crisogono, and S. Lorenzo in Lucina. Perhaps the continued reluctance to provide these grandiose and costly churches with *campanili* reflects traditional Roman conservatism, an affinity for early Christian forms and a corresponding reluctance to adopt a radical and distinctly foreign innovation. It may not be coincidence that the large majority of the bell towers in the city, and all the really large ones, appeared only after the end of the investiture controversy in 1122 – almost immediately so, in the case of S. Maria in Cosmedin – when popes and eminent prelates, among them the chamberlain Alfanus at S. Maria in Cosmedin, embraced a more stridently imperious vision of the Church's place at the head of Christian society. It is hard not to see the *campanili* that subsequently proliferated as the urban exclamation points of an ascendant Church.[38]

Further, in an age when towers were becoming prime status symbols, the Church may simply have wanted to compete with its noble neighbors, the more so from the 1140s on, when a broad cross section of the Roman middling and upper classes established their Senate and communal government in defiance of the popes. Though bell towers were never to match private towers in numbers, nor to equal the very largest in height and bulk, in other respects they competed on favorable terms. They were unparalleled in the ornateness of their architecture, their elegant windows and intricate cornices, and in the richness of their exterior ornament, which often included colorful plaques of polished marble and glazed pottery of Islamic manufacture inserted into their brickwork (Figs. 6.23 and 6.28, above). And, of course, they were 'armed' with bells that transformed the urban soundscape. By the end of the 12th century, no Roman living anywhere inside the walls was out of range of bells pealing throughout the day, every day of the year, calling the faithful to prayer, sounding the annual round of liturgies and feasts, and making time itself an emanation of the Church, an audible token of its capacity to dictate the pacing and rhythms of daily life. Little wonder, then, that the new communal palace established in the mid 12th century on the Capitoline, where the Senate henceforth met, was soon provided with its own bells, to mark communal time and summon popular assemblies. Like towers, bells in medieval Rome were inevitably politicized things.[39]

Underlying all these various assertions of ecclesiastical power and prestige, however, was a still more sweeping topographical revolution accomplished under Paschal II and his immediate successors, which (literally) laid the groundwork for all the rest. It had gone mostly unremarked until Federico Guidobaldi connected a scattered array of archaeological dots in a groundbreaking article published in 2014. In the preceding chapters, we have already seen that ground levels in the Show Area and other frequented zones of the city center stayed near their ancient and late antique levels throughout the early Middle Ages, even in places where ancient pavements were removed and houses built in the 8th – 10th centuries, as in the forums of Trajan and Nerva. Yet today, ancient/early medieval levels in low-lying areas are far below ground level, often by as much as 5 m or more. In a wide swath from S. Clemente and the Colosseum in the east, across the Show Area, and on to the Campus Martius in the west, excavations of ancient and early medieval sites produce deep pits sunk far below modern street level, from which today's visitors peer down; think of Largo Argentina, for example, or the view of the imperial forums from the Via dei Fori Imperiali. What Guidobaldi has artfully shown is that, in a whole slew of sites in this central swath (but sometimes also beyond it, from S. Crisogono in Trastevere to S. Pudenziana in the valley between the Quirinal and Esquiline hills), the bulk of the increase in ground levels occurred in a matter of decades. The submersion and consequent disappearance of ancient/early medieval Rome, in other words, now looks in many cases not to have transpired incrementally over the centuries due to the slow buildup of alluvial soils washed down from the hills or deposited by Tiber floods, or the inexorable accumulation of waste, as has been generally assumed. Rather, it resulted from a coordinated series of interventions on a massive scale, involving the systematic infilling of low-lying areas with vast quantities of earth and rubble, that seems to have begun under Paschal II and continued under his successors.

Though the many examples adduced by Guidobaldi are not always beyond question, in terms both of the proposed extent and the exact chronology of ground-level rise, their cumulative effect is powerful. Starting in the east (to cite only some of Guidobaldi's more compelling case studies), there is S. Clemente, where the floor of the early-12th-century upper church is c. 4 m above the highest paving levels of the 5th-century church below – a building, let it be recalled, that was still being shored up and decorated with new frescoes scant decades before it was replaced (Fig. 6.21, above). In the Forum, evidence for several meters' worth of 12th-century increase comes from a number of sites. The remodeled S. Adriano of c. 1101–02 had a floor c. 3.4 m above the preceding pavement, which had been in continuous use from the 3rd century, when Diocletian rebuilt the Senate House, and the 7th century, when it became a church. The 12th-century church of S. Maria *de inferno* rose over the old Oratory of the Forty Martyrs a full 4.5 m above the early medieval levels of the 9th/10th centuries. The house in the Basilica Aemilia and the larger one that once faced it across the Via Sacra, both built directly on the ancient paving in the 9th century, were submerged by 3–4 m of fill, again in the 12th century, as were the 9th-century houses in the Forum of Nerva. Just beyond, in the area of Piazza Venezia, the final tract of the Via Lata rose close to 3 m over its early medieval surface during the 12th century, if not in a single bound then at least within a few generations, along with the land on both sides of the street, including the area of the Hadrianic auditoriums (Fig. 6.30). Farther west, at the Crypta Balbi, a single layer some 2.5 m thick was deposited around 1100, raising levels more than they had increased in the entire preceding millennium; a new block of upper-class housing centered on a tower was then built on the new surface, facing onto today's Via delle Botteghe Oscure. The ground nearby at Largo Argentina also seems to have jumped c. 2 m above early medieval levels early in the 12th century.[40]

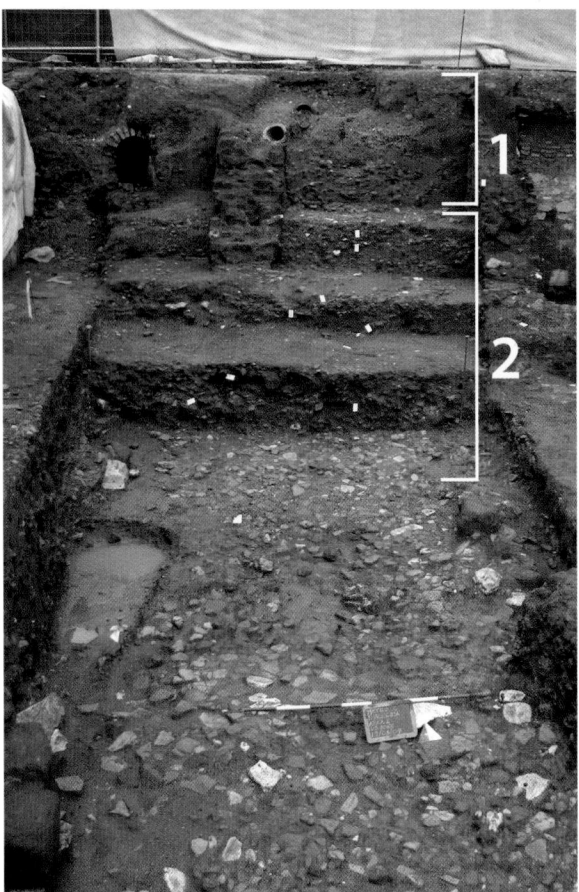

Figure 6.30 The Via Lata at Piazza Venezia. Bracket 2 comprises 12th-century elevations of the road; bracket 1 encompasses subsequent increases in ground level from the 13th century to the present. (Modified from Serlorenzi and De Luca 2015, fig. 8; photo courtesy of the authors/SSABAP di Roma.)

These and other sites collectively make for a strong case that the 12th century opened with a systematic effort to transform ample tracts of the cityscape by rebuilding them well above their former levels. One might wonder whether Paschal II was quite as much the driving force as Guidobaldi suggests, and whether instead more of the credit might belong to Paschal's wealthier and less harried successors in the decades after the Concordat of Worms, Callixtus II, Honorius II, and the rivals Anacletus II and Innocent II. But it is clear that transformative strides were made during the first half of the 12th century; and the only good explanation for the creation of such anomalously thick layers of fill in such a brief span is intentional deposition. New religious and domestic architecture would no longer take shape in and among the blasted wrecks of a bygone age, but rather safely atop them. The thousand-year-old ruins that until then had threatened collapse, damaged buildings and blocked streets when they did collapse, and trapped swampy pools of muck undrained by long-blocked sewers, became the solution to the problem. By razing and/or leveling off ruins and spreading the rubble evenly, the masterminds behind this feat of urban engineering created a solid base for future urban development. Atop the fill, new roads and churches and residential neighborhoods took shape, less exposed to flooding and, for the first time, largely independent of the contours of the ancient city now buried far beneath them. Such a process is clearly apparent, for example, in the Hadrianic auditoriums by Piazza Venezia, whose massive concrete vaults had collapsed in the earthquake of 847. The resulting heaps of rubble lay where they fell in an impassible, uninhabitable jumble until the 12th century, when they were leveled and infilled to create a flat, well-drained surface several meters above the 9th-century levels, where a new residential neighborhood then grew up.[41]

For Guidobaldi, one main objective of this leveling and raising was to facilitate movement through the city via a network of improved streets that were both drier than their predecessors and unencumbered by the massive piles of ancient rubble that had littered the city and obstructed circulation along its existing roads. He is undoubtedly right. At the Crypta Balbi, along Via delle Botteghe Oscure, it is even possible to show that the c. 2.5 m of 12th-century fill was deposited in, and only in, the vicinity of the street itself, such that the ground farther back behind the new houses built along the south side of the road was left at its original level. And it is remarkable how many of the best-documented instances of raising and filling cluster athwart the main processional routes through the city center that connected the Lateran to the Vatican, which ran through what Étienne Hubert already perceived to be the most densely settled swath of the later medieval city.[42]

Beginning from the Lateran, this central axis followed the *via maior* past S. Clemente to the Colosseum, where it bifurcated into two main processional itineraries. The southern branch skirted the north flank of the Colosseum, turned into the Forum along the Via Sacra, via the Arch of Titus, and exited through the Arch of Septimius Severus onto the Argiletum; from there it curved around the northern slopes of the Capitoline Hill and went past S. Marco, then on along today's Via delle Botteghe Oscure past the Crypta Balbi and Largo Argentina, and thence through the central Campus Martius, passing south of the Pantheon and Piazza Navona, before turning right onto the final stretch of the ancient Via Triumphalis/*porticus maximae* along today's Via del Banco di Santo Spirito to the Ponte Sant'Angelo and the Vatican beyond. This was the most prestigious ceremonial itinerary of all, followed (inter alia) by popes returning to the Lateran from St. Peter's on Easter Monday, and on the occasion of the *possesso*, wherein a newly crowned pope rode from Saint Peter's to be formally seated at the Lateran Palace, processing along a festively decorated itinerary spanned by dozens of temporary triumphal arches. By the early 11th century, as we have seen, the stretch running through the Campus Martius was being called the "Papal Way" (*via Pontificalis*, later the *via Papalis*). As for the northern branch, after diverging at the Colosseum, it followed the northern periphery of the forums of Peace and Nerva, went up today's Salita del Grillo behind the Markets of Trajan and down the far slope of the Quirinal past SS. Apostoli, crossed the Via Lata near S. Maria in Via Lata, and wended its way through the northern Campus Martius to Ponte Sant'Angelo. Among the ceremonies that unfolded along this route was the procession to St. Peter's for the Easter Monday service. A glance at the map will show how closely many of the known instances of ground-raising correspond with these routes, above all with the main, southern processional itinerary (Fig. 6.31). The old axis of the Via Triumphalis/*porticus maximae* through the southern Campus Martius, meanwhile, stopped hosting papal processions over the course of the 12th century. Interestingly, the environs of this road seem not to have been artificially elevated, though levels continued slowly, gradually to increase as detritus

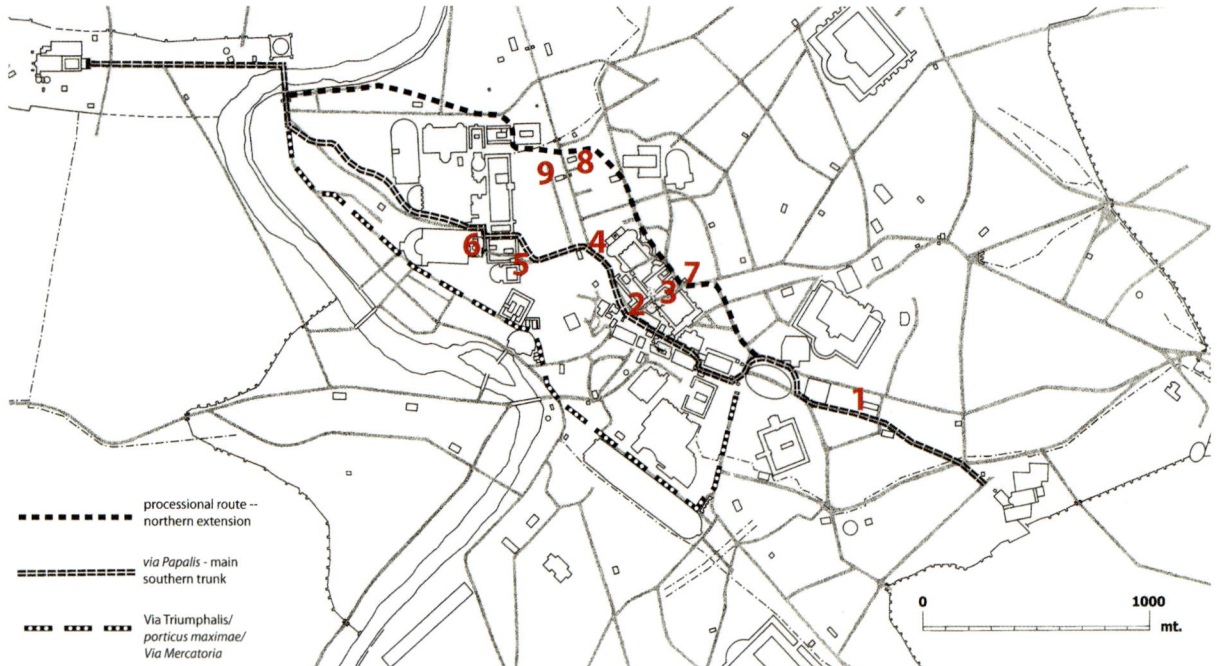

Figure 6.31 Sites with certain or probable evidence of substantial 12th-century increases in ground levels located in close proximity to the main later medieval processional routes between the Lateran and St. Peter's. (All the numbered sites are discussed in Guidobaldi 2014.) 1: S. Clemente; 2: Forum – S. Adriano; 3: Forum of Nerva; 4: Piazza Venezia; 5: Crypta Balbi; 6: Largo Argentina – S. Nicola in Calcarario; 7: SS. Quirico e Giulitta; 8: S. Marcello; 9: S. Maria in Via Lata/S. Ciriaco. (Author.)

accumulated. The popes left it, after some seven centuries of ceremonial use, to the merchants and artisans whose stalls packed the remnants of its ancient colonnades and overflowed into the street.[43]

That the Church was the driving force behind Guidobaldi's "very extensive urban intervention" can hardly be doubted. This is already *a priori* likely for the simple reason that popes and the urban prefects who governed in their name were the preeminent civic authorities in the early 12th century. But the distribution and particulars of the interventions themselves also point to the involvement of the Church at all levels of planning and execution. The demolitions and earthmoving served to improve access to venerable cult sites and to facilitate movement (notably processional movement) between them across formerly treacherous, low-lying areas. Further, the process of razing, infilling, and ground-raising in certain locales was manifestly achieved in cooperation with the eminent prelates who sponsored the new churches that – immediately – rose atop the fill. S. Clemente is one example where the razing of the old church, the raising of ground levels, and the erection of the new basilica comprise a single, coordinated project – the intentional destruction of the old church only makes sense if the subsequent stages in the process were already planned. Another is S. Crisogono in Trastevere, where exactly the same sequence repeated itself: the late antique basilica was leveled and rubble fill 4–5 meters thick spread across the site, upon which John of Crema's new basilica was straightaway built. The latter instance also makes clear how targeted these ground-raising initiatives were: Nothing comparable occurred at the nearby *tituli* of S. Maria in Trastevere, where the 12th-century church is only slightly elevated over the previous one, and S. Cecilia, also restored under Paschal II, where the pavement-level of the 9th-century church is unchanged to this day. The difference is that these two were situated on higher, dryer ground, while S. Crisogono lay in a deep depression, running perpendicular to the Tiber along the course of today's Viale di Trastevere, that was inevitably subject to regular flooding. That depression no longer exists because it was filled in and brought to the level of the surrounding ground in the early 12th century.[44]

Since the 12th century, interestingly, S. Crisogono and its surroundings have remained at more or less the same level – no continuous, uncontrolled accumulations here! Around Via Lata at Piazza Venezia, too, the levels attained during the 12th–13th century phase of rapid expansion changed little for centuries thereafter – 19th-century quotas are only some 50 cm higher than those of the 13th. At the Crypta Balbi, the elevations along Via delle Botteghe Oscure have hardly risen since the 12th century. In all these cases, the 12th-century interventions were decisive and lasting. Across those areas of the low-lying Tiber floodplain where the heart of the later medieval city took shape, the transfiguration begun under Paschal II established the 'natural' topographical contours that persist up to the present. It may not be much of an exaggeration to say that the formation of Rome's later medieval nucleus, in the shape it eventually took, was made possible by the ground-scaping campaigns of the earlier 12th century. The replacement of swampy, rubble-choked morasses with better-drained, unobstructed expanses of well-graded land laid the groundwork, very literally, for the improved roads, the grand churches and *campanili*, and also the more robust, densely packed residences that proliferated from the 12th century on.[45]

By the early 1140s, then, the Church had attained new heights of power and prestige, both internationally and at home. Its preeminence on the Roman scene was more apparent with every passing year. The popes and cardinals responsible for a passel of splendid new churches were freely ransacking Rome's ancient monuments for their choicest spoils, like the spectacular set of granite columns from the Baths of Caracalla installed at S. Maria in Trastevere – possibly the last such matching set available anywhere in the city. Canon Benedict of St. Peter's was putting the final touches on his handbook (*ordo*) of papal ceremonial, meticulously cataloguing and describing the yearly round of occasions when the popes projected the spectacle of their majesty across Rome, processing through the streets robed in imperial purple, often crowned, accompanied by a dazzling coterie of high dignitaries and ceremonial attendants. The processions themselves crossed whole neighborhoods recently raised, on papal initiative, above the muck of the Tiber floodplain, wending along improved roads that connected a glittering constellation of new and restored churches.

And then, just when the ascending trajectory of the Church must have seemed unstoppable, it was brusquely checked. In 1143–4, the Church's Roman neighbors brought it back to earth and reminded the pope that the regent of Christendom was nonetheless the resident of an earthly city animated by forces well beyond his control. Long-smoldering tensions between the papacy and elements of the Roman populace anxious for greater autonomy in managing civic affairs flamed into open hostility in 1143, when Innocent II offered unexpectedly lenient terms to the nearby town of Tivoli, thereby depriving the Roman militia of the rich plunder it expected after routing the Tivolesi in battle. An autonomous civic commune was proclaimed, governed by a Senate composed of some fifty-six members, elected in public assembly and corporately invested with supreme legislative, financial, and judicial authority, not to mention control over Rome's physical patrimony, its infrastructure and monuments and public spaces. The motivators and instigators of the upstart regime came from the ranks of the landowning minor nobility and the more successful of the mercantile, manufacturing, and professional classes, an upper echelon of Roman society that probably comprised a few hundred families in all.[46]

From its earliest years, the communal government moved to assert, and indeed to flaunt, its control over public buildings and infrastructure. In the time-honored tradition of Roman rulers (lay or ecclesiastical), it set to work putting its stamp on existing monuments and building others *ex novo*. It thus proclaimed in no uncertain terms its intent to supplant the Church as the legitimate owner and steward of the public patrimony of the city. Already in 1149, we see the Senate proudly writing to Conrad III to inform the German sovereign that it was in the process of refurbishing the Milvian Bridge and fortifying it with "most strong" walls of mortared stone, which it expected soon to be complete. This way, the senators told Conrad, whenever he wished to visit the city, he might do so without having to traverse Ponte Sant'Angelo, "so that the Pierleoni will not be able to harm you at Castel Sant'Angelo, as they had agreed with the pope [Eugene III, r. 1145–53] and the Sicilian [Roger II, Norman king of Sicily]."[47]

All the complications of the Roman political scene in the later 12th century are here in microcosm. As usual, looming over everything are the external powers, German emperor and Norman king, ready to be played against each other by competing Roman interests. Then, there is the very upper crust of the nobility, the Pierleoni and Frangipane in particular, who still supported the Church that had helped make their fortune through grants of land, offices, and other privileges (witness the Pierleoni occupation of Castel Sant'Angelo itself!). They initially remained aloof from the upstart nobles and medium elites of the commune, whose resentment of the established magnates in fact looks to have been one of the factors that motivated the "restoration" of the Senate in the first place. The new commune rallied and combined the energies of the rest of upper-class Rome into a cohesive force capable of speaking for itself and confronting head-on the popes and their Pierleoni and Frangipane backers. But the Senate needed material trappings to match its sovereign pretensions. Probably even before its refurbishment of the Milvian Bridge, therefore, the Senate had also begun work on its permanent meeting place atop the Capitoline, on the site where the much-altered Palazzo Senatorio still stands today. Already by 1151, this senatorial palace was sufficiently complete to host fifty senators gathered "on the Campidoglio, in the new council chamber (*consistorio novo*) of the palace, in the seventh year of the restoration or renewal of the sacred Senate" to confirm a commercial treaty between Rome – whose collective interests the Senate now claimed to represent – and Pisa.[48]

Shortly thereafter, the communal authorities took in hand the largest and most critical piece of infrastructure of all, the Aurelian Wall. The Senate sponsored the first recorded program of renovations since the time of Leo IV, three centuries earlier. The work is recorded in an inscription dated to 1157 that was installed on the interior façade of Porta Metronia, where surviving tracts of *opus vittatum* masonry characteristic of the mid-12th century attest to the considerable extent of the reconstruction that occurred there. The inscription left no doubt about where the responsibility for the renovation of Rome's defenses lay: "in the year 1157 of the incarnation of our lord Jesus Christ, the SPQR restored these walls ruined by age" (Fig. 6.32). There follow the names of ten individual senators. In a city where the commissioning of inscriptions had been for centuries a virtual monopoly of the Church, the very act of displaying publically the 'communal' inscription was an unmistakable challenge. In 1191, the ruling senator, Benedetto *Carushomo*, would reiterate the

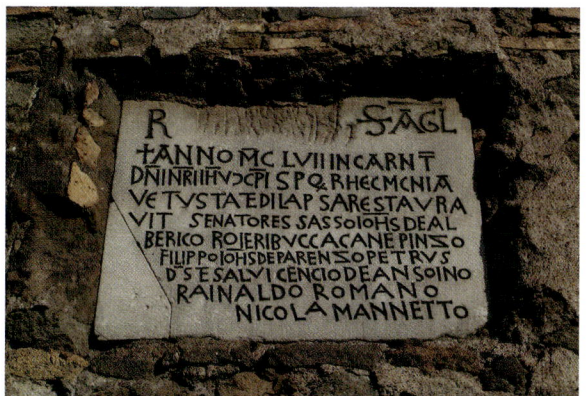

Figure 6.32 Copy of the dedicatory inscription of 1157 *in situ* on the interior façade of Porta Metronia (the original is in the Capitoline Museums). (Author.)

challenge after restoring the Pons Cestius at the Tiber Island, an intervention he commemorated with a monumental inscription still visible today over the central arch of the bridge. Along with the interventions at the Milvian Bridge and the Pons Cestius, the reconstruction of Porta Metronia (and almost certainly other parts of the circuit, too, unattested by inscriptions) points to the eagerness of the communal authorities to appropriate the critical pieces of infrastructure – city walls and gates, roads and bridges – on which access to, and therefore control over, the city center depended.[49]

The walls, above all, were critical. Control over them inevitably entailed control over the flows of people and goods circulating between the city center and the world beyond, always via the gates in the circuit. It further entailed command of considerable revenues in the form of tolls and taxes, which were naturally levied at the gates in the circuit, as they had been since its construction in the 3rd century. It was a superb customs barrier, an unbroken cordon traversable only via its fifteen-odd remaining gates, all of which could be closed at night or whenever they were not being manned by troops or customs officials in the employ of the governing authorities. Until the 12th century, those authorities had consistently turned their control over the gates to the profit of the Church (or individual religious institutions), which from the 5th century through the 11th is the only known beneficiary of the revenues collected there.[50]

It is therefore very striking how rapidly the situation changed after the establishment of the communal government: almost immediately upon its inception, the Senate took control of the revenues collected from the gates in the wall. The key text is the second commercial treaty signed between Rome and Pisa in 1174, which stipulates that Pisan merchants approaching Rome were to pay all their dues and taxes at the city gates, including tax on the merchandise they were bringing to market, and "that [portion] which the Senate has been accustomed to take from the grain, as [in the treaty of] 20 years ago." The reference to the prior treaty suggests that the Senate had already asserted its authority over the walls, the gates, and the dues collected there by the 1150s, just as it was restoring the Porta Metronia and commemorating the effort with the proud inscription bearing the names of ten individual senators – the only extant building inscription from the walls in all the years between the 5th century and the 15th. The newly restored city walls were thus not only the most visible and imposing token of the Senate's usurpation of control over Rome's monumental fabric. They were also the means by which the Senate established its legal claim to the public revenues of the city, in the form of taxes and tolls and customs-dues; and they very materially enhanced the ability of the commune and its agents to collect those funds at the gates of the wall. For the next two centuries and more, until the final suppression of communal government in 1398, the municipal authorities would regularly (albeit not always successfully) assert their control over the walls, the gates, and the revenues collected there.[51]

Such considerations, practical and symbolic alike, help to explain the continuing eagerness of the communal authorities to play a leading role in repairing and maintaining the city walls, especially during the heyday of republican government in the first century or so of its existence. A series of documents emitted between the 1180s and the mid-13th century demonstrates the communal government's ongoing commitment to maintaining the circuit and keeping it under communal jurisdiction. All are records of judicial proceedings (civil justice, too, passed from ecclesiastical into communal hands) or contracts that include mention of the fines to be levied on violators of the stipulated terms. The documents specify that the fines, assessed in gold, were to be paid to the Senate and wholly or partly used for repairing the city walls; the surviving exemplars date to 1186, 1201, 1212, 1214, 1224, 1231, 1235 (three times), 1244, and 1258.[52]

There are ample material traces in the walls themselves to show where some of the money collected by the communal authorities for the preservation of the circuit may have been spent. Apart from the closely dated reconstruction of Porta Metronia, there are numerous tracts of masonry at widely scattered points around the perimeter that can be approximately dated to the first century or so after the restoration of the Senate, thanks to the more refined understanding of later medieval masonry types developed in recent decades. These tracts include not only minor patching, but also very substantial interventions involving the partial or total reconstruction of entire towers and sections of curtain wall. Those repairs executed in a sort of *opus vittatum* masonry, typically with single courses of irregularly shaped chunks of stone alternating with one or more courses of brick, as at Porta Metronia, are characteristic of the 12th century (Fig. 6.33). There are more numerous and extensive tracts, including whole towers and sections of curtain wall between towers, faced with cobbles

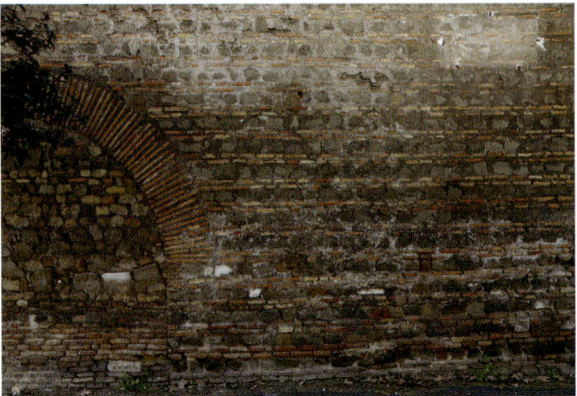

Figure 6.33 12th-century *opus vittatum* on the exterior façade of Porta Metronia (note the immured arch of the gateway at left). (Author.)

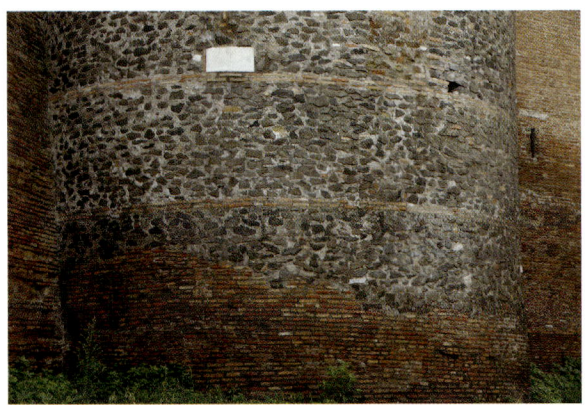

Figure 6.34 Aurelian Wall, Tower K2, by Porta Latina, reconstructed in the early 13th century. (Author.)

of hard black leucite or white limestone, which mostly belong to the later 12th or earlier 13th centuries (Fig. 6.34). There is very little of the most common masonry type of the middle and later 13th century, which consists of small, roughly rectangular blocks of tuff laid in generally even, well-leveled courses, in the manner of brickwork. The documentary corpus and the material analysis thus appear to corroborate each other quite well in indicating the first century of communal government, c. 1150–1250, as a period when unusual amounts of care and labor (and money!) were lavished on the city walls. Nothing of similar magnitude had been attempted since the mid 9th century under Leo IV, nor would be again for another two centuries thereafter, until the pontificate of Nicholas V (r. 1447–55). The leaders of the early commune evidently recognized that the Aurelian Wall was critical to the success of their project. In appropriating Rome's largest, most imposing ancient monument, they proclaimed the legitimacy of their regime, enhanced their control over the city center, and helped fill the civic coffers, all of which amply justified the effort and treasure lavished on the upkeep of the circuit.[53]

The communal government devised various other ways of projecting its authority over the built environment, too. In a remarkable judgment issued in 1162, the Senate confirmed the Column of Trajan in the possession of the monastery of S. Ciriaco in Via Lata, but reserved for itself a kind of eminent domain over the monument, invoking the "public honor of the Roman people" to stipulate that the death penalty would apply to anyone who damaged the precious relic of antiquity. The Senate thus cast itself as the preserver and guardian of the glories of imperial Rome, and in the process delivered what looks suspiciously like a rebuke, and a challenge, to the prime despoilers of precious antiquities: the eminent prelates who, in the days when the Church reigned supreme, had so zealously pillaged storied monuments for the materials to build the likes of S. Crisogono and S. Maria in Trastevere.[54]

By the early 13th century, the communal authorities had extended their purview beyond public monuments and infrastructure to include all of the built environment. They established what would now be called a department of public works and sanitation under the command of three functionaries called the *Magistri edificiorum Urbis*, the "masters of the buildings of the City." These officials were certainly operating by the 1220s, when they first appear among the extant communal records in a sentence issued in 1227, which puts their number at three and magniloquently qualifies them as "the masters established and constituted by the most ample Senate and people of Rome over all questions pertaining to the buildings, walls, houses, streets and piazzas and boundaries, and over all other questions pertaining to the exercise of their office." It is noteworthy that this earliest extant sentence of the *Magistri edificiorum* was issued in response to a boundary dispute between three churches, wherein S. Maria Nova as plaintiff charged that the nearby churches of SS. Giovanni e Paolo and SS. Abdon e Sennen had infringed on some of its land. Ecclesiastical properties, too, came under the jurisdiction of the *Magistri edificiorum*, and were recognized as so doing by the clerics who brought their complaints before the civil authorities.[55]

In sum: In a peculiar historical inversion, after less than a half-century of glory in the period c. 1100–43, the post-reform Church saw its authority in and over the city of Rome challenged and eroded, just as its international prestige and power to shape events on the world stage were reaching new heights. A broad cross section of the nobility and propertied classes, corporately represented in the Senate and institutions of communal government, became a force to rival and sometimes exceed the Church in its capacity to shape the urban fabric in the broadest sense. From the mid 12th century until the end of the 14th, the civil authorities exercised substantial, albeit not uninterrupted, authority over the city's walls, its roads and bridges, its public spaces and monuments. By the early 13th (at the latest), they had further insinuated themselves into the most mundane corners of the cityscape, where the *Magistri edificiorum* and their subordinates could be found regulating everything from the improper disposal of waste and private encroachment on roads and piazzas to contretemps between neighbors over the maintenance of a party wall or the placement of a fence.

Religious art and architecture continued to flourish at Rome, to be sure, across much of the later 12th and 13th centuries, but these were localized commissions, sumptuous nodes scattered across a cityscape that even the most formidable popes could no longer reliably shape according to their designs – not even one of the stature of Innocent III (r. 1198–1216), a scion of the aristocratic Conti di Segni family. The most galvanic personality to occupy the papal throne since Gregory VII, and the driving force behind the Fourth Lateran Council in 1215, Innocent left an enduring legacy as an ecclesiastical administrator and shaper of canon law. He projected sovereign might and imperiousness. But his capacity to transform the city center, to obliterate and create anew anywhere and everywhere, did not approach that of Paschal II and his immediate successors. Innocent concentrated his efforts on the great martyrial shrines on the urban periphery, especially St. Peter's and the Borgo, where he reworked the 4th-century apse mosaic in the basilica, expanded and fortified the adjacent papal residence, and founded the hospital of S. Spirito in Sassia by the banks of the Tiber. Elsewhere, he established a smaller hospice at the Lateran, and set in motion the complete remodeling of the apse mosaic at St. Paul's. Otherwise, the most notable project launched during his pontificate was the transformation of the 6th-century basilica of S. Lorenzo *fuori le mura*, a project sponsored by its titular cardinal, Cencius *camerarius*, the future Pope Honorius III. The old building was more than doubled in length with the addition of a new, three-aisled basilica at the west end of the 6th-century church, the apse of which was razed to create a continuous interior space, now entered from the west instead of the east; and a new cloister was annexed to south flank of the church (Fig. 6.35). But neither Innocent nor his successors, Honorius III (r. 1216–27) and Gregory IX (r. 1227–41), attempted much outside of the Lateran and the great martyrial shrines on the periphery. Inside the city walls, more monumental churches were built or transformed under Paschal II alone than under all three combined.[56]

The artistic ambitions of Innocent and the popes who followed him in the first half of the 13th century were complicated by simmering tensions between the Church and the proponents of increased communal autonomy, which at times flared into open conflict, as during the early years of Innocent's pontificate. In the first years of the 13th century, the prominent nobleman and ex-senator Giovanni Capocci united the local adversaries of the pope and rallied them to oppose efforts by the papal party to usurp control of the organs of communal government and put the election of Rome's senator into the hands of the pope. (From 1191 on, "senator" became the title of the one or, from 1238, two individuals who served as a kind of chief executive of the larger governing councils, now called the "special assembly" and the "general assembly.") Though Innocent's party prevailed over its local opponents by 1205, the champions of communal independence reasserted themselves periodically over the following decades, with steady support from a circle of leading noble families opposed, for one reason or another, to the Church's temporal dominion over the city.[57]

One apparent consequence of the dogged persistence of local challenges to papal rule at Rome was the growing preference of the popes and the Curia for the fortified enclave of the Vatican Borgo, safely across the river from the city center and shielded by its Leonine walls and the hulking pile of Castel Sant'Angelo. The primitive nucleus around which today's sprawling Vatican palace would grow up over the centuries was begun under Eugene III (r. 1145–53), surely not coincidentally in the years immediately following the establishment of the commune, when the need for a defensible base outside the city center became pressing. In the early years of his reign, the embattled Innocent III then expanded

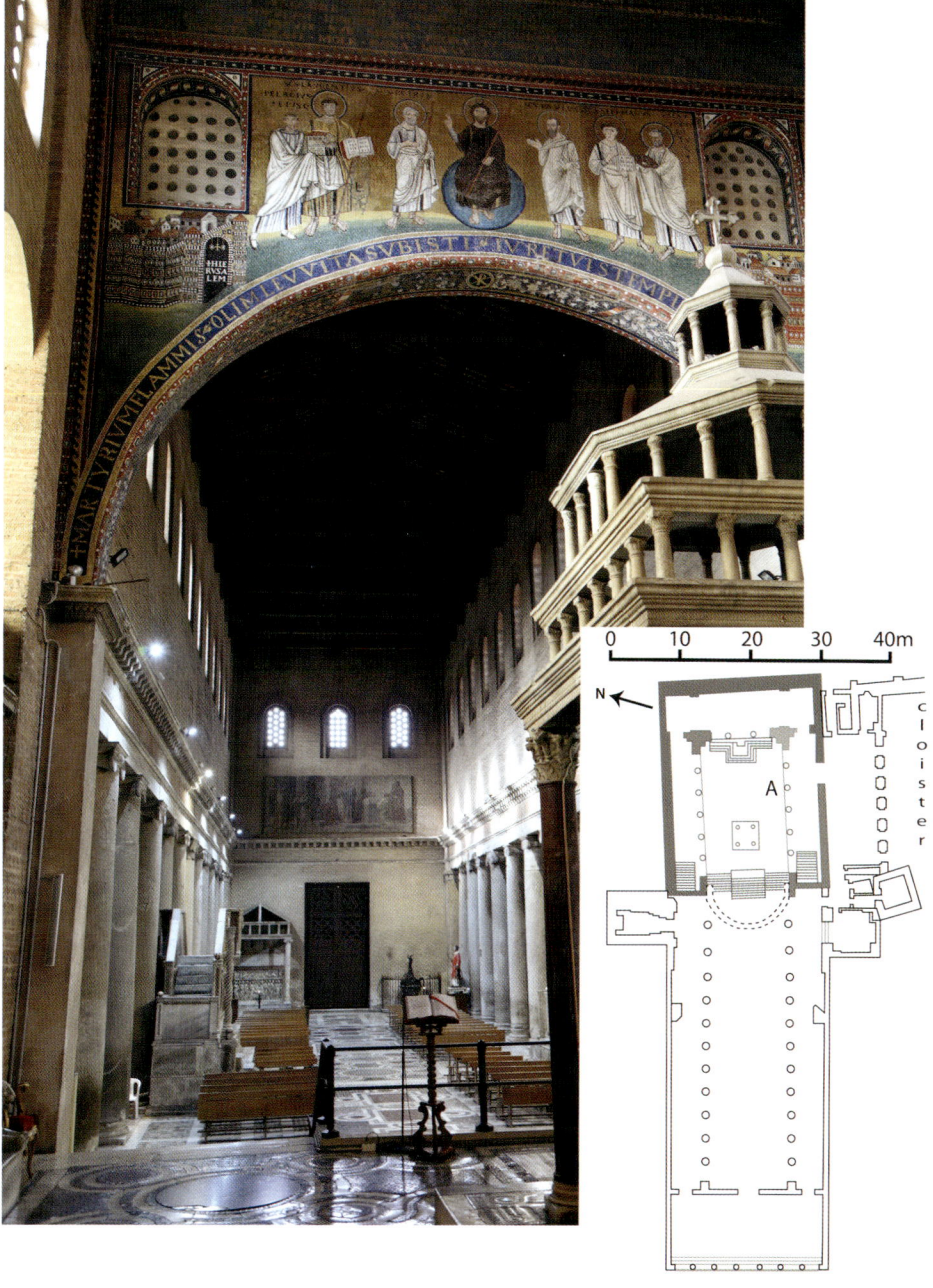

Figure 6.35 S. Lorenzo *fuori le mura*, looking from the 6th-century nave into the 13th-century church. On the inset plan, the 6th-century church is in grey at top; the apse demolished at the time of the 13th-century extension appears in dotted lines. A on the plan shows the point of view of the photo. (Author.)

Eugene's palace into a complex capable of hosting the whole apparatus of the papal court and bureaucracy, complete with chapels, kitchens and storerooms, and accommodations for various officials and servants, all protected by walls and towers. Another major expansion followed under Nicholas III (r. 1277–80), which included the building of an enclosed passageway, the *passetto*, atop the old Leonine Walls to provide a secure connection between the palace and the fortress of Castel Sant'Angelo (Fig. 6.36). By this time, the Vatican was well on its way to supplanting the

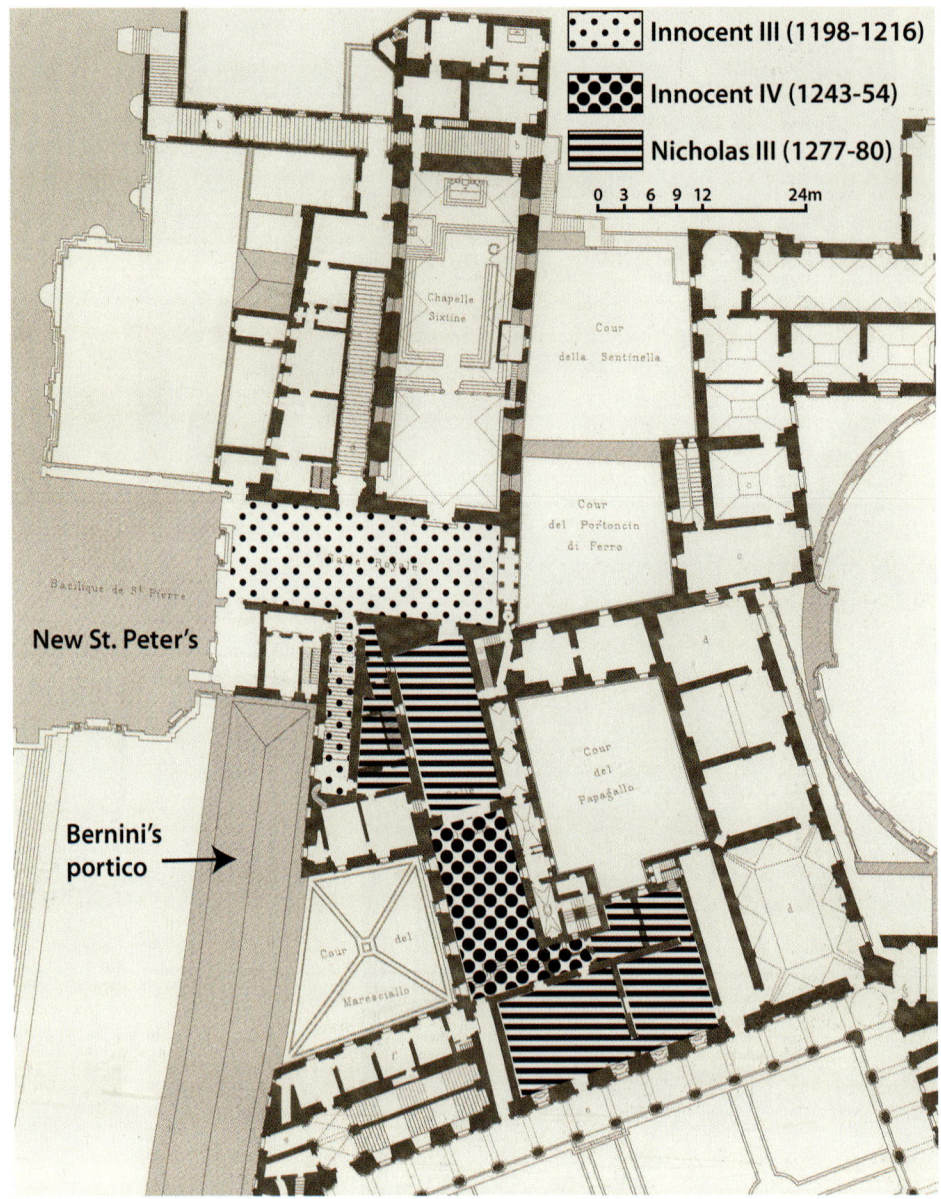

Figure 6.36 Detail of Paul Letaruoilly's plan of the Vatican palace (Letaruoilly 1882, vol. I: *Ensemble des batiments*, pl. 6), with the 12th- and 13th-century structures highlighted. Identification of building phases based on Le Pogam 2005, fig. 9. (Author.)

Lateran palace as the primary urban seat of the papacy, though the transition was only completed in the 15th century, after the return from Avignon.[58]

A second consequence was the acceleration of a trend with roots stretching back to the beginnings of the reform period: the growing inclination of the popes and their court to absent themselves from Rome entirely. In the later 11th and 12th centuries, these absences had mostly been compulsory, the result of conflicts between rival contenders for the papacy and their partisans among the local nobility, or between popes and Hohenstaufen kings, or popes and the Roman commune. Starting with Innocent III, however, even the most secure pontiffs regularly chose to avoid the summer heat, disease, crowds, and unrest of

Rome, not so much running for their lives as preferring to reside in the small cities of the papal domains – Anagni, Viterbo, Rieti, Orvieto, and Perugia in particular. The lengthening absences of the papacy from Rome culminated in the move to Avignon for most of the 14th century, but even before then, reigning popes had already chosen to absent themselves from the city for more than half of the period 1198–1304.[59]

The more the universalist vision of the papacy prevailed, the more tenuous the popes' relationship with, and grounding in, the city of Rome itself became. "Where the pope is, there is Rome" (*ubi papa, ibi Roma*): the idea began to gain currency from the later 12th century, and was being explicitly stated by the mid-13th. Even when the popes were in Rome, moreover, they became a more remote presence, detached from the quotidian hurly-burly of the city center. They paraded less frequently through its streets and interacted less with the Roman populace. The crucial series of liturgical innovations occurred, again, with Innocent III, under whom papal ceremony became an increasingly private, inward-looking affair, largely confined to members of the Curia and conducted within the confines of whichever palace the pope happened to be residing in, at Rome or otherwise. By the time the popes settled in Avignon in the early 14th century, they rarely left the palace to interact with the townspeople at all, save on the occasion of their coronation procession. The urban seat and its inhabitants had been marginalized. The *Ordo Romanus* of Cencius *camerarius*, with its meticulous descriptions of papal processions along Roman streets festooned with garlands and tapestries, spanned by honorary arches, and packed to the gills with raucous crowds of onlookers, verged on obsolescence already when it appeared in 1192. The dense yearly round of public ritual and processional ceremony that had embedded popes in the spatiotemporal fabric of their capital since late antiquity was on the wane, and with it the spectacle of pontiffs parading in the triumphal guise of purple-clad, crowned Roman emperors.[60]

Meanwhile, effective power within the urban collective passed increasingly into the hands of a small circle of superelite families, the so-called "barons of the City" (*barones Urbis*) – families that never relaxed their vigilance or left for distant parts, because there were prizes enough in wealth and power to be had in Rome and its environs to occupy their expansionist energies over the course of many generations. From the first half of the 13th century until the middle of the 14th, their wealth and influence grew virtually unchecked. Along the way, they inserted themselves into the highest echelons of the Church and the communal government: as senators, cardinals, and sometimes popes, they exercised a preponderant influence over local politics and administration, which they in turn used to enrich and empower their families still more. Their capacity to shape the cityscape and the lives of its inhabitants grew apace, as we shall see in Chapter 7.

Chapter 7

1230–1420

Barons, Babylonian Captivity, and Black Death: The Apogee and Agony of Late Medieval Rome

THERE IS SUBSTANTIAL CONSENSUS that the years around 1230 represent a sociopolitical inflection point at Rome, when the "barons" began definitively to surpass the rest of the urban nobility and constitute themselves as a class apart – the *barones Urbis* as opposed to the ordinary *nobiles Urbis*. This local superelite, never exceeding 12–15 families, would exercise "a crushing hegemony over Roman political life" for more than a century, until the popular backlash that crystallized around Cola di Rienzo in 1347. Even then, their eclipse was temporary. Across the period c. 1230–1420, the barons were the most consistently influential actors on the Roman stage. Whether as cardinals (and sometimes popes), senators, or 'private' agents, they would play an outsized role in shaping – for better and for worse – the urban environment for the rest of the Middle Ages: for better, in that baronial patrons sponsored a preponderance of the most impressive monuments and artistic commissions attempted in Rome; for worse, in that they subverted the mechanisms of communal government and made Rome the arena for their bloody rivalries. Barricaded into ever-more imposing urban fortresses, supported by private armies, and sustained by the human and material resources of their expansive territorial holdings, the baronial houses jockeyed for control over Rome and its surroundings, dragging much of the populace along with them into the fray.

A few of the baronial clans, the Anguillara, Normanni, and Sant'Eustachio, built gradually on the success they enjoyed already during the 12th century to supersede their peers among the urban nobility by the 13th. But the majority achieved their extraordinary wealth and power thanks in large part to the

Church, or better to individual popes and cardinals who, for motives of kinship or interest, abetted the rise of favored clans. The roots of the phenomenon lie in the half-century c. 1188–1241, when the near-monopoly of foreigners on the papacy was interrupted after a century and a half (recall that between 1046 and 1188, locals had reigned for only 15 years). Starting with Clement III (r. 1188–91) and continuing through Gregory IX (r. 1227–41), a series of popes from Rome or Lazio continuously occupied the papal throne. They did so at a time when the Church was growing further in international prestige and administrative cohesion, and at the same time expanding and tightening its control over its dominions in central Italy, which by the 1280s would stretch from southern Lazio all the way north to Romagna, via Umbria and Le Marche – from Terracina to Bologna. Their ability to elevate those they favored grew accordingly.[2]

These local popes promptly began to elevate relatives and allies to leading positions in the Curia, the cardinalate above all. The 13th century was the great age of Roman cardinals, who at times accounted for half of the college of cardinals, and usually comprised at least a quarter of the group. And as the century progressed, cardinals of local extraction came to be drawn almost exclusively from the baronial families. At the conclave of 1292 that elected Celestine V, for example, six of the twelve cardinals present (and six of the eleven alive at the end) were Roman barons: three Orsini, two Colonna, and one Boccamazza. These Roman prelates enjoyed numerous advantages over their foreign peers. Because they were usually elected younger and died later, being more resistant to the rigors of the local climate, they tended to remain in office much longer. They were brought up and educated to know all the intricacies of the Roman scene and the workings of the ecclesiastical administration. And they had a local power base sustained by networks of relatives, allies, and clients able to provide anything from money to armed retainers in case of need. Their ability to dispense patronage and accumulate riches and property for themselves and their families was thus unrivalled. They gave lucrative ecclesiastical prebends and benefices to family members and allies of the cloth, who often (contrary to canon law) obtained dispensations to hold many such sinecures together, often a dozen or more. But most importantly, they trafficked in land and castles.[3]

In Rome and its environs, and throughout the modern region of Lazio, the Church was still by far the largest landholder in the 13th century, as it had been since the early Middle Ages; and control of land (and fortified towns and villages) remained the principal source of wealth, and of the political, military, and social power that control of such wealth entailed. By conceding long-term or perpetual leases on Church holdings to Roman families on favorable terms, or otherwise helping them to acquire full legal title to territories made available by sale, alienation, or judicial forfeiture, popes and cardinals were able to make the fortunes of the families closest to them, and in the process to ensure the support of powerful allies. The ascent of the Orsini began when Celestine III (r. 1191–8) gave several strategically located castles in the valley of the Aniene to his nephew, Orso, and Orso's two sons. Over the next century, the Orsini would expand from this base to control immense territories and dozens of castles in Lazio and beyond, with considerable help from successive generations of Orsini Cardinals and the Orsini pope, Nicholas III (r. 1277–80). Innocent III launched his own minor noble family, the Conti from Segni in southern Lazio, along with the Annibaldi, who were related by marriage, conceding to siblings and nephews and in-laws an assortment of urban fortresses and rural estates that set both families up for success in the generations to come. Later in the 13th century, the Boccamazza, Romani, Savelli, and Caetani families would all be 'made' from the moment one of their number became cardinal or pope. In the case of the Colonna, it was the (unrelated) Pope Nicholas IV (r. 1287–92) whose favors lifted the already powerful family to a position of preeminence rivaled only by the Orsini and, for a time, the Caetani, whose star rose with the election and fell with the death of the formidable Boniface VIII Caetani (r. 1294–1303).[4]

Once established and backed by powerful patrons, baronial houses had all the more occasion to further expand their holdings. The key to establishing a family's fortunes on a solid and lasting basis was the exercise of seigneurial rights over the fortified villages, or "castles" (*castelli* in Italian, *castra* or *castella* in Latin, comprising a walled nucleus of settlement and its surrounding territory), that proliferated starting some 20–25 km outside the city walls. (Closer to the city, sparsely populated agricultural estates called *casali* predominated, most of which were controlled by 'ordinary' upper-class families.) While lesser families might hold one or two *castelli*, the leading baronial clans accumulated them by the dozen, and proceeded to extract a steady stream of cash and goods from the inhabitants of the lands their *castelli* controlled. They found refuge there when necessary, in bristling strongholds from which they could defy their enemies indefinitely and marshal their forces against rival families or the communal authorities. And they drew from them the manpower for armed retinues, private armies many hundreds strong that provided the brute force on which the baronial families depended to survive and compete effectively against their rivals. As of c. 1250, the Roman barons together controlled about 60 *castelli*; by the early 14th century, the number had soared past 200, with some three-quarters located in Lazio and the rest scattered still farther afield. Their control over wide swaths of the countryside, with all the human and material resources available there, set the barons apart from everyone else.[5]

These structural advantages helped the barons to go from strength to strength. Displacing the lesser urban-based nobles and the successful mercantile and professional classes who had been the backbone of the early communal regime, they occupied the leading municipal office, the senatorate, with startling regularity from the 1230s on. Among the 168 individuals of Roman origin known to have held the senatorate between 1230 and 1347, Sandro Carocci counts 50 members of the Orsini family, 28 Annibaldi, 24 Colonna, 17 Conti, 15 Savelli, 8 Stefaneschi, and 5 Anguillara, a total of 147 out of 168 that is all the more remarkable given that not one member of these families is attested in the position before 1220. Outside of Rome, barons also frequently served as commanders of papal forces and rectors of the ecclesiastical provinces into which the Papal States were divided, positions that offered further opportunities for self- and family-aggrandizement.[6]

In terms of both Rome's urban evolution and the barons' impact thereon, the period c. 1230–1420 breaks roughly into two phases, with the dividing line falling around 1300. The first phase saw more of the steady expansion that had proceeded apace from the early 12th century on. As Rome's hold on its surrounding territory strengthened, more wealth and produce poured in. Along with the nobility, the "medium elite" of successful artisans and merchants and landowners prospered, population grew, and the densely populated neighborhoods in the west of the city expanded and densified. As real estate prices rose, more and larger houses were built, crowding closer together and beginning to form long rows of conjoined facades fronting onto the more desirable streets, as we saw in the Chapter 6. Communal government grew in elaboration and efficiency, and the *Magistri edificiorum* worked to regulate new development and protect public buildings and spaces. Capable foreign senators, such as Brancaleone degli Andalò in the 1250s and Charles of Anjou during his three senatorates between the 1260s and the 1280s, were often able to check the worst excesses of the barons, and the papacy too exercised a stabilizing influence. In the middle decades of the 13th century, Rome thus hovered around its medieval apex of size and prosperity. Though no preserved records conduce to hard figures, there is something of a consensus that at its demographic peak c. 1250–1300, the city had somewhere between 40,000 and 80,000 inhabitants.[7]

By the 1280s, however, the pace of growth was tailing off. Property values stagnated, and less new development occurred. In part, this slowing reflects broader trends common to Italy and much of western Europe. After centuries of largely uninterrupted expansion, population in many areas had, simply, reached a saturation point beyond which the available food supplies and resources did not permit it to grow. Moreover, a worldwide cooling trend now called the Little Ice Age was beginning, which reduced crop yields and put existing populations under pressure. At Rome, the tightening grip of the barons on political office and the economy – on the means of production in the city and its environs – reduced the resources and opportunities available to everyone else. The dynamism of the Roman mercantile classes, the *mercatores Romani*, diminished, and profits concentrated in the hands of the privileged few. But the heaviest blow came with the removal of the Curia in 1305. Clement V, the French pope elected in that year, never set foot in Rome, preferring instead to establish himself in Avignon, which became the primary seat of the papacy until 1377.[8]

Worsening economic recession and administrative instability ensued upon the departure of the popes and the Curia from the Papal States. If growth was already slowing in the decades just prior to 1305, thereafter there was full-blown contraction. The merchants and artisans and producers who supplied the needs of the Curia lost their best customer. The incoming stream of pilgrims and foreign dignitaries diminished, along with the money these visitors injected into the local economy. In a Curia increasingly dominated by Frenchmen, there were fewer cardinalates and other plum positions for the offspring of Roman families, and those who did achieve high ecclesiastical office mostly lived (and spent their money) far from home. For their part, French popes and cardinals based in Avignon commissioned few works of art and architecture in Rome. And with the Curia absent, the only remaining force sufficient to rein in the barons was removed. Bereft of any guiding authority capable of repressing baronial excesses or imposing its will on the collective, the city experienced protracted periods of near-anarchy. The barons fought each other and squeezed the rest for whatever they could take, the city center fragmented between armed camps held by rival factions, and chronic lawlessness and violence ensued.[9]

Then, in 1348, just as the anti-baronial movement catalyzed by Cola di Rienzo was gathering momentum, the Black Death struck at Rome, where (in line with estimates for other Italian and European cities) it presumably killed a third or more of the population. When it receded with the coming of winter, population numbers may have approached the lows of the 9th and 10th centuries. While the more dire estimates of 20,000–25,000 may be too low, even the optimists rarely venture to suggest more than 30,000–35,000 were left. A sizeable fraction of all the residences occupied at the end of the 13th century must have lain vacant, and many will have remained so into the 15th century: There were regular recurrences of plague for over a century after the initial outbreak (in 1363, 1374, 1390, and so on), and not until the decades after 1420 is there a priori cause to expect sustained demographic recovery. The first census that offers a reliable estimate of the Roman population dates as late as 1527, at which point the number had climbed to c. 60,000, following a century of steady growth. Only then, in the early 16th century, were the population levels achieved in the 13th century again equaled or exceeded.[10]

In political and administrative terms, however, the middle of the 14th century saw some improvement on the preceding decades. For a decade after the anti-baronial revolution inspired by Cola di Rienzo starting in 1347, the local balance of power seesawed back and forth between the barons and a coalition of opponents drawn from a wide cross section of society. The latter prevailed, and a new communal government with broad popular support, the Felice Società dei Balestrieri e Pavesati, took over in 1358 and ruled into the 1390s. Led by seven annually elected officials called *banderesi*, the regime counted for armed support on a corps of 1,500 citizen-crossbowmen (*balestrieri*) and 1,500 men-at-arms equipped with swords and large shields (*pavesati*, because such equipment was associated with Pavia in Lombardy, a metallurgical center). The barons were forbidden from taking any part in urban politics and banished to their rural castles. A new code of municipal statues was published in 1363, which put a high premium on the maintenance of law and order (including the imposition of extra-harsh penalties for crimes committed by barons) and responsible stewardship of the city's buildings and infrastructure.[11]

The absence of the Curia and periodic recurrences of plague continued to weigh, however, and the communal authorities insistently petitioned for the return of the papacy to what they insisted was its rightful home. Their efforts came to fruition in 1377, after years of negotiations with Pope Gregory XI (r. 1370–8) that involved substantial financial and statutory concessions on the part of the Felice Società. But Pope Gregory died less than a year after he brought the Curia back to Rome, and by the end of 1378, two rival popes had been elected to succeed him: the Neapolitan Urban VI, who resided at Rome, and the Genevan Clement VII, who reestablished his court at Avignon. The result was the so-called Great Western Schism. From 1378 until 1417, there were at least two and occasionally as many as three rival popes, each supported by a substantial chunk of western Christendom. One always resided in Rome and the Papal States, but brought few of the benefits the Romans had expected. Their divided inheritance, along with the cost and difficulties of combatting their opponents, left all the schismatic popes weakened, embattled, and impoverished.

The general state of political and economic instability was compounded at Rome by unrest and sporadic violent conflicts that continued across the decades of the schism, fomented both by local antagonists and external powers. Consequently, little was spent on art, architecture, and even essential maintenance of infrastructure and civic monuments. The one signal political success of Urban VI's successor, Boniface IX (r. 1389–1404), was the final suppression in 1398–9 of the Felice Società, which ended autonomous communal government for good. The barons returned to the city and to the Curia in force, lending added impetus to the cycle of factional strife. The combination of civic tumults and unremedied decay left the cityscape in a state of almost unremitting material squalor by the early 15th century. Until the schism ended with the election of Martin V, of the baronial Colonna family, at the Council of Constance in 1417, and the new pope's triumphal return to Rome in 1420, few might have imagined that everything within the embrace of the Aurelian Wall might again become an urban collective under a stable governing regime.[12]

With this broad-brush historical panorama of Rome's last two medieval centuries in mind, we turn to the evolution of the cityscape, starting with a word on sources and methods. Relative to the earlier Middle Ages, there are more written sources available to the student of late medieval Rome, but the textual record is still very patchy. Narrative histories and chronicles are fewer than one might expect, such that we lack detailed information for much of the period c. 1230–1420; and we depend heavily on a single text for much of the rest, where we see only what the author chose to notice and are often unable to corroborate the account by reference to parallel narratives. As for the archival sources, more contracts than ever are preserved in ecclesiastical (and occasionally private) collections, but, as in the preceding period, the spatial coverage of the documents is spotty. Starting in the second half of the 14th century, however, there are also the protocols (*protocolli*) of the Roman notaries, albums containing compilations of the contracts written up by *notai*, professionals who combined something of the modern solicitor and notary, and often became eminent figures in municipal politics in their own right (Cola di Rienzo himself started as a *notaio*). Privately hired but publicly sanctioned, they were employed in any business that required a legally binding contract between two parties, many involving the sale or transfer of real estate and other assets, commodities, and services. The first mostly preserved collection of municipal statutes, that of 1363, opens another window onto the sociopolitical and physical contours of the urban environment, and other such compilations would follow.[13]

Useful as these and other sources can be, they do not permit most corners of the cityscape to be reconstructed or envisioned in detail, and the surviving depictions produced before the later 15th century offer little further assistance. Views of Rome range from the largely fanciful (e.g. the anonymous, late 13th-century image of the city in the shape of a lion; see Fig. 7.16, below) to the highly stylized (e.g. Fra Paolino's oval-shaped 'maps' of the 1320s and 1330s [Fig. 7.1], or Pol de Limbourg's bird's-eye panorama in the *Très Riches Heures du Duc de Berry*, of c. 1415). While fascinating for what they show about how Rome was imagined, they add little to our understanding of urban topography.[14]

As for the physical fabric of the late medieval city, what presents itself for study is largely what remains visible in the present day. In this sense, the period presents challenges and possibilities different from those available to the student of the early Middle Ages. Scholarly approaches tend to involve less archaeology, in the traditional sense of the word, and more history of art and architecture – more on the structures, objects, and art that survive above ground, and less on those that lie buried. The problems of doing scientific archaeology in the heart of modern Rome aside, across most of the later medieval city, centered as we know in the low-lying plain between the Capitoline and the Vatican, late medieval levels are frequently close enough to the surface that there is little to excavate. As we saw in Chapter 6, after the rapid increases of the 12th century, ground levels stabilized across much of the late medieval city center, from the Show Area and the Campus Martius to Trastevere. Relative to the early medieval centuries, therefore, more of what was built in the 13th and 14th centuries sits above today's street levels, incorporated into the living fabric of the modern city.

It is no coincidence that specialists in later medieval Rome have been leaders in the emergent discipline of "archaeology of architecture" – the close study of extant architectural remains, which aims to distinguish and sequence all building phases of a given structure, to analyze the technologies and materials involved in its facture, and ideally then to inquire into the social and environmental factors that helped determine the shape it ultimately took. This brings us back to the story of Roman construction techniques, which we pick up where we left off, in Chapter 5, in the

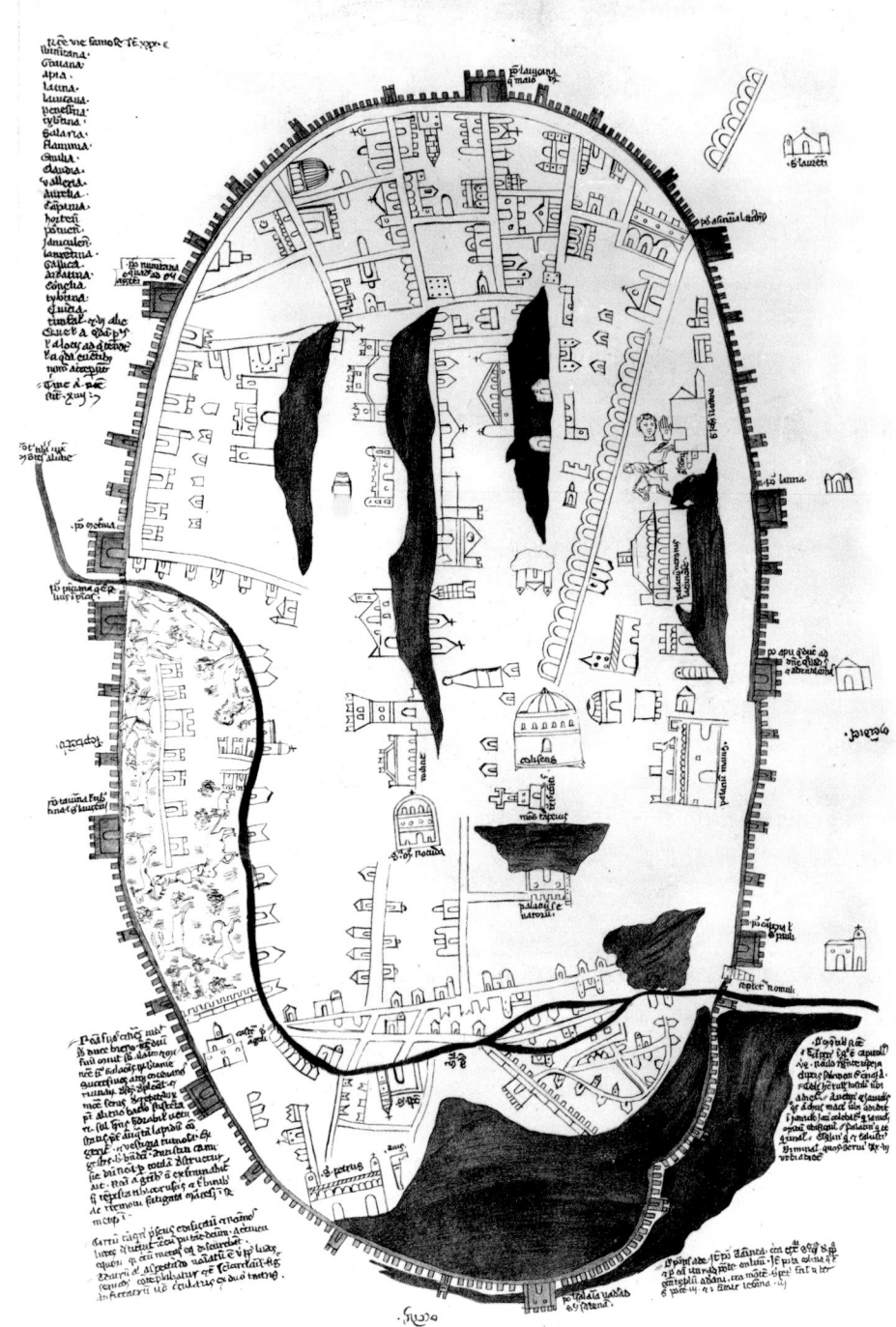

Figure 7.1 The second iteration of Fra Paolino's map of Rome, c. 1330s, which resembles the earlier version of c. 1320. (BAV Vat. Lat. 1960; image courtesy of The American Academy in Rome, Fototeca Unione, Roma.PIR.83.)

early 11th century. By covering the full span from the early 11th through the early 15th century all together, we can link this and the preceding chapter into a continuous historical arc that covers all of Rome's parabolic growth curve across the later Middle Ages – a progression characterized by relatively steady expansion from the early 11th century to a peak in the 13th, followed by contraction across the 14th and early 15th centuries.[15]

The building boom that began more sporadically in the 11th century, gathered steam from the early 12th, and peaked in the 13th brought with it new types of masonry, new ways of building and facing walls that are recognizably different from those that prevailed before. As for the early Middle Ages, such evolutions in the physical characteristics of walls can (and should!) be seen as fossilized traces of changes in the building industry itself: in the way materials were sourced, shaped, and assembled into standing walls; in the technical training and tools available to builders; in the priorities of patrons and the resources available to them at various times. These evolutions can also, consequently, be physical indexes of socioeconomic and even political developments over the long term. Hence, the study of building techniques is useful not only for topographers and archaeologists interested in dating more closely the structures they study and assessing the transformations of the urban fabric over time; it can also help to illuminate big-picture aspects of social and economic history.

By the 11th century, then, Rome's most characteristic types of early medieval masonry had gone out of fashion. The brickwork employed in many of the more prestigious monuments of the Carolingian era, with its meandering courses of heterogeneous and often fragmentary bricks, was already little used after the 9th century. The more widely diffused ersatz *opus quadratum* in sizeable blocks of recycled peperino and tuff, sometimes transitioning at higher elevations into smaller blocks combined with brick to fill the interstices, was gone by the early 11th century. These styles were eventually supplanted by medieval variations on what the ancients called *opus caementicium*. Most of the mass and thickness of such walls consisted of a more or less solid core composed of a mortared-rubble aggregate obtained by mixing chunks of stone with large quantities of lime-pozzolana mortar. The resulting mixture could be layered or poured between thin curtains

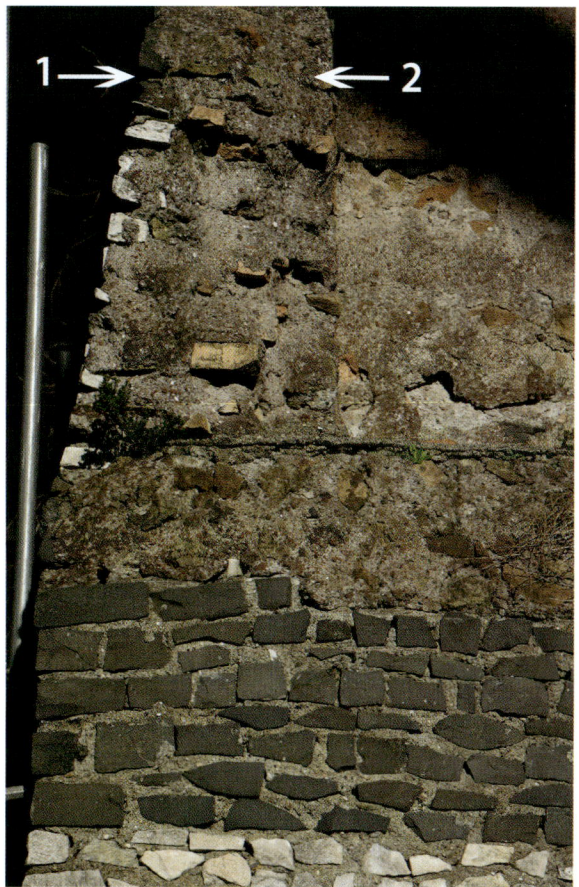

Figure 7.2 Transverse section (upper left) of an *opus caementicium* wall at the Tor de' Conti. 1: facing stones; 2: mortar and rubble core. (Author.)

of stone or brick masonry that became the interior and exterior facings of the finished wall. The curtains were built up gradually and progressively filled with the liquid concrete slurry, which conformed and bonded with the curtains' interior surfaces before it solidified (Fig. 7.2). In ancient as well as later medieval Rome, walls in *opus caementicium* differed in the materials and techniques used to assemble their visible facings, which changed over time and can be dated accordingly.[16]

From the 11th century into the 14th, Roman builders produced latter-day variants of several types prevalent in antiquity, from the later republic through late antiquity (2nd century BC – 7th AD). The most basic, ad hoc facing technique is what the ancients called *opus incertum*, wherein

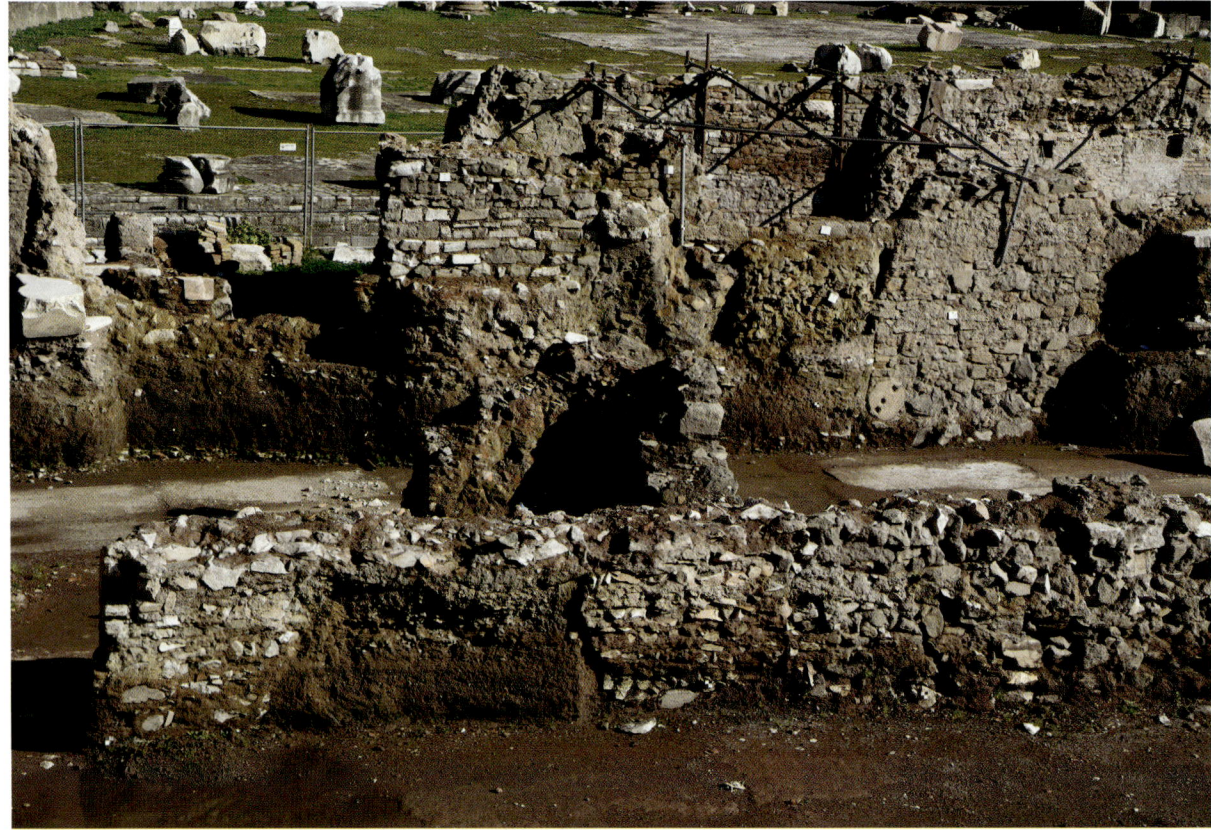

Figure 7.3 11th-century *opus incertum* walls in the Forum of Trajan. (Author.)

the concrete core is faced in irregularly shaped pieces of stone, roughly plumb only on their exterior surfaces, laid without horizontal coursing or regular patterning of any sort. The first method employed in ancient Rome (2nd century BC), its appearance derives from the seemingly cursory attention given to the selection and finishing of the facing materials. Building history repeated itself in the 11th century, when the first new walls consisting mostly of a mortared-rubble core were again faced with an apparently miscellaneous jumble of small stones. Some of the earliest occurrences of the technique appear in the neighborhood that grew up after the mid 10th century in the Forum of Trajan, where most of the house plots seem first to have been developed in the decades after c. 1000 (Fig. 7.3).[17]

There is considerably more surviving masonry from the 12th century, when the pace of construction accelerated. Some structures were still faced with irregularly shaped chunks of stone, usually relatively soft varieties of tuff and peperino. Others featured small, oblong cobbles of harder stone, black (volcanic leucite or sedimentary flint) or white (marble or limestone), which were more durable and lent themselves better to laying in some approximation of horizontal coursing. This technique never appears in churches, but was commonly used in residential buildings and defensive structures, including both private towers and repairs to the city walls. A striking late example, probably from around 1200, is the wide bands of alternating black and white stone at the base of the Tor de' Conti, by the Forum of Nerva, which are mirrored in the nearby façade of the Annibaldi residence atop the "Salita dei Borgia" by Piazza S. Francesca di Paola (Fig. 6.14, above).[18]

After being little used in the 10th and earlier 11th centuries, brick made a strong comeback by the 12th. Almost all of it was recycled, usually laboriously hacked from the facings of ancient monuments. It was used mainly in two ways, both of which recall techniques common in later ancient Rome. Facings in alternating bands of brick and stone blocklets (*opus vittatum* or *listatum*) proliferate for the first time since the 7th century. 12th-century work differs most noticeably from its late antique antecedents in its stone courses, where the blocks tend to be larger and more heterogeneous in shape and size than the roughly rectangular *tufelli* typically used in late antiquity. Examples include the outer walls of the atrium at S. Clemente and the left arm of the transept at S. Bartolomeo all'Isola, both from the first half of 12th century, and various repairs to the Aurelian Wall, among them the restorations at Porta Metronia datable to 1157 thanks to the inscription appended to the gate (Fig. 6.33, above).[19]

But the 12th century also saw the return of walls faced entirely in brick, usually executed to a higher standard than those of the later 8th and 9th centuries, when brick was last commonly used. More care was taken in the selection and sorting of the recycled bricks, which were laid in well-leveled, consistently spaced horizontal courses – the work of experienced masons operating with a tool kit that included both the horizontal level and the plumb line (both usually ignored by early medieval bricklayers, judging from their preserved efforts). The best work approximates the appearance and regularity of ancient brickwork, as the medieval builders evidently intended. Such brickwork appears in, for example, Rome's 20-odd 12th-century bell-towers; churches such as S. Clemente, S. Maria in Trastevere, and S. Lorenzo in Lucina; the outer courtyard and entrance porch at S. Cosimato in Trastevere (Fig. 7.4); and the surviving bottom floors of the remarkably ornate tower house near

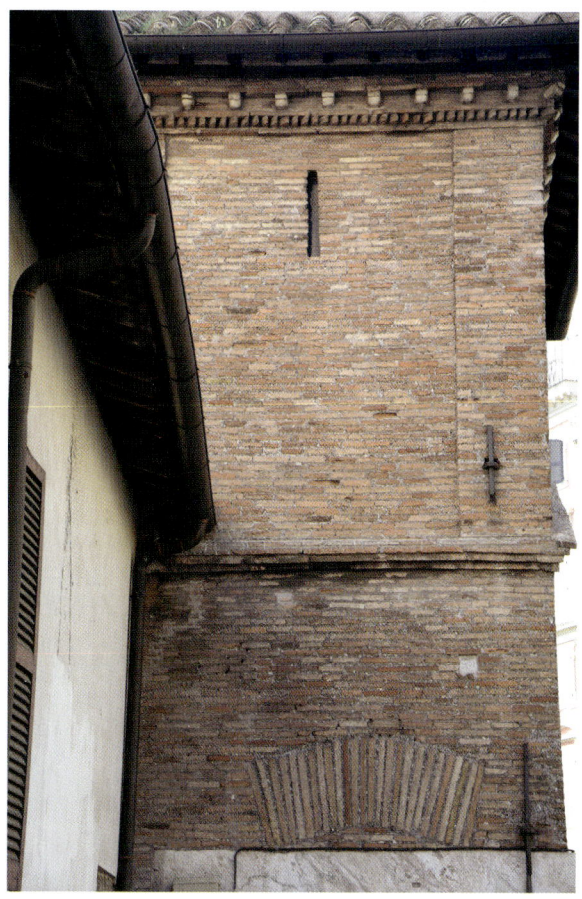

Figure 7.4 The N facing of the entrance porch at S. Cosimato, early 12th century. (Author.)

S. Maria in Cosmedin known as the "Casa dei Crescenzi," where the extensive use of high-quality ancient *spolia* makes manifest the patron's desire to revive the glories of antiquity (Figs. 7.5–7.6). The high technical standards attained by the brickwork in these and other 12th-century monuments is a telling indicator of an expanding, increasingly professionalized building industry at Rome. For the first time in centuries, there was regular demand for substantial new buildings, enough to provide steady work for experienced master builders capable of working to exacting specifications. Called *muratores*, these expert masons worked alongside other trained professionals with complementary skills whose numbers also grew across the 12th and 13th centuries, notably the marble-workers (*marmorarii*) and the carpenters (*carpentarii*).[20]

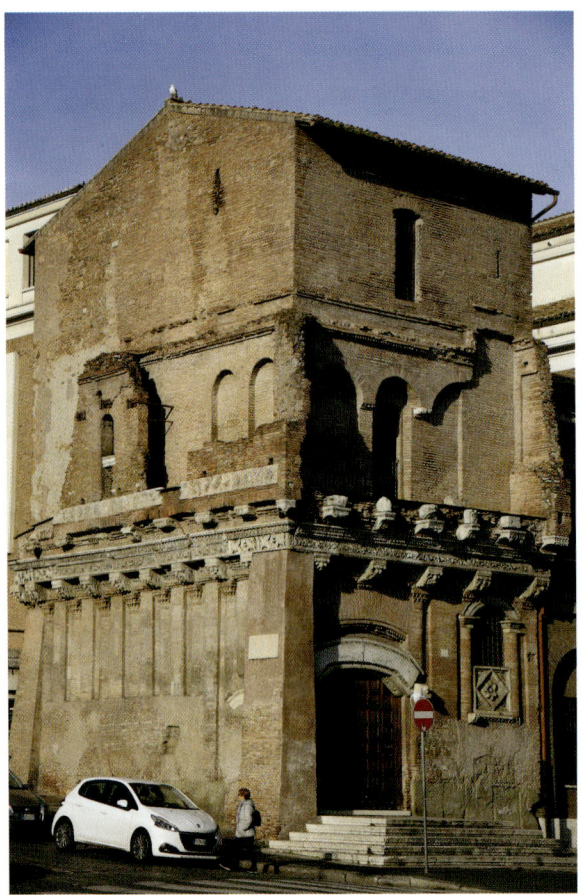

Figure 7.5 The so-called "Casa dei Crescenzi," probably mid-12th century. (Author.)

In the 13th century, the *muratores* preferred to work in a narrower range of styles than their predecessors. Facings in *opus incertum*, *opus vittatum*, and small cobbles of black leucite or whitish limestone all went out of fashion between the later 12th and the early 13th centuries, roughly in that order. Brick remained a material of choice for churches and *campanili*, and sometimes for residential buildings and towers, or parts thereof – ground floors and exterior walls often got durable (and ancient Roman–looking) facings in brick, while upper stories and interior walls were finished in a new masonry style that emerged in the first half of the 13th century and proliferated from mid-century on. As an alternative to brick, masons used small blocks of comparatively soft tuff (*tufelli*) cut into brick-shaped rectangles, typically c. 4.5–9 cm high and two to three times their height in length. The blocks used in single projects tend to be fairly uniform, especially in thickness, such that builders were readily able to achieve regular horizontal coursing. The parts of the monastery and cardinal's palace at SS. Quattro Coronati built in the second quarter of

Figure 7.6 Detail of the S wall of the Casa dei Crescenzi: 12th-century brickwork incorporating abundant ancient spolia. (Author.)

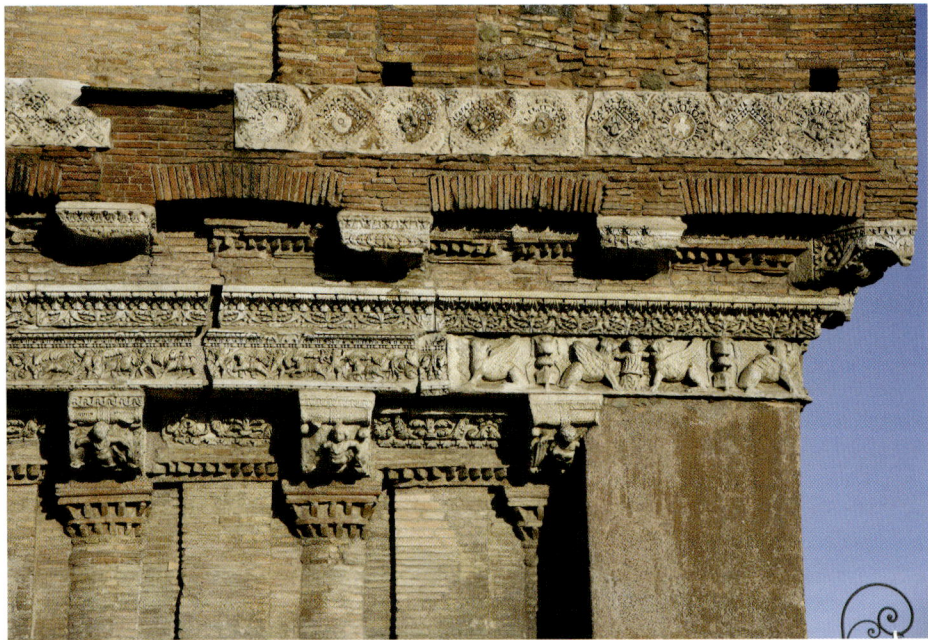

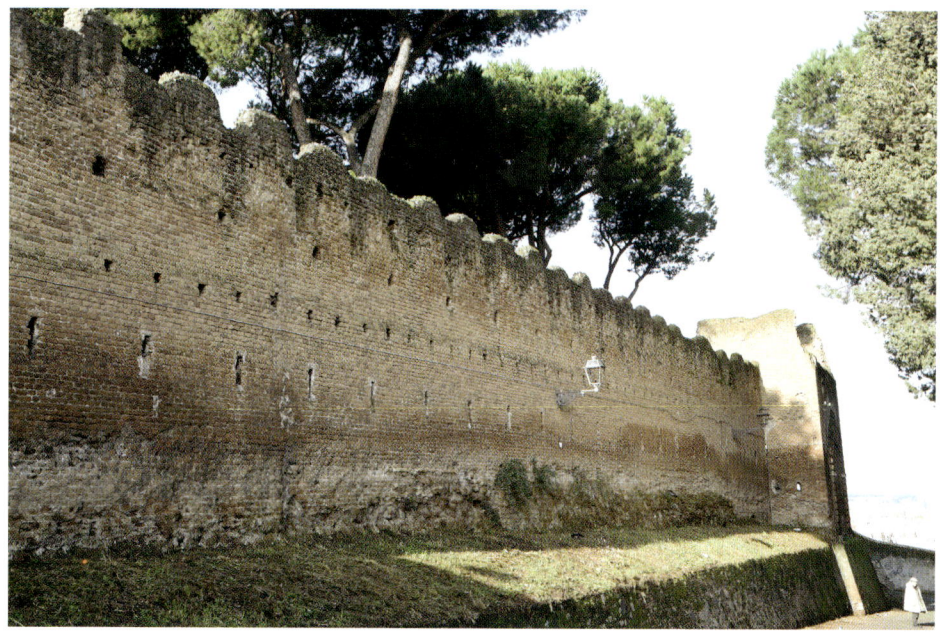

Figure 7.7 Rocca Savella, exterior of the eastern perimeter, overlooking the Clivo di Rocca Savella. (Author.)

the 13th century are a typical early example of the technique, which was progressively refined in the second half of the century, reaching an apogee of geometrical regularity in, for example, the perimeter walls of the fortified Savelli compound on the Aventine, from the 1280s (Fig. 7.7). The style predominated not only inside the city, but also throughout the Roman countryside within a radius of about 40 km of the center, an area corresponding quite closely with the *districtus Urbis*, the territory administered directly from Rome.[21]

This progression toward more homogenous, semi-standardized facing materials in the 13th century parallels the evolution of facings in the later Roman republic, when the jumble of jagged stone chunks typical of the 2nd century BC gradually gave way, in the 1st, to carefully shaped cubes of uniform size laid in the 'net' pattern of *opus reticulatum*. I suspect that the causes of the evolution in both periods were broadly similar. As the pace of construction accelerated and the numbers of professional masons at work grew, there was a corresponding increase in demand for standardized construction materials that could be quickly and efficiently employed in rising walls. And with demand came supply: an industry grew up dedicated to quarrying (or otherwise sourcing) and cutting to shape the finished building components that builders needed. Though some 13th-century *tufelli* came from recycled material, growing quantities were produced with freshly quarried stone, as can be deduced from the presence of very large structures faced in a uniform variety of stone evidently obtained from a single source, such as the perimeter walls of the Rocca Savella on the Aventine. By the 13th and 14th centuries, then, the needs of Roman builders had finally begun to outstrip the quantities of recycled building materials that the city's ancient ruins could supply, which suggests a second motive for making prefabricated *tufelli* that were essentially brick substitutes made of cut stone instead of fired clay. It would seem that for all but the most wealthy and powerful patrons, it was becoming more difficult to obtain recycled brick in quantity. Structures such as the baths of Caracalla and Trajan, or the imperial palaces on

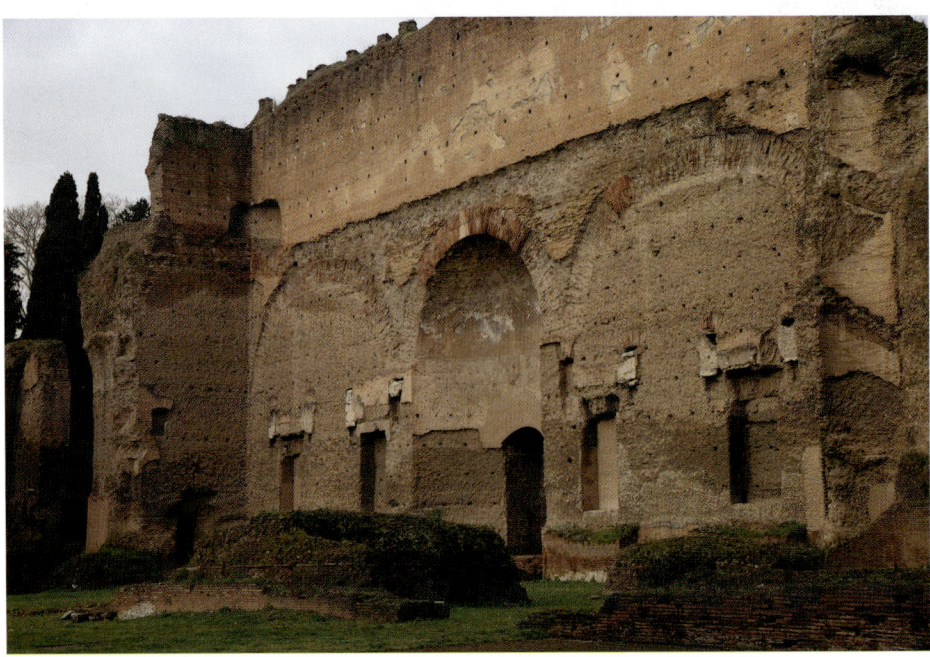

Figure 7.8 The outer precinct wall of the Baths of Caracalla, methodically stripped of its brick facing up to some 12 m above ground level. (Author.)

the Palatine, already appeared much as they do today, stripped down to the concrete core (Fig. 7.8). The ancient monuments that remained undespoiled, meanwhile, were under the control of the Church, the communal authorities, or the most powerful noble clans, leaving little for everyone else.[22]

As brickmaking was hardly an unknown skill in the 13th century, the choice to use stone instead of new brick was evidently just that – a choice, perhaps dictated by motives of cost or expediency. The firing *en masse* of brick requires huge amounts of fuel (wood or charcoal), whence later medieval Romans may simply have preferred to reserve the limited quantities of wood available within Roman territory for other purposes, as a building material in its own right, for example, or for heating. Some bricks were in fact made from the 12th century on, usually in specialized shapes needed for features such as decorative cornices and moldings; and roof tiles, which rarely survive intact to be recycled, were produced in the vast quantities needed to cover, essentially, all the inhabited quarters of the city. But mortared stone facings over a concrete and rubble core predominated in rising walls from the 13th century until the mid 15th, when new bricks finally began to be made in quantity.[23]

Over the course of the 14th century, however, the geometric consistency of these facings decreased markedly. Less care was taken in shaping the stone facing components, which grew steadily larger while also becoming less uniform in shape and less consistent in size, making it more difficult for builders to reproduce the evenly spaced, well-leveled coursing of the preceding period. The irregularity of the blocks in turn prompted more abundant use of mortar in thicker beds to compensate for the inconsistencies of the facing stones. The walls of the Caetani palace by the suburban Mausoleum of Caecilia Metella on the Via Appia, from c. 1302–3, are still in the 13th-century tradition, though the *tufelli* are somewhat less homogenous and occasionally interspersed with other fragments (Fig. 7.9). By the time parts of the Vatican walls were repaired

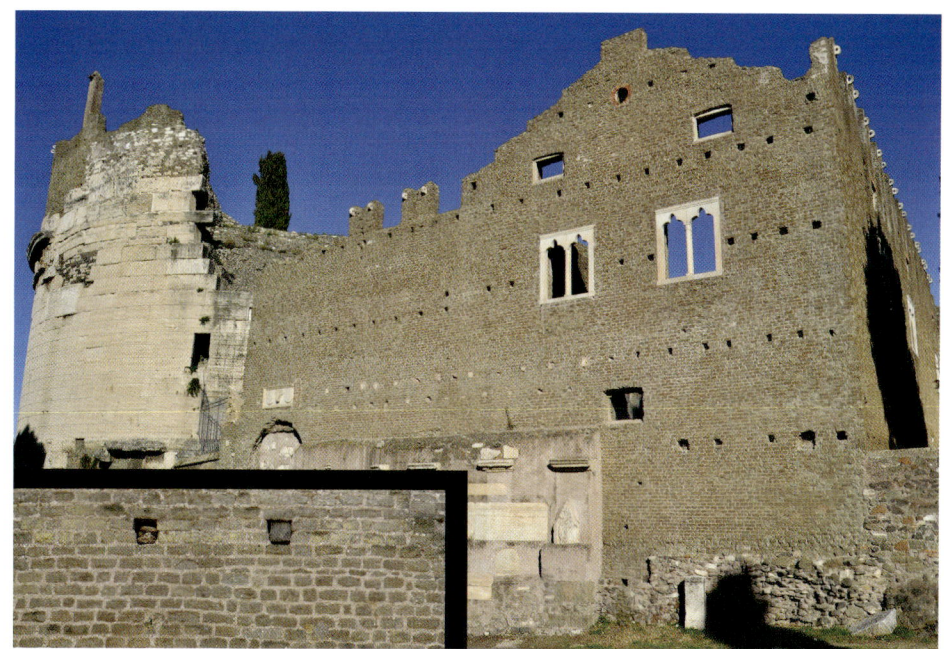

Figure 7.9 The Caetani palace on the Via Appia, incorporating (at left) the 1st-century BC mausoleum of Caecilia Metella; inset: detail of the masonry in *tufelli*. (Author.)

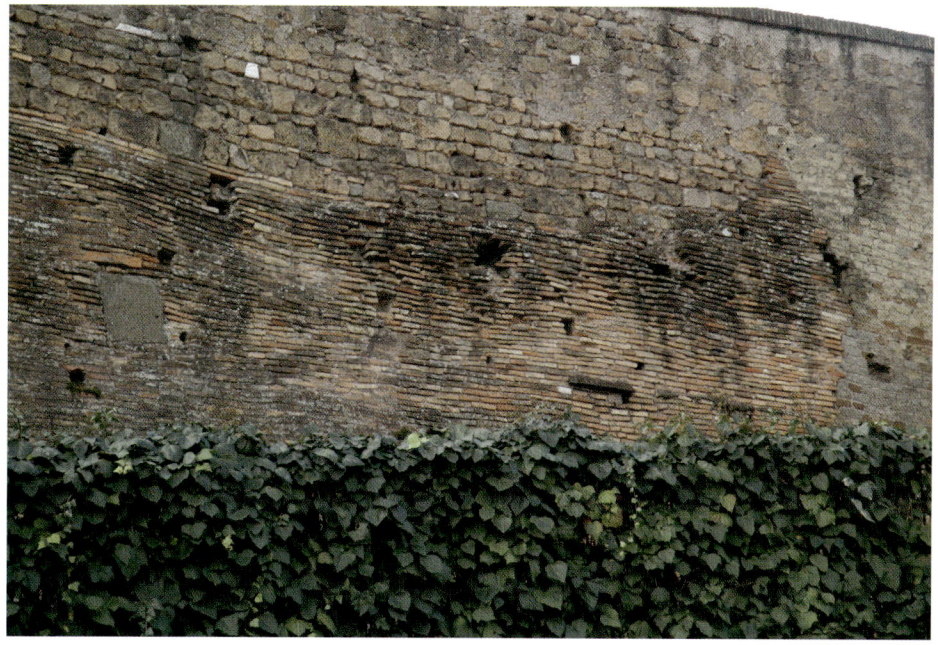

Figure 7.10 The interior of the Leonine circuit (north side) in the Vatican gardens. Original, undulating brickwork of the 9th century below with masonry of the later 14th century above. (Author.)

in (probably) the 1370s, however, the builders were working with a varied assemblage of mostly larger blocks whose disparities in size and shape obviated any possibility of regular coursing (Fig. 7.10).[24]

We should be wary of adducing facile equivalences between the diminishing regularity of mortared masonry and the broader processes of contraction at work in 14th-century Rome, and it bears stressing that 14th-century walls manifestly still 'worked,' as various edifices built then that still stand today demonstrate. But the differences between 13th and 14th-century masonry are, I think, a revealing indicator of changing social and economic conditions. When the construction industry was thriving during the 13th century, patrons were able to rely on experienced professionals who used semi-standardized, mass-produced components to build quickly and efficiently, the better to meet the burgeoning demands of the urban market. In the 14th century, by contrast, as the economy stagnated and population declined, demand for new construction diminished; while some skilled builders continued to operate, they relied on more heterogeneous materials that were less carefully worked prior to use. Given that it is faster and easier to build masonry walls using relatively uniform components (when they are readily available), we might presume that the move away from such components reflects a decline in their ready availability. As construction became a more occasional and therefore ad hoc process, the ancillary industries that had supported builders in the 13th century consequently waned, among them the sector devoted to sourcing and shaping *tufelli* and other building materials.

Let us return, then, to the built environment in the 13th century, and in particular to the activities of the barons, whose preponderant impact on urban topography and institutions alike is hard to overstate. By the second half of the century, a handful of families occupied all of the most imposing ancient monuments in the city, which they used as fortified residences. They also built additional residential compounds of unusual size and defensive potency that resembled rural castles or fortified villages uprooted and transplanted inside the city walls, as contemporaries recognized – while everyone else, nobles and prelates included, was said to dwell in a (perhaps fortified) "house" (*domus* or *turris*) or "palace" (*palatium*), the baronial strongholds are "castles" or "fortresses" (*castra, munitiones, fortilitia*) in the sources. Like rural castles, these complexes included enough facilities and amenities to ensure they could hold out for weeks or months even if besieged or cut off from the outside world: sleeping quarters for dozens or hundreds of retainers, chapels, baths, wells and cisterns, stables, storerooms for grain and other essential supplies. As the barons grew in wealth and influence, their urban fortresses grew along with them, reaching new heights of size and elaboration during the second half of the 13th century.[25]

The Conti controlled the slopes of the Quirinal, overlooking the Forum, from their twin fortresses of the Tor de' Conti, in the Forum of Nerva, and the Torre delle Milizie, atop the Markets of Trajan. At the end of the 13th century, under Boniface VIII, the Caetani would take over the Torre delle Milizie and expand the castle that surrounded it; parts of the fortified circuit wall in *tufelli* masonry still loom over Via Quattro Novembre. The Colosseum itself was shared between the long-established Frangipane and the rising Annibaldi family, which obtained title to half of the building in 1244. In the 12th century, the Frangipane had walled up extensive sections of the outer arcades to create a fortified perimeter that enclosed residential and utility spaces on two levels within, and attached a fortified, multistory tower block to the exterior of the oval at its eastern extremity, facing toward the Lateran; the roof gave access to a wooden fighting platform extending all along the lower, southern perimeter of the oval (Fig. 7.11). Around the amphitheater was a scatter of other towers and fortified residences under Frangipane control that stretched all the way to the summit of the Palatine. At the Theater of Marcellus, where the Savelli supplanted the Pierleoni in the 13th century, the exterior arcades of the upper levels had likewise been blocked to create enclosed spaces within, and there were multistory structures inside the arena. The

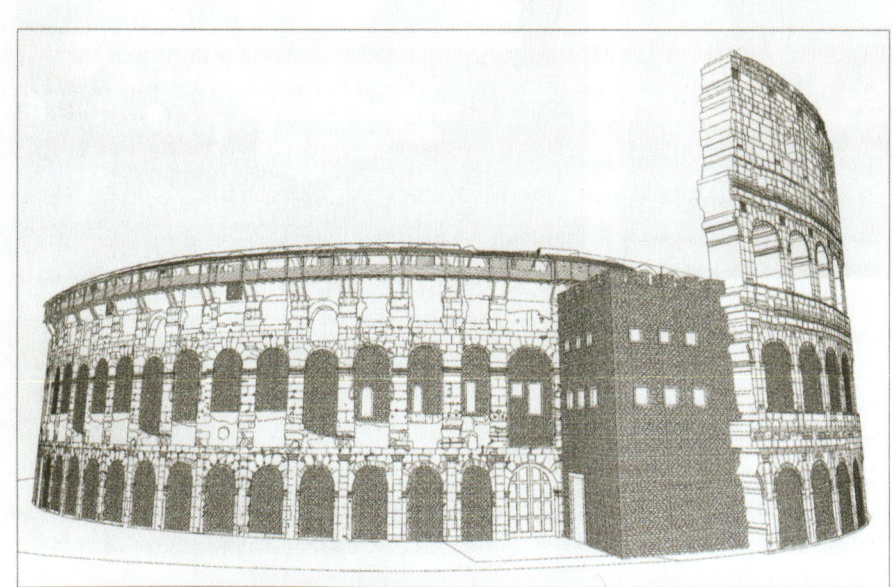

Figure 7.11 The Frangipane fortified compound in the SE sector of the Colosseum, as of the first half of the 13th century. (Delfino 2018, fig. 11.)

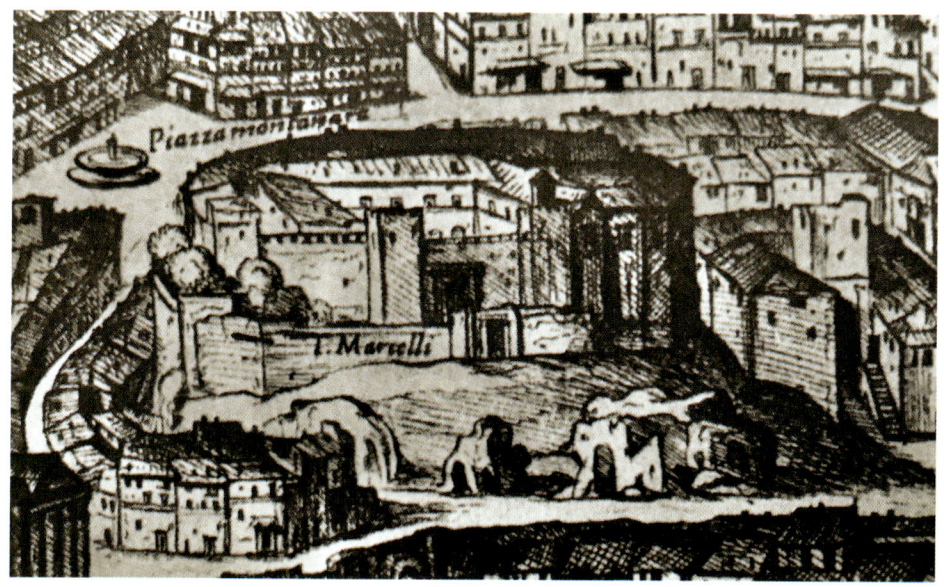

Figure 7.12 The Theater of Marcellus in Antonio Tempesta's 1593 plan of Rome. Note the turreted wall enclosing the arena. (Courtesy American Academy in Rome, Fototeca Unione.)

chord of the semicircle, facing the river, was closed off by powerful walls and towers that 16th-century depictions show reaching close to the full height of the seating tiers (Fig. 7.12).[26]

The second Savelli stronghold looked out across the *Ripa Graeca* toward the Theater of Marcellus from the summit of the Aventine, adjacent to S. Sabina. The only baronial fortress in Rome to preserve much of its original perimeter, it deserves a closer look. Unlike many compounds that arose piecemeal over the course of generations, the "Rocca Savella" was a unitary

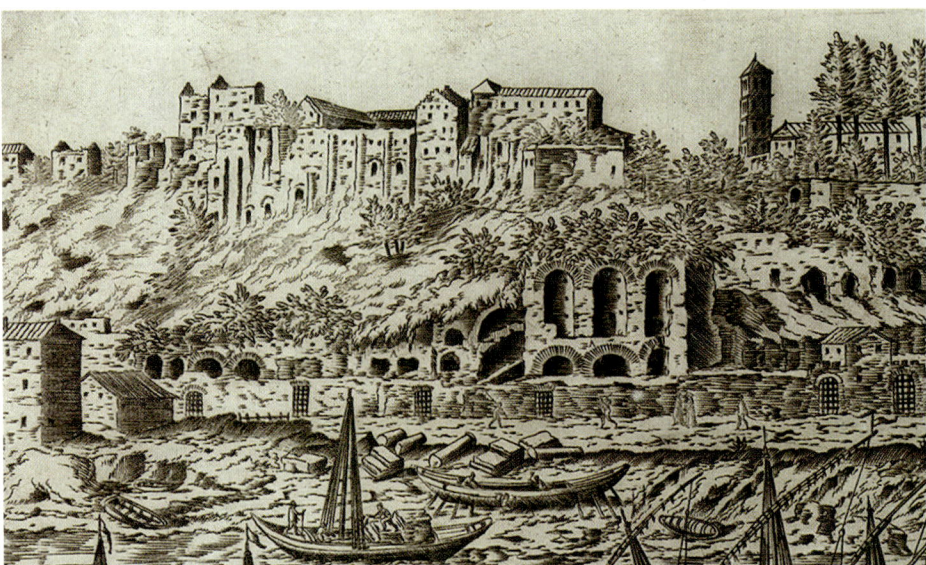

Figure 7.13 Detail of Étienne Dupérac's c. 1570 *veduta* of the Aventine (early 17th-century reprint). SS. Bonifacio ed Alessio is at upper right; the remains of the Savelli fortified compound attached to the church and monastery of S. Sabina is upper center. (Courtesy British School at Rome Library digital collections, tapri-L611.D9.023).

project sponsored by a single patron, the eminent cardinal Giacomo Savelli. Work probably began around 1280 and must have been largely complete by the time Savelli became Pope Honorius IV (r. 1285–7), given that he chose to base himself in the new family fortress during his papacy. The now-vanished residential wing rose close to the basilica and monastery of S. Sabina. Traces of the foundations and early modern sketches reveal an imposing block of conjoined edifices with an irregular profile, punctuated by at least two residential towers, all gravitating around an interior courtyard (Fig. 7.13). The structures around its perimeter included a colonnaded loggia and a large, rectangular great hall. This complex was enclosed within the much more extensive fortified perimeter, a slightly irregular quadrangle with sides approximately 100 m long, that still encloses what is now the Giardino degli Aranci. Built in concrete faced with *tufelli*, the crenellated circuit wall reached at least 6–7 m in height and was reinforced in places by projecting quadrangular towers. The largest studded the east flank of the circuit, looming over the narrow lane (today's Clivo di Rocca Savella) that climbs up from the Tiber embankments below (Fig. 7.7, above). Towering over the *Ripa Graeca* on its commanding eminence, the Rocca Savella was both a safe haven and a proud assertion of Savelli might and prestige, a pledge in stone that the family was there to stay.[27]

But the two most enduringly powerful families were the Orsini and the Colonna, whose perpetual enmity was a defining feature of local politics (and conflicts) for centuries, from the 13th well into the 15th. The Colonna dominated from the northern Campus Martius eastward to the hills of Monti, roughly speaking beyond a diagonal line running from the Mausoleum of Augustus in the northwest to SS. Apostoli in the southeast. The mausoleum itself, which they controlled by the 1210s, was one of their principal fortresses. Its massively thick concrete drum provided both security against attack and a lofty pedestal to keep the structures built atop it above the reach of even the most disastrous floods of the Tiber. The other Colonna stronghold was Montecitorio, where the parliament building now stands, an artificial eminence created by the deposition of huge quantities of broken transport amphorae in the late Roman period. As at the Mausoleum of Augustus, the Colonna were firmly installed here by the 1210s. They eventually surrounded the hill with a turreted perimeter wall, inside of which, again raised well above floodwaters, were more towers, living and service buildings, and so on. From the summits of the towers on Montecitorio and the Mausoleum of Augustus, the Colonna could look south upon the principal bastions of the Orsini, who occupied the southern half of the Campus Martius, a zone of crucial strategic value that included the main routes between the city center and the Vatican: the ancient Via Triumphalis/*porticus maximae*, and the medieval Via Papalis, which roughly paralleled the old route a few hundred meters farther north (Fig. 7.14).[28]

To hold this critical swath of the city, the Orsini developed an especially potent chain of strongpoints that eventually stretched from today's S. Carlo ai Catinari, near Largo Argentina, all the way to Castel Sant'Angelo. The original nucleus of the Orsini holdings was at the Theater of Pompey, parts of which had been acquired by Orsini ancestors already in the 1140s. By the later 13th century, one branch of the family controlled all of the theater, atop which stood one of the highest towers in Rome, the renowned Arpacata (or Arpacasa). By then, the theater itself was attached to a sprawling fortified enclosure that stretched southwest to the present church of S. Carlo ai Catinari along the northern flank of the *porticus maximae* (today's Via dei

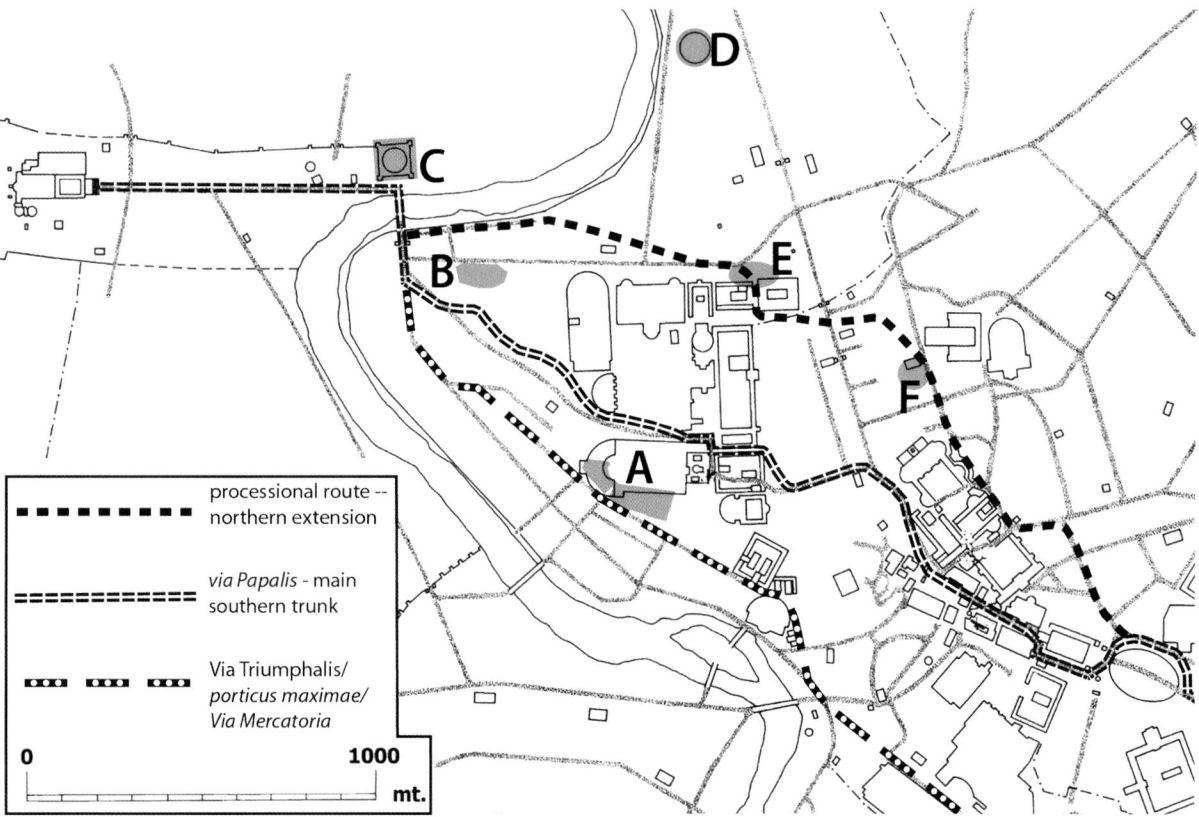

Figure 7.14 Detail of Fig. 6.31, showing the main roads and processional routes across the Campus Martius; the shaded areas indicate the principal Orsini (A, B, C) and Colonna (D, E, F) strongholds as of the late 13th century. A: Theater of Pompey – *turris pertundata* compound; B: Montegiordano; C: Castel Sant'Angelo; D: Mausoleum of Augustus; E: Montecitorio; F: SS. Apostoli. A final important axis of movement is the straight street that runs E – W just north of Monte Giordano, along the line of today's Via dei Coronari (between 'B' and 'E' on plan). It is evident how well-placed the Orsini strongholds were to control movement along all these routes, and thus also to command communications between the city center and the Vatican across the river. (Author.)

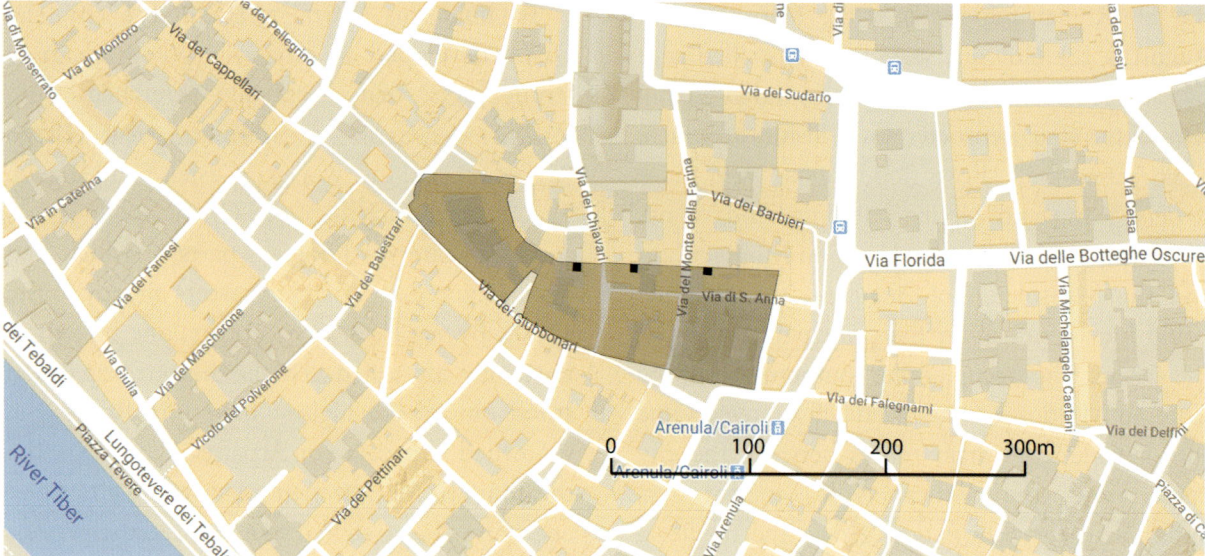

Figure 7.15 The area of the Orsini compound (shaded) between the Theater of Pompey and today's S. Carlo ai Catinari overlaid on today's map of the southern Campus Martius. The three partially extant towers along the north flank are indicated in black. (Google Maps/author, based on the reconstruction of Bosman 1990, fig. 1.)

Giubbonari). The irregular oblong of the compound measured some 300 meters long by 70 wide, and was anchored at its far end, at S. Carlo, by another massive tower, the *turris pertundata*. The remains of at least three more towers that once reinforced the north flank of the fortified perimeter have been identified in the fabric of later residential buildings (Fig. 7.15). The Orsini were thus in a position to control what was still one of the principal routes between the Capitoline and the Vatican; now a bustling commercial thoroughfare, the *porticus maximae* had changed its common name to the Via Mercatoria, "Market Street," for the many shops and stalls that lined its course.[29]

A second branch of the family was based farther west at Montegiordano, another hill composed of discarded Roman amphorae that rose from the floodplain of the Tiber, sited close enough to the bridgehead of Ponte Sant'Angelo to dominate all the main roads that converged on the bridge – the Via Mercatoria, the Via Papalis, and a third still farther north by the banks of the Tiber, the latter two of which hosted all the ecclesiastical processions between the city center and St. Peter's. Like the Colonna fortress at Montecitorio, this eminence was covered with residences and service buildings, all encircled by a potent perimeter wall reinforced with towers. When the Orsini pope, Nicholas III, put Castel Sant'Angelo under the control of his family in 1278, the Orsini stranglehold on communications between the Vatican and the rest of Rome was complete. Their control of the Theater of Pompey and its attached 'castle', Montegiordano, and (for a time) Castel Sant'Angelo ensured Orsini predominance in the southern Campus Martius for the rest of the Middle Ages. Command of this central, densely populated part of the late medieval *abitato*, in turn, helps to explain how the Orsini managed to stay at the top of the baronial hierarchy for centuries.[30]

Fanciful as it is, the late 13th-century manuscript image of Rome in the shape of a lion is revealing in one important respect (Fig. 7.16). The only features shown inside the walls are a handful of clearly baronial fortresses, including two labeled as the Colosseum and a "theater,"

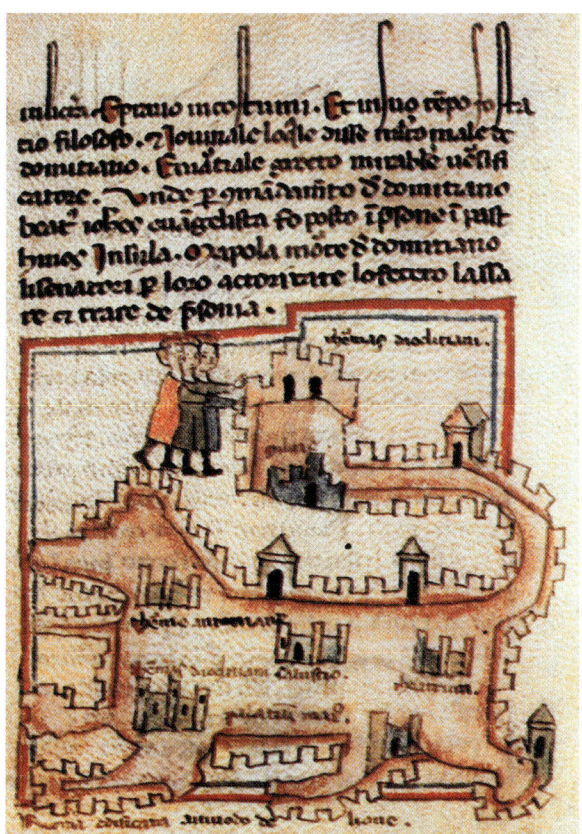

Figure 7.16 Late 13th-century depiction of Rome in the shape of a lion. (Staats- und Universitätsbibliothek Hamburg, Cod. in scrin. 151, fol. 107v.)

presumably that of either Marcellus or Pompey; all appear as imposing castles surrounded by high, tower-studded walls. The artist's conception of Rome as a single large wall encircling a group of fortified enclaves is an understandable way for a late medieval observer to perceive the cityscape. It bears repeating that the baronial fortresses were only the centerpieces of much more extensive areas under the preponderant influence of individual families – the Frangipane and then the Annibaldi from the Colosseum to the summit of the Palatine; the Savelli from the *Ripa Graeca* to the Aventine; the Conti and Caetani in the Subura; the Stefaneschi in Trastevere; the Colonna and Orsini in the northern and southern Campus Martius, respectively, and so on. As the decades passed, such families bought up more houses and towers around their principal fortresses, which they leased to retainers and clients who helped consolidate and expand the patron family's territory. From the late 13th century, it became customary for baronial tenants to paint the family's coat of arms on the facades of their houses and shops, such that entire neighborhoods came to be colored with the red bars and rose of the Orsini, the white column of the Colonna, the red lions rampant of the Annibaldi, and so on. By the first half of the 14th century, it was difficult to go far in Rome without knowing where one stood, and by whose sufferance one stood there. With the anti-baronial reaction that set in under Cola di Rienzo and the popular regime that followed, the display of baronial coats of arms was expressly prohibited, the better to show that Rome was no longer meant to be a gaggle of antagonistic feudal seigneuries cooped up together inside the city walls, like cats in a sack.[31]

In addition to their anomalous size and commanding locations, the barons' urban castles also increasingly distinguished themselves from the residences of lesser nobles by their overtly fortified appearance. Over the course of the 13th century, the residences of the minor nobility and the "medium elites" of prosperous merchants and professionals were in fact becoming distinctly more comfortable and less militarized in aspect, though they often still incorporated one or more towers. Interior spaces grew larger and more elegant; bigger windows brought more air and light to rooms on upper floors, where colonnaded loggias and balconies proliferated. Though usually heavily restored and often incorporated into later structures, parts of hundreds of such houses survive today across the late medieval *abitato*, from the foot of the Capitoline and the *Ripa Graeca* on into the southern Campus Martius, and across the river in Trastevere (Fig. 7.17).[32]

Inside their fortress walls, the upper crust of the nobility also had sumptuous living spaces at their disposal. The residential wings of the

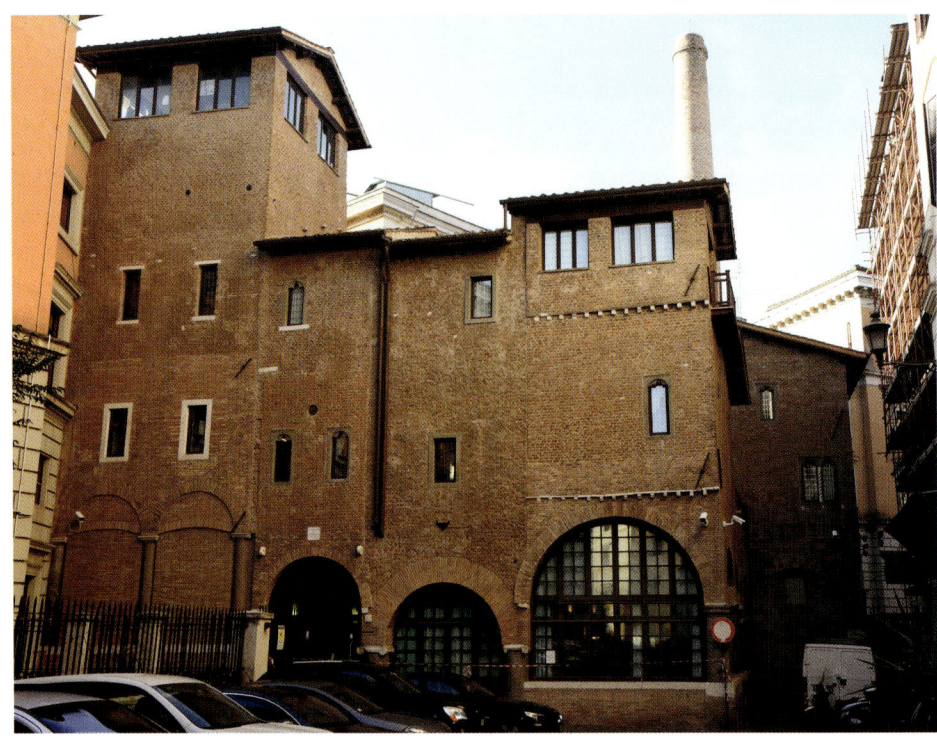

Figure 7.17 A continuous row of (heavily restored) 13th-century houses, all with ground-floor porticoes, in Via di Santa Maria in Monticelli. (Author.)

baronial compounds have mostly disappeared along with the fortifications, however. The best way to imagine the domestic arrangements is to examine the residences of Roman cardinals, who tended to live much like their baronial kin. As their wealth and influence grew during the 13th century, these cardinal-barons expanded the residences attached to various titular churches into imposing palaces with luxurious interiors that had much in common with the 'castles' inhabited by their lay relatives. The residences at S. Maria in Cosmedin, Sant'Angelo in Pescheria, S. Maria in Trastevere, SS. Giovanni e Paolo; S. Lorenzo in Lucina, S. Clemente, and SS. Quattro Coronati, among others, were all transformed and expanded on the initiative of Roman cardinals accustomed to princely standards of living (Fig. 7.18).[33]

The palace at SS. Quattro Coronati, overlooking the main route between the Colosseum and the Lateran (today's Via dei SS. Quattro), is an especially well-preserved example of the type. The existing residential wing along the north side of the 12th-century church was transformed into the imposing edifice visible today during the tenure of Innocent III's nephew, Stefano Conti, cardinal from 1216 until his death in 1254. He may have received the property already upon his promotion in 1216, but the bulk of the rebuilding dates to the 1240s, when Conti is certainly attested as residing there. The new palace rose as a series of distinct blocks along the steep northern slope of the Caelian hill, at a commanding elevation over the road below. Its salients and rientrants largely conform to the contours of the 9th-century structures built under Leo IV (whose basilica, recall, was both wider and much longer than its 12th-century successor), which were incorporated into the foundations of the 13th-century constructions.[34]

The complex gravitated around two bulky, reinforced blocks of rooms, essentially squat

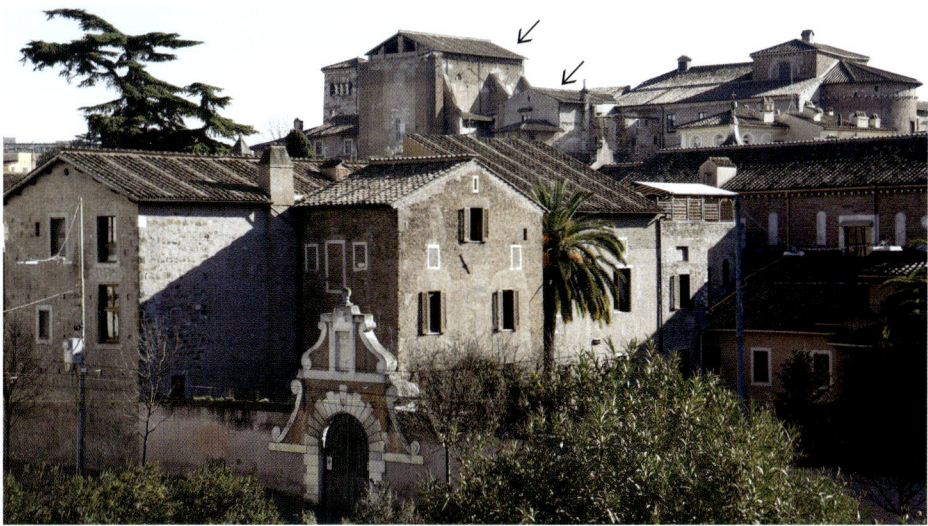

Figure 7.18 Two predominantly 13th-century cardinals' palaces. In the foreground is the residence attached to S. Clemente (the church is visible at far right with its nave wall in shade); above looms the palace at SS. Quattro Coronati, whose apse is visible at upper right. The arrows indicate the two main residential blocks in the SS. Quattro palace – the taller is the Torre Maggiore. (Author.)

towers, both of which were accessed from the protected confines of the two courtyards that fronted the 12th-century church (Fig. 7.19). Their exterior-facing walls were thick and impermeable, with only narrow slits to let in light on the lower levels, and larger apertures above. The smaller tower ("torre minore"), to the west, was two stories high, with a vaulted upper chamber and a flat roof originally topped with a crenellated parapet. Its strong walls of mortared masonry, faced partly in *tufelli* and partly in roughly squared fragments of marble, are typical of the first half of the 13th century. The ground floor, with its massive hearth, probably housed kitchens and other service quarters, while the upper floor may have been the private sleeping quarters of the cardinal himself. To the east, across a small courtyard that was later roofed over, is the still more massive Torre Maggiore, an irregular rectangle some 20 meters long by 15 wide on its exterior. The lower two-thirds are faced in fine brick masonry, regular and with thin beds of mortar characteristic of the mid 13th century; the upper third is of one build with the rest, but faced with finely cut, evenly laid *tufelli*. It has four stories, two of them downslope below the floor level of the basilica and its front courtyards. A smaller tower block projects off its east side, built at the same time but walled off from the main block. The Torre Maggiore's road-facing northern façade rises more than 26 meters above ground level, and is reinforced by thick projecting buttresses. Now covered with a pitched roof, it initially culminated in a flat platform; surviving sockets for flagpoles near the summit indicate that it stands close to its original height.[35]

The Torre Maggiore contained the grandest, most public spaces in the palace. The ground (third) floor was divided into three vaulted chambers, one of which was the cardinal's palace-chapel. This is the famous S. Silvestro chapel, with its cycle of frescoes that reprise the tale of the *Acta Silvestri* and the Donation of Constantine: Pope Sylvester cures Constantine of leprosy, so the emperor bequeaths all his sovereign rights to the pope (Fig. 7.20). The date of the fresco program is assured by an *in situ* inscription commemorating the chapel's consecration in 1246, which names Stefano Conti as the patron

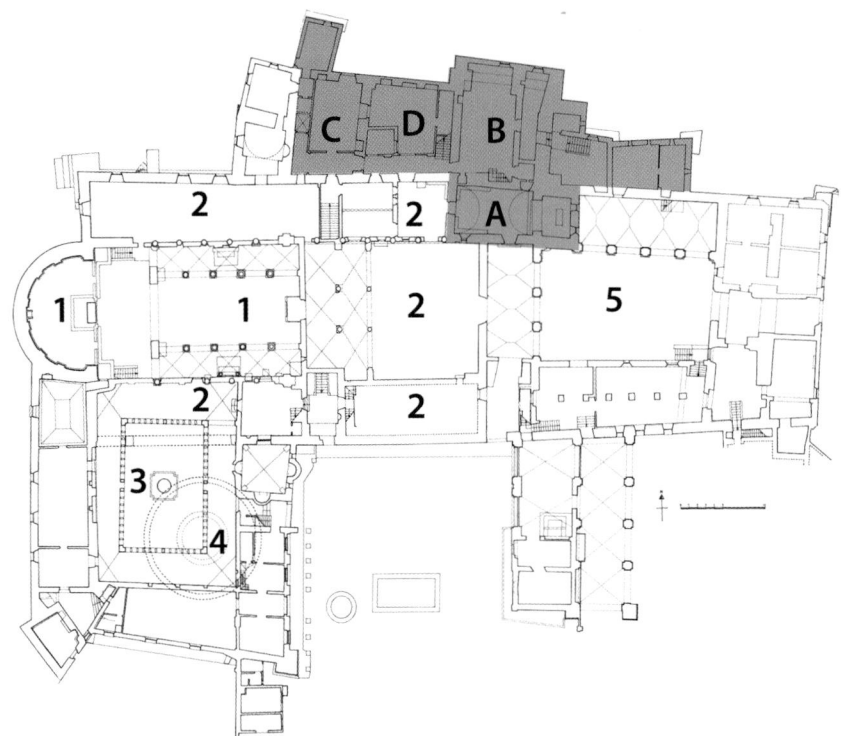

Figure 7.19 The SS. Quattro Coronati complex (letters indicate principal features of the 13th-century cardinal's palace, shaded). A: San Silvestro chapel; B: Torre Maggiore, with the Aula Gotica on the top floor; C: "torre minore"; D: courtyard. 1: the 12th-century church; 2: parts of 9th-century church left out of the 12th-century reconstruction (incorporated into later monastery and cardinal's palace); 3: 12th-century cloister; 4: round 5th-century baptistery destroyed in 1084; 5: atrium of 9th-century church. (Plan courtesy of Lia Barelli, adapted by author.)

of both the chapel and the new residential wing. The chapel was thus painted at a time when the Church was especially anxious to assert its supremacy over the secular arm. In 1244, Innocent IV had fled into virtual exile in France because of his feud with Barbarossa's grandson, Frederick II, leaving Rome in the hands of his chosen vicar, Cardinal Conti himself. In their pointed suggestion that the pope, and thus also the cardinal he appointed to serve in his stead, were Rome's rightful masters, the new frescoes radiated polemical intent.[36]

The top (fourth) story comprised a single grand hall, a rectangle some 17.5 meters by 9 on the interior, divided into two cross-vaulted bays that peak 11.5 m above the floor. The walls and ceiling of this room, the so-called Aula Gotica, are covered in a splendid cycle of frescoes that can now be appreciated in much of its original splendor, following removal of overpainting and cleaning in the 1990s. It is one of those concatenations of allegory and erudite arcana beloved of highly educated medieval minds (like Stefano Conti), a sort of compendium of antiquarian curiosities, cosmology, and natural philosophy. The lower register is mostly lost, but much remains of the frescoes above the springing of the vaults. On the vaults themselves, there are telamons perching on capitals, personifications of the seasons and winds, a seascape, and constellations and signs of the zodiac. On the walls of the southern bay, the lowest register had personifications of the cardinal vices, now mostly lost. Above are depictions of the twelve months, represented by a labor for each month, with playful erotes cavorting in the interstices; higher still were personifications of the seven liberal arts, of which five remain: grammar, geometry, music,

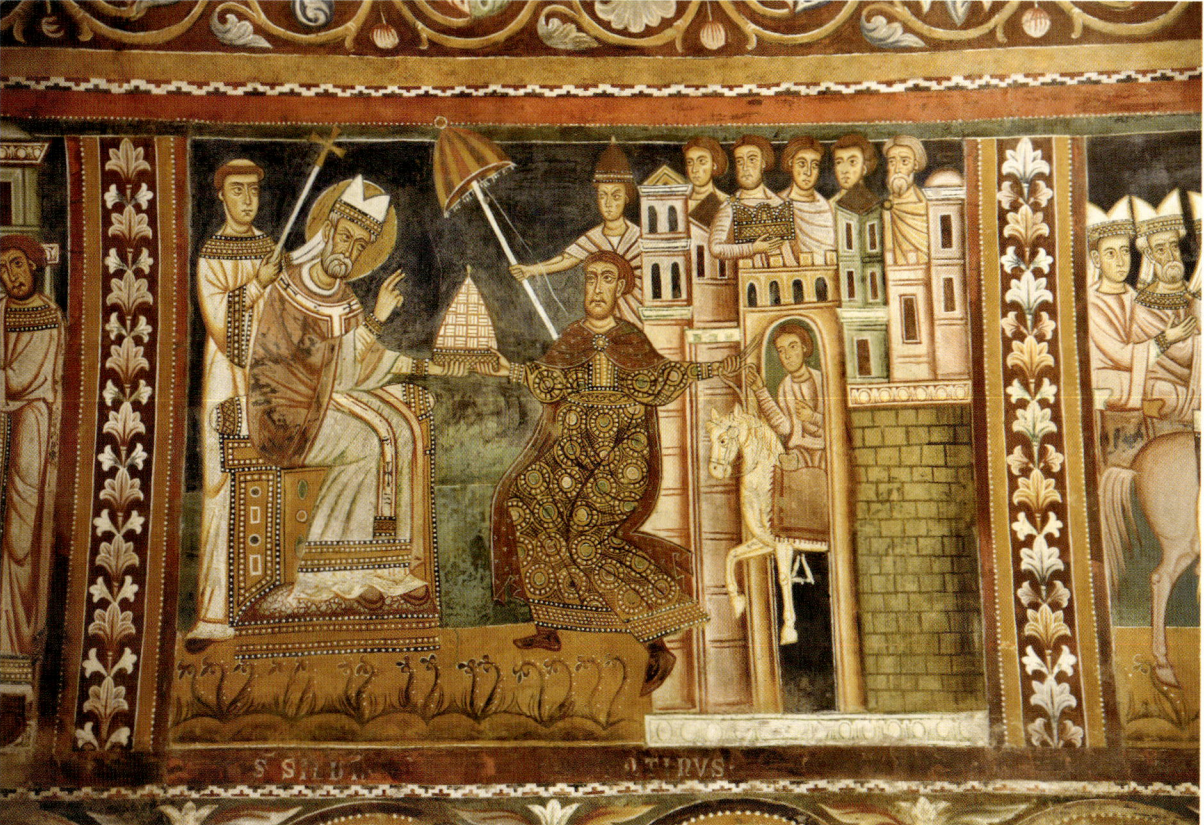

Figure 7.20 S. Silvestro chapel, north wall: Constantine hands over his crown to Pope Sylvester. (Author.)

arithmetic, and astronomy (Fig. 7.21). In the north bay, the side (east and west) walls teem with personifications of the virtues and beatitudes. On the north wall, the visual focus of the hall as a whole, the main register comprises standing prophets and doctors of the church, with Solomon at their center. In the arch above is Mithras slaying the bull(!), flanked by allegories of the Sun and Moon. All in all, the Aula Gotica is the most complete extant example of a great hall in the residence of a Roman *grand seigneur*. In its rich program of largely profane imagery, it recalls the decorative schemes favored by lay nobles of the period, scattered fragments of which survive. It was here that Cardinal Conti, papal *vicarius*, doubtless did his receiving and banqueting, and performed his judicial functions – the prominence of Solomon, the Old Testament judge *par excellence*, strongly suggests that the space functioned as a courtroom, as does the cosmological thrust of the fresco program as a whole: Righteous rulers and adjudicators rightly enjoy the bounty of the earth.[37]

After Cardinal Conti died in 1254, his grand palace remained a privileged residence for the rest of the 13th century, when it belonged to a series of especially eminent cardinals, starting with the potent Ottaviano degli Ubaldini in the later 1250s. The strength of its defenses and its position close to the Lateran made it a secure refuge in times of need as well as a most desirable abode, both for its owners and for distinguished guests. When the Brescian Emanuele Maggi was deposed from the senatorate in 1257, he fled there for safety. Charles of Anjou took up residence during his stay in Rome in 1265. The future Boniface VIII, Benedetto Caetani, dwelled there from 1285 until he became pope in 1294; in

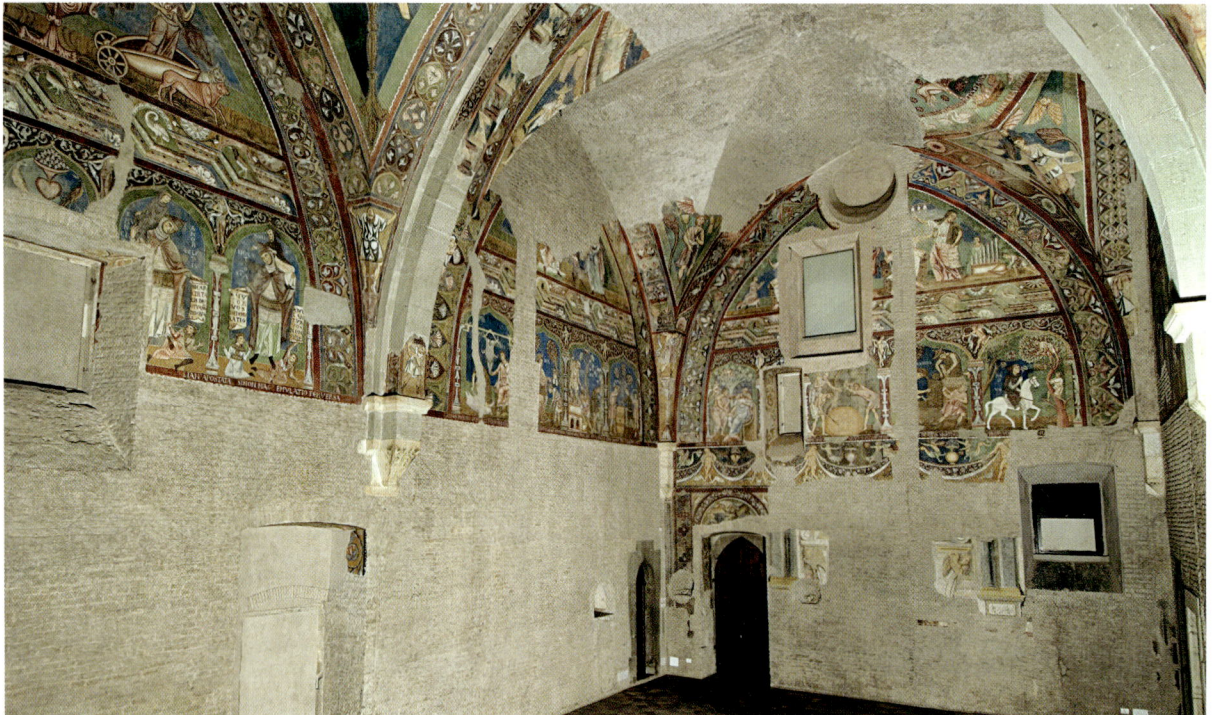

Figure 7.21 The Aula Gotica: view from the north bay into the south. (Courtesy of Lia Barelli and the Monache Agostiniane di Santi Quattro Coronati.)

the following year, he gave it to his nephew, Cardinal Francesco Caetani, who seems to have held it until his death in 1313. Like so much of Rome's ecclesiastical patrimony, however, the complex suffered after the removal of the Curia to Avignon. After Caetani's death, it was given to a series of absent French cardinals who allowed it to fall into disrepair, and was stably reoccupied and restored only after the return of Martin V in 1420. Its first resident was the Spanish cardinal Alfonso Carillo (1423–34), whose renovations, evidently necessitated by long neglect, are commemorated in a surviving inscription.[38]

As for sacred architecture, the middle decades of the 13th century saw few noteworthy commissions. The 1230s and 1240s were marked by tensions between the Church and Frederick II, the last great Hohenstaufen emperor, and between the Church and local proponents of communal autonomy, all of which encouraged the popes to avoid Rome and diminished curial patronage of Roman churches. The death of Frederick II in 1250 led to further decades of political turmoil, as his heirs contended with the Angevins for the kingdoms of Sicily and Naples. The popes were leading players in the unfolding political drama, and the climate at Rome was so charged that they and the Curia were absent from the city more than ever. Innocent IV (r. 1243–54) fled Rome for Lyon after clashing with Frederick II in 1244, and did not set foot in the capital again until 1253. Alexander IV (r. 1254–61), Urban IV (r. 1261–4), and especially Clement IV (r. 1265–8) all preferred the relatively secure Viterbo to Rome. After a hotly disputed conclave during which the papal throne lay vacant for almost three years, Clement IV's successor, Gregory X (r. 1271–6), would spend much of his pontificate in his native France. With the popes mostly absent and otherwise preoccupied with war and high politics, and the Roman cardinals concentrating their creative energies on their own palatial residences, there was little impetus toward costly prodigies of ecclesiastical art and architecture.³⁹

All this would change in the last quarter of the 13th century, when Rome shone again, briefly but brilliantly, as the artistic epicenter of the Italian peninsula. In contrast to the period 1227–77, when the popes were completely absent from the city during twenty-nine of the fifty-one years, only six years of the twenty-six between 1278 and 1303 passed without a papal sojourn in the capital. And three of the popes who ruled during that quarter-century were Roman barons: Nicholas III Orsini (r. 1277–80), Honorius IV Savelli (r. 1285–7), and Boniface VIII Caetani (r. 1294–1303). Monumental art and architecture flourished as they had not since the earlier 12th century, and would not again until the mid 15th. For a brief moment, the ambitions of rich and assertive popes and cardinals from the Roman baronial families were matched by the genius of an inspired group of artists. Along with the Tuscans Arnolfo di Cambio and Giotto, who made regular appearances in the city, there were the three leading lights of the so-called Roman School: Filippo Rusuti, Jacopo Torriti, and Pietro Cavallini, all active in Rome in the period c. -1280–1310. Working in fresco and mosaic, these Roman masters used pioneering advances in the treatment of color, shading, and perspective to imbue their compositions with volume and spatial depth, prefiguring and helping to inspire the move toward naturalism now associated with Giotto and the beginnings of the Tuscan Renaissance. Had the removal of the Curia to Avignon not dispersed them abroad in search of other patrons, Rome might well have joined or indeed surpassed Florence as the artistic cradle of the Renaissance.⁴⁰

The season of Roman flourishing opened during the pontificate of Nicholas III Orsini, a worldly and imperious promoter of the Church's temporal sovereignty and universalizing mission in the mold of Innocent III. In the less than four years he reigned, Nicholas III bodily inserted himself into some of the most symbolically charged loci in the city. He expanded and fortified the papal palace at the Vatican, as we have already seen. He may well have commissioned the frescoes in the council chamber (*aula conciliare*) on the top floor of the communal palace on the Capitoline, and more certainly adorned the façade overlooking the piazza with painted shields bearing the Orsini arms, presumably when he himself became the ruling senator of the Commune for a year in 1278–9, replacing Charles of Anjou.⁴¹

But the most impressive of the Orsini pope's surviving commissions is the restoration of the Sancta Sanctorum chapel in the Lateran palace, home of the most prestigious collection of relics in Christendom, among them the heads of Saints Peter and Paul. The project was directed by a member of the Cosmati family (a *magister Cosmatus* is commemorated in an inscription on the marble doorjamb of the entrance), and involved the complete redecoration of the interior of the 8th-century chapel with new sculpted furnishings, mosaics, and an extensive cycle of frescoes. Following cleaning and restoration in the early 1990s, the frescoes can again be appreciated in much of their original splendor. The cross vaults of the ceiling bear the signs of the four evangelists silhouetted against a deep-blue background pricked with gilded stars. On the upper registers of three walls are five scenes of martyrdom, four featuring the Roman saints Peter, Paul, Lawrence, and Agnes, along with the protomartyr Stephen. Next to Stephen, Nicholas of Myra, the pope's namesake, performs a miracle for the three poor girls. On the fourth wall, above the altar, Nicholas himself, flanked by Saints Peter and Paul, offers a likeness of his chapel to Christ (Fig. 7.22). The pope is shown in a convincing portrait likeness, a striking

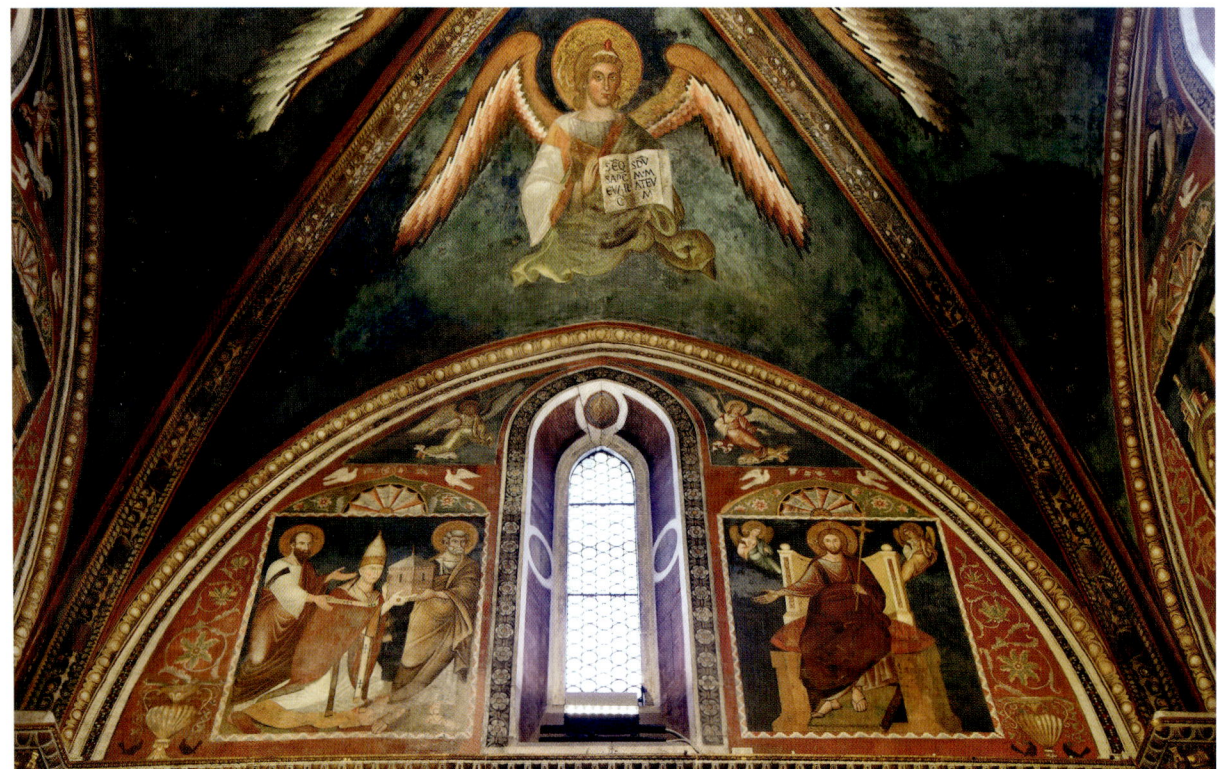

Figure 7.22 The Sancta Sanctorum chapel: upper register of east (altar) wall and vaulting. In the left-hand panel, Pope Nicholas III, flanked by Peter and Paul, offers a simulacrum of the chapel to Christ, enthroned in the panel at right. (Author.)

innovation that has led some to propose a youthful Torriti as the painter of the scene. A false gallery runs below the scenes on all four walls, with seven arcuated niches per side framing standing figures of saints and doctors of the Church. On the vaulting above the altar niche, visible only to the pope officiating at the altar, are mosaics with a central bust of Christ supported by angels, beneath which Peter and Paul, Agnes, and Lawrence reappear. The renovated chapel thus embodies a potent vision of a universal Church, founded on the blood of Roman martyr-saints and led by a Roman pope; "it displays with crystalline clarity [Nicholas III's] vision of the Roman and Apostolic Church, an Orsini version of the universalism of Innocent III and a clear anticipation of the soon-to-come Boniface VIII," as Serena Romano has put it.[42]

Construction of the two most monumental churches built at Rome across the period 1230–1420 also began during or very close to Nicholas III's reign. These were to become the Roman headquarters of two of the great mendicant orders that burst onto the scene in the 13th century: the Dominicans and the Franciscans. Work began first on the new Franciscan church of S. Maria in Aracoeli, located on the northern summit of the Capitoline Hill on the spot where, according to ancient tradition, Emperor Augustus had seen a celestial vision of the Virgin Mary and Jesus at the time of Jesus' birth. A porphyry sarcophagus on the spot was supposed to be the "Aracoeli," an altar – the first Christian altar in the world – erected by Augustus following his vision. A small oratory seems to have been built over the site already by c. 500, which was replaced by a 9th-century basilica that was rebuilt in the 12th, on a north–south orientation with the altar near the sanctuary at the north end. In 1249, Pope Innocent IV gave the property to the

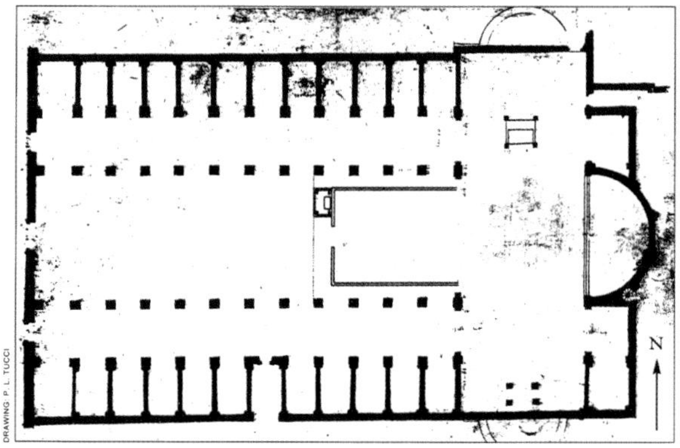

Figure 7.23 The c. 1500 Spada plan of S. Maria in Aracoeli, with the Felici Tabernacle, mentioned below, added along the outer face of the presbytery. (Bolgia 2005, fig. 5.)

most dynamic of the upstart mendicant orders, the Franciscans, who made it their principal Roman base.[43]

As Claudia Bolgia has now elegantly shown, the 12th-century church remained in use throughout the 1250s and 1260s; only in the 1270s was it demolished to prepare for the erection of its successor. Work on the present building seems to have begun c. 1276–9 and to have been mostly complete by the later 1290s (Fig. 7.23). The new basilica was very large, at c. 65 m long (exclusive of the apse) and 30 m wide, exclusive of the later side chapels. Room was made for it by changing the orientation of the previous church from north–south to east–west, such that the foundations of the old basilica were used for the transept of the new church. With the new Aracoeli, the Gothic style finally made a late, partial appearance in a Roman church, a century and more after taking root across much of western Europe. But the enduring Roman attachment to the architectural vernacular of the city's early Christian churches made for a sort of hybrid: a typical Roman transept basilica built in brick-faced concrete, timber-roofed, with a monoapsidal nave flanked by colonnaded side aisles, but with a veneer of Gothic refinements. The clerestory windows and the apse arch have ogival (pointed) arches, as probably did the nave arcades until they were redone in the 16th century with their current round profile. The clerestory windows feature Gothic stone tracery, among the first of its kind to appear in Rome, as do the rose windows of the façade and the transept arms. The exterior of the apse was pentagonal, with each facet set off by pilasters and topped with a pointed gable, an arrangement typical of Franciscan churches that was meant to evoke the Holy Sepulcher in Jerusalem. On the interior, however, the dome of the apse was the standard Roman spherical type, framed by twin sets of monumental ancient columns, one supporting the apse arch and the other the triumphal arch. Its frescoes depicting the miraculous vision of Augustus were said by Vasari, who saw them shortly before the apse was torn down in the 1570s and replaced by the current structure, to be Cavallini's best work in Rome.[44]

The grand new basilica stood, by design, at the epicenter of communal life in Rome; indeed, one of Innocent IV's reasons for giving the site to the Franciscans may have been to establish the rising order at the heart of the civic commune, right next to the senatorial palace. The old church and its attached cloisters had already been used for meetings of the Senate and the popular assemblies, a tradition that would continue in the new building. The summit of the Capitoline was also the seat of communal justice, where trials were held and punishments meted out to the condemned; public proclamations were read out here; it was the site of the main weekly market and the repository of the city's standard weights and measures, and so on. These and other civic routines subsequently unfolded in the shadow of the new church, or even inside of it: guardianship hearings for the children of widows were conducted near the south entrance that fronted onto the central piazza; the albums of the urban notaries were stored inside under lock and key.

The Aracoeli consequently became a focal point for the commemorative energies of Roman grandees, to the point that its interior can be read as a kind of barometer of evolving familial and political dynamics across the 14th century and beyond. Even before construction was complete, holders of high municipal office and scions of the baronial families were vying for space in the new building, installing family chapels and funerary monuments. The grandest chapel of all belonged to the Savelli family. Occupying the full width of the south transept, it was acquired in the 1290s by the senator Pandolfo Savelli, brother of Honorius IV (r. 1285–7), the next Roman pope after Nicholas III. Pandolfo was buried there in an opulent tomb when he died in 1296, soon to be joined by other members of the family. The Savelli crest was everywhere: on the tombs, the floor, the wrought-iron gate to the chapel, and, more visibly still, on mosaic shields high up on the exterior of the south transept, overlooking the Capitoline piazza. The Colonna had a chapel nearby, its interior adorned with mosaics bearing the family crest, as did other baronial families. In the second half of the 14th century, the anti-baronial reaction and the regime of the Felice Società brought new protagonists to the fore, families like that of Francesco Felici, a notary and leading member of the popular regime. In 1372, Felici erected a two-story marble tabernacle in the center of the nave, installing in it both the arms of Cola di Rienzo and the Aracoeli's ancient painted icon of Mary that was credited with ending the plague of 1348 (Fig. 7.24). He and his descendants were buried in this 'communal' shrine, a monument built to stare down the baronial chapels that surrounded it, furnished with a 'popular' icon to rival the greatest relics in the papal collection.[45]

The second major new church was the Dominican basilica of S. Maria sopra Minerva, near the Pantheon. The small existing church was razed after the Dominicans were given the property in 1275, and work on the new basilica and its attached cloister commenced around 1280. (In June of that year, Nicholas III wrote a letter to the

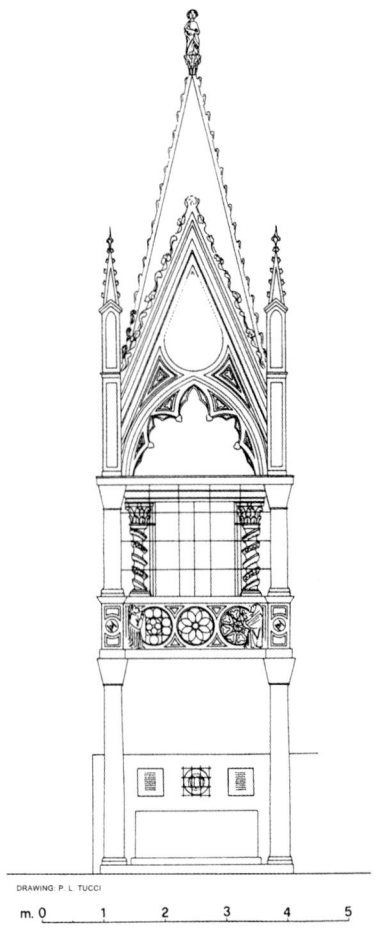

Figure 7.24 Claudia Bolgia's reconstruction of the Felici tabernacle. (Bolgia 2005, fig. 9.)

senators Giovanni Colonna and Pandolfo Savelli to encourage them to contribute communal funds to the project.) Financed mostly by a trickle of donations and bequests, the project took many decades to complete. The vaulted choir and high, slightly projecting transept seem to have been finished by around 1300, when members of the Orsini and other prominent families were already being buried there, but the remainder of the nave took much longer, rising in fitful stages over several decades and reaching completion only around mid-century.

At almost eighty meters long (exclusive of the apse) and almost thirty meters wide, the finished building was one of the largest churches inside the walls, comparable in size to S. Maria Maggiore. Though Gothic in its architectural refinements (high transept, pointed arches, quadrifoil pilasters in the nave), in structural terms, it was essentially another transept basilica in the late antique tradition – Roman conservatism again! Its stout concrete walls, faced in a mixture of brick and *tufelli*, were topped by a wooden trussed roof over the nave, while the apse and transept were covered with concrete vaults. Unusually, the clerestory walls of the nave had no windows, such that the interior was lit primarily via large windows in the exterior walls of the side aisles. By the 15th century, when chapels had been built all along the exterior flanks of both side aisles, the interior must have been very dark (Fig. 7.25). Perhaps in part for this reason, extensive modifications were made in the middle decades of the 15th century. The nave was covered with concrete groin vaults, and windows were cut into the clerestory level. The façade, until then left rough, got the fine travertine facing it retains today.[46]

The interior, in its current form the product of the extensive renovations conducted from 1848 to 1855, has been remodeled so many times that little trace of its late medieval decoration and furnishings remains. But surviving tombstones and written documentation make it clear that the new Dominican church, like the Aracoeli, was from its inception a premiere venue for elite display. The Orsini and Colonna both built chapels by the mid 14th century, the Savelli followed around the end of the century, and members of the lesser nobility (and other wealthy Romans) were amply represented, too. In part perhaps because they were built for the new mendicant orders, with funds provided by a wide range of donors, both the Aracoeli and the Minerva thus functioned as 'communal' spaces of self-representation (and competition), and never fell under the sway of any single family. In this respect, they differed from the many venerable urban churches that came to function virtually as family chapels for the great baronial clans. It was in such churches that baronial cardinals sponsored many of the masterpieces of Rome's late 13th-century artistic flowering.[47]

One example is S. Maria in Trastevere under the patronage of the Stefaneschi, the predominant baronial family in Trastevere in the later 1200s. In the mid-1290s, Cardinal Giacopo Stefaneschi and his brother, Bertoldo, commissioned Pietro Cavallini to decorate the hemicycle of the apse with a mosaic cycle of scenes from the life of the Virgin. A central, dedicatory panel directly behind the altar immortalized the patronage of the Stefaneschi for posterity: Saints Peter and Paul flank a roundel with the Virgin and Child, beneath which Bertoldo Stefaneschi, identified by name, kneels in prayer next to a shield bearing the Stefaneschi arms (Fig. 7.26). Cavallini used pronounced highlights and shading to imbue his figures with sculptural weight and volume. He gave them individualized features and poses, and attempted a range of three-quarter profiles and foreshortening, even showing the occasional figure nearly from behind. Such features recur in Cavallini's spectacular fresco of the Last Judgement on the interior of the façade at S. Cecilia in Trastevere, of c. 1293, which may also have been commissioned by the Stefaneschi, though their patronage here is far from certain. In the upper register, an enthroned Christ surrounded by a halo of angels is flanked by Mary,

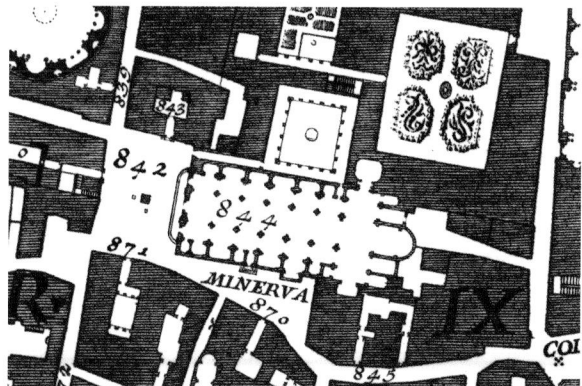

Figure 7.25 S. Maria sopra Minerva on Nolli's 1748 plan of Rome.

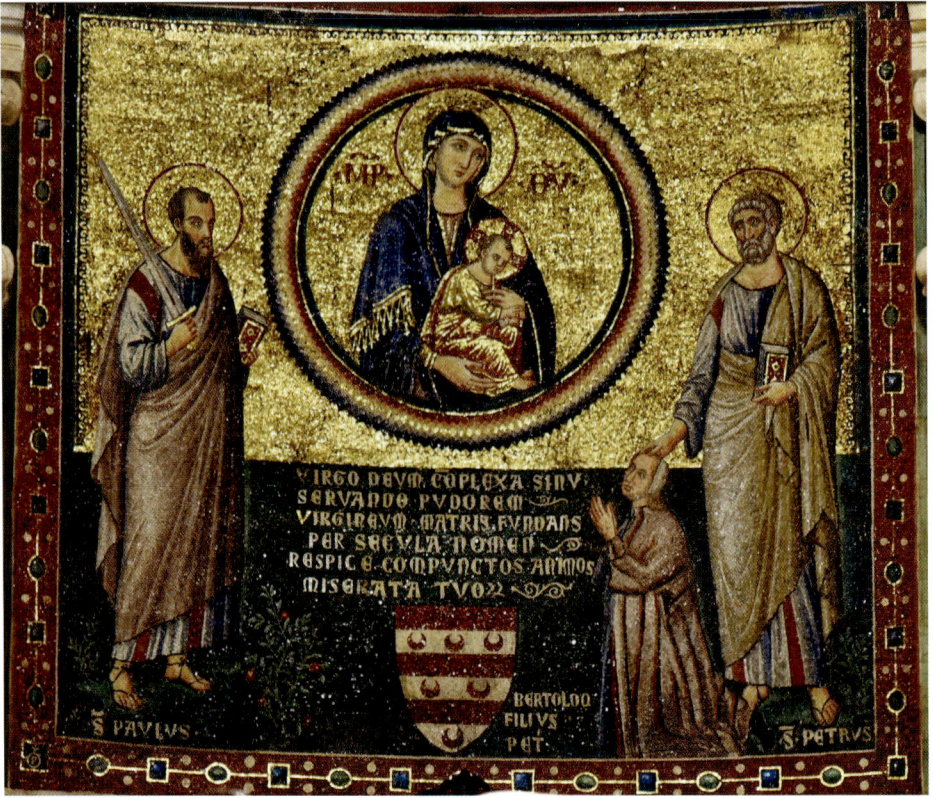

Figure 7.26 Cavallini's dedicatory panel in the center of the hemicycle of the apse at S. Maria in Trastevere. (Author.)

John the Baptist, and the twelve enthroned apostles, all set against a deep blue background. Below, angels lead the blessed, on the left, toward a central altar; to the right, angels herd the naked damned toward the demons and fires of hell (Fig. 7.27).[48]

The preeminent monument to the patronage of a single family is S. Maria Maggiore, located in the heart of Colonna territory by one of the family's principal residences. Starting under Nicholas IV (r. 1288–92), the first Franciscan pope and a close ally of the Colonna, the old basilica was transformed into a showpiece of the most current trends in Gothic art and architecture. The works involved both ends of the building, and seem to have been mostly complete by 1297, when Boniface VIII declared war on the Colonna family and banished them all from Rome, Cardinals Giacomo and Pietro included. In the east, the façade was restored and faced with a cycle of mosaics by Filippo Rusuti. In the west, a new transept was added that rose to the full height of the nave, in the manner of the great Gothic cathedrals of northern Europe, and the apse was rebuilt and adorned on both its interior and exterior surfaces with mosaics by Jacopo Torriti.

The mosaic in the conch of the apse centers on a roundel within which Christ and Mary sit enthroned on a blue background dotted with stars. Two kneeling figures, set against a gold ground, face each other across the roundel, Pope Nicholas in scarlet on the left, and the potent Cardinal Giacomo Colonna in blue on the right. Behind the two kneeling donors stand larger figures of (ancient) saints and (much more recent) Franciscan luminaries in their brown habits: Saints Peter, Paul, and Francis behind the pope on the left, and John the Baptist, John

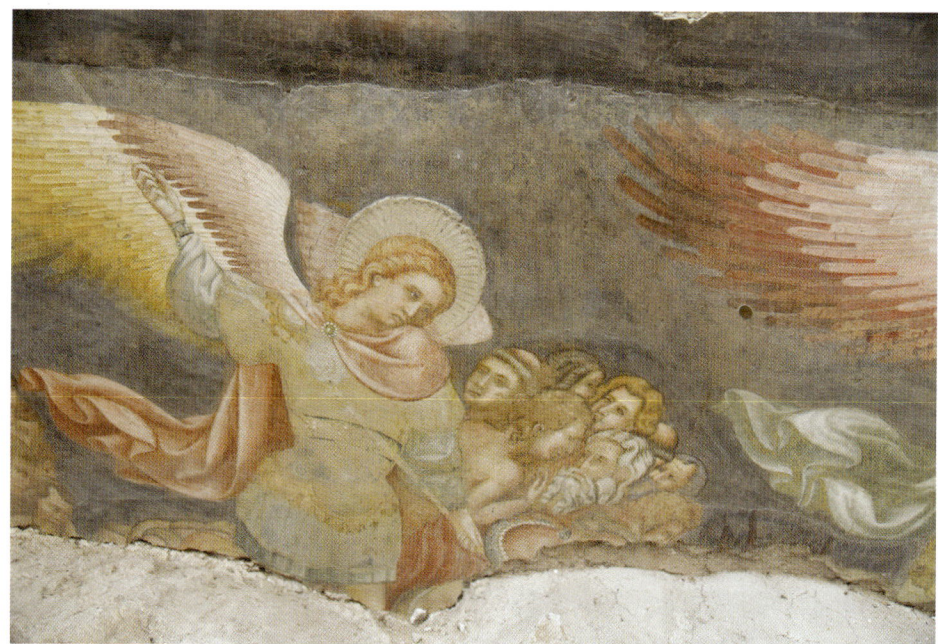

Figure 7.27 S. Cecilia in Trastevere, counter-façade, lower register: An angel drives a group of the damned toward hell. (Author.)

the Evangelist, and St. Anthony of Padua behind Cardinal Colonna on the right (Fig. 7.28). Though completed years after Nicholas IV died in 1292 (it is signed by Torriti and dated to 1295/96), the mosaic thus proclaimed for the ages the special relationship, the unity of intent, that subsisted between the Colonna family and the Franciscan pope.[49]

The Colonnas' appropriation of the visual and decorative focal point of the interior repeated itself at the entrance of the church, where Rusuti's mosaics unfold in two superimposed registers across the exterior of the façade. The upper register partially reprises the schema of the apse. It centers on a mandorla with an enthroned Christ on a starry blue background, flanked by standing saints and donors set against a gold ground. The arches of the loggia added to the façade in the 18th century have obscured some of the standing figures, among them (again) Giacomo Colonna, who once appeared between Mary and the central medallion, just above an inscription that identified him. Another donor presumably appeared in the corresponding position on the right of the medallion, now also obscured by the springing of an arch; he may have been the other serving Colonna Cardinal, Pietro, or Giovanni Colonna, senator of Rome circa 1290–1. The lower register depicts the visions and miracles that preceded the founding of the basilica itself, all set in deep pictorial spaces defined by complex architectural backgrounds. Here, too, the Colonna presence is manifest: Four Colonna coats of arms, each flanked by a cardinal's hat, surround the round window at the center of the façade, set directly above the main entrance to the nave and below the roundel of Christ.[50]

The prestige that accrued to the Colonna family through its remodeling of Rome's second-most prestigious intramural basilica can only have been enhanced by what was transpiring nearby at the Lateran cathedral, which S. Maria Maggiore faced along what is now Via Merulana. In both architectural form and decoration, the Lateran was evolving into a larger cousin of

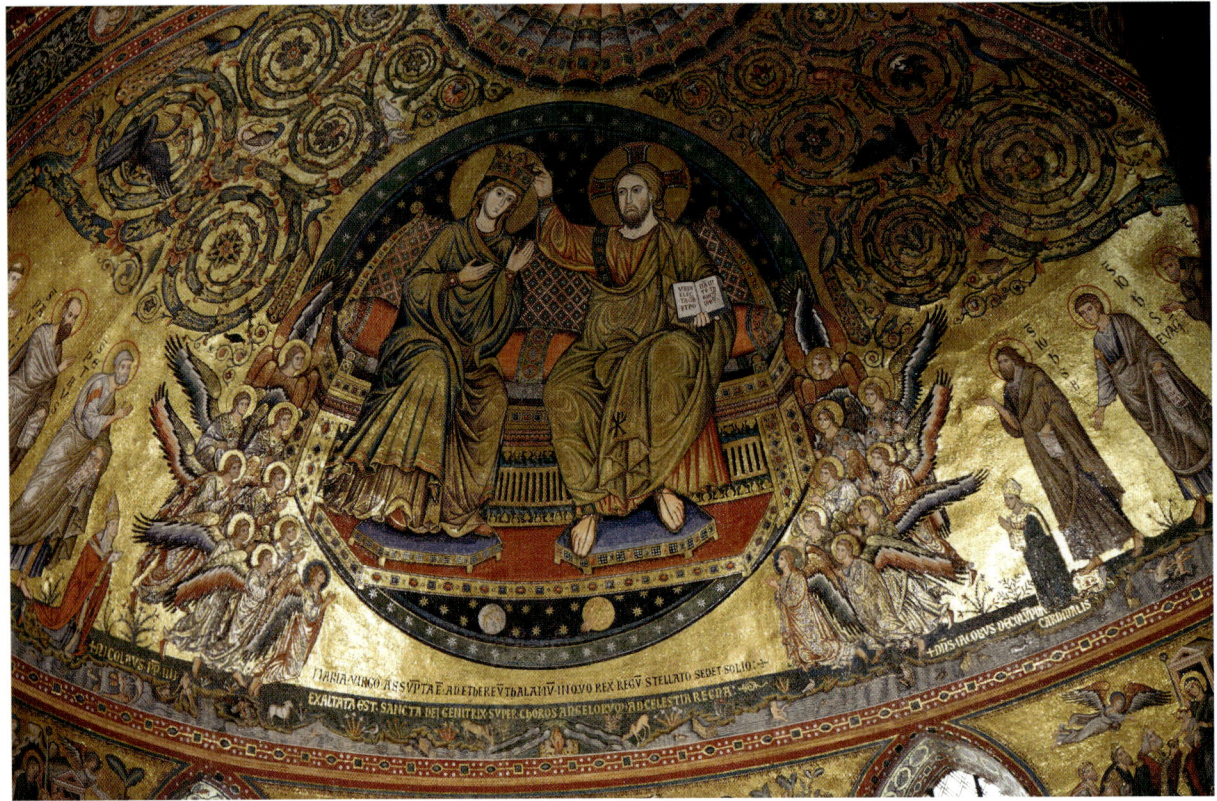

Figure 7.28 Torriti's apse mosaic at S. Maria Maggiore. Note the small kneeling figures of Pope Nicholas IV (at far left, in front of St. Peter) and Giacomo Colonna (far right, in front of John the Baptist). (Author.)

S. Maria. It looks, in fact, as though the remodeling of both churches was conceived as part of a cohesive scheme, which envisioned similar architectural modifications and sumptuous new mosaics in each location. The kinship between the two projects was further proclaimed by the common involvement of Torriti, who also directed the mosaic program at the Lateran. Work probably began slightly earlier at the Lateran than at S. Maria, given that the apse mosaic at the former was complete by 1291, according to the dated mosaic 'signature' of Torriti.[51]

Here, too, the west end of the Constantinian basilica got a modernizing makeover designed to imbue the ancient church with new Gothic splendor. Nicholas IV's architects, probably led by Torriti himself, demolished the original apse and built a new one, semicircular on the interior but polygonal on the exterior (like those at S. Maria Maggiore and the Aracoeli), which opened onto a lower outer ambulatory, also hexagonal; and they built a soaring new transept that reached to the height of the nave. Torriti and his *bottega* of mosaicists then went to work in the loftier, better-lit spaces that resulted. Though much restored in the late 19th century, the original composition in the apse is substantially unchanged. Above, a bust of Christ, surrounded by angels, floats on a deep blue background. In the main register below, nine figures silhouetted against a gold background face each other across a central cross with the four rivers of paradise spouting from its base. At left are Saints Paul and Peter, the smaller figure of St. Francis, and Mary, who presents a still smaller, kneeling figure of Nicholas IV in his papal robes. Facing them on the right are John the Baptist, a smaller Anthony of Padua in Franciscan habit, John the Evangelist, and St. Andrew. As at S. Maria Maggiore, the timeless themes of the universal Church entered into a Franciscan-inflected present.[52]

Work on the transept and the façade doubtless continued into the pontificate of Boniface VIII, which otherwise marks the waning of the Roman 'proto-Renaissance.' Preoccupied with other concerns during his tempestuous reign, among them the all-out war he waged against the Colonna and their allies starting in 1297, Boniface himself left few enduring works. His most substantial project was a new colonnaded loggia at the Lateran, the "loggia delle benedizioni," attached to the façade of the palace that overlooked the *campus Lateranensis* where crowds gathered. The rear wall, frescoed perhaps by Cavallini (only a small fragment remains), showed the pope in just such a colonnaded loggia, surrounded by members of the Curia, in the act of blessing a crowd of the faithful below (Fig. 7.29). Work probably began in 1300, the year of the first Jubilee, when Romans and foreigners alike were offered remission for all their sins after performing days of penitential visits (fifteen days for foreigners, thirty for Romans) to the shrines of the martyrs. Many thousands made the trip to Rome, bringing both donations for the Church and business for the Romans who catered to their needs. In retrospect, the festive Jubilee (by all accounts, a great success) and Boniface's loggia seem a final flourish on two decades of outstanding creative fervor, which stand out all the more starkly in contrast to the relative barrenness of the following century.[53]

The list of major artistic and architectural commissions for the years 1305–1420 is, indeed, strikingly short, especially after the 1320s. The most notable civic monument produced during the whole period is the monumental marble staircase from the foot of the Capitoline to the Aracoeli. It was built in 1348, with contributions from the masses of the faithful, in thanks for the end of the plague (Fig. 7.30). Though the list of ecclesiastical projects is longer, and all churches required a ceaseless round of maintenance whose importance we tend to underestimate, it is still quite sparse; and most of the work that did occur focused on the major basilicas. Giotto was in action at St. Peter's around 1310, painting frescoes inside the church and collaborating with Roman masters on a cycle of mosaics in the atrium. Only fragments were saved when Old St. Peter's was demolished in the 16th century: a couple of frescoed saints' heads from the interior of the basilica, and bits of the Navicella mosaic in the atrium. From Avignon, Pope John XXII sent money for a new program of mosaics on the façade of St. Paul's, executed circa 1325–30 by the *bottega* of the aging Cavallini. It was the last grand cycle of mosaics of the Middle Ages at Rome. The Lateran basilica burned calamitously in 1308, requiring major repairs to the roof and the interior colonnades; the roof was still being reconstructed in the 1320s, and the repairs were

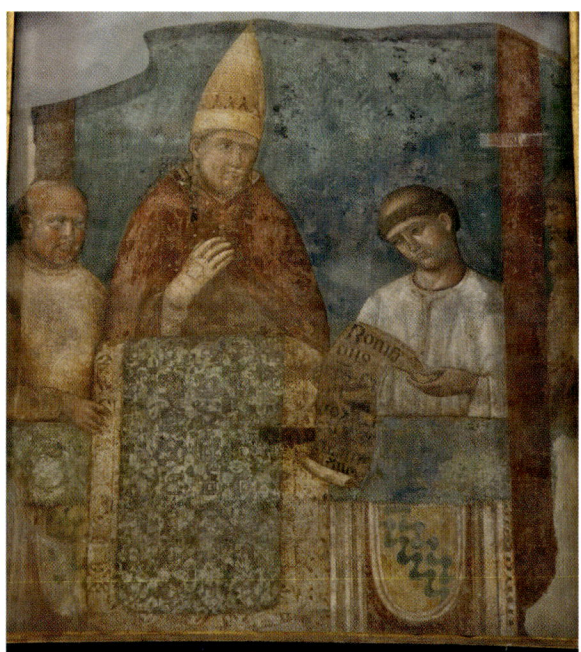

Figure 7.29 The surviving fragment of the frescoes of the Loggia delle Benedizioni, today preserved inside the Lateran cathedral: Boniface VIII reads from the bull proclaiming the jubilee of 1300. Note the prominent Caetani coat-of-arms on the parapet at lower right. (Author.)

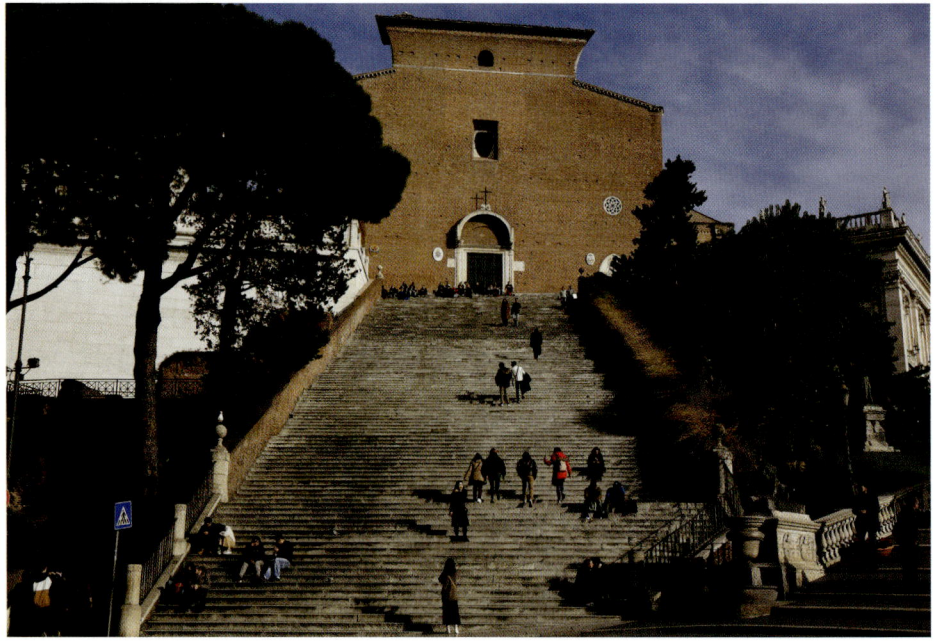

Figure 7.30 The monumental stairway leading to S. Maria in Aracoeli. (Author.)

only finished during the pontificate of Benedict XII (1334–42), who also funded the reconstruction of the roof at St. Peter's. The Lateran would burn again in 1361, after which another decade of work was required to put it back into working order. As the project neared completion, Gregory XI commissioned the extant two-story Gothic tabernacle over the high altar, into which the heads of Saints Peter and Paul were inserted after being removed from the Sancta Sanctorum chapel. Elsewhere, S. Maria Maggiore got its very impressive *campanile*, at seventy-five meters high the tallest in the city, in the 1370s. Another symbolically potent project occurred just after the submission of the commune to the Church in 1398, when Boniface IX (r. 1389–1404) fortified the senatorial palace on the Capitoline and enlarged the tower on the north end of the façade, overlooking the Forum, which still bears the pope's arms (Fig. 7.31). The building that epitomized the institutions of the autonomous commune thus became a bastion of the Church.[54]

For a sense of the quantitative and qualitative decline in artistic commissions, it suffices to peruse the final volume of the recent *La pittura medievale a Roma 312 – 1431*, the most comprehensive catalogue yet produced of extant paintings and mosaics done in Rome in the years 1288–1431. The scarcity of works datable to the years circa 1330–1420 in particular is very striking, the more so relative to the richness of the preceding and following periods. There is a bare trickle of frescoes from a smattering of churches and monasteries, and still less from residential *palazzi* and civic buildings. Those works that survive, moreover, are limited in scale and of generally indifferent quality. Few existing buildings were extensively redecorated, and few new ones were built that required ambitious decorative programs.[55]

But if few grand monuments for the ages took shape in 14th-century Rome, life hardly stood still. Romans went on with their lives and their work, confronted the straitened conditions imposed by the departure of the Curia and the subsequent outbreaks of plague, and in the process transformed the city center into a more compact and in some respects more vital urban nucleus. The challenges of the 14th century

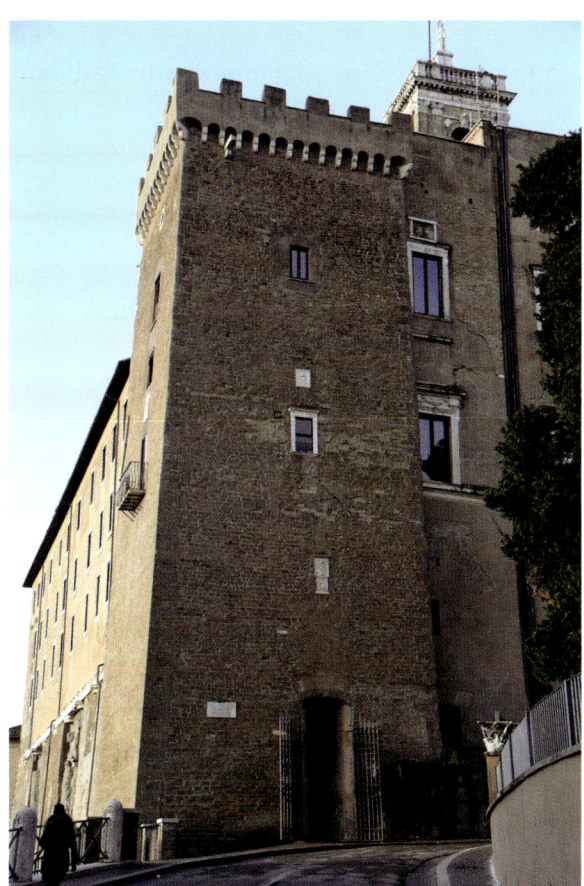

Figure 7.31 The tower of Boniface IX at the NW corner of the senatorial palace. His coat of arms appears on the two marble plaques between the entrance and the lower of the two windows; above, between the two windows, is a plaque with the arms of Nicholas V (r. 1447–55). (Author.)

papacy for Avignon, the tail dissipated, evidently because the disappearance of the whole apparatus of ecclesiastical governance from the Lateran deprived the surrounding area of its principal economic motor. Those who had made their living or otherwise benefited from proximity to the Curia gravitated westward toward the Campus Martius and the Vatican, where those pilgrims and other foreign visitors who came to Rome despite the absence of the popes continued to congregate. The fate of the eastern 'tail' was sealed after 1377, when the repatriated Curia neglected the Lateran in favor of the much safer residence at the Vatican, where teams of builders promptly got to work restoring the walls of the Borgo within months of Gregory XI's arrival. Though the schismatic popes of the period 1378–1417 had nothing like the disposable income or prestige of their successors from Martin V on, their preference for the Vatican doubtless helped to draw any remaining waverers westward. A schismatic Curia was a considerable improvement on no Curia at all, and still a potent economic force. In 1381, for example, we find the Curia contracting with a Roman merchant to supply 1,000 florins' worth of meat, a sum that would have sufficed to buy ten town houses in the city center at current prices.[56]

Signs of this westward shift of remaining clusters of population from the eastern fringes to the Tiber bend are easily discerned. Take, for example, the case of the blacksmiths (*ferrarii*) who clustered near the Colosseum and the basilica of Maxentius in the 12th and 13th centuries. Their collegiate church, S. Maria *de ferrariis*, was located between the Colosseum and the Baths of Titus, overlooking the *via maior*. First attested in 1173, we find it again in Cencius *camerarius*' *Ordo Romanus* of 1192, which lists the compensation it received for the temporary arches and incense burners it installed along the processional route from the Lateran during Easter week. It still appears as a functioning church served by

seem indeed to have given new impetus to the concentration of population in and around the Tiber bend, which culminated only in the 14th and 15th centuries. Krautheimer's 'medieval' *abitato*, that is, had only just fully coagulated by the time we see it in maps and *vedute* produced from the later 15th century on.

This centripetal flow of people is best observed in relation to the substantial 'tail' of settlement that until the 14th century still extended to the eastern edge of the city, from the Colosseum to the Lateran along the line of the *via maior*, the great processional route between the cathedral and the city center. After the departure of the a resident priest in the Turin Catalogue, a list of Roman churches compiled c. 1320, but must have been abandoned entirely soon thereafter, as it is described as defunct and ruinous in the time of Pope Eugene IV (r. 1431–47). There is no sign of blacksmiths still operating along the *via maior* in the 14th century, by which time they were mostly concentrated in the densely populated quarters just west of the Capitoline, in the *rioni* of Ripa and S. Angelo. A second example is the *campsores*, specialists who combined the functions of money changers, bankers, and assayers, whose steady westward migration paralleled that of the smiths. Whereas many had practiced between the Basilica of Maxentius and the Colosseum in the 12th and 13th centuries, the notarial registers indicate that by the later 14th century, they concentrated between the Capitoline and the Vatican, in the city's busiest commercial spaces: the piazza at the entrance of St. Peter's; Ponte Sant'Angelo; the market square in front of the Pantheon; and around the Capitoline, both on the Forum-side at S. Adriano and along the Via Mercatoria at S. Angelo in Pescheria. The other inhabitants of the eastern 'tail' evidently migrated along with the smiths and the money changers, leaving desolate the corridor along the *via maior* between the Colosseum and the Lateran: the road itself is described as ruined and nearly impassable by the 1380s, and in 1386, we find the communal authorities offering incentives to encourage the reoccupation of the whole corridor, evidently in vain. With the Curia spending more and more time at the Vatican, there was simply no good reason to live so far east of the city center.[57]

Indeed, the final emptying out of most of the remaining population centers in the east may help to explain why the main settled zones from the Capitoline to the Vatican show such considerable signs of vitality notwithstanding the assorted traumas of the 14th century. Though Rome's total population undoubtedly shrank, that is, an ever-growing proportion of those who remained piled into the vicinity of the Tiber bend. Notwithstanding the removal of the Curia to Avignon; the baronial abuses, civic misgovernment, and periods of near-anarchy typical of the first half of the century; the plague of 1348 and its subsequent recurrences; the major earthquake of 1349; and a host of other damaging events and conjunctures besides, plenty of people remained to keep the *abitato* teeming with activity.

A great deal of that activity flourished along the long corridor between the Capitoline and the Ponte Sant'Angelo – and the Vatican beyond – that largely corresponded with the route of the ancient Via Triumphalis/*porticus maximae*, which by the 14th century was commonly called the Via Mercatoria, "Market Street," as we have seen. The commercial vitality of this corridor in the later Middle Ages was rooted in its connections to natural topography and surviving nodes of ancient infrastructure – to the Tiber itself and the last three ancient bridges that remained passable. The southeastern and northwestern extremities of the rough diagonal it traces across the Campus Martius were anchored on the Tiber itself, at the points where the only surviving ancient bridges stood: in the northwest, the Ponte Sant'Angelo; and in the southeast, the Pons Aemilius, called the Pons Maior in the Middle Ages, and the passage across the Tiber Island via the Pons Cestius and Pons Fabricius, both serving the area of the *Ripa Graeca*. These crossings, both north and south, were conveniently (and not coincidentally) located close to the city's two principal river ports. The largest and busiest was the southern port, the Ripa Romea or Ripa Grande, located in Trastevere downstream of the two southern river crossings, where goods traveling to and from the seaports at the mouth of the Tiber were loaded and unloaded. The roads from both bridgeheads on the left bank ran toward the initial tract of the Via

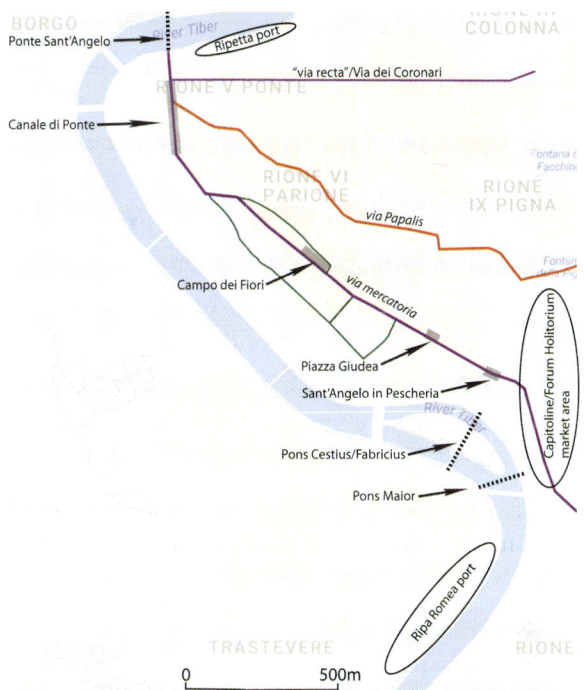

Figure 7.32 Principal ports, markets, and river crossings in the late Middle Ages. (Google Maps/Author.)

Mercatoria at the foot of the Capitoline, near the Theater of Marcellus. As for the northern port, the Ripetta, it extended along the left (city-side) bank of the Tiber just upstream of Ponte Sant'Angelo, and served mostly for goods coming downstream from upper Lazio and Umbria (Fig. 7.32).[58]

Given the Via Mercatoria's close connections to the two river ports and all the surviving Tiber bridges, then, it is little wonder that the explosive, largely unregulated economic boom of the 11th–13th centuries transformed what remained of the stately colonnades of the *porticus maximae* into a warren of shops and stalls and workspaces, or that a succession of thriving markets had developed along its path across the Campus Martius by the 14th century. The *Ripa Graeca* at the southeast terminus of the route had been a major commercial center since antiquity, when it encompassed the Forum Boarium and Forum Holitorium, and it remained so throughout the Middle Ages. Just to the north, the Capitoline piazza and the western slopes of the hill, where the grand staircase now stands, hosted the main Saturday market, where producers and artisans from across the city came to hawk their wares. The market flourished after the Capitoline became the seat of communal government in the 1140s, transforming the area into the political as well as the economic hub of the Roman commune.[59]

The traveler leaving the Capitoline and setting out for the Vatican along the Via Mercatoria proper encountered a host of other bustling commercial hubs. First, there was the meat market that occupied the ground-level arcades of the Theater of Marcellus and spilled over into neighboring structures. Next came the fish market at S. Angelo in Pescheria (from which the church takes its name), where fishmongers displayed their wares on marble slabs in the colonnades of the Porticus Octaviae; then Piazza Giudea, the main marketplace for the city's Jewish community, which was clustering in the surrounding neighborhood probably already in the 12th and 13th centuries. Farther on, just past the Orsini stronghold at the Theater of Pompey, there was the large piazza of the Campo de' Fiori, occupying approximately the same area it does today. In addition to foodstuffs and various manufactures, this was Rome's main market for horses, many of which were stabled in the vicinity. Still more market stalls and shops clustered along the Canale di Ponte at the approaches to Ponte Sant'Angelo, along with growing numbers of money changers and bankers. Across the bridge, there was the old portico leading to St. Peter's, still lined with houses and shops, that led directly to the *platea* (piazza) in front of the basilica, another busy market that catered especially to the crowds of pilgrims and foreign visitors who gathered in the Borgo.[60]

There were other markets and commercial quarters, of course, both in the Tiber bend and beyond. The piazza in front of the Pantheon was a haven for both merchants and money changers in the 14th century; there was another meat market at the Forum and the Forum of Nerva, and so on. But the corridor running from the Capitoline to St. Peter's was the pulsing commercial artery of late medieval Rome, and all signs are that it was as bustling as ever in the later 14th century. The notarial registers show merchants and artisans and bankers operating in profusion all along the Via Mercatoria and its extension across the river toward St. Peter's. Pressure for space remained great, such that the *Magistri edificiorum* and other responsible bodies were called to intervene in order to reduce crowding and rein in unauthorized encroachments on public spaces and private property alike. Business increased further with the return of the Curia in 1377, and still more after the end of the schism in 1417.[61]

And the successful merchants, artisans, and professionals crowding into the Tiber bend continued to spend money and advertise their success, notably in constructing family chapels and other ostentatious funerary monuments. Many of these chapels and tombs sprouted up in prestigious and fashionable churches, alongside those of the nobility and the barons. The Aracoeli and S. Maria sopra Minerva were especially popular, but upper-middling families left their mark at a host of other places: SS. Sergio e Bacco, S. Angelo in Pescheria, S. Maria *ad martyres* (the Pantheon), S. Maria in Via Lata, and SS. Apostoli, to name but a few (see above, Fig. 7.24). The mercantile and professional classes also worked to embellish and expand their residences, hiring builders and marble-workers expert in sourcing and working fine building materials (stone blocks, columns, colored marbles, and so on) recovered from ancient structures. These interventions were generally modest in scale, however, which explains why relatively little trace remains of them today. Those houses that survive have been remodeled countless times over the centuries, while the original art and furnishings of the funerary chapels have almost all disappeared in the course of subsequent renovations that left them with the Renaissance and Baroque veneers they have today. The fact remains, however, that the 14th (and early 15th) century was not a time of unmitigated involution and squalor; on the contrary, life clearly went on, and in some cases flourished, amidst the chaos. But such patronage of art and architecture as occurred generally involved small-scale initiatives on the part of individual families or patrons. The point holds also for the nobility, the clergy, and the communal authorities, none of which showed much appetite for grandiose projects.[62]

This inability or unwillingness to 'think big,' as it were, is apparent also with regard to the upkeep of public spaces, monuments, and infrastructure, which was spotty at best throughout the period c. 1305–1420. The Statutes of 1363 show that the popular government of the Felice Società at least aspired to keep piazzas, roads and bridges, and the waters of the Aqua Virgo and Aqua Marana in working order, and there is a single mention in the 1370s of repairs to a small section of the city walls. But the age-old difficulty of maintaining Rome's extensive built environment with the sparse human and material resources available remained, and was in fact compounded by demographic decline and economic stagnation. For much of the 14th century, even elementary stewardship of public works fell into abeyance. For the first half-century after the popes left for Avignon, in fact, there is not a single preserved sentence of the *Magistri edificiorum*. Documents attesting to their efforts to preserve the decorum of the cityscape recur frequently up to 1306, and again after 1361 (perhaps significantly, just after the Felice Società came to power), which suggests that the total absence of similar sentences from the period 1307–60 reflects a real hiatus in their activities.

With the departure of the Curia and the virtual baronial stranglehold on urban politics and institutions that ensued, relatively little effort was made to maintain the urban fabric on behalf of the collective.[63]

By the beginning of the 15th century, then, the consequences of a full millennium of spotty and insufficient upkeep of the ancient urban fabric were everywhere more apparent than ever; and the degradation was compounded by the disastrous political conditions that prevailed during the first two decades of the new century. In Avignon, Pope Benedict XIII (r. 1394–1423) reigned. Boniface IX (r. 1389–1404), Innocent VII (r. 1404–6), and Alexander V (r. 1406–15) reigned at Rome. From 1409 to 1415, yet a third line of claimants based itself in Pisa, with Alexander V (r. 1409–10) and John XXIII (r. 1410–15). All three factions had support among the Roman barons, who had returned to the city in force after 1398, and among the royalty of Europe. King Ladislas of Naples, allied with the Colonna and Annibaldi families, among others, opposed the Roman line of popes, which most of the Orsini magnates supported. Ladislas himself took the city in 1408, leaving parts of it in the hands of his backers until 1411, when Ladislas' rival for the throne of Naples, Louis II of Anjou, descended on Rome and personally installed the rival 'Pisan' pontiff John XXIII at the Vatican. As kings, foreign *condottieri*, Roman barons, and shifting coalitions of the urban populace thus vied for control of Rome and the Church across most of the first two decades of the 15th century, the city became an almost perpetual battleground.[64]

The local ramifications of these simmering conflicts appear most vividly in the "Roman diary" (*Diario Romano*) of current events written by a canon of St. Peter's, Antonio di Pietro dello Schiavo, the surviving portions of which span the years 1404–17. The Vatican Borgo and the adjoining regions of the Campus Martius were the scene of particularly intense fighting. In 1405, the pro-Neapolitan garrison of Castel Sant'Angelo sortied across Ponte Sant'Angelo into the northern Campus Martius, much of which was put to the torch. Returning to their fortress, they kept the area under cannon fire from the ramparts (*Diario*, pp. 10–11). Cannons and a trebuchet from Castel Sant'Angelo again bombarded the *rione* of Ponte, across the river, in 1415; defenders returned fire from the opposite bank (p. 96). The Borgo was sacked and burnt twice, in 1409 and 1413 (pp. 44; 79), and witnessed pillaging and fighting on many other occasions. Elsewhere, the Aurelian Wall was pierced and broken down at various points around its perimeter: near Porta S. Lorenzo and then by Monte Testaccio in 1407 (pp. 17; 26); at S. Croce in Gerusalemme in 1413 (p. 79). The ancient gate-castles on the interior of the gates became the site of pitched battles and sieges. In 1410, the castles at the Portae S. Lorenzo, Maggiore, Appia, and S. Paolo were all tenaciously held by the Colonna and their Neapolitan allies against Pope Alexander V and his Orsini supporters (Fig. 7.33). Paolo Orsini took large cannon from Castel Sant'Angelo and used them to batter all the fortresses into submission, sometimes in the face of return fire from inside the gates. The last stronghold taken, Porta Maggiore, fell in February of 1411 after a siege lasting a month (pp. 55–7).

And so on. Much of the city, including some of its most populous regions, was thus reduced to a blasted shell where the conditions of daily life were parlous in the extreme. There were incessant episodes of famine and pestilence. Wolves lurked in the gardens of the Vatican (p. 65). The lion traditionally kept in a cage on the Capitoline escaped from captivity in 1414 and took to the streets, where it fed on easy prey, mostly children, until it was finally tracked down and killed (p. 95). In 1414, when the charred and shattered Borgo was filled with homeless refugees sheltering in St. Peter's and S. Spirito in Sassia, there was

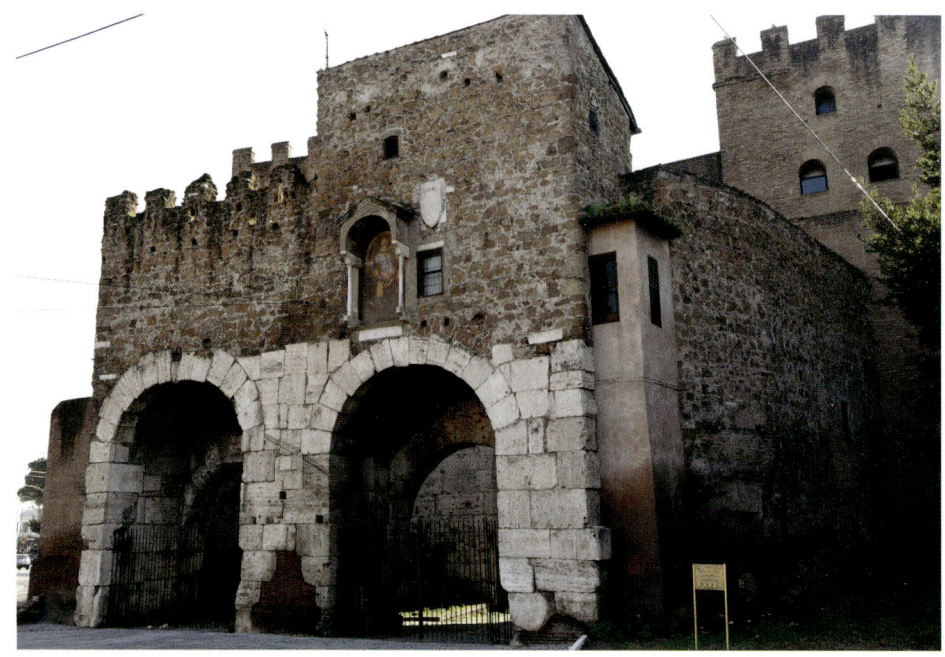

Figure 7.33 The gate-castle inside Porta Ostiense. (Author.)

no oil to light the lamps in St. Peter's for the festival of Peter and Paul on June 29 (p. 87). Killings in the streets and gruesome executions were a daily occurrence.[65]

Out of these agonies, however, and perhaps to an extent because of them, the seeds of renewal eventually sprouted. Rome and all of Christendom could not stay forever torn between three rival Curias. In 1415, both Italian claimants to the papacy voluntarily abdicated, paving the way for the election of Martin V Colonna at the Council of Constance in 1417. The legitimacy of the long-reigning Martin V and his successors was never successfully challenged, nor was their decision to bring the Curia back to Rome, where nearly all could agree it belonged. And, having decided to make Rome their capital, the popes of the early Renaissance committed themselves to consolidating their authority over the city and restoring as much of its physical fabric as possible. Even before Martin V made his triumphal entry into Rome in November, 1420, he had assembled and funded a committee tasked with renovating urban churches. In the ensuing decades, the political and administrative climate stabilized enough to permit the popes and their agents to exert effective, enduring control over the cityscape, and in the process to start shaping the Rome of the Renaissance.[66]

EPILOGUE

Rome and Pope Nicholas V (1447–55)

IN DECEMBER 1450, AS the festive and very successful Jubilee year was drawing to a close, tragedy famously struck at Ponte Sant'Angelo. It was evening, and thousands of pilgrims were coming back from the Borgo to their lodgings across the river. As the flow of pedestrians on the congested roadway over the bridge slowed and stopped, those behind continued to push ahead; in the resulting squeeze, the parapets of the bridge gave way and some 200 people died, either crushed above or drowned in the waters below. Pope Nicholas V Parentucelli reacted decisively in the wake of the disaster. He expropriated the shops and stalls that packed the approaches to the bridge on the Campus Martius side (using some of the piles of cash collected during the Jubilee to compensate the proprietors), and leveled them to create an open esplanade hundreds of meters long and dozens of meters wide, with the road running through the center. Around the periphery of this sort of grand boulevard, the Canale di Ponte, rose regular rows of new shops for the bankers and merchants who crowded into this strategic crossing-point between the Borgo and the city center. In addition to alleviating the traffic problems along the bridge, the new space was meant to confront everyone headed toward the Vatican with a framed panorama of the papal fortress at Castel Sant'Angelo, which loomed all the more impressively on the far side of the bridge after Nicholas heightened the tower atop the drum and added new towers to its outer perimeter.[1]

But Nicholas' scheme to improve road connections between the Borgo and the city center went far beyond the Canale di Ponte. His next step was to commission an expanded edition of the statutes of the *Magistri edificiorum et stratarum*, last issued in Latin in 1410. Published in Italian, in 1452, as the *statuti de li maestri de li edefitij di Roma*, the revised compilation gave much broader responsibilities to the Masters of buildings and streets, and bolstered their authority with the sovereign mandate of the pope himself. As Orietta Verdi has put it, "The new version ... of 1452 effectively constituted the legal basis for the restructuring of the capital in the manner intended by the pope ... From that moment on, the Masters would have been able to exercise a more attentive surveillance over buildings, to concede permits for the use of public space upon papal concession, to remove whatever obstructed circulation along roads, to promote and accomplish the paving of main streets and improvements to the precarious network of urban sewers."[2]

The *maestri de li edefitij* were directed to attend especially closely to three streets, each carefully identified in the Statutes of 1452, which traversed the Campus Martius in the form of a trident that converged on the Canale di Ponte itself: in the south, the ancient route successively known as the Via Triumphalis, *porticus maximae*, Via Mercatoria, and, by 1452, "Pilgrim's Way" (Via del Pellegrino; how many names in almost two millennia, how many different incarnations!), from S. Angelo in Pescheria; in the middle, the meandering, medieval section of the Via Papalis from the Capitoline; and in the north, the ancient Via Recta – "straight street" –, today's Via dei Coronari, from the Via Lata, the main route toward the Vatican for anyone arriving in Rome from the north along the Via Flaminia – Via Lata (Fig. 7.32, above). The Masters of the Streets were supposed to widen and improve these routes by aggressively removing obstructions and encroaching structures; ensuring that trash was collected at least once a week during the hottest summer months; and compelling the owners of adjacent properties to install paving at their own expense. Although these provisions ideally extended to other streets and public spaces also, it is the "three principal streets" that matter most – the ones that traversed the populous heart of the *abitato* between the Capitoline and the river and connected the city center with the Borgo and St. Peter's. The Nicholine interventions helped to improve the décor and functionality of the street network serving the ever more crowded neighborhoods in the Tiber bend, certainly. But the project also served more ambitious ends: It linked the papal enclave at the Vatican with the 'other' Rome in the Tiber bend into a conjoined whole, and proclaimed the renewal of benevolent (but pervasive, even immanent) papal sovereignty throughout the city.[3]

Yet change, particularly constructive change, almost always comes slowly in Rome. The chaotic immensity of the cityscape tends to frustrate even determined efforts at urban renewal, or otherwise to absorb them with barely a ripple. One might sooner build Rome in a day – a new Rome, from scratch – than remake the existing one; and the 15th century was no exception to the broader rule. While the popes who again ruled over the ancient capital began to operate on a grander scale than their medieval predecessors, they were anything but miracle workers. The end of the schism and the return of the unified Curia established the basic preconditions needed for farther-reaching programs of urban renewal, but hardly sufficed to achieve quick and comprehensive results. Nobody ever achieved revolutionary change in the span of a single pontificate. Nonetheless, Nicholas V's eight years on the throne (1447–55) are a milestone in Rome's passage from the Middle Ages toward early modernity, albeit one whose conceptual and material implications mostly became apparent only in retrospect.

Nicholas' immediate predecessors, Martin V and Eugene IV, sought to enhance the décor of their capital, too, to be sure. They and other members of the Curia renovated some (but by no means most!) of the city's hundreds of dilapidated churches, improved the palaces they dwelled in, and patched up critical faults in infrastructure such as water channels, roads and bridges, and the city walls. But these interventions were scattered and isolated; they were ad hoc responses to localized problems. In modern bureaucratese, one would say they were reactive rather than proactive measures. They amounted to a haphazard sprinkling of drops in the enormous Roman bucket. Nicholas V's great leap was to conceptualize the city as a unitary topographical ensemble, an assemblage of interdependent components, and consequently to operate in ways intended to recondition the whole. The reconditioning of the whole, in turn, was meant to make Rome into a vision of papal sovereignty embodied, and as such a worthy capital for all Christendom, as supreme among cities as the pope was among rulers. Nicholas was able to think in such terms thanks to his formation among the humanist circles of early *Quattrocento* Florence, and his personal exposure to some of the leading lights of the age: Poggio Bracciolini, whose *De varietate Fortunae* contains a precocious attempt at empirical, citywide analysis of Rome's ancient monuments; Flavio Biondo, whose *Roma instaurata* presents a coherent urbanistic vision for the new Rome due to arise from the ruins of antiquity; and, of course, Leon Battista Alberti, who proposed a transformational understanding of the role architecture and urban space might play in the formation of good citizens and enlightened civic government. And we know that Nicholas V was indeed thinking in such terms thanks to another Florentine humanist and long-time associate of the pope, Giannozzo Manetti, whose posthumous biography of Nicholas, written shortly after the latter's death in 1455, is broadly acknowledged to reflect quite closely the pope's ideas about how – and why – Rome was to be transformed.[4]

Though many of his initiatives remained incomplete at his death, after eight years in power, and many others never made it past the planning stages, what Nicholas accomplished is impressive enough in its own right. In terms of infrastructure and civic architecture, his initiatives went well beyond improvements to streets and public spaces. He rebuilt the Trevi Fountain. He expanded the fortifications of Castel Sant'Angelo, as we have already seen. Atop the Capitoline, he enlarged and further fortified the senatorial palace, and rebuilt the Palazzo dei Conservatori, across the piazza from the Aracoeli, in its current form. (Travelers along two of the three repristinated avenues through the Campus Martius were thus confronted at both ends, Castel Sant'Angelo and Capitoline, with newly enlarged monuments to the temporal sway of the papacy.) Nicholas also accomplished probably the single most extensive campaign of repairs to the Aurelian Wall since Leo IV in the 9th century, conspicuous traces of which survive in various points around the perimeter, especially in the southern part of the circuit, between today's Bastione Ardeatino and the Tiber. The more substantial restorations conspicuously identify their patron: The eastern tower of the Porta Tiburtina and four other rebuilt towers all feature marble plaques with Nicholas' papal arms, as does a section of curtain wall between Porta Appia and Porta Ostiense, where the characters N PP V (*Nicolaus Papa V*) are outlined in brick in the masonry underneath the plaque (Fig. 8.1). In thus breaking an epigraphic silence that had lasted for more than a millennium, save the lone inscription of 1157, Nicholas made manifest the restoration of papal authority over the structure best suited to proclaim Rome the citadel of Christendom, the terrestrial analogue of Heavenly Jerusalem.[5]

In the ecclesiastical sphere, Nicholas set out to restore all forty of Rome's stational churches, the lynchpins of the annual liturgical cycle, and a number of other churches besides. He restored the papal residence by S. Maria Maggiore. But he reserved the most thought and energy for St. Peter's and the Borgo, which he intended to transform into an awe-inspiring model of rational urban planning; a glorious citadel of the restored

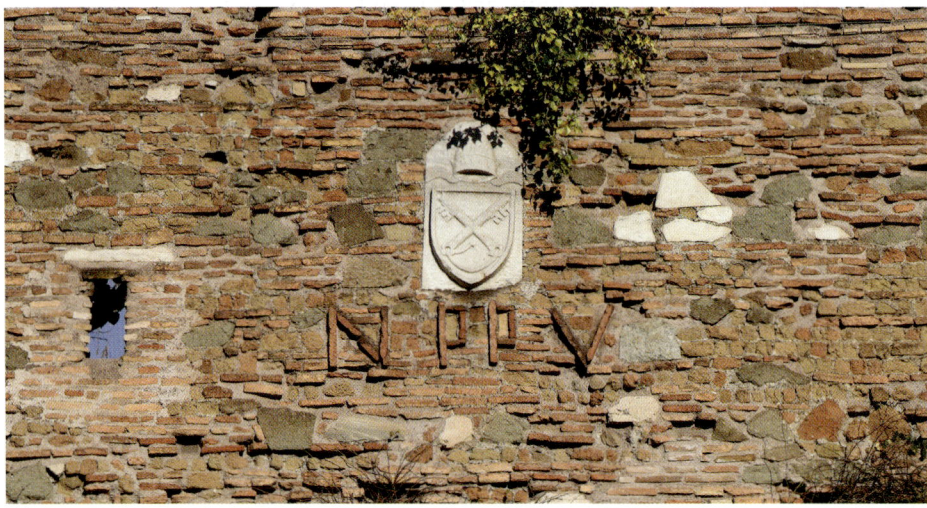

Figure 8.1 The papal arms and "inscription" of Nicholas V on a repaired curtain (L16-17) of the Aurelian Wall, between Porta Appia and Porta Ostiense. (Author.)

papacy, connected to but spatially and formally distinct from the city center across the river. He succeeded in building a new wing onto the Vatican palace, the single largest addition yet made to the complex, and enclosing it within a new walled salient that projected northward off the existing circuit. He created the original nucleus of the Vatican library. He involved (perhaps) Alberti himself in a project to straighten and reinforce the rising walls of the nave and side aisles at St. Peter's, parts of which were dangerously far out of plumb.[6]

Even so, Nicholas' most ambitious schemes to remake the Borgo remained unrealized upon his death in 1455. Manetti's biography offers the most expansive vision of the intended program of works, which grew further in scale when the quantity of donations collected during the Jubilee year was tabulated. The project envisioned the transformation of the three streets that led lengthwise through the Borgo from the river to St. Peter's into wide avenues, each 'zoned' for discrete functions and activities, which would thus have reprised the schema of the three avenues leading through the Campus Martius to the far end of the Ponte Sant'Angelo. All three roads were to have debouched into a vast new piazza fronting St. Peter's, which would have been realized by demolishing acres' worth of shops and houses. The existing transept and apse of the basilica itself were to be razed and replaced by much grander structures extending well west of the existing apse, covering much of the area eventually occupied by the new basilica built in the 16th century. (The foundations of the new apse, laid outside the existing one, were well underway when Nicholas died, having reached a height of 13 *palmi* – approximately a meter – above ground; they were subsequently incorporated into the foundations of New St. Peter's.) A huge dome was even planned for the crossing of the new transept.[7]

As it turned out, however, St. Peter's and the Borgo were left looking little different after Nicholas than before him. Even his efforts to widen and improve the streets through the Campus Martius evidently met with indifferent success, given that Sixtus IV (r. 1471–84) was back at work only 30 years later to clear and widen the same roads, the Canale di Ponte included, with more lasting results than Nicholas achieved. In the short term, Roman inertia mostly prevailed again. Nicholas did not himself remodel the cityscape in profound and lasting ways. And yet the moment he presided over was transformational nonetheless. Nearly all of his grand designs would be realized in some form over the following couple of centuries. More to the point, his pontificate forever reshaped – expanded – the boundaries of the conceivable. None of the succeeding popes who ruled Rome until 1870 would ever again be able to consider the city as anything but an integrated whole, a single canvas on which to trace their urban designs. Rome's congeries of antique churches remodeled into showpieces of Renaissance and Baroque fashion; its grand *palazzi* and scenically orchestrated *piazze*; its long, straight avenues cut through dense medieval neighborhoods, receding to distant obelisks and artfully framed landmarks: All recognizably descend from the urban visions given currency by Nicholas V and his circle of erudite advisors. So in particular does the Borgo, of course, where the gargantuan 16th-century St. Peter's, Bernini's 17th-century colonnades and piazza in front, even the 20th-century Via della Conciliazione from the Tiber to the façade of the Basilica, respond to invitations left by Nicholas and his architects.[8]

As for Nicholas himself, he butted up against the same elemental facts of Roman life faced by everyone who had presided over the city during the preceding millennium. Like the last western emperors, Gothic kings, Byzantine governors, popes, nobles, senators, barons, *banderesi*, and popes again, he found his capacity to reshape the urban fabric blunted by the messy realities of a place that was too big to fix, too dangerous to ignore, too important to abandon. Every urbanistic initiative contemplated or implemented by Pope Parentucelli and his successors was deeply conditioned by monuments and artificial topography either created or preserved during the medieval millennium. What survived of the ancient city had been conserved, and usually also more or less profoundly reconfigured, as a result of choices made by medieval Romans, mighty and humble alike. All the rest of the urban ensemble, the large majority by the 15th century, was a product of the medieval centuries themselves. Far more than the cultured, classicizing aesthetes of the Renaissance and after liked to acknowledge, the Rome they inherited was mostly a creation of the Middle Ages.

LIST OF ABBREVIATIONS (PRIMARY SOURCES, JOURNALS, FREQUENTLY CITED VOLUMES)

Acta IRN	*Acta ad Archaeologiam et Artium Historiam Pertinentia*
AE	*Année Épigraphique*
AJA	*American Journal of Archaeology*
ARID	*Analecta Romana Instituti Danici*
AnTard	*Antiquité Tardive*
ASRSP	*Archivio della Società Romana di Storia Patria*
BullCom	*Bullettino della Commissione Archeologica Communale di Roma*
CBCR	*Corpus Basilicarum Christianarum Romae.* R. Krautheimer, S. Corbett, and W. Frankl, 5 vols., Rome, 1937–77.
CCSL	*Corpus Christianorum Series Latina*
CSA VII	*Corpus della scultura altomedievale, VII:La diocesi di Roma*. 7 vols., Spoleto, 1974–2015.
CDMA	*Carte del monastero dei SS. Cosma e Damiano in Mica Aurea, I:secoli X e XI*. P. Fedele, P. Pavan (eds.), Codice diplomatico di Roma e della regione romana 1, Rome, 1981.
Codice Diplomatico	*Codice Diplomatico del Senato Romano dal MCXLIV al MCCCXLVII*, vol. 1. F. Bartoloni (ed.), FSI 87, Rome, 1948.
CIC	*Corpus Iuris Civilis.* T. Mommsen et al. (eds.); revised edition W. Kunkel, 3 vols., Heidelberg, 1954. Trans. S. P. Scott, *The Civil Law*, 7 vols., Cincinnati, 1932. For the Novellae, see now D. J. D. Miller and P. Sarris, *The Novels of Justinian. A Complete Annotated English Translation*, Cambridge, 2018.
CJ	*Codex Justinianus*
Dig.	*Digestum*
Inst.	*Institutiones*
Nov.	*Novellae*
CIL	*Corpus Inscriptionum Latinarum*
CSEL	*Corpus Scriptorum Ecclesiasticorum Latinarum*
CSPV	"Cartario di S. Pietro in Vaticano." L. Schiaparelli (ed.), ASRSP 24 (1901), pp. 393–496.
CTh.	*Codex Theodosianus. Theodosiani Libri XVI cum Constitutionibus Sirmondianis et Leges Novellae ad Theodosianum Pertinentes.* T. Mommsen and P. M. Meyer (eds.), 2 vols., Berlin, 1905. Trans. C. Pharr, *The Theodosian Code and Novels and the Sirmondian Constitutions, a Translation with a Commentary, Glossary and Bibliography*, Princeton, 1952.
DBI	*Dizionario biografico degli italiani*
FSI	*Fonti per la Storia d'Italia*
GR	*S. Gregorii Magni Registrum epistolarum.* D. Norberg (ed.), 2 vols., CCSL 140-140A, Turnhout, 1982. Trans. J. R. C. Martyn, *The Letters of Gregory the Great*, 3 vols., Turnhout, 2004.
ICUR	*Inscriptiones Christianae Urbis Romae.* G. B. De Rossi (ed.), 3 vols., Rome, 1861–8.
ICUR, n.s.	*Inscriptiones Christianae Urbis Romae, nova series.* A. Ferrua and A. Silvagni (eds.), 6 vols., Rome and Vatican City, 1922–75.
ILCV	*Inscriptiones Latinae Christianae Veteres.* E. Diehl (ed.), 3 vols., Berlin, 1924–31.
JRA	*Journal of Roman Archaeology*
JRS	*Journal of Roman Studies*
KSRM	P. C. Claussen et al., *Die Kirchen der Stadt Rom im Mittelalter 1050–1300*, 3 vols. (2002, 2008, 2010), Stuttgart.
Le piante	*Le piante di Roma.* P. A. Frutaz (ed.), 3 vols., Rome, 1962.
LC	*Liber Censuum Ecclesiae Romanae.* P. Fabre and L. Duchesne (eds.), *Le Liber Censuum de l'Église romaine*, 2 vols., Paris, 1910.
LCL	Loeb Classical Library
LD	*Liber diurnus Romanorum pontificum.* H. Foerster (ed.), Bern, 1958.
LP	*Liber Pontificalis.* L. Duchesne (ed.), with additions by C. Vogel, *Le Liber Pontificalis. Texte, introduction et commentaire*, 3 vols., Paris, 1955–7. Trans.

	R. Davis, *The Book of Pontiffs (Liber Pontificalis)*, 3rd ed., Liverpool, 2010 (to 715 AD); *The Lives of the Eighth-Century Popes (Liber Pontificalis)*, 2nd ed., Liverpool, 2008 (715–817 AD); *The Lives of the Ninth-Century Popes (Liber Pontificalis)*, Liverpool, 1996 (817–91 AD).	RIASA	*Rivista dell'istituto nazionale d'archeologia e storia dell'arte*
		RF	*Il Regesto di Farfa*. I. Giorgi and U. Balzani (eds.), 5 vols., Rome, 1879–1914.
		RIS²	*Rerum Italicarum Scriptores. Raccolta degli storici italiani dal Cinquecento al millecinquecento ordinata da Antonio Ludovico Muratori*, 34 vols., Città di Castello – Bologna, 1900–75.
LTUR	*Lexicon Topographicum Urbis Romae*. M. Steinby (ed.), 6 vols., Rome, 1993–8.		
Mansi	G. D. Mansi, *Sacrorum conciliorum, nova et amplissima collectio*, reprint Graz, 1960–1.	Röm. Mitth.	*Mittheilungen des kaiserlich deutschen archaeologischen Instituts. Römische Abteilung*
MEFR	*Mélanges d'Archeologie e d'Histoire* (École française de Rome; 1881–1970)	RömQSchr.	*Römische Quartalschrift für christliche Altertumskunde und Kunstgeschichte*
MEFRA	*Mélanges de l'École française de Rome. Antiquité* (1971–)	RSAA	"Regesto dell'abbazia di Sant'Alessio all'Aventino." A. Monaci (ed.) ASRSP 27 (1904), pp. 351–98; 28 (1905), pp. 151–200; 395–449.
MEFRM	*Mélanges de l'École française de Rome. Moyen Âge* (1971–)		
MGH	*Monumenta Germaniae Historica*	SMCM	*Cartario di Santa Maria in Campo Marzio (986–1199)*. E. Carusi (ed.), Miscellanea della Società romana di storia patria 17, Rome, 1948.
AA:	*Auctores Antiquissimi*		
EP:	*Epistulae*		
SRG:	*Scriptores Rerum Germanicarum*		
SRL:	*Scriptores Rerum Langobardicarum*	SMVL	*Ecclesiae S. Mariae in Via Lata Tabularium*. L. M. Hartmann (ed.), 3 vols., Vienna, 1895–1913.
SRM:	*Scriptores Rerum Merovingicarum*		
SS:	*Scriptores*		
NSc	*Atti della Accademia Nazionale dei Lincei. Notizie degli scavi di antichità*	S. Sisto	*Le più antiche carte del convento di San Sisto in Roma (905–1300)*. C. Carbonetti Vendittelli (ed.), Codice diplomatico di Roma e della regione romana 4, Rome, 1987.
PBSR	*Papers of the British School at Rome*		
PL	J.-P. Migne (ed.), *Patrologia Latina*		
PMR	*La pittura medievale a Roma 312–1431, Corpus*. M. Andaloro and S. Romano (eds.), 6 vols., Milan. Published so far are vol. 1 (2006); vol. 4 (2006); vol. 5 (2012); vol. 6 (2017).	SC	*Sources Chrétiennes*
		Settimane del CISAM	*Settimane di studio del Centro Italiano di Studi sull'Alto Medioevo*
		TSMN	"Tabularium S. Mariae Novae ab an. 982 ad an. 1200." P. Fedele (ed.), ASRSP 23 (1900), pp. 171–237; 24 (1901), pp. 159–96; 25 (1902), pp. 169–209; 26 (1903), pp. 21–141.
PSMT	"Le pergamene di S. Maria in Trastevere: Storia del fondo ed edizione delle pergamene anteriori al 1200." P. Radiciotti (ed.), MEFRM 122.2 (2010), pp. 279–317.		
RAC	*Rivista di Archeologia Cristiana*	VZ	*Codice topografico della città di Roma*. R. Valentini and G. Zucchetti (eds.), 4 vols., Rome, 1940–53.
Rend PontAc	*Rendiconti della Pontificia Accademia Romana di Archeologia* (Serie III)		

NOTES

INTRODUCTION

1. For all of the preceding, see Otto of Freising, *Gesta Frederici I. imperatoris*, 2.28–33; also *LP* 2, pp. 390–2. "Arab gold" refers to subsidies allegedly sent by the Norman kings of Sicily (the island, formerly under Muslim rule, still had a large Muslim population) to support local factions hostile to Barbarossa and the growth of Hohenstaufen power in Rome and Italy.
2. On Legnano and its repercussions, see Grillo 2012.
3. Alexander excommunicates Frederick: *LP* 2, p. 403; Frederick's Roman campaign of 1166: *LP* 2, pp. 415–18.
4. For the quote, see Otto of Freising, *Gesta Frederici I. imperatoris*, 2.29: *romana virtus indomita cuncta perdomuit*. On the Donation of Constantine, see below at Ch. 3. The classic study on the legal and theoretical underpinnings of papal claims to temporal sovereignty is Ullmann 1970.
5. *Continentia tecta*: e.g., *CIC Dig.* 50.16.139 (Ulpian), with Goodman 2007, pp. 13–18; 46–59.
6. Cf. Montaubin 2006.
7. On the idea and the ideal of Rome in the Middle Ages, Arturo Graf's *Roma nella memoria e nelle immaginazioni del medio evo* (2 vols., Turin, 1882–3) is still essential reading. See also Schramm 1929; Giardina and Vauchez 2000; Settis 2001; Dieffenbach 2002; Bolgia, McKitterick, and Osborne (eds.) 2011.
8. The current state of the art on the reuse of ancient *spolia* during the Middle Ages is the encyclopedic Pensabene 2015; more briefly, see also, e.g., Kinney 2013. On floor pavements in particular, see Guidobaldi and Guiglia Guidobaldi 1983 for the early Middle Ages, and Claussen 1987 on the later Middle Ages. The 12th-century *Mirabilia Urbis Romae* and its various later medieval derivatives are full of fantastic legends and stories of monsters and demons, and further examples abound, going back to the Roman saints' lives written starting in the 5th and 6th centuries.
9. On the use, reuse, and interpretation of ancient remains in the later Middle Ages, see, for example, Di Santo 2009; Maire Vigueur 2010, pp. 437–90. For Trastevere's peri-urban status, see Wickham 2014, pp. 128–9. Roman dialects: Trifone 2008; 2012, pp. 155–64. Still in more recent times, the spoken language of Monti, the region comprising the ancient Subura and much of the Esquiline and Oppian hills, was distinguishable from that of Trastevere, for example.
10. Krautheimer 1980, pp. 68–9. For the abundant evidence against 6th-century contraction of settlement to the Campus Martius and Trastevere, treated in detail below, see Hubert 1990; Coates-Stephens 1996; Meneghini and Santangeli Valenzani 2004, pp. 31–48. Excavations in the imperial forums: Meneghini and Santangeli Valenzani 2007; Meneghini 2009.

11. Coates-Stephens 1997; 1998; 1999; 2003; Santangeli Valenzani 2002; 2004.
12. The most comprehensive presentation of the finds from the Crypta Balbi excavations comes in two hefty volumes: Arena et al. (eds.) 2001; Paroli and Vendittelli (eds.) 2004. For a shorter synthesis, see Manacorda 2001, with L. Vendittelli 2010 for some updates. On the dating and typologies of Forum Ware, see Romei 1992; Mazzucato 1993.
13. Hubert 1990. On later medieval building typologies and construction techniques, see, e.g., D. Esposito 1998; Montelli 2011. Towers and aristocratic residences: Carpegna Falconieri 1994; Bianchi 1998. Markets and commerce: Modigliani 1998; and – covering the entirety of the Middle Ages – Molinari, Santangeli Valenzani, and Spera 2015.
14. Recent historical syntheses: Wickham 2014 for the 10th–12th centuries; Maire Vigueur 2010 for the 12th–14th centuries. On Rome's 'normalization' relative to other medieval Italian cities, also Wickham 2015. Other groundbreaking historical studies on later medieval Rome include – but are by no means limited to – Carocci 1993a and 1993b on the upper nobility; Carocci and Vendittelli 2004 and 2013 on the social and economic structures of the Roman countryside; Carpegna Falconieri 2002a on the urban clergy; and on the papacy, and the practical and symbolic elaboration of papal government and administration, the numerous studies by Agostino Paravicini Bagliani (e.g. Paravicini Bagliani 2005 and 2008); Herklotz 2000; Twyman 2002.
15. The syntheses produced since Krautheimer, especially those in English, tend to read (at best) as abbreviated versions of *Profile of a City*: e.g., Hetherington 1994; Magnuson 2004. Meneghini and Santangeli Valenzani 2004 remains crucial for the early Middle Ages, as do Arena et al. (eds.) 2001; Paroli and Vendittelli 2004. One valuable recent study that does cover the full span of the Middle Ages is Carbonetti Vendittelli, Carocci, and Molinari 2017, though it is a very condensed treatment that, further, treats political/institutional/social history more than urbanism/architecture/topography (there are some 40 pages devoted specifically to the cityscape: see pp. 1–21 and 169–86). The most noteworthy recent English-language treatment of Roman urbanism over the *longue durée* is Taylor, Rinne, and Kostof 2016, but this is no replacement for Krautheimer: in its gallop from prehistory to the 20th century, it devotes only about 100, albeit valuable, pages to the medieval millennium. Finally, to maintain that Krautheimer's knowledge of ecclesiastical architecture remains unsurpassed is not to say that considerable advances have not been made since his day, some by towering figures in the field such as Sible de Blaauw and Peter Cornelius Claussen; some of Krautheimer's methodological inclinations have also been searchingly questioned, e.g., in McCurrach 2011.
16. On Rome's urban fabric, its pagan temples included, remaining substantially unaltered up to c. 400, see, e.g., Meneghini 2003, esp. pp. 1049–54.
17. The transformations, institutional and topographical, that swept Rome in the decades after 1420 are treated at somewhat greater length below in the epilogue; useful recent overviews include McCahill 2013 and Esch 2016.

1 THE ETERNAL CITY ON THE BRINK

1. I rely on Nordh's 1949 edition of the Regionary Catalogues; see also VZ vol. 1, pp. 63–258. For discussion of these texts, see also Chastagnol 1996 and Arce 1999. On the Severan Marble Plan, Carettoni et al. 1960, updated in Rodriguez-Almeida 1981, are the main sources. Stanford University's online *Forma Urbis* project is more up to date (the process of identifying and placing various fragments of the plan continues apace) and includes scans of all the surviving fragments and many other useful tools and reconstructions; at the time of writing, the URL was https://formaurbis.stanford.edu . All of the buildings and features recorded in the Regionary Catalogues and the Severan Marble Plan, and many more besides, have individual entries in M. Steinby (ed.), *Lexicon Topographicum Urbis Romae* (6 vols., Rome, 1993–2001; hereafter *LTUR*); this should be consulted for more information (and bibliography) on all the features I mention in the following topographical excursus. See also Richardson 1992; Claridge 2010; Coarelli 2014. Except where I diverge substantially from or add to the entries in *LTUR*, I do not give citations for the individual features I mention below. All quoted descriptions come from the Regionary Catalogues, unless otherwise specified. All names given in italics appear as such in the Regionary Catalogues, though I sometimes put them in their nominative forms.
2. "Show Area": Krautheimer 1980, pp. 12–13 and *passim*.
3. Domitian's paranoia: Suetonius, *Vita Domitiani*, 14. On the topography of the Palatine from its origins through the construction of the imperial palaces, see Coarelli 2012.

4. On the early development of the Forum area, see Coarelli 1983 and 1985; for its late antique configuration, as it was rebuilt chiefly after the fire of 283, see Bauer 1996, pp. 7–80; Coarelli 1999; Kalas 2015; Machado 2019, pp. 95–123.
5. The closure of the Temple of Vesta was part and parcel of Theodosius' (r. 379–95) broader efforts to end pagan worship in all its public manifestations, a vast topic whose particulars continue to inspire debate; on the Vestals in particular, see Lizzi Testa 2007; also Brown 2012, pp. 104–9. Alan Cameron's exquisitely learned and much-discussed attempt to argue that paganism was effectively dead in Rome and elsewhere long before Theodosius has left many unconvinced, myself included (Cameron 2011).
6. See Albertson 2001 on the colossus of Nero; also Marlowe 2006 on the statue and its surroundings in the 4th century. The tale of the 24-elephant team hauling the colossus to its new location appears in the late-4th-century *Scriptores Historiae Augustae* (*Vita Hadriani*, 19.12).
7. On all the imperial forums, see the overviews of Bauer 1996, pp. 81–100; Meneghini and Santangeli Valenzani 2007. On the Forum of Trajan, see also Packer 2001; Forum of Peace, Tucci 2017; Forum of Augustus, Spannagel 1999; Forum of Caesar, Amici 1991; see also Zanker 1988 on the forums of both Caesar and Augustus.
8. On the number of recipients of the grain dole in the imperial period, see Lo Cascio 1997. From the 3rd century, when baked loaves distributed at numerous points across the city supplanted the original ration of unmilled grain, the *Porticus Minucia* lost its original function. On grain distribution in the earlier empire, see Virlouvet 1995; on bread in the later empire, Tengström 1974; and on both phases, see also Rickman 1980, pp. 156–217.
9. Valuable surveys of the Campus Martius and its monuments include Castagnoli 1947; La Rocca 1984; Coarelli 1997; Jacobs and Conlin 2015. *Insula Felices*: Tertullian, *Adversus Valentinianos* 7. On the *ciconiae nixae* and the subsidized wine unloaded there for distribution in the 4th century, see Rougé 1957; Durliat 1990, pp. 348–51; Virlouvet 1995, pp. 51–9.
10. On the ancient topography of the Forum Boarium area, see Coarelli 1988; for the Circus Maximus and its immediate surroundings, Marcattili 2009; also Humphrey 1986, pp. 56–294.
11. Aguilera Martín 2002 comprehensively surveys the commercial quarter along the Tiber by the Aventine; on Monte Testaccio, see also Rodriguez-Almeida 1984. On Trajan's port facilities at Portus, at the Tiber mouth, see Keay et al. (eds.) 2005; and more broadly on the city's maritime connections, Keay (ed.) 2012.
12. A book-length study of ancient Trastevere is still sorely lacking. For now, see the summary treatment of Azzena 2010; also Palmer 1981. The mechanics of grain distribution are treated above in n. 8.
13. "Greenbelt": Krautheimer 1980, pp. 16–17 and *passim*. Mills on the Janiculum, and their role in the provisioning of the city: Durliat 1990, pp. 42–51; Wilson 2000.
14. On the Colosseum, its surroundings, and the spectacle industry more generally, see Rea (ed.) 2002; Beard and Hopkins 2005; Rea, Romano, and Santangeli Valenzani (eds.) 2017.
15. On the architecture and functioning of the baths of Trajan and Rome's other grandest public baths, see the overviews of Nielsen 1992 and DeLaine 2018. The largest of them probably catered to some 8,000–10,000 patrons per day (Lo Cascio 2000, p. 245).
16. Much archaeology has been done on the Caelian since the late 19th century; for syntheses of its sumptuous late antique mansions and various other features, see Colini 1944, and now especially Pavolini 2004 and 2006.
17. On Aurelian's temple-forum (*templum Solis*), see Moneti 1990; the whole complex attained an east-west length of some 280m and a width of 92, according to the 16th-century plans made by Palladio.
18. Magister Gregorius, *Narracio de mirabilibus urbis Romae*, ch. 17. The Baths of Caracalla are exhaustively dissected in one of the great monographs devoted to a single monument (DeLaine 1997). On Rome's water supply, the *De aquaeductu urbis Romae* of Frontinus, the official in charge of the aqueducts under Trajan, is the principal ancient source. Modern studies of Rome's water supply include Bruun 1991; Evans 1994 (with an English translation of Frontinus); de Kleijn 2001; see also K. Rinne's *Aquae Urbis Romae* online resource: www3.iath.virginia.edu/waters/. On the greenbelt, start with Cima and La Rocca (eds.) 1998; also Hartswick 2004 for an in-depth look at the Horti Sallustiani.
19. Nordh 1949, pp. 97–106. The significance of the over 46,000 *insulae* mentioned in this passage is much debated, particularly by those interested in its possible relevance to Rome's total population. I follow Elio Lo Cascio (1997, pp. 58–63) in thinking that it does not denote specifically residential units, but rather refers to the total number of discrete properties of any type under separate ownership, rather like taxable property units in the modern world.

20. Notwithstanding their relentless litanies of figures and details, the Regionary Catalogues inevitably give an incomplete and partial glimpse of a dynamic place that evolved with every passing year. The Catalogues, too, were updated and reworked over time, such that the Rome they present is actually a hybrid creation. An early draft of the *Curiosum* probably dates to the beginning of the 4th century, after the dedication of Diocletian's triumphal arch (the *arcus novus*) over the Via Lata c. 303, but before Constantine took Rome in 312 and razed the camp of the horse-guards (*equites singulares*) in reprisal for their support of Maxentius. (As the catalog mentions both features, one version should date to the decade when they coexisted.) Yet it was updated at least as late as 357, when the tallest of Rome's Egyptian obelisks was erected in the Circus Maximus, where the catalog puts it. In its current form, then, the *Curiosum* (like the *Notitia*) presents an imaginary Rome, an impossible composite, Calvinoesque "invisible city" where the obelisk and the camp of the horse-guards coexist, as they never did in Roman time and space.
21. Storey 2013 is a handy overview of residential building in imperial Rome.
22. Constantius II's tour in 357: Ammianus Marcellinus, *Res Gestae*, 16.10.13–17.
23. See Cameron 2011, with the further references cited there, for the expansion and empowerment of imperially sponsored Christianity over the course of the 4th century (though I think he overestimates the speed and completeness with which traditional religious observance and beliefs declined; cf. Harris 2016). Other English-language classics on the topic include MacMullen 1984 and Lane Fox 1987; and on Constantine specifically, Lenski 2016.
24. Krautheimer citation: 1980, pp. 35–6. Decrees on the preservation of temples in Rome/Italy: *CTh.* 16.3.3 (342); 16.10.15 (399); 16.10.19 (407).
25. All three churches are amply covered in Krautheimer 1980; the *CBCR*; and Brandenburg 2005, among many others. On the *basilica Salvatoris*, now St. John Lateran, see also de Blaauw 1994, pp. 109–60; St. Peter's: McKitterick et al. 2013; St. Paul's: Camerlenghi 2018, esp. pp. 41–81.
26. The most comprehensive treatment of the early institutional evolution of the Church of Rome remains Pietri 1976. For overviews of church building in the century after Constantine, in addition to Krautheimer 1980, pp. 18–45, see Reekmans 1989; Fiocchi Nicolai 2001, pp. 50–105; Brandenburg 2005. Specifically on the Via Ardeatina basilica, see Fiocchi Nicolai et al. 1995–6; Fiocchi Nicolai, Mastrorilli, and Vella 2016. Extrapolating from the number of corpses recovered in the excavated portion of the Via Ardeatina basilica, the excavators calculate that the tombs beneath the floor, most of which received multiple burials, would alone have contained some 2,350 bodies; far more were originally present in tombs above floor-level and in the various graves and burial chapels located in the immediate vicinity (Fiocchi Nicolai and Vella 2016–17, p. 305).
27. Remarkably, there is still no comprehensive study of Rome's early baptisteries; for the known 4th-and 5th-century examples, see Barelli, Pugliese, and Sadori 2007–8, pp. 87–8; Brandt 2017, p. 18, with the bibliography cited there. The earliest known baptistery attached to a titular church seems to be the one at S. Anastasia, attributed by an inscription to the patronage of Longinianus, urban prefect in 400–2: see Cerrito 2011, p. 351; the new *titulus* of Vestina (now S. Vitale) also had a baptistery from the time of its building in the early 5th century (Kinney 2017, p. 71). The relatively recently discovered baptistery at SS. Quattro Coronati, datable to the mid-5th century and visible in Fig. 7.19, is discussed in detail in Barelli, Pugliese, and Sadori 2007–8, pp. 78–93.
28. For a very sensible discussion of *tituli* and the main scholarly viewpoints thereon, see Hillner 2007, with whom I agree that the term *titulus* should signify an irrevocable concession of legal proprietorship to the Church. Useful surveys of Rome's titular churches include, after the foundational Kirsch 1918, Geertman 1975, pp. 143–53; Guidobaldi 2000; Saxer 2001, pp. 553–71. The *CBCR* remains an important resource for their early configuration and documented remains, though it is often supplanted by more recent monographic studies on individual churches, examples of which appear in the following notes. The forthcoming Rome-centered volumes of the *Corpus Architecturae Religiosae Europeae (saec. IV – VX)*, starting with Guidobaldi, Miele, and Cecalupo 2021, will soon be essential reading for all of Rome's early medieval churches, titular and otherwise. Priests of the Roman *tituli* who signed the acts of the council of 499: *MGH AA* 12, pp. 410–15.
29. S. Clemente: Guidobaldi 1992; Brandenburg 2005, pp. 142–51; *titulus Pammachii*/SS. Giovanni e Paolo: *CBCR* 1, pp. 265–300; Acconci, Astolfi, and Englen (eds.) 2020; and on the structures beneath the church, Englen et al. (eds.) 2014; Fiocchi Nicolai 2019b. Whether the large, Christian-owned *domus* beneath SS. Giovanni e Paolo was used as a "house church" for public Christian services before the upper church was built in the first half of the 5th century is

impossible to determine for certain (strong views continue to be expressed on both sides of the question), though I think the balace of the evidence suggests that it was (cf. Fiocchi Nicolai 2019b, *contra*, e.g., Brenk 1995).

30. S. Pudenziana: *CBCR* 3, pp. 280–305; Angelelli 2010. The now-lost inscription that accompanied the apse mosaic probably shows that it was done soon after 410 (and not later than 417), to commemorate the church's deliverance from Alaric's Goths; see Schlatter 1989. S. Anastasia: Cerrito 2011.

31. Marazzi 2000, at p. 35; see also Noble 2001, pp. 45–9. On the relative invisibility, or at least unobtrusiveness, of Rome's early churches, cf. Krautheimer 1980, pp. 18–19; 30–1.

2   401–552

1. Urban population figures for late medieval Italy: Hubert 2009. See below on Roman population estimates for the 5th and 6th centuries.

2. *CTh*. 14.4.4. On this text, as well as those of 414, 419, and 452 discussed below, see Mazzarino 1951, pp. 217–47; Lo Cascio 1997, pp. 63–76.

3. E.g., Lo Cascio 1997, pp. 73–5 ("certainly not less than" 600,000–700,000); Mazzarino (1951, p. 237) imagines 800,000 or more. Durliat, despite his different interpretation of the figures for the pork dole, nonetheless proposes about 800,000 (1990, pp. 116–17). As for the identity of the recipients, Mazzarino (1951, pp. 235–6) thinks they were adult males; Lo Cascio (1997, pp. 73–5) similarly imagines that the individual ration was meant to cover the needs of each adult male recipient's underage and female dependents. For the proportion of adult males to women and children, Julius Beloch's 19th-century comparative data for preindustrial cities in Europe gave 796 women and 137 children for every 1000 males over the age of 10 (cited at Mazzarino 1951, p. 237).

4. Durliat 1990, pp. 90–109, *contra* Lo Cascio 1997, pp. 69–70.

5. Senatorial estates: Jones 1964, pp. 554–62; Matthews 1975, pp. 23–31. Senatorial *domus* at Rome: the survey of Guidobaldi 1986 remains essential; see also Guidobaldi 1999; Ensoli and La Rocca (eds.) 2000, pp. 147–60; Machado 2019, pp. 201–30. Hillner 2003 argues that the concept of a senatorial "family house" passed stably down from generation to generation in the male line obscures the often messier dynamics of alienation and transferal of properties between families or different branches of the same family.

6. Cozza 1987; Dey 2011; Medri et al. (eds.) 2017.

7. Inscription of Nicomachus to Arcadius: *CIL* 6, 40798. Fragmentary inscription commemorating a restoration of the forum of Caesar: *CIL* 6, 41384; D'ambrosio 2009, p. 469. Statues: Camodeca and Solin 2000, no. 48 (Claudian); *CIL* 6, 1731=1195 (silvered statue of Stilicho); *CIL* 6, 31987 (*fides* and *virtus* of the soldiery). Triumphal arches: Liverani 2004; 2007a; 2007b. The inscription on the arch of Arcadius, Honorius, and Theodosius II fronting the Pons Aelius is *CIL* 6, 1196.

8. On the events of 408–10 and their consequences at Rome, start with Lipps, Machado, and von Rummel (eds.) 2013. Among the ancient sources, the best account is Zosimus, *Hist. nov.*, 5.37–51; 6.6–13 (also for the gold and silver statues); also, e.g., Olympiodorus, fragments 5–14 (Blockley, vol. 2, pp. 157–74). On the *fastigium* at the Lateran, see *LP* 1, p. 172 (for Constantine's original dedication: the structure was covered with 2,025 Roman pounds of silver plate, equivalent to about 1,450 imperial pounds, or 658 kg, and crowned by solid silver statues that weighed another 1,760 Roman pounds); for its removal by the Goths and replacement by Valentinian III in the 430s, see *LP* 1, p. 233, with Bauer 2013. On the vexed question of the precise configuration of the Lateran *fastigium* (which might also, though less probably, have been a ciborium over the altar rather than a screen in front of it), see Brandt 2016. Good surveys of the ancient accounts of the sieges and sack of Rome include Mathisen 2013a; Courcelle 1964, pp. 50–77.

9. Regarding the numbers of deaths at Rome during the siege years 408–10, with ample comparative data for urban epidemics in 19th-century contexts, see Meneghini 2013; and more broadly on the proliferation of intramural burials from the 6th century, after much sparser beginnings in the 5th, see Meneghini and Santangeli Valenzani 1993 and 1995; Costambeys 2001. Zosimus (*Hist. nov.* 5.39) explicitly says that Romans were compelled to bury bodies inside the walls while besieged by Alaric (cf. also Augustine, *De civ. Dei* 1.12, on the impossibility of burying all the victims of famine and sickness). However, a couple of extant inscriptions from extramural cemeteries, datable precisely to the periods of Alaric's sieges, indicate that at least some bodies were disposed of in the traditional places even at the height of the conflict (on the inscriptions, see Fiocchi Nicolai 2012, p. 287, who consequently proposes *contra* Meneghini 2013 that extramural burials were allowed to continue during the sieges). Fiocchi Nicolai (2012) shows that the really dramatic

shift in burial practice that occurred at Rome in the decades around 400 was the abandonment of the catacombs in favor of suburban churches and martyrial shrines and their associated *sub divo* cemeteries, apparently because Christians increasingly wanted to be buried near the relics of the saints, and the crowds of praying faithful who thronged their prestigious shrines; interestingly, however, the final abandonment of the catacombs seems to correspond, on the basis of epigraphic evidence at least, precisely to the period of Alaric's sieges. Regarding the burial at the Marmorata, plausibly but not positively associated with the events of 408–10, see R. Meneghini in *BullCom* 91.2 (1986), pp. 594–5; Meneghini 2013, pp. 405–6. Rea (ed.) 2002, pp. 85–125 presents the burials and the associated archaeological levels at the Colosseum in their full complexity – the vexed stratigraphy of the burials makes dating difficult, but some at least seemingly precede the restoration of the esplanade, whose dating to the years 417–23 derives from the fragmentary inscription *CIL* 6, 32085. Meneghini (2013, pp. 405–6) suggests that as many as 40 burials may belong to the pre-417–23 phase, though this number is certainly debatable and may be on the high side (cf. Meneghini and Santangeli Valenzani 2004, p. 116, where the 5th-century burials are numbered at 35 on the basis of the artifact assemblages found in them). On the switch to intramural cemeteries in the 6th and 7th centuries, see Ch. 3, below.

10. On hoards and other signs of trauma associated with the events of 408–10, the syntheses of Spera 2012 and Spera 2013 are very useful; see also various contributions in Lipps, Machado, and von Rummel (eds.) 2013. One such hoard may be the famous "Esquiline Treasure," a collection of exceptionally high-quality silver objects found in the 1790s near the church of S. Lucia in Selci, hastily hidden around the beginning of the 5th century and never recovered (Painter 2000).

11. House of Sallust: Procopius, *Wars* 3.2.24. Senate House and Forum of Caesar: Corsaro et al. 2013. Basilica Aemilia: Meneghini and Santangeli Valenzani 2004, p. 157; Spera 2013, pp. 175 and 183–4; Lipps 2013 offers a different interpretation of the phases of destruction, but does acknowledge some early 5th-century fire damage. Jerusalem spoils: Procopius says the treasures from the Jewish Temple carried off in 410 were still kept in the Visigothic treasury at Carcassonne in the 6th century (*Wars* 5.12.41–2). Generally on the 1990s–2000s excavations in the imperial forums (and the lack of damage attributable to 410 across most of the area), see Meneghini and Santangeli Valenzani 2004, pp. 157–75; id. 2007, pp. 115–22.

12. For the archaeology of the house of the Valerii, see Pavolini 2013, p. 163, with the prior scholarship cited there. (Parts of the complex would eventually be reoccupied, but by much humbler users engaged in workaday activities.) Julia Hillner (2003, pp. 140–3) shows that the case for associating this particular property with the residence of Melania and Pinianus described in the textual account (Gerontius, *Vita Melaniae iunioris*, chaps. 14 and 19) is less clear-cut than traditionally assumed, but the standard view may be right nonetheless.

13. Quaranta et al. 2013, pp. 189–92.

14. Aventine: Quaranta et al. 2013, pp. 192–5. Caelian: Pavolini 2004; Pavolini 2013; specifically on the Basilica Hilariana, see also Palazzo and Pavolini (eds.) 2013; Calabria et al. 2015. Generally on the architecture and building history of S. Stefano, see Brandenburg 1998 and 2000; also Lissi Caronna 2000 and Martin 2004 on the complex stratigraphy of the layers immediately beneath the church, which seem to include two separate phases of infilling of the derelict Castra Peregrina (the first at the beginning of the 5th century, and the second in connection with the building of the church), along with some traces of an intermediate phase of occupation in the first half of the 5th century. *Dendrophori* and edict of 415: *CTh*. 16.10.20.

15. Fogagnolo 2013, citing additional hints of destruction and abandonment in the neighborhood that may be connected to the events of 410.

16. On the sources that report the earthquake of 408, see Tucci 2017, p. 629; on the floods of 398 and 411, Le Gall 1953, p. 29.

17. The constitution of 419 is *CTh*. 14.4.10. There is no dispute about the figure of 120,000 beneficiaries: see, e.g., Mazzarino 1951, pp. 228–9; Durliat 1990, p. 107; Lo Cascio 1997, pp. 64–5.

18. Olympiodorus, fragment 25 (Blockley, vol. 2, pp. 188–9: [Albinus] ἔφραψε γὰρ ἐν μιᾷ ἡμέρᾳ τετέχθαι ἀριθμὸν χιλιάδων δεκατεσσάρων), with Durliat 1990, pp. 107–8; for an alternative interpretation of the 14,000, see Lo Cascio 2013, pp. 412–14, who suggests, as does Blockley in his translation, that 14,000 people *per day* were being inscribed on the city's census rolls, which is impossibly high: at this rate, population would have grown by over 5,000,000 per year!

19. On 5th-century emperors at Rome: Gillett 2001; McEvoy 2010; Humphries 2012; Spera 2019. Burial at St. Peter's: Johnson 2009, pp. 167–74; McEvoy 2013.

20. *Secretarium Senatus*: *CIL* 6, 1718. Restoration of Senate House: *CIL* 6, 41378 and 41386. *Atrium Libertatis*: Fraschetti 1999, pp. 175–212. *Tabernae* in Forum of Caesar: Corsaro et al. 2013, pp. 127–30. Not far away, along the bustling final stretch of the Via Lata at today's Piazza Venezia, another row of *tabernae* also lost their original function and were given over to smelting and metalworking activities at the beginning of the 6th century (Saguì and Serlorenzi 2008, pp. 182–4).

21. The prevalent view of the Basilica Aemilia has the exterior row of shops (*tabernae*) facing the Forum restored after 410, such that the ruined interior was less visible: see Bauer 1996, pp. 32–5; Meneghini and Santangeli Valenzani 2004, p. 157; Spera 2013, pp. 175 and 183–4. Johannes Lipps (2013) has recently argued that these shops were actually restored a century earlier and left ruinous after 410, in which case a far more obviously blasted wreck thereafter defined the north side of the main forum plaza; I find this hard to believe, the more so because in 416 Probianus apparently also set up statues in the façade of the Basilica Aemilia (Bauer 1996, p. 35, with *CIL* 6, 1658a-b), which is therefore hard to imagine in ruins at the time. On the Basilica Julia, see Bauer 1996, pp. 29–30, with *CIL* 6, 1658c-d and 31886. For the statues in both the Julia and the Aemilia, see also Kalas 2015, pp. 105–24.

22. *Casas seu tuguria*: *CTh*. 14.14.1; Theater of Pompey: *CIL* 6, 1191 and 1193. Largo Argentina: Meneghini and Santangeli Valenzani 2004, p. 201. Faustus inscription: *CIL* 6, 1676.

23. Portico/exedra of the Theater of Balbus: Manacorda and Saguì 1995. *Porticus Minucia frumentaria*: Manacorda 1993 and 2001, pp. 42–9. Stadium of Domitian: Molinari 2014.

24. Colosseum: Rea (ed.) 2002, pp. 130–8; Circus Maximus: Lim 1999, esp. pp. 280–1. The last attested games in the Colosseum are in 523 (Cassiodorus, *Variae* 5.42); the last race in the Circus Maximus in 549 (Procopius, *Wars* 8.37.4). Baths of Decius: *CIL* 6, 1703. Baths of Constantine: *CIL* 6, 1750. Baths of Caracalla and of Diocletian: Spera 2013, pp. 177–8. Baths of Agrippa and of Nero: Sidonius Apollinaris, *Carm.* 23, 495–6. Both of these older baths had been extensively rebuilt in the more recent past: those of Nero under Alexander Severus (r. 222–35), and those of Agrippa in the 330s or 340s, as the study of Guidobaldi and Conte 2011–12 now convincingly shows. The Baths of Trajan, on the other hand, seem to have ceased functioning in the mid 5th century, when the channel linking the baths to its massive water-storage cisterns became blocked and was never reopened; see Meneghini 2003, pp. 1055–6. Aqueduct maintenance is discussed below.

25. Minerva in the *atrium Minervae*: *CIL* 6, 526 = 1664; Bauer 2001, pp. 87–8; Orlandi 2012, pp. 295–6. Fraschetti (1999, pp. 157–63) thinks Aginatius Faustus was undoubtedly Christian, but traditionalist enough to restore what by then appeared a venerable talisman long purged of pagan taint. A number of laws provided for preserving temples as civic adornments or putting them to other uses, once they had been purged of all pagan cult: see *CTh*. 16.10.15 and 16.10.18, both of 399; *CTh*. 16.10.19 (407); Theodoric was still attempting to preserve Roman temples in 510–11 (Cassiodorus, *Variae* 3.31.4).

26. Valentinian's gifts to St. Peter's, St. Paul's, and the Lateran: *LP* 1, pp. 233–4, with Bauer 2013 on the Lateran *fastigium*. Generally on imperial patronage of Roman churches under Valentinian III, see, e.g., Humphries 2007, p. 43; Thacker 2013, pp. 147–8; Kinney 2017, pp. 77–80. Regarding Valentinian's concession of, presumably, land for S. Lorenzo, the notice comes from *LP* 1, p. 234: *fecit* [Sixtus III] *autem basilicam sancto Laurentio, quod Valentinianus Augustus concessit*. Brandt 2012, pp. 145–7 outlines the long and ongoing debate between those who would identify the site in question with either S. Lorenzo *fuori le mura* or S. Lorenzo in Lucina; Brant sides with S. Lorenzo *flm*, but I think the question remains open. In either case, the fact of imperial patronage remains. On the mosaics of the triumphal arch and the program of restorations at St. Paul's under Leo I, who repaired the roof, strengthened the transept, and added a new altar over the tomb of the apostle with an enclosed presbytery around it, see Camerlenghi 2018, pp. 83–102. The earthquake in question would be the well-known event of 443. The (many times reworked) mosaic of the triumphal arch still bears an inscription commemorating Galla Placidia and Leo's collaboration: PLACIDIAE PIA MENS OPERIS DECUS HOMNE PATERNI | GAUDET PONTIFICIS STUDIO SPLENDERE LEONIS.

27. *CBCR* 4, pp. 72–98; Brandenburg 2005, pp. 167–76; *PMR* 1, pp. 292–304. For the quote, Krautheimer 1980, p. 45.

28. Construction over remains of *domus* abandoned around 410: Liverani 2010; Liverani 2013, pp. 279–86. On the architecture, see *CBCR* 3, pp. 1–60; de Blaauw 1994; Kinney 2010, pp. 72–5; and on the mosaics, *PMR* 1, pp. 306–46; Lidova 2015. The trabeated colonnades ran counter to the prevailing fashion for arcades, which appears to have begun with the arcaded colonnades of Rome's grandest

imperially sponsored basilica, St. Paul's (built c. 386–404), after which arcades rapidly proliferated (S. Cecilia, S. Vitale, S. Sabina, S. Pietro in Vincoli, etc.); cf. Camerlenghi 2018, p. 56. The fashion for arcades may also, however, have resulted from the difficulty and expense of acquiring the massive architrave blocks needed for trabeated entablatures – in fact the trabeations at Santa Maria Maggiore are merely wooden beams, while the real work of supporting the clerestory is done by the usual arcades in brick, here artfully concealed with stucco and mosaics to give the impression of a more classicizing, flat entablature.

29. Dedicatory inscription of Sixtus III: *ICUR* 2, p. 110, no. 67; p. 124, no. 3. Inscription commemorating Eudoxia's patronage: *ICLV* 1, p. 1779, with Rausa 2004, pp. 546–7. The inscription of Licinia Eudoxia claims that that her patronage of the new church came in fulfillment of the desires of her parents, the eastern imperial couple Theodosius II and Aelia Eudoxia, who presumably gave the property to the Church; the inscription probably dates to Licinia Eudoxia's first visit to Rome in 439/40, though work on the church may well have continued into the 440s. The inscription does not specify exactly what Licinia Eudoxia did, but her support was presumably financial. On the structure, see *CBCR* 3, pp. 179–234; and for the identification of the site with the *Curia athletarum* and the complex question of the phases preceding the creation of the existing basilica in the second quarter of the 5th century, Rausa 2004, pp. 544–50.

30. On the remains under S. Sabina, see Spera 2013, p. 175; on S. Maria Maggiore and S. Pietro in Vincoli, see the preceding two notes. An analogous example comes from Trastevere, where the *titulus* of S. Cecilia rose, in the first half of the 5th century, atop the remains of a 2nd-century insula that seems to have gone out of use around the time of the Gothic sack of 410: see Fogagnolo 2013, pp. 158–9. Regarding Roman senators' relatively seamless transition from traditional modes of civic euergetism and religious benefaction to Christian ones, a process well advanced by the 420s and 430s, see, e.g., Matthews 1975, pp. 352–76; Marazzi 2000, pp. 35–7; Machado 2019, pp. 162–200; see also Lizzi Testa 2004, pp. 99–100 for a lengthy list of 'Christian' projects sponsored by Roman aristocrats. On the total absence of evidence for Roman aristocrats involving themselves in constructing churches until the very end of the 4th century, see also Pietri 1976, pp. 83–4; 558–67.

31. Rufenus: Bauer 2013, pp. 265–6. Edicts governing spoliation of old buildings: *CTh.* 15.1.19 (AD 376); 15.1.21 (380); 15.1.37 (398). A decree issued by Majorian, in 458, gave precise guidelines for the reuse of materials from older public buildings judged to be irreparable. The materials were to be employed only in other public buildings, and only after the Senate had consulted and passed its findings to the emperor for final approval (*CTh. Nov. Maj.* 4.3, with Fauvinet-Ranson 2006, pp. 242–3). Krautheimer (1980, p. 66) strangely got the sense of this law completely wrong, claiming that it sanctioned unregulated pillaging ("spoliation was legalized") and that it shows, essentially, the government throwing up its hands in despair. In many cases, of course, dilapidated buildings were haphazardly and illegally mined for their materials, in just the sort of abuses laws such as Majorian's were meant to curb. On the probability that the matching column sets at S. Sabina and San Pietro in Vincoli each came from a single, methodically disassembled public building, see Kinney 2010, pp. 69–71; Bauer 2013, pp. 265–6; Pensabene 2015, p. 31. More generally on the likelihood of an organized system of spoliation under government control, see, e.g., Ward-Perkins 1984, p. 203 and ff.; Christie 2001, pp. 118–19; see also Spera 2015 on archaeological evidence for late antique *spolia* depots. The twenty-four matching *pavonazzetto* columns at St. Paul's are another example of magnificent components sourced from a single important building, possibly the *Porticus Liviae*: see *LTUR* 4, pp. 127–9 (C. Panella); Brandenburg 2005, p. 193.

32. *CTh. Nov. Val.* 36.1–2.

33. Mazzarino (1951, p. 230) evidently assumed that the additional quantity in 419 was negligible: he has beneficiaries increasing from 120,000 to c. 141,000, and thus a population increase of over 15 percent between 419 and 452. On the stabilization of the Roman population prior to 452, see also Lo Cascio 2013, pp. 417–18. Another text worth mentioning in the context of Rome's demographic stabilization in the first half of the 5th century is Valentinian's *Novella* 5 (*CTh.*, vol. 2), of 440, which ordains that the Greek merchants called *pantapoli* be readmitted to Rome (locals' fear of competition had evidently driven them out), in order to ensure that the material needs of an ideally growing population could be properly satisfied: *Idcirco hoc edicto singuli universique cognoscant pantapolis ad urbem Romam redeundi negotiandique licentiam restitutam, ut cura pervigili ubertas populo ministretur et in rebus suspectis a maiore multitudine civitas possit habitari.*

34. Mazzarino and Lo Cascio: see the preceding note. Durliat 1990, pp. 94–104.

35. Romans to guard and repair city walls: *CTh. Nov. Val.* 5.2–3; Italians to arm themselves against Vandal threat: *CTh. Nov. Val.* 9. Earthquake of 443: *Fasti Vindobonenses Priores* (*s. a.* 443, *MGH AA* 9, p. 301), with Guidoboni and Molin 1989, pp. 199–201. For a historical overview of these developments, see Merrills and Miles 2010, pp. 111–16.

36. Murder of Aëtius: Priscus, fragment 30.1 (Blockley, vol. 2, pp. 327–33); Procopius, *Wars* 3.4.24–8. Capitol despoiled: Procopius, *Wars* 3.5.4; Zosimus, *Historia nova*, 5.38.5. Other accounts of the disastrous events of 455 at Rome: Prosper of Aquitaine, *Epitoma Chronicon, s. a.* 455 (Prosper ends his chronicle in 455, as if to suggest that the old order terminated there); Jordanes, *Romana*, 334. Good recent overviews of these events include Humphries 2000, pp. 526–8; Oppedisano 2013, pp. 55–70; Roberto 2017.

37. McEvoy's recent discussion of Roman politics in the two decades after 455 justly stresses how impoverished and chaotic the city seems to have been (McEvoy 2017). I think Salzman 2017 too optimistic about the numbers, independence, wealth, and international connections of the Roman senatorial elite as a whole after 455 – a few families did quite well; most did poorly or disappeared entirely. For the Vandal raids and conquest of the islands, see Merrills and Miles 2010, pp. 116–40.

38. On the treaty of 442, the probability that Valentinian III signed it in large part to guarantee Rome's African grain supply, and the final rupture following Petronius Maximus's seizure of power, see Vera 2004, p. 154; Conant 2012, pp. 22–31; also Caliri 2004, pp. 1704–10 for more on the causes and consequences of the interruption in African grain supplies in the mid 5th century. On the archaeological evidence for the decline (but by no means disappearance) of transport amphorae from Africa in the later 5th century, and the rise of imports from south Italy/Sicily and the eastern Mediterranean, see, e.g., Casalini 2015, esp. pp. 540–5; Wickham 2005, pp. 709–12; and, more cautiously, Panella and Saguì 2001, pp. 776–90; cf. also McCormick 2001, pp. 100–1. As grain was not shipped in pots, however, the ceramic record can only serve as a partial, albeit essential, proxy for such archaeologically invisible commodities. As for foodstuffs bought and sold on the open market, Domenico Vera has recently argued forcefully that such commerce always accounted for more of the calories consumed at Rome (and elsewhere), relative to the *annona*, than nearly all scholars have assumed; see esp. Vera 2010, pp. 6–9. He may be right, but the fact remains that Africa had for centuries supplied Rome with most of the grain and oil both sold on the open market *and* distributed via the *annona*, and there was simply no good way to compensate for the loss of the richest grain-producing (and tax-paying) provinces in the western Empire.

39. Ricimer's sack: John of Antioch, fragments 207 and 209; Malalas, *Chron.* 14.26; Procopius, *Wars* 3.5.1–8, with Roberto 2012, pp. 157–96 and Roberto 2017. On the period 454–76 at Rome, see McEvoy 2017; and more broadly on Ricimer's career, MacGeorge 2002, pp. 165–268.

40. The year 455 as tipping point: Marcellinus *comes, s. a.* 455 (*MGH AA* 11, p. 86); see also above at n. 36 for Prosper of Aquitaine ending his Chronicle in 455. For an overview of the material evidence for the pace of 5th-century contraction, see Panella 2013, along with the sources cited in the following note.

41. Houses under the Ospedale Militare: Pavolini 2013, pp. 172–5; also pp. 179–80 for broader signs of decay and abandonment on the Caelian from the mid 5th century; house in Piazza dei Cinquecento: Meneghini and Santangeli Valenzani 1996, pp. 63–9; Meneghini 1999, pp. 171–5. House under Palazzo Altemps: De Angelis d'Ossat 2005. *Domus* in Vicus Caprarius: Insalaco 2005, pp. 32–5. *Domus* under the new Rinascente: Baumgartner 2017 for an overview of the area; Acampora 2017 on the ruin of the *domus* around the mid 5th century. *Domus* under the padiglione Pio Piacentini: Martines 2015, esp. pp. 269–70. For a more synthetic overview of upper-class dwellings at Rome in the 5th century, see Santangeli Valenzani 2012, who points to the second half of the 5th century as the period when the pace of decay and abandonment increased considerably, as does, e.g., Meneghini 2003, p. 1057.

42. See above at nn. 20–23; also Meneghini 2003, pp. 1056–67, and specifically on the Basilica Aemilia, Pensabene 2015, p. 159.

43. Oxford database: www.laststatues.classics.ox.ac.uk. For an overview of the Roman evidence, see Machado 2010b and 2016a, esp. p. 124 on the numbers of inscribed bases – not including statues without bases probably datable to the 5th century – alone, which results in a somewhat different picture from the one I present here, though the disparity between the first half of the 5th century and the second half remains marked; one should also keep an eye peeled for the appearance of Robert Coates-Stephens' long-awaited book on the end of honorary statues.

44. Machado 2010a; Ward-Perkins and Machado 2013; and Machado 2016b all detail the end of the practice of dedicating honorary statues in Italy, and the relative resilience of the Roman statue habit. On the wholesale pillaging of Roman statues in 455, see Roberto 2017.

45. Orlandi 2010; Orlandi 2012; Orlandi 2013, p. 345 for the lines quoted.
46. On S. Stefano as "der letzte Großbau der Antike in Rom," see Brandenburg 2000, who prefers to date construction to around the 460s; it was dedicated by Pope Simplicius (r. 468–83). On the chronology of the strata beneath the church and the resulting possibility that construction was underway already in the 440s or 450s, see Lissi Caronna 2000 and Martin 2004.
47. Regarding the dynamics of building patronage in later 5th-century Rome, see, e.g., Mathison 2013b; Roberto 2013. S. Agata was originally probably dedicated to Christ, possibly along with the apostles; the dedication changed when Pope Gregory I reconsecrated the formerly Arian church at the end of the 6th century. The best treatment of the building is now Aimone 2016. For Ricimer's dedication, destroyed when the apse collapsed in 1589, see also Orlandi 2009; Mathisen 2013b; and on the structure, also Hülsen et al. 1924, pp. 103–12. This church is but one of the examples that gives the lie to Krautheimer's bald statement that "by the second third of the fifth century ... church building in Rome became both the exclusive prerogative and the responsibility of the papacy alone" (1980, p. 34) – for other 6th- and 7th-century churches in whose foundation the popes played a secondary part at best, see Chapter 3, below.
48. Valila inscription from S. Andrea (now lost): see *ICUR* 2, p. 436, no. 115 = *ILCV* 1785 = *CIL* 6, 41402, with *LP* 1, p. 249; Roberto 2013. On the structure of the church itself, *CBCR* 1, pp. 64–5, with *PMR* 1, pp. 247–52 on the 4th-century *opus sectile* revetments; also Kalas 2013. Among the few other churches founded in the late 5th century were the original incarnations of S. Bibiana and S. Martino ai Monti (but the latter probably dates to shortly after 500, under Pope Symmachus I (r. 498–514); both were completely rebuilt later on, such that their original configuration is unknown, though it is quite certain that S. Bibiana at least, like S. Andrea, made extensive use of preexisting structures: see Costambeys 2001, p. 178 and n. 36.
49. Regarding the steady influx of immigrants needed to sustain Rome's bloated population numbers in the imperial period, see Holleran 2011. On the causes and effects of Italian demographic decline in late antiquity, the countryside very much included, see the thought-provoking analysis of Giovannini 2010.
50. Political and administrative dynamics of Odoacer's reign: MacGeorge 2002, pp. 269–93; Caliri 2017. For the situation at Rome and relations between Odoacer and the Senate: Chastagnol 1966; Orlandi 2010, also for Odoacer's (nonimperial) titles in Roman inscriptions; Caliri 2017, pp. 113–21.
51. See Caliri 2017, pp. 151–60 on the events of 489–93. Writing in the 8th century, Paul the Deacon claimed that Odoacer fled to Rome with some remaining troops after his initial defeat by Theodoric in 489, where he proceeded to burn and pillage the surrounding countryside when the Romans locked him out of the city (*Historia Romana* 15.17). If the episode happened (and it appears only in this one late source), the city center was nonetheless spared. On the (questionable) notion of a Theodorican "Indian summer," see La Rocca 1993, pp. 454–5; Marazzi 2016, p. 106.
52. Roman Senate under Ostrogothic rule: La Rocca and Oppedisano 2016; Radtke 2016; also Porena 2019 on the central role played by the leading senator, the *prior senatus*, in the administration of the city and the tutelage of its monuments. Continuing games and races: Cameron and Schauer 1982; Lim 1999; Orlandi 2001; Fauvinet-Ranson 2006, pp. 380–9.
53. "Abominable earthquake": *CIL* 6, 1716a-b, with Guidoboni and Molin 1989, pp. 201–2; Galadini et al. 2018, pp. 321–2. The inscription might also date to 508, in which case the repairs in question would have occurred under Theodoric, but I think 484 likelier. On the infilling of the arena substructures, see Rea (ed.) 2002, p. 127 (and pp. 126–38 for the architectural history of the building from 411 through the last recorded games held there, in 519 and 523; see also Rea 1999). Over 70 percent of the columns from the upper-level colonnade were found buried beneath the arena floor. Generally on the later 5th- and early-6th-century senatorial place inscriptions, see Rea (ed.) 2002, pp. 143–50; Orlandi 2004.
54. Forum of Augustus: Meneghini and Santangeli Valenzani 1996, pp. 78–81; 2004, pp. 179–80; Meneghini and Santangeli Valenzani (eds.) 2010, pp. 143–8. There are three possibilities for the Decius in question: Caecina Mavortius Basilius Decius, consul in 486; Decius Albinus, consul in 493 and praetorian prefect 500–3; or Flavius Decius, consul in 529. It should be said, however, that Lucrezia Spera has expressed doubts about the date of the inscription based both on its wording and letter forms, suggesting that it was more likely carved *before* the column was erected; in this case, there would be little reason to think that the Forum of Augustus was a precocious outlier, ruined and despoiled long before the adjoining forums of Caesar, Augustus, and Trajan were in the 9th century (Spera 2015, pp. 252–3). Forum of Peace: Procopius, *Wars*

55. 8.21.11–12, with Meneghini 2003, pp. 1053–4; Santangeli Valenzani and Meneghini 2007, pp. 115–17; Meneghini 2009, pp. 198–9. Palatine: Augenti 1996, pp. 17–45; Augenti 2000. More broadly on the condition of the city in Odoacer's day, see, e.g., Marazzi 2007.

55. Theodoric, Cassiodorus, and the Ostrogothic kingdom are the subject of a spate of recent scholarship, much in English, that tends to emphasize the continuities – real or vaunted – that Italy's Ostrogothic rulers sought to establish with their imperial predecessors: see, for example, Barnish and Marazzi (eds.) 2007; Bjornlie 2013; Arnold, Bjornlie, and Sessa (eds.) 2016. Arnold 2014, however, goes too far in making of Theodoric a latter-day Roman emperor. Fauvinet-Ranson 2006 is essential on urban culture and civic upkeep in Ostrogothic Italy – on Rome see esp. pp. 226–55, with the tables on pp. 256–8; also Pani Ermini 1995; Marazzi 2007. Theodoric's visit to Rome in 500: *Anonymi Valesiani pars posterior* 12.65–7, with Liverani 2007b, pp. 91–2; Fraschetti 1999, p. 257.

56. *Portus Licini*: Cassiodorus, *Variae* 1.25.2, of AD 509–10. For the brick stamps of Theodoric at all the locations mentioned (there are also others of his successor, Athalaric, and several other presumed Ostrogothic-era officials), see *CIL* 15, nos. 1663–70 (and 1671–5 for bricks of Athalaric); Steinby 1986, pp. 114–15 and 140–1; Steinby 2001, pp. 138–9 and 142–3; Fauvinet-Ranson 2006, p. 258. Restoration of the Baths of Constantine is somewhat less certain, as perhaps only one Theodorican brick has been recovered there, from an exedra in the perimeter wall: see *LTUR* 5, p. 49, with *CIL* 15, 1665a (but Steinby 1986, p. 115 indicates more than one). La Rocca 1993, pp. 475–6 stresses the ideological significance of Theodoric's stamped bricks.

57. *Secretarium Senatus, atrium Libertatis*, and Capitol(?): see *CIL* 6, 1794 = 40807, with Fraschetti 1999, pp. 175–217; Moralee 2018, p. 64. Theater of Balbus: Fauvinet Ranson 2006, pp. 246–7. Other sources mention Theodoric's work on the city walls, the imperial palace, and "public buildings" in general: see *Anonymi Valesiani pars posterior*, 12.65–7; Cassiodorus, *Chronica, s. a.* 500 (*MGH AA* 11, p. 160); Isidore of Seville, *Historia Gothorum, s. a.* 513 (*MGH AA* 11, p. 283).

58. On the mention of "temples" (*templa*), certainly in reference to ancient temples rather than churches, see Ward-Perkins 1984, p. 89.

59. Ennodius, *Panegyricus* 11.56: *Illa ipsa mater civitatum Roma iuveniscit marcida senectutis membra resecando*. The inscription at the Colosseum remains in situ on the wall of the outer ambulatory and was clearly carved after the adjacent sections of the ambulatory had come down; it names a *v(ir) s(pectabilis) Gerontius*, apparently the senator who lived from 467 to 523: see Rea (ed.) 2002, pp. 153–9; Orlandi 2004, pp. 532–4. Columns from the Temple of Sol: Moneti 1993. For these and other examples of dismantling, see also Meneghini and Santangeli Valenzani 2004, pp. 70–2. The encyclopedic Pensabene 2015 is the most comprehensive survey of reuse in late antique and medieval Rome.

60. Regarding the complete absence of churches in the *Variae*, see La Rocca 1993, p. 465. On the three basilicas attributed to Symmachus, see *LP* 1, p. 262, with Guiglia 2016, pp. 113–16 (and pp. 116–25 on the more limited initiatives of his successors during the rest of the first half of the 6th century). The possibility of a new Symmachan basilica at S. Agnese appears especially dubious; more likely is an intervention on the existing 4th-century funerary basilica. On Symmachus' efforts to improve the facilities for pilgrims and the poor at the great extramural sanctuaries of St. Peter's, St. Paul's, and S. Lorenzo, and on the Honorian basilicas of S. Agnese and S. Pancrazio, see Chapter 3, below. The sweeping panorama traced in Reekmans 1989 gives a good sense of the enormous disparity that existed, from the 6th century on, between Rome's diminished population on the one hand and the size and sheer numbers of Roman churches on the other.

61. The only textual notice of SS. Cosma e Damiano's foundation is *LP* 1, p. 279. The best treatment of the complex is Tucci 2017, pp. 627–78; see also *CBCR* 1, pp. 137–43; *LTUR* 1, pp. 324–5. It is not impossible that Theodoric himself gave the property to Pope Felix in the brief interval between the pope's accession and the old king's death (cf. Tucci 2017, p. 641), but the concession makes much better sense as the doing of Amalasunta, who strove to effect a rapprochement with the court in Constantinople as well as with Rome. The church's dedication to Cosmas and Damian probably betokens a date after Justinian became emperor in 527, as it was Justinian who zealously promoted the cult of these two eastern healer saints; see Brenk 2006; Maskinarec 2018, pp. 32–7.

62. On the gap between Theodoric's carefully cultivated image as a builder and restorer, and the more limited – though hardly negligible – extent of the work actually undertaken, the classic study is La Rocca 1993; see also Marazzi 2016, pp. 105–13.

63. There are many "ifs" inherent in these calculations. Some unspecified part of the meat delivered in 535 was beef, which would make the quantity of pork somewhat lower (my 'high' calculation of 24,000 rations assumes that the portion in beef was negligible). Durliat 1990, pp. 104–7 inclines to c. 15,000; Lo Cascio 2013, p. 418 thinks no more than c. 20,000. As for grain, the main difficulty is that the Anonymous Valesianus (12.67) says Theodoric's 120,000 *modii* was an annual quantity (*MGH AA* 9, p. 324): *Donavit populo Romano et pauperibus annonas singulis annis centum viginti milia modios*. But grain and pork had traditionally been distributed on a monthly basis, in which case 120,000 *modii* would have sufficed for only 2,000 monthly 5-*modius* rations over the 12 months of the year, a number so low that one doubts whether Theodoric or his chroniclers would have bothered to vaunt it. Perhaps the text is corrupt, or perhaps the Anonymous Valesianus confused a monthly or one-time allotment for an annual one (for another take on the Anonymous Valesianus' evident confusion here, see Barnish 1987, p. 161). Certainly this quantity is far too small to represent the *annual* total of Rome's grain allotment, but assuming it supplemented an existing ration and went to all eligible recipients, it should still bear some calculable relationship to the total number of beneficiaries. On grain and pork as the two subsidized commodities still distributed under Ostrogothic rule, under the supervision of the *praefectus annonae*, see Cassiodorus, *Variae* 6.18.

64. Lo Cascio (2013, pp. 417–18) has also recently stressed the accelerated rate of population loss after 455, on which see also, e.g., Meneghini and Santangeli Valenzani 2004, p. 21.

65. On Theodoric's divergent approach to Rome and the northern Italian cities, see La Rocca 1993, at pp. 479–82; Fauvinet Ranson 2006, pp. 255–65.

66. For the events leading into the Gothic War, see Humphries 2000, pp. 532–5; Vitiello 2014, with Procopius' account of events at *Wars* 5.2–5.

67. The guesstimates for subsequent periods are presented in the following chapters.

68. Many of the aqueducts were subsequently repaired, in one case possibly starting before the end of the Gothic War: an inscription from Vicarello, by Lago di Bracciano, indicates repairs to the Aqua Traiana carried out under Belisarius himself, though the fragmentary inscription, now lost, was perhaps misidentified (*CIL* 11, 3298, with Coates-Stephens 1998, p. 173, n. 18). In any case, a number of the aqueducts cut by the Goths were working again by Gregory the Great's time (r. 590–604), as discussed in Chapter 3.

3 552–705

1. For the citation, see Krautheimer 1980, p. 46; see further p. 33, also demonstrably incorrect: "[after Constantine] No emperor ever returned to Rome to take up permanent residence there." On the renewed presence of emperors in 5th-century Rome, their extended (years-long) periods of residence in the city, and the continued predominance of the civil administration in Roman affairs, see Gillett 2001; Humphries 2007 and 2012; McEvoy 2017. Classic takes on the 5th-century elaboration of papal (and Roman) spiritual primacy include Ullmann 1960; Paschoud 1967, esp. pp. 319–22; Pietri 1976, esp. pp. 645–51. On Leo I, see also, e.g., Wessel 2008; Neil 2009.

2. The political and administrative structures of Byzantine Italy are detailed in T. Brown 1984. Other valuable overviews include Guillou 1988 and Zanini 1998, pp. 33–104. Bertolini 1941 is still the most thorough historical treatment of Roman politics under Byzantine rule. More recently, see Delogu 2000a, 2000b, and 2001; also Llewellyn 1993, pp. 141–72. On the decline and disappearance of the Senate, T. Brown 1984, pp. 21–37. Humphries 2007, pp. 21–5 and 56–8 is good on the events of 603 at the Lateran, which are described in a document attached to the letter collection (*Registrum*) of Pope Gregory I: see vol. 2, appendix 8 (Norberg ed., p. 1101). On continuing imperial control of Rome's monumental patrimony through the 7th century, see Meneghini and Santangeli Valenzani 2004, pp. 53–4; Coates-Stephens 2006a and 2006b; Humphries 2007, pp. 53–6.

3. Deportation of Vigilius: *LP* 1, p. 297; Deportation of Martin: in addition to *LP* 1, p. 338, see esp. Martin's own considerably more detailed account in his Letters 14 and 15 (*PL* 87, cols. 198–202). In Pope Agatho's (r. 678–81) time, an induction fee was still paid directly to the emperor (*LP* 1, pp. 354–5), while Pope Sergius I paid the Exarch the hefty fee of 100 pounds of gold for official sanction of his election in 687 (*LP* 1, p. 372).

4. Generally on the continuing subservience of the papacy to the empire in all but doctrinal matters, see Delogu 2000a, pp. 198–9; Delogu 2000b, pp. 93–5; Humphries 2007, esp. pp. 55–6.

5. The best edition of the Donation of Constantine is H. Fuhrmann (ed.), *Das Constitutum Constantini* (*MGH Fontes iuris germanici antiqui in usum scholarum separatim editi* 10, Hanover, 1968). The text is traditionally dated to the second half of the 8th century, with some preference for the pontificate

of Paul I (757–67); for an overview of the question, see Noble 1984, pp. 134–7; Arnaldi 1987, pp. 141–7; Nelson and Goodson 2010. Hartmann (2006, pp. 182–93) suggests putting it a bit later, in the papacy of Hadrian I (r. 772–95). Johannes Fried (2007) now seeks to overturn the traditional understanding entirely, arguing that the document is a Frankish product of the mid 9th century; while Fried's sophisticated reading of the document deserves close attention, I still incline toward the standard view.

6. The omissions of the *LP* are considered in, e.g., Bauer 2004, pp. 27–38; Coates-Stephens 2006a and 2006b.

7. On Rome's robust trade and international connections in the 7th century, see Delogu 2000b, pp. 96–100; Panella and Saguì 2001, pp. 791–813; Saguì 2002; Wickham 2005, pp. 712; 735–6.

8. For the text of the Pragmatic Sanction, see *CIC Nov.* pp. 799–802, with the perceptive analysis of Archi 1981. Exiled/abducted proprietors: Chs. 3–4; contracts and documents lost or destroyed: Ch. 7; missing slaves: Ch. 16; missing nuns: Ch. 17; continuation of the *annona*: Ch. 22; public buildings at Rome: Ch. 25 (p. 802): *Ut fabricae publicae serventur. Consuetudines etiam et privilegia Romanae civitatis vel publicarum fabricarum reparationi vel alveo Tiberino vel foro vel aut portui Romano sive reparationi formarum concessa servari praecepimus, ita videlicet, ut ex isdem tantummodo titulis, ex quibus delegata fuerunt, praestentur.*

9. Generally on these Roman projects, Zanini 1998, pp. 182–6. On the Ponte Salario, see also Ward-Perkins 1984, p. 48; Coates-Stephens 2006a, pp. 149–50, also for the other bridges probably restored. The inscription commemorating Narses' rebuilding of Ponte Salario in 565 is *CIL* 6, 1199. On the Aurelian Wall, see Dey 2011, pp. 54–6; 292–7; and on the 6th-century brick vaults of tower J 17, Vitti 2013.

10. For the epitaph of Plato, father of John VII and *curator palatii Urbis Romae*, see *ICUR* 2.1, p. 442, no. 152; also *LP* 1, p. 386, n. 1. He died in 686/87. Narses' residence on the Palatine: Andreas Agnellus, *Liber Pontificalis Ecclesiae Ravennatis*, chap. 95. Visiting exarch in 653: Letter 15 of Pope Martin (Migne, PL 87, cols. 199–202). Visit of Constans II in 663: Paul the Deacon, *Historia Langobardorum*, 5.11; also *LP* 1, pp. 343–4; on the likelihood of his residence on the Palatine, Augenti 1996, pp. 46–52, also for continuing occupation by Rome's Byzantine administrators. Icons in palatine chapel of Caesarius: Gregory I, *Registrum*, vol. 2, Appendix 8 (Norberg ed., p. 1101), with Humphries 2007, pp. 21–5, and on the chapel itself, Spera 2017. On curators of the aqueducts, see below at n. 12.

11. Conversion of Pantheon: *LP* 1, p. 317. Temple of Venus and Rome: *LP* 1, p. 323. Despoiling of the Pantheon, etc. under Constans II: *LP* 1, pp. 343–4; cf. Paul the Deacon, *Historia Langobardorum*, 5.11. Generally on the events of 663, see Coates-Stephens 2017, pp. 204–9. Six columns for Gregory III's chapel: *LP* 1, p. 417.

12. *Registrum* 12.6: *Praeterea ante aliquantum temporis experientiae tuae praeceperamus, ut apud eminentissimum filium nostrum praefectum ageret, quatenus cura formarum committi Augusto viro clarissimo debuisset, pro eo quod omnino sollicitus atque strenuus vir est; et ita hactenus distulisti, ut nobis nec, quid egeris, indicaris; et ideo apud eundem eminentissimum filium nostrum vel modo omni agere intentione festina, ut formae praedicto clarissimo viro per omnia committantur, quatenus sollicitudine sua aliquid in eas valeat reparare.*

13. Assertions that popes from Gregory I on took the lead in stewarding Rome's physical plant (including aqueducts): Krautheimer 1980, pp. 59–61; 69–71 – at p. 60, he oddly calls Byzantine officials in Rome "a powerless and inefficient, if at times rapacious, nuisance" (powerless and rapacious?), while at p. 69, we read that "The Church was the only efficient organization left to maintain the economic, social, and indeed the political fabric of Rome"; Noble 1984, p. 10; T. S. Brown 1984, p. 12. Useful correctives to this view include Delogu 2000b, pp. 83–4 and 94; Delogu 2001, pp. 10–12; Marazzi 2001, pp. 43–6; Coates-Stephens 2006a, p. 151; Humphries 2007, pp. 55–6. As Delogu (2000a, p. 199) has put it, "The popes took part in the administration of their city, like every bishop did in the Byzantine empire, but they did not possess any independent right of secular government, not even as actual substitutes of the Byzantine administrators," which is exactly right. On the interpolated passage in the Life of Honorius, see *LP* 1, p. 327, and p. cxcv on the date of the earliest manuscript where it appears. For the aqueducts restored under Hadrian I, see *LP* 1, pp. 503–4.

14. Coates-Stephens 2006a, pp. 150–1. The 8th-century papal projects enumerated in the *LP* are discussed in the following chapter.

15. Gregory's letter of 602: see above at n. 12. Coates-Stephens 2011 is an excellent overview of the Forum in the Byzantine period; see esp. pp. 389–90 on the Basilica Aemilia floors, and 397–401 on the Column of Phokas. Also, e.g., Guiglia Guidobaldi 1983 for the Basilica Aemilia; and for the Column of Phokas, Giuliani and Verduchi 1987, pp. 174–7; Kalas 2017. The dedicatory inscription of the column is *CIL* 6, 1200; dated to August 1, 608, it states that the

exarch Smaragdus set up a gilded statue of Phokas: *Smaragdus . . . hanc statuam maiestatis eius auri splendore fulgentem huic sublimi columnae ad perennem ipsius gloriam imposuit ac dedicavit*. Ward-Perkins 1984, pp. 47–8 is especially pessimistic regarding the efficacy of the Byzantine administration in maintaining Rome's physical plant. More broadly on the Forum in the Byzantine period, see also Serlorenzi 2016; Spera 2016b.

16. On late antique masonry styles at Rome, see the sources cited below at n. 18; on technical continuity into the 7th century, see also Meneghini and Santangeli Valenzani 2004, 135.

17. S. Lorenzo: *CBCR* 2, pp. 1–146; S. Agnese: *CBCR* 1, pp. 14–39; S. Pancrazio: *CBCR* 3, pp. 154–75; also Brandenburg 2005, pp. 236–48, on all three. Though there are those who still consider possible a 6th-century date for S. Pancrazio, the majority opinion (rightly, I think) attributes the current church to the reign of Honorius, as also in the case of S. Agnese; on the question, see Guiglia 2016, pp. 113–14. My point about the prevalence of *opus vittatum* into the 7th century is made more fully in Dey 2019.

18. Generally on late antique masonry in Rome and the building industry that produced it, see Heres 1982; Cecchelli (ed.) 2001; Santangeli Valenzani 2002; Meneghini and Santangeli Valenzani 2004, pp. 133–42; D. Esposito 2014. More broadly on material and technical continuities with the late antique past into the 7th century, see also Santangeli Valenzani 2003.

19. For the presentation of these likely interventions of the 6th–7th century, we await the publication of the proceedings of the conference on the medieval phases of the Aurelian Wall held in October 2017 (Le Mura Aureliane nella storia di Roma, 2: Da Onorio a Nicolò V), in particular the contribution of A. Molinari, N. Giannini, and D. Mercuri.

20. On this central zone of concentrated Byzantine presence, see Coates-Stephens 2006a and 2006b; Maskarinec 2018, pp. 27–99; also Marchetti Longhi 1938 on the *Ripa Graeca* in later centuries.

21. The name *porticus maximae* appears in the dedicatory inscription of a triumphal arch over the road, from c. AD 380, which commemorates the extension of the flanking porticoes up to the one remaining river crossing toward the Vatican, the Ponte S. Angelo. Preserved only in the late 8th-century manuscript (*Codex Einsiedlensis* 326) that contains the Einsiedeln Itineraries, the inscription says that the arch served "to conclude the entire work of the *porticus maximae*": see Walser 1987, p. 75 = *CIL* 6, 1184 (c. AD 380): *Imperatores caesares ddd nnn Gratianus Valentinianus et Theodosius pii felices semper Auggg arcum ad concludendum opus omne porticuum maximarum aeterni nominis sui pecunia propria fieri ornariq. iusserunt*. The continuation of the portico from the far side of Ponte S. Angelo to St. Peter's is first mentioned by Procopius in the mid 6th century (*Wars* 5.22.21). Lucrezia Spera has made the strongest case in favor of dating it as early as the late 4th century, in connection with the *porticus maximae*: see Spera 2011a, pp. 1317–21; 2013, pp. 164–7; also Dey 2015, pp. 69–73. Back toward the city center, the route was lined with prestigious ancient monuments, too: the theaters of Marcellus and Pompey, with the Porticus Octaviae and Porticus Philippi between them; dozens of temples, including the three now incorporated into the church of S. Nicola in Carcere; triumphal arches, and so on; for all the premedieval features, and the close association with triumphal processions, see Popkin 2016. In modern terms, the route follows Via dei Cerchi from the Circus Maximus, past S. Anastasia and down toward the Tiber, bending right near the round temple of Hercules and proceeding along Via del Teatro di Marcello to the Theater of Marcellus, where it curves around the theater onto Via di Pescheria, coasting the colonnades of the Porticus Octaviae. From there, it plunges straight through the southern Campus Martius on the line Via di Pescheria – Via del Pianto – Via dei Giubbonari, skirts the Theater of Pompey just before crossing the Campo de Fiori, and continues on along Via dei Cappellari as far as Via dei Banchi Vecchi, where it doglegs right toward the river crossing at Ponte S. Angelo. The Einsiedeln Itineraries' repeated mentions of porticoes suggest that the basic architectural cohesion of the route, between the Theater of Pompey and the Circus Maximus, remained apparent to the 8th-century compiler; see especially Lanciani 1891, cols. 509–13. Also significant is the subsequent reference, in the continuation of the same itinerary, to the porticoes of the Circus Maximus as the *porticum maximum* (Walser 1987, p. 205; cf. Lanciani 1891, cols. 514–16). When we remember that the transcription of the inscription from the triumphal arch that commemorates the completion of the *porticus maximae* was recorded in the same manuscript (Walser 1987, p. 75), it starts to look as though the 8th-century author/compiler still perceived the colonnades leading to the arch near Ponte S. Angelo on the one hand, and on the other, the arcades of the Circus Maximus, halfway across the city, as parts of a much greater whole – the *porticus maximae*. Note that the course of the route shown in

Figure 3.7 is approximate in places, as, for example, between the Circus Maximus and the Theater of Marcellus; in antiquity, the route may indeed have run through the Theater of Marcellus itself (for the case in favor of the idea, see Monterroso 2009), but by the time of the Einsiedeln Itineraries, it passed between the Portico of Octavia and the partially collapsed outer ambulatory of the theater, as shown here.

22. In the Einsiedeln Itineraries, the church is connected directly with this portico: *Et sic per porticum maximum usque ad Anastasiam* (Walser 1987, p. 175). For the installation of the regionary crosses at S. Anastasia, see *Itinerarium Salisburgense* (VZ 2, p. 120): *Basilica quae appellatur Sancta Anastasia, ubi cruces servantur quae portantur per stationes*, with Montauban 2009, p. 19. Baldovin 1987, pp. 143–66 is essential on the stational liturgy (and stational crosses) at Rome; see also Saxer 1989; de Blaauw 1994, pp. 53–85. S. Anastasia stood near the foot of the *scalae Caci*, one of the main routes leading (steeply) up to the top of the Palatine (on the route, see *LTUR* 4, pp. 239–40).

23. Text of Canon Benedict's *Ordo*: *LC* 2, pp. 141–74; the relevant section is at p. 145. *Gallatorum*: Marchetti Longhi 1924. On the ancient *kalatores* and the possible site of their *schola* in the Roman Forum, near the Regia, see Coarelli 1983, pp. 178–82; Carnabucci 2012, pp. 99–104.

24. After veering right near the temple of Portunus (*ante templum Sibillae*), the road passed between the *templum Ciceronis* on the left and the *porticus Crinorum* on the right, according to Canon Benedict (*LC* 2, p. 145). The *templum Ciceronis* ("Temple of Cicero"), probably one of the temples under the 12th-century church of S. Nicola in Carcere, took its name from the prison located in the immediate vicinity, which also gave S. Nicola its epithet (in Carcere – "at the Prison"). This prison was itself named for the *Tullianum*, part of the old *carcer Mamertinus* in the Roman Forum; by Benedict's time, the *Tullianum* of the prison had been conflated with the legendary orator Tullius Cicero, leading to the idea of a "Temple of Cicero" by the prison (Bartoli 1926–7; Kinney 2007, p. 246). Both the 12th-century *Mirabilia urbis Romae* and the *Graphia aureae urbis Romae* make the connection between Cicero and the prison *in Tulliano* explicit: see *LC* 1, p. 272 (*Mirabilia*): *In Alephanto, templum Sibille, et templum Ciceronis in Tulliano*; VZ vol. 3, p. 94 (*Graphia*): *In Elephanto templum Sibillae, et templum Ciceronis ubi nunc est domus filiorum Petri Leonis. Ibi est carcer Tullianus, ubi est ecclesia Sancti Nicholai*. Prison mentioned in the *LP* Life of Hadrian: *LP* I, p. 490: *Deductique Elefanto, in carcere publico, illic quoram universo populo examinati sunt*. Earlier mentions of a prison in this location put it *in circo Flaminio*, meaning close to the Theater of Marcellus (Fraschetti 1999, pp. 229–30). Marchetti Longhi argued plausibly that the *carcer ad Arcum Stellae* mentioned in the *LP* Life of Stephen I (r. 254–7) is the prison in question, which would also date it back at least to the 6th century, when this section of the *LP* was written: see *LP* I, p. 154, with Marchetti Longhi 1924–5, pp. 171 and 181–2. The original Tullianum in the Forum seems to have been transformed into a shrine by the 7th century, evidently because of its reputation as the place where St. Peter had been imprisoned: see Thacker 2014, p. 111. Various conjugations of the Greek verb *krinein* (to judge), or inflections of the related nouns for 'judgment' (*krisis, krima*) and 'judge' (*krites*) might easily have been creatively Latinized into a genitive plural *crinorum*.

25. *Ordo Romanus* 1, ch. 126, p. 108: *Discendente autem ad presbiterium episcopi ... post episcopos presbiteri, deinde monachi, deinde scola, deinde milites draconarii, id est qui signa portant*. On the *banda* and *signa* this corps carried, and the possibility that the regionary crosses were among them, see Twyman 2002, pp. 73–4; also *LP* 1, p. 497, where the *signa* are explicitly stated to be crosses. The 12th-century Basel *Ordo* still calls the banner bearers in the papal cortege *drachonarii* (Basel *Ordo* 3.9; see Schimmelpfennig 1968, p. 68); and they were still based in the area in 1192, when they appear in the *Liber Censuum* (*LC* 1, p. 306) as the *schola* of the *Bandonarii ... Caccabarii*. The toponym *ad Caccavari* is given in the *Mirabilia* (*LC* 1, p. 272) as adjacent to the *templum Craticule*, which Canon Benedict himself puts in the immediate vicinity of the *insula Militena et drachonariorum* (*LC* 2, p. 245: *et transiens ante templum Craticule et ante insulam Militenam et drachonariorum*); for the location of this *schola* at San Carlo ai Catinari, see Duchesne at *LC* 1, p. 316, n. 29.

26. S. Anastasia is first attested as the repository for the regionary crosses under Byzantine rule, that is; the church dates to the 4th century (see Ch. 1, at n. 30). On the Mese in Constantinople, see Dey 2015, pp. 77–84, with the prior bibliography cited there.

27. See the discussion of all three of these foundations in Maskarinec 2018, pp. 77–93. S. Giorgio in the Life of Zacharias: *LP* 1, p. 434. The later interpolation in the Life of Leo II (r. 682–3; *LP* 1, p. 360), which claims him as the founder, is suspicious to say the least, but may at least accurately reflect the date of its construction. Among those who suppose that S. Nicola was founded in the Byzantine period, see, for example, Marchetti Longhi 1976, pp. 11–12;

Palombi 2006, pp. 25–6. On *diaconiae* and similar charitable foundations, see below.

28. On all of these foundations, and the various archaeological, art-historical, and textual clues that suggest they were established in the Byzantine era, see Coates-Stephens 2006a, pp. 154–63; Coates-Stephens 2011, pp. 405–7; Maskarinec 2018, pp. 27–52. The small church in the Basilica Julia provisionally identified as S. Maria in Cannapara may actually date somewhat later, to the 8th or even the 9th century; its sparse remains were excavated and mostly removed in the 19th century, which makes a final resolution of the problem unlikely: see Maetzke 1991, pp. 80–5; Meneghini and Santangeli Valenzani 2004, p. 168. Another small church, just recently excavated, was installed by the 7th century in the remains of another monumental public building at the foot of the Palatine, just across the Via Sacra from the Temple of Venus and Rome: see Saguì and Cante 2015.

29. *Xenodochium* of Belisarius: *LP* 1, p. 296. This one foundation aside, the *LP* "contains not a single reference to a new-built ecclesiastical establishment by any Byzantine, emperor or empress, lay or cleric, government official or private person," as Coates-Stephens has put it (2006a, p. 155). On the monastery of the Tre Fontane, see Ferrari 1957, pp. 33–48, and now Fiocchi Nicolai 2019a on remains of sculptural furnishings preserved on-site that suggest a foundation date during the period of Narses' ascendancy in the 550s and 560s, which makes Benedict of Soracte's claim (*Chronicon*, p. 33) that Narses founded the monastery more plausible than many have thought in the past. On the strong possibility that Narses also founded S. Maria Antiqua, see, e.g., Coates-Stephens 2006b, pp. 306–9; Bordi 2016a, p. 40. The church of S. Giovanni a Porta Latina, dated by Krautheimer (1980, p. 68) and Heres (1982, pp. 145–6) toward the mid 6th century on technical grounds, is another monumental project plausibly associated with the patronage of Narses (see Fiocchi Nicolai 2019a, p. 315, with n. 96), as is SS. Apostoli, on which see below at n. 34.

30. S. Adriano: Bordi 2011; S. Maria Antiqua: Andaloro, Bordi, and Morganti (eds.) 2016; Chapel of the Forty Martyrs: Coates-Stephens, forthcoming; SS. Sergio e Bacco: Bonfioli 1974.

31. Others to note the importance of continuing cooperation between Church and state include T. Brown 1984, pp. 175–7; Humphries 2007, pp. 53–6.

32. On SS. Giovanni e Paolo, see *LTUR* 3, pp. 105–7; Acconci, Astolfi, and Englen (eds.) 2020. For the inscription, *ICUR* 2, pp. 322 and 440. On the others, see above at Ch. 1. The most extensive early-medieval list of Roman churches and monasteries comes in the *LP* Life of Leo III (r. 795–816), which includes a list of donations Leo made in 807 to some 107 Roman churches, monasteries, and charitable institutions, all punctually enumerated. The *LP* records the foundation of well under half. On the list, see Geertman 1975, pp. 82–129, and below at Ch. 4.

33. See now Machado 2019 on senatorial deportment and engagement with the cityscape up until the Gothic War. The first pope known to be of senatorial rank was Vigilius (r. 537–55), who is called the son of a consul (*LP* 1, p. 296). The *LP* claims his two immediate successors, Pelagius I and John III, came from similarly exalted families.

34. The *LP* says that SS. Apostoli was begun (*initiata est*) shortly before the death of Pelagius I (r. 556–61), and that John III (r. 561–74) completed (*perfecit*) and dedicated it (see *LP* 1, pp. 303 and 305). Even here, however, 'state' involvement in the form of that avid patron of religious institutions, Narses, is often suspected, in part because Pelagius I was Narses' candidate for the papacy, and also for the church's conspicuously 'Byzantinizing' plan – the trilobed form of its three apses is a typically Byzantine configuration common in the eastern Mediterranean but otherwise almost completely unknown at Rome. On the structure, see *CBCR* 1, pp. 77–83; Kinney 2010, p. 84. Extramural churches: Pelagius II builds S. Lorenzo *a fundamento* (*LP* 1, p. 309); Honorius I builds S. Agnese on Via Nomentana, S. Pancrazio on Via Aurelia, and S. Ciriaco on Via Ostiense *a solo* (*LP* 1, pp. 323–4), plus a fourth 20 miles away near Tibur (S. Severino); Theodore I (r. 642–9) builds S. Valentino on Via Flaminia *a solo* (*LP* 1, pp. 332–3); Sergius I (r. 687–701) rebuilds *a solo* the oratory of S. Andrea on Via Labicana (*LP* 1, p. 376). Other possible examples of new or extensively rebuilt extramural churches: Pelagius II's *ad corpum* basilica of Saint Hermes on the Via Salaria (*LP* 1, p. 309); Boniface V's *ad corpus* basilica of Saint Nicomedes on the Via Nomentana (*LP* 1, p. 321). The *LP* claims more generically that John III (r. 561–74) "cherished and restored" (*amavit et restauravit*) the cemetery churches around the Roman periphery, which had doubtless suffered badly during the Gothic War.

35. Though ascetic communities are known at Rome by the later 4th century, the first entities actually called monasteries appear, later, in the *LP*; all papal projects (naturally, given the source that reports them), they adjoined martyrial basilicas outside the walls. The first is the *monasterium in catacumbas* at S. Sebastiano on

the Via Appia under Sixtus III (r. 432–40; *LP* 1, p. 234), soon followed by the first monasteries at St. Peter's under Leo I (*LP* 1, p. 239) and S. Lorenzo under Hilarus (*LP* 1, p. 245). On these three, see Ferrari 1957, pp. 163–5; 166–72; 182–9, respectively. Symmachus' housing for the poor: *LP* 1, p. 263: *Item ad beatum Petrum et beatum Paulum et sanctum Laurentium pauperibus habitacula construxit*; more broadly on his improvements at St. Peter's and St. Paul's, Guiglia 2016, pp. 109–13. The recent excavations along the south flank of St. Paul's have uncovered the corner of a substantial building in mortared brick masonry, datable to around 500 and supplied with water via a masonry channel and lead pipes, which the excavators propose to identify with Symmachus' accommodations for the poor; see Spera 2011b, p. 132. Broadly on Rome's earliest monasteries, in addition to the seminal Ferrari 1957, see Giuntella 2001. On the development of the extramural sanctuaries over the *longue durée*, the overviews of Reekmans 1968 and Pani Ermini 1989 remain essential; more recently, see Fiocchi Nicolai 2001 and 2003, esp. 939–43; Thacker 2014; cf. also Krautheimer 1980, pp. 54; 80–7.

36. The intramural activities of Honorius I, for example, present a marked contrast with the four extramural churches he built from the ground up (*a solo*). Inside the walls, he exclusively adapted existing buildings, converting the Senate House into S. Adriano, and the audience hall of a grand *domus* in the Subura into today's S. Lucia in Selci (*LP* 1, p. 324). At S. Lucia, there is no evidence of any structural modifications made upon its transformation into a church (Serlorenzi 2004, p. 362). For the buildings converted in and around the Forum, see above at n. 30.

37. *Ptochium* of Pelagius: *LP* 1, p. 309. Monastery of Gregory I: *LP* 1, p. 312, with Ferrari 1957, pp. 138–51. Boniface IV: *LP* 1, p. 317, with Ferrari 1957, pp. 76–7; Honorius I: *LP* 1, p. 324 (also p. 506), with Ferrari 1957, pp. 159–62; Adeodatus: *LP* 1, p. 347.

38. Ascetic communities founded by Roman noblewomen: Jerome, Letter 127, with Dunn 2000, pp. 46–56. *Hospitale* founded by noblewoman Fabiola (died 399): Jerome, Letter 77.6; *xenodochium* of Pammachius: Jerome, Letter 66.11; 77.10. Other 5th- and early 6th-century senatorial initiatives include a monastery called the *boetiana* (*LP* 1, p. 348) possibly founded by Boethius (d. 525) himself; the monastery of S. Stefano Maior at St. Peter's, founded by Galla, daughter of the early 6th-century senator Aurelius Symmachus; a *xenodochium* installed near the Crypta Balbi by the Anicii family, and another *xenodochium* founded by the Valerii family that may be associated with remains in the markets of Trajan; see Santangeli Valenzani 1996–7; 2014 at pp. 70–3 (p. 72 for the quote). On the identity of religious benefactors in the Byzantine period, see also Coates-Stephens 2006a and 2006b.

39. Marrou (1940, pp. 97–8) and Bertolini (1947, pp. 61–74) long ago stressed the apparent connection of *diaconiae/xenodochia* with both population clusters and transport infrastructure; see also Santangeli Valenzani and Meneghini 2004, pp. 78–80. On the locations of all known early medieval *diaconiae* and *xenodochia*, see Santangeli Valenzani 1996–7; Giuntella 2001; on Leo III's donations to *diaconiae* (as all charitable foundations were generically called by his time) in 807, see *LP* 2, pp. 21–2, with Geertman 1975, pp. 111–14.

40. On the spatial distribution of the *tituli*, see Guidobaldi 2000; Saxer 2001, at pp. 553–71; also Pani Ermini 2000 on the demographic pull exerted by *tituli* and other churches.

41. Krautheimer 1980, pp. 62–5. To be fair, Krautheimer's view on the early contraction of the *abitato* to the Tiber bend represented what was common opinion into the 1990s – Coates-Stephens 1996, p. 239 lists some of the illustrious others who concurred. Krautheimer acknowledged that his 90,000 is based on the "guesswork" of the *Enciclopedia Italiana* (note on p. 339), and proposed that population had tripled since the end of the Gothic War: "After the Gothic siege, no more than 30,000 were left and possibly fewer, until by Gregory's time refugees from the Longobards swelled the figure to perhaps 90,000." But there is simply no way to gauge the effect of the Lombard invasion on Rome's population, much less whether population tripled as a result.

42. On the superabundance of older residential buildings for Rome's remaining population, cf. Meneghini and Santangeli Valenzani 2004, p. 224. Visible portions of a few *insulae* survive even today, and bits of many more are incorporated into medieval and later constructions, where they are often difficult to see and document. Quilici 1982–3 documents imperial-period *insulae* preserved to at least 2 stories/6–7 meters' elevation incorporated into 12th-century constructions in Via Capodiferro; nearby in Via di San Paolo alla Regola, he has identified Roman-period remains that reach four stories high in places (two now below ground, and two above built into the medieval and early modern structures fronting the street); see Quilici 1986–7, at p. 252. In addition to noting the *a priori* likelihood that surviving ancient buildings more than sufficed to house early medieval Romans, Coates-Stephens 1996, pp. 245ff. outlines a wide range of

archaeological evidence for the continuing use and adaptation of older structures. On the *insula* of the Aracoeli, see also Santangeli Valenzani 2011a, p. 75, who likewise points to the occupation of ancient structures through the Middle Ages and beyond. But the durability of Roman *insulae* is better demonstrated at nearby Ostia, where many of them still stand to two and even three stories in height, having been abandoned in late antiquity and never reoccupied or modified thereafter.

43. Hubert 1990, pp. 74–81 and *passim*; Coates-Stephens 1996, esp. the distribution map of textually attested early medieval residential occupation at p. 240; also Pani Ermini 2001, pp. 306–10.

44. For Rome's early medieval "leopard-skin" distribution of settlement, see Meneghini and Santangeli Valenzani 2004, pp. 213–16. Dey 2011, pp. 199–205, stresses the importance of proximity to aqueducts and throughroads. On the four aqueducts repaired in the 8th century, see Coates-Stephens 2003a, with Ch. 4, below.

45. For some of the more recent perspectives on the organization and functions of Rome's early medieval charitable institutions, see Durliat 1990, pp. 164–83; Falsiedi 1995; Santangeli Valenzani 1996–7 and 2014; Giuntella 2001; Dey 2008. For the phrase *monasteriis diaconiae*, see *LP* 1, p. 364 (Benedict II, r. 684–5); *LP* 1, p. 367 (John V, r. 685–6); *LP* 1, p. 369 (Conon, r. 686–7); *LP* 1, p. 410 (Gregory II, 715–31). Regarding Rome's earliest charitable centers as independent initiatives by noble patrons, see above at n. 38.

46. All the sources cited in the preceding note discuss the changed situation in the 8th century, when charitable centers came under direct papal control.

47. Grain from Egypt under Benedict I: *LP* 1, p. 308. For a range of views on how and why the civic *annona* ended at Rome, see, for example, Arnaldi 1986; Durliat 1990, at pp. 137–48; Delogu 2000b, at pp. 83–4; see esp. note 2 for an effective rebuttal of Durliat's idea (1990, pp. 164–83) that Church distributions replaced the civic *annona* on a similar scale. But Arnaldi, Durliat, and Delogu all concur in putting the collapse of the civic *annona* in the first half of the 7th century. On Emperor Heraclius apparently terminating the civic *annona* at Constantinople in c. 618, during the empire's death struggle with Persia, see Patlagean 1977, pp. 185–6. It is hard to imagine that a Byzantine state no longer willing to devote precious resources to feeding Constantinople would have chosen to keep feeding Rome on a substantial scale.

48. On the differing institutional profile of the civic *annona* and Church charity, and the diversity of the recipients each was meant to benefit, see Veyne 1976, pp. 44–67; Patlagean 1977; P. Brown 1992, pp. 89–103; P. Brown 2002. See Dey 2008, pp. 405–8 for the sources' consistent focus on the poor, sick, and pilgrims as the main beneficiaries of the services provided at *xenodochia*, *diaconiae*, etc. On Hadrian's program to feed the poor at the Lateran, see *LP* 1, p. 502. Pope Stephen I's (r. 752–7) new *xenodochium in Platanis* was also meant to feed 100 beggars on a daily basis (*LP* 1, pp. 440–1); even if all of Rome's *xenodochiae* and *diaconiae* each fed a similar number – and 100 is probably on the high side – the total number of recipients of Church charity will not have exceeded a few thousands, only a small percentage (almost certainly under 10 percent) of the Roman population. (Basing himself on similar premises, Paolo Delogu hypothetically calculated that in Gregory the Great's day, the Church was providing for about 8,500 clerics and needy poor, who of course represented only a fraction of Rome's total population – see Delogu 2010 [1993], pp. 237–9.)

49. In the Life of Hadrian I (*LP* 1, p. 506), there is mention of *diaconiae* offering baths to the poor once a week; the *privilegium* for the founding of a *diaconia* in the 8th-century *Liber Diurnus* also puts bathing among the services provided (Foerster ed., p. 261). For more on the spiritual and practical implications of the baths provided by charitable centers, see Falsiedi 1995, pp. 104–6; Giuntella 2001, pp. 674–7; more generally on Church-run baths in Rome, also Stasolla 2002. The archaeology and occupational history of Rome's major bath complexes (especially those of Trajan, Caracalla, and Diocletian/Maximian, but also, e.g., of Constantine on the Quirinal and Decius on the Aventine) is far too complex to treat here in detail; generally on their partial or complete abandonment by the later 6th century, see Meneghini and Santangeli Valenzani 2004, pp. 68–70.

50. Justinian's defunding of public games and entertainments: Procopius, *Historia Arcana* 26.8–11. Cassiodorus on the size of Rome's arenas: *Variae* 11.39.2, with Ch. 2 above on the dismantling of the Colosseum. On the lack of evidence for traditional spectacles at Rome after the Gothic War, and the abandonment or repurposing of old entertainment venues, see Ward-Perkins 1984, pp. 92–118; Lim 1999, pp. 280–1; more broadly on the end of classical spectacle culture, see also Inglebert 2006; Pinon 2014.

51. Dugast 2007, pp. 12–13 also thinks we underestimate the extent to which games and group entertainments continued on into the Middle Ages, at Rome and elsewhere; Ward-Perkins (1984, pp. 116–17) calls

attention to later use of old arenas for public spectacles (coronations, executions, etc.), as even in ruins they often remained the best urban venues in which to assemble a large crowd. On Roman games and contests in the later Middle Ages, see Di Santo 2016, pp. 19–30. For the transformation and reuse of the superstructures of the Stadium of Domitian from the later 4th century through the 7th, see the contributions of D'Annoville – Ferri and Molinari in Bernard (ed.) 2014. The church of S. Agnese was built before the late 8th century, when it first appears in the Einsiedeln Itineraries – see Sotinel in Bernard (ed.) 2014. On the stadium's later medieval history as the *Campus Agonis*, see M. Vendittelli 2014.

52. On the *pomerium*, the Aurelian Wall, and burials, see Dey 2011, pp. 209–13. Broadly on pre-Christian approaches to the dead, and the juridical tradition regarding burial outside the city limits, see Vismara 1999; the English-language classic on the topic is Toynbee 1971. I say the Goths "complicated" rather than "entirely prevented" access to the extramural cemeteries because of the compelling arguments presented in Fiocchi Nicolai 2012 – see Ch. 2, above, for discussion of the 5th-century intramural burials.

53. For the rise of intramural burial in all of Italy and beyond, see Fiocchi Nicolai 2003. At Rome, Meneghini and Santangeli Valenzani's effort to catalogue the first wave of intramural burials made a crucial contribution to understanding the timing of the move toward intramural burial (Meneghini and Santangeli Valenzani 1993; Meneghini 1995); the additional burials since found have broadly tended to reinforce their preliminary chronology: see Nieddu 2003; Meneghini and Santangeli Valenzani 2004, pp. 103–25; Molinari 2014, pp. 268–9. On the changing mentalities and beliefs that made cohabitation with the dead desirable, see P. Brown 1981, pp. 3–8; Lambert 1997; Cantino Wataghin and Lambert 1998, pp. 107–8; Fiocchi Nicolai 2001, p. 137.

54. Burials at the Colosseum: above, Ch. 2, n. 9. Stadium of Domitian: n. 51, above. Generally on the distribution pattern of early medieval burials across Rome, see Pani Ermini 2001, pp. 282–5; Meneghini and Santangeli Valenzani 2004, pp. 103–25, with the map at p. 104, showing almost no funerary areas in all of the Tiber bend west of Piazza Navona; also Meneghini and Santangeli Valenzani 1993 for the correspondence between burials and settlement. Systematic burial at churches from the later 8th century: Fiocchi Nicolai 2003, p. 954; Meneghini and Santangeli Valenzani 2004, p. 124.

55. On all of these points, see Meneghini and Santangeli Valenzani 1993, at pp. 107–9.

56. Broadly on the Crypta Balbi excavations, see Arena et al. (eds.) 2001, and the contributions of L. Vendittelli, Ricci, Saguì – Coletti, and Romei, in Paroli and Vendittelli (eds.) 2004, with the briefer synthesis of Manacorda 2001. On the possible connection with the monastery later known as S. Lorenzo in Pallacinis, Manacorda and Saguì 1995; Manacorda 2001, pp. 50–2. Specifically on the late 7th-century deposit at the Crypta Balbi, see, e.g., Saguì and Rovelli 1998, pp. 175–81; Arena et al. (eds.) 2001, pp. 259–63 (F. Marazzi).

57. On both the transport amphorae and the tablewares, see Panella and Saguì 2001, pp. 791–813; Saguì 2001 and 2002.

58. On the coins from the Crypta Balbi and other contemporary contexts, see Rovelli 1998; 2000; 2001, pp. 824–32; 2013. On the transformation of the old Hadrianic *Athenaeum* by Piazza Venezia into a space for metalworking, which perhaps included the (state-run) mint where bronze coinage was produced from the later 6th century to the early 8th, see Serlorenzi 2013, pp. 74–80; Serlorenzi et al. 2017.

59. The most extensive publication of these finds is Arena et al. (eds.) 2001, at pp. 331–443.

60. On the Hadrianic (early 2nd century AD) auditoriums at Piazza Venezia, approximately one-and-a-half of which have been excavated, see Serlorenzi 2013, pp. 74–80; Serlorenzi et al. 2017. Among the many other sites that now corroborate the sequences of coins and imported ceramics from 7th-century contexts at the Crypta Balbi, see Munzi *et al.* on the Palatine (several sites, including the *domus Tiberiana*; the Bastione Farnesiano, and the Vigna Barberini); Molinari on the Forum; and Fontana *et al.* on the Aventine (largo Arrigo VII), all in Paroli and Vendittelli (eds.) 2004.

4 705–882

1. For the political and institutional framework, in addition to the still-fundamental Noble 1984, see also the briefer, updated overviews of Noble 2000 and 2001; the syntheses of Delogu 2000a, 2000b, and 2001; Carpegna Falconieri 2012, among many others. *Pace* Noble, one might better speak of a (papal) "Republic of the Romans" than a "Republic of St. Peter," as Paolo Delogu has pointed out to me, since the former appears much more frequently in the sources and better reflects the pope's role as leader of a flourishing Roman collective that always comprised considerably more than the Church and its possessions – see also Delogu 2015.

2. See Bertolini 1968; Noble 1984, pp. 1–18; Delogu 2000b, pp. 100–2 on the 7th-century doctrinal squabbles between Rome and Constantinople. Specifically on the Lateran Council of 649, monotheletism, and Martin I's arrest and deportation, see *LP* 1, pp. 336–8, with Llewellyn 1993, pp. 146–56; Economou 2007, pp. 113–57. T. Brown 1984, pp. 144–58 is good on the political and military situation in Italy following the Muslim expansion out of Arabia in the 630s.
3. Quinisext Council (*in Trullo*) of 692 and the imperial *protospatharius* Zacharias' abortive attempt to arrest Sergius: *LP* 1, pp. 372–3, with Llewellyn 1993, pp. 160–1. First papal coins: Morrison and Barrandon 1988; Rovelli 1998, pp. 79–91; Fusconi 2016, pp. 5–8. Papal supervision of the monasteries of the *diaconia* first appears three years before Sergius' accession, in the biography of Benedict II (r. 684–5; *LP* 1, p. 364); see above, Ch. 3, at n. 45.
4. Arena et al. (eds.) 2001, pp. 498–514.
5. Provenance of the ceramics from the early 8th-century deposit: Saguì, Ricci, and Romei 1997, pp. 42–6; Panella and Saguì 2001, pp. 813–15; Romei 2004, pp. 283–5. Impact of the Muslim conquest of North Africa and fall of Carthage in 698: Delogu 2000b, p. 100; Delogu 2010, pp. 76–7; Wickham 2005, pp. 735–6.
6. For signs in the ceramic record of Rome's increasing reliance on regional produce (from Lazio and Campania) over the course of the 8th century, see, in addition to the references in the preceding note, Patterson 1993; Arthur 1993; and broadly on Rome's early 8th-century contraction and isolation, also Durliat 1990, p. 155; Delogu 2001, pp. 27–33. Prigent 2004, pp. 580–6 is a convenient summary of the numismatic evidence, on which see also Rovelli 2000; 2001, pp. 837–41; and more broadly on the shortage of precious metal in Rome starting under Pope Zacharias, Delogu 1988b.
7. On the iconoclast movement in the East, which gained steam from the mid 720s and officially became orthodoxy in 754, see Brubaker and Haldon 2011.
8. The papacy's declining dependence on Constantinople comes through clearly in the diminishing length of the interregna between the death of one pope and the consecration of his successor, as reported by the *LP*. Into the 680s, interregna of a year or longer were common, because official confirmation of all popes-elect still came directly from the emperor in Constantinople. From 685 through 731, approval of new popes-elect devolved on the exarch in Ravenna, such that interregna were reduced to intervals of between one and three months. The great shift came from 741, when Pope Zacharias (r. 741–52) was elevated in the record time of 8 days, while his successor Stephen (752–7) was anointed only 12 days after Zacharias' death. Though neither the *LP* nor any other source explicitly proclaims the change, from 741 on, it is apparent that no distant imperial official signed off on the Romans' choice of pope.
9. *LP* 1, p. 385: *basilicam itaque sanctae Dei genetricis qui Antiqua vocatur pictura decoravit, illicque ambonem noviter fecit et super eandem ecclesiam episcopium quantum ad se construere maluit, illicque pontificati sui tempus vitam finivit*. Bertolini 1941, pp. 410–12 sees well the biographer's reproving tone. Archaeological remains of John's possible *episcopium*: Carboni 2016 (and below). Spera 2016a, pp. 396–409 exhaustively reviews past scholarly views on the motives and significance of the move to the Palatine, which she, too, views as an ostentatious, symbolically pregnant assertion of the popes' growing presence on the Roman scene.
10. *LP* 1, p. 385: *Fecit vero et imagines per diversas ecclesias quas, quicumque nosse desiderat in eis eius vultum depictum repperiet*. John's oratory at St. Peter's: Ballardini and Pogliani 2013; frescoes at S. Maria Antiqua: Nordhagen 1968; Andaloro 2016; at the Oratory of the Forty Martyrs: Nordhagen 1968, pp. 84–5; Bordi 2016b, esp. pp. 279–82. Noble 2001, pp. 57–8 notes the apparent novelty of John VII's living portraits; see also pp. 66–7 on the iconographical innovations beginning in John's reign that presented the popes as answering directly to Mary (and/or Christ), as opposed to any secular sovereign. On the square halo as a signifier of a portrait likeness, see Osborne 1979.
11. *LP* 1, p. 388: *Qui* [Sisinnius] *et calcarias pro restauratione murorum iussit dequoquere*. We can leave aside the singular mention of Honorius I restoring the Aqua Traiana on the Janiculum around 630, for the reasons given in Ch. 3 at n. 13.
12. Gregory II's unfinished wall repairs: *LP* 1, p. 396. Attempts on his life, and resistance of Roman militia: *LP* 1, pp. 403–4; Paul the Deacon, *Historia Langobardorum* 6.49. Gregory III's wall repairs: *LP* 1, p. 420; for his outreach to the Franks in 739, see also *Codex Carolinus*, nos. 1–2. The *LP* later says (*LP* 1, p. 444) that Gregory II was actually the first to appeal to the Franks for aid, which is not impossible, given his feud with Constantinople, but see Duchesne's comments at *LP* 1, p. 457, n. 17. For more on the early 8th-century papal repairs to the wall, see Dey 2011, pp. 245–8, with Noble 1984, pp. 1–60 on the broader historical situation.

13. Transfer of the estates of *Nymphas* and *Normias* from the imperial domain to the Church in the 740s, under Zacharias: *LP* 1, p. 433. Gregory III's use of his own money for repairs to the wall: *LP* 1, p. 420: *alimonia quoque artificum et pretium ad emendum calcem de proprio tribuit*. The strength of Byzantine governmental institutions right up until 751 is probably overstressed by Llewellyn 1986, but the point stands that they continued to exist and command respect. Even after the fall of Ravenna, the presumption of nominal Byzantine sovereignty persisted for another couple of decades, while the popes waited to see how the Frankish alliance developed; see, for example, *LP* 1, p. 444, with Noble 1984, pp. 71–98.
14. On Gregory III's architectural commissions, see *LP* 1, pp. 417–21, with Coates Stephens 1997, pp. 191–5; Bauer 2004, pp. 39–40; also 49–58 on the political context and subtexts of Gregory's building program.
15. Possible residence of John VII at the *domus Tiberiana*: Carboni 2016, esp. pp. 90–5; also Spera 2016a, pp. 397–400. Even if the structures are not those of John VII, they should nonetheless represent the state of the art in Roman construction around 700: the prestigious location alone suggests that the complex was an important commission undertaken by leading civic authorities. Gregory II's monastery at St. Paul's: Spera, Esposito and Giorgi 2011. On both, see also Dey 2019.
16. Dey 2019.
17. I here summarize arguments I make at greater length in Dey 2019. On the *ius publicum* in the 740s, see above at n. 13. Laws in the Theodosian and Justinianic Codes regulating (and generally forbidding) the despoliation of old buildings: *CTh*.15.1.19; 15.1.37; *CJ* (*CIC*, vol. 2), 8.11.9; 8.11.13.
18. Pani Ermini 1992, pp. 503–7; Coates-Stephens 1995; Barelli, Fabbri and Asciutti 2005, pp. 62–3; Spera 2016a, pp. 412–19.
19. Historical overviews: Bertolini 1941, pp. 547–698; Noble 1984, pp. 71–183; Noble 2001; Arnaldi 1987; Delogu 1988a (updated in Italian translation as Delogu 2010, pp. 259–87); Llewellyn 1993, pp. 206–45.
20. *LP* 1, pp. 468–80.
21. Two *xenodochia* at the Vatican: *LP* 1, p. 441; four restored *xenodochia* and the new one *in Platana*: *ibid.* pp. 440–1; fourth monastery at St. Peter's: *ibid.* p. 451; oratory of St. Petronilla and restorations to the atrium of St. Peter's: *ibid.* p. 455; bell tower: *ibid.* p. 454, with de Blaauw 1993, pp. 371–2.
22. S. Angelo in Pescheria inscription: Bauer 2004, pp. 192–3 and n. 1069; remains of the church and *diaconia*: Meneghini 1997; Meneghini and Santangeli-Valenzani 2004, pp. 84–91. I think 755 more probable than 770 because Theodotus, already a mature man when he decorated his chapel at S. Maria Antiqua in the 740s, is likelier to have been still alive and vigorous in 755 than in 770. The second example involves the remains of a small church that now lie beneath the Via delle Botteghe Oscure near the Crypta Balbi, a structure with three apses in a trilobed configuration that is typical of "Byzantine" churches elsewhere but almost unprecedented at Rome (the 6th-century church of SS. Apostoli is the notable exception). This is S. Lucia *de Calcarario*, now plausibly associated with the church earlier known as S. Lucia *in xenodochio Anichiorum*, thus the one attached to the *xenodochium* that was founded in the 5th or 6th century by one of Rome's leading senatorial families. The masonry of the surviving remains of the church, however, is the classic type of the mid 8th century and later: lower courses in large, recycled blocks of tuff and undulating courses of brick above, which in fact very closely resembles that at S. Angelo in Pescheria. Ceci and Santangeli Valenzani 2016 make a strong, albeit circumstantial, case that this is one of the charitable centers rebuilt in Stephen II's time, and along with S. Angelo in Pescheria one of the earliest examples of the new-style masonry that proliferated after the papal takeover in Rome.
23. Theodotus chapel at S. Maria Antiqua, where the portrait of Theodotus also labels him *dux* and *primicerius*: Bordi 2016c. Toubert 2001 is excellent on the interrelationships between, and interpermeability of, the pontifical bureaucracy and the Roman nobility in the 8th century; see also Noble 1984, pp. 184–211, and Carpegna Falconieri 2012 on the progressive "Romanization" of descendants of the Byzantine ruling class, many of whom lived in the *Ripa Graeca* for centuries after the end of Byzantine rule. On the Greek community at Rome, see also von Falkenhausen 2015. For the *LP*'s protestations of Hadrian I's *romanitas*, and his family connection to his uncle Theodotus, see *LP* 1, p. 486: *Hadrianus, natione Romanus, ex patre Theodoro, de regione Via lata* [...] *Vir valde praeclarus et nobilissimi generis prosapia ortus atque potentissimis romanis parentibus editus* [...] *Hic namque beatissimus vir, defuncto eius genitore atque parvulus suae nobilissimae genetrici relictus, studiose a proprio thio Theodoto dudum consule et duce, postmodum vero primicerio sanctae nostrae ecclesiae, post antedictae suae genetricis obitum nutritus atque educatus est.*
24. On all of Paul's initiatives, see *LP* 1, pp. 464–5. Saxer 1989, pp. 1020–3 lists the earliest translations of relics

from extramural cemeteries into the city. See also Bellardini and Delogu 2003, pp. 209–14; Bauer 2004, pp. 121–47, esp. 129–32 on the preserved inscriptions from Paul's house-monastery listing the various saints whose bones he installed there.

25. Noble 2001, p. 54. Highlights of the vast literature on the building projects that accompanied the papal takeover of Rome that culminated under Hadrian I and Leo III include Geertman 1975 and Geertman (ed.) 2003 (see esp. Bauer's contribution); Bauer 2004; also Krautheimer 1980, pp. 109–42; Pani Ermini 1992.

26. On the absorption of the old imperial fiscal lands by the Church after the mid 8th century, see esp. Marazzi 1998, pp. 274–80; cf. Wickham 2014, pp. 57–8.

27. For the figures, see Noble 2001, pp. 54–5. More broadly on the sources of papal wealth and the influx of precious metals (and other commodities) into Rome from the later 8th century through the mid 9th, see also Noble 2000; Delogu 1988a and 1988b; and on silks, Phillips 1988. Papal silver *denarii* on the Carolingian standard: Rovelli 2001, pp. 842–9, who makes it clear that the papal coins were minted in limited numbers and were useful only for high-value transactions. Noble 2001, pp. 72–83 is good on the symbolic dimensions of the papal coinage. Papal silver coins continued to be struck at Rome into Benedict VII's pontificate (974–83), after which no more coins were minted locally until the first communal issues appeared c. 1180; Romans in the interim made do with limited quantities of issues from Pavia and other northern Italian cities such as Lucca and Venice (Rovelli 2010).

28. Wall repair of 776: *LP* 1, p. 501; wall repair of 790, *LP* 1, p. 513, with Dey 2011, pp. 248–60. 12,000 blocks used to restore Vatican portico: *LP* 1, p. 507, and p. 508 on the porticoes to St. Paul's and S. Lorenzo. (The admittedly awkward Latin of the *LP* suggests not that Hadrian "built a protecting embankment" along the Tiber by Castel S. Angelo, as Krautheimer 1980, pp. 111–12 has it, but rather that he reused stones from the old river embankment in the portico itself.) Geertman 1975, pp. 7–36 reconstructs the chronology of these interventions.

29. Hadrian's aqueduct repairs: *LP* 1, pp. 503–5. Some think the Aqua Iobia of the *LP* is the main line of the Aqua Marcia-Tepula-Julia on the Esquiline and Quirinal Hills (e.g. Hubert 1990, p. 77) but this seems unlikely. Hubert himself acknowledges that the early medieval texts that mention it never show the Esquiline-Quirinal branch flowing, and Coates-Stephens is very likely right that the line in question is the southern branch running from the Marcia to the Porta Appia, on past the Baths of Caracalla, and down to the Tiber, as the Einsiedeln Itineraries say it is (Route 10, Walser 1987, p. 200; Route 12, Walser 1987, p. 205: *Inde ad Portam Appiam. ibi Forma Iopia quae venit de Marsia, et currit usque ad ripam*), though it may in fact be another aqueduct entirely, the *aqua alessandrina* of the Regionary Catalogues, which does indeed intersect the Marcia on a roughly north–south bearing but seems to be a separate line: see Coates-Stephens 1999, pp. 219–23.

30. On all four aqueducts, see Coates-Stephens 2003a and 2003b. On the Aurelian Wall, see also Coates-Stephens 1998 and 1999; Mancini 2001, pp. 37–53. Leo IV is the last early medieval pope known to have restored the Wall; Nicholas I is the last reported to have repaired aqueducts (see preceding note). For the two towers in question (M14 between Porta Ostiensis and the Tiber; H14 by Porta Metronia), see Coates-Stephens 1995; generally on both types of masonry, see Meneghini and Santangeli Valenzani 2004, pp. 135–40; Barelli, Fabbri, and Asciutti 2005; Barelli 2012a.

31. Traveling master builders: Galetti 1994, pp. 475–6. *Vestiarius/vestararius* and the organization of papal building projects: Geertman 1975, pp. 34–5; Noble 1984, p. 226; Dey 2011, pp. 251–2. References to workers conscripted across the papal territories in central Italy: *LP* 1, p. 513 (c. 790); *LP* 2, p. 123 (c. 850). Inscriptions from the Leonine walls at the Vatican: Pani Ermini 1992, figs. 16–17; Gibson and Ward-Perkins 1979, pp. 32–3.

32. Expansion of the Vatican neighborhood from the later 8th century: Krautheimer 1980, pp. 161–9; Giuntella 1985; Pani Ermini 2001, pp. 317–23. On the Vatican *scholae*, all of which are first mentioned under Leo III in 799 (*LP* 2, p. 6), see also Perraymond 1979. The *burgus* of the English is first named as such in the *LP* life of Paschal I (*LP* 2, p. 53): *ita est omnis illorum* [sc. *gentis Anglorum*] *habitatio, quae in eorum lingua burgus dicitur*; cf. Belli Barsali 1976, p. 202. Carolingian residence at the Vatican: Brühl 1954; Marazzi 1994, p. 263 and n. 37; Bauer 2004, p. 177.

33. Among the many recent works that deal with the topography and functions of the Lateran *patriarchium* in the 8th and 9th centuries, see Noble 1984, pp. 212–30; Noble 2001, pp. 51–3; 68–72; Bauer 2004, pp. 61–79; McClendon 2005, pp. 123–7; Luchterhandt 2006, 2014, and 2015; Liverani 2012; Ballardini 2015. Zacharias' additions are described at *LP* 1, p. 432; Osborne 2011 proposes to identify possible remnants of Zacharias' *triclinium*.

34. See Ch. 3, above, on the Donation of Constantine. Hadrian's works at the Lateran: *LP* 1, pp. 501–3. For

the convincing hypothesis that the ancient statues were moved to the Lataran piazza in the second half of the 8th century, see Herklotz 2000, esp. pp. 57–87. The statues were likely moved after c. 750, as only then would the popes have had the right to take them, and before c. 800, when Charlemagne seems to have evoked the sculptural collection at the Lateran at his new palace in Aachen. The first explicit attestations of the she-wolf and the equestrian Marcus Aurelius at the Lateran, however, come only in 10th-century authors. The wolf appears – as the toponym *ad lupam* in the Lateran piazza – c. 900 in the *De imperatoria potestate in urbe Roma libellus* (p. 199), and in the later 10th century in Benedict of Soracte, *Chronicon*, p. 145, here with regard to events of the first half of the 9th century. Both call the wolf *mater Romanorum*. As the she-wolf in the Capitoline Museum has now been thermoluminescence and radiocarbon dated to the high or late Middle Ages (Calcagnile 2014, pp. 118–20), it would seem not to be the one in question, though debate continues. The equestrian statue, the *caballus Constantini*, is mentioned in connection with events of 966 and 985 (*LP* 2, pp. 252 and 259).

35. The quotation is at Ballardini 2015, p. 913. *Triclinium* of 797/98: *LP* 2, pp. 3–4; second *triclinium* of 801/02: *LP* 2, p. 11; on both, see Luchterhandt 2006, pp. 179–85; Luchterhandt 2014, pp. 13–21; Ballardini 2015, pp. 918–27; and on the mosaic of the *triclinium maius* in particular, Luchterhandt 1999. See also *LP* 2, pp. 28–9 for additional work carried out under Leo III. On the chronology of the two *triclinia*, see Geertman 1975, pp. 40 and 43, respectively.

36. On the parallels between the Lateran and the imperial palace, see especially Luchterhandt 2006; Luchterhandt 2014; but also e.g. McClendon 2006, pp. 123–7; Ballardini 2015, at pp. 923–6. The parallel for the equestrian statue in Rome is the equestrian statue of Justinian in the Augusteion in Constantinople, on which see studies X and XI in Mango 1993. On the Sancta Sanctorum chest of Leo III and reliquaries of Paschal I, see Galland 2004; Thunø 2015, pp. 17–23; 157–78. The *LP* first calls the Lateran complex a *palatium* in reference to the year 827 (*LP* 2, p. 71); the first source ever to use the term is, not surprisingly, the Donation of Constantine itself: see Fuhrmann (ed.), pp. 84; 86.

37. See Krautheimer 1942, and for a more recent take on St. Peter's and other early Christian churches as models for 8th- and 9th-century churches in Rome, de Blaauw 2014. On the methodological pitfalls and blind spots of Krautheimer's comparative/typological approach to Roman "copying" of earlier architectural models, however, see the perceptive historiographical analysis of McCurrach 2011.

38. S. Prassede: *CBCR* 3, pp. 235–62; S. Cecilia: *CBCR* 1, pp. 95–112; S. Maria in Domnica: *CBCR* 2, pp. 311–24; also Krautheimer 1980, pp. 122–40 on all three, along with others built in the first half of the 9th century (S. Marco at Piazza Venezia; SS. Quattro Coronati between the Colosseum and the Lateran; S. Martino ai Monti on the Esquiline; S. Susanna on the Quirinal, etc.). On annular crypts, see also de Blaauw 1994, pp. 530–9; de Blaauw 2014; Goodson 2007; Guidobaldi and Sabbi 2016; cf. also Krautheimer 1980, p. 86. For the proposal that Gregory did much the same at St. Paul's as at St. Peter's, see Camerlenghi 2018, pp. 108–12.

39. See *LP* 2, pp. 54–6 on all three of Paschal's churches. Thunø 2015 discusses the apse mosaics in detail; Goodson 2010 surveys Paschal's building activities and situates them within the wider political and theological currents of his pontificate. Paschal claimed to have brought the bones of thousands more martyrs to S. Prassede also, many of whom are listed by name in the preserved marble inscription he installed in the church, on which see Nilgen 1974. Renewed debate about the acceptability of religious imagery was stimulated in the Carolingian West by the publication of the *Libri Carolini* in the early 790s; the reinstatement of iconoclasm as official orthodoxy in Byzantium in 815 (and until 843, when it was repudiated for good) presumably gave Paschal still more pressing reason to reassert Roman support for images. In addition to Brubaker and Haldon 2011 on the East, see also Deliyannis 1996 on the West.

40. On all of the sites discussed here, Marazzi 1994 is fundamental. On the fortification of St. Peter's and St. Paul's, see also Belli Barsali 1976.

41. *LP* 2, pp. 281–2, with Pani Ermini 1992, pp. 518–19; Paroli 1993, pp. 170–2. The remains of the circuit, heavily restored over the centuries and now only partially preserved, have yet to be properly studied.

42. Saracen raid on Rome of 846: *LP* 2, pp. 99–101, with Marazzi 1994, pp. 252–7; Llewellyn 1993, pp. 256–65. Leo's repairs to the Aurelian Wall: *LP* 2, p. 115.

43. The building and dedication of the Vatican circuit is recounted at length at *LP* 2, pp. 123–5. Gibson and Ward-Perkins 1979 and 1983 provide detailed analysis of the standing remains; see also Pani Ermini 1992, pp. 514–18; Meneghini and Santangeli Valenzani 2004, pp. 63–5. Other parts of the circuit, particularly on the interior facings, were built with recycled blocks of tuff. Saracen prisoners: *LP* 2, p. 119. Two inscriptions survive that commemorate sections of the wall and towers built by teams from two different Church

estates/*domuscultae*: Pani Ermini 1992, figs. 16–17; Gibson and Ward-Perkins 1979, pp. 32–3.

44. Marazzi 1994, pp. 260–4, and 276 for the text of the inscriptions (also *ICUR* 2.1, p. 324); Llewellyn 1993, pp. 264–5.

45. Portus: *LP* 2, pp. 125–7; Leopolis: *LP* 2, pp. 131–2. The remains of Leopolis have been extensively studied since the 1990s: see Gentili, Somma, and Stasolla 2016–17. The precise extent of the early medieval circuit is unknown, but it apparently enclosed an area of 3–4 ha.

46. Belli Barsali 1976, pp. 208–9; Marazzi 1994, pp. 269–71. Inscription: *ICUR* 2.1, p. 326; Marazzi 1994, p. 277: *hic murus salvator adest invictaque porta | quae reprobos arcet suscipit atque pios | hanc proceres intrate senes iuvenesque togati | plebsque sacrata Dei limina sancta petens | quam praesul domini patravi rite Iohannes |qui nitidis fulsit moribus at meritis |praesulis octavi Dei nomine facta Iohannis |ecce Iohannipolis urbs veneranda cluit*. Recent excavations have shed some light on the topographical evolution of the inhabited quarter around St. Paul's, which emerged in the later 5th century and flourished into the 10th, when it was largely abandoned; see Spera 2011b. For John VIII's papacy as the end of an era, see Arnaldi 1990; also e.g. Wickham 2000, at p. 159, with Patlagean 1974 on the conception of Roman society as a triad of clergy, nobles, and commoners (*populus*) that emerged from the mid 8th century.

47. On the proposed demographic progression from c. 50,000–60,000 in the early 7th century to 20,000–30,000 by the 9th, see Meneghini and Santangeli 2004, pp. 22–4. Wickham 2005, p. 736 likewise estimates c. 20,000–25,000 for the 9th century. We await systematic study of medieval floods, and more generally of the relationship between the city and the Tiber, along the lines of Le Gall 1953 and Aldrete 2007 for ancient Rome (up to c. 400 AD). But clearly the frequency and spatial extent of the ancient floods documented by Le Gall and Aldrete hardly diminished in the Middle Ages, when the detrimental effects of flooding if anything increased, for the reasons cited just below; Anna Esposito's contributions on Tiber floods at the very end of the Middle Ages show how frequent and destructive such events were in the 15th and 16th centuries (A. Esposito 2010, with the prior works cited at nn. 1–2). On the early medieval floods cited in the *LP*, see *LP* 1, p. 399 (716); p. 513 (791); *LP* 2, pp. 91–2 (845); p. 145 (856); pp. 153–4 (860).

48. 12,000 blocks from embankments: above at n. 28. Sewers and drains blocked already in the 4th and 5th centuries: e.g. Filippi 2013, pp. 140–1 (Campus Martius); at the Baths of Trajan by c. 450 (Meneghini 2003, pp. 1055–6); at the Colosseum starting in the 4th century (Facchin, Rea, and Santangeli Valenzani [eds.] 2018, pp. 55; 85); along the northeast slope of the Palatine by c. 500 (Casalini 2015, p. 545). Further blockages in the 9th century: Serlorenzi 2010, pp. 134–5 (Via Lata at Piazza Venezia); Meneghini and Santangeli Valenzani 2004, p. 183 (Forum of Trajan).

49. Reams have been written about the Einsiedeln Itineraries and their implications for Roman street networks in the early Middle Ages: see *inter alia* Lanciani 1891; Bauer 1997; Santangeli Valenzani 2001b; Bellardini and Delogu 2003; Del Lungo 2004; Meneghini 2017, pp. 286–7. The best edition of the text is Walser 1987; see also *VZ* 2, pp. 155–201.

50. Steadily rising levels along the Via Triumphalis are documented at, for example, the Theater of Marcellus (Fidenzoni 1970, p. 73) and the Porticus Octaviae (Ciancio Rossetto 2008). Via Sacra: Meneghini and Santangeli Valenzani 2004, pp. 172–4; Argiletum: *ibid*. p. 175; Via Lata: Serlorenzi 2010, pp. 134–5; Serlorenzi and De Luca 2015, p. 501. On surviving paved roads in the 10th–13th centuries, see Hubert 1990, pp. 105–10; more broadly on the condition of city streets in the Middle Ages, see Meneghini 2017 and (specifically on the early Middle Ages) Esch 2008.

51. Early medieval earthquakes at Rome: *LP* 1, p. 319 (618); *LP* 2, p. 9 (801); *LP* 2, p. 108 (847), with Guidoboni and Molin 1989, p. 202; Galli and Molin 2013, sections 2.5–2.7, also for more examples of damage attributable to the quakes of 801 and, especially, 847. Galadini et al. 2018 tend to be more cautious of linking cases of structural damage to particular seismic events mentioned in the sources, but stress the cumulative damage wrought on aging ancient monuments by the quakes attested between the 5th century and the 9th (pp. 343–5); their assessment of the evidence also points to the quake of 847 having been especially destructive (pp. 330–7). S. Maria Antiqua: Ward-Perkins 1984, pp. 222–3. Crypta Balbi: Arena et al. (eds.) 2001, p. 595; Manacorda 2001, p. 55. Auditoriums at Piazza Venezia: Serlorenzi 2010, p. 148; Serlorenzi 2013, pp. 84–5 —the quake also opened large fissures in the walls of the auditoriums, and caused the partial collapse of nearby Roman-period *insulae* along the Via Lata. Basilica Ulpia: Galli and Molin 2013, section 2.7. For collapses at the Basilica Hilariana and the Crypta Balbi that may be connected to the earlier quake of 618, see also Rovelli 2013.

52. As there is next to no archaeological or textual evidence for residential building in the 7th and 8th centuries, all this remains hypothetical. On the likelihood of upper-class families residing in older *domus* at least through the 7th century, albeit in considerably less luxury than their 4th-century predecessors, see Meneghini and Santangeli Valenzani 2004, pp. 32–3; Meneghini 2009, p. 207; Santangeli Valenzani 2011a, *passim*. Certainly there is archaeological evidence for the abandonment of solidly built ancient structures once damaged beyond early medieval Romans' limited capacity for repair, though of course we cannot know how or where the displaced residents re-housed themselves. In the *insulae* along the Via Lata recently excavated during the Metro C works at Piazza Venezia, for example, spaces inhabited for centuries were abandoned because of heavy damage apparently caused by the earthquake of 847: see Saguì and Serlorenzi 2008, pp. 188–9; Serlorenzi 2010, pp. 136; 144.

53. On all of the preceding, see Santangeli Valenzani 2015b; on the total quantities of various types of stone employed in the Forum of Trajan, also Bianchi and Meneghini 2002.

54. Piles of architectural *spolia* in the Forum of Peace: Santangeli Valenzani 2015b, pp. 340–1 (also on the systematic, regulated character of the spoliation process). On the 6th-century deposits in the Forum of Peace, and the possibility that the Temple of Mars in the Forum of Augustus was also being dismantled at a similarly early date, see the sources cited above at Ch. 2, n. 54.

55. For a summary of the situation in the forums of both Caesar and Trajan, see Santangeli Valenzani 2001a; Meneghini and Santangeli Valenzani 2004, pp. 175–88. The two small 9th-century shacks in the Forum of Caesar whose outlines were clearly traceable during the excavations of 2004–5 measured 7.7 × 2.8 m and 4.7 × 2.8 m; it is not clear whether these were dwellings or rather workspaces related to the new agricultural uses of the surrounding area. Paleobotanical analysis shows that the garden crops grown in the first half of the 9th century included lettuce, cabbage, coriander, mint, white mustard, and green anise (Meneghini 2009, pp. 203–4). On the gardens and orchards in the Forum of Caesar, see also Meneghini and Santangeli Valenzani 2004, pp. 127–9.

56. Calculations regarding the paving of Trajan's Forum: Meneghini and Santangeli Valenzani 2004, p. 183; *ibid.* on the possibility that the dismantling occurred in connection with the building of Leo IV's wall around the Vatican. Not all of the original pavers were still *in situ* at the time of their removal, but most were, and the gaps had been repaired not long before, suggesting that the decision to dismantle came quite suddenly and unexpectedly.

57. Meneghini and Santangeli Valenzani 1996; Meneghini 2009, pp. 208–11. Like the date of the dismantling of the Temple of Augustus (see above, Ch. 2) the date of the installation of the monastery on its podium is complicated. The monastery is first mentioned in 955 in a bull issued by Pope Agapetus II (Kehr 1906, p. 70), but sculpted furnishings and architectural elements reused in the late medieval rebuilding of the monastic church, which are assumed to come from (and be coeval with) the original church on the same site, are dated to the 9th century (*CSA VII*, vol. 2, pp. 59–77). Early medieval stratigraphic sequences in the forum plaza: Meneghini and Santangeli Valenzani (eds.) 2010, pp. 149–51.

58. Broadly on the condition of the imperial forums in the early Middle Ages, see Santangeli Valenzani 1999; 2001a; Meneghini and Santangeli Valenzani 2004, pp. 175–88; 2007, pp. 115–58. The Argiletum was a sufficiently important road in ancient times that the Forum of Nerva, which replaced its initial tract between the Forum Romanum and the Subura, was commonly known as the *forum transitorium*, the "throughway-forum." The alignment of the Column of Phokas with the road in the early 7th century, such that the column was the main visual focus for all traffic entering the Forum Romanum along the Argiletum, is one sign of the street's lasting importance; its continued use and successive rises in level from the 9th century on are outlined in Meneghini 2017, pp. 289–91. On the 9th-century transformation of the forum, and the houses themselves, see the following note.

59. For all the preceding points on the two houses and their surroundings, see Santangeli Valenzani 1999; 2000; Meneghini and Santangeli Valenzani 2004, pp. 34–7. More broadly on the development and distribution of the *curtes* in Rome from the 9th century, see Santangeli Valenzani 2008 and 2015, with the discussion below in Ch. 5.

60. For these and other signs of residential construction in the Forum, see Meneghini and Santangeli Valenzani 2004, pp. 164–75. Coates-Stephens 1996 surveys traces of early medieval housing elsewhere in the city.

61. Giuliani and Verduchi 1987, pp. 173–87; Maetzke 1991, pp. 76–92. Note that in antiquity, the road along the southern flank of the Forum plaza may properly have been the Via Sacra, but by the early Middle Ages, the northern road had definitively usurped this title. The Diocletianic (or Tetrarchic)

reconstruction of the Forum following the fire of 283 appears to have been the critical moment of change that saw the northern road monumentalized while the southern was marginalized: see Giuliani and Verduchi 1987, pp. 185–7; and more broadly Kalas 2015, pp. 30–45.

62. The *LP* (1, p. 512) does not specify which temple collapsed onto the original SS. Sergius and Bacchus; if it is not the Temple of Vespasian, then it was the adjacent Temple of Concord. Meneghini 1997, p. 51 makes similar points about the preservation of the ancient buildings surrounding the Forum plaza into the 9th century. See also Ward-Perkins 1984, pp. 222–3 on Santa Maria Nova as the first important building erected at the Forum since antiquity.

5   THE LONG TWILIGHT OF THE EARLY MIDDLE AGES

1. The closest thing to a "monumental edifice" that survives from this period is the church of S. Maria in Pallara on the Palatine, on which see below. Robert Coates-Stephens has compiled the most exhaustive list to date of ecclesiastical building projects for the years 860–1000; while his meticulous synthesis of the written and material evidence makes the period less bereft of activity than it once seemed, the fact remains that buildings attributable to these years were evidently relatively modest in terms of both scale and artistic ambition (Coates-Stephens 1997, pp. 205–22). Valuable historical and historiographical perspectives on the era in its entirety include Brezzi 1947, pp. 83–217; Toubert 1973, pp. 963–1038; Arnaldi 1991; Llewellyn 1993, pp. 286–315; Wickham 2000 and 2015; Marazzi 2001, pp. 57–69; Delogu 2015.
2. On John VIII's wall at St. Paul's, see the preceding chapter. Aurelian Wall: Dey 2011, pp. 271–8. Final repairs to the aqueducts: the Sabbatina was repaired under Gregory IV (*LP* 2, p. 77) and Nicholas I (*LP* 2, p. 164 – the branch-line to the Vatican); the Iobia/Jovia under Sergius II (*LP* 2, p. 91) and Nicholas I (*LP* 2, p. 154; it is called the *Iocia* here). But references in archival documents show that the Claudia (at Porta Maggiore) functioned into the 11th century, at least as late as 1006 (*RS* 104, with Coates-Stephens 2004, pp. 122–5; Hubert 1990, pp. 75–8). The Traiana looks to have been out of service already before 1005, when a section in Trastevere by SS. Cosma e Damiano in *Mica Aurea* is called the *forma antiqua ... ubi olim fuerunt aquimoles tres* (Pflugk Harttung 1881–3, vol. 2, no. 93, p. 57). *Domus* with oratory at the Lateran: *LP* 2, p. 166; decorated under Hadrian II: *LP* 2, p. 176. The unique and otherwise unsupported claim of Bonizo of Sutri, writing in the late 11th century, that John X (r. 914–28) erected a basilica in the Lateran palace (*aedificavit basilicam in palatio lateranensi*) has generally, probably rightly, been treated with skepticism; on the question, see Pollio 2016, p. 247. S. Maria Nova: *LP* 2, p. 158 (it is first mentioned in the life of Benedict III, r. 855–8, where it is attributed to Leo IV).
3. Population: Meneghini and Santangeli Valenzani 2004, pp. 23–4; Wickham 2000, pp. 162–5; Wickham 2014, p. 112. Wickham strongly states the case also for Rome's continued superiority in population, wealth, and socioeconomic complexity into the 11th century. Thereafter, first Milan and later other north-central cities such as Pisa, Florence, and Venice would surpass it.
4. As far as I know, there is not a single scholarly survey dedicated specifically to Rome's urban trajectory in the 10th century. Meneghini and Santangeli Valenzani 2004 remains the best synthesis, though there is less on the 10th century than on the 5th–9th, for simple lack of material evidence. The eventual publication of the papers of the COVID-19-delayed "Roma X secolo" conference organized by Manuela Gianandrea and Xavier Barral i Altet should help to fill the void. On the disappearance of the Augustan regions and the emergence of the new *rioni*, see below, Ch. 6, at n. 10.
5. On the unusual chaos of the years 870/80–910, and the systemic repercussions thereof, see, for example, Toubert 1973, pp. 311–13; 968–74; Arnaldi 1991; Wickham 2014, pp. 20–3.
6. John VIII's letters: *Registrum Iohannis VIII papae*, E. Caspar (ed.), *MGH EP* 7.1–2. From 891 until the second half of the 11th century, many of the entries for individual popes included in later compilations (and assembled in the second volume of Duchesne's edition of the *LP*) shrink to a single sentence or two. The most informative sources for events in Rome and its surroundings in the period covered in this chapter, notwithstanding their many defects and distortions, are Liutprand of Cremona (the *Antapodosis* and *Historia Ottonis*), and Benedict of Soracte's *Chronicon*. Next in importance are Hugo of Farfa's *Destructio monasterii Farfensis*; Gregory of Catino's *Chronicon Farfense*; and the *Chronicon* of Regino of Prum, with its later continuation up to 967.
7. *LP* 1, p. 175: *factiosorum tyrannide liberius solito seviente*. As for projects sponsored by other actors in the later 9th century, there is also very little. One might mention the transformation of the small republican temple of Portunus in the *Ripa Graeca* into the

church of S. Maria *Secundicerii* (or *de secundicerio*) very probably by the *secundicerius* Stephen in the early years of John VIII's pontificate (c. 872–6); the intervention apparently consisted chiefly in covering the interior of the cella with a cycle of frescoes, fragments of which remain today. (A painted dedication mentioning a Stephanus and dating the intervention to the reign of John VIII, now lost, was copied in the 16th century.) On the identification of this church and its patron, see Osborne 1988; cf. Bianchi 2015, p. 21. On the frescoes, Del Buono 2010.

8. Lateran sack: *LP* 2, p. 192; Stephen's gifts: pp. 194–5. A Church council in 898 already treated pillaging upon the death of a pope as an established and lamentable reality: see Mansi, vol. 18, p. 226.

9. On the "Cadaver Synod" of 898 and its aftermath, see Duhr 1932; Arnaldi 1951; Llewellyn 1993, pp. 289–300; and Sansterre 1997 more broadly on the life and career of Formosus.

10. Broadly on the political and institutional situation in north-central Italy, see, for example, Tabacco 1991. For the period of the "Saracen" and "Magyar" incursions in Lazio: Brezzi 1947, pp. 105–19; Toubert 1973, pp. 311–13; 970–4. A few examples of archival references to rural depredations by "pagans" or "Saracens" or "barbarians": *S. Sisto*, n. 1 (905); *RF*, n. 348 (934); Pflugk Harttung 1881–3, vol. 2, p. 58 (1005); see also, e.g., Hugo of Farfa's *Destructio monasterii Farfensis*; Benedict of Soracte, *Chronicon*, pp. 167–8.

11. On the chaos and impoverishment of the years around 900, cf. Wickham 2000, pp. 158–9. While there is no way to quantify the decline in the amounts of foreign cash – precious metals and other portable forms of wealth – that had flooded into Church coffers in particular at the height of Carolingian power in Italy (see above at Ch. 4, n. 27), there can be no doubt that far less was arriving from the late 9th century on. Thereafter, there is no evidence of abundant papal largesse distributed to churches and other religious institutions, much less of architectural patronage on a grand scale. Papal silver coinage declined in quantity and fineness until disappearing entirely after the 970s, presumably as local stocks of silver diminished. Thereafter, only a few coins from 'foreign' mints (Pavia, Pisa, Venice, etc.) continued to circulate (Rovelli 2010); and most of the coins found in 10th-century contexts at Rome are in fact Anglo-Saxon silver pennies, which presumably trickled into the city in the purses of those enterprising pilgrims who still came (Naismith 2014). Collapse of Lateran roof: *LP* 2, p. 229. Failure to procure new roof beams: Mansi, vol. 18, col. 233. One wonders if there is a connection between these "malicious people" and the Muslim raiders who sacked and gutted the great abbey of Farfa, itself located near prime timber country, in the same year. Repairs under Sergius III (confirmed by inscriptions transcribed before they were lost): *LP* 2, pp. 236–7. On timber-sourcing for Roman roofs, see Graham and Squatriti 2019.

12. Life and career of Theophylact: Brezzi 1947, pp. 99–108; Toubert 1973, pp. 968–74.

13. On Otto III's career and the chronology (and motives) of his Roman sojourns, see Althoff 2003; also Santangeli Valenzani 2001 on the place of Otto's residence in Rome, more likely to have been the Aventine than the Palatine as traditionally assumed.

14. For much more on all of the preceding, see the sources cited above at n. 1. Wickham 2014 goes so far as to proclaim the period 906–63 "the longest stable period in Roman history across the entire Middle Ages, until the end of the Avignon schism" (p. 25). On the noble families who controlled Rome in the 10th and early 11th centuries, start with Wickham 2014, pp. 186–220 (with ample citations of previous scholarship, notably Toubert 1973 and Toubert 2001); see also Wickham's historical overview at pp. 20–9.

15. Toubert 1973, pp. 963–1038; Toubert 2001; Wickham 2014, pp. 186–204. On the origins of the Roman *militia*, and the formation of the durable group of aristocratic families that captained it, see also Carpegna Falconieri 2012.

16. I thank Riccardo Santangeli Valenzani for pushing me to articulate my reasons for suspecting limited recovery already in the mid-to-late 10th century; and certainly he is right to remind me that there is little indication of rising prosperity translating into monumental interventions in the built environment until well into the 11th century. Regarding Rome's economic isolation (or autarchy, if one prefers) and the lack of evidence for 10th-century imports, see Romei 2004. On the recent historiographical trend toward antedating to well before 1000 the beginnings of the high medieval economic and demographic boom, at least in certain privileged regions of Italy and western Europe, see Franceschi 2017, pp. 5–9, with the extensive bibliography included there; for consistent signs of economic and demographic growth in northern Italian cities already by the first half of the 10th century, see Cirelli 2013. On the abundant production of glazed ceramics in 10th-century Rome, see Romei 2001 and 2004.

17. Two scholars who provide an object lesson in the exhaustive use of archival documents to reconstruct

the material contours of Roman society in the 10th–11th centuries are Étienne Hubert and Chris Wickham: see esp. Hubert 1990 and Wickham 2014. Both include compendious lists of the extant collections of documents, published and otherwise, as does Toubert 1973, pp. 3–37. On the 10th-century replacement of papyrus, which almost never survives, with parchment, which very often does, see Carbonetti Vendittelli 2011.

18. Coates-Stephens 2004, p. 116; for his analysis of the Porta Maggiore neighborhood during the period of the Subiaco documents, including the meager physical/archaeological remains, see pp. 115–25. The documents are all published in the *Registrum Sublacense*.

19. *Parietinis desertis*: e.g. *RS* 113 (919 or 934); *Terra sationale/sementaricia*: e.g. *RS* 112 (919 [or 934?]), *RS* 46 (966); *RS* 118–19 (966); *RS* 104 (1006); "land to be given over to pasture" (*terra ad pratum faciendum*): *RS* 38 (956); other, larger pastures (and grainfields) between Porta Maggiore and Porta Tiburtina mentioned at *RS* 46 (966) and elsewhere; cucumber plot (*ortuo cucummerario*): *RS* 118 (966).

20. The most informative documents are, in chronological order: *RS* 27 (924); *RS* 17 (936), p. 48; *RS* 121 (937); *RS* 122 (952); *RS* 12 (958), p. 29; *RS* 5 (967); *RS* 14 (973), p. 36; *RS* 104 (1006).

21. Description of the *domus maior* in 924 (*RS* 27): *Idest domus maiore signino opere Cum inferioribus et superioribus suis a solo et usque ad summum tectum Cum oratorio sancti christi martyis theodori et corticella ante se et Introito et exoito suo et via publica et cum omnibus ad eas pertinentibus. Nec non et parietinis destructis de post se Simulque et ortuo maiore cum diversis arboribus pomarum* ... Marozia's purchase of the main house in 937: *RS* 121. Marozia's donation to Subiaco in 952, with the detailed description of the properties: *RS* 122; also *RS* 104, of 1006, with Santangeli Valenzani 2008, pp. 239–40. As Santangeli Valenzani says, Marozia's amalgamation of neighboring properties into a larger nucleus looks to parallel the strategies being used elsewhere in Rome by prominent nobles in the 10th century, who thus obtained the space necessary to establish their residential *curtes* and stake out local zones of influence. For the reconstruction of the configuration of the conjoined properties donated by Marozia, see Coates-Stephens 2004, pp. 122–5, also for the conjecture that the dwellings sat on the podium of the mausoleum.

22. Houses formerly belonging to the *primicerius* Sergius: *RS* 122; house of Ursus *bledanu*: ibid.; properties of Iohannis and Stephano *de grifi*: *RS* 12, p. 29 (958):

domoras quas fuerunt de iohannis et stephano de grifi. Cum corte et pergule atque ortuo Iuxta forma claudia et vinea clusura in integro cum arboribus pomarum cum criptis Iuxta via quae ducit ad ierusalem; also *RS* 14, p. 36 (973); *RS* 9, p. 18 (926) and *RS* 5, p. 6 (967) mention only the house of Iohannis *de grifi/crifi*, who was already defunct by 926. On the two houses "under" the aqueduct, see *RS* 17, p. 49: *domoras duas solaratas tegulicias et scandolicias cum corte et ortuo ... Posita rome regione tertia iuxta porta maiore subtus forma claudia*, with the discussion of the houses in the Forum of Nerva in Chapter 4.

23. The essential topographical study of the area from antiquity through the 10th century is Coates-Stephens 2004, pp. 9–115.

24. For the archaeology of the Caelian from the Roman period through the early Middle Ages, see Colini 1944 and especially now Pavolini 2006, with the additional references listed there (e.g. Pavolini 2004); on the importance of the streets connected to still-functioning gates in the walls, see also Dey 2011, pp. 199–202. S. Erasmo first appears as a monastery in the *LP* Life of Adeodatus (r. 672–6), in a passage that leaves some doubt about whether it was founded then or earlier: *LP* 1, p. 346, with Ferrari 1957, pp. 119–31.

25. Annexation to Subiaco: *RS* 24 (938), p. 63: *monasterium Sancti herasmi cum cellis seu domoras et parietinis in circuitu et cum omnibus suis edificiis atque ortuis seu terris sationalis cum arboribus olivarum et ceteras arbores pomarum in circuitu predicti monasterii et cum omnibus ad eum generaliter et in integro permanentibus positum roma regione Secunda ante venerabili titulo sancti Christi protomartyris stephani In predicto celio monte ; et inter affines ab uno latere corte de georgio viro magnifico et via publica atque domucella de petrus vir honestus et domucellas de plures homines atque parietinis et criptis seu terra de urso sementaricia qui vocatur centum scuta et a secundo latere terra sementaricia de leone religioso presbitero seu via publica que ducit in decennias et a tertio latere terra sementaricia de heredibus adriano quoddam de banneo neapolim seu et ortuo vineato de sergia nobili femina et a quarto latere domucella In qua est oratorio sanctorum cosme et damiani et via publica* ... House with oratory of Cosmas and Damian donated to monastery in 978: *RS* 114, p. 161: *Idest domus integram tiguliciam et solaratam cum inferioribus et superioribus a solo usque ad summum tectum In quo est oratorium sanctorum martyrum Christi cosme et damiana Cum corte infra eadem domo et cum ortuo ante se In quo est arborem ficulneam seu corte ante In quo est pergula et introitu per porta maiore a via publica ... posita rome regione*

secunda iuxta forma Claudia. This house, in turn, was entirely surrounded by fields and gardens mostly owned by the monasteries of S. Erasmo and S. Saba (*ibid.*): *Affines ab huno latere ortuo maiore de monasterio sancti sabe et a secundo suprascripta via publica et a tertio ortuo maiore et terra de monasterio sancti herasmi Iuris eiusdem*.

26. House mentioned in 965: *RS* 90, p. 135: *domus integram tiguliciam solaratam ... cum curte ante se in quo est pergula atque puteum et scala marmorea et cum introito suo nec non et ortuo maiore iuxta se et de post se in integro vineato Cum diversis arboribus pomarum simulque et criptis cum usu aque et cum omnibus ad eas pertinentibus posita rome regione secunda iuxta decennias ; Et inter affines a duobus lateribus vie publice Unam que ducit at portam mitrobi et aliam que ducit a lateranensis sacri palatii iuxta suprascripta decennias*. One-story *domus terrinea* near S. Stefano with a roof partly of tile and partly of wooden shingles (*domus terrinea tigulicia et scandolicia*): *RS* 91 (1003); another by Porta Metronia (*RS* 88, also of 1003): *domus terrinea una in integra tigulicia et scandolicia cum clibano intra se cum corte et pergola vineata ante se*.

27. *RS* 87, p. 132 (A contract for a three-generation lease from the *vestararius* Pipinus to the subdeacon Romanus): *Idest terra vacante modica quod est clusura una super se in integro ad domum faciendam et orticello abente in medio aquam vibam inter criptas et alia terra vacante et cum omnibus ad eas pertinentibus Posita rome regione secunda ... Et inter affines ab huno latere parietina deserta Iuris monasterii sancti herasmi Et ab alio latere via publica que vadit ad portam mitrobi et a tertio latera fistula qui ducit aquam vivam Et a quarto latere parietinas desertas quem tenere videtur theoduli honesta femina iusta decennias*.

28. Expanding vine cultivation on the Caelian: A house sold in 965 located *iuxta decennias* has a vineyard (*RS* 90); in 967, the monastery leased a tract of land to a priest of S. Sisto with the express provision that he turn it into a vineyard, complete with chestnut poles for the vines, within three years (*RS* 88); in 978, the monastery leased another vineyard (with fruit and olive trees) to Iohannes, *mansionarius* at the Lateran (*RS* 59); others appear at *RS* 91 (1003). By 1011, a vineyard *in decennias* was flanked on two sides by other vineyards, all lining the road to Porta Metronia and all, apparently, provided with a constant supply of water via a pipe or conduit from the Aqua Claudia (*RS* 85). In this last document of 1011, only the vineyard sandwiched between the other two is specified as having a constant supply of water, but it is hard to see how a line running downhill from the Claudia (and thus more or less parallel to the road) could not have supplied the adjoining properties as well: *Idest clausura de vinea cum arboribus olive et arbores ficulneas omnesque fructiferas et ciruteta cum aqua omni tempore Posita in decennia Et abet affines ab uno latere via qui ducitur in portu Et a secondo latere terra et vinea nettoni A tertio latere vinea sancti benedicti A quarto latere suprascripta decennia via publica*. This would seem to show the Aqua Claudia still flowing in 1011, five years after it is last explicitly said to be in service in *RS* 104.

29. *RS* 103 (943) and *RS* 80 (968) show only grainfields, trees, and pasture outside the gate. After *RS* 84, of 993, vineyards appear in *RS* 86 (1008, land leased by the monastery to tenants charged with planting vineyards); *RS* 100 (1021); *RS* 102 (1024, another plot provisionally intended to be planted with vines); *RS* 106 (1024, a vineyard bordered on at least two other sides by vineyards); the vineyards in *RS* 101 (1034), *RS* 98 (1035), and 99 (1035) are all completely surrounded by others.

30. Raising and repaving of the *via capitis Africae* in c. 800: Pavolini 1993, p. 57. Recall that in Chapter 4, we saw similar roadbeds in gravel and sherds replace the Roman pavers along the Argiletum and the Via Sacra at the Forum, and the final stretch of the Via Lata nearby at Piazza Venezia, all during the course of the 9th century. First and last mentions of the conduit down to Porta Metronia: *RS* 87 (857), where the term *fistula* appears, and *RS* 85 (1011). Fishpond and marsh along the walls just outside Porta Metronia: *RS* 84 (993).

31. Cf. Hubert 1990, pp. 76–8.

32. Last mentions of the Claudia in use: see above at n. 28; the last document relevant to the areas in question is *RS* 183, of 1057. On Paschal II's canal to the Lateran, see *LP* 2, pp. 323 and 379, with Coates-Stephens 2004, pp. 125–6; Capelli 2015; Giannini 2015; Dey 2020a, pp. 160–1. The canal continued on from the Lateran along the outside of Aurelian Wall, turning into the city at Porta Metronia and flowing, as the Acqua Marana, down to the Tiber by way of the Circus Maximus, thus serving as a partial substitute for the defunct Claudia and Iobia aqueducts.

33. As Santangeli Valenzani points out (2018, p. 215), S. Maria Nova's apparent majority ownership of the Colosseum depends on the fact that the surviving documents come from its archive; and other religious institutions besides the two mentioned therein may also have owned parts of the structure and its surroundings, as did some individual proprietors. On the eleven documents relevant to the occupation of the Colosseum produced between 1038 and 1232, see also Greco 2018. Contract of 1038: *TSMN* 10. For material traces of medieval occupation and the scars left on the

standing masonry of the building, see Rea (ed.) 2002, pp. 218–30. The results of the 2011–15 excavations are reported summarily in Santangeli Valenzani and Facchin 2017, and extensively in Facchin, Rea, and Santangeli Valenzani (eds.) 2018.

34. Bordi 2017, pp. 79–82; also Santangeli Valenzani and Facchin 2017, p. 69 on the surrounding churches.
35. Regarding the identity of Petrus *medicus*, who seems to have come from Siena and perhaps received his medical training there, see the interesting suggestions in Manacorda 2007, pp. 8–13.
36. On the structure and date of the building, see Pollio 2014; also Coates-Stephens 1997, pp. 207; 221 (also for the quote), who concurs that it is better to postdate its typical early medieval masonry (in both tuff blocks below and undulating courses of brick above) to the 10th century than to antedate the building itself (*contra* Augenti 1996, pp. 65–6). On the continuation of 8th–9th century-style *opus quadratum* through the 10th, see Santangeli Valenzani 2011a, p. 113 for a chunk in the Forum of Nerva stratigraphically dated to the beginning of the 11th; also Meneghini 2009, p. 225 for the first appearance in the 11th century of new masonry types in the Forum of Trajan, where the 'old' style still prevailed in the 10th. On the fresco program at S. Maria, the essential study is Marchiori 2007, reprised in Marchiori 2009; she concurs that both structure and decorative program should belong to the same period, in the later 10th century (e.g. 2009, pp. 229–30). There was probably an earlier shrine dedicated to S. Sebastian on the site, which would have been replaced by the current edifice.
37. Traffic bound for the Lateran from the Forum passed the Basilica of Maxentius and the podium of the Temple of Venus and Rome on the left, traversed the Arch of Titus, and turned sharply left at the Colosseum, coasting its northern flank on a paved road laid in the 6th century atop rising layers of fill at the base of the Oppian Hill. This final stretch of the route to the Lateran, later known as the *via maior*, was repaved at a higher level in the 8th century, perhaps in connection with Pope Zacharias' restorations at the Lateran in the 740s: see Rea (ed.) 2002, 271–2; 279–82; and on the papal processions, Twyman 2002, pp. 175–87; Wickham 2014, pp. 332–48. Gardens and building lots at the Basilica of Maxentius/Basilica Nova (still called the *domus noba* at this time): *TSMN* 13 (1042) and 15 (1052). Houses abutting or atop the podium of the Temple of Venus and Rome (called the *Templum Romuli* in the documents): *TSMN* 1 (982): the two-story house being rented adjoins two other residences that are not described in detail. Crypts: *TSMN* 4 (1017), a crypt with a wooden roof by the Temple of Venus and Rome; 5 (1018) another wooden-roofed crypt facing onto the Via Sacra, abutting others. *TSMN* 3 (1011) may refer to the lease of half the concrete apse of the Temple of Venus and Rome itself; a nearby limekiln was perhaps burning marbles from the temple itself.
38. Wickham 2014, pp. 259–320 on the "medium elite"; specifically on this neighborhood, see pp. 124–6; 292–305. *Prior schole errariorum*: *TSMN* 6 (1025). Also *TSMN* 1 (982), 4 (1017), 5 (1018) for bronzesmiths; *TSMN* 1 (982) for an ironsmith. First appearance of the Frangipane family in the area in 1039: *TSMN* 11, with Fedele 1910, pp. 499–500.
39. Signs of gradually growing prosperity and economic activity going well back into the 10th century at Rome fit well with the current tendency to place the origins of the medieval demographic and economic boom, in Italy and beyond, well before the traditional date of c. 1000, at least in certain privileged locales. On the state of the question, see Franceschi 2017, pp. 5–9.
40. Forum of Augustus: Meneghini 2009, Meneghini and Santangeli Valenzani (eds.) 2010, pp. 149–52. Forum of Nerva: Meneghini and Santangeli Valenzani (2004), pp. 175–9; Meneghini 2009, pp. 220–1.
41. Santangeli Valenzani 2008, p. 235; Meneghini 2009, pp. 211–12. On the dating of S. Basilio, see Ch. 4, n. 57.
42. Meneghini and Santangeli Valenzani 2007, pp. 144–50; Meneghini 2009, pp. 215–19; Santangeli Valenzani 2011a, pp. 58–60.
43. Meneghini and Santangeli Valenzani 2007, pp. 151–3; Meneghini 2009, pp. 212–15. The pottery used for the fill may have come from Monte Testaccio. Recent excavations at the Nuovo Mercato di Testaccio indicate that the mountain of potsherds was being selectively mined for materials suitable for construction projects from the 4th century into the 18th: see De Luca and Serlorenzi 2015, p. 500.
44. *Campus* of Kaloleus: Santangeli Valenzani 2008, pp. 244–5; 2011a, p. 97. Kaloleus at Alberic's *curtis* at SS. Apostoli in 942: *RS* 155; still living in 963: *RS* 93; dead by 967: *RS* 3. Property in the *campo de quondam Kaloleoni* in 1004: *SMVL* 26. Alberic's residence is said to be directly connected to SS. Apostoli also at *RF* 637 (of 1013), when the master of the house was Alberic's homonymous descendent Alberic III. *Ascesa Proti*: Meneghini 2009, p. 217. For Leo's residence *de regione quae vocatur Clivo Argentarii*, *LP* 2, p. 246.
45. The 10th-century peak of settlement in the imperial forums: Meneghini 2009, p. 219. Abandonment and degradation at forums of Caesar and Nerva, respectively: Meneghini and Santangeli Valenzani

46. Virgili and Battistelli 1999, pp. 252–3. Flood of 860: *LP* 2, pp. 153–4.
47. The neighborhood appears as *scorticlaro* already in 998 (*RF* 425), and consistently thereafter as *scorticlari, scorticlarios, scorticlaria*, etc. *RF* 426 (998) names two churches, one dedicated to Mary and the other to Benedict, inside the Terme Alessandrine; both were the object of a property dispute with the priests of the nearby church of S. Eustachio, eventually resolved in favor of Farfa. Elsewhere, these churches are described as a single monastic oratory dedicated to Mary, Benedict, and Blaise, e.g. *RF* 425 (998); *RF* 616 (1011); *RF* 652 (1011). In 1011, another oratory dedicated to the Savior located "by or inside the Terme Alessandrine" (*iuxta thermas alexandrinas vel deintus*) was given to Farfa. A third nearby church dedicated to S. Symeon appears at *RF* 506 (1017). Houses surrounded by or constructed within antique structures: *RF* 658 (1012): *domo maiori solorata scandolicia undique a muro antiquo circumclusa*; *RF* 667 (1013): *idest domum unam soloratam, in ruinis positam*; *RF* 506 (1017) refers to a site with "ancient walls suitable for building a house" (*in qua stare videntur parietini ad domum faciendam*); in the same document we also find the *curtis* installed in a single chamber of the baths, next to which was another grand vaulted space called a *triclinium*, both clearly said to be located inside the baths themselves: *Idest terram cum parietinis antiquis qui sunt triclinia duo, unum sinino opere coopertum et aliud in quo est domus et curtis cum puteo aquae vivae, et arboribus ficulnearum, et arcu qui est aedificatus in ipsis parietinis … Positas romae regione nona in scorticlari intra thermas alexandrinas*. On the dimensions of Nero's bath complex (a rectangle measuring roughly 200 × 170m), which had been reconstructed under Alexander Severus (r. 222–35), whence the name, see *LTUR* 4, pp. 60–2.
48. Hubert 1990, pp. 74–83; 142–3 already stressed the comparable density of settlement in the Campus Martius relative to other parts of the city in the 10th and 11th centuries. A few examples of large areas of open land, pasturage, cultivated fields, etc.: *RF* 441 (the open expanse inside the stadium of Domitian itself, donated to Farfa in 999); *RF* 524 (1019; an undeveloped and apparently extensive *terra* next to another such *terra*); *RF* 658 (1012; a *terra sementaricia*). For the documents in the archive of S. Maria in Via Lata detailing the creation of contiguous housing lots on the land of SS. Ciriaco e Nicola, see *SMVL* 41, 42, 43 (all of 1019); 74 (1042) records the renewal of a lease on another recently built house in the same area. On this initiative, and the broader phenomenon of planned 'housing developments' on the lands of great proprietors to which it belongs, see e.g. Hubert 1990, pp. 134–41; 2001, pp. 163–8; Santangeli Valenzani 2011a, pp. 91–2 (also for the parallels with the forums of Caesar and Trajan); Wickham 2014, pp. 129–31.
49. For the 10th- and 11th-century levels at the Crypta Balbi, with their relative lack of signs of activity of any kind, graves and ceramics apart, see L. Vendittelli 2004; 2010. On the locations of 10th-century *curtes* belonging to Rome's leading aristocrats, see Santangeli Valenzani 2008; 2011a, pp. 93–7; cf. also the maps plotting the locations of all early medieval housing known from both texts and archaeology in Coates-Stephens 1996, at pp. 240–3, where again the Tiber Bend is conspicuously empty. On the Aventine as an important zone of aristocratic settlement through the 10th century, see Hubert 1990, esp. pp. 181–4; Santangeli Valenzani 2015a, pp. 140–1.
50. First attestation of the name *via Pontificalis* in 1017: *RF* 506, p. 217. On the earlier growth of the Vatican neighborhood and the building of the Leonine Wall, see Ch. 4.
51. For the vast constellation of properties, in and around the *civitas Leonina* and elsewhere, that Leo IV gave to the St. Peter's-adjacent monastery of S. Martino alone in 854, see *CSPV* 2. The convent of SS. Ciriaco e Nicola in Via Lata is one example of a religious foundation elsewhere in the city that owned substantial properties in the area; see *SMVL* 36 (1014); *SMVL* 72 (1042); *SMVL* 152 (1129). Houses ranged two rows deep against the façade of the atrium at St. Peter's: *CSPV* 10 (1030); houses two deep along the *porticus maior* at the *burgo Saxonorum*, and a house facing onto the main road with two shops in the portico itself: *CSPV* 12 (1041). *CSPV* 13 (1043) shows another house directly attached (*coniuncta*) to the portico, with a shop in the portico. Another house adjoining the *porticus maior* appears in *SMVL* 36 (1014). On the topography and economy of the region generally, see Wickham 2014, pp. 134–41.
52. *SMVL* 36 (1014) mentions the one *domus solarata* with a tile roof. Roofs and/or external staircases in wood: *CSPV* 10 (1030; roof and stairs); *CSPV* 12 (1041; roof of *domus terrinea*); *CSPV* 13 (1043; roofs of two *domus solaratae*, one with stairs).
53. The Vatican neighborhood also lacks mentions of undeveloped plots strewn with (ancient) stone rubble reusable as building material, which occasionally appear

across the Tiber: e.g. *RF* 761 (1042; a *terram vacantam cum tufo infra se* by the Terme Alessandrine).

54. On the urban fabric of Trastevere in the 10th and 11th centuries, see Annoscia, De Mincis and Taviani 2010, esp. pp. 188–93. For the foundation of SS. Cosma e Damiano *in mica aurea* in 936–44, see Santangeli Valenzani 2008, pp. 241–2. Its archive preserves a few valuable documents relating to central Trastevere in the period prior to 1050. See *CDMA* 34 (1029) for a house bordered by a crypt and two open plots (*terra*); the neighboring proprietors included a shoemaker and a blacksmith; in *CDMA* 51 (1046), there is a crypt bordered on two sides by other crypts. In 1005, the cloister walls of the monastery continued to be surrounded by gardens, pastures, and orchards (Pflugk Harttung 1881–3, vol. 2, no. 93, p. 57; there were some houses as well), as they still were in 1049 (*CDMA* 52). Floating water mills on the Tiber: *CDMA* 1 (948/49; on the Tiber Island, called the *insula lycaonia* in the Middle Ages); *SMVL* 6b (974); *SMVL* 54 (1029; a mill flanked on both sides by other mills); *CDMA* 38 (1033; another mill bracketed by others, on the Trastevere side). On these mills, and their increasing importance as the last aqueducts failed (most critically the Aqua Traiana), see Squatriti 1998, pp. 126–59; Meneghini and Santangeli Valenzani 2004, pp. 129–32. The earliest textual evidence for floating mills comes from Procopius (*Wars* 5.19.19–28), who describes how, in 537, after the Goths cut the Aqua Traiana and thus stopped the mills on the Janiculum, Belisarius devised a system of floating mills on boats strung across the Tiber. Fishponds: e.g. *PSMT* 4 (1063), mentioning three contiguous *piscariae* along the riverbank near the Ponte Rotto.

55. S. Maria Antiqua atrium: Osborne 1987, pp. 200–19 (there is also evidence of a second campaign of frescoes executed apparently in the 11th century). There are, to be sure, other bits and pieces of church decoration from the 10th and early 11th centuries; I single out for mention S. Maria Antiqua and the fresco fragment from the Colosseum because they plausibly relate to 'new' foundations – to a new phase of occupation at S. Maria Antiqua, and perhaps to the construction of a new church by the Colosseum. The rest consist mainly of frescoes, often limited in extent, added to older churches, among them S. Saba, S. Maria in Via Lata, SS. Quirico e Giulitta, S. Adriano in the Forum, S. Clemente, and (probably) S. Urbano alla Caffarella, if Bordi and others are right to place the interior redecoration of this converted Roman temple outside the walls near the Via Appia early rather than late in the 11th century (see Bordi 2016d, p. 41, with further bibliography cited there). In addition to Bordi 2016d, pp. 39–43, see also Osborne 2004 for a partial inventory of these 10th- and 11th-century initiatives. A fragmentary inscription applied to an ancient architrave now at S. Sabina records a restoration undertaken by Theodora, wife of Theophylact, in the early 10th century, of what was probably a church, perhaps SS. Alessio e Bonifacio on the Aventine: see Santangeli Valenzani 2015a, pp. 139–40.

56. Even at the Lateran, the dominant focus of papal patronage in the 10th century, little of note occurred after Sergius III. John IX (r. 914–28) restored the venerable *Acheiropoieta* icon of Christ, and possibly repainted some rooms in the Lateran palace, if Benedict of Soracte is to be believed. John XII (r. 955–64) installed a small oratory *cum* sacristy inside the southern end of the entrance portico of the basilica. John XIII (r. 965–72) installed the cathedral's first known bell, which he christened *Iohannes*(!); there is no way of knowing whether this bell was housed in a solid belfry or some sort of wooden scaffold. All these interventions, including those away from the Lateran, are listed in the recent synthesis of Giorgia Pollio (2016), an accomplished 10th-century specialist who is attempting to be exhaustive! On the structural repairs to the Lateran basilica, see also *KSRM* 2, pp. 29–30, with *VZ* 3, pp. 368–71 on Sergius's repairs to the basilica and endowment of furnishings as listed in the *Descriptio Lateranensis Ecclesiae*. Gandolfo 2016, pp. 258–9 doubts that the tomb or monument to John XIII was a papal commission, in which case the number of plausible 10th-century papal commissions outside the Lateran drops to two.

57. The other three, all likewise founded in or shortly after Alberic's time, are S. Maria in Pallara (by Petrus *medicus*), the subsidiary of Subiaco in the *curtis* at Porta Maggiore discussed above, and (probably) S. Lorenzo in Miranda (was Miranda the name of the noble foundress?) at the temple of Antoninus and Faustina in the Forum. When we see that Benedetto *campanino* personally chose the abbot of his new community (*RF* 439), the suspicion grows that these monasteries were, first and foremost, vehicles for the prosecution of family politics under a different guise, as Santangeli Valenzani has noted (2011b, pp. 279–80). The essential studies on all these foundations are now Santangeli Valenzani 2011b and 2015. On the architectural evolution and surviving remains of SS. Cosma e Damiano in Mica Aurea, see Barclay Lloyd and Bull-Simonsen Einaudi 1998.

58. *Domus* bought by Louis II: Hubert 1990, p. 183; Meneghini and Santangeli Valenzani 2004, p. 41; the

document is now at last published in a critical edition: see A. Pratesi and P. Cherubini (eds.), *Liber Instrumentorum seu Chronicon Monasterii Casaurensis* (*FSI, Rerum Italicarum Scriptores*, 3rd series, 14, vol. 3; Rome, 2018). *Curtis* at Largo Argentina: Meneghini and Santangeli Valenzani 2004, pp. 41–4; Santangeli Valenzani 2011a, pp. 86–7. Santangeli Valenzani 1994 presents numerous archival photos of the early medieval remains excavated in the 1920s. On the dating of the features associated with the first phase of the church, see De Nuccio 2002.

59. S. Maria in Campo Carlèo: Meneghini 1992; Meneghini 2001, pp. 164–5. S. Lorenzo *de ascesa*: Meneghini 2009, p. 217. Churches *de curte, in curtis*, etc.: Santangeli Valenzani 2008, pp. 232–3. Alberic himself seems to have used the venerable (6th-century) church of SS. Apostoli as kind of *curtis*-chapel for his nearby residence, making public appearances and holding assemblies there (Santangeli Valenzani 2015a, pp. 142–4).

60. On *incastellamento* in Lazio, Toubert 1973 (pp. 303–68 and *passim*) remains fundamental; see also the updated perspective in Wickham 2014, pp. 42–52. For the rest, see Hubert 1990, pp. 179–89; Santangeli Valenzani 2008 and 2015.

61. Along with the sources cited in the preceding note, see Marazzi 2001, pp. 53–66; Manacorda 2006; Di Santo 2009, pp. 28–9; 33–43 for different facets, social and topographical, of the fragmentation of Rome's residential fabric and the appearance of more closed (and fortified) residential paradigms. For the earliest attested private towers in the later 11th century, see Hubert 1990, pp. 184–9; Carpegna Falconieri 1994; Yawn 2016, pp. 88–92.

6 1046–1230

1. The removal of the papacy and the cardinalate from the purview of the local nobility accompanied other critical initiatives that had dramatic and lasting impact. A conciliar decree of 1059, aimed at excluding lay interference in papal elections, put the responsibility for selecting new popes exclusively in the hands of the cardinal bishops, soon to be joined by cardinal priests and deacons. It was the beginning of the College of Cardinals as we know it now, as an exalted coterie of princes of the Church who serve as its governing body and executive council. Other priorities of the reformers given legal substance at the council of 1059, and repeated elsewhere, included the enforcement of clerical celibacy, and vigorous prohibitions against the sale of Church offices, and against lay investiture of ecclesiastics. The protocols and administrative structures of the Catholic Church as they exist today, its autonomous governing structures and its ecumenical pretensions, too, were largely born of the sweeping restructuring accomplished during the first century of the reform period. On the first of the German reform popes, Clement II, including the events leading up to his election in 1046, Gresser 2007; decree of 1059: Jasper 1986; College of Cardinals: Klewitz 1957, pp. 9–134. Broader overviews of the reform movement: Goez 2000 and Stroll 2012, among many others.

2. On the near-exclusion of Romans from the upper levels of Church administration from the mid-11th century, and the redrawing of the Roman nobility's social and political horizons that this shift entailed, see Carocci 2006, esp. pp. 17–25; also, e.g., Brezzi 1947, pp. 221–40; Toubert 1973, pp. 1038–68.

3. On all of the preceding, Blumenthal 1988, esp. pp. 45–113, is a fine starting point; see also Stroll 2012.

4. Gregory VII himself expounded his vision of papal supremacy in the Roman imperial mold in the *Dictatus papae*, a list of 27 brief propositions, included in the Register of his letters for the year 1075, that shaped prevailing conceptions of papal sovereignty for centuries to come (Caspar ed., *Das Registrum Gregors VII*, vol. 1, pp. 201–8). Notable studies on Gregory's life and works include Cowdrey 1998 and Blumenthal 2001. On Guibert/Clement III, the longest reigning and most formidable of the antipopes, who was in control at Rome for most of the period 1084–99, see also Ziese 1982.

5. See Carocci 2006, pp. 17–25; Wickham 2014, pp. 28–33 and 245–6, both indebted to the pioneering work of Laura Moscati on the rising, urban-based 'new' nobility (Moscati 1980, esp. pp. 121–51). On the rural possessions of the old nobility, see also Toubert 1973, 1026–31.

6. On the end of the aqueducts, see above, Ch. 5, n. 2. As pleasant and useful an amenity as aqueduct water was, however, it bears recalling that the eastern half of the city, like the rest, teemed with cisterns, wells, and springs – the end of the aqueducts did not preclude access to potable water, in short. See Squatriti 1998, p. 22 on the importance of wells already in the early Middle Ages, when more of the aqueducts still functioned, with the distribution map of known early medieval wells in Coates-Stephens 2003a, p. 93. Hamilton 2003 prudently questions whether the effects of the Norman descent on Rome in 1084 were as catastrophic as contemporaries tended to claim, but certainly there

were significant episodes of burning and destruction on the Caelian, as for example at SS. Quattro Coronati, where new signs of catastrophic fire damage have recently turned up in connection with the paleo-Christian baptistery (Barelli, Pugliese, and Sadori 2007–8, pp. 92–3).

7. Essential salt-pans at the mouth of the Tiber: Wickham 2014, pp. 100–9. On Rome's expanding commerce and the merchants who spread across the Tyrrhenian coasts of Italy and S. France, especially from the 12th century, see, e.g., Moscati 1980, pp. 153–73; Maire Vigueur 2001, pp. 128–32; and on the attractions of the Capitoline from the mid 12th century, Maire Vigueur 2010, pp. 38–44.

8. Regarding the growing topographical pull of the Vatican *borgo* and its effect on settlement in contiguous regions, cf. Wickham 2014, pp. 137–40; Paravicini Bagliani 2015.

9. On the spatial distribution of the families mentioned, see Moscati 1980, pp. 128–40; also Wickham 2014, pp. 220–77.

10. Hubert 1990, pp. 70–4; 86–96; Hubert 2001, pp. 176–8; Carpegna Falconieri 2014; Wickham 2014, pp. 120–2; also pp. 259–320 for in-depth discussion of the social and economic matrix of various *rioni*.

11. Dating and forms of thick- and sparse-glazed wares: Paroli 1990; Romei 2001.

12. All of the preceding is based on the data plotted in Rascaglia and Russo 2015, a valuable synthesis of recorded urban find-spots of glazed ceramics datable between c. 800 and the end of the Middle Ages; my chronological distribution maps are all based on theirs. For more on the forms and typological evolution of thick- and sparse-glazed wares, see Romei 1992; Mazzucato 1993. On the new types that prevailed from the 13th century on, see the relevant contributions in Ricci and Vendittelli (eds.) 2010; Panuzzi 2011.

13. Rascaglia and Russo 2015, pp. 205–10.

14. The sources of the dated tower contracts are as follows: *CDMA* 70 (1069); *PSMT* 6 (1073); *SMCM* 17 (1076); *SMVL* 115 (1086); *ibid.* 121 (1094); *SMCM* 28 (1117); *SMVL* 152 (1129); *Annales Camaldulenses* vol. 3, appendix, n. 271 (1145); Archivio Storico Capitolare, Archivio Orsini II A 13, marzo, 4 (1149); *SMVL* 185 (1155); *SMCM* 60 (1192). Note that the large majority of these towers are located in Trastevere and the Campus Martius. On the underrepresentation of towers in the documentary record, cf. Carpegna Falconieri 1994, p. 6.

15. Hubert 1990, pp. 179–89 is characteristically clear and concise on the new residential forms and towers that emerged after c. 1050. Yawn 2016 is good on the political and social context of the initial move toward fortified residences and towers in the later 11th century; cf. also Hubert 1990, p. 180. Cadalus in 1062: *LP* 2, p. 337; the tower was later destroyed by Gregory VII (*LP* 2, p. 362), who thus had his revenge on Cencius for abducting him from Christmas mass in 1075, on which see *LP* 2, p. 282. Urban II in 1093/94: Brezzi 1947, pp. 274–5; Yawn 2016, p. 92. Frangipane towers and fortified houses: Hubert 1990, pp. 188–9; for the tower in the Circus Maximus they acquired in 1145, *Annales Camaldulenses*, vol. 3, p. 289 and appendix, n. 271.

16. Though Katermaa-Ottela 1981 has been caught in various errors (see, e.g., Bianchi 1998, pp. 31–2; 50; 256), her attempt to catalog and date all towers known both from physical remains and written sources remains the most complete accounting available (the digital *Forma Urbis* project cited below at n. 19 deals only with physical remains). The chronological panorama she presents, while undoubtedly imprecise, is plausible in its general outlines. On early towers before c. 1150 as only occasional refuges, see Hubert 1990, pp. 185–6; broadly on the transformation of ancient monuments into medieval fortresses, di Santo 2009.

17. Hubert 1990, pp. 185–9. See Katermaa-Ottela 1981, pp. 22–69 for the chronological accounting of tower foundations, with the summary tables at p. 70. On the *casatorre*-paradigm outside of Rome, see e.g. Settia 1986.

18. On all of these facts and figures, see Giannini 2016, pp. 297–304.

19. "Capocci" towers: Bianchi 1998, pp. 3–98; Torre dei Grassi: *ibid.*, pp. 213–35; Torre del Papito: *ibid.*, pp. 243–96. For the Torre dei Margana, Torre della Scimmia/degli Scapucci, Torre del Grillo, Torre dei Borgia, and all the rest, refer to the medieval *Forma Urbis* database hosted by the University of Rome "Tor Vergata": http://archeologiamedievale.uniroma2.it/progetti/roma-medievale/ . On the Torre delle Milizie, Tor de' Conti, and their surroundings, see Meneghini 2009, pp. 221–5; also Bernacchio and Meneghini 1994 for full architectural analysis of the Torre delle Milizie; and Cusanno 1988 on the Tor de' Conti. Carocci 1993b, p. 171 makes the case that both were built by the Conti family upon Innocent III becoming pope.

20. Magister Gregorius, *Narracio de mirabilibus urbis Romae*, c. 1: *Vehemencius igitur admirandam censeo tocius Urbis inspectionem, ubi tanta seges turrium, tot edificia palatiorum, quot nulli hominum contigit enumerare*. The towers seen by Master Gregory would also have included dozens of church bell-

towers, which started to proliferate in the 12th century (see below), thus with a few generations' delay relative to those of the nobility. Destruction of towers by Brancaleone: Matthew Paris, *Chronica Majora*, vol. 5, p. 709: *Brancaleo, videns insolentiam et superbiam nobelium romanorum non posse aliter reprimi nisi castra eorum, quae erant quasi spoliatorum carceres, prosternerentur, dirui fecit eorundem nobilium turres circiter centum et quadraginta*, with Dupré Theseider 1952, pp. 47–9; Carocci 1993a, pp. 37–8. For discussion of *incastellamento*, see above, Ch. 5, at n. 60.

21. See generally Carpegna Falconieri 1994; the rapid decline in donations by noble families to the Church after c. 1050 was already well seen by Moscati 1980, pp. 108–9. For more on the *contrade* and their eventual amalgamation into larger regions (*rioni*), the latter all first attested between the 10th and 12th centuries, see Carpegna Falconieri 2014.

22. Over 150 houses in 1194: *SMCM* 62.

23. For the situation in the 12th and 13th centuries, see Hubert 1990, pp. 138–66. Earliest party wall in 1199: *SMCM* 66. The extant remains of house-porticoes are surveyed in Pensabene 2008. In some especially prestigious areas, the formation of continuous files of houses was well under way already in the 13th century: along the final stretch of the Via Lata at Piazza Venezia, for example, recent archaeological investigations have shown that rows of contiguous, apparently multistory dwellings began to form early in the 13th century, and were largely complete by century's end: see Saguì and Serlorenzi 2008, pp. 189–91.

24. On S. Maria de Portico, later known as S. Galla, see Barclay Lloyd 1981 and Acconci 1991, and on the inscription, Riccioni 2005; Blennow 2011, pp. 19–26. It appears as *Santa Maria de lo Portico* as early as 1108 (Hülson 1927, pp. 359–60). S. Maria in Cappella: Hülsen 1927, pp. 322–3; Blennow 2011, pp. 35–9.

25. S. Pudenziana: Gandolfo 2016, p. 261. S. Cecilia: *KSRM* 1, pp. 227–9; Blennow 2011, pp. 27–35. A striking total of seven new altars was consecrated at S. Cecilia in the period 1073–98, during the years when Desiderius was first cardinal priest (from 1059) and then pope (Urban II, r. 1088–99). S. Cosimato: *KSRM* 1, p. 248; S. Biagio alla Pagnotta: *KSRM* 1, pp. 177–8.

26. On the S. Clemente frescoes, see *PMR* 4, pp. 120–50; also the thought-provoking study of Yawn 2012, with the ample prior bibliography cited there. The dating of the frescoes at S. Urbano alla Caffarella is disputed, though they are almost certainly of the 11th century. There is a growing tendency to place them earlier than the 1080s or 1090s, where Noreen 2001 and others before her wanted them, possibly as early as 1011 (Bordi 2016d, p. 41), or maybe closer to mid-century (Romano 2012); in any case, the point about medium elite patrons stands.

27. On the (mutually reinforcing) congeries of ceremony and symbols, images and architecture deployed by 12th-century popes, see (among many others) Stroll 1991; Claussen 1992, pp. 99–118; Herklotz 2000; Twyman 2002; Paravacini Bagliani 2005; *PMR* 4, pp. 163–82; also the sources cited below at n. 43. Herklotz has called the enhanced symbolic and ceremonial repertoire of the reform papacy after the mid-11th century a "theatrical production of what was claimed in the Donation of Constantine" (2000, p. 32).

28. S. Adriano: *KSRM* 1, pp. 20–38. As for S. Bartolomeo in Isola, a foundation date of 1113 is indicated by a dedicatory inscription of that year preserved over the central doorway, assuming it relates to the completion of the extant church, the next written mention of which comes only in the 1160s. See *KSRM* 1, pp. 132–67, esp. pp. 146–9, where Claussen tentatively inclines in favor of the earlier construction date; on the archaeological indicators, see Di Manzano, Cecchelli, and Milella 2006–7. S. Maria in Monticelli: Hülsen 1927, pp. 349–50. The *LP* (2, p. 305) reports that Paschal II consecrated it; Innocent II reconsecrated it in 1143, according to an inscription still extant in the church.

29. S. Gregorio Magno: *KSRM* 3, pp. 187–213, esp. 189–90 on the date. SS. Quattro Coronati: Barelli 2009. The original church occupied an existing apsidal hall by 400 or so; it was rebuilt under Leo IV in the mid-9th century. On cosmatesque pavements and Rome's later medieval *marmorarii* in general, see Glass 1980; Claussen 1987; Del Bufalo 2010. Pavements from the first half of the 12th century, before the appearance of the Cosmati family, are technically "pre-cosmatesque."

30. On the dating of the church and its probable completion within the lifetime of Anastasius, see Barclay Lloyd 1986; *KSRM* 1, pp. 302–4. Cosmati pavement: *KSRM* 1, pp. 316–25; choir: pp. 325–33; throne, pp. 342–3.

31. Hélène Toubert's treatment of the mosaic is still essential (Hubert 1970, pp. 122–54); see also Riccioni 2006; *PMR* 4, pp. 209–18. The acanthus scrolls clearly echo those in the right-hand apse in the atrium of the Lateran baptistery; and similar figures of shepherds, birds, etc. also appear in the Lateran baptistery, on which see *PMR* 1, pp. 348–57. The Lateran apse featured a cross of life (*PMR* 6, pp. 53–4), but still closer parallels to the central cross are those extant in the apses of S. Pudenziana, S. Stefano Rotondo, and SS. Nereo ed Achilleo.

32. For the new wing of the palace with the frescoes of Callixtus II, see esp. Herklotz 2000, pp. 95–158; also Stroll 1991, pp. 16–34. In the adjacent chapel of St. Nicholas of Myra, Innocent II would later (c. 1140) depict Emperor Lothar II as a vassal receiving his crown by concession of the pope, with an accompanying inscription proclaiming as much, all of which infuriated Barbarossa when he saw it in the 1150s (Rahewin, *Gesta Federici* 3.10, with Stroll 1991, pp. 188–92). On S. Maria in Cosmedin, see Giovenale 1927; Stroll 1991, pp. 2–15. Two altars were consecrated by Callixtus II in 1123, presumably when the restoration project was at least well under way (Blennow 2011, pp. 65–72). S. Nicola in Carcere: Palombi 2006; and on the inscription commemorating the consecration of the church in 1128, Blennow 2011, pp. 88–92.

33. S. Crisogono: *KSRM* 1, pp. 386–411; Claussen 2016, pp. 283–5; and on the two surviving consecrative inscriptions of 1123 (an oratory) and 1127 (an altar), both mentioning John of Crema as patron, Blennow 2011, pp. 76–88. On the symbolic and conceptual implications of the ostentatious reuse of ancient *spolia* in the 12th century, see also Kinney 2011.

34. Another project worth mentioning is the massive, arcaded transverse wall running the length of the transept at S. Paul's – essentially a kind of second triumphal arch, richly decorated in fresco – that was inserted to stabilize the structure and facilitate reroofing, probably under the antipope Anacletus II (r. 1130–8); see Camerlenghi 2018, pp. 153–9. The extant churches aside, a further sign of the frenetic activity of the years c. 1110–30 is the number of preserved inscriptions recording ecclesiastical patronage (consecrations of churches, and altars, chapels, etc. added to existing churches) – the twelve that Blennow (2011, pp. 234–5) counts for the years 1110–29 are the most of any twenty-year span in the period she covers (1050–1263); with the exception of the years 1240–59, no other twenty-year period comes close. S. Maria in Trastevere: Kinney 1975 and 1986; also Di Fazio 2014, and on the mosaics of the apse and triumphal arch, *PMR* 4, pp. 305–11. For the alternative hypothesis, see Perchuk 2016, whose arguments, while not conclusive, are cogent and appealing. S. Maria Nova/S. Francesca Romana: *KSRM* 1, pp. 466–87; also *PMR* 4, pp. 335–43 for the mosaics.

35. Priester 1990, *passim* (for her proposal that the first towers appeared after 1120, starting with S. Maria in Cosmedin, see esp. pp. 71–3). Nicoletta Giannini has been kind enough to discuss the earlier bell towers with me, and to explain her convincing reasons for dating them before 1100 (in addition to their technical characteristics, these towers have stratigraphic relationships with later constructions, frescoes, etc. of the – earlier – 12th century, which they must predate). A full presentation of the data will have to await the publication of Giannini's online digital *Forma Urbis* of medieval Rome and its accompanying volume, which are expected to appear by 2021 (http://archeologiamedievale.uniroma2.it/progetti/roma-medievale/). On the vanished towers at S. Valentino and S. Biagio alla Pagnotta, see de Blaauw 1993, pp. 372–3.

36. Quoted passage at Priester 1990, p. 10. Placement of towers: *ibid.* pp. 11–13; dimensions and heights: pp. 15–16, with table I on p. 299.

37. Stephens II's bells at St. Peter's: *LP* 1, p. 454: *beatissimus papa fecit super basilicam beati Pertri apostoli turrem, quam ex parte inauravit et ex parte argento investivit, in quo tribus posuit campanis, qui clero et populum ad officium Dei invitarent*, with de Blaauw 1993, pp. 371–2, *contra CBCR* 5, p. 175, where a wooden structure on the roof is envisioned. Leo IV's bells at S. Andrea: *LP* 2, p. 119. Lateran bell christened in 968 by John XIII: Pollio 2016, p. 249. The tower at the Lateran struck by lightning in 1118 (*LP* 2, p. 301) would then almost certainly be a full-fledged *campanile* rather than a simple early medieval-type wooden belfry – Priester (1990, p. 61), de Blaauw (1993, p. 373), and Claussen (*KSRM* 2, p. 90) are all inclined to agree. On the remains of the late-8th-century tower inside the monastic enclosure at St. Paul's, see Spera, Esposito, and Giorgi 2011, p. 20; I thank Lucrezia Spera for discussing with me the excavators' conclusions about the structure's function.

38. On the origins of bell towers and their early incarnations in Italy before 1100, see Priester 1990, pp. 115–80 (again, however, she downplays the evidence for masonry towers at Rome before c. 1100); Trevisan 2007. For the seven Roman towers apparently datable on the basis of literary or epigraphic testimony, see Priester 1990, pp. 62–3 and 212–97; on the rest, pp. 64–9 and table IV on p. 304. Regarding Rome's relative slowness to adopt bell towers, and the surge in tower-building after the 1120s/1130s, see Priester 1990, pp. 70–6 and 189–210 (she, too, inclines toward seeing them as manifestations of the pride and power of the reform Church in the period after 1122, as does Claussen 1992, pp. 117–18). More recently, Claussen's grand survey of churches c. 1050–1300 (*KSRM* vols. 1–3) carefully addresses the evidence for bell towers at the

churches it currently covers, pending the much-anticipated appearance of the final volumes.

39. On bells and the Roman soundscape, see esp. de Blaauw 1993; also Atkinson 2016, much of whose discussion of the immersive aural presence of bells in late medieval Florence applies, *mutatis mutandis*, to Rome already from the later 12th century on. On the new Senatorial palace on the Capitoline, already functioning by 1151, see below. Whether it had bells from the beginning is unknown. After 1200, its bell was the famous Patarina taken as booty from Viterbo; and popular assemblies in the piazza fronting the palace are regularly said to be convened to the sound of tolling bells from the 1230s on: see *Codice Diplomatico* 75 (1233); 81 (1235); 84 (1235); 128 (1255); 136 (1257). On the architectural and decorative refinements of the Roman *campanili*, see Priester 1990, pp. 18–51.

40. Guidobaldi 2014, *passim*, on all the preceding points.

41. Smoothing and infilling of collapsed vaults of the Hadrianic auditoriums: Serlorenzi 2010, p. 149. On the new houses that began to rise on both sides of the Via Lata in the later 12th century, and to meld into continuous rows over the course of the 13th, see Saguì and Serlorenzi 2008, pp. 189–91; Serlorenzi 2010, p. 138.

42. Distribution of fill along Via delle Botteghe Oscure: Guidobaldi 2014, p. 590. On the new houses, also L. Vendittelli 2004, esp. pp. 223–7; and for other examples of new housing built atop the new layers of fill, for example near S. Cosimato in Trastevere and in Via Capodiferro in the Campus Martius, see Giannini 2015, pp. 26–7. Centrality of Lateran–Vatican axis in terms of settlement and viability: Hubert 1990, p. 106.

43. Cf. Guidobaldi 2014, pp. 599–603; Giannini 2015, pp. 24–5. For more on papal ceremonial and the processional routes, see Schimmelpfennig 1992 and 2006; Herklotz 2000, pp. 41–57 (with particular emphasis on the Lateran complex and its role as starting and finishing point of processional ceremonies); Wickham 2014, pp. 321–84; Paravicini Bagliani 2015a and 2015b. On the *via Pontificalis* in particular, and the abandonment of the old Via Triumphalis by papal processions, see also Dey 2020b. The Via Triumphalis is still indicated as the route for the Christmas Eve procession from S. Anastasia to St. Peter's in canon Benedict's *ordo* of c. 1143 (*LC* 2, p. 145), but is totally absent from the next Roman *ordines* of 1189 and 1192 (Cardinal Albinus' *Gesta pauperis scholaris*, of 1189: *LC* 2, pp. 87–137; and the *Ordo Romanus* of Cencius *camerarius*, of 1192: *LC* 1, pp. 290–316). First appearance of the name *via Pontificalis*, in 1017: *RF* 506.

44. S. Crisogono and Trastevere: Guidobaldi 2014, pp. 591–2; 598.

45. Ground levels at Piazza Venezia: Serlorenzi 2010, p. 138; Crypta Balbi: L. Vendittelli 2010, pp. 18–19. The situation at S. Crisogono is apparent at a glance.

46. Important recent contributions on the formation of the commune and the identity of the Romans who brought it into being and governed it include Maire Vigueur 2001; Wickham 2014, at e.g. pp. 220–77; Wickham 2015, pp. 119–60. Brezzi 1947, pp. 317–39 is still worth reading.

47. On the politics of communal building projects, see the excellent Baumgärtner 1989 and 2004. Senate's letter of 1149: *Codice Diplomatico* 5, p. 5: *Sciatis praeterea quia pontem Mulvium extra Urbem parum longe, per tempora multa pro imperatorum contrario destructum, nos, ut exercitus vester per eum transire queat, ne Petri Leonis per castellum Sancti Angeli vobis nocere possint, ut statuerant cum papa et Siculo, magno conamine restauramus et in parvi temporis spacio muro fortissimo et silicibus iuvante Deo complebitur*.

48. Continued support of the Pierleoni and Frangipane (and some other leading families) for the papacy against the upstart supporters of the commune: Moscati 1980, pp. 141–3; Ellis 1998; Wickham 2014, p. 434. The one prominent exception in the early years of the commune was Giordano Pierleoni, brother of Innocent II's sworn enemy Anacletus II; he supported the Senate from the beginning, probably for readily imaginable personal reasons, and replaced Innocent's urban prefect as *patricius* of Rome in 1144 (Moscati 1980, pp. 143–6). New senatorial palace: *Codice Diplomatico* 11: *in Capitolio, in consistorio novo palatii in renovationis vero seu restaurationis sacri senatus anno . vii*. On the architectural history of the Senatorial Palace from the 12th century through the 15th, many particulars of which remain unknown or debated, see Pietrangeli 1960; Bedon 2008, pp. 9–23.

49. The full text of the inscription reads: R(EGIO) S(ANCTI) A(N)G(E)L(I) | ANNO MCLVII INCARNAT(IONIS) D(OMI)NI N(OST)RI IH(ES)U CHR(IST)I SPQR HEC MENIA | VETUSTATE DILAPSA RESTAURA | VIT SENATORES SASSO IOH(ANNE)S DE AL | BERICO ROIERI BUCCACANE PINZO / FILIPPO IOH(ANNE)S DE PARENZO PETRUS / D(EU)STESALVI CENCIO DE ANSOINO | RAINALDO ROMANO | NICOLA MANNETTO (Silvagni 1943, tav. XXV, no. 5). Note, however, my use of the term "recorded": while the Senate's campaign is the first since Leo IV attested by written evidence, it is beyond question that repairs to the wall were carried out at various times in the intervening 300 years, some of which are now

beginning to be identified; for examples, see Molinari and Giannini 2014 and 2015; Giannini 2016). On both the Porta Metronia inscription and that of Benedetto *Carushomo* (the latter considerably more accomplished and classicizing than the former), see now Bolle 2019, pp. 226–38. For the Church's virtual monopoly on epigraphic display at Rome until the 12th century, when other actors gradually began to assert themselves, see Annoscia 2010, esp. pp. 133–6.

50. Wall as customs barrier since its inception: Dey 2011, p. 108; Palmer 1980, pp. 219–20. I know of only four instances relating to the 5th–11th centuries, but they are unanimous. In the early 5th century, some of the take from Porta Nomentana went to S. Vitale (*LP* 1, p. 222); in the 8th century, Rome's gates were staffed by customs agents of the Church (*LD*, p. 268); in 996, half the revenues from the Porta San Paolo went to the monastery of S. Alessio on the Aventine (*RSAA* 5, p. 372); and in 1099, the Porta Nomentana reappears, this time as the property of S. Ciriaco at the Baths of Diocletian, which must mean that this church controlled the money collected there (Kehr 1900, p. 282). In the three cases where a gate is connected to a specific church, the practice seems to have been to allocate gate-dues to places located near, or along roads leading to, the gate whence the money came.

51. Treaty of 1174: *Codice Diplomatico* 29, p. 52: *liceat eis* [sc. pisanis] *omnibus libere et secure negotiari in Urbe et eius districtu sine aliqua diricatura, preter antiquam dirictturam a viginti annis retro et excepto quod de frumento senatus tollere consuevit similiter a viginti annis retro*. It goes on to specify that taxes on the goods being carried by Pisan merchants are only to be collected when they are carried inside the walls for the purpose of being sold on the urban market (*ibid*.): *salvo si per portas murorum Urbis illas vendendas portaverint, quod supra dictam tribuant dirictturam*. The communal statues of 1363 continue to presume the authority of the communal government over the gates and the revenues collected there (Bk. 2, ch. 130; see Re 1880, p. 156).

52. The first example, of 1186, approximated by most of the others, reads: *Si quis autem senator vel aliqua alia persona contra hec que prescripta sunt, aliquo modo venire temptaverit vel fecerit, incidat in penam senatui pro refectione huius inclite Urbis murorum duarum librarum auri* (Bartoloni 1948, no. 40, p. 68). Thereafter, *Codice Diplomatico* 55 (1201), 68 (2012), 70 (1214), 72 (1224), 74 (1231); 81, 83, 86 (1235), 108 (1244); and 1258, on which see Baumgärtner 2004, p. 279. For complicating factors, including occasional episodes of papal interest in the walls in the later 12th century, see Dey 2020a.

53. On all three types and their chronology and characteristics, in addition to the more detailed excursus on late medieval masonry styles below in Ch. 7, see D. Esposito 1998, esp. pp. 30–5, D. Esposito 2016; Montelli 2011, pp. 46–57; 157–71. For samples from the Aurelian Wall itself, see Mancini 2001, 65–8; Dey 2020a. For more on the peaks and valleys in maintenance and refurbishment of the Wall between the 9th century and the 15th, see Dey 2020a.

54. See *Codice Diplomatico* 18, pp. 26–7: . . . *salvo honore publico Urbis eidem colupne n[e] unquam per aliquam personam obtentu investimenti huius restitutionis diruatur aut minuatur, sed ut est ad honorem ipsius ecclesie et totius populi Romani integra et incorrupta permaneat, dum mundus durat, sic eius stante figura*, with Baumgärtner 1989, pp. 37–9. Baumgärtner 2004, pp. 285–9 discusses the communal approach to the stewardship of ancient monuments in more detail.

55. First extant sentence issued by the *Magistri edificiorum* in 1227: Fedele 1908, republished as *Codice Diplomatico* 73: *Petrus Malapilii dativus iudex, Iohannes Tineosus et Petrus Mannetti positi et constituti magistri ab amplissimo senatu et populo Romano super omnibus questionibus hedificiorum, mur[orum], dom[o] rum, viarum et platearum adque divisionum et super omnibus aliis questionibus ad officium magistratus pertinentibus* . . . For the other surviving documents pertaining to the *Magistri edificiorum*, and broadly on the organization and responsibilities of their office, see Schiaparelli 1902; Carbonetti Vendittelli 1990 and 1993. As the communal archives at Rome were lost long ago, a disproportionate number of the few communal documents that survive pertain to religious institutions, which kept copies of documents relevant to their affairs in their own archives. The Roman commune (and the *Magistri edificiorum*) devoted considerably more attention to questions involving lay proprietors, relative to ecclesiastical proprietors, than the extant texts would suggest, but the fact remains that Church property fell broadly under communal jurisdiction, even from as early as 1162 in the case of the Column of Trajan.

56. On Innocent III's works and legacy, see Sommerlechner (ed.) 2003, esp. Iacobini's chapter on his architectural commissions (pp. 1261–91), for which see also, e.g., Krautheimer 1980, pp. 203–6; Pace 2016, pp. 299–305 (also pp. 305–7 on the few major projects accomplished under Honorius III and Gregory IX). Expansion and fortification of Vatican palace: *Gesta Innocentii III*, ch. 146. Apse mosaic at St. Peter's: *PMR* 5, pp. 62–6. Innocent earmarked funds for the apse mosaic at St. Paul's (*Gesta*

Innocentii III, ch. 145) and doubtless set the project in motion, but it was still ongoing in 1218, two years after his death, under his successor Honorius III (*PMR* 5, pp. 13–15; 77–87; Camerlenghi 2018, pp. 163–6). Other initiatives of Innocent's pontificate include the renovation of the small church of SS. Sergio e Bacco in the Forum, Innocent's former titular church, and the construction of a convent at S. Sisto. On S. Lorenzo, see *KSRM* 3, pp. 317–527. The great expansion began while Cencius was still cardinal, under Innocent II, but continued well into his pontificate as Honorius III. The reign of Honorius III saw more artistic and architectural activity, much sponsored by cardinals, than those of both Innocent III and Gregory IX. Highlights include the splendid cloisters at the Lateran and St. Paul's, both by the workshop of the *marmorarius* Vassaletto (Pistilli 1991, pp. 30–41). Another important commission perhaps begun under Honorius III is the mosaics on the façade of S. Maria in Trastevere, on which see *PMR* 5, pp. 72–4. The single major project that Gregory IX is known to have sponsored in the 14 long years of his pontificate is the restoration (or complete refashioning?) of the mosaics on the façade of St. Peter's (*PMR* 5, pp. 16–17; 113–16). In sum: while some of these commissions are (or were) spectacular artistic *tours de force*, milestones in the history of medieval art and architecture that do much to illuminate the ideological and theological currents of their time, their collective impact on the cityscape was less than transformative.

57. For the evolving structures of communal government in the later 12th and early 13th centuries, see Bartoloni 1946, esp. pp. 50–65; Brezzi 1947, Maire Vigueur 2001, pp. 124–32. Giovanni Capocci: see Paravicini Bagliani in *DBI* vol. 18 (1975), pp. 596–8, with Brezzi 1947, pp. 393–401; Di Santo 2016, pp. 195–210, on the conflict between Innocent III and the partisans of the autonomous commune; the most expansive contemporary source is the *Gesta Innocentii III*, c. 125–43. On the more or less constant state of tension and conflict that persisted between papacy and commune from the mid-12th century to the mid-13th, notwithstanding a long series of (provisional and usually ephemeral) pacts and accords, cf. Brentano 1974, pp. 93–136; Carocci 1999, pp. 49–52; Maire Vigueur 2001, pp. 131–2.

58. First Vatican palace of Eugene III: *LP* 2, p. 387: *fecit unum palatium apud sanctum Petrum*. Surviving traces of Eugene's works have yet to be identified, but papal letters and other documents show him and his successors immediately starting to reside at the new residence with some frequency (Ehrle and Egger 1935, pp. 31–3; Steinke 1984, pp. 32–4). Major expansion under Innocent III: see esp. *Gesta Innocentii III*, c. 147: *Quia vero non honorabile sed utile censuit, ut summus pontifex eciam apud sanctum Petrum palacium dignum haberet, fecit ibi fieri domos istas de novo: capellaniam, cameram et capellam, panettariam, butilleriam, coquina et marescalciam; domos cancellarii, camerarii et helemosinarii; aulam autem confirmari praecepit, ac refici longiam, totumque palacium claudi muris, et super portas erigi turres*, with Steinke 1984, pp. 39–47; Monciatti 2005, pp. 96–108. Second major expansion under Nicholas III: Steinke 1984, pp. 49–66; Le Pogam 2005, pp. 62–72; Monciatti 2005, pp. 115–82. See also *PMR* 5, pp. 220–5 on the sections of the palace that preserve bits of 13th-century frescoes. According to the calculations of Le Pogam (2005, p. 16), in the years 1254–1304, the Curia was in residence at the Lateran for 1,856 days, and at the Vatican for 1,714 (both easily surpassed by the 2,679 days it spent at Orvieto and the 2,209 at Viterbo); see also Montaubin 2006, pp. 398–400 on the growing prominence of the Vatican.

59. Papal absences from Rome in the period 1198–1304, starting with Innocent III: Paravicini Bagliani 2015b, pp. 19–21; on the motives for these extended absences from the city, see also e.g. Paravicini Bagliani 2004.

60. *Ubi Papa, ibi Roma*: Paravicini Bagliani 2015b, pp. 19–21. Constriction of public papal ceremonial under Innocent III: Schimmelpfennig 1974, pp. 225–6; Paravicini Bagliani 2015b, pp. 16–19; cf. also Carpegna Falconieri 2002a, esp. pp. 235–41, who notes that already from the early 12th century, the popes and the Curia, bent on their universalizing mission, increasingly left the performance of stational liturgy in the hands of the urban clergy, the humble parish priests who came to be perceived as more and more distinct from, and inferior in dignity to, the prelates in the Curia. Papal ceremony at Avignon: Schimmelpfennig 1990. *Ordo Romanus* of Cencius *camerarius*: *LC* 1, pp. 290–316.

7 1230–1420

1. Carocci 1993a is the most exhaustive study of the Roman barons. See also (among many others) Carocci 1999, pp. 177–90; Maire Vigueur 2010, pp. 241–69; M. Vendittelli 2015, pp. 34–7. On the years around 1230 as a turning point, see, e.g., Carocci 1993a, 34–7 ("crushing hegemony" quote at p. 35); Maire Vigueur 2010, p. 217; Carbonetti Vendittelli 2015, 297. See below on the division of the cityscape into baronial zones of control.

2. On the critical support provided by popes and cardinals to baronial families, see above all Carocci 1999; also Carocci 1993a, pp. 29–34 and *passim*. Waley 1961 and Partner 1972 remain essential for the expansion and consolidation of the Papal States in the 13th century; cf. also Carocci 1999, pp. 40–6.

3. Conclave of 1292: Dupré Theseider 1952, pp. 271–3. Structural advantages enjoyed by Roman cardinals: Carocci 1999, pp. 78–83 and *passim*.

4. On the expansion of Roman territorial control in the 12th and 13th centuries, and the growing wealth urban-based nobles (and others) derived from the countryside, see Carocci and Vendittelli 2004; 2013; also, e.g., Maire Vigueur 2010, pp. 73–115. Carocci 1993a traces the rise and subsequent fortunes of all the baronial families; see also Maire Vigueur 2010, pp. 241–304. Specifically on the Orsini, the best documented of the baronial families thanks to the survival of the family archive, see also the important monograph of Allegrezza 1998.

5. On *castelli/castra* and their distribution in the Roman hinterland, see Carocci and Vendittelli 2004, pp. 23–52. On the large agricultural estates called *casali* that predominated within c. 20–25 km of the walls, *ibid.* pp. 11–22 and *passim*; D. Esposito 2005. Also centered on a fortified nucleus, they had far fewer permanent residents than most *castelli*, usually only a handful of families. Numbers of *castelli* controlled by the barons: Carocci 1999, pp. 176–7.

6. Barons in the senatorate: Carocci 1993a, p. 35; cf. Maire Vigueur 2001, pp. 132–4. On the displacement of lesser noble families, see also, e.g., Carocci and Vendittelli 2004, pp. 201–4; Maire Vigueur 2010, pp. 217–22.

7. On the growing intensity of Roman exploitation of the surrounding countryside after c. 1150, see the sources cited above at n. 4. Housing density and the *Magistri edificiorum*: see above, Ch. 6. On civic government in the later 13th century, and the senatorates of Brancaleone and Charles of Anjou, see Dupré Theseider 1952, pp. 3–254. Population estimates for late medieval Rome, which are now again rising together with scholars' appreciation of the dynamism of the Roman economy: Hubert 2008, p. 248 (40,000–80,000); Maire Vigueur 2010, pp. 36–7 (at least 50,000).

8. On demographic trends in late medieval Italy, and the stagnation that set in by the last decades of the 13th century, see the lucid synthesis of Hubert 2009; also Menant 2011, pp. 125–32; and more broadly on the causes and timing of the slowing European economy, Menant 2017. For the situation at Rome, see also Hubert 2001, pp. 142–8; Carocci and Vendittelli 2001, pp. 88–99. After an anomalously warm period c. 950–1250, which corresponds quite closely with the period of rapid population increase in Europe, temperatures began to drop steadily, reaching anomalous lows by the 15th century (Headrick 2012; Hoffmann 2014, pp. 323–9).

9. For the local causes and repercussions of the move to Avignon, see Dupré Theseider 1952, pp. 377–422; Quaglioni (ed.) 1994; Carocci and Vendittelli 2001, pp. 99–108; 2004, pp. 52–8. Among the bleak descriptions of 14th-century Rome that attribute the prevailing lawlessness and dysfunctionality of urban institutions to the depredations of the barons, see, e.g., Bartolo da Sassoferrato, *Tractatus de regimine civitatis* (ed. Quaglioni 1983, p. 152); Anonimo Romano, *Cronica*, c. 18 (ed. Porta 1981, p. 111). Maire Vigueur (2001, pp. 132–8) justly calls attention to the occasional reactions against baronial supremacy, but acknowledges nonetheless the pervasiveness of baronial influence and its damaging effects on the cohesion of the urban collective. Hubert 2001, pp. 174–5 points to abundant signs of declining population during the first half of the 14th century, even before the arrival of the Black Death.

10. Regarding the post–Black Death population figures, A. Esposito 1998, p. 38 imagines c. 20,000 following the second outbreak of plague in 1363, accepted by, e.g., Hubert 2001, p. 175; Esch 1969, p. 209 imagines "at most" 25,000 in the late 14th century. For the more optimistic minimum of c. 30,000–35,000, see Maire Vigueur 2010, pp. 36–8. Census (*Descriptio Urbis*) of 1527: Lee 1985.

11. On Cola di Rienzo and the civic politics of his era, see Musto 2003; Rehberg and Modigliani 2004. Felice Società: Maire Vigueur 2008b; 2010, pp. 352–68. For the Municipal Statutes of 1363, see below at n. 13.

12. Rollo-Koster and Izbicki (eds.) 2009 is a useful introduction to the Great Western Schism in its broad European context. Regarding the fall of the communal regime in 1398 and the failed popular revolt against Pope Boniface IX in 1399, after which lasting Curial control over municipal government was established, see Esch 1969, pp. 209–76; *id.* 2007. On the end of the schism and the return of Martin V in 1420, Esch 2016, pp. 70–80. On the myriad causes and ramifications of urban conflict at Rome in the late Middle Ages, see also Di Santo 2016.

13. Some of the most useful narrative sources include the *Vita Gregorii papae IX*, which opens a vivid window onto the Roman scene in the 1230s; the *Cronica* of Matthew Paris (Luard ed., vol. 5) for the regime of Brancaleone degli Andalò in the 1250s; the Roman-

born Saba Malaspina's *Rerum Sicularum historia*, which contains much precious information on events in Rome in the years 1250–85; the memorably vivid vernacular history (*Cronica*) of the Anonimo Romano for the second quarter of the 14th century; and, for the period 1404–17, the equally vivid, albeit less stylistically accomplished, Roman "diary" of Antonio di Pietro dello Schiavo. Roman notarial protocols: Lori Sanfilippo 1988; Nussdorfer 2016; and for a practical demonstration of the sorts of topographical information that can be gleaned from the protocols, many of which remain unpublished, Lori Sanfilippo 2001. The Municipal Statutes of 1363 are published in C. Re 1883; on the date of the compilation, see Bolgia 2017, pp. 353–5 (*contra* Carbonetti Vendittelli 1993, pp. 15–16, who proposed anticipating the date of publication to c. 1360). Dupré Theseider 1952, pp. 727–32 lists the main primary sources bearing on Roman affairs in the 13th and 14th centuries.

14. On the anonymous late 13th-century image of Rome as a lion, see Maddalo 1990, p. 22 and plate I; for the 'maps' of Fra Paolino and Pol de Limbourg, see *Le piante*, vol. 2, tavv. 143/145 and 148, respectively. More broadly on late medieval images of Rome, see Maddalò 1990; Parlato 2001; and on the cartographic revolution that began in the mid 15th century, Westfall 1974, pp. 85–92; Maier 2015, pp. 19–48.

15. On the "archaeology of architecture," see in particular the annual installments of the journal *Archeologia dell'Architettura*, born in 1996 as an offshoot of the journal *Archeologia Medievale* and still dedicated in large part to the Middle Ages.

16. For the technical characteristics of medieval *opus caementicium* with stone facings, see D. Esposito 1998, pp. 105–21.

17. As D. Esposito has said (1998, pp. 23–6), the later medieval recurrence of ancient masonry styles looks to be part and parcel of the conscious emulation and "revival" of antiquity characteristic of the later Middle Ages more broadly; cf. also D. Esposito 2015. Early examples of "*opus incertum*" in the Forum of Trajan: Meneghini 2009, pp. 225–6. A second sample of probable 11th-century *opus incertum* appears at the base of a tower near the Theater of Marcellus: see Giannini 2016, p. 301 with fig. 11 on p. 302.

18. Regarding the use of these facings in small cobbles of hard stone in nonecclesiastical architecture, see Giannini 2015, p. 28; the more ornate banded types seem to be associated in particular with leading noble families, whose taste for ostentation in their urban milieus is apparent; see Giannini 2016, pp. 301–2 (also on the Conti tower and the nearby residence in Piazza S. Francesca di Paola, which probably belonged to the Annibaldi family, close allies of the Conti at the beginning of the 13th century).

19. Montelli 2011, pp. 46–9; 158–68.

20. "Renaissance" of ancient-style brick masonry in the 12th century: Montelli 2011, pp. 46–9; and 219–25 on the use of brick in Roman *campanili* in particular, on which see also Priester 1991. On the structure and technical characteristics of the Casa dei Crescenzi, see Chiovelli 2015, with Bianchi 2015, pp. 26–31 on the inscription over the door and its bearing on the dating of the structure. Like Bianchi, Montelli 2011, pp. 43–5, and Wickham 2014, p. 237 incline toward a date in the mid-12th century, as does Rolle 2019, pp. 256–7, who makes a strong case that the patron was a senator active in the first decades after the *renovatio Senatus*. Regarding the increasing professionalism and specialization of Roman builders, cf. D. Esposito 1998, pp. 183–9; Montelli 2011, pp. 225–33; and on the complementary skills of the *muratores*, *marmorarii*, and *carpentarii*, also Lori Sanfilippo 2001, pp. 228–53.

21. Generally on the situation in the 13th century, see Barclay Lloyd 1985, pp. 238–44; Montelli 2011, pp. 50–7; D. Esposito 2015, pp. 246–9. On civil and residential buildings with external facings in brick and interiors in *tufelli*, also Bernacchio 2002, pp. 134–5. The seminal study on the new forms of *petit appareil* facings that emerged in the 13th century is D. Esposito 1998. 13th-century phases at SS. Quattro Coronati: Barelli 2012b, pp. 58–65. Savelli fortress on the Aventine: Le Pogam 2005, pp. 298–332. For the use of masonry "a tufelli" across the territory under Roman political control, the *Districtus Urbis*, see D. Esposito 1998, pp. 171–224 – the correspondence is so close that the distribution of this distinctively Roman masonry style across the 13th to 15th centuries helps to define the boundaries of the territory administered directly by the urban authorities.

22. On the sources of stone used for *tufelli* and the production of the finished product, D. Esposito 1998, pp. 121–40. Cf. Barclay Lloyd 1985, p. 242 on the apparently increasing scarcity of recyclable brick from the 13th century. On the homogeneity of the reddish tuff employed in the walls of the Rocca Savelli, see Le Pogam 2005, p. 298.

23. On the scarcity of new brick at Rome until the later 15th century, albeit with exceptions, cf. Montelli 2011, pp. 63–8; and pp. 114–28 on production of specialized forms, roof tiles, etc. in and around Rome.

24. Caetani Palace: D. Esposito 2008. Repairs to Vatican walls: D. Esposito 2015, pp. 247–48.

25. Overviews of barons' urban fortresses, which peaked in numbers, size, and sophistication from the 1260s on: Carocci 1993b and 2004; Carocci in Di Santo 2009, pp. 149–65; Maire Vigueur 2008; and specifically on the adaptation of older monuments, also Di Santo 2009.

26. On the surviving walls and other components of the 13th-century 'castle' at the Torre delle Milizie, which passed first from the Conti to the Annibaldi before it went to the Caetani, see Bernacchio and Meneghini 1994, pp. 32–6; Di Santo 2009, pp. 76–80; also Di Santo 2016, pp. 204–9 more generally on the residences of the allied Conti and Annibaldi families in the area. Tor de' Conti: Meneghini 2009, pp. 224–25; Carocci (1999, p. 112; in Di Santo 2009, pp. 152–3) is more certain than Meneghini that both the first phase of the Torre delle Milizie and the Tor de' Conti were built with funding and crucial support from Innocent III Conti in the first years of the 13th century. Frangipane and Annibaldi at the Colosseum: Di Santo 2009, pp. 103–5 (and 95–110 on the broader network of Frangipane fortifications in the area, some of which subsequently passed to the Annibaldi); Santangeli Valenzani and Facchin 2017, pp. 66–9; and esp. Delfino 2018 for the reconstruction of the tower block and wooden fighting platform. Pierleoni and Savelli at the Theater of Marcellus: Marchetti Longhi 1976, pp. 22–31; Di Santo 2009, pp. 117–20.

27. Le Pogam 2004 and 2005, pp. 275–343.

28. Mausoleum of Augustus: di Santo 2009, pp. 55–7; Montecitorio: Carocci 1993b, p. 170, also on the final family strongpoint at SS. Apostoli, about whose configuration little is known. On the Via Triumphalis and the Via Papalis in this period, see Dey 2020a.

29. Orsini fortifications at and around the Theater of Pompey: Bosman 1990 and 1995; Di Santo 2009, pp. 121–5. On the Via Mercatoria, see also Modigliani 1998, pp. 9–11; 145–209.

30. The Orsini are the subject of a valuable monograph that deals thoroughly with both their urban properties and their holdings elsewhere (Allegrezza 1998); on the consolidation of their urban fortresses and zones of influence during the 13th century, see esp. pp. 4–17. On Montegiordano, see also e.g. Maire Vigueur 2008a, p. 142; on Castel Sant'Angelo, C. D'Onofrio 1978; Carocci 1993b, p. 173.

31. On the zones of family influence in Rome, in addition to the sources cited above at nn. 25–6, see also the monographic excursus on Rome's thirteen leading baronial families in Carocci 1993a, pp. 299–431. Buildings adorned with baronial coats of arms, and subsequent prohibitions: Carocci 1993b, p. 150; Carpegna Falconieri 2002b, p. 81.

32. With regard to the residences of 'ordinary' middle- and upper-class Romans, the digital *Forma Urbis* project conducted by Roma Tre University has now identified and catalogued remains of over 300 houses built in the 12th and 13th centuries; for preliminary results, see Molinari and Giannini 2014 and 2015; Giannini 2016. See also e.g. Hubert 1990, pp. 169–232; Maire Vigueur 2010, pp. 402–10.

33. On the urban palaces inhabited by cardinals (and popes), see generally Monciatti (ed.) 2004; Monciatti 2005, pp. 57–89; Le Pogam 2005; Brancone 2010.

34. On the 12th-century rebuilding of the basilica, see above, Ch. 6. Barelli 1998 is essential on the structure of the palace, but see also Brancone 2010, pp. 75–80.

35. On all of the preceding, see Barelli 1998.

36. Among the many discussions of the iconographical program of the chapel, see *PMR* 5, pp. 191–9, with extensive prior bibliography.

37. For the Aula Gotica, suffice it to cite *PMR* 5, pp. 22–3 and 137–76, with the excellent illustrations and critical apparatus included there. Other examples of 13th-century palatial interiors: at S. Clemente, a tower block in fine brick masonry similar to the Torre Maggiore at SS. Quattro Coronati was added to the cardinal's residence by Cardinal Raniero Capocci (r. 1216–50); the frescoes that adorned its top story have recently been uncovered and dated by Serena Romano to the first half of the 13th century (Romano 2004). The wing of the Vatican palace that centers on the so-called "Tower of Innocent III" and an adjacent hall, which may actually have been built and decorated somewhat later, under Innocent IV c. 1253–4, preserves parts of its interior decoration (Le Pogam 2004, pp. 59–62; 72–3; Monciatti 2005, pp. 96–108). As for interior spaces potentially sponsored and occupied by lay patrons, there are the very fragmentary frescoes with floral and animal motifs in the top floor of the Palazzo Comunale on the Capitoline (the "aula conciliare"), which may have been executed under Brancaleone degli Andalò in the 1250s, but might better date to the senatorate of Pope Nicholas III in 1278–9 (*PMR* 5, pp. 312–15, but see also Bedon 2008, pp. 9–11 on the possibility that Brancaleone expanded the palace and built the "aula conciliare"); and the mid-13th-century frescoes recently uncovered in a 13th-century house by Piazza Lovatelli, featuring scenes of daily life and hunting, as well as a series of fantastic animals (*PMR* 5, pp. 131–2).

38. Barelli 1998, pp. 113–14; 122.

39. For the political dramas of the era, see the relevant sections of Brezzi 1947 and Dupré Theseider 1952. On

39. (cont.) the marked slowing of important ecclesiastical commissions in the middle decades of the 13th century, see *PMR* 5, pp. 16–22; Gardner 2014, pp. 227–43, esp. 242–3; Pace 2016, pp. 307–8.

40. The principal extant works at Rome of all three masters of the Roman School are thoroughly presented in *PMR* 6; see p. 148 on Rusuti's stylistic affinities with Giotto. On these artists and the Roman moment of creative flourishing more generally, see also Ladner 1970, pp. 209–96; Krautheimer 1980, pp. 203–28; Tomei 1991; Gardner 2014, pp. 245–302; Pace 2016, pp. 308–24. Papal absences from Rome: Paravicini Bagliani 2004; Carocci 2004, pp. 26–7.

41. On the political and ideological tenor of Nicholas III's reign, see e.g. Waley 1961, pp. 189–201; Allegrezza 1998, pp. 15–41; on his artistic patronage, Tomei 1995. On the frescoes of the *aula conciliare* in the Palazzo Comunale, probably but not certainly commissioned during the senatorate of Nicholas III, see *PMR* 5, pp. 312–15.

42. *PMR* 5, p. 336: "Niccolò … espose con cristallina chiarezza la propria visione della Chiesa Romana e Apostolica, edizione orsiniana dell'universalismo innocenziano e antefatto indubitabile del poco più tardo Bonifacio VIII." On the full decorative program of the chapel as it appears following the recent restoration, see Romano 1995; *PMR* 5, pp. 321–38.

43. Bolgia 2017, pp. 22–89.

44. On all of the preceding, see Bolgia 2017, now the definitive study of the Aracoeli, who stresses the innovative features of the building more than I do here. For Bolgia's demonstration that work on the new church did not begin in the 1250s, as used to be assumed, see esp. pp. 99–116; and for the configuration of the late 13th-century building, all built in a single construction campaign extending over some 20 years, pp. 146–289. For the previous view that put its construction primarily in the 1250s and 1260s, see e.g. Tosti-Croce 1991, pp. 85–95.

45. Bolgia 2005; Bolgia 2017, pp. 290–393. On the surviving mosaics of the Colonna chapel, also *PMR* 6, pp. 152–4.

46. The principal monograph on the church is Palmerio and Villetti 1989. See pp. 43–65 for the textual sources and the chronology of the various construction phases (p. 43 for Nicholas III's letter to the senators); and pp. 69–118 for the 13th–15th-century building phases.

47. Palmerio and Villetti 1989, pp. 149–63 on the noble families active at the Minerva in the 14th and 15th centuries.

48. Mosaics at S. Maria: *PMR* 6, pp. 171–82; Last Judgment at S. Cecilia: *PMR* 6, pp. 80–93, with careful consideration of the unresolved question of patronage.

49. On the rebuilding of the apse and transept, see de Blaauw 1994, pp. 359–65. Mosaics: Gardner 2014, pp. 261–7; *PMR* 6, pp. 116–27 (interior); *PMR* 6, pp. 127–30 (surviving fragments from the exterior).

50. Gardner 2014, pp. 272–8; *PMR* 6, pp. 137–51; both concur that the façade, like the rest of the mosaic program, is likelier to have been completed by 1297, before the banishment of the Colonna, than after their rehabilitation in 1305 following the death of Boniface VIII. The upper register includes a remarkably prominent 'signature' of Rusuti, unaccompanied by a date, at the bottom of the central medallion of Christ. On the conflict between Boniface VIII and the Colonna, see Dupré Theseider 1952, pp. 307–36.

51. On the kinship between the two projects, in addition to the sources cited in the following note, cf. Pace 2016, pp. 313–17.

52. On the reconstruction of the apse and transept, see *KSRM* 2, pp. 92–117 (apse and ambulatory); 150–7 (transept); also Morbidelli 2010, esp. pp. 52–4. Both show that the transept is likelier to have been built under Nicholas IV than earlier in the 13th century, as some (e.g. de Blaauw 1994, pp. 221–7) have proposed. Apse mosaic: *KSRM* 2, pp. 104–13; Gardner 2014, pp. 256–61; *PMR* 6, pp. 49–56.

53. Broadly on art, politics, and society at Rome under Boniface VIII: Tosti-Croce (ed.) 2000; Andaloro, Maddalo, and Miglio (eds.) 2009. On the Jubilee of 1300, also e.g. Dupré Theseider 1952, pp. 337–52. Loggia delle benedizioni: Gardner 2014, pp. 289–92; Pace 2016, pp. 323–4; *PMR* 6, pp. 208–12.

54. Aracoeli staircase: Bolgia 2017, pp. 208–10. Giotto's Navicella mosaic and frescoes at St. Peter's: *PMR* 6, pp. 246–63 and 287–9, respectively. Façade mosaics at St. Paul's: Bolgia 2016, pp. 334–9; *PMR* 6, pp. 310–15. Lateran fire of 1308 and lengthy repairs: *KSRM* 2, pp. 34–5; Bolgia 2016, pp. 332–3. Reconstruction of roof at St. Peter's: Ceratti 1915. Lateran fire of 1361, repairs and new tabernacle: *KSRM* 2, pp. 170–7; Bolgia 2016, pp. 343–8. Campanile at S. Maria Maggiore: Bolgia 2016, p. 350. Boniface IX's additions to the Capitoline palace: Bedon 2008, pp. 18–21; Bolgia 2016, p. 252.

55. *PMR* 6; for the period after c. 1330, see esp. pp. 316ff.

56. Various entries regarding repairs to the Vatican walls and gates in 1377 are preserved in the account registers of the Curia. Repairs to the walls: Archiv. Vat. Intr. et Exit. 345, fol. 109v.: *Dicta die (4a Martii) fuerunt soluti ibidem Bocachio Pererio de Urbe deducendi sibi super certa quantitate muri quam debet facere inter portam Pertusii in Roma et portam Viterbii ipso per manus dni. Petri de Morteriis recipiente* (Kirsch 1898, p. 226); *Guillermo sub die 7a presentis mensis, Santo Laurentii*

et Iohanni Iacobini fusteriis de Urbe facientibus certa cadafalla supra muros extendentes se de porta Pertusii ad portam Sancti Spiritus in Urbe, deducendi de pretio dictorum cadafallorum, 55 flor. currentes Rome, valentes computati ut supra 53 flor. camere 14 sol. 6 den. Urbis (Kirsch 1898, p. 226); *Guillermo sub die predicta 7a presentis mensis, Bocachio Pererio de Urbe deducendi de pretio sive salario quod debet recipere a camera ratione reparationis muri se extendentis a supradicta porta usque ad portam Sancti Spiritus de Urbe, 40 flor. currentes Rome 38 flor. camere 37 sol. Urbis* (Kirsch 1898, pp. 226–7). Repair of the gate at the bridgehead of Ponte Sant'Angelo: Archiv. Vat. Intr. et Exit. 345, fol. 245 (Müntz 1891, 127–30): *Die XXII dicti mensis fuerunt soluti ibidem (apud Romam) Hugolino de Bononia servienti armorum domini nostri Papae pro quatuordecim libris, undecim solidis et sex denariis monete Urbis, sibi debitis pro certis reparationibus per eum factis fieri in porta ponti Sancti Angeli de Urbe, ante recessum domini nostri ad Anagniam, solvente domino Vicethesaurario, VI flor Cam., VI den. mon. Urbe.* 1,000 florins' worth of meat for the Curia in 1381: Lori Sanfilippo 2001, p. 270.

57. For S. Maria *de ferrariis* and the westward migration of the blacksmiths, see Lori Sanfilippo 2001, pp. 220–1. The Turin Catalogue is published in Hülsen 1927, pp. 19–43. *Campsores*: Lori Sanfilippo 2001, pp. 166–72. Conditions of *via maior* in 1380s: Esch 1969, pp. 209–10. Communal government's attempt to promote reurbanization of the *via maior* corridor in 1386: Lori Sanfilippo 2001, p. 113. In the late 1440s, Nicholas V would again try to encourage resettlement of the desolate zone between the Colosseum and the Lateran; see Westfall 1974, p. 106. The declining quantities of ceramics in the area from the 14th century on (see above at Ch. 6, n. 13) is another revealing index of dwindling population.

58. On the two southern crossings in the Middle Ages, see Marchetti Longhi 1938. The Ripa Grande port is the subject of the excellent monograph of Palermo 1979. Palermo 1990 focuses on the Roman grain trade and shows *inter alia* that overseas grain exports were a flourishing sector of the later medieval economy, thus helping to dismantle the shibboleth that Rome was a "consumer city" that produced little of note. Porto di Ripetta: Modigliani 1998, pp. 197–209.

59. Modigliani 1998, pp. 29–55; Modigliani 2011, pp. 27–35; Maire Vigueur 2010, pp. 38–44.

60. Fish market at S. Angelo: Modigliani 1998, pp. 61–75; Piazza Giudea: *ibid.*, pp. 57–61 (the chronology of the formation of the Jewish quarter here remains vexed, but there was clearly a thriving community in the 14th and 15th centuries that had presumably coagulated rather earlier; for more on the Jewish community at the end of the Middle Ages, see A. Esposito 1995); Campo de' Fiori: *ibid.*, pp. 84–7; 176–97; Canale di Ponte: *ibid.*, pp. 197–209; Borgo: *ibid.*, pp. 259–84.

61. For the various concentrations of mercantile and commercial activity along the course of the Via Mercatoria, as indicated by the notarial registers and other sources, see Lori Sanfilippo 2001, *passim*. The *Magistri edificiorum* intervened to ensure the safety and practicability of the Via Mercatoria and its continuation to St. Peter's in 1306, when they directed the *ospedale* of S. Spirito to clean a trash-strewn plot adjoining the main road to St. Peter's, and in 1382, when they checked to ensure that the stalls (*banche*) installed in front of a house along the Canale di Ponte on the approaches to Ponte Sant'Angelo, by the church of S. Celso, did not impede the flow of traffic along the route: see Schiaparelli 1902, doc. 11 (pp. 53–5) and Carbonetti Venditelli 1990, doc. 5 (pp. 181–3), respectively. Generally on the increasing wealth and economic vitality of Rome in the 15th century, see e.g. Modigliani 1998 and 2011; Esch 2016, pp. 264–88.

62. On the chapels at S. Maria sopra Minerva and their patrons, see Palmerio 1989, pp. 141–86; at S. Maria in Aracoeli, Bolgia 2017, pp. 309–48; on the rest, Lori Sanfilippo 2001, *passim*; also Bock 2019. Roman builders and the sourcing of building materials for reuse in houses and other constructions: Lori Sanfilippo 2001, pp. 228–53. On 14th-century expansion and consolidation of family compounds, often comprising multiple attached or proximate structures, see Broise and Maire Vigueur 1983.

63. Statutes of 1363, maintenance of roads and/or bridges: Bk. 2, ch. 135; 190; 194; 196, etc.; watercourses: Bk. 2, ch. 188–9; the Trevi Fountain: Bk. 3, ch. 126–7. The one instance of 14th-century repairs to the Aurelian Wall that I know of refers to "a broken and ruined bit [*particula*] of the wall of the city near St. John Lateran"; the text comes to us from a transcription of the original document published by Torrigio in 1641, cited in Corvisieri 1877, p. 87 (also Mancini 2001, 64–5). For all known sentences of the *Magistri edificiorum* (and their dates), see Carbonetti Venditelli 1993, pp. 33–8. For more on the stewardship of public buildings and infrastructure in the 14th century, see Baumgärtner 2004, pp. 280–4. The popes occasionally also sent money from Avignon for civic maintenance, as in the case of the 1,450 florins dispatched by Pope Urban V (r. 1362–70) to repair the important Roman bridge (the ancient *pons Aemilius*, called the *pons maior* or Ponte S. Maria in the Middle Ages) just south of the Tiber Island (Renouard 1941, p. 347).

64. Useful overviews of the complex political situation include G. Ortalli in *DBI* vol. 59 (2003), pp. 195–204; Richardson 2013, pp. 39–94; Esch 2016, pp. 70–4; Rollo-Koster 2019. On the condition of the cityscape around 1400, see e.g. Esch 1969, pp. 209–15.
65. Generally on the depictions of violence in Antonio di Pietro dello Schiavo and other Roman "diaries" and chronicles of the 15th century, see Di Santo 2016, pp. 305–21.
66. On the conjoined projects of administrative reform and urban renewal that unfolded in the decades after 1420, see Partner 1958; Westfall 1974; Burroughs 1990; McCahill 2013, along with the dossier of texts pertaining to curial patronage of art and architecture collected in Müntz 1878.

EPILOGUE

1. The disaster of 1450 is reported (including the figure of c. 200 dead) in the 'official' biography written shortly after Nicholas V's death by his longtime friend and contemporary, Giannozzo Manetti (*De vita ac gestis Nicolai quinti summi pontificis*, Bk. 2, 11–15). On the Canale di Ponte project, see also Burroughs 1982; Modigliani 1998, pp. 90–4, with the documents in Müntz 1878, pp. 140–1; 154.
2. Verdi 1997, p. 57: "La nuova stesura degli statuti dei maestri nel 1452 costituì difatti la base normativa per la risistemazione della capitale nella direzione auspicata dal pontefice ... Da quel momento in poi i maestri sarebbero stati in grado di esercitare una sorveglianza più vigile sulle edificazioni, di rilasciare dietro autorizzazione pontificia licenze di suolo pubblico, di procedere alla rimozione di quanto era d'intralcio alla viabilità, di promuovere e realizzare la pavimentazione delle strade principali e la sistemazione della precaria rete fognaria cittadina." The prologue explicitly invokes the supreme authority of the pope and specifies that the new edition of the statutes was compiled at his instance: "li statuti ... novamente facti de mandato de la sanctità de nostro signore papa Nicolò quinto" (Re 1920, p. 88).
3. On the statutes of 1452, Nicholas' program of street improvements, and its place in his larger political and urbanistic designs, see Magnussen 1958, pp. 34–41; Spezzaferro 1973; Burroughs 1990, pp. 72–98; Ait 1991; Verdi 1997, pp. 44–59. Valtieri 1992 and Cafà 2010 more closely scrutinize the material and also the social contours of the Via Papalis and Canale di Ponte in the generations after Nicholas V. The 1452 statutes are published in E. Re 1920 (and those of 1410 in Scaccia Scarafoni 1927). The "three principal streets" are named and described in Ch. 32 of the 1452 statutes, which prescribes at least weekly cleaning during the four summer months (May–August): *Et quando non si potesse fare per tutta la terra, almeno si faccia per queste tre strade principali : cioè dallo Canale de Ponte in sino ad Sancto Agnilo Piscivendolo, dallo Canale de Ponte per via Papale in sino ad Campitoglio, dallo Canale de Ponte per la via ritta in sino alla Magdalena* (E. Re 1920, p. 99). Other provisions for cleaning streets and public spaces, prohibiting unauthorized waste disposal, etc.: Chs. 29–31; 33–8; 40–2; Removal of obstructions and abusive constructions from public spaces and streets: Chs. 22–6; 28; 39; street paving: Ch. 27.
4. On the composition and editorial slant, as it were, of Manetti's *De vita ac gestis Nicolai quinti summi pontificis*, see esp. Modigliani 2009 (along with her critical edition of the text, of 2005); on its relative faithfulness to Nicholas' thoughts and intentions, see also, e.g., Westfall 1974, pp. 17–19; Miglio 2001, p. 52. Note, further, that while Nicholas knew Alberti and presumably absorbed something of the latter's expansive, holistic conception of urban topography, it is unlikely that Alberti was the guiding spirit behind Nicholas' plans for Rome (as, e.g., Westfall 1974 proposed), and indeed probable that Alberti was less than impressed with at least some of the pope's urbanistic initiatives; see the searching critiques of Tafuri 1992, Ch. 2, and Miglio 2001, themselves, however, nuanced and in part corrected in Modigliani 2009, pp. 542–55. Generally on Nicholas' education and cultural formation, see Coluccia 1998, esp. pp. 244–81 on Biondo, Bracciolini, Alberti, and the rest of the Roman circle whose ideas helped shape his project of urban renewal. The section of Bracciolini's *De varietate Fortunae* devoted to Roman topography appears at VZ 4, pp. 223–45; Biondo's *Roma instaurata* is VZ 4, pp. 247–323; Alberti's *Descriptio urbis Romae* is VZ 4, pp. 209–22.
5. Broadly on all these projects, see Westfall 1974; Burroughs 1990. The renovation of the Aurelian Wall looks to have been finished well before he died; see Modigliani 2009, pp. 523–5. On the areas implicated in the restoration campaign and the form of the repairs, see Cassanelli, Delfini, and Fonti 1974, pp. 89–102; Mancini 2001, pp. 69–73. Three of the towers are in Sector M, between Porta Ostiense and the Tiber; the fourth is in Sector F near Porta Tiburtina; the curtain is L16-17 (sectors and alphanumeric designators as in Mancini 2001 and Dey 2011). Regarding Nicholine Rome as the terrestrial analogue of Celestial Jerusalem, see Cassanelli, Delfini, and Fonti 1974, pp. 101–2; Burroughs 1990, pp. 185–90; Miglio 1993, p. 14.

6. For the work actually done at St. Peter's, and the possibility of Alberti's involvement therein, Modigliani 2009, pp. 532–42; see also Magnussen 1958, Frommel 1997, and, on the additions to the papal palace, Magnussen 1958, pp. 115–26; Westfall 1974, pp. 129–65.
7. Regarding the schemes for St. Peter's and the Borgo, see Manetti, *De vita ac gestis Nicolai quinti*, Bk. 2, with Magnussen 1958, pp. 65–97 (Borgo) and 163–214 (St. Peter's); Westfall 1974, pp. 103–27; Burroughs 1990, pp. 140–245; Modigliani 2009, pp. 526–32.
8. Sixtus IV's new campaign of street clearance and beautification: Ait 1991; Verdi 1997, pp. 68–81; Blondin 2005.

REFERENCES

EDITIONS

Agnellus, Andreas. *Liber pontificalis ecclesiae Ravennatis.* D. M. Deliyannis (ed.), *Corpus Christianorum. Continuatio Medievalis,* vol. 199, Turnhout, 2006. Trans. D. M. Deliyannis, *The Book of Pontiffs of the Church of Ravenna,* Washington, DC, 2004.

Ammianus Marcellinus. *Res Gestae.* W. Seyfarth (ed.), *Ammiani Marcellini rerum gestarum libri qui supersunt,* 2 vols., Leipzig (Teubner), 1968. Trans. J. C. Rolfe, *Ammianus Marcellinus. History,* 3 vols., Cambridge, MA, 1939–50 (*LCL* vols. 300, 315, 331).

Annales Camaldulenses Ordinis Sancti Benedicti. J. B. Mittarelli and D. A. Costadoni (eds.), 9 vols., Venice, 1755–73.

Anonimo Romano. *Cronica.* G. Porta (ed.), Milan, 1979.

Anonymi Valesiani pars posterior. T. Mommsen (ed.), *MGH AA* 9.1, Berlin, 1892, pp. 306–28. Trans. J. C. Rolfe, *Excerpta Valesiana* (included in *Ammianus Marcellinus. History,* vol. 3), Cambridge, MA, 1939 (*LCL* vol. 331).

Antonio di Pietro dello Schiavo. *Il diario romano di Antonio di Pietro dello Schiavo: dal 19 ottobre 1404 al 25 settembre 1417.* F. Isoldi (ed.), *RIS*² 24.5, Città di Castello, 1917, pp. 3–112.

Augustine. *De civitate Dei.* B. Dombart and A. Kalb (eds.), 2 vols., Stuttgart (Teubner), 1993. Trans. W. Babcock, *The City of God,* 2 vols., Hyde Park, NY, 2012.

Bartolo da Sassoferrato. *Tractatus de regimine civitatis.* D. Quaglioni (ed.), *Politica e diritto nel Trecento italiano: il "De tyranno" di Bartolo da Sassoferrato (1314–1357),* Florence, 1983, 149–70. Trans. D. Robinson, *Bartolus of Saxoferrato. On the Government of a City,* Toronto, 2012 (online at: http://individual.utoronto.ca/jwrobinson/translations/bartolus_de-regimine-ciuitatis.pdf).

Benedict of Soracte. *Chronicon.* G. Zucchetti (ed.), *Il Chronicon di Benedetto monaco di S. Andrea del Soratte e il Libellus de imperatoria potestate in urbe Roma,* FSI 55, Rome, 1920.

Blockley, R. C. (ed. and trans.) *The Fragmentary Classicising Historians of the Later Roman Empire,* 2 vols., Liverpool, 1981–3.

Cassiodorus Senator. *Chronica.* T. Mommsen (ed.), *MGH AA* 11.2, Berlin, 1894, pp. 109–61.

Cassiodorus Senator. *Variae.* A. Giardina et al. (eds.), *Cassiodoro Varie,* 6 vols., Rome, 2014–19. Trans. (partial) S. J. B. Barnish, *Cassiodorus: Variae,* Liverpool, 1992; somewhat less abridged is T. Hodgkin, *The Letters of Cassiodorus,* London, 1886.

Codex Carolinus. W. Gundlach (ed.), *MGH EP* 3, Berlin, 1892, pp. 469–657. Trans. (partial) P. D. King, *Charlemagne: Translated Sources,* Kendal, 1987.

Curiosum urbis Romae; Notitia urbis Romae. A. Nordh (ed.), *Libellus de regionibus urbis Romae,* Rome, 1949.

De imperatoria potestate in urbe Roma libellus. G. Zucchetti (ed.), *Il Chronicon di Benedetto monaco di S. Andrea del*

Soratte e il Libellus de imperatoria potestate in urbe Roma, Rome, 1920, pp. 188–210.

Descriptio Lateranensis Ecclesiae. VZ 3, pp. 319–73.

Donation of Constantine (Constitutum Constantini). H. Fuhrmann (ed.), *Das Constitutum Constantini (MGH Fontes iuris germanici antiqui in usum scholarum separatim editi* 10), Hanover, 1968. Trans. online at: https://sourcebooks.fordham.edu/source/donatconst.asp.

Einsiedeln Itineraries. G. Walser (ed.), *Die Einsiedler Inschriftensammlung und der Pilgerführer durch Rom (Codex Einsiedlensis 326)*, Stuttgart, 1987.

Ennodius. *Panegyricus dictus clementissimo regi Theoderico.* C. Rohr (ed. and trans.), *Der Theoderich-Panegyricus des Ennodius, MGH Studien und Texte*, vol. 12, Hanover, 1995. Trans. B. S. Haase, online at: https://ruor.uottawa.ca/bitstream/10393/7776/1/MM75012.PDF

Frontinus. *De aquaeductu urbis Romae.* C. Kunderewicz (ed.), Stuttgart – Leipzig (Teubner), 1998. Trans. Evans 1994, pp. 13–52.

Gerontius. *Vita Melaniae iunioris.* D. Gorce (ed. and trans.), *Vie de Sainte Mélanie, SC* 90, Paris, 1962. Trans. E. A. Clark, *Life of Melania the Younger*, New York, 1984.

Graphia aureae urbis Romae. VZ 3, pp. 67–110.

Gregory VII, Pope. *Registrum.* E. Caspar (ed.), *Das Register Gregors VII, MGH Epistolae Selectae* 2.1–2, Berlin, 1920–3. Trans. H. E. G. Cowdrey, *The Register of Gregory VII, 1073–1085*, Oxford, 2002.

Gregory of Catino. *Chronicon Farfense.* U. Balzani (ed.), *Il Chronicon Farfense di Gregorio di Catino*, Rome, 1903.

Hugo of Farfa. *Destructio monasterii Farfensis.* U. Balzani (ed.), *Il Chronicon Farfense di Gregorio di Catino*, Rome, 1903, pp. 27–51.

Innocent III, Pope. *Gesta Innocentii III.* D. Gress-Wright (ed.), *The Gesta Innocentii III: Text, Introduction and Commentary*, Ph.D. Diss., Bryn Mawr College, 1981. Trans. J. M. Powell, *The Deeds of Pope Innocent III by an unknown author*, Washington, DC, 2004.

Isidore of Seville. *Historia Gothorum Wandalorum Sueborum.* T. Mommsen (ed.), *MGH AA* 11.2, Berlin, 1894, pp. 241–303. Trans. G. Donini and G. B. Ford, *Isidore of Seville's History of the Kings of the Goths, Vandals and Suevi*, Leiden, 1966.

Itinerarium Salisburgense. See: *Notitia ecclesiarum urbis Romae.*

Jerome, Saint. *Epistulae.* J. Labourt (ed. and trans.), *Saint Jérôme. Lettres*, 8 vols., Paris (Budé), 1949–63. Trans. (partial) F. A. Wright, *Jerome. Select Letters*, Cambridge, MA, 1933 (*LCL* vol. 262).

John of Antioch. *Chronica.* U. Roberto (ed. and trans.), *Iohannis Antiocheni ex Historia chronica*, Berlin – New York, 2005.

John VIII, Pope. *Registrum Iohannis VIII papae.* E. Caspar (ed.), *MGH EP* 7, Berlin, 1928.

Jordanes. *Romana.* T. Mommsen (ed.), *MGA AA* 5, Berlin, 1882, pp. 1–52.

Liutprand of Cremona. *Antapodosis.* J. Becker (ed.), *MGH SS in usum scholarum separatim editi* 41, Hanover – Leipzig, 1915, pp. 1–158. Trans. P. Squatriti, *The Complete Works of Liudprand of Cremona*, Washington, DC, 2007.

Liutprand of Cremona. *Historia Ottonis.* J. Becker (ed.), *MGH in usum scholarum separatim editi* 41, Hanover – Leipzig, 1915, pp. 159–75. Trans. P. Squatriti, *The Complete Works of Liudprand of Cremona*, Washington, DC, 2007.

Magister Gregorius ("Master Gregory"). *Narracio de mirabilibus urbis Romae.* C. Nardella (ed. and trans.), *Il fascino di Roma nel Medioevo. Le 'Meraviglie di Roma' di maestro Gregorio*, Rome, 2nd ed., 2007. Trans. J. Osborne, *Magister Gregorius, The marvels of Rome*, Toronto, 1987.

Malalas, John. *Ioannis Malalae Chronographia.* J. Thurn (ed.), *Corpus Fontium Historiae Byzantinae* 35, Berlin – New York, 2000. Trans. E. Jeffreys, M. Jeffreys, and R. Scott, *The Chronicle of John Malalas*, Melbourne, 1986.

Manetti, Giannozzo. *Iannotii Manetti De vita ac gestis Nicolai quinti summi pontificis.* A. Modigliani (ed.), *Fonti per la Storia dell'Italia Medievale – Rerum Italicarum Scriptores* 6, Rome, 2005. Partial trans. in C. Smith and J. F. O'Connor, *Building the Kingdom: Giannozzo Manetti on the Material and Spiritual Edifice*, Washington, DC, 2007.

Matthew Paris. *Matthaei Parisiensis monachi Sancti Albani chronica majora.* H. R. Luard (ed.), *Rerum britannicarum medii aevi scriptores* 57, 7 vols., London, 1872–83. Trans. J. A. Giles, *Matthew Paris's English history from the year 1235 to 1273*, 3 vols., London, 1852–4.

Mirabilia urbis Romae. Duchesne (ed.), *LC* 1, pp. 262–83; also VZ 3, pp. 3–65. Trans. F. M. Nichols, *The Marvels of Rome*, 2nd ed., New York, 1986 [1889].

Notitia ecclesiarum urbis Romae. VZ 2, pp. 67–99.

Notitia urbis Romae. See: *Curiosum urbis Romae.*

Otto of Freising. *Chronica.* A. Hofmeister (ed.), *MGH SS in usum scholarum separatim editi* 45, Hanover – Leipzig, 1912. Trans. C. Mierow, *The Two Cities: a Chronicle of Universal History to the Year 1146 A.D.*, New York, 1953 (reprint 2002).

Otto of Freising. *Gesta Frederici I. imperatoris*, Books 1–2. G. Waitz (ed.), *MGH SS in usum scholarum separatim editi* 46, Hanover, 1912. Trans. C. Mierow, *The deeds of Frederick Barbarossa*, New York, 1953 (reprint 2004).

Paul the Deacon. *Historia Romana.* A. Crivelucci (ed.), *FSI* 51, Rome, 1914.

Paul the Deacon. *Historia Langobardorum.* L. Capo (ed. and trans.), *Storia dei Longobardi*, Milan, 1992. Trans.

W. D. Foulke, *History of the Lombards*, Philadelphia, 2003 [1907].

Procopius. *De bellis*. J. Haury and G. Wirth (eds.), *Procopii Caesariensis opera omnia*, vols. 1–2, Leipzig (Teubner), 1962–3. Trans. H. B. Dewing, *Procopius, History of the Wars*, 5 vols., Cambridge, MA, 1914–28 (*LCL* vols. 48, 81, 107, 173, 217).

Procopius. *Historia arcana*. J. Haury and G. Wirth (eds.), *Procopii Caesariensis opera omnia*, vol. 3, Leipzig (Teubner), 1963. Trans. H. B. Dewing, *The Anecdota or Secret History*, Cambridge, MA, 1935 (*LCL* vol. 290).

Prosper of Aquitaine. *Epitoma Chronicon*. T. Mommsen (ed.), *MGH AA* 9.1, Berlin, 1892, pp. 341–485. Trans. A. C. Murray, *From Roman to Merovingian Gaul: A Reader*, Ontario, 2003, pp. 62–76.

Rahewin. *Gesta Frederici I. imperatoris*, Books 3–4. G. Waitz (ed.), *MGH SS in usum scholarum separatim editi* 46, Hanover, 1912. Trans. C. Mierow, *The Deeds of Frederick Barbarossa*, New York, 1953 (reprint 2004).

Regino of Prum. *Chronicon*. F. Kurze (ed.), *Reginonis abbatis prumiensis Chronicon cum continuatione treverensi, MGH SRG in usum scholarum separatim editi* 50, Hanover, 1890. Trans. S. MacLean, *History and Politics in Late Carolingian and Ottonian Europe: The Chronicle of Regino of Prüm and Adalbert of Magdeburg*, Manchester, 2009.

Saba Malaspina. *Rerum Sicularum historia*. F. De Rosa (ed. and trans.), *Storia delle cose di Sicilia*, Cassino, 2014.

Scriptores historiae Augustae. E. Pohl (ed.), 2 vols., Leipzig (Teubner), 1965. Trans. D. Magie, *Historia Augusta*, 3 vols., Cambridge, MA, 1921–32 (*LCL* vols. 139, 140, 263).

Suetonius. *De vita Caesarum*. M. Ihm (ed.), Leipzig – Berlin (Teubner), 1923. Trans. J. C. Rolfe, *Lives of the Caesars*, 2 vols., Cambridge, MA, 1914 (*LCL* vols. 31, 38).

Tertullian. *Adversus Valentinianos*. A. Kroymann (ed.), *CCSL* 2, Turnhout, 1954, pp. 751–78. Trans. M. T. Riley, Stanford Ph.D. Diss., 1971. Online at: www.tertullian.org/articles/riley_adv_val/riley_00_index.htm

Vita Gregorii papae IX. *LC* 2, pp. 18–36.

Zosimus. *Historia nova*. L. Mendelssohn (ed.), *Zosimi comitis et exadvocati fisci Historia nova*, Leipzig (Teubner), 1887. Trans R. T. Ridley, *Zosimus, New History*, Canberra, 1982.

SECONDARY LITERATURE

Acampora, L. (2017) "Frequentazione e abbandoni dal IV all'VIII secolo," in Baumgartner (ed.), pp. 147–57.

Acconci, A. (1991) "Le vicende storico-monumentali della chiesa di S. Maria in Portico," *Giornata di studi su Santa Galla*, Rome, pp. 89–119.

Acconci, A., F. Astolfi, and A. Englen (eds.) (2020) *Caelius II. Pars Superior. La basilica dei santi Giovanni e Paolo*, Rome.

Aguilera Martín, A. (2002). *El Monte Testaccio e la llanura subaventina. Topografía extra portam Trigeminam*, Rome.

Aimone, M. (2016) "'Spelunca aliquando pravitatis hereticae.' Ric erche sulla basilica romana di Sant'Agata dei Goti," *Reti Medievali Rivista* 17.2. DOI 10.6092/1593-2214/515.

Ait, I. (1991) "Strade cittadine: Atteggiamenti mentali e comportamenti a Roma nel XV secolo," *Studi Storici* 32.4, pp. 877–88.

Albertson, F. C. (2001) "Zenodorus' 'Colossus of Nero,'" *MAAR* 46, pp. 95–118.

Aldrete, G. (2007) *Floods of the Tiber in Ancient Rome*, Baltimore.

Allegrezza, F. (1998) *Organizzazione del potere e dinamiche familiari: gli Orsini dal Duecento agli inizi del Quattrocento*, Rome.

Althoff, G. (2003) *Otto III*, University Park, PA [German ed. 1996].

Amici, C. (1991) *Il foro di Cesare*, Florence.

Andaloro, M. (2006) *L'orizzonte tardoantico e le nuove immagini 312–468 (La pittura medievale a Roma 312–1431, Corpus, vol. 1)*, Milan.

Andaloro, M. (2016) "I cantieri di Giovanni VII," in Andaloro, Bordi, and Morganti (eds.), pp. 212–19.

Andaloro, M., S. Maddalo, and M. Miglio (eds.) (2009) *Frammenti di memoria: Roma, Giotto e Bonifacio VIII*, Rome.

Andaloro, M., G. Bordi, and G. Morganti (eds.) (2016) *Santa Maria Antiqua tra Roma e Bisanzio*, Milan.

Angelelli, C. (2010) *La basilica titolare di S. Pudenziana: Nuove ricerche*, Vatican City.

Angelelli, W., and S. Romano (eds.) (2019) *La linea d'ombra: Roma 1378–1420*, Rome.

Annoscia, G. M. (2010) "Scritture esposte di committenza pontificia (XII secolo) in tre chiese dei rioni VI e VIII di Roma," *Temporis Signa* 5, pp. 133–47.

Annoscia, G. M., E. De Minicis, and M. Taviani (2010) "Case, strade e pozzi nel Trastevere medievale," in Pani Ermini and Travaglini (eds.), pp. 183–99.

Arce, J. (1999) "El inventario de Roma: Curiosum y Notitia," in Harris (ed.), pp. 15–22.

Archi, G. G. (1981) "Pragmatica sanctio pro petitione Vigilii," in *id.*, *Scritti di diritto romano*, vol. 3, Milan, pp. 1971–2010.

Arena, M. S. et al. (eds.) (2001) *Roma dall'antichità al medioevo. Archeologia e storia nel Museo Nazionale Romano Crypta Balbi*, Rome.

Arnaldi, G. (1951) "Papa Formoso e gli imperatori della casa di Spoleto," *Annali della Facoltà di Lettere e Filosofia della Università di Napoli* 1, pp. 85–104.

Arnaldi, G. (1981) "Il papato e l'ideologia del potere imperiale," *Settimane del CISAM* 27, pp. 341–407.

Arnaldi, G. (1986) "L'approvvigionamento di Roma e l'amministrazione del 'patrimonio di san Pietro' al tempo di Gregorio Magno," *Studi Romani* 34, pp. 25–39.

Arnaldi, G. (1987) *Le origini dello stato della chiesa*, Turin.

Arnaldi, G. (1990) *Natale 875: politica, ecclesiologia, cultura del papato altomedievale*, Vol. 1, Rome.

Arnaldi, G. (1991) "Mito e realtà del secolo X romano e papale," *Settimane del CISAM* 38, pp. 27–53.

Arnold, J. J. (2014) *Theoderic and the Roman Imperial Restoration*, Cambridge.

Arnold, J. J., M. S. Bjornlie, and K. Sessa (eds.) (2016) *A Companion to Ostrogothic Italy*, Turnhout.

Arthur, P. (1993) "Early Medieval Amphorae, the Duchy of Naples and the Food Supply of Rome," *PBSR* 61, pp. 231–44.

Augenti, A. (1996) *Il palatino nel medioevo. Archeologia e topografia (secoli VI–XIII)*, Rome.

Augenti, A. (2000) "Continuity and Discontinuity in a Seat of Power: the Palatine Hill from the Fifth to the Tenth Century," in J. Smith (ed.), *Early Medieval Rome and the Christian West, Essays in Honour of Donald A. Bullough*, Leiden and Boston, pp. 43–54.

Azzena, G. (2010) "Il Trastevere in età romana," in Pani Ermini and Travaglini (eds.), pp. 1–33.

Baldovin, J. F. (1987) *The Urban Character of Christian Worship. The Origins, Development and Meaning of Stational Liturgy*, Rome.

Ballardini, A., and P. Pogliani (2013) "A reconstruction of the oratory of John VII (705–07)," in McKitterick *et al.* (eds.), pp. 190–213.

Ballardini, A. (2015) "'In antiquissimo ac venerabili Lateranensi palatio': la residenza dei pontefici secondo il *Liber Pontificalis*," *Settimane del CISAM* 62, pp. 889–927.

Barbiera, I., and G. Dalla Zuanna (2007) "Le dinamiche della popolazione nell'Italia medievale. Nuovi riscontri su documenti e reperti archeologici," *Archeologia Medievale* 24, pp. 19–42.

Barclay Lloyd, J. (1981) "The Medieval Church of S. Maria in Portico in Rome," *RömQSchr.* 76, pp. 95–107.

Barclay Lloyd, J. (1985) "Masonry Techniques in Medieval Rome, c. 1080–1300," *PBSR* 53, pp. 225–76.

Barclay Lloyd, J. (1986) "The Building History of the Medieval Church of S. Clemente in Rome," *JSAH* 45.3, pp. 197–223.

Barclay-Lloyd, J., and K. Bull-Simonsen Einaudi (1998) *SS. Cosma e Damiano in Mica Aurea. Architettura, storia e storiografia di un monastero romano soppresso*, Rome.

Barelli, L. (1998) "Il palazzo cardinalizio dei Ss. Quattro Coronati a Roma nel basso medieoevo," in Z. Mari, M. T. Petrara, and M. Sperandio (eds.), *Il Lazio tra antichità e medioevo: studi in onore di Jean Coste*, Rome, pp. 111–24.

Barelli, L, (2009) *Il complesso monumentale dei Ss. Quattro Coronati a Roma*, Rome.

Barelli, L. (2012a) "Construction Methods in Carolingian Rome (Eighth – Ninth Centuries)," in R. Carvais, A. Guillerme, V. Nègre, and J. Sakarovitch (eds.), *Nuts & Bolts of Construction History*, Paris, vol. 2, pp. 135–41.

Barelli, L. (2012b) "Il supposto *palatium dormidorii*: analisi storico-tecnica in vista di un auspicabile restauro," in L. Barelli and R. Pugliese (eds.), *Dal cantiere dei Ss. Quattro Coronati a Roma. Note di storia e restauro per Giovanni Carbonara*, Rome, pp. 53–74.

Barelli, L., M. C. Fabbri, and M. Asciutti (2005) "Lettura storico-tecnica di una muratura altomedievale: *l'opus quadratum* a Roma nei secoli VIII e IX," in D. Fiorani and D. Esposito (eds.), *Techniche costruttive dell'edilizia storica. Conoscere per conservare*, Rome, pp. 59–76.

Barelli, L., R. Pugliese, and L. Sadori (2007–08) "Nuovi dati dallo scavo del chiostro del complesso dei Ss. Quattro Coronati a Roma," *RendPontAc* 80, pp. 77–121.

Barnish, S. B. J. (1987) "Pigs, Plebeians and *Potentes*: Rome's Economic Hinterland c. 350–600 A.D.," *PBSR* 55, pp. 157–85.

Barnish, S. B. J., and F. Marazzi (eds.) (2007) *The Ostrogoths. From the Migration Period to the Sixth Century*, Woodbridge.

Bartoli, A. (1926–27) "I templi del Foro Olitorio e la diaconia di S. Nicola in 'in carcere,'" *RendPontAc* 5, pp. 213–26.

Bartoloni, F. (1946) "Per la storia del Senato Romano nei secoli XII e XIII," *Bullettino dell'Istituto Storico Italiano per il Medio Evo e Archivio Muratoriano* 60, pp. 1–108.

Bauer, F. A. (1996) *Stadt, Platz und Denkmal in der Spätantike*, Mainz.

Bauer, F. A. (1997) "Das Bild der Stadt Rom in karolingischer Zeit: Der Anonymus Einsidlensis," *RömQSchr* 92, pp. 190–229.

Bauer, F. A. (2001) "Beatitudo temporum. Die Gegenwart der Vergangenheit im Stadtbild des spätantiken Rom," in F. A. Bauer and N. Zimmermann (eds.), *Epochenwandel? Kunst und Kultur zwischen Antike und Mittelalter*, Mainz, pp. 75–94.

Bauer, F. A. (2003) "Il rinnovamento di Roma sotto Adriano I alla luce del *Liber Pontificalis*. Immagine e realtà," in Geertman (ed.), pp. 189–203.

Bauer, F. A. (2004) *Das Bild der Stadt Rom im Frühmittelalter. Papststiftungen im Spiegel des Liber Pontificalis von Gregor dem Dritten bis zu Leo dem Dritten*, Wiesbaden.

Bauer, F. A. (2013) "Sacheggi e distruzioni nell'anno 410?," in Lipps, Machado, and von Rummel (eds.), pp. 259–75.

Baumgärtner, I. "Rombeherrschung und Romerneuerung. Die römische Kommune im 12. Jahrhundert," *Quellen und Forschungen aus italienischen Archiven und Bibliotheken* 69, pp. 27–79.

Baumgärtner, I. (2004) "Kommunale Bauplanung in Rom. Urkunden, Inschriften und Statuten vom 12. bis 14. Jahrhundert," in M. Stolleis and R. Wolff (eds.), *La bellezza della città. Stadtrecht und Stadtgestaltung im Italien des Mittelalters und der Renaissance*, Tübingen, pp. 269–301.

Baumgartner, M. (ed.) (2017) *Roma Rinascente: La città antica tra Quirinale e Pincio*, Rome.

Baumgartner, M. (2017) "La città antica tra quirinale e Pincio: evoluzione di un contesto urbano," in Baumgartner (ed.), pp. 41–52.

Beard, M., and K. Hopkins (2005) *The Colosseum*, Cambridge, MA.

Bedon, A. (2008) *Il Campidoglio. Storia di un monumento civile nella Roma papale*, Milan.

Bellardini, D., and P. Delogu (2003). "Liber Pontificalis e altre fonti: la topografia di Roma nell'VIII secolo," in Geertman (ed.), pp. 205–23.

Belli Barsali, I. (1976) "Sulla topografia di Roma in periodo carolingio: la 'Civitas Leoniana' e la Giovannipoli," in *Roma e l'età carolingia. Atti delle giornate di studio 3–8 maggio 1976*, Rome, pp. 201–14.

Bernacchio, N. (2002) "L'ospedale dei Cavalieri di S. Giovanni di Gerusalemme a Roma," *Arte Medievale* (n.s.) 1.1, pp. 127–48.

Bernacchio, N., and R. Meneghini (1994) "Roma-Mercati di Traiano: Nuovi dati Strutturali sulla Torre delle Milizie," *Archeologia Medievale* 21, pp. 31–56.

Bernard, J.-F. (ed.) (2014) *Piazza Navona, ou Place Navone, la plus belle et la plus grande: du stade de Domitien à la place moderne, histoire d'une évolution urbaine*, Rome.

Bertolini, O. (1941) *Roma di fronte a Bisanzio e ai Longobardi*, Bologna.

Bertolini, O. (1947) "Per la storia delle diaconie romane nell'alto medio evo sino alla fine del secolo VIII," *ASRSP* 70, pp. 1–141.

Bertolini, O. (1968) "Riflessi politici delle controversie religiose con bisanzio nelle vicende del secolo VII in Italia," in O. Bertolini, *Scritti scelti di storia medievale*, vol. 2, Livorno, pp. 265–308.

Bianchi, E., and R. Meneghini (2002) "Il cantiere costruttivo del Foro di Traiano," *Röm. Mitth.* 109, pp. 395–417.

Bianchi, L. (1998) *Case e torri medioevali a Roma: Documentazione, storia e sopravvivenza di edifici medioevali nel tessuto urbano di Roma*, Rome.

Bianchi, L. (2015) "*Surgit in astra domus sublimis*: note sulla topografia antica e medievale fra Tevere e Foro Boario," *Bollettino del Centro di Studi per la Storia dell'Architttura* 45–52 (2008–2015), pp. 11–37.

Bjornlie, M. S. (2013) *Politics and Tradition between Rome, Ravenna and Constantinople: A Study of Cassiodorus and the* Variae, Cambridge.

Blennow, A. H. (2011) *The Latin Consecrative Inscriptions in Prose of Churches and Altars in Rome 1046–1263*, Rome.

Blondin, J. E. (2005) "Power Made Visible: Pope Sixtus IV as *Urbis restaurator* in Quattrocento Rome," *The Catholic Historical Review* 91, pp. 1–25.

Blumenthal, U.-R. (1988) *The Investiture Controversy*, Philadelphia.

Blumenthal, U.-R. (2001) *Gregor VII. Papst zwischen Canossa und Kirchenreform*, Darmstadt.

Bock, N. (2019) "*Artisti anonimi romani. Monumenti funebri e scultura all'epoca di Bonifacio IX*," in Angelelli and Romano (eds.), pp. 305–26.

Bolgia, C. (2005) "The Felici Icon Tabernacle (1372) at S. Maria in Aracoeli, Reconstructed: Lay Patronage, Sculpture, and Marian Devotion in Trecento Rome," *Journal of the Warburg and Courtald Institutes* 68, pp. 27–72.

Bolgia, C. (2016) "Il XIV secolo: da Benedetto XI (1303–1304) a Bonifacio IX (1389–1404)," in D'Onofrio (ed.), pp. 331–59.

Bolgia, C. (2017) *Reclaiming the Roman Capitol: Santa Maria in Aracoeli from the Altar of Augustus to the Franciscans, c. 500–1450*, London and New York.

Bolgia, C., R. McKitterick, and J. Osborne (eds.) (2011) *Rome across Time and Space: Cultural Transmission and the Exchange of Ideas, c. 500–1400*, Cambridge and New York.

Bolle, K. (2019) "Die Kommune Rom und ihre Inschriften. Ein Blick aus althistorischer Perspektive," in K. Bolle, M. van der Höh, and N. Jaspert (eds.), *Inschriftenkulturen im kommunalen Italien: Traditionen, Brüche, Neuanfänge*, Berlin, pp. 225–66.

Bonfioli, M. (1974) "La diaconia dei Ss. Sergio e Bacco nel foro romano: fonti e problemi," *RAC* 50, pp. 55–85.

Bordi, G. (2011) "Committenza laica nella chiesa di Sant'Adriano al foro romano nell'Altomedioevo," in C. A. Quintavalle, *Medioevo: i committenti, Atti del XIII Convegno Internazionale di Studi (Parma, 21–26 settembre 2010)*, Bologna, pp. 63–75.

Bordi, G. (2016a) "Santa Maria Antiqua attraverso i palinsesti pittorici," in Andaloro, Bordi, and Morganti (eds.), pp. 34–52.

Bordi, G. (2016b) "Dall'Oratorio dei Quaranta Martiri a Santa Maria *de inferno*," in Andaloro, Bordi, and Morganti (eds.), pp. 278–87.

Bordi, G. (2016c) "La cappella del *primicerius* Teodoto," in Andaloro, Bordi, and Morganti (eds.), pp. 260–69.

Bordi, G. (2016d) "Laïcs, nobles et parvenus dans la peinture murale. Rome du VIIIe au XIIe siècle," *Les Cahiers de Saint-Michel de Cuxa* 47, pp. 37–44.

Bordi, G. (2017) "Fino al terremoto del 1349: immagine della città e cristianizzazione dentro e fuori il Colosseo," in Rea, Romano, and Santangeli-Valenzani (eds.), pp. 76–91.

Bosman, F. (1990) "Una torre medievale a Via Monte della Farina: ricerche topografiche e analisi della struttura," *Archeologia Medievale* 17, pp. 633–60.

Bosman, F. (1995) "Incastellamento urbano a Roma: Il caso degli Orsini," in N. Christie (ed.), *Settlement and Economy in Italy 1500 BC–AD 1500*, Oxford, pp. 499–507.

Brancone, V. (2010) *Le* domus *dei cardinali nella Roma del Duecento: Gioielli, mobili, libri*, Rome.

Brandenburg, H. (1998) *Die Kirche S. Stefano Rotondo in Rom. Bautypologie und Architektursymbolik in der spätantiken und frühchristlichen Architektur*, Berlin and Boston.

Brandenburg, H. (2000) "S. Stefano Rotondo: Der letzte Großbau der Antike in Rom. Die Tipologie des Baues. Die Ausstattung der Kirche. Die kunstgeschichtliches Stellung des Kirchenbaues und seiner ausstattung," in Brandenburg and Pál (eds.), pp. 35–65.

Brandenburg, H., and J. Pál (eds.) (2000) *Santo Stefano Rotondo in Roma: Archeologia, storia dell'arte, restauro / Archäologie, Bauforschung, Geschichte*, Wiesbaden.

Brandenburg, H. (2005) *Ancient Churches of Rome from the Fourth to the Seventh Century. The Dawn of Christian Architecture in the West*, Turnhout.

Brandt, O. (2012) "The Early Christian Basilica of San Lorenzo in Lucina," in O. Brandt (ed.), *San Lorenzo in Lucina – The Transformations of a Roman Quarter (Acta Instituti Romani Regni Sueciae,* Series in 4°, 61), Stockholm, pp. 123–54.

Brandt, O. (2016) "L'improbabile legame delle colonne di bronzo al Laterano con il *fastigium* costantiniano," *RAC* 92, pp. 117–36.

Brandt, O. (2017) "*Battisteri paleocristiani in Italia: monumentalità per la città episcopale,*" in J. Beltrán de Heredia and C. Godoy Fernández (eds.), *La dualitat de baptisteris el les ciutats episcopals del cristianisme tardoantic*, Barcelona, pp. 9–30.

Brandt, O., and P. Pergola (eds.) (2011) *Marmoribus vestita. Miscellanea in onore di Federico Guidobaldi*, 2 vols., Vatican City.

Brenk, B. (1995) "Microstoria sotto la Chiesa dei SS. Giovanni e Paolo: la cristianizzazione di una casa privata," *RIASA, serie III*, 18, pp. 169–206.

Brenk, B. (2006) "Zur Einführung des Kultes der heiligen Kosmas und Damian in Rom," *Theologische Zeitschrift* 62, pp. 303–20.

Brentano, R. (1974) *Rome before Avignon: A Social History of Thirteenth-Century Rome*, Berkeley.

Brezzi, P. (1947) *Roma e l'impero medioevale (774–1252)*, Bologna.

Broise, H. and J.-C. Maire Vigueur (1983) "Strutture famigliari, spazio domestico e architettura civile a Roma alla fine del Medioevo," in *Storia dell'arte italiana*, vol. 12, *Momenti di architettura*, Turin, pp. 97–160.

Brown, P. (1992) *Power and Persuasion in Late Antiquity: Towards a Christian Empire*, Madison, WI.

Brown, P. (2002) *Poverty and Leadership in the Later Roman Empire*, Hanover, NH.

Brown, P. (2012) *Through the Eye of a Needle. Wealth, the Fall of Rome, and the Making of Christianity in the West, 350–550 AD*, Princeton.

Brown, T. S. (1984) *Gentlemen and Officers. Imperial Administration and Aristocratic Power in Byzantine Italy A.D. 554–800*, Rome.

Brubaker, L., and J. Haldon (2011) *Byzantium in the Iconoclast Era c. 680 – 850: A History*, Cambridge.

Bruun, C. (1991) *The Water Supply of Ancient Rome*, Helsinki.

Burroughs, C. (1982) "Below the Angel: An Urbanistic Project in the Rome of Pope Nicholas V," *Journal of the Warburg and Courtauld Institutes* 45, pp. 94–124.

Burroughs, C. (1990) *From Signs to Design. Environmental Process and Reform in Early Renaissance Rome*, Cambridge, MA and London.

Cafà, V. (2010) "The via Papalis in Early Cinquecento Rome: a Contested Space between Roman Families and Curials," *Urban History* 37.3, pp. 434–51.

Calabria, M. E. *et al.* (2015) "Produzioni artigianali nella Basilica Hilariana sul Celio fra tarda antichità e alto medioevo," in Molinari, Spera, and Santangeli Valenzani (eds.), pp. 173–93.

Calcagnile, L. (2014) "Tecniche nucleari di analisi e datazione dei beni culturali con l'acceleratore tandetron del CEDAD," *Conservation Science in Cultural Heritage* 14, pp. 113–23.

Caliri, E. (2004) "*Praedia pistoria* e *possessores* africani in età vandalica: A proposito di Valentiniano III, *Nov.* 34," in M. Khanoussi, P. Ruggieri, and C. Vismara (eds.) *Africa Romana. Ai confini dell'impero: contatti, scambi, conflitti*, vol. 3, Rome, pp. 1693–1710.

Caliri, E. (2017) *Praecellentissimus rex. Odoacre tra storia e storiografia*, Rome.

Camerlenghi, N. (2018) *St. Paul's Outside the Walls. A Roman Basilica, from Antiquity to the Modern Era*, Cambridge and New York.

Cameron, A. (2011) *The Last Pagans of Rome*, Oxford and New York.
Cameron, A., and D. Schauer (1982) "The Last Consul: Basilius and His Diptych," *JRS* 72, pp. 126–45.
Camodeca, G., and H. Solin (2000) *Catalogo delle iscrizioni latine del Museo nazionale di Napoli (ILMN)*, Vol. 1, *Roma e Latium*, Naples.
Cantino Wataghin, G., and C. Lambert (1998) "Sepolture e città. L'Italia settentrionale tra IV e VIII secolo," in G. P. Brogiolo and G. Cantino Wataghin (eds.), *Sepolture tra IV e VIII secolo. 7° seminario sul tardo antico e l'alto medioevo in Italia centro settentrionale*, Mantua, pp. 89–114.
Capelli, G. (2015) "La Marrana dell'acqua mariana. Un corso d'acqua al servizio dei papi," *Italian Journal of Groundwater* (2015), pp. 79–82.
Carbonetti Vendittelli, C. (1990) "Documentazione inedita riguardante i *magistri edificiorum Urbis* e l'attività della loro curia nei secoli XIII e XIV," *ASRSP* 113, pp. 169–88.
Carbonetti Vendittelli, C. (1993) "La curia dei magistri edificiorum Urbis nei secoli XIII e XIV e la sua documentazione," in É. Hubert (ed.), *Rome aux XIIIe et XIVe siècles/Roma nei secoli XIII–XIV. Cinque saggi*, Rome, pp. 3–42.
Carbonetti Vendittelli, C. (2011) "I supporti scrittorii della documentazione : l'uso del papiro," in Martin, Peters-Custot, and Prigent (eds.), pp. 87–115.
Carbonetti Vendittelli, C. (2015) "Le scritture del comune di Roma nei secoli XII–XIII," in C. Carbonetti, S. Lucà, and M. Signorini (eds.), *Roma e il suo territorio nel medioevo. Le fonti scritte tra tradizione e innovazione*, Spoleto, pp. 293–342.
Carbonetti Vendittelli, C., S. Carocci, and A. Molinari (2017) *Roma*, Spoleto.
Carboni, C. (2016) "Un complesso altomedievale nel cuore della *domus tiberiana*," in Andaloro, Bordi and Morganti (eds.), pp. 86–96.
Carettoni, G., A. M. Colini, L. Cozza, and G. Gatti (1960) *La pianta marmorea di Roma antica*, Rome.
Carnabucci, E. (2012) *Regia. Nuovi dati archeologici dagli appunti inediti di Giacomo Boni*, *LTUR* Supplement 5, Rome.
Carocci, S. (1993a) *Baroni di Roma. Dominazioni signorili e lignaggi aristocratici nel duecento e nel primo trecento*, Rome.
Carocci, S. (1993b) "Baroni in città. Considerazioni sull'insediamento e i diritti urbani della grande nobiltà," in É. Hubert (ed.), *Rome aux XIIIe et XIVe siècles/Roma nei secoli XIII–XIV. Cinque saggi*, Rome, pp. 137–74.
Carocci, S. (1999) *Il nepotismo nel medioevo. Papi, cardinali e famiglie nobili*, Rome.
Carocci, S. (2004) "Insediamento aristocratico e residenze cardinalizie a Roma fra XII e XIV secolo," in Monciatti (ed.), pp. 17–28.
Carocci, S. (2006) "Nobiltà romana e nobiltà italiana nel medioevo centrale, parallelismi e contrasti," in S. Carocci (ed.), *La nobiltà romana nel medioevo*, Rome, pp. 15–42.
Carocci, S., and M. Vendittelli (2001) "Società ed economia (1050–1420)," in Vauchez (ed.), pp. 71–116.
Carocci, S., and M. Vendittelli (2004) *L'origine della campagna romana. Casali, castelli e villaggi nel XII e XIII secolo*, Rome.
Carocci, S., and M. Vendittelli (2013) "Proprietà fondiaria, organizzazione produttiva e società cittadina (secoli XII–XIII). Un percorso di ricerche, da Tomassetti ad oggi," in L. Pani Ermini and P. Sommella (eds.), *Giuseppe Tomassetti a cento anni dalla morte e la sua opera sulla campagna romana*, Rome, pp. 183–201.
Carpegna Falconieri, T. di (1994) "Torri, complessi e consorterie. Alcune riflessioni sul sistema abitativo dell'aristocrazia romana nei secoli XI–XII," *Rivista Storica del Lazio* 2, pp. 3–15.
Carpegna Falconieri, T. di (2001) "Giovanni di Crescenzio," *DBI* 56, pp. 1–4.
Carpegna Falconieri, T. di (2002a) *Il clero di Roma nel medioevo : istituzioni e politica cittadina*, Rome.
Carpegna Falconieri, T. di (2002b) *Cola di Rienzo*, Rome.
Carpegna Falconieri, T. di (2012) "La *militia* a Roma. Il formarsi di una nuova aristocrazia (secoli VII–VIII)," in Martin, Peters-Custot, and Prigent (eds.), pp. 559–83.
Carpegna Falconieri, T. di (2014) "Sulle prime attestazioni dei nomi dei rioni nel medioevo," *Strenna dei Romanisti* 75, pp. 73–84.
Casalini, M. (2015) "Roma e il Mediterraneo dal IV al VI secolo," in E. Cirelli, F. Diosono, and H. Patterson (eds.), *Le forme della crisi: Produzioni ceramiche e commerci nell'Italia centrale tra Romani e Longobardi (III–VIII secolo d.C.)*, Bologna, pp. 535–46.
Cassanelli, L., G. Delfini, and D. Fonti (1974) *Le mura di Roma. L'architettura militare nella storia urbana*, Rome.
Castagnoli, F. (1947) "Il Campo Marzio nell'antichità," *Atti della Accademia Nazionale dei Lincei. Memorie* 8.1, pp. 93–193.
Cecchelli, M. (2001) "Le strutture murarie di Roma tra IV e VII secolo," in M. Cecchelli (ed.), *Materiali e tecniche dell'edilizia paleocristiana a Roma*, Rome, pp. 11–101.
Ceci, M., and R. Santangeli Valenzani (2016) "La chiesa di s. Lucia *de Calcarario*. Nuovi dati dalle indagini a via delle Botteghe Oscure," in A. Ferrandes and G. Pardini (eds.), *Le regole del gioco. Tracce archeologiche, racconti, studi in onore di Clementina Panella*, Rome, pp. 235–48.
Cerrati M. V. (1915) "Il tetto della Basilica Vaticana rifatto per opera di Benedetto XII," *MEFR* 35, pp. 81–117.
Cerrito, A. (2011) "Contributo allo studio del *titulus Anastasiae*," in Brandt and Pergola (eds.), pp. 345–71.

Chastagnol, A. (1966) *Le sénat romain sous le règne d'Odoacre. Recherches sur l'épigraphie du Colisée au V siècle*, Bonn.

Chastagnol, A. (1996) "Les régionnieres de Rome," *Entretiens Hardt* 42, pp. 179–92.

Chiovelli, R. (2015) "La struttura medievale dell'edificio tra crolli e ricostruzioni," *Bollettino del Centro di Studi per la Storia dell'Archittura* 45–52 (2008–2015), pp. 39–61.

Christie, N. (2001) "War and order: urban remodeling and defensive strategy in late Roman Italy," in L. Lavan (ed.), *Recent Research in Late-Antique Urbanism*, Portsmouth, RI, pp. 106–22.

Ciancio Rossetto, P. (2008) "Portico d'Ottavia – Sant'Angelo in Pescheria : nuove acquisizioni sulle fasi medievali," *RAC* 84, pp. 415–37.

Cima, M. and E. La Rocca (eds.) (1998) *Horti romani*, Rome.

Cirelli, E. (2013) "Le città dell'Italia del nord nell'epoca dei re (888–962 AD)," in M. Valenti and C. Wickham (eds.), *Italia, 888–962: una svolta*, Turnhout, pp. 131–68.

Claridge, A. (2010) *Rome. An Oxford Archaeological Guide*, 2nd ed., Oxford.

Claussen, P.C. (1987) *Magistri doctissimi romani: Die römischen Marmorkünstler des Mittelalters*, Stuttgart.

Claussen, P.C. (1992) "*Renovatio Romae*. Erneuererungsphasen römischer Architektur im 11. und 12. Jahrhundert," in Schimmelpfennig and Schmugge (eds.), pp. 87–125.

Claussen, P.C. (2016) "Il XII secolo. Da Pasquale II (1099–1118) a Celestino III (1191–98)," in D'Onofrio (ed.), pp. 275–98.

Coarelli, F. (1983) *Il Foro Romano*, vol. 1: *Periodo arcaico*, Rome.

Coarelli, F. (1985) *Il Foro Romano*, vol. 2: *Periodo repubblicano e augusteo*, Rome.

Coarelli, F. (1988) *Il Foro Boario dalle origini alla fine della repubblica*, Rome.

Coarelli, F. (1997) *Il Campo Marzio dalle origini alla fine della repubblica*, Rome.

Coarelli, F. (1999) "L'edilizia pubblica in età tetrarchica," in Harris (ed.), pp. 23–33.

Coarelli, F. (2012) *Palatium: il Palatino dalle origini all'impero*, Rome.

Coarelli, F. (2014) *Rome and Environs. An Archaeological Guide* (updated edition, Berkeley – Los Angeles – London).

Coates-Stephens, R. (1995). "Quattro torri alto-medievali delle Mura Aureliane," *Archeologia Medievale* 22, pp. 501–17.

Coates-Stephens, R. (1996) "Housing in early medieval Rome A.D. 500–1000," *PBSR* 64, pp. 239–60.

Coates-Stephens, R. (1997) "Dark Age Architecture in Rome," *PBSR* 65, pp. 177–232.

Coates-Stephens, R. (1998) "The Walls and Aqueducts of Rome in the Early Middle Ages," *JRS* 88, pp. 166–78.

Coates-Stephens, R. (1999) "Le ricostruzioni altomedievali delle mura aureliane e degli acquedotti," *MEFRM* 111.1, pp. 209–25.

Coates-Stephens, R. (2003a) "The Water-Supply of Early Medieval Rome," *Acta Instituti Romani Finlandiae* 31, pp. 81–113.

Coates-Stephens, R. (2003b). "The Water-Supply of Rome from Late Antiquity to the Early Middle Ages," *Acta IRN* 17, pp. 165–86.

Coates-Stephens, R. (2004) *Porta Maggiore monument and landscape. Archaeology and Topography of the southern Esquiline from the Late Republican period to the present*, Rome.

Coates-Stephens, R. (2006a) "Byzantine building patronage in post-reconquest Rome," in Ghilardi, Goddard and Porena (eds.), pp. 149–66.

Coates-Stephens, R. (2006b) "La committenza edilizia a Roma dopo la riconquista," in A. Augenti (ed.), *Le città italiane tra la tarda Antichità e l'alto Medioevo. Atti del convegno (Ravenna, 26–28 febbraio 2004)*, Florence, pp. 299–316.

Coates-Stephens, R. (2011) "The Roman Forum in the Byzantine Period," in Brandt and Pergola (eds.), pp. 385–408.

Coates-Stephens, R. (2017) "The Byzantine Sack of Rome," *AnTard* 25, pp. 191–212.

Coates-Stephens, R. (forthcoming) "The Oratory of the Forty Martyrs," in E. Rubery, G. Bordi and J. Osborne (eds.), *Santa Maria Antiqua: The Sistine Chapel of the Early Middle Ages*, Turnhout.

Colini, A. (1944) *Storia e topografia del Celio nell'antichità*, RendPontAc 7, Rome.

Coluccia, G.L. (1998) *Niccolò V umanista: papa e riformatore : Renovatio politica e morale*, Venice.

Conant, J. (2012) *Staying Roman. Conquest and Identity in Africa and the Mediterranean, 439–700*, Cambridge.

Corsaro, A., A. Delfino, I. De Luca, and R. Meneghini (2013) "Nuovi dati archeologici per la storia del Foro di Cesare tra la fine del IV e la metà del V secolo," in Lipps, Machado, and von Rummel (eds.), pp. 123–36.

Corvisieri, C. (1877) "Delle Posterule tiberine tra la Porta Flaminia ed il Ponte Gianicolense," *ASRSP* 1, pp. 79–121; 137–70.

Costambeys, M. (2001) "Burial Topography and the Power of the Church in Fifth- and Sixth-Century Rome," *PBSR* 69, pp. 169–89.

Courcelle, P. (1964) *Histoire littéraire des grandes invasions germaniques*, 3rd ed., Paris.

Cowdrey, H.E.J. (1998) *Pope Gregory VII, 1073–1085*, Oxford.

Cozza, L. (1987) "Osservazioni sulle Mura Aureliane a Roma," *ARID* 16, pp. 25–52.

Curran, J. (2000) *Pagan City and Christian Capital: Rome in the Fourth Century*, Oxford.

Cusanno, A.M. (1988) "Turris comitum. Vicende storiche ed ipotesi sulla 'torre della città,'" *L'Urbe* 5–6, pp. 20–38.

D'ambrosio, E. (2009) "Nuovi dati epigrafici," *Scienze dell'Antichità* 15, pp. 463–72.

De Angelis d'Ossat, M. (2005) "Gli scavi urbani nell'area di Palazzo Altemps a Roma: la *domus* tardoimperiale," in F. Morandini and F. Rossi (eds.), *Domus romane: dallo scavo alla valorizzazione*, Milan, pp. 239–46.

de Blaauw, S. (1993) "*Campanae supra urbem*: sull'uso delle campane nella Roma medievale," *Rivista di Storia della Chiesa in Italia* 47, pp. 367–414.

de Blaauw, S. (1994) *Cultus et decor: liturgia e architettura nella Roma tardoantica e medievale : Basilica Salvatoris, Sanctae Mariae, Sancti Petri*, Vatican City.

de Blaauw, S. (2014) "Liturgical Features of Roman Churches: Manifestations of the Church of Rome?," *Settimane del CISAM* 61, pp. 321–37.

de Kleijn, G. (2001) *The Water Supply of Ancient Rome: City Area, Water, and Population*, Leiden and Boston.

DeLaine, J. (1997) *The Baths of Caracalla. A Study in the Design, Construction and Economics of Large-Scale Building Projects in Imperial Rome*, Portsmouth, RI.

DeLaine, J. (2018) "The Imperial *Thermae*," in C. Holleran and A. Claridge (eds.), *A Companion to the City of Rome*, London and New York, pp. 325–42.

Del Bufalo, D. (2010) *Marmorari magistri romani*, Rome.

Del Buono, G. (2010) "Giovanni VIII e le pitture di Santa Maria de Secundicerio a Roma: realizzazione artistica di un progetto ecumenico," *Rendiconti dell'Accademia Nazionale dei Lincei, Classe di Scienze Morali, Storiche e Filologiche*, series 9, vol. 21, pp. 513–68.

Delfino, A. (2018) "La fortezza dei Frangipane al Colosseo: un'ipotesi ricostruttiva," in Facchin, Rea, and Santangeli Valenzani (eds.), pp. 32–51.

Deliyannis, D. (1996) "Agnellus of Ravenna and Iconoclasm: Theology and Politics in a Ninth-Century Historical Text," *Speculum* 71, pp. 559–76.

Del Lungo, S. (2004) *Roma in età carolingia e gli scritti dell'Anonimo Augiense*, Rome.

Delogu, P. (1988a) "The Rebirth of Rome in the Eighth and Ninth Centuries," in Hobley and Hodges (eds.), *The Rebirth of Towns in the West AD 700–1050*, London, pp. 33–42.

Delogu, P. (1988b) "Oro e argento in Roma tra il VII ed il IX secolo," in *Cultura e Società nell'Italia medievale. Studi per Paolo Brezzi* (Studi Storici, vols. 184–7), Rome, pp. 173–93.

Delogu P. (2000a) "The Papacy, Rome and the Wider World in the Seventh and Eighth Centuries," in J. Smith (ed.), pp. 197–220.

Delogu, P. (2000b) "Solium imperii – urbs ecclesiae. Roma fra la tarda antichità e l'alto medioevo," in J. M. Gurt and G. Ripoll (eds.), *Sedes regiae (ann. 400–800)*, Barcelona, pp. 83–108.

Delogu, P. (2001) "Il passaggio dall'antichità al Medioevo," in Vauchez (ed.), pp. 3–40.

Delogu, P. (2010) *Le origini del medioevo*, Rome.

Delogu, P. (2015) "I romani e l'Impero (VII–X secolo)," in West-Harling (ed.), pp. 191–225.

Delogu, P., and L. Paroli (eds.) (1993) *La Storia economica di Roma nell'alto medioevo alla luce dei recenti scavi archeologici. Atti del Seminario Roma 2–3 aprile 1992*, Florence.

Delogu, P., and S. Gasparri (eds.) (2010) *Le trasformazioni del V secolo. L'Italia, i barbari, e l'Occidente romano*, Turnhout.

De Nuccio, M. (2002) "La cripta semianulare di San Nicola de' Calcarario e la scultura altomedievale rinvenuta nell'area sacra di Largo Argentina," in Guidobaldi and Guiglia Guidobaldi (eds.), pp. 891–911.

Dey, H. (2008) "*Diaconiae, Xenodochia, Hospitalia* and Monasteries: 'Social Security' and the Meaning of Monasticism in Early Medieval Rome," *Early Medieval Europe* 16.4, pp. 398–422.

Dey, H. (2011) *The Aurelian Wall and the Refashioning of Imperial Rome, AD 271–855*, Cambridge.

Dey, H. (2015) *The Afterlife of the Roman City: Architecture and Ceremony in Late Antiquity and the Early Middle Ages*, Cambridge.

Dey, H. (2019) "Politics, Patronage, and the Transmission of Construction Techniques in Early Medieval Rome, c. 650–750," *PBSR* 87, pp. 177–205.

Dey, H. (2020a) "Popes, Senators, Barons, and Popes Again: The Aurelian Wall from the 12th to the 15th Century," in E. Intagliata, C. Courault, and S. Barker (eds.), *City Walls in Late Antiquity: An Empire-Wide Perspective*, Oxford and Philadelphia, pp. 157–73.

Dey, H. (2020b) Landscape Change and Ceremonial Praxis in Medieval Rome: From the Via Triumphalis to the Via Papalis," in J. Beasley and G. Farquat (eds.), *Landscapes of Pre-Industrial Urbanism*, pp. 57–84.

di Bernardino, A., G. Pilara, and L. Spera (eds.) (2012) *Roma e il sacco del 410. Realtà, interpretazione, mito*, Rome.

Dieffenbach, S. (2002) "Beobachtungen zum antiken Rom im hohen Mittelalter: Städtische Topographie als Herrschafts- und Erinnerungsraum," *RömQSchr* 97, pp. 40–88.

Di Fazio, C., and S. Guidone (2014) "Disiecta membra nella basilica di S. Maria in Trastevere," *Archeologia Classica* 65, pp. 227–54.

Di Manzano, P., M. Cecchelli, and A. Milella (2006–7) "Indagini archeologiche nella chiesa di S. Bartolomeo all'Isola Tiberina," *RendPontAc* 79, pp. 125–76.

Di Santo, A. (2009) *Monumenti antichi fortezze medievali. Il riutilizzo degli antichi monumenti nell'edilizia aristocratica di roma (VIII–XIV secolo)*, Rome.

Di Santo, A. (2016) *Guerre di torri. Violenza e conflitto a Roma tra 1200 e 1500*, Rome.

D'Onofrio, C. (1978) *Castel S. Angelo e Borgo tra Roma e Papato*, Rome.

D'Onofrio, M. (ed.) (2016) *La committenza artistica dei papi a Roma nel Medioevo*, Rome.

Dugast, F. (2007) "Spectacles et édifices de spectacles dans l'Antiquité tardive," *AnTard* 15, pp. 11–20.

Duhr, J. (1932) "Le concile de Ravenna en 898. La rehabilitation du pape Formose," *Recherches de science religieuse* 22, pp. 541–79.

Dunn, M. (2000) *The Emergence of Monasticism: From the Desert Fathers to the Early Middle Ages*, Oxford.

Dupré Theseider, E. (1952) *Roma dal Comune di Popolo alla Signoria pontificia (1252–1377)*, Bologna.

Durliat, J. (1990) *De la ville antique à la ville Byzantine: le problème des subsistances*, Rome.

Economou, A. (1997) *Byzantine Rome and Greek Popes: Eastern Influences on Rome and the Papacy from Gregory the Great to Zacharias, A.D. 590–752*, Lanham, MD.

Ehrle, F., and H. Egger (1935) *Der vaticanische Palast in seiner Entwicklung bis zur Mitte des XV. Jahrhunderts*, Vatican City.

Ellis, M. R. (1998) "Landscape and Power: The Frangipani Family and Their Clients in the Twelfth-Century Roman Forum," in J. Hill and M. Swan (eds.), *The Community, the Family and the Saint: Patterns of Power in Early Medieval Europe*, Turnhout, pp. 61–76.

Englen, A., R. Santolini, M. G. Fileticì, P. Palazzo, and C. Pavolini (eds.) (2014) *Caelius II. Pars Inferior. Le Case Romane sotto la Basilica dei Ss. Giovanni e Paolo*, Rome.

Ensoli, S., and E. La Rocca (eds.) (2000) *Aurea Roma: dalla città pagana alla città cristiana*, Rome.

Esch, A. (1969) *Bonifaz IX. und der Kirchenstaat*, Tübingen.

Esch, A. (2007) "Dalla Roma comunale alla Roma papale: La fine del libero comune," *ASRSP* 130, pp. 1–16.

Esch, A. (2008) "Straßenzustand und Verkehr in Stadtgebiet und Umgebung Roms im Übergang von der Spätantike zum Frühmittelalter, 5.–8. Jh.," *Palilia* 18, pp. 218–37.

Esch. A. (2016) *Rom vom Mittelalter zum Renaissance*, Munich.

Esposito, A. (1995) *Un'altra Roma: Minoranze nazionali e comunità ebraiche tra Medioevo e Rinascimento*, Rome.

Esposito, A. (1998) "La popolazione romana dalla fine del sec. XIV al Sacco: caratteri e forme di un'evoluzione demografica," in E. Sonnino (ed.), *Popolazione e società a Roma dal medioevo all'età contemporanea*, Rome, pp. 37–49.

Esposito, A. (2010) "Il Tevere e Roma," in M. Matheus et al. (eds.), *Le calamità ambientale nel tardo medioevo europeo: Realtà, percezioni, reazioni*, Florence, pp. 257–75.

Esposito, D. (1998) *Tecniche costruttive murarie medievali. Murature 'a tufelli' in area romana*, Rome.

Esposito, D. (2005) *Architettura e costruzione dei casali e costruzione dei casali della Campagna Romana fra XII e XIV secolo*, Rome.

Esposito, D. (2008) "Alcune note sull'insediamento fortificato di Capodibove," in A. Mazzon (ed.), *Scritti per Isa. Raccolta di studi offerti a Isa Lori Sanfilippo*, Rome, pp. 369–93.

Esposito, D. (2014) "Il cantiere e le opere murarie in Roma tra Tardoantico e alto Medioevo," in G. P. Brogiolo (ed.) *Tecniche costruttive e cicli edilizi tra VI e IX secolo, fra oriente e occidente* (*Archeologia dell'Architettura*, vol. 18), Florence, pp. 80–7.

Esposito, D. (2015) "Tecniche murarie e organizzazione del cantiere a Roma e in area romana nei secoli XII–XIV: alcuni indicatori," in Molinari, Santangeli Valenzani, and Spera (eds.), pp. 345–54.

Evans, H. B. (1994) *Water Distribution in Ancient Rome. The Evidence of Frontinus*, Ann Arbor.

Facchin, G., R. Rea, and R. Santangeli Valenzani (eds.) (2018) *Anfiteatro Flavio / trasformazioni e riusi*, Milan.

Falesiedi, U. (1995) *Le diaconie. I servizi assistenziali nella Chiesa antica*, Rome.

Fauvinet-Ranson, V. (2006) *Decor civitatis, decor Italiae. Monuments, travaux publics et spectacles au VI siècle d'après les variae de Cassiodore*, Bari.

Fedele, P. (1908) "Il più antico documento dei 'Magistri aedificiorum Urbis' e 'Donna Comitissa,'" in *Miscellanea per nozze Crocioni-Ruscelloni*, Rome, pp. 147–55.

Fedele, P. (1910) "Sull'origine dei Frangipane," *ASRSP* 33, pp. 493–506.

Ferrari, G. (1957) *Early Roman monasteries. Notes for the History of the Monasteries and Convents at Rome from the V through the X Century*, Vatican City.

Fidenzoni, P. (1970) *Il Teatro di Marcello*, Rome.

Fiocchi Nicolai, V. (2001) *Strutture funerarie ed edifici di culto paleocristiani di Roma dal IV al VI secolo*, Vatican City.

Fiocchi Nicolai, V. (2003) "Elementi di trasformazione dello spazio funerario tra tarda antichità ed alto medioevo," *Settimane del CISAM* 50, pp. 921–69.

Fiocchi Nicolai, V. (2012) "Il sacco dei Goti e la fine delle catacombe: un mito storiografico?," in di Bernardino, Pilara, and Spera (eds.), pp. 283–310.

Fiocchi Nicolai, V. (2019a) "Un pluteo 'bizantino' dalle Tre Fontane a Roma. A proposito delle origini del monastero *ad Aquas Salvias* e del luogo del martirio di Paolo," in G. Archetti et al. (eds.), *"Colligere fragmenta" Studi in onore di Marcello Rotili per il suo 70° genetliaco*, Spoleto, pp. 291–317.

Fiocchi Nicolai, V. (2019b) "A proposito di *Caelius II*: Ancora sul santuario martiriale dei SS. Giovanni e Paolo al Celio," *RAC* 95, pp. 281–326.

Fiocchi Nicolai, V., M. P. Del Moro, D. Nuzzo, and L. Spera (1995–96) "La nuova basilica circiforme della via Ardeatina," *RendPontAc* 68, pp. 69–233.

Fiocchi Nicolai, V., D. Mastrorilli, and A. Vella (2016) "Le campagne di scavo 2007–2012 nella basilica a deambulatorio della via Ardeatina (S. Marco). Note preliminari," in O. Brandt and V. Fiocchi Nicolai (eds.), *Costantino e i Costantinidi. L'innovazione costantiniana, le sue radici e i suoi sviluppi. Acta XVI Congressus Internationalis Archaeologiae Christianae (Romae, 22–28.9.2013)*, Vatican City, pp. 2063–90.

Fiocchi Nicolai, V., and A. Vella (2016–17) "Nuove ricerche nella basilica di papa Marco sulla via Ardeatina: la tomba 'dei gioielli' e il riuso di un acquedotto romano," *RendPontAc* 89, pp. 299–366.

Fogagnolo, S. (2013) "Testimonianze del sacco del 410 in un cantiere edilizio a Trastevere (Conservatorio di San Pasquale Baylon)," in Lipps, Machado, and von Rummel (eds.), pp. 151–61.

Franceschi, F. (2017) "La crescita economica dell'occidente medievale: un tema storico non ancora esaurito. Introduzione," in *La crescita economica dell'occidente medievale: un tema storico non ancora esaurito. Pistoia, 14–17 maggio 2015*, Rome, pp. 1–24.

Francovich, R. (2002) "Changing Structures of Settlements," in C. La Rocca (ed.), *Italy in the Early Middle Ages*, Oxford, pp. 144–67.

Fraschetti, A. (1999) *La conversione : da Roma pagana a Roma cristiana*, Rome and Bari.

Fried, J. (2007) *Donation of Constantine and Constitutum Constantini. The Misinterpretation of a Fiction and its Original Meaning*, Berlin and New York.

Frommel, C. L. (1997) "Il San Pietro di Nicolò V," in G. Spagnesi (ed.), *L'architettura della basilica di San Pietro. Storia e costruzione*, Rome, pp. 103–10.

Fusconi, G. (2016) *La zecca di Roma. Le prime coniazioni pontificie e gli antiquiores*, Rome (*Bollettino di Numismatica on-line, Materiali* 39).

Galadini, F. et al. (2018) "Archaeoseismological evidence of past earthquakes in Rome (fifth to ninth century A.D.) used to quantify dating uncertainties and coseismic damage," *Natural Hazards* 94, pp. 319–48.

Galland, B. (2004) *Les authentiques de reliques du Sancta Sanctorum*, Vatican City.

Galli, P. A. C., and D. Molin (2013) "Beyond the Damage Threshold: the Historic Earthquakes of Rome," *Bulletin of Earthquake Engineering* 12.3.

Gandolfo, F. (2016) "l'XI secolo: da Silvestro II (999–1003) ad Urbano II (1088–1099)," in D'Onofrio (ed.), pp. 255–73.

Gardner, J. (2014) *The Roman Crucible. The Artistic Patronage of the Papacy 1198–1304*, Munich.

Geertman, H. (1975) *More veterum. Il 'Liber Pontificalis' e gli edifici ecclesiastici di Roma nella tarda antichità e nell'alto medioevo*, Groningen.

Geertman, H. (ed.) (2003) *Il Liber Pontificalis e la storia materiale*, Rome.

Gentili, M. D., M. C. Somma, and F. R. Stasolla (2016–17) "*Ad locum optimum valdeque munitum*: nuovi dati sulla fondazione di Leopoli-Cencelle," *RendPontAc* 89, pp. 367–406.

Ghilardi, M., C. Goddard, and P. Porena (eds.), *Les cités de l'Italie tardo-antique (IVe–VIe siècle). Institutions, économie, société, culture et religion*, Rome.

Giannini, N. (2015) "Leggere la città attraverso i dati materiali. L'esempio del fosso della Marana e le trasformazioni urbanistiche di Roma tra XI e XIII secolo," in C. Bonardi (ed.), *Fare urbanistica tra XI e XIV secolo* (*Storia dell'Urbanistica* 7/2015), Rome, pp. 15–32.

Giannini, N. (2016) "Abitare a Roma nel Medioevo. Dall'edilizia civile allo spazio urbano, primi risultati della ricerca," *Archeologia Medievale* 43, pp. 289–307.

Giardina, A., and A. Vauchez (2000) *Rome, l'idée et le mythe: du Moyen Age à nos jours*, Paris.

Gibson, S., and B. Ward-Perkins (1979) "The Surviving Remains of the Leonine Wall," *PBSR* 47, pp. 30–57.

Gibson, S., and B. Ward-Perkins (1983) "The Surviving Remains of the Leonine Wall. Part II: The Passetto," *PBSR* 51, pp. 222–39.

Gillett, A. (2001) "Rome, Ravenna and the Emperors," *PBSR* 69, pp. 131–67.

Giovenale, G. B. (1927) *La basilica di S. Maria in Cosmedin*, Rome.

Giovannini, F. (2010) "Le trasformazioni demografiche in Italia tra IV e V secolo," in Delogu and Gasparri (eds.), pp. 215–38.

Giuliani, C., and P. Verduchi (1987) *L'area centrale del Foro Romano*, Florence.

Giuntella, A. M. (1985). "'Spazio cristiano' e città altomedievale: l'esempio della *civitas leoniana*," in *Atti del VI Congresso Nazionale di Archeologia Cristiana (Pesaro – Ancona 19–23 settembre 1983)*, pp. 309–25.

Giuntella, A. M. (2001) "Gli spazi dell'assistenza e della meditazione," *Settimane del CISAM* 48, pp. 639–91.

Glass, D. (1980) *Studies in Cosmatesque Pavements*, Oxford.

Goez, W. (2000) *Kirchenreform und Investiturstreit 910–1122*, Stuttgart.

Goodman, P. J. (2007) *The Roman City and Its Periphery: from Rome to Gaul*, London – New York.

Goodson, C. (2007) "Building for Bodies. The Architecture of Saint Veneration in Early Medieval Rome," in É. Ó. Carraghain and C. Neuman de Vegvar (eds.), *Roma Felix – Formation and Reflections of Medieval Rome*, Aldershot and Burlington, VT, pp. 51–79.

Goodson, C. (2010) *The Rome of Pope Paschal I: papal power, urban renovation, church rebuilding and relic translation, 817–824*, Cambridge and New York.

Goodson, C., and J. Nelson (2010) "The Roman Contexts of the Donation of Constantine," *EME* 18.4, pp. 446–67.

Graf, A. (1882–83) *Roma nella memoria e nelle immaginazioni del medio evo*, 2 vols., Turin.

Graham, B., and P. Squatriti (2019) "Roofing Rome: Church Coverings and Power in the Postclassical City," in Y. Kim and A. McLaughlin (eds.), *Cities and Saints in Late Antiquity*, Turnhout, pp. 189–219.

Greco, R. (2018) "L'insediamento medievale attraverso i dati d'archivio," in Facchin, Rea, and Santangeli Valenzani (eds.), pp. 25–31.

Gresser, G. (2007) *Clemens II. Der erste deutsche Reformpapst*, Paderborn.

Grillo, P. (2012) *Legnano 1176: Una battaglia per la libertà*, Rome and Bari.

Guidobaldi, F. (1986) "L'edilizia abitativa unifamiliare nella Roma tardoantica," in A. Giardina (ed.), *Società romana e impero tardoantico*, vol. 2, Rome, pp. 165–237.

Guidobaldi, F. (1992) *San Clemente. Gli edifici romani, la basilica paleocristiana e le fasi altomedievali*, Rome.

Guidobaldi, F. (1999) "Le domus tardoantiche di Roma come 'sensori' delle trasformazioni culturali e sociali," in Harris (ed.), pp. 53–68.

Guidobaldi, F. (2000) "L'organizzazione dei *tituli* nello spazio urbano," in Pani Ermini (ed.), pp. 123–9.

Guidobaldi, F. (2014) "Un estesissimo intervento urbanistico nella Roma dell'inizio del XII secolo e la parziale perdita della 'memoria topografica' della città antica," *MEFRM online* 126.2, pp. 1–47.

Guidobaldi, F., and A. Guiglia Guidobaldi (1983) *Pavimenti marmorei di Roma dal IV al IX secolo* (Studi di antichità cristiana, 36), Vatican City.

Guidobaldi, F., and A. Guiglia Guidobaldi (eds.) (2002) *Ecclesiae urbis. Atti del Congresso Internazionale di Studi sulle chiese di Roma (IV–X secolo)*, 3 vols., Vatican City.

Guidobaldi, F., and G. Conte (2011–12) "La parte centrale delle terme di Agrippa nel Campo Marzio: una totale o parziale ricostruzione *a fundamentis* in età tardocostantiniana," *RAC* 87–8, pp. 175–208.

Guidobaldi, F., and L. Sabbi (2016) "Cripte semianulari e altri ambienti devozionali ipogei o semipogei delle chiese di Roma dall'età paleocristiana al medioevo: aspetti tipologici e cronologia," *RAC* 88, pp. 443–556.

Guidobaldi, F., A. Miele, and C. Cecalupo (2021) *Corpus Architecturae Religiosae Europeae* (saec. IV–X), Vol. II. Italia, 2a. *Roma dentro le mura, Regiones I–IV*, Zagreb – Vatican City.

Guidoboni, E., and D. Molin (1989) "Effetto fonti effetto monumenti a Roma: i terremoti dall'antichità a oggi," in E. Guidoboni (ed.), *I terremoti prima del Mille in Italia e nell'area mediterranea*, Bologna, pp. 194–223.

Guiglia, A. (2016) "Il VI secolo: da Simmaco (498–514) a Gregorio Magno (590–604)," in D'Onofrio (ed.), pp. 109–43.

Guiglia Guidobaldi, A. (1983) "I pavimenti in opus sectile della Basilica Emilia: Testimonianze bizantine a Roma nel VI secolo," in *III Colloquio Internazionale sul Mosaico Antico*, vol. 2, Ravenna, pp. 505–13.

Guillou, A. (1988) "L'Italia bizantina dall'invasione longobarda alla caduta di Ravenna," in A. Guillou and F. Burgarella (eds.), *L'Italia bizantina. Dall'esarcato di Ravenna al tema di Sicilia*, Turin, pp. 3–122.

Hamilton, L. I. (2003) "Memory, Symbol and Arson: Was Rome 'Sacked' in 1084?," *Speculum* 78, pp. 378–99.

Harris, W. V. (ed.) (1999) *The Transformations of Urbs Roma in Late Antiquity*, Portsmouth, RI.

Harris, W. V. (2016) "Religion on the Battlefield: from the Saxa Rubra to the Frigidus," in V. Gasparini (ed.), *Miscellanea di studi storico-religiosi in onore dell'80° anniversario di Filippo Coarelli*, Stuttgart, pp. 437–50.

Hartmann, F. (2006) *Hadrian I (772–795). Frühmittelalterliches Adelspapsttum und die Lösung Roms vom byzantinischen Kaiser*, Stuttgart.

Hartswick, K. J. (2004) *The Gardens of Sallust. A Changing Landscape*, Austin, TX.

Headrick, D. (2012) "The Medieval World, 500 to 1500 CE," in J. R. McNeill and E. S. Mauldin (eds.), *A Companion to Global Environmental History*, Hoboken, NJ, pp. 39–56.

Heres, T. L. (1982) *Paries. A Proposal for a Dating System of Late-Antique Masonry Structures in Rome and Ostia*, Amsterdam.

Herklotz, I. (2000) *Gli eredi di Costantino. Il papato, il Laterano e la propaganda visiva nel XII secolo*, Rome.

Hetherington, P. (1994) *Medieval Rome. A Portrait of the City and Its Life*, London.

Hillner, J. (2003) "*Domus*, Family, and Inheritance: The Senatorial Family House in Late Antique Rome," *JRS* 93, pp. 129–45.

Hillner, J. (2007) "Families, Patronage, and the Titular Churches of Rome, c. 300 – c. 600," in C. Cooper and J. Hillner (eds.), *Religion, Dynasty and Patronage in Early Christian Rome, 300–900*, Cambridge, pp. 225–61.

Hoffmann, R. C. (2014) *An Environmental History of Medieval Europe*, Cambridge.

Holleran, C. (2011) "Migration and the Urban Economy of Rome," in C. Holleran and A. Pudsey (eds.), *Demography and the Graeco-Roman World: New Insights and Approaches*, Cambridge, pp. 155–80.

Hubert, É. (1990) *Espace urbain et habitat à Rome du X siècle à la fin du XIII siècle*, Rome.

Hubert, É. (2001) "L'organizzazione territoriale e l'urbanizzazione," in Vauchez (ed.), pp. 159–86.

Hubert, É. (2008) "La diversité socio-économique des quartiers romains : l'indicateur du marché immobilier (XIIe–XIVe siècle)," in A. Béranger, É. Hubert, and M. Royo (eds.), *Rome des quartiers: des vici aux rioni. Cadres institutionnels, pratiques sociales et requalifications entre Antiquité et époque moderne*, Paris, pp. 247–60.

Hubert, É. (2009) "Urbanizzazione, immigrazione e cittadinanza (XII–metà XIV secolo). Alcune considerazioni generali," in *La costruzione della città comunale italiana (secoli XII–inizio XIV)*, Pistoia, pp. 131–45.

Hülsen, C. (1927) *Le chiese di Roma nel Medio Evo: cataloghi ed appunti*, Rome.

Hülsen, C., C. Cecchelli, G. Giovannoni, U. Monneret de Villard, and A. Muñoz, *S. Agata dei Goti* (Rome, 1924).

Humphrey, J. H. (1986) *Roman Circuses: Arenas for Chariot Racing*, London.

Humphries, M. (2000) "Italy 425–605," *The Cambridge Ancient History* (2nd ed.), vol. 14, pp. 525–51.

Humphries, M. (2007) "From Emperor to Pope? Ceremonial, Space, and Authority at Rome from Constantine to Gregory the Great," in K. Cooper and J. Hillner (eds.), *Religion, Dynasty and Patronage in Early Christian Rome, 300–900*, Cambridge, pp. 21–58.

Humphries, M. (2012) "Valentinian III and the City of Rome (AD 425–455): Patronage, Politics and Power," in L. Grig and G. Kelly (eds.), *Two Romes: Rome and Constantinople in Late Antiquity*, Oxford, pp. 161–82.

Inglebert, H. (2006) "Conclusions. Périodiser l'antiquité tardive," in Ghilardi, Goddard, and Porena (eds.), pp. 359–66.

Insalaco, A. (2005) *La città dell'acqua: archeologia sotterranea a Fontana di Trevi*, Milan.

Jacobs, P. W., and D. A. Conlin (2015) *Campus Martius: The Field of Mars in the Life of Ancient Rome*, Cambridge and New York.

Jasper, D. (1986) *Das Papstwahldekret von 1059. Überlieferung und Textgestalt*, Sigmaringen.

Johnson, M. J. (2009) *The Roman Imperial Mausoleum in Late Antiquity*, Cambridge.

Jones, A. H. M. (1964) *The Later Roman Empire 284–602: A Social, Economic and Administrative Survey*, 2 vols., Oxford.

Kalas, G. (2013) "Architecture and Élite Identity in Late Antique Rome: Appropriating the Past at Sant'Andrea Catabarbara," *PBSR* 81, pp. 279–302.

Kalas, G. (2015) *The Restoration of the Roman Forum in Late Antiquity. Transforming Public Space*, Austin.

Kalas, G. (2017) "The Divisive Politics of Phocas (602–610) and the Last Imperial Monument of Rome," *AnTard* 25, pp. 173–90.

Katermaa-Ottela, A. (1981) *Le casetorri medievali in Roma*, Helsinki.

Keay, S., M. Millett, L. Paroli, and K. Strutt (eds.) (2005) *Portus. An Archaeological Survey of the Port of Imperial Rome*, London.

Keay, S. (ed.) (2012) *Rome, Portus, and the Mediterranean*, London.

Kehr, P. F. (1906) *Regesta Pontificum Romanorum. Italia Pontificia*, vol. I: Roma, Berlin.

Kessler, H., and J. Zacharias (2000) *Rome 1300: On the Path of the Pilgrim*, New Haven and London.

Kinney, D. (1975) "S. Maria in Trastevere from Its Founding to 1215," Ph.D. diss., New York University.

Kinney, D. (1986) "Spolia from the Baths of Caracalla in Sta. Maria in Trastevere," *The Art Bulletin* 68.3, pp. 379–97.

Kinney, D. (2007) "Fact and Fiction in the *Mirabilia urbis Romae*," in É.Ó. Carraghain and C. Neuman de Vegvar (eds.), *Roma Felix – Formation and Reflections of Medieval Rome*, Aldershot and Burlington, VT, pp. 235–52.

Kinney, D. (2010) "Edilizia di culto Cristiano a Roma e in Italia centrale dalla metà del IV al VII secolo," in S. de Blaauw (ed.), *Storia dell'architettura italiana: Da Costantino a Carlo Magno*, Milan, pp. 54–97.

Kinney, D. (2011) "Spolia as Signifiers in Twelfth-Century Rome," *Hortus Artium Medievalium* 17, pp. 151–66.

Kinney, D. (2013) "Spoliation in Medieval Rome," in S. Altekamp, C. Marcks-Jacobs, and P. Seiler (eds.), *Perspektiven der Spolienforschung: Spoliierung und Transposition*, Boston, pp. 261–86.

Kinney, D. (2017) "Expanding the Christian Footprint: Church Building in the City and the *Suburbium*," in I. Foletti and M. Gianandrea (eds.), *The Fifth Century in Rome: Art, Liturgy, Patronage*, Rome, pp. 65–97.

Kirsch, J. P. (1898) *Die Rückkehr der Päpste Urban V. und Gregor XI. von Avignon nach Rom, Auszüge aus den Kameralregistern des Vatikanischen Archivs*, Paderborn.

Kirsch, J. P. (1918) *Die römischen Titelkirche im Altertum*, Paderborn.

Klewitz, H. W. (1957) *Reformpapsttum und Kardinalcolleg*, Darmstadt.

Krautheimer, R. (1942) "The Carolingian Revival of Early Christian Architecture," *The Art Bulletin* 24, pp. 1–38.

Krautheimer, R. (1980) *Rome, Profile of a City, 312–1308*, Princeton.

Ladner, G. B. (1970) *Die Papstbildnisse des Altertums und des Mittelalters*, vol. 2: *Von Innozenz II zu Benedikt XI*, Vatican City.

Lambert, C. (1997) "Le sepolture in urbe nella norma e nella prassi (tarda antichità – alto medioevo)," in L. Paroli (ed.), *L'Italia centro-settentrionale in età longobarda. Atti del Convegno Ascoli Piceno, 6–7 ottobre 1995*, Florence, pp. 285–93.

Lanciani, R. (1891) "L'Itinerario di Einsiedeln e l'Ordine di Benedetto Canonico," *Monumenti Antichi R. Accademia dei Lincei* 1, cols. 437–552.

Lanciani, R. (1988) *Forma Urbis Romae*, Rome [1893–1901].

Lane Fox, R. (1987) *Pagans and Christians in the Mediterranean World from the Second Century AD to the Conversion of Constantine*, New York.

La Rocca, A., and F. Oppedisano (2016) *Il senato romano nell'Italia ostrogota*, Rome.

La Rocca, C. (1993) "Una prudente maschera 'antiqua.' La politica edilizia di Teoderico," in *Teoderico il Grande e i Goti d'Italia. Atti del 13 Congresso internazionale di studi sull'Alto Medioevo*, Spoleto, pp. 451–515.

La Rocca, E. (1984) *La riva a mezzaluna: culti, agoni, monumenti funerari presso il Tevere nel Campo Marzio occidentale*, Rome.

Lee, E. (1985) *Descriptio Urbis. The Roman Census of 1527*, Rome.

Le Gall, J. (1953) *Le Tibre, fleuve de Rome, dans l'antiquité*, Paris.

Lenski, N. (2016) *Constantine and the Cities: Imperial Authority and Civic Politics*, Philadelphia.

Le Pogam, P.-Y. (2004) "Cantieri e residenze dei papi nella seconda metà del XIII secolo. Il caso del 'Castello Savelli' sull'Aventino," in Monciatti (ed.), pp. 77–87.

Le Pogam, P.-Y. (2005) *De la "cité de dieu" au "palais du pape": Les résidences pontificales dans la seconde moitié du XIIIe siècle (1254–1304)*, Rome.

Letaruoilly, P. (1882) *Le Vatican et la Basilique de Saint-Pierre de Rome*, 2 vols., Paris.

Lidova, M. (2015) "The Imperial Theotokos: Revealing the Concept of Early Christian Imagery in Santa Maria Maggiore in Rome," *Convivium* 2.2, pp. 60–81.

Lim, R. (1999) "People as Power: Games, Munificence and Contested Topography," in Harris (ed.), pp. 265–81.

Lipps, J. (2013) "Alarichs Goten auf dem Forum Romanum? Überlegungen zu Gestalt, Chronologie und Verständnis der spätantiken Platzanlage," in Lipps, Machado, and von Rummel (eds.), pp. 103–22.

Lipps, J., C. Machado, and P. von Rummel (eds.) (2013) *The Sack of Rome in 410 AD. The Event, Its Context and Its Impact*, Wiesbaden.

Lissi Caronna, E. (2000) "Edifici, fasi edilizie, demolizioni, riempimenti nell'area della basilica di S. Stefano Rotondo," in Brandenburg and Pál (eds.), pp. 29–33.

Liverani, P. (2004) "Arco di Onorio. Arco di Portogallo," *BullCom* 105, 351–70.

Liverani, P. (2007a) "Dal trionfo pagano all'adventus cristiano: percorsi della Roma imperiale," *Anales de arqueología cordobesa* 18, pp. 385–400.

Liverani, P. (2007b) "Victors and Pilgrims in Late Antiquity and the Early Middle Ages," *Fragmenta* 1, pp. 83–102.

Liverani, P. (2010) "Osservazioni sulla domus sotto S. Maria Maggiore a Roma e alla sua relazione con la basilica," *Röm. Mitth.* 116, pp. 459–67.

Liverani, P. (2012) "L'episcopio lateranense dalle origini all'alto medioevo," in S. Balcon-Berry, J.-P. Caillet, and D. Sandron (eds.), *Des domus ecclesiae aux palais épiscopaux. Actes du colloque tenu à Autun du 26 au 28 novembre 2009*, Turnhout, 2012, pp. 119–131.

Liverani, P. (2013) "Alarico in Laterano e sull'Esquilino," in Lipps, Machado, and von Rummel (eds.), pp. 277–92.

Lizzi Testa, R. (2004) *Senatori, popolo, papi. Il governo di Roma al tempo dei Valentiniani*, Bari.

Lizzi Testa, R. (2007) "Christian Emperors, Vestal Virgins and Priestly Colleges: Reconsidering the End of Paganism," *AnTard* 15 (2007), pp. 251–62.

Llewellyn, P. (1986) "The Popes and the Constitution in the Eighth Century," *The English Historical Review* 101, pp. 42–67.

Llewellyn, P. (1993) *Rome in the Dark Ages*, 2nd ed., New York [1971].

Lo Cascio, E. (1997) "Le procedure di *recensus* dalla tarda reppublica al tardo antico e il calcolo della popolazione di Roma," in *La Rome impérial. Démographie et logistique. Actes de la table ronde (Rome, 25 mars 1994)*, Rome, pp. 3–76.

Lo Cascio, E. (2000) *Roma imperiale: Una metropoli antica*, Rome. Studi superiori (Carocci editore); 391. Mondo romano. Rome.

Lo Cascio, E. (2013) "La popolazione di Roma prima e dopo il 410," in Lipps, Machado, and von Rummel (eds.), pp. 411–21.

Lori Sanfilippo, I. (1988) "I protocolli notarili romani del Trecento," *ASRSP* 110, pp. 99–150.

Lori Sanfilippo, I. (2001) *La Roma dei romani: Arti, mestieri e professioni nella Roma del Trecento*, Rome.

Luchterhandt, M. (1999) "Famulus Petri – Karl der Große in den römischen Mosaikbildern Leos III," in C. Stiegemann and M. Wemhoff (eds.), *799. Kunst und*

Kultur der Karolingerzeit. Karl der Große und Leo III. in Paderborn, Paderborn, pp. 55–70.

Luchterhandt, M. (2006) "Stolz und Vorurteil. Der Westen und die byzantinische Hofkultur im Frühmittelalter," in F. A. Bauer (ed.), *Visualisierungen von Herrschaft frühmittelalterliche Residenzen. Gestalt und Zeremoniell*, Istanbul, pp. 171–211.

Luchterhandt, M. (2014) "Konvergenzen und Divergenzen im profanen Kulturaustausch des Frühmittelalters. Die Karolinger und der päpstliche Hof um 800," *Aachener Kunstblätter* 65, pp. 8–33.

Luchterhandt, M. (2015) "Vom Haus des Bischofs zum Locus Sanctus: Der Lateranpalast im kulturellen Gedächtnis des römischen Mittelalters," in M. Featherstone et al. (eds.), *The Emperor's house. Palaces from Augustus to the Age of Absolutism*, Berlin, pp. 73–92.

MacGeorge, P. (2002) *Late Roman Warlords*, Oxford.

Machado, C. (2010a) "Public Monuments and Civic Life: The End of the Statue Habit in Italy," in Delogu and Gasparri (eds.), pp. 237–57.

Machado, C. (2010b) "The City as Stage. Aristocratic Commemorations in Late Antique Rome," in C. Sotinel and E. Rébillard (eds.), *Les frontières du profane dans l'antiquité tardive*, Rome, pp. 287–317.

Machado, C. (2016a) "Rome," in Smith and Ward-Perkins (eds.), pp. 121–35.

Machado, C. (2016b) "Italy," in Smith and Ward-Perkins (eds.), pp. 43–55.

Machado, C. (2019) *Urban Space and Aristocratic Power in Late Antique Rome, AD 270–535*, Oxford.

MacMullen, R. (1984) *Christianizing the Roman Empire (A.D. 100–400)*, New Haven and London.

Maddalo, S. (1990) *In figura Romae: Immagini di Roma nel libro medievale*, Rome.

Maetzke, G. (1991) "La struttura stratigrafica dell'area nordoccidentale del Foro Romano come appare dai recenti interventi di scavo," *Archeologia Medievale* 18, pp. 43–200.

Magnusen, T. (1958) *Studies in Roman Quattrocento Architecture*, Rome.

Magnuson, T. (2004) *The Urban Transformation of Medieval Rome, 312–1420*, Stockholm.

Maier, J. (2015) *Rome Measured and Imagined: Early Modern Maps of the Eternal City*, Chicago.

Maire Vigueur, J.-C. (2001) "Il comune romano," in Vauchez (ed.), pp. 117–57.

Maire Vigueur, J.-C. (2008a) "Guerres et fortifications dans la Rome communale," in P. Cressier (ed.), *Castrum 8. Le château et la ville. Espaces et réseaux (VIe–XIIIe siècle)*, Madrid and Rome, pp. 311–23.

Maire Vigueur, J.-C. (2008b) "La Felice Societas dei balestrieri e dei pavesati a Roma: una società popolare e i suoi ufficiali," in *Scritti per Isa. Raccolta di studi offerti a Isa Lori Sanfilippo*, Rome, pp. 377–406.

Maire Vigueur, J.-C. (2010) *L'autre Rome. Une histoire des Romains à l'époque communale (XIIe–XIVe siècle)*, Paris.

Manacorda, D. (1993) "Trasformazioni dell'abitato nel Campo Marzio: l'area della 'Porticus Minucia'," in Paroli and Delogu (eds.), pp. 31–51.

Manacorda, D. and L. Saguì (1995) "L'esedra della Crypta Balbi e il monastero di S. Lorenzo in Pallacinis," *Archeologia laziale* 12, pp. 121–34.

Manacorda, D. (2001) *Crypta Balbi: archeologia e storia di un paesaggio urbano*, Milan.

Manacorda, D. (2006) "Castra e burgi a Roma nell'alto medioevo," in S. Carocci (ed.), *La nobiltà romana nel medioevo*, Rome, pp. 97–135.

Manacorda, D. (2007) "Siena e Roma nell'alto Medioevo: Qualche lume sui secoli bui," *MEFRM* 119.1, pp. 5–23.

Mancini, R. (2001) *Le mura aureliane di Roma. Atalante di un palinsesto murario*, Rome.

Mango, C. (1993) *Studies on Constantinople*, Aldershot.

Marazzi, F. (1991) "Il conflitto fra Leone III Isaurico e il papato fra il 725 e il 733, e il 'definitivo' inizio del medioevo a Roma: un'ipotesi in discussione," *PBSR* 59, pp. 231–57.

Marazzi, F. (1993) "Roma, il Lazio, il Mediterraneo: relazioni fra economia e politica dal VII al IX secolo," in Delogu and Paroli (eds.), pp. 267–85.

Marazzi, F. (1994) "Le 'città nuove' pontificie e l'insediamento laziale nel IX secolo," in R. Francovich and G. Noyé (eds.), *La storia dell'alto medioevo italiano (VI–X secolo) alla luce dell'archeologia*, Florence, pp. 251–77.

Marazzi, F. (2000) "Rome in Transition. Economic and Political Change in the Fourth and Fifth Centuries," in J. Smith (ed.), pp. 21–41.

Marazzi, F. (2001) "Aristocrazia e società (secoli VI–XI)," in Vauchez (ed.), pp. 41–69.

Marazzi, F. (2007) "The Last Rome: From the End of the Fifth to the End of the Sixth Century," in Barnish and Marazzi (eds.), pp. 279–302.

Marazzi, F. (2016) "Ostrogothic Cities," in Arnold, Bjornlie, and Sessa (eds.), pp. 98–120.

Marcattili, F. (2009) *Circo Massimo. Architetture, funzioni, culti, ideologia*, Rome.

Marchetti Longhi, G. (1924) "Porticus Gallatorum," *BullCom* 52, pp. 176–240.

Marchetti Longhi, G. (1924–5) "'Arcus Stillans' e 'Balneum Pelagi'. Note di topografia medioevale di Roma," *RendPontAc* 3, pp. 143–90.

Marchetti Longhi, G. (1938) "Il quartiere Greco-orientale di Roma nell'antichità e nel medio evo," *Atti del IV congresso Nazionale di Studi Romani*, vol. 1, Rome, pp. 169–85.

Marchetti Longhi, G. (1976) "Il Mons Fabiorum. Note di topografia medioevale di Roma," *ASRSP* 99, pp. 5–69.

Marchiori, L. (2007) *Art and Reform in Tenth-Century Rome – The Paintings of S. Maria in Pallara*, Ph.D. thesis, Queen's University (available online at: https://qspace.library.queensu.ca/handle/1974/908).

Marchiori, L. (2009) "Medieval Wall Painting in the Church of Santa Maria in Pallara, Rome: the Use of Objective Dating Criteria," *PBSR* 77, pp. 225–55.

Marlowe, E. (2006) "Framing the Sun: The Arch of Constantine and the Roman Cityscape," *The Art Bulletin* 88.2, pp. 223–42.

Marrou, H.-I. (1940) "L'origine orientale des diaconies romaines," *MEFR* 57, pp. 95–142.

Martin, A. (2004) "Santo Stefano Rotondo: stratigrafia e materiali," in Paroli and Vendittelli (eds.), pp. 506–16.

Martin, J.-M., A. Peters-Custot, and V. Prigent (eds.) (2011) *L'héritage byzantin en Italie (VIIIe–XIIe siècle)*, 2 vols., Rome.

Martines, M. (2015) "*Domus* sul versante sudoccidentale del Pincio. Lo scavo," *Bollettino di Archeologia On Line* 6, pp. 257–70.

Maskarinec, M. (2018) *City of Saints. Rebuilding Rome in the Early Middle Ages*, Philadelphia.

Mathisen, R. (2013a) "*Roma a Gothis Alarico duce capta est*. Ancient Accounts of the Sack of Rome in 410 CE," in Lipps, Machado, and von Rummel (eds.), pp. 87–102.

Mathisen, R. (2013b) "Ricimer's Church in Rome: How an Arian Barbarian Prospered in a Nicene World," in N. Lenski and A. Cain (eds.), *The Power of Religion in Late Antiquity*, Burlington, pp. 307–25.

Matthews, J. F. (1975) *Western Aristocracies and Imperial Court AD 364–425*, Oxford.

Matthiae, G. (1954) "La cultura artistica in Roma nel secolo IX," *RIASA* 3 (n.s.), pp. 257–74.

Mazzarino, S. (1951) *Aspetti sociali del quarto secolo. Ricerche di storia tardo-romana*, Rome.

Mazzucato, O. (1993) *Tipologie e tecniche della ceramica a vetrina pesante. IX–X secolo*, Rome.

McCahill, E. (2013) *Reviving the Eternal City: Rome and the Papal Court, 1420–1447*, Cambridge, MA and London.

McClendon, C. B. (2005) *The Origins of Medieval Architecture: Building in Europe, AD 600–900*, New Haven.

McCormick, M. (2001) *Origins of the European Economy. Communications and Commerce AD 300–900*, Cambridge.

McCurrach, C. (2011) "'Renovatio' Reconsidered: Richard Krautheimer and the Iconography of Architecture," Gesta 50.1, pp. 41–69.

McEvoy, M. (2010) "Rome and the Transformation of the Imperial Office in the Late Fourth to Mid-Fifth Centuries AD," *PBSR* 79, pp. 151–92.

McEvoy, M. (2013) "The Mausoleum of Honorius. Late Roman Imperial Christianity and the City of Rome in the Fifth Century," in McKitterick *et al.* (eds.), pp. 119–36.

McEvoy, M. (2017) "Shadow Emperors and the Choice of Rome (455–476 AD)," *AnTard* 25, pp. 95–112.

McKitterick, R., R. Osborne, C. M. Richardson, and J. Story (eds.) (2013) *Old Saint Peter's, Rome*, Cambridge.

Medri, M. *et al.* (eds.) (2017) *Le Mura Aureliane nella Storia di Roma, vol. 1: Da Aureliano a Onorio*, Rome (electronic publication, Roma TrE-Press).

Menant, F. (2011) *L'Italia dei comuni (1100–1350)*, Rome (French ed. 2010).

Menant, F. (2017) "'Fine della crescita o inizio della crisi?'," in *La crescita economica dell'occidente medievale: un tema storico non ancora esaurito*, Rome, pp. 409–22.

Meneghini, R. (1992) "Roma. Ricerche nel Foro di Traiano. Nuovi dati archeologici e d'archivio riguardanti le vicende del monumento e la chiesa di S. Maria in Campo Carlèo," *Archeologia Medievale* 19, pp. 409–36.

Meneghini, R. (1995). "Sepolture intramuranee a Roma tra V e VII secolo d.C. – aggiornamenti e considerazioni," *Archeologia Medievale* 22, pp. 283–90.

Meneghini, R. (1997) "Edilizia pubblica e riuso dei monumenti classici a Roma nell'altomedievo: l'area dei templi di Apollo Sosiano e Bellona e la diaconia di Sant'Angelo in Pescheria," in *I Congresso Nazionale di Archeologia Medievale*, Florence, pp. 51–7.

Meneghini, R. (1999) "Edilizia pubblica e privata nella Roma altomedievale. Due episodi di riuso," *MEFRM* 111.1, pp. 171–82.

Meneghini, R. (2001) "Il foro di Traiano nel Medioevo," *MEFRM* 113.1, pp. 149–72.

Meneghini, R. (2003) "La trasformazione dello spazio pubblico a Roma tra tarda antichità e alto medioevo, *MEFRM* 115.2, pp. 1049–62.

Meneghini, R. (2009) *I Fori Imperiali e i Mercati di Traiano. Storia e descrizione dei monumenti alla luce degli studi e degli scavi recenti*, Rome.

Meneghini, R. (2013) "Le vicende del 408–10 e la comparsa delle sepolture urbane a Roma," in Lipps, Machado, and von Rummel (eds.), pp. 403–9.

Meneghini, R. (2017) "Le strade di Roma nel medioevo," in S. Altekamp, C. Marcks-Jacobs, and P. Seiler (eds.), *Perspektiven der Spolienforschung 2. Zentren und Konjunkturen der Spoliierung*, Berlin, pp. 283–309.

Meneghini, R., and R. Santangeli Valenzani (1993) "Sepolture intramuranee e paesaggio urbano a Roma tra V e VII secolo," in Delogu and Paroli (eds.), pp. 89–111.

Meneghini, R., and R. Santangeli Valenzani (1996) "Episodi di trasformazione del paesaggio urbano nella Roma altomedievale attraverso l'analisi di due contesti: un isolato in Piazza dei Cinquecento e l'area dei fori imperiali," *Archeologia Medievale* 23, pp. 53–99.

Meneghini, R., and R. Santangeli Valenzani (2004) *Roma nell'altomedioevo. Topografia e urbanistica della città dal V al X secolo*, Rome.

Meneghini, R., and R. Santangeli Valenzani (2007) *I Fori Imperiali. Gli scavi del Comune di Roma (1991–2007)*, Rome.

Meneghini, R., and R. Santangeli Valenzani (eds.) (2010) *Scavi dei Fori Imperiali. Il Foro di Augusto. L'area centrale*, Rome.

Merrils, A., and R. Miles (2010) *The Vandals*, Chichester.

Miglio, M. (1993) *Scritture, scrittori e storia, II: Città e corte a Roma nel Quattrocento*, Rome.

Miglio, M. (2001) "Nicolò V, Leon Battista Alberti, Roma," in *Leon Battista Alberti e il Quattrocento. Studi in onore di Cecil Grayson e Ernst Gombrich. Atti del Convegno internazionale, Mantova 29–31 ottobre 1998*, Florence, pp. 47–64.

Modigliani, A. (1998) *Mercati, botteghe e spazi di commercio a Roma tra Medioevo ed età moderna*, Rome.

Modigliani, A. (2009) "*ad urbana tandem aedificia veniamus*. La *Vita Nicolai quinti* di Giannozzo Manetti: una rilettura," in A. Calzona *et al.* (eds.), *Leon Battista Alberti. Architetture e committenti*, Florence, pp. 513–59.

Modigliani, A. (2011) "Mercati, botteghe e spazi di commercio nella Roma tardo-medievale," in R. Padovano (ed.), *Mercati, arti e fiere storiche di Roma e del Lazio*, Rome, pp. 27–69.

Molinari, A. (2014) "Gli scavi al n. 62 di Piazza Navona tra 'microstorie' e 'grandi narrazioni' (secoli V–XV)," in Bernard (ed.), pp. 263–74.

Molinari, A., and N. Giannini (2014) "Un archivio digitale dell'edilizia civile medievale di Roma," in E. De Minicis (ed.), *Case e torri medievali IV. Indagini sui centri dell'Italia meridionale ed insulare (sec. XI–XV), Campania, Basilicata, Puglia, Calabria, Sicilia e Sardegna*, Rome, pp. 334–40.

Molinari, A., and N. Giannini (2015) "La costruzione della *Forma Urbis* digitale di Roma medievale: il progetto dell'università di Roma Tor Vergata," in M. Serlorenzi and G. Leoni (eds.), *Il SITAR nella Rete della ricerca italiana. Verso la conoscenza archeologica condivisa* (*Archeologia e Calcolatori* Supplemento 7), Rome, pp. 213–25.

Molinari, A., L. Spera, and R. Santangeli Valenzani (eds.) (2015) *L'archeologia della produzione a Roma. Atti del Convegno Internazionale di Studi Roma 27–29 marzo 2014*, Rome.

Monciatti, A. (ed.) (2004) *Domus et splendida palatia. Residenze papali e cardinalizie a Roma fra XII e XV secolo*, Pisa.

Monciatti, A. (2005) *Il Palazzo Vaticano nel medioevo*, Florence.

Moneti, A. (1990) "Posizione e aspetti del 'tempio' del sole di Aureliano a Roma," *Palladio* 6, pp. 9–24.

Moneti, A. (1993) "La Santa Sofia di Giustiniano e il tempio del Sole di Aureliano, *ARID* 21, pp. 153–71.

Montaubin, P. (2006) "De l'an mil à la Renaissance : de qui donc Rome fut-elle la capitale?," in *Actes des congrès de la Société des historiens médiévistes de l'enseignement supérieur public, 36ᵉ congrès, Istanbul, 2005. Les villes capitales au Moyen Age*, Paris, pp. 391–428.

Montaubin, P. (2009) "*Pater urbis et orbis*. Les cortèges pontificaux dans la Rome médiévale (VIIIᵉ–XIVᵉ siècles)," *Rivista di Storia della Chiesa in Italia* 63.1, pp. 9–47.

Montelli, E. (2011) *Tecniche costruttive murarie medievali: mattoni e laterizi in Roma e nel Lazio fra X e XV secolo*, Rome.

Monterroso, A. "Via triumphalis per theatrum Marcelli, símbolos de arquitectura en la forma urbis marmorea," *Revue archéologique* 2009.1 (n° 47), pp. 3–51.

Moralee, J. (2018) *Rome's Holy Mountain: The Capitoline Hill in Late Antiquity*, Oxford.

Morbidelli, M. (2010) *L'abside di S. Giovanni in Laterano: una questione controversa*, Rome.

Morrison, C., and J.-N. Barrandon (1988) "La trouvaille de monnaies d'argent byzantines de Rome (VIIᵉ–VIIIᵉ siècles): analyses et chronologie," *Revue Numismatique*, 6th Series, vol. 30, pp. 149–65.

Moscati, L. (1980) *Alle origini del comune romano : economia, società, istituzioni*, Rome.

Müntz, E. (1878) *Les Arts à la cour des papes pendant le XVᵉ et le XVIᵉ siècle: Recueil des documents inédits tirés des archives et des bibliothèques Romaines, part 1: Martin V – Pie II (1417–1464)*, Paris.

Müntz, E. (1891) "Lavori d'arte fatti eseguire a Roma dai Papi d'Avignone," *Archivio Storico dell'Arte* 4, 127–30.

Musto, R. G. (2003) *Apocalypse in Rome: Cola di Rienzo and the Politics of the New Age*, Berkely, Los Angeles, and London.

Naismith R., (2014) "Peter's Pence and Before: Numismatic Links between Anglo-Saxon England and Rome," in Tinti (ed.), pp. 217–53.

Neil, B. (2009) *Leo the Great*, Abdingdon and New York.

Nieddu, A. M. (2003) "L'utilizzazione funeraria del suburbio nei secoli V e VI," in Pergola *et al.* (eds.), pp. 545–606.

Nielsen, I. (1992) Thermae et Balnea: *The Architecture and Cultural History of Roman Public Baths*, Aarhus.

Nilgen, U. (1974) "Die grosse Reliquieninschrift von Santa Prassede: Eine quellenkritische Untersuchung zur Zeno-Kapelle," *Römische Quartalschrift für christliche Altertumskunde und Kirchengeschichte* 69, pp. 7–29.

Noble, T. F. X. (1984) *The Republic of St. Peter. The Birth of the Papal State, 680–825*, Philadelphia.

Noble, T. F. X. (2000) "Paradoxes and Possibilities in the Sources for Roman Society in the Early Middle Ages," in J. Smith (ed.), pp. 55–83.

Noble, T. F. X. (2001) "Topography, Celebration, and Power: The Making of a Papal Rome in the Eighth and Ninth Centuries," in F. Theuws, M. de Jong, and C. Van Rhijn (eds.), *Topographies of Power in the Early Middle Ages*, Leiden, pp. 45–91.

Nordh, A. (1949) *Libellus de regionibus urbis Romae*, Rome.

Nordhagen, P. J. (1968) *The Frescoes of John VII (A.D. 705–707) in S. Maria Antiqua in Rome (Acta IRN 3)*, Rome.

Noreen, K. (2001) "Lay Patronage and the Creation of Papal Sanctity during the Gregorian Reform: the Case of Sant'Urbano alla Caffarella, Rome," *Gesta* 99, pp. 39–59.

Nussdorfer, L. (2016) "Roman Notarial Records Between Market and State," in L. Corens, K. Peters, and A. Walsham (eds.), *The Social History of the Archive: Record Keeping in Early Modern Europe*, Oxford, pp. 71–89.

Oppedisano, F. (2013) *L'impero d'Occidente negli anni di Maioriano*, Rome.

Orlandi, S. (2001) "I loca del Colosseo," in A. La Regina (ed.), *Sangue e arena*, Milan, pp. 89–103.

Orlandi, S. (2004) *Epigrafia anfiteatrale dell'Occidente Romano. VI. Roma. Anfiteatri e strutture annesse con una nuova edizione e commento delle iscrizioni del Colosseo*, Rome.

Orlandi, S. (2009) L'iscrizione di Flavius Ricimer in S. Agata dei Goti a Roma, in M. Rotili (ed.), *Tardo Antico e Alto Medioevo: filologia, storia, archeologia, arte*, Naples, pp. 215–23.

Orlandi, S. (2010) "L'epigrafia romano sotto il regno di Odoacre," in G. Bonamente and R. Lizzi (eds.), *Istituzioni, carismi ed esercizio del potere (IV–VI secolo d. C.)*, Bari, pp. 331–8.

Orlandi, S. (2012) "Passato e presente nell'epigrafia tardoantica di Roma," in R. Behrwald and C. Witschel (eds.), *Rom in der Spätantike. Historische Erinnerung im städtischen Raum*, Stuttgart, pp. 293–307.

Orlandi, S. (2013) "Le tracce del passaggio di Alarico nelle fonti epigrafiche," in Lipps, Machado, and von Rummel (eds.), pp. 335–51.

Osborne, J. (1979) "The Portrait of Leo VI at San Clemente, Rome: a Re-examination of the So-Called 'Square Nimbus' in Medieval Art," *PBSR* 47, pp. 58–65.

Osborne, J. (1987) "The Atrium of S. Maria Antiqua, Rome: A History in Art," *PBSR* 55, pp. 183–223.

Osborne, J. (1988) "A Note on the Medieval Name of the So-Called 'Temple of Fortuna Virilis' at Rome," *PBSR* 56, pp. 210–12.

Osborne, J. (2004) "Framing Sacred Space. Eleventh-Century Mural Painting in the Churches of Rome," *ARID* 30, pp. 137–54.

Osborne, J. (2011) "The Early Medieval Painting of St. Augustine in the Lateran Palace," in Brandt and Pergola (eds.), pp. 993–1002.

Pace, V. (2016) "Il XIII secolo: da Innocenzo III (1198–1216) a Bonifacio VIII," in D'Onofrio (ed.), pp. 299–329.

Packer, J. (2001) *The Forum of Trajan in Rome: A Study of the Monuments in Brief*, Berkeley – Los Angeles.

Painter, K. S. (2000) "Il tesoro dell'Esquilino," in Ensoli and La Rocca 2000, pp. 140–6.

Palazzo, P., and C. Pavolini (eds.) (2013) *Gli dèi propizi. La Basilica Hilariana nel contesto dello scavo dell'Ospedale Militare Celio (1987–2000)*, Rome.

Palermo, L. (1979) *Il porto di Roma nel XIV e XV secolo*, Rome.

Palermo, L. (1990) *Mercati di grano a Roma tra medioevo e rinascimento*, vol. I, *Il mercato distrettuale di grano in età comunale*, Rome.

Palladino, S. (1996) "Le terme Eleniane a Roma," *MEFRA* 108.2, pp. 855–71.

Palmer, R. E. A. (1980) "Customs on Market Goods Imported into the City of Rome," *MAAR* 36, pp. 217–33.

Palmer, R. E. A. (1981) "The Topography and Social History of Rome's Trastevere (Southern Sector)," *Proceedings of the American Philosophical Society* 125, pp. 368–97.

Palmerio, G., and G. Villetti (1989) *Storia edilizia di Santa Maria sopra Minerva in Roma*, Rome.

Palombi, A. (2006) *La basilica di San Nicola in Carcere. Il complesso architettonico dei tre templi del Foro Olitorio*, Rome.

Panella, C. (2013) "Roma e gli altri. La cultura materiale al tempo del sacco di Alarico," in Machado, Lipps, and von Rummel (eds.), pp. 365–402.

Panella, C., and L. Saguì (2001) "Consumo e produzione a Roma tra tardoantico e altomedioevo: le merci, i contesti," *Settimane del CISAM* 48, pp. 757–818.

Pani Ermini, L. (1989) "Santuario e città fra tarda antichità e alto medioevo," *Settimane del CISAM* 36, pp. 837–77.

Pani Ermini, L. (1992) "*Renovatio murorum*: tra programma urbanistico e restauro conservativo: Roma e il ducato romano," *Settimane del CISAM* 39, pp. 485–530.

Pani Ermini, L. (1995). "Forma urbis e renovatio murorum in età teodoriciana," in A. Carile (ed.), *Teoderico e i Goti tra Oriente e Occidente*, Ravenna, pp. 171–225.

Pani Ermini, L. (2000) "Lo 'spazio cristiano' nella Roma del primo millennio," in Pani Ermini (ed.), pp. 15–37.

Pani Ermini, L. (ed.) (2000) *Christiana loca. Lo spazio cristiano a Roma del primo millennio*, 2 vols., Rome.

Pani Ermini, L. (2001) "Forma Urbis: Lo spazio urbano tra VI e IX secolo," *Settimane del CISAM* 48, pp. 255–323.

Pani Ermini, L., and C. Travaglini (eds.) (2010) *Trastevere. Un'analisi di lungo periodo. Atti del Convegno di Studio – Roma 13–14 marzo 2008*, 2 vols., Rome.

Panuzzi, S. (2011) "Le prime ceramiche rivestite da mensa nell'area laziale: innovazioni tecnologiche e continuità produttive," in *La ceramica nei periodi di transizione. Novità e persistenze nel Mediterraneo tra XII e XVI secolo. Atti del XLIII Convegno Internazionale della Ceramica*, Florence, pp. 103–16.

Paravicini Bagliani, A. (2004) "La mobilità della corte papale nel Duecento. Cura corporis e vita di corte," in Monciatti (ed.), pp. 29–42.

Paravicini Bagliani, A. (2005) *Le Chiavi e la Tiara. Immagini e simboli del papato medievale*, 2nd ed., Rome.

Paravicini Bagliani, A. (2008) *Il potere del papa. Corporeità, autorappresentazione, simboli*, Florence.

Paravicini Bagliani, A. (2015a) "La corte dei papi nei secoli XI e XII: ritualità e autorappresentazione," *Settimane del CISAM* 62, pp. 259–77.

Paravicini-Bagliani, A. (2015b) "Il papato medievale, Roma e lo spazio," in C. Carbonetti, S. Lucà, and M. Signorini (eds.), *Roma e il suo territorio nel medioevo. Le fonti scritte fra tradizione e innovazione*, Spoleto, pp. 1–22.

Parlato, E. (2001) "Vista da Nord: immagini di Roma dal Medioevo al Quattrocento," in F. Troncarelli (ed.), *Roma. Memoria e oblio*, Rome, pp. 198–207.

Paroli, L. (1990) "Ceramica a vetrina pesante altomedievale (Forum Ware) e medievale (Sparse Glazed). Altre invetriate tardo-antiche e altomedievali," in L. Paroli and L. Saguì (eds.), *Archeologia urbana a Roma: il progetto della Crypta balbi, vol. 5: L'esedra della Crypta Balbi nel Medioevo (XI–XV secolo)*, Florence, pp. 314–56.

Paroli, L. (1993) "Ostia nella tarda antichità e nell'alto medioevo," in Paroli and Delogu (eds.), pp. 153–75.

Paroli, L., and L. Vendittelli (eds.) (2004) *Roma dall'antichità al medioevo II. Contesti tardoantichi e altomedievali*, Rome.

Partner, P. (1958) *The Papal State under Martin V: The Administration and Government of the Temporal Power in the Early Fifteenth Century*, London.

Partner, P. (1972) *The Lands of St. Peter: The Papal State in the Middle Ages and Early Renaissance*, London.

Paschoud, F. (1967) *Roma Aeterna. Études sur le patriotisme romain dans l'occident latin a l'époque des grandes invasions*, Neuchâtel.

Patlagean, É. (1974) "Les armes et la cité à Rome du VIIe au IXe siècle, et le modèle européen des trois fonctions sociales," *MEFRM* 86, pp. 25–62.

Patlagean, É. (1977) *Pauvreté économique e pauvreté social à Byzance, 4e–7e siècles*, Paris.

Patterson, H. (1993) "Un aspetto dell'economia di Roma e della Campagna Romana nell'altomedieovo: l'evidenza della ceramica," in Paroli and Delogu (eds.), pp. 309–31.

Pavolini, C. (1993) "L'area del Celio fra l'antichità e il medioevo alla luce delle recenti indagini archeologiche," in Delogu and Paroli (eds.), pp. 53–70.

Pavolini, C. (2004) "Aspetti del Celio fra il V e l'VIII–IX secolo," in Paroli and Vendittelli (eds.), pp. 418–34.

Pavolini, C. (2006) *Archeologia e topografia della regione II (Celio): un aggiornamento sessant'anni dopo Colini*, Rome.

Pavolini, C. (2013) "Le conseguenze del Sacco di Alarico sul Celio," in Lipps, Machado, and von Rummel (eds.), pp. 163–83.

Pensabene, P. (2008) "I portici nelle case medievali di Roma," in J.-F. Bernard, P. Bernardi, and D. Esposito (eds.), *Il reimpiego in architettura*, Rome, pp. 67–93.

Pensabene, P. (2015) *Roma su Roma. Reimpiego architettonico, recupero dell'antico e trasformazioni urbane tra il III e il XIII secolo*, Rome.

Perchuk, A. L. (2016) "Schismatic (Re)Visions: Sant'Elia near Nepi and Sta. Maria in Trastevere in Rome, 1120–1143," *Gesta* 55.2, pp. 179–212.

Pergola, P., R. Santangeli Valenzani, and R. Volpe (eds.) (2003) *Suburbium: il suburbio di Roma dalla crisi del sistema delle ville a Gregorio Magno*, Rome.

Perraymond, M. (1979) "Le *scholae peregrinorum* nel borgo di San Pietro," *Romanobarbarica* 4, pp. 183–200.

Pflugk Harttung, J. von (1881–3) *Acta pontificum romanorum inedita*, 3 vols., Tübingen and Stuttgart.

Phillips, L. (1988) "A Note on the Gifts of Leo III to the Churches of Rome," *Ephemerides Liturgicae* 102, pp. 72–8.

Pietrangeli, C. (1960) "Il Palazzo senatorio nel medioevo," *Capitolium* 35.1, pp. 3–19.

Pietri, C. (1976) *Roma christiana: recherches sur l'Église de Rome, son organisation, sa politique, son idéologie de Miltiade à Sixte III (311–440)*, 2 vols., Paris.

Pinon, P. (2014) "La conservation des édifices de spectacle antiques dans les espaces urbains," in Bernard (ed.), pp. 255–62.

Pistilli, P. F. (1991) "L'architettura tra il 1198 e il 1254," in Romanini (ed.) 1991, pp. 1–71.

Pollio, G. (2014) "Alcuni suggerimenti sull'aspetto della chiesa di Santa Maria in Pallara nel Medioevo attraverso le fonti," in V. Carmelitti and A. Trivellone (eds.), *Un medioevo in lungo e in largo: da Bisanzio all'Occidente (VI–XVI secolo); studi per Valentino Pace*, Rome, pp. 51–8.

Pollio, G. (2016) "Il X secolo: da Benedetto IV (900–903) a Gregorio V (996–999)," in D'Onofrio (ed.), pp. 239–54.

Popkin, M. L. (2016) *The Architecture of the Roman Triumph. Monuments, Memory, and Identity*, Cambridge.

Porena, P. (2019) "Il '*prior / caput senatus*' in occidente: aspetti del primato dell'aristocrazia di Roma dopo il 476," *Latinitas, nova series*, 7.2, pp. 25–50.

Priester, A. (1990) "*The Bell Towers of Medieval Rome and the Architecture of Renovatio*," Ph.D. diss., Princeton University.

Prigent V. (2004) "Les empereurs isauriens et la confiscation des patrimoines pontificaux d'Italie du Sud," *MEFRM* 116.2, pp. 557–94.

Quaglioni, D. (ed.) (1994) *La crisi del Trecento e il papato avignonese (1274–1378)*, Milan.

Quaranta, P., R. Pardi, B. Ciarrocchi, and A. Capodiferro (2013) "Il 'giorno dopo' all'Aventino," in Lipps, Machado, and von Rummel (eds.), pp. 185–213.

Quilici, L. (1982–83) "Strutture antiche e medioevali nelle case all'imbocco di via Capodiferro," *BullCom* 88, pp. 255–68.

Quilici, L. (1986–87) "Roma. Via di S. Paolo alla Regola. Scavo e recupero di edifici antichi e medioevali," *NSc* 1986–7, pp. 175–416.

Radtke, C. (2016) "The Senate at Rome in Ostrogothic Italy," in Arnold, Bjornlie, and Sessa (eds.), pp. 121–46.

Rascaglia, G., and J. Russo (2015) "La ceramica medievale di Roma: organizzazione produttiva e mercati (VIII–XV secolo)," in Molinari, Santangeli Valenzani, and Spera (eds.), pp. 189–218.

Rausa, F. (2004) "I luoghi dell'agonismo nella Roma imperiale: L'edificio della *Curia athletarum*," *Röm. Mitth.* 111, pp. 537–53.

Re, C. (1883) *Statuti della città di Roma del secolo XIV*, Roma.

Re, E. (1920) "Maestri di strada," *ASRSP* 43, pp. 86–102.

Rea, R. (1999) "Il Colosseo. Destrutturazione e riuso tra IV e VIII secolo," *MEFRM* 111.1, pp. 183–95.

Rea, R. (ed.) (2002) *Rota Colisei. La valle del Colosseo attraverso i secoli*, Milan.

Rea, R., S. Romano, and R. Santangeli Valenzani (eds.) (2017) *Colosseo*, Milan.

Reekmans, L. (1968). "L'implantation monumentale chrétienne dans la zone suburbaine de Rome du IVe au IXe siècle," *RAC* 44, pp. 173–207.

Reekmans, L. (1989) "L'implantation monumentale chrétienne dans le paysage urbain de Rome de 300 à 850," in *Actes du XIe congrès international d'archéologie chrétienne. Lyon, Vienne, Grenoble, Genève, Aoste, 21–28 septembre 1986*, Rome, pp. 861–915.

Rehberg, A., and A. Modigliani (2004) *Cola di Rienzo e il Comune di Roma*, 2 vols., Rome.

Renouard, Y. (1941) *Les relations des papes d'Avignon et des compagnies commerciales et bancaires de 1316 à 1378*, Paris.

Ricci, M., and L. Vendittelli (eds.) (2010) *Museo nazionale romano – Crypta Balbi. Ceramiche medievali e moderne, I: Ceramiche medievali e del primo rinascimento (1000–1530)*, Milan.

Riccioni, S. (2005) "Gli altari di S. Galla e di S. Pantaleo. Una 'lettura' in chiave riformiana dell'antico," *Hortus Artium Medievalium* 11, pp. 189–99.

Riccioni, S. (2006) *Il mosaico apsidale di S. Clemente a Roma: "Exemplum" della chiesa riformata*, Spoleto.

Richardson, L. (1992) *A New Topographical Dictionary of Ancient Rome*, Baltimore.

Rickman, G. (1980) *The Corn Supply of Ancient Rome*, Oxford.

Roberto, U. (2012) *Roma capta. Il Sacco della città dai Galli ai Lanzichenecchi*, Rome.

Roberto, U. (2013) "Strategie di integrazione e lotta politica a Roma alla fine dell'impero: la carriera di Fl. Valila tra Ricimero e Odoacre," in N. Cusumano and D. Motta (eds.), *Xenia. Studi in onore di Lia Marino*, Caltanissetta and Rome, pp. 247–61.

Roberto, U. (2017) "Dépouiller Rome? Genséric, Avitus et les statues en 455," *Revue historique* 684, pp. 775–801.

Rodriguez-Almeida, E. (1981) *Forma urbis marmorea. Aggiornamento generale 1980*, Rome.

Rodriguez-Almeida, E. (1984) *Il monte Testaccio: ambiente, storia, materiali*, Rome.

Rollo-Koster, J. (2019) "*Rome during the Schism: The Long Carnival*," in Angelelli and Romano (eds.), pp. 41–52.

Rollo-Koster, J., and T. M. Izbicki (eds.) (2009) *A Companion to the Great Western Schism (1378–1417)*, Leiden – Boston.

Romanini, A. M. (ed.) (1991) *Roma nel Duecento. L'arte nella città dei papi da Innocenzo III a Bonifacio VIII*, Turin.

Romano, S. (1995) "Il Sancta Sanctorum: Gli affreschi," in C. Pietrangeli (ed.), *Sancta sanctorum*, Milan, pp. 38–125.

Romano, S. (2004) "Nuovi affreschi nella residenza di S. Clemente a Roma: gli anni dei 'quattro cardinali,'" in Monciatti (ed.), pp. 59–76.

Romano, S. (2012) "Gli affreschi di S. Urbano alla Caffarella: qualche elemento di discussione," *Arte medievale*, IV serie – anno II, pp. 77–94.

Romei, D. (1992) "La ceramica a vetrina pesante altomedievale nella stratigrafia dell'esedra della Crypta Balbi," in L. Paroli (ed.), *La ceramica invetriata tardoantica e altomedievale in Italia*, Florence, pp. 378–93.

Romei, D. (2001) "Il deposito del X secolo nell'esedra della Crypta Balbi. Ceramica a vetrina pesante (Forum Ware).

Ceramica a vetrina pesante a macchia (Sparse Glazed)," in Arena *et al.* (eds.), pp. 524–7.

Romei, D. (2004) "Produzione e circolazione dei manufatti ceramici a Roma nell'alto medioevo," in Paroli and Venditelli (eds.), pp. 278–311.

Rougé, J. (1957) "Ad ciconias nixas," *Revue des Études Anciennes* 59, pp. 320–8.

Rovelli, A. (1998) "La circolazione monetaria a Roma nei secoli VII e VIII. Nuovi dati per la storia economica di Roma nell'alto medioevo," in P. Delogu (ed.), *Roma medievale. Aggiornamenti*, Florence, pp. 79–91.

Rovelli, A. (2000) "Monetary Circulation in Byzantine and Carolingian Rome: a Reconsideration in the Light of Recent Archaeological Data," in Smith (ed.), pp. 85–99.

Rovelli, A. (2001) "Emissione e uso della moneta: le testimonianze scritte e archeologiche," *Settimane del CISAM* 48, pp. 821–52.

Rovelli, A. (2010) "Nuove zecche e circolazione monetaria tra X e XIII secolo: L'esempio del Lazio e della Toscana," *Archeologia Medievale* 37, pp. 263–70.

Rovelli, A. (2013) "Ostrogoti e bizantini a Roma. Brevi note sulle circolazione del bronzo minuto nei contesti urbani dell'Italia centro-meridionale," in *Atti del 4° Congresso Nazionale di Numismatica*, Taranto, pp. 305–19.

Royo, M., É. Hubert, and A. Béranger (eds.) (2008) *"Rome des quartiers": des vici au rioni. Cadres institutionnels, pratiques sociales, et requalifications entre Antiquité et époque moderne*, Paris.

Russell, A. (2014) "Memory and Movement in the Roman Fora from Antiquity to Metro C," *Journal of the Society of Architectural Historians* 73.4, pp. 478–506.

Saguì, L. (2001) "Roma e il Mediterraneo: la circolazione delle merci," in Arena *et al.* (eds.), pp. 62–8.

Saguì, L. (2002) "Roma, i centri privilegiati e la lunga durata della tarda antichità. Dati archeologici dal deposito di VII secolo nell'esedra della Crypta Balbi," *Archeologia Medievale* 29, pp. 7–42.

Saguì, L., M. Ricci, and D. Romei (1997) "Nuovi dati ceramologici per la storia economica di Roma tra VII e VIII secolo," in *La céramique médiévale en Méditerranée*, Aix-en-Provence, pp. 35–48.

Saguì L., and A. Rovelli (1998) "Residualità, non residualità, continuità di circolazione. Alcuni esempi dalla Crypta Balbi," in *I materiali residui nello scavo archeologico. Testi preliminari e Atti della tavola rotonda organizzata dall'École française de Rome e dalla Sezione romana "Nino Lamboglia" dell'Istituto internazionale di studi liguri*, Rome, pp. 173–95.

Saguì, L., and M. Serlorenzi (eds.) (2008) "Roma, piazza Venezia. L'indagine archeologica per la realizzazione della metropolitana. Le fasi medievali e moderne," *Archeologia Medievale* 25, pp. 175–98.

Saguì, L., and M. Cante (2015) "Archeologia e architettura nell'area delle 'Terme di Elagabalo,' alle pendici nord-orientali del Palatino. Dagli isolati giulio-claudii alla chiesa paleocristiana," *Thiasos* 4, pp. 37–75.

Salzman, M. R. (2017) "Emperors and Elites in Rome after the Vandal Sack of 455," *AnTard* 25, pp. 243–62.

Sansterre, J-M. (1997) "Formoso," *DBI* vol. 69, pp. 55–61.

Santangeli Valenzani, R. (1994) "Tra la Porticus Minucia e il Calcarario. L'Area Sacra di Largo Argentina nell'Altomedioevo," *Archeologia Medievale* 21, pp. 57–98.

Santangeli Valenzani, R. (1996–7) "Pellegrini, senatori e papi. Gli *xenodochia* a Roma tra il V e il IX secolo," *RIASA, serie III*, 19–20, pp. 203–26.

Santangeli Valenzani, R. (1999). "Strade, case e orti nell'alto medioevo del foro di Nerva," *MEFRM* 111.1, pp. 163–9.

Santangeli Valenzani, R. (2000) "Residential building in early medieval Rome," in J. Smith (ed.), pp. 101–12.

Santangeli Valenzani, R. (2001) "I Fori Imperiali nel Medioevo," *Röm. Mitth.* 108, pp. 269–83.

Santangeli Valenzani, R. (2001b) "L'Itinerario di Einsiedeln," in Arena *et al.* (eds.), pp. 154–9.

Santangeli Valenzani, R. (2001c) "La residenza di Ottone III sul Palatino: un mito storiografico?," *BullCom* 102, pp. 163–8.

Santangeli Valenzani, R. (2002) "Il cantiere altomedievale. Competenze tecniche, organizzazione del lavoro e struttura sociale," *Röm. Mitth.* 109, pp. 419–26.

Santangeli Valenzani, R. (2003) "Struttura economica e ruoli sociali a Roma nell'altomedioevo: una lettura archeologica," *Acta IRN* 17, pp. 115–26.

Santangeli Valenzani, R. (2004) "Abitare a Roma nell'alto medioevo," in L. Paroli and L. Vendittelli (eds.), *Roma dall'antichità al medioevo II. Contesti tardoantichi e altomedievali*, Rome, pp. 41–59.

Santangeli Valenzani, R. (2008) "L'insediamento aristocratico a Roma nel IX–X secolo," in Royo, Hubert, and Béranger (eds.), pp. 229–45.

Santangeli Valenzani, R. (2011a) *Edilizia residenziale in Italia nell'altomedioevo*, Rome.

Santangeli Valenzani, R. (2011b) "Aristocratic Euergetism and Urban Monasteries in Tenth Century Rome," in H. Dey and E. Fentress (eds.), *Western Monasticism ante litteram. The Spaces of Monastic Observance in Late Antiquity and the Early Middle Ages*, Turhout, pp. 273–87.

Santangeli Valenzani, R. (2012) "I quartieri residenziali. Deprezzamento, crisi e mutamenti proprietari delle *domus* aristocratiche," in di Bernardino, Pilara, and Spera (eds.), pp. 219–27.

Santangeli Valenzani, R. (2014) "Hosting Foreigners in Early Medieval Rome: From *xenodochia* to *scholae peregrinorum*," in Tinti (ed.), pp. 69–88.

Santangeli Valenzani, R. (2015a) "Topografia del potere a Roma nel X secolo," in West-Harling (ed.), pp. 135–48.

Santangeli Valenzani, R. (2015b) "Calcare ed altre tracce di cantiere, cave e smontaggi sistematici degli edifici antichi," in Molinari, Santangeli Valenzani, and Spera (eds.), pp. 335–44.

Santangeli Valenzani, R. (2018) "*In amphiteatrum quod nuncupatur Coloseum.* Il Colosseo nel medioevo: dalla microstoria alla storia urbana," in Facchin, Rea, and Santangeli Valenzani (eds.), pp. 14–24.

Santangeli Valenzani, R., and G. Facchin (2017) "Il Colosseo nel medioevo tra baroni, preti e mercanti," in Rea, Romano, and Santangeli Valenzani (eds.), pp. 66–75.

Saxer, V. (1989) "L'utilisation par la liturgie de l'espace urbain et suburbain: l'example de Rome dans l'Antiquité et le Haut Moyen Âge," in *Actes du XIe congrès international d'archéologie chrétienne*, Rome, pp. 917–1033.

Saxer, V. (2001) "La chiesa di Roma dal V al X secolo: amministrazione centrale e organizzazione territoriale," *Settimane del CISAM* 48, pp. 493–632.

Scaccia Scarafoni, C. (1927) "L'antico Statuto dei 'Magistri Stratarum'," *ASRSP* 50, pp. 239–308.

Schiaparelli, L. (1902) "Alcuni documenti dei magistri aedificiorum urbis (secoli XIII e XIV)," *ASRSP* 25, pp. 5–60.

Schimmelpfennig, B. (1968) "Ein bisher unbekannter Text zur Wahl, Konsekration und Krönung des Papstes im 12. Jahrhundert," *Archivum Historiae Pontificiae* 6, pp. 43–70.

Schimmelpfennig, B. (1974) "Die Krönung des Papstes im Mittelalter dargestellt am Beispiel der Krönung Pius' II. (3. 9. 1458)," *Quellen und Forschungen aus Italienischen Archiven und Bibliotheken* 54, pp. 192–270.

Schimmelpfennig, B. (1990) "Papal Coronations in Avignon," in J. M. Bak (ed.), *Coronations. Medieval and Early Modern Monarchic Ritual*, Berkeley, pp. 179–96.

Schimmelpfennig, B. (1992) "Die Bedeutung Roms im päpstlichen Zeremoniell," in Schimmelpfennig and Schmugge (eds.), pp. 47–61.

Schimmelpfennig, B. (2006) "Zum päpstlichen Zeremoniell in der Zeit des Investiturstreits," in C. Stiegemann and M. Wemhoff (eds.), *Canossa 1077 Erschütterung der Welt*, vol. 1: Essays, Munich, pp. 111–16.

Schimmelpfennig, B., and L. Schmugge (eds.) (1992) *Rom im hohen Mittelalter. Studien zu den Romvorstellungen und zur Rompolitik vom 10. Bis 12. Jahrhundert*, Sigmarigen.

Schlatter, F. W. (1989) "The Text in the Mosaic at Santa Pudenziana," *Vigiliae Christianae* 43.2, pp. 155–65.

Schramm, P. (1929) *Kaiser, Rom und Renovatio*, 2 vols., Leipzig.

Serlorenzi, M. (2004) "Santa Lucia in Selcis. Lettura del palinsesto murario di un edificio a continuità di vita," in Paroli and Vendittelli (eds.), pp. 350–79.

Serlorenzi, M. (2010) "Le testimonianze medievali nei cantieri di Piazza Venezia," in R. Egidi, F. Filippi, and S. Martone (eds.), *Archeologia e infrastrutture. I; tracciato fondamentale della linea C della Metropolitana di Roma: prime indagini archeologiche*, Florence, pp. 131–65.

Serlorenzi, M. (2013) "L'area dell'*athenaeum* in età medievale e moderna," *Bollettino di Archeologia On Line* 4, pp. 72–94.

Serlorenzi, M. (2016) "All'origine del medioevo: passeggiando nel Foro romano," in Andaloro, Bordi, and Morganti (eds.), pp. 110–29.

Serlorenzi, M., and I. De Luca (eds.) (2015) "Piazza Venezia. Indagini archeologiche della metropolitana: ceramica a vetrina pesante dalle stratigrafie altomedievali," in Stasolla and Annoscia (eds.), pp. 495–520.

Serlorenzi, M., G. Ricci, I. de Luca, L. Anguilano, V. La Salvia, and F. Marani (2017) "Il contesto archeologico dell'Athenaeum di Adriano tra tardo antico ed alto medioevo: una possibile zecca di VI-fine VII/prima metà VIII secolo?," in G. Pardini, N. Parise, and F. Marani (eds.), *Numismatica e Archeologia. Monete, stratigrafie e contesti. Dati a confronto*, Rome, pp. 369–403.

Settia, A. A. (1986) "La casa forte urbana nell'Italia centro settentrionale. Lo sviluppo di un modello," in *La Maison forte au moyen âge*, Paris, pp. 325–30.

Settis, S. (2001) "Roma fuori di Roma: periferie della memoria," *Settimane del CISAM* 48, pp. 991–1013.

Silvagni, A. (1943) *Monumenta epigraphica Christiana saeculo XIII antiquiora quae in Italiae finibus adhuc extant*, vol. 1: Roma, Vatican City.

Smith, J. (ed.) (2000) *Early Medieval Rome and the Christian West. Essays in Honour of Donald A. Bullough*, Leiden and Boston.

Smith, R. R. R., and B. Ward-Perkins (eds.) (2016) *The Last Statues of Antiquity*, Oxford.

Sommerlechner, A. (ed.) (2003) *Innocenzo III: urbs et orbis*, 2 vols., Rome.

Spannagel, M. (1999) *Exemplaria Principis. Untersuchungen zu Entstehung und Ausstattung des Augustusforums*, Heidelberg.

Spera, L., D. Esposito, and E. Giorgi (2011) "Costruire a Roma nel medioevo: evidenze di cantiere dallo scavo a San Paolo fuori le mura," *Archeologia dell'architettura* 16, pp. 19–33.

Spera, L. (2011a) "Osservazioni sulle porticus dei santuari martiriali a Roma. Assetti architettonico-urbanistici e questioni cronologiche," in Brandt and Pergola (eds.), pp. 1299–1330.

Spera, L. (2011b) "Dalla tomba alla 'città' di Paolo: profilo topografico della Johannipolis," in O. Bucarelli and M. M. Morales (eds.), *Paulo apostolo martyri. L'apostolo San Paolo nella storia, nell'arte e nell'archeologia*, Rome, pp. 119–61.

Spera, L. (2012) "La realtà archeologica: restauro degli edifici pubblici e riassetto urbano dopo il sacco," in A. Di Berardino, G. Pilara, and L. Spera (eds.), *Roma e il sacco del 410: realtà, interpretazione, mito*, Vatican City, pp. 113–55.

Spera, L. (2013) "Roma, gli imperatori e i barbari nel V secolo," in I. Baldini and S. Cosentino (eds.), *Romania Gothica I: Potere e politica nell'età della famiglia teodosiana (395–455). I linguaggi dell'impero, le identità dei barbari*, Bari, pp. 163–93.

Spera, L. (2015) "A proposito di quattro blocchi di pavonazzetto con iscrizioni da un'officina marmoraria nell'area del Quirinale," in A. Serra (ed.), *Miscellanea in onore di Patrizia Serafin*, Rome, pp. 249–71.

Spera, L. (2016a) "Il papato e Roma nell'VIII secolo. Rileggere la 'svolta' istituzionale attraverso la documentazione archeologica," *RAC* 92, pp. 393–430.

Spera, L. (2016b) "La cristianizzazione del Foro romano e del Palatino. Prima e dopo Giovanni VII," in Andaloro, Bordi, and Morganti (eds.), pp. 96–109.

Spera, L. (2017) "Note sull'oratorio di San Cesareo al Palatino," *RAC* 93, pp. 505–60.

Spera, L. (2019) "Roma, il suburbio e gli imperatori nel V secolo. Archeologia di un ritorno," *Archeologia Classica* 70, pp. 455–98.

Spezzaferro, L. (1973) "La politica urbanistica dei Papi e le origini di via Giulia," in L. Salerno, L. Spezzaferro, and M. Tafuri, *Via Giulia. Una utopia urbanistica del 500*, Rome, pp. 15–64.

Squatriti, P. (1998) *Water and Society in Early Medieval Italy*, Cambridge.

Stasolla, F. R. (2002) "Balnea ed edifici di culto: relazioni e trasformazioni tra tarda antichità e alto medioevo," in Guidobaldi and Guiglia Guidobaldi (eds.), pp. 143–51.

Stasolla, F. R., and G. M. Annoscia (eds.) (2015) *Le ceramiche di Roma e del Lazio in età medievale e moderna. La polifunzionalità nella ceramica medievale*, Rome.

Steinby, E. M. (1986) "L'industria laterizia di Roma nel tardo impero," in A. Giardina (ed.), *Società romana e impero tardoantico*, vol. 2, Rome, pp. 99–164.

Steinby, E. M. (2001) "La cronologia delle 'figlinae' tardoantiche," in M. Cecchelli (ed.), *Materiali e tecniche dell'edilizia paleocristiana a Roma*, Rome, pp. 127–50.

Steinke, K. B. (1984) *Die mittelalterlichen Vatikanpaläste und ihre Kapellen. Baugeschichtliche Untersuchung anhand der schriftlichen Quellen*, Vatican City.

Storey, G. R. (2013) "Housing and Domestic Architecture," in P. Erdkamp (ed.), *The Cambridge Companion to Ancient Rome*, Cambridge and New York, pp. 151–68.

Stroll, M. (1991) *Symbols as Power: The Papacy Following the Investiture Contest*, Leiden.

Stroll, M. (2012) *Popes and Antipopes. The Politics of Eleventh Century* [sic] *Church Reform*, Leiden and Boston.

Tabacco, G. (1991) "Regno, impero e aristocrazie nell'Italia postcarolingia," *Settimane del CISAM* 38, pp. 243–69.

Tafuri, M. (1992) *Ricerca del Rinascimento: principi, città, architetti*, Turin.

Taylor, R., K. Rinne, and S. Kostof (2016) *Rome. An Urban History from Antiquity to the Present*, Cambridge.

Tengström, E. (1974) *Bread for the People (Acta instituti romani regni sueciae in 8°, vol. 12)*, Stockholm.

Thacker, A. (2013) "Popes, Emperors and Clergy at Old Saint Peter's from the Fourth to the Eighth Century," in McKitterick et al. (eds.), pp. 137–56.

Thacker, A. (2014) "Rome: The Pilgrims' City in the Seventh Century," in Tinti (ed.), pp. 89–139.

Thunø, E. (2002) *Image and Relic. Mediating the Sacred in Early Medieval Rome*, Rome.

Thunø, E. (2015) *The Apse Mosaic in Early Medieval Rome: Time, Network, and Repetition*, Cambridge and New York.

Tinti F. (ed.) (2014) *England and Rome in the Early Middle Ages: Pilgrimage, Art, and Politics*, Turnhout.

Tomei, A. "La pittura e le arte suntuarie: Da Alessandro IV a Bonifacio VIII (1254–1303)," in Romanini (ed.), pp. 321–404.

Tomei, A. (1995) "Un modello di committenza papale: Niccolo III e Roma," in Carlo Pietrangeli (ed.), *Sancta Sanctorum*, Milan, pp. 192–201.

Tosti-Croce, M. R. (1991) "L'architettura tra il 1254 e il 1308," in Romanini (ed.), pp. 73–143.

Tosti-Croce, M. R. (ed.) (2000) *Bonifacio VIII e il suo tempo. Anno 1300 il primo Giubileo*, Milan.

Toubert, H. (1970) "Le renouveau paléochrétien à Rome au début du XIIe siècle," *Cahiers Archeologiques* 20, pp. 99–154.

Toubert, P. (1973) *Les structures du Latium médiéval*, 2 vols., Rome.

Toubert, P. (2001) "*Scrinium* et *Palatium*: la formation de la bureaucratie romano-pontificale aux VIIIe – IXe siècles," *Settimane del CISAM* 48, pp. 57–117.

Toynbee, J. M. C. (1971) *Death and Burial in the Roman World*, London.

Trevisan, G. (2007) "Campane e campanili nell'altomedioevo (secoli VIII-XI)," in S. Lusuardi Siena and E. Neri (eds.), *Del fondere campane. Dall'archeologia alla produzione*, Florence, pp. 135–48.

Trifone, P. (2008) *Storia linguistica di Roma*, Rome.

Trifone, P. (2012) "Le città, capitali della varietà linguistica," in C. Marazzini (ed.), *Italia dei territori e Italia del futuro: Varietà e mutamento nello spazio linguistico italiano*, Florence, pp. 151–76.

Tucci, P.L. (2017) *The Temple of Peace in Rome*, 2 vols., Cambridge.

Twyman, S. (2002) *Papal Ceremonial at Rome in the Twelfth Century*, London.

Ullmann, W. (1960) "Leo I and the Theme of Papal Primacy," *Journal of Theological Studies*, new series 11, pp. 25–51.

Ullmann, W. (1970) *The Growth of Papal Government in the Middle Ages: a Study in the Ideological Relation of Clerical to Lay Power*, 3rd ed., London.

Valtieri, S. (1992) "Il ruolo dell'area compresa nell'ansa del Tevere nelle strategie papali dal Medioevo fino al XV secolo," in C. Bozzoni, G. Carbonara, and G. Villetti (ed.), *Saggi in onore di Renato Bonelli*, Rome, pp. 335–44.

Vauchez, A. (ed.) (2001) *Roma medievale*. (*Storia di Roma dall'antichità a oggi*, vol. 2), Rome and Bari.

Vendittelli, L. (2004) "*Crypta Balbi*: stato e prospettive della ricerca archeologica nel complesso," in Paroli and Vendittelli (eds.), pp. 222–30.

Vendittelli, L. (2010) "La ricerca archeologica nel sito," in Ricci and Vendittelli (eds.), pp. 9–23.

Vendittelli, M. (2014) "Il Campus Agonis nei secoli centrali del medioevo: proprietà, insediamenti, usi sociali," in Bernard (ed.), pp. 459–69.

Vendittelli, M. (2015) "Istituzioni, società, economia a Roma tra XII e XIII secolo," in C. Carbonetti, S. Lucà, and M. Signorini (eds.), *Roma e il suo territorio nel medioevo. Le fonti scritti tra tradizione e innovazione*, Spoleto, pp. 23–37.

Vera, D. (2004) "Panis Ostiensis adque fiscalis: vecchie e nuove questioni di storia annonaria romana," in R. Lizzi Testa and J.-M. Carrié (eds.), *Humana sapit. Études d'antiquité tardive offertes à Lellia Cracco Ruggini*, Turnhout, pp. 341–56.

Vera, D. (2010) "Fisco, annona e commercio nel Mediterraneo tardoantico: Destini incrociati o vite parallele?," in S. Menchelli *et al.* (eds.), *LRCW3 Late Roman Coarse Wares, Cooking Wares and Amphorae in the Mediterranean: Archaeology and Archaeometry. Comparison between Western and Eastern Mediterranean. Volume I*, Oxford, pp. 1–18.

Verdi, O. (1997) *Maestri di edifici e di strade a Roma nel secolo XV. Fonti e problemi*, Rome.

Veyne, P. (1976) *Le pain et le cirque. Sociologie historique d'un pluralisme politique*, Paris.

Virgili, P., and P. Battistelli (1999) "Indagini in piazza della Rotonda e sulla fronte del Pantheon," *BullCom* 100, pp. 137–54.

Virlouvet, C. (1995). Tessera frumentaria. *Les procédures de la distribution du blé public à Rome à la fin de la république et au début de l'empire*, Rome.

Vismara, G. (1999) "La città dei morti nella tradizione del diritto romano," *Studi Medievali*, 3rd series, 40, pp. 499–514.

Vitiello, M. (2014) *Theodahad. A Platonic King at the Collapse of Ostrogothic Italy*, Toronto.

Vitti, P. (2013) "Tradizione romana e tradizione bizantina nelle tecniche costruttive delle volte fra V e VI secolo: il caso delle Mura Aureliane," *Archeologia dell'Architettura* 18, pp. 88–113.

von Falkenhausen, V. (2015) "Roma greca. Greci e civiltà greca a Roma nel medioevo," in C. Carbonetti, S. Lucà, and M. Signorini (eds.), *Roma e il suo territorio nel medioevo. Le fonti scritti tra tradizione e innovazione*, Spoleto, pp. 39–72.

Waley, D. (1961) *The Papal State in the Thirteenth Century*, London.

Ward Perkins, B. (1984) *From Classical Antiquity to the Middle Ages. Urban Public Building in Northern and Central Italy AD 300–850*, Oxford.

Ward-Perkins, B., and C. Machado (2013) "410 and the End of New Statuary in Italy," in Lipps, Machado, and von Rummel (eds.), pp. 353–63.

Wessel, S. (2008) *Leo the Great and the Spiritual Rebuilding of a Universal Rome*, Leiden and Boston.

Westfall, C. W. (1974) *In This Most Perfect Paradise: Alberti, Nicholas V and the Invention of Conscious Urban Planning in Rome, 1447–55*, College Park, PA.

West-Harling, V. (ed.) (2015) *Three Empires, Three Cities: Identity, Material Culture and Legitimacy in Venice, Ravenna and Rome, 750–1000*, Turnhout.

Wickham C. (2000) "The Romans according to their Malign Custom: Rome in Italy in the Late Ninth and Tenth Centuries," in Smith (ed.), pp. 151–67.

Wickham, C. (2005) *Framing the Early Middle Ages: Europe and the Mediterranean 400–800*, Oxford.

Wickham, C. (2014) *Medieval Rome. Stability and Crisis of a City, 900–1150*, Oxford and New York.

Wickham, C. (2015) *Sleepwalking into a New World. The Emergence of Italian City Communes in the Twelfth Century*, Princeton.

Wilson, A. (2000) "The Water-Mills on the Janiculum," *MAAR* 45, pp. 219–46.

Yawn, L. (2012) "Clement's New Clothes. The Destruction of Old S. Clemente in Rome, the Eleventh-Century Frescoes, and the Cult of (Anti)Pope Clement III," *Reti Medievali Rivista* 13.1, pp. 1–34.

Yawn, L. (2016) "Public Access, Action, and Display in Rome of the Later *anni mille*," in J. Gadeyne and G. Smith (eds.), *Perspectives on Public Space in Rome, from Antiquity to the Present Day*, London and New York, pp. 85–105.

Zanini, E. (1998) *Le Italie bizantine*, Bari.

Zanker, P. (1988) *The Power of Images in the Age of Augustus*, Ann Arbor.

Ziese, J. (1982) *Wibert von Ravenna. Der Gegenpapst Clemens III (1084–1100)*, Stuttgart.

INDEX

Adelspapsttum, 171, 186
Adeodatus, Pope, 87
Aëtius, Flavius, general, 52
Agatho, Pope, 273
Aistulf, King of the Lombards, 110
Alaric I, King of the Visigoths, 36
    sacks Rome in 410, 37
Alberic I, Duke of Spoleto, 141
Alberic II, *princeps Romanorum*, 142, 148, 159, 167, 294
Alberti, Leon Battista, 257–8
Albinus, urban prefect, 42
Alexander II, Pope, 172, 189
Alexander III, Pope, 2, 196
Alexander IV, Pope, 238
Alexander V, Pope, 253
Alfanus *camerarius*, 194, 200
Amalasunta, Queen of the Ostrogoths, 64, 66
Ammianus Marcellinus, 25
Anacletus II, antipope, 195, 297, 298
Anastasius, Cardinal, 192–4
Anastasius, Pope, 85
Annibaldi family, 187, 215, 253, 302
annona, 34–5, 42, 51–2, 65, 72
    end of, 93–4
Anonimo Romano, 301–6
Anonymous Valesianus, 273
Anthemius, Emperor, 54
Antiochus, prefect of Italy, 72
aqueducts, 7, 23, 46, 62, 67, 75, 91, 115, 173
    Acqua Marana, 151, 252

aqua alessandrina, 283
Aqua Antoniniana, 24
Aqua Claudia, 22, 91, 115, 120, 146, 147–8, 151
Aqua Jovia (Iobia), 91, 115, 137, 151
Aqua Marcia-Tepula-Julia, 283
Aqua Sabbatina. *See* aqueducts: Aqua Traiana
Aqua Traiana, 20, 75, 91, 115, 137, 164, 273
Aqua Virgo, 18, 91, 115, 137, 252
Arcadius, Emperor, 37
archaeology, medieval
    methods and practices, 5–6, 41, 89, 144, 201–4, 219
arches, triumphal, 37
Arcionii family, 187
arcus Constantini, 20
Argiletum, 127, 131, 203
ascesa Proti, 159
Athalaric, King of the Ostrogoths, 66
atrium Libertatis, 43, 62
atrium Minervae, 11, 46
Aula Gotica, 236–8
Aurelian Wall, 3, 35–6, 62, 67, 73, 79, 95, 107, 115, 117, 124, 137, 148, 206–9, 223, 253, 257, 305
    Porta Appia, 73, 76, 253
    Porta Asinaria (S. Giovanni), 151
    Porta Maggiore, 145–8, 253
    Porta Metronia, 148–50, 206–7
    Porta Ostiensis (S. Paolo), 253

    Porta Tiburtina (S. Lorenzo), 107, 253, 257
Aurelian, Emperor, 23
Aventine Hill, 40, 162, 228–30
Avignon, removal of papacy to, 8–9, 213, 217
Avitus, Emperor, 54

Ballardini, Antonella, 119
baptisteries, 29
    Lateran, 77, 193
    S. Anastasia, 265
    S. Vitale, 265
    SS. Quattro Coronati, 265, 295
Barbarossa. *See* Frederick I, King/Emperor
barons (*barones Urbis*), 213–16, 253
    urban strongholds of, 228–34
Bartolo da Sassoferrato, 301
Basilica Aemilia, 15, 39, 44, 55, 62, 75, 133, 202
basilica argentaria, 16
Basilica Hilariana, 40, 178
Basilica Julia, 15, 44, 134
basilica nova. *See* Basilica of Maxentius
Basilica of Junius Bassus, 58
Basilica of Maxentius, 15, 30, 156
basilica Salvatoris. *See* churches: Lateran Basilica (St. John Lateran)
Basilica Ulpia, 17, 48, 128
Baths of Agrippa, 18, 46
Baths of Caracalla, 24, 46, 62, 196, 279
Baths of Constantine, 46, 62, 279
Baths of Decius, 46, 279

Baths of Diocletian, 24, 46, 279
Baths of Nero, 46, 161
Baths of Titus, 22
Baths of Trajan, 22, 23, 97, 268, 279
Belisarius, 66, 67
    founds a *xenodochium*, 84
bell towers. *See* churches: *campanili* (bell towers)
Benedetto *campanino*, 165, 167
Benedetto *Carushomo*, 206
Benedict IX, Pope, 171
Benedict of Soracte, 84
Benedict X, antipope, 172
Benedict XII, Pope, 248
Benedict, canon of St. Peter's, 80, 205
Berardi family, 174
Boethius, senator, 278
Bolgia, Claudia, 241
Boniface IV, Pope, 74, 83, 87
Boniface IX, Pope, 218, 248, 253
Boniface VIII, Pope, 216, 237, 244, 247
Bordi, Giulia, 153, 293
Borgo. *See* Vatican
Brancaleone degli Andalò, 185, 217, 303
brick stamps
    of Athalaric, 272
    of Theodoric, 62
bridges
    Pons Cestius, 164, 207, 250
    Pons Fabricius, 164, 174, 250
    Pons Iudaeorum, 174
    Pons Maior, 164, 174, 250, 305
    Ponte Lucano, 73
    Ponte Mammolo, 73
    Ponte Milvio, 206
    Ponte Nomentano, 73
    Ponte Salario, 73
    Ponte Sant'Angelo, 2, 79, 124, 162, 181, 203, 250, 251, 255–6
burials
    at cemetery-basilicas, 27–8
    distribution and characteristics of, 94–6
    first intramural instances of, 38

Cadalus of Parma, antipope, 172, 181
Caelian Hill, 22, 39–40, 148–51, 178, 191–4
Caetani family, 216, 228
    Francesco Caetani, Cardinal, 238
    palace on the Via Appia (Capodibove), 226
Callixtus II, Pope, 194
Campo de' Fiori, 251
campsores, 250
campus Agonis. See Piazza Navona
campus Agrippae, 23
campus Bruttianus et Codetanus, 20
campus Kaloleonis, 158

campus Lateranensis, 119, 247
Campus Martius, 17–19, 44, 89, 96, 160–2, 174, 177, 178, 203–4, 230–2, 248–50, 253, 256, 295
Canale di Ponte, 251, 255–6
Cannapara, 134
Capitoline Hill, 14, 240–2, 251, 257
Capocci family, 183
    Giovanni Capocci, 210
    Raniero Capocci, Cardinal, 303
carcer Mamertinus, 276
Carocci, Sandro, 216
Carolingian Renaissance, 121
Carpegna Falconieri, Tommaso di, 185
casali, 216
Cassiodorus Senator
    Variae, 61–3, 64
    Variae, 65
Castel Sant'Angelo, 67, 115, 124, 164, 181, 206, 210, 232, 253, 255
castelli, 216
Castra Misenatium, 21
Castra Peregrina, 40
Cavallini, Pietro, 239, 241, 243–4, 247
Celestine II, Pope, 47
Celestine III, Pope, 215
Cencius *camerarius*, 213, 249 *See also* Honorius III, Pope
Cencius *praefecti Stephani*, 181
ceramics, 7, 176
    8th-century decline in imports, 104
    African Red Slip (ARS), 98, 104
    Byzantine era, 96
    Forum Ware, 7, 176–7
    maiolica, 179
    Roman proto-maiolica, 179
    sparse-glazed ware, 7, 177–8
Charlemagne, King of the Franks, 110
    palace at Aachen, 284
Charles of Anjou, 217, 237
Charles the Bald, Emperor, 141
charters, 144, 181
    Registrum Sublacense, 145–51
Church of Rome
    5th-century assertion of ecclesiastical primacy, 69–70
    5th-century church-building, 46–51
    8th-century architectural patronage, 105–8, 111–20
    8th-century break with Byzantium, 102–4
    9th-century architectural patronage, 120–5
    9th-century privatization of public spaces, 135–6
    10th/11th-century architectural patronage, 165

    10th-century 'crisis' of, 139–42
    11th-century architectural patronage, 188–9
    12th-century architectural patronage, 190–205
    12th-century cityscaping initiatives, 201–5
    13th/14th-century architectural patronage, 238–48
    15th-century architectural patronage, 255–9
    administrative apparatus in Byzantine period, 70–1
    charitable activities in the early Middle Ages, 93–4
    Christianization of Roman Forum, 82–5
    Great Reform movement, 171–3, 185–7
    late antique expansion of, 25–32
    Lateran bureaucracy, 143
    patrimonium Sancti Petri, 114
    under Byzantine rule, 74–5
churches
    annular crypt, 121
    campanili (bell-towers), 198–201, 223
    cemetery-basilicas, 27–8
    Forty Martyrs of Sebaste, Oratory of, 83, 85, 106, 202
    Lateran Basilica (St. John Lateran), 26, 38, 46, 87, 115, 141, 165, 245–7
    S. Adriano, 70, 82, 84, 166, 191, 201, 293
    S. Agata dei Goti, 57
    S. Agnese, 277
    S. Agnese fuori le mura, 27, 63, 77
    S. Agnese in Agone, 94
    S. Anastasia, 26, 31, 79–80, 276
    S. Andrea (on Via Labicana), 277
    S. Andrea in Catabarbara, 58
    S. Angelo in Pescheria, 111, 251, 252
    S. Balbina, 31
    S. Bartolomeo all'Isola, 191, 223
    S. Biagio alla Pagnotta, 189
    S. Bibiana, 271
    S. Cecilia, 40, 121–3, 189, 205, 243, 269
    S. Ciriaco, 277
    S. Clemente, 30, 57, 189, 192–4, 201, 204, 223, 293
    S. Cosimato, 189, 223
    S. Crisogono, 121, 194–5, 204
    S. Ermete (on Via Salaria), 277
    S. Francesca Romana. *See* churches: S. Maria Nova
    S. Giovanni a Porta Latina, 277
    S. Gregorio Magno, 192
    S. Lorenzo *de ascesa*, 168
    S. Lorenzo fuori le mura, 27, 46, 77, 86, 210
    S. Lorenzo in Damaso, 85, 89
    S. Lorenzo in Lucina, 46, 223
    S. Lorenzo in Miranda, 293

churches (cont.)
    S. Lucia *de Calcarario*, 282
    S. Lucia in Selci, 278
    S. Lucia *in xenodochio Anichiorum*, 282
    S. Marco, 26, 31, 85, 284
    S. Maria *ad martyres*. *See* churches: Pantheon
    S. Maria Antiqua, 78, 83, 84, 105–6, 111, 128, 165
    S. Maria *de ferarriis*, 249
    S. Maria *de inferno*, 202
    S. Maria degli Angeli, 24
    S. Maria in Aquiro, 108
    S. Maria in Aracoeli, 240–2, 252
    S. Maria in Campo Carlèo, 168
    S. Maria in Cannapara, 83
    S. Maria in Cappella, 189
    S. Maria in Cosmedin, 82, 194
    S. Maria in Domnica, 121–3, 148
    S. Maria *in gradibus*, chapel of, 165
    S. Maria in Monticelli, 191
    S. Maria in Pallara, 153–5, 165, 293
    S. Maria in Portico, 189
    S. Maria in Trastevere, 85, 195–8, 204, 205, 223, 243, 300
    S. Maria in Via Lata, 252, 293
    S. Maria Maggiore, 47–8, 51, 87, 244–5, 248
    S. Maria Nova, 135, 152, 155–6, 196
    S. Maria *Secundicerii*, 288
    S. Maria sopra Minerva, 242–3, 252
    S. Martina, 83
    S. Martino ai Monti, 63, 271, 284
    S. Nicola *de Calcarario*, 167
    S. Nicola in Carcere, 81, 194, 276
    S. Nicomede (on Via Nomentana), 277
    S. Pancrazio, 63, 121, 275, 277
    S. Pietro in Vincoli (*titulus Apostolorum*), 46, 48–9, 51
    S. Prassede, 121–3
    S. Pudenziana (*titulus Pudentis*), 31, 189, 296
    S. Saba, 293
    S. Sabina, 47, 51
    S. Salvatore *in rota Colisei*, 153
    S. Sebastiano (*basilica Apostolorum*), 27
    S. Sebastiano al Palatino. *See* churches: S. Maria in Pallara
    S. Silvestro chapel (at SS. 4 Coronati), 235
    S. Silvestro in Capite, 85, 113
    S. Spirito in Sassia, 210, 253
    S. Stefano Rotondo, 40, 57, 148, 296
    S. Susanna, 284
    S. Teodoro, 83
    S. Urbano alla Caffarella, 190, 293
    S. Valentino, 277
    S. Venanzio chapel, 77
    S. Vitale (*titulus Vestinae*), 57, 85
    Sancta Sanctorum chapel, 120
    SS. Alessio e Bonifacio, 293
    SS. Apostoli, 86, 158, 252, 294
    SS. Cosma e Damiano, 63–4, 82, 130
    SS. Giovanni e Paolo (*titulus Pammachii*), 30, 57, 85, 148
    SS. Marcellino e Pietro, 108
    SS. Marcellino e Pietro flm, 27
    SS. Nereo ed Achilleo, 296
    SS. Quattro Coronati, 31, 192–3, 224, 284
    SS. Quattro Coronati (cardinal's palace), 234–8
    SS. Quirico e Giulitta, 293
    SS. Sergio e Bacco, 83, 85, 252, 300
    SS. Sergio e Bacco (at the Vatican), 108
    St. Paul's, 26, 28, 46, 86, 125, 137, 165, 210, 247, 269, 278, 297
    St. Peter's, 2, 26, 46, 79, 86, 106, 113, 124, 166, 247, 253, 257–8, 300
    St. Petronilla, chapel of, 111, 113
    St. Theodore, oratory of (at Porta Maggiore), 146
    titular churches (*tituli*), 88, 95
    titular churches (*tituli*), definition and characteristics of, 28–31, 85
    titulus Crescentianae, 85
    Via Ardeatina, funerary basilica, 27–8
ciconiae nixae, 18
Circus Flaminius, 18
Circus Maximus, 20, 44, 94, 181, 275
cityscape, definition of, 5
civitas Leonina. *See* Vatican, walls of
Clement II, Pope, 171
Clement IV, Pope, 238
Clement V, Pope, 217
clivus Scauri, 148
Coates-Stephens, Robert, 75, 90, 115, 145, 155, 270
coinage
    first communal issues, 283
    first papal issues, 104
    in the 10th century, 288
    in the Byzantine era, 98, 104
    of Pope Hadrian I, 114
Cola di Rienzo, 217–8, 242
College of Cardinals, 294
Colonna family, 216, 230–1, 244–5, 253
    chapel at Aracoeli, 242
    chapel at S. Maria sopra Minerva, 243
    Giacomo Colonna, Cardinal, 244–5
    Giovanni Colonna, senator, 245
    Pietro Colonna, Cardinal, 244
Colosseum, 21, 44
    6th-century spoliation of, 63
    early medieval burials at, 95
    end of traditional spectacles at, 94
    Frangipane and Annibaldi fortresses at, 228
    high medieval occupation of, 152
    late antique cemetery at, 38
    senatorial inscriptions at, 60
colossus of Nero, 16
column of Marcus Aurelius, 18
column of Phokas, 75, 286
column of Trajan, 17, 209
Concordat of Worms, 190, 194, 202
Conrad III, King/Emperor, 206
Constans II, Emperor, 74
Constantine I, Emperor, 3, 23, 26, 28, 121
Constantinople, 70
    Church council "in Trullo," 104
    Cosmidion monastery, 82
    Hagia Sophia, 63
    imperial palace, 120
    Mese, 81
Constantius II, Emperor, 25
constitutio pragmatica. *See* Pragmatic Sanction
construction techniques, 76–9, 108–10, 115–17, 154–5, 164, 208, 219–28
    opus caementicium, 221–2
    opus incertum, 221
    opus latericium, 29, 116, 223
    opus quadratum, 111, 131, 154, 167, 221
    opus sectile, 192–3, 196
    opus signinum, 146
    opus vittatum, 30, 76–9, 89, 108, 206, 208, 223
    tufelli, 183, 224–8
Conti family, 185, 215, 228
    Stefano Conti, Cardinal, 234–7
contrade, 139, 175
    Calderario, 174
    contrada de Arcionibus, 187
    S. Eustachio, 174
cosmatesque pavements. *See* construction techniques: *opus sectile*
Crescentius *murcapullo*, 150
Crescenzi family, 143, 173
Crypta Balbi, 7, 44, 62, 72, 96–100, 104–5, 128, 162, 202, 203, 205
cryptae, 152, 156, 161, 164
curatores, 73, 75
Curia athletarum, 48
Curia Senatus, 11, 39, 43, 46, 62, 70
Curiosum urbis Romae regionum XIIII. *See* Regionary Catalogues

Dark Ages, historiography of, 6, 72, 99, 137–8, 143
De varietate Fortunae (Poggio Bracciolini), 257
Decius *patricius*, 60
Delogu, Paolo, 274, 280

demographics
    population decline in late antiquity, 33–5, 42, 51–2, 58–9, 64–6
    population decline in the late Middle Ages, 217–18
    population growth in the 11th century, 161–2
    population growth in the high Middle Ages, 144, 217
    population in the 10th century, 138
    population in the 8th-9th centuries, 126
    settlement distribution in the 10th century, 138, 159–64
    settlement distribution in the early Middle Ages, 87–9, 90–1, 115
    settlement distribution in the high Middle Ages, 173–9
    settlement distribution in the late Middle Ages, 248–50
dendrophori, 40
Descriptio Lateranensis Ecclesiae, 165, 293
Desiderius of Montecassino, 189
Desiderius, King of the Lombards, 110
diaconiae, 81–2, 87–8, 91–2, 93–4
    S. Angelo in Pescheria, 111
    S. Giorgio in Velabro, 82
    S. Maria in Cosmedin, 82
    S. Nicola in Carcere, 82
    SS. Sergio e Bacco, 134
Diario Romano (Antonio di Pietro dello Schiavo), 253
domus (senatorial), 22, 25, 35, 54, 62
    "House of Sallust," 39
    at Vicus Caprarius, 54
    domus Philippi, 22
    domus Victiliana, 22
    in Piazza dei Cinquecento, 54
    in Via del Tempio di Diana, 40
    of the Valerii, 39
domus Augustana, 61
domus Tiberiana, 61, 106, 108
domuscultae, 105, 111, 124
Donation of Constantine, 3, 71, 119, 172, 191, 235
Durliat, Jean, 35, 52, 93

earthquakes, 41, 46, 52, 59, 60, 128, 135
Edict of Milan, 3, 8
Einsiedeln Itineraries, 126–7, 275, 276
Emporium. *See* Porticus Aemilia
Ennodius of Pavia, 63
epigraphy
    5th-century building inscriptions, 56
    5th-century dedications of statues, 55–6
    senatorial inscriptions at Colosseum, 60
    12th-century building inscriptions, 206–7

Epiphanius, Flavius Annius Eucharius, urban prefect, 43
Esquiline Hill, 145–8
Eugene III, Pope, 206, 210
Eugene IV, Pope, 256
Eugenius (usurper), 26

Faustus, Acilius Anicius Aginatius, urban prefect, 46
Faustus, Anicius Acilius Glabrio, urban prefect, 44
Felice Società dei Balestrieri e Pavesati, 218, 252
Felici tabernacle (S. Maria in Aracoeli), 242
Felix IV, Pope, 64
ferrarii, 249
Flavian Amphitheater. *See* Colosseum
floods, 41, 96, 126, 160
Formosus, Pope, 140
forum transitorium. See forums: Nerva, forum of
forums
    Augustus, forum of, 16, 60, 131, 156
    Caesar, forum of, 16, 43, 129–30, 157
    Forum Boarium, 19, 79, 251
    Forum Holitorium, 19, 79, 251
    Forum Romanum, 10, 11–16, 64, 75, 82–4, 127, 133–5, 155–6, 201, 252, 292
    forum suarium, 23
    Nerva, forum of, 16, 130, 131–3, 157, 202, 252, 291
    Peace, forum of (*templum Pacis*), 10, 16, 39, 61, 64, 129–30, 157
    Trajan, forum of, 16, 37, 60, 128, 129–31, 157–9, 168, 222, 291
Frangipane family, 156, 173, 174, 181, 206, 228
Franks, 118
    alliance with papacy, 110
    waning of Italian hegemony (late 9th century), 140–2
Frederick I, King/Emperor, 1–3, 172, 297
Frederick II, King/Emperor, 238

Galla Placidia, Empress, 46
gardens, 20, 23
    Horti Sallustiani, 39
Genseric, King of the Vandals, 53
Gerontius, *Life of Melania*, 40
Gerontius, *vir spectabilis*, 272
Giannini, Nicoletta, 183, 198, 297
Giotto, 239, 247
Glycerius, Emperor, 54
Golden House (*domus aurea*), 22
Gothic War, 66–8
Great Western Schism, 9, 218, 253
Gregoriopolis (Ostia), 124

Gregory I, Pope, 74, 86, 87, 121
Gregory II, Pope, 105, 107, 108
Gregory III, Pope, 74, 107–8
Gregory IV, Pope, 123
Gregory IX, Pope, 210, 300
Gregory VII, Pope, 172, 181, 189
    Dictatus Papae, 294
Gregory X, Pope, 238
Gregory XI, Pope, 218, 248, 249
Guibert of Ravenna, antipope, 172, 190
Guidobaldi, Federico, 201–4

Hadrian I, Pope, 81, 93, 110, 113, 114–15, 117, 200
Hadrian II, Pope, 138
Hadrian IV, Pope, 1–3
Helena, Empress (mother of Constantine), 23
Henry III, King/Emperor, 171–2
Henry IV, King/Emperor, 172–3
Henry V, King/Emperor, 190, 194
Heraclius, Emperor, 74
Hilarus, Pope, 86
Hildebrand, archdeacon. *See* Gregory VII, Pope
Honorius I, Pope, 63, 74, 75, 77, 83, 87, 277–2
Honorius III, Pope, 210, 300
Honorius IV, Pope, 230, 242
Honorius, Emperor, 23, 42–4
Horrea Galbes et Aniciana, 20
Hubert, Étienne, 7, 90, 182–3, 187, 203

iconoclasm, 105, 123
incastellamento, 168, 185
Innocent I, Pope, 85
Innocent II, Pope, 195, 205, 297
Innocent III, Pope, 184, 209–10, 213, 303
Innocent IV, Pope, 238, 240, 303
Innocent VII, Pope, 253
insulae, 25, 40, 302–10
    in Via Capodiferro, 278
    in Via di San Paolo alla Regola, 278
    insula Felicles, 18
    insula militena et drachonarii, 81
    insula of the Aracoeli, 89
Iohannipolis, 125, 137
Itinerarium Salisburgense, 80

Janiculum Hill, 75, 91, 115
John III, Pope, 86, 277
John IX, Pope, 140–1, 293
John of Crema, 195, 204
John VII, Pope, 104–6, 108
John VIII, Pope, 125, 137, 139, 288
John XII, Pope, 293
John XIII, Pope, 142, 165, 200, 293
John XV, Pope, 166

John XXII, Pope, 247
Julian "the Apostate," Emperor, 26
Julius Nepos, Emperor, 54
Justin I, Emperor, 93
Justin II, Emperor, 84
Justinian I, Emperor, 66, 72–3, 94
Justinianic Code (*Corpus Iuris Civilis*), 109

kalatores, 276
Kaloleus (10th-century aristocrat), 158, 168
Katermaa-Ottela, Aino, 181
Krautheimer, Richard, 6–8, 9, 26, 47, 69, 71, 89, 90, 121, 249, 250, 269, 274, 283

La pittura medievale a Roma 312–1431 (M. Andaloro and S. Romano eds.), 248
Ladislas, King of Naples, 253
Largo Argentina, 44, 167–8, 183, 202
Lateran palace, 118–20, 138, 140, 151, 156, 192, 194, 203, 249
   loggia delle benedizioni, 247
   Sancta Sanctorum chapel, 239
Leo I, Pope, 46, 70, 86
Leo III, Emperor, 105, 107
Leo III, Pope, 119–20, 277
Leo IV, Pope, 124–5, 128, 135, 163
Leo VIII, Pope, 142, 159
Leopolis, 125
Liber Pontificalis
   historiography of, 71–2, 75, 139
Licinia Eudoxia, Empress, 48
Liutprand, King of the Lombards, 107
Lo Cascio, Elio, 34–5, 52, 65
Lombards
   besiege Rome in 756, 110, 113
   invade Italy in 560s, 71
Longinianus, Flavius Macrobius, urban prefect, 36
Lothar I, King/Emperor, 124
Lothar II, King/Emperor, 297
Louis II of Anjou, 253
Ludus Magnus, 21

Magistri edificiorum, 209, 252, 255–6
Majorian, Emperor, 269
Manetti, Giannozzo, 257–8
Marazzi, Federico, 32
Marchetti Longhi, Giuseppe, 80
Marchiori, Laura, 155
Marcus, Pope, 28
Markets of Trajan, 184, 278
marmorarii, 192, 223
   magister Cosmatus, 239
   Vassaletto, 300
Marozia, Roman noblewoman/nun, 147
Marozia, *senatrix Romanorum*, 142
Martin I, Pope, 70, 103

Martin V, Pope, 9, 218, 238, 254, 256
Master Gregory (Magister Gregorius), 185
mausoleum of Augustus, 18, 230
mausoleum of Hadrian. *See* Castel Sant'Angelo
Mazzarino, Santo, 34, 65
Meneghini, Roberto, 60, 159, 168
monasteries, 167, 277
   "monasteries of the *diaconia*," 91–2
   boetiana, 278
   in houses of early medieval popes, 87–8
   monasterium in catacumbas, 277
   monasterium maior sancti Petri, 86
   S. Andrea, 87
   S. Basilio, 131, 156
   S. Erasmo, 148–50
   S. Lorenzo *in Pallacinis*, 280
   S. Maria in Aventino, 167
   S. Maria in Campo Marzio, 188
   S. Silvestro in Capite, 113, 188
   S. Sisto, 300
   S. Stefano Maior, 278
   SS. Benedetto e Scolastica (Subiaco), 145
   SS. Ciriaco e Nicola, 161–2, 167, 187, 209
   SS. Cosma e Damiano *in mica aurea*, 165, 167, 188
   St. Paul's fuori le mura, 108
   Tre Fontane (*ad aquas salvias*), 84
Montecitorio, 230
Montegiordano, 232
municipal statutes of 1363, 219, 252
municipal statutes of 1452, 256
Muñoz, Antonio, 47
muratores, 223

Naples
   diaconiae at, 92
Narses, general, 72–4
   founds churches, 84, 277
Nicholas I, Pope, 137
Nicholas II, Pope, 172, 199
Nicholas III, Pope, 211, 215, 239–40, 242, 303
Nicholas IV, Pope, 216, 244–7
Nicholas V, Pope, 255–9, 305
Nicomachus the Younger, Virius Flavius, urban prefect, 37
Noble, T. F. X., 104, 113
Normans
   kingdom of southern Italy, 172
   sack of Rome in 1084, 173, 191
notaries (*notai*), 219
Notitia urbis Romae. *See* Regionary Catalogues

obsonium, 42, 52, 65

Octavian (Pope John XII), son of Alberic, 142
Odeum of Domitian, 18
Odo of Cluny, 167
Odoacer, 54, 59–60
Olympiodorus of Thebes, 42
Oppian Hill, 22, 48, 291
opus listatum. *See* construction techniques: *opus vittatum*
Ordines Romani, 81
Orlandi, Silvia, 56
Orsini family, 215, 231–2, 253
   chapel at S. Maria sopra Minerva, 243
Ostia, 123
Otto I, King/Emperor, 142
Otto III, King/Emperor, 142
Otto of Freising, Bishop, 1–2

Palatine Hill, 11, 61, 73–4, 80, 105–6, 108, 181
Palladius, Praetorian Prefect of Italy, 42
Pantheon. *See* temples: Pantheon
Papareschi family, 174
Paschal I, Pope, 120–3
Paschal II, Pope, 190–4, 201–4
Paul I, Pope, 113
Pelagius I, Pope, 277
Pelagius II, Pope, 87
Perchuk, Alison, 196
Petronius Maximus, Emperor, 53
Petrus *consul et dux*, 167
Petrus *medicus*, 154, 167
Phokas, Emperor, 70, 74
Piazza Giudea, 251
Piazza Navona, 18, 94, 177
Piazza Venezia, 202
   Hadrianic auditoriums at, 100–1, 128, 203
Pierleoni family, 173–4, 194, 196, 206
   Giordano Pierleoni, 298
Pincian Hill, 23
Pippin II, King of the Franks, 110
plagues
   Black Death, 217–18
   in late antiquity, 38
plans of Rome, 219
Plato, *curator palatii*, 74, 106
pomerium, 95
Pons Aemilius. *See* bridges: Pons Maior
porticus absidata, 16
Porticus Aemilia, 20
porticus Crinorum, 81
porticus curva, 62
porticus Divorum, 18
porticus Fabarius, 20
porticus Gallatorum, 80
porticus maior (S. Petri), 115, 126, 163, 251

porticus maximae, 79–82, 111, 127, 189, 203–4, 231–2, 250, 251, 256
porticus Minucia vetus et frumentaria, 18, 44, 162
Porticus Octaviae, 18, 183, 251, 275
Porticus of Meleager, 18
Porticus of the Argonauts, 18
porticus Philippi, 18, 275
Portus, 20, 125
Portus Licini, 62
praefectus annonae, 273
Pragmatic Sanction of 554, 72–3
Priester, Ann, 198–200
primates romani, 143
Probianus, Gabinius Vettius, urban prefect, 44
processional ceremonies, 79–82, 203–4, 213
Procopius of Caesarea, 39, 66–7, 94, 270, 310
ptochium, 87, 92

Ravenna, 70
  church-building at, 63
Regia, 133
Regionary Catalogues, 10–25
relics
  intramural translations of, 113, 122
residential architecture *see also* domus (senatorial); *insulae*; tower houses (*casetorri*)
  baronial strongholds, 228–34
  cardinals' palaces, 234–9
  curtes, 133, 149, 159, 161–2, 167–8
  in the 10th century, 145–50, 157–9, 168–9
  in the 9th century, 128–34
  in the 13th century, 233
  in the Byzantine period, 89–90
  in the high Middle Ages, 187–8
Ricimer, *magister militum*, 46, 54, 57
  sacks Rome in 455, 54
rioni, 139, 175, 187
Ripa Graeca, 19, 79, 81, 178, 250, 251
Ripa Grande, 164, 174, 250
Ripa Romea. *See* Ripa Grande
Ripetta (river port), 174, 251
Rocca Savella, 225, 228–30
Roma instaurata (Flavio Biondo), 257
Rome, Profile of a City (Richard Krautheimer), 6–8, 126, 138
Romulus Augustulus, Emperor, 54, 59
Rostra, 11, 133, 134
Rusuti, Filippo, 239, 244–5

Saepta Julia, 18
Salita dei Borgia, 222
Sant'Eustachio family, 174, 187

Santangeli Valenzani, Riccardo, 60, 87, 131, 158, 167, 288
Saracens
  attacks on Rome in the 840s, 124
  sack *Centumcellae* in 813, 125
  settlements in Italy, 141
Savelli family, 228–30
  chapel at S. Maria sopra Minerva, 243
  chapel at the Aracoeli, 242
  Pandolfo Savelli, 242
schola Anglorum, 118
scorticlari, 161
secretarium Senatus, 43, 62
Senate House. *See* Curia Senatus
Senate of Rome, ancient, 44
  5th-century impoverishment of, 53
  charitable foundations in late antiquity, 87
  dissolution of, 70, 86
  role under Odoacer and Theodoric, 60
  support for usurper Eugenius, 26
Senate of Rome, medieval, 1–3, 200
  senatorial palace, 201, 206, 239, 248, 257, 303
Septizodium, 181
Sergius I, Pope, 104, 273, 277
Sergius III, Pope, 140, 142, 165
Sergius *primicerius*, 146
Severan Marble Plan, 10
Show Area, 11, 15, 17, 21, 25, 26, 28, 31, 37, 39, 44, 60, 64, 82, 85, 86, 87, 94, 96, 106, 129, 135, 136, 151–60, 176, 177, 179, 201
Sidonius Apollinaris, 46
Simplicius, Pope, 40, 58
Sisinnius, Pope, 106
Sixtus III, Pope, 46–9
Sixtus IV, Pope, 258
Smaragdus, Exarch, 75
Spera, Lucrezia, 271, 275, 297
spolia, 62, 109–10, 195–6, 205, 223
  9th-century spoliation of public monuments, 129–31
  in 5th-century churches, 50–1
Stadium of Domitian, 44, 292
  as locus of medieval spectacle, 94
  early medieval burials at, 95
statuary
  dedications in late antiquity, 37
  dedicatory inscriptions of, 55–6
  Marcus Aurelius at the Lateran, 119
  she-wolf at the Lateran, 119
Stefaneschi family, 243–4
  Bertoldo Stefaneschi, 243
  Giacopo Stefaneschi, Cardinal, 243
Stephen II, Pope, 110, 111–13
Stephen III, Pope, 111
Stephen *secundicerius*, 288

Stephen V, Pope, 140
Stephen VI, Pope, 140
Stilicho, *magister utriusque militiae*, 36–7
suarii, 34–5, 52
Subura, 16, 183
Sylvester I, Pope, 71
Symmachus, Aurelius Anicius, urban prefect, 44
Symmachus, Pope, 63, 86

Tebaldi family, 174
Temple of Peace/*templum Pacis*. *See* forums:Peace, forum of
temples
  Antoninus and Faustina, temple of, 293
  Antoninus Pius, temple of, 15
  Apollo, temple of, 111
  Bellona, temple of, 111
  Caesar, temple of the Divine, 133
  Castor and Pollux, temple of, 15
  Claudius, temple of the Divine (Claudianum), 22
  Concord, temple of, 287
  Elagabalus, temple of, 61
  Hadrian, temple of, 18
  Hercules, round temple of, 20
  Isis and Serapis, temple of, 18
  Jupiter Optimus Maximus, temple of, 14, 53, 62
  Marcus Aurelius, temple of, 18
  Mars *ultor*, temple of, 16, 60, 131, 156
  Minerva Chalcidica, temple of, 18
  Minerva, temple of (in forum of Nerva), 130
  Pantheon, 18, 74, 160–1, 251, 252
  Portunus, temple of, 20, 276, 287
  preservation of in late antiquity, 46
  Saturn, Temple of, 14
  Sun, temple of the (*templum Solis*), 23, 63
  Trajan, temple of the Divine, 16, 130
  Venus and Rome, temple of, 15, 74, 128, 135, 156
  Venus *genetrix*, temple of, 16, 130
  Vespasian, temple of, 134
  Vesta, temple of, 15
Terme Alessandrine. *See* Baths of Nero
Testaccio, 20, 253, 291
The Republic of St. Peter (T. F. X. Noble), 104
Theater of Balbus, 18, 44, 62
Theater of Marcellus, 18, 228, 251, 275
Theater of Pompey, 18, 44, 62, 231, 275
Theodora, wife of Theophylact, 142, 293
Theodoric, King of the Ostrogoths, 54, 61–4
Theodosian Code (*Codex Theodosianus*), 51, 109

Theodosius I, Emperor, 26
Theodotus *dux* and *primicerius*, 111–13
Theophylact, *vestararius*, 142–3, 169
Tor de' Conti, 184, 222, 228
Torre delle Milizie, 184, 228
Torriti, Jacopo, 239–40, 244–7
Totila, King of the Ostrogoths, 67, 73
Toto, Duke of Nepi, 111
tower-houses (*casetorri*), 181–7
    Casa dei Crescenzi, 223
Trastevere, 20, 40, 67, 89, 164–5, 174, 295
Trevi Fountain, 257
Triumphal Way. *See* Via Triumphalis
Tullianum, 276
Turin Catalogue, 250
turris pertundata, 232
Tuscolani family, 143, 169, 172–3

Urban II, Pope, 181
Urban IV, Pope, 238
Urban V, Pope, 305
Urban VI, Pope, 218

Valentinian III, Emperor, 43, 46, 52–3
Valila, Flavius, *magister militum*, 58
Vandals
    conquest of North Africa, 52–3
    sack of Rome in 455, 53–6
Vatican, 174, 210, 251, 253–4, 257–8
    in the 8th century, 118
    in the 10th–11th centuries, 162–4
    papal palace, 210–12, 303
    passetto, 211
    walls of, 2, 124–5, 163, 226, 249
    water supply to, 115
Velabrum, 20
Vera, Domenico, 270
Verdi, Orietta, 256
vestararius, 117, 142
Via Caelemontana, 22, 148–9, 151
via capitis Africae, 22, 148, 151
Via del Pellegrino, 256
Via Flaminia. *See* Via Lata
Via Lata, 17, 18, 23, 84, 88, 127, 157, 188, 202, 204–5, 256, 296
via maior, 127, 155, 193, 203, 249–50
Via Mercatoria, 232, 250–1, 256
Via Papalis, 162, 203, 231, 256
Via Recta, 256
Via Sacra, 15, 127, 133, 155, 202, 286
Via Tiburtina, 127
Via Triumphalis, 18, 79–82, 111, 127, 203–4, 250, 256
viability (roads), 126–8, 203–4, 256
Vicus Iugarius, 134
vigiles, 20, 22–3, 25
Vigilius, Pope, 70, 72, 277
vineyards
    10th/11th-century expansion of, 150
Vitalian, Pope, 74
Vitigis, King of the Ostrogoths, 67
Vitti, Paolo, 73

water mills, 20, 75, 146–7, 164
Wickham, Chris, 156

xenodochia, 87–8, 92, 93–4, 111
    at Portus, 87
    in Platana, 111, 279
    of Belisarius, 84
    of the Anicii, 278, 282
    of the Valerii, 278

Zacharias, Pope, 105, 107, 118, 281
Zosimus, 38